Lecture Notes in Computer Science 16174

The series Lecture Notes in Computer Science (LNCS), including its subseries Lecture Notes in Artificial Intelligence (LNAI) and Lecture Notes in Bioinformatics (LNBI), has established itself as a medium for the publication of new developments in computer science and information technology research, teaching, and education.

LNCS enjoys close cooperation with the computer science R & D community, the series counts many renowned academics among its volume editors and paper authors, and collaborates with prestigious societies. Its mission is to serve this international community by providing an invaluable service, mainly focused on the publication of conference and workshop proceedings and postproceedings. LNCS commenced publication in 1973.

Christian Wallraven · Ran He · Brian Lovell ·
Prithwi Chakraborty
Editors

Pattern Recognition and Computer Vision

8th Asian Conference on Pattern Recognition, ACPR 2025
Gold Coast, QLD, Australia, November 10–13, 2025
Proceedings, Part I

Editors
Christian Wallraven
Korea University
Seoul, Korea (Republic of)

Ran He
Chinese Academy of Sciences
Beijing, China

Brian Lovell
The University of Queensland, Australia
Brisbane, QLD, Australia

Prithwi Chakraborty
Southern Cross University
Sydney, NSW, Australia

ISSN 0302-9743 ISSN 1611-3349 (electronic)
Lecture Notes in Computer Science
ISBN 978-981-95-4394-6 ISBN 978-981-95-4395-3 (eBook)
https://doi.org/10.1007/978-981-95-4395-3

This Springer imprint is published by the registered company Springer Nature Singapore Pte Ltd.
The registered company address is: 152 Beach Road, #21-01/04 Gateway East, Singapore 189721, Singapore

Preface

Pattern recognition stands at the core of artificial intelligence and has been evolving significantly in the past decades. What began as the study of fundamental algorithms has grown into a driving force behind transformative technologies reshaping how we live, work, and connect. From enabling machines to see and understand the world to empowering breakthroughs in healthcare, education, and science, pattern recognition has become a cornerstone of human progress in the digital age.

These proceedings include high-quality original research papers presented at the 8th Asian Conference on Pattern Recognition (ACPR 2025), which was successfully held in Gold Coast, Australia, from November 10th to November 13th, 2025. The conference provided a timely platform for researchers, practitioners, and students from around the world to meet physically in the beautiful Gold Coast to share their latest findings, exchange ideas, and foster collaborations that will shape the future of pattern recognition technologies.

ACPR 2025 was the eighth conference of its series since it was launched in 2011 in Beijing, followed by ACPR 2013 in Okinawa, Japan, ACPR 2015 in Kuala Lumpur, Malaysia, ACPR 2017 in Nanjing, China, ACPR 2019 in Auckland, New Zealand, ACPR 2021 in Jeju Island, South Korea, and ACPR 2023 in Kitakyushu, Japan. As we know, ACPR was initiated to promote pattern recognition theories, technologies, and applications in the Asia-Pacific region. Over the years, it has actually welcomed authors from all over the world. This year, we had participants from 16 countries.

ACPR 2025 focused on four important areas of pattern recognition: pattern recognition and machine learning; computer vision and robot vision; signal, speech, and video processing; and document, media processing, and interaction, covering various technical aspects.

ACPR 2025 received 118 submissions from 16 countries. The program chairs invited 136 program committee members and additional reviewers. Each paper was single-blindly reviewed by at least three reviewers. This rigorous procedure ensured an unbiased review. The review committee made a hard decision to accept 35 oral presentation papers and 25 poster papers. This resulted in an acceptance rate of 29.7% for oral presentation and 21.2% for poster presentation, a total acceptance rate of 50.9%.

The technical program of ACPR was scheduled over four days (10–13 November 2025), including three tutorials and one workshop, three keynote speeches, seven oral sessions, and one poster session.

The keynote speeches were provided by internationally renowned professors. Alison Noble, from the University of Oxford, UK, talked on "Healthcare AI Imaging Algorithms and Systems in the new Era of Humans and AI working together". Shijian Lu, from Nanyang Technological University, Singapore, talked on "Sustainable AI via Image Generation and Cross-Domain Transfer". Chin-Teng Lin, from the University of Technology Sydney, Australia, talked on "Brain Computer Interface in Augmented Reality and Metaverse".

Organizing a conference is challenging, requiring teamwork, intensive coordination, and collaboration from different geolocations and time zones. We would like to thank all organizing committee members for their hard work, with guidance from the steering committee. The program chairs, organizing chairs, publication chairs, publicity chairs, workshop chairs, tutorial chairs, sponsorship chair, finance chair, and webmaster all led their respective committees and worked together closely to make ACPR 2025 successful. Our special thanks go to the reviewers for constructive comments to improve the papers. We thank all the authors who submitted their papers, which is the most important part of a scientific conference. Finally, we would like to acknowledge the volunteers and students from our local organizers.

Alan Wee-Chung Liew
Cheng-Lin Liu
Dacheng Tao
Brian Lovell
Ran He
Christian Wallraven

Organization

Steering Committee

Seong-Whan Lee	Korea University, South Korea
Cheng-Lin Liu	Chinese Academy of Sciences, China
Umapada Pal	Indian Statistical Institute, Kolkata, India
Tieniu Tan	Nanjing University, China
Yasushi Yagi	Osaka University, Japan

General Chairs

Alan Wee-Chung Liew	Griffith University, Australia
Cheng-Lin Liu	Chinese Academy of Sciences, China
Dacheng Tao	Nanyang Technological University, Singapore

Program Chairs

Brian Lovell	University of Queensland, Australia
Ran He	Chinese Academy of Science, China
Christian Wallraven	Korea University, South Korea

Organizing Chairs

Ali Reza Alaei	Southern Cross University, Australia
Anwaar Ul-Haq	Central Queensland University, Australia
Partha Pratim Roy	IIT Roorkee, India
Yanming Zhu	Griffith University, Australia

Workshop Chairs

Xiao Bai	Beihang University, China
Lihong Zheng	Charles Sturt University, Australia
Xiaoyi Jiang	University of Münster, Germany
Reza Ghanbarzadeh	Southern Cross University, Australia

Tutorial Chairs

Vinh Bui	Southern Cross University, Australia
Venu Govindaraju	University at Buffalo, USA
Mohammed Awrangjeb	Griffith University, Australia
Can Wang	Griffith University, Australia

Publicity Chairs

Umapada Pal	Indian Statistical Institute, Kolkata, India
Yuta Nakashima	Osaka University, Japan
Unsang Park	Sogang University, South Korea
Shijian Lu	Nanyang Technological University, Singapore
Brendan McCane	University of Otago, New Zealand

Sponsorship Chair

Michael Blumenstein	University of Technology Sydney, Australia

Publication Chairs

Haifeng Shen	Southern Cross University, Australia
Fahimeh Alaei	Southern Cross University, Australia
Prithwi Chakraborty	Southern Cross University, Australia

Award Chair

Jun Zhou	Griffith University, Australia

Finance Chair

Tony Adriaansen	Marab Pty Ltd., Australia

Webmaster

Mohammad Ala Uddin Azad Southern Cross University, Australia

Contents – Part I

Contents – Part II

Finding Outliers in a Haystack: Anomaly Detection for Large Pointcloud Scenes

Ryan Faulkner[1(✉)], Luke Haub[2], Simon Ratcliffe[2], and Tat-Jun Chin[1]

[1] University of Adelaide, Adelaide, Australia
ryjamesfaulkner@gmail.com
[2] Maptek, Glenside, Australia

Abstract. LiDAR scanning in outdoor scenes acquires accurate distance measurements over wide areas, producing large-scale point clouds. Application examples for this data include robotics, automotive vehicles, and land surveillance. During such applications, outlier objects from outside the training data will inevitably appear. Our research contributes a novel approach to open-set segmentation, leveraging the learnings of object defect-detection research. We also draw on the Mamba architecture's strong performance in utilising long-range dependencies and scalability to large data. Combining both, we create a reconstruction based approach for the task of outdoor scene open-set segmentation. We show that our approach improves performance not only when applied to our own open-set segmentation method, but also when applied to existing methods. Furthermore we contribute a Mamba based architecture which is competitive with existing voxel-convolution based methods on challenging, large-scale pointclouds.

Keywords: 3D Vision · Scene Understanding · Anomaly Detection · Open Set Segmentation

1 Introduction

Understanding large pointcloud scenes is an important goal for a variety of applications, from self-driving vehicles or drones, to general land surveillance. Accurate three-dimensional data can be obtained from Light Detection and Ranging (LiDAR) scanners, offering geometric information and precision which a two dimensional camera cannot. However between the structure of the data, and the potential scale, with millions of points and objects over a hundred meters apart, processing these LiDAR scans can be difficult. Furthermore, when the context of a practical application is as uncontrolled and diverse as an outdoor scene, there will inevitably be anomalous objects which were not in the training data. Identifying these unknown anomalies when they appear is essential to the reliable application of theoretical architectures and methods to real-world applications.

Existing "Anomaly Detection" research can be grouped into two distinct categories. Either detecting defects and flaws when examining a single object

C. Wallraven et al. (Eds.): ACPR 2025, LNCS 16174, pp. 1–15, 2026.
https://doi.org/10.1007/978-981-95-4395-3_1

at a time [10,17], or identifying unknown objects which were not present in the training data, in a scene context [3,6,8]. We develop a novel approach to open-set segmentation, developed by approaching the problem of anomalous object detection from both of these perspectives.

Instead of defining the problem as either "Identifying *outliers* within a consistent object" or "Identifying *unknown* objects not present in training" we combine the two, and define the problem as "Identifying *unknown outliers* in a scene". Our paper puts forward that by training a reconstruction step using only known classes in a scene, we have developed an architecture which achieves superior performance at detecting unknown objects (anomalies).

In this paper we provide:

- One mamba-based architecture for reconstructing a scene's "default context" trained only on known objects.
- A second architecture for the task of anomaly detection. Our mamba backbone contrasts to existing voxel convolution based methods.
- Analysis and ablation testing provides the first exploration of how Mamba, which boasts high efficiency and ability to utilise long-range dependencies in data, applies to the field of anomaly detection for large-scale point cloud data.
- We propose a novel method for creating synthetic anomalies to support training.

2 Related Work

2.1 Open-Set Segmentation for Point Cloud Scenes

There are some methods which fall outside of machine learning/AI which identify anomalous objects. These include representing the data as a graph, within which "outliers" can be identified [7]. Alternatively, using predefined matrices and equations (instead of learned ones) to extract object features from the data with which to identify clear outliers (robust principle component analysis) [2]. This paper focuses on and compares against other machine-learning methods, including the expansion of the task from simply anomaly detection, to also applying semantic segmentation to the point cloud scene.

This task of open-set segmentation for point clouds has been explored previously [3,6], using voxel-based architectures such as Cylinder3D [21]. One of the key challenges for this area is training a network when almost by definition, the training data should not have any examples of anomalous objects. Cen et al. [3] approach this by using known instance labels in the training data to create synthetic anomalies during training, and demonstrate improved results on unknown (real) anomalies during testing.

As these existing methods however do not include anything like our reconstruction step, in our experiments we test our method against existing ones both with and without our reconstruction step added for a more thorough analysis. We also propose an alternative way to augment object instances which we demonstrate creates better synthetic anomalies for training.

2.2 Mamba for Point Cloud Scene Understanding

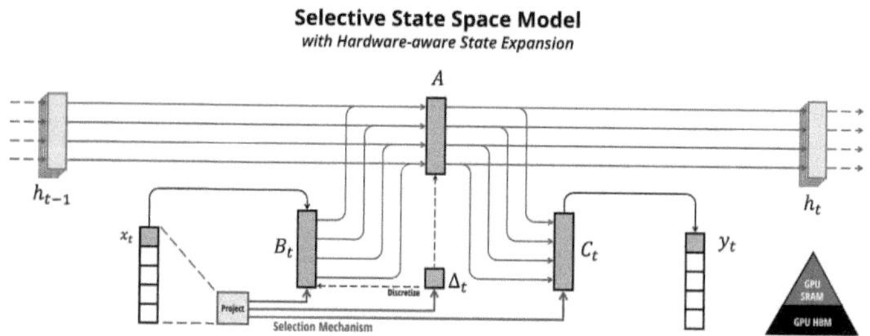

Fig. 1. A visual diagram of the Selective State Space Model which forms the core of a Mamba block, from the Mamba paper [9].

Originating as a method for sequencing of dna, time, or large language models, Mamba [5,9] builds on the combined bases of Recurrent Neural Networks and State Space Models. It is able to store a "hidden state" of information (referred to as h in Fig. 1) while sequentially processing the data. The details of how much the hidden should both be updated, and be utilised, during the processing of each datapoint x_t, determined by applying learned weights to x_t, shown as blue lines in Fig. 1. This process allows a network to selectively store only useful information long-term while processing a sequence, while still being computationally efficient (with all computationally expensive steps capable of being performed in parallel on a GPU). Together this gives Mamba a powerful ability to model long-range dependencies, as well as efficient scalability to large datasets. For applications where data can be very large in scale such as outdoor-scene pointclouds, this makes it a very suitable architecture to use as a backbone.

Most computer-vision applications such as Vision Mamba [20] first flatten the data into a sequence, then apply each block in both directions (forwards and backwards) to allow the network to learn and apply long-range dependencies in both directions.

Applied to vision tasks ranging from those with causal data like video sequences [11,18] to less causal ones like denoising or densification of static point clouds [4,19], the architecture's effectiveness as a backbone, especially on large datasets such as LiDAR point clouds, has already been firmly established outside the context of anomaly detection.

Closed-set segmentation has also already shown success, either supplementing Mamba with "K Nearest Neighbour" [12,14] or Octree convolutions [13] to extract close-range dependencies.

In the context of single-object, RGB image defect-detection, Mamba has been used previously [10,17]. Two notable contrasts from this in our method are that we do not rely on pre-trained RGB networks such as ResNet (making our method more applicable to non-standard data types). We also investigate the challenging open-set, large-scale scene segmentation task instead of single-object defect detection.

2.3 Reconstruction for Anomaly Detection

Reconstruction as a preprocessing step is common for defect detection [10] where a robust, pretrained, ResNet or similar can be used. Outside of this scope however, the use of reconstruction is rare. In examples where it has been used for open-set [8,16], it uses predicted semantic labels as the reconstruction base. For example, Biase et al. [8] use a GAN to reconstruct a 2D image from their predicted semantic labels. Such a reconstruction will diverge from the input where there are inconsistencies in a given class (e.g. cars being different colours), or errors in the semantic prediction being used as a base (e.g. mislabeling one uncommon class for another).

We argue it is more effective to train an autoencoder to encode and decode the original input, removing any reliance on predicted semantic labels. This allows the autoencoder to learn to reconstruct a scene's "default context", directly assisting with outlier detection. This is inspired by reconstruction steps in single-object defect-detection which will fail to recreate scratches, blemishes, or other defects, aiding in their identification.

3 Method

Our two separate architectures are shown in Fig. 2. We define each point cloud $\mathcal{P}$, as having an (inconsistent) number of points N, such that $\mathcal{P} = \{\mathbf{p}_i\}_{i=1}^N$. First, a learned reconstruction of the scene $\widetilde{\mathcal{P}} = \{\widetilde{\mathbf{p}_i}\}_{i=1}^N$ is generated. We find relying on the inconsistencies between this reconstruction and the original values (RGB, Intensity, XYZ), improves performance, especially for detection of out-of-set anomalies.

The final result for the task of open-set segmentation is defined as two sets of predicted labels, the semantic class prediction $\mathcal{C}$ where $\mathcal{C} = \{\mathbf{c}_i\}_{i=1}^N$, and a separate anomaly score $\mathcal{A}$, where $\mathcal{A} = \{\mathbf{a}_i\}_{i=1}^N$. The class prediction is an integer from 0 to k, where k is the number of classes in the training data, excluding any anomaly classes (real or synthetic) used to train for anomaly detection. The anomaly score is a single value from 0 to 1. We provide a Mamba-based anomaly detection architecture, in contrast to convolutional backbones such as the Cylinder3D [21], used by REAL [3] and DOSS [6]. Our architecture generates for a point cloud $\mathcal{P}$ both semantic class predictions $\mathcal{C}$, as well as an anomaly score $\mathcal{A}$.

The groundtruth class labels for each point are $\mathcal{G}$ where $\mathcal{G} = \{\mathbf{g}_i\}_{i=1}^N$. In training and testing these labels are mapped and masked to either $\mathcal{G}_A$ or $\mathcal{G}_c$ to be used as the groundtruth for anomaly detection or semantic class prediction respectively.

To ensure both robust performance as well as scientifically rigorous experiments, the training data undergoes masking of three different types. Unknown

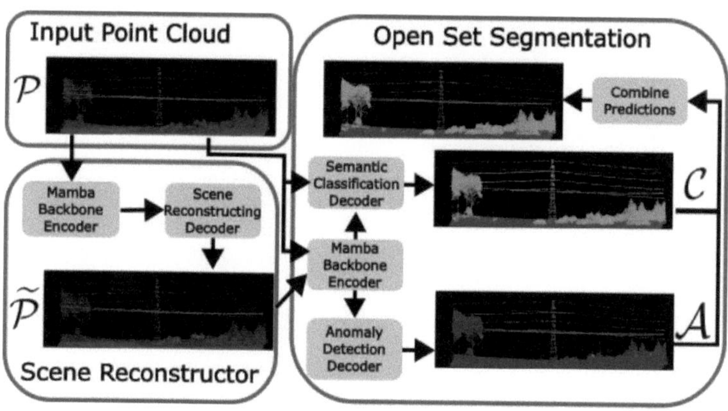

Fig. 2. High level diagram of our overall method for inference. Our scene reconstructor can be separated out to assist any existing anomaly detection architecture, not just our MambaAD. Red points are anomalous, brown are ground, green is vegetation. For anomaly vs in-set, blue points are in-set. (Color figure online)

objects to be used during testing must be completely hidden during training, the removal of such points is defined as $k()$ such that $\mathcal{P}_{known} = k(\mathcal{P})$. For training the semantic segmentation, the "known" anomalous points (either synthetic anomalies for KITTI or a defined subset of anomalies in ECLAIR) are also removed to create an anomaly-free scene we refer to as the "default context". This process defined as $d()$, $\mathcal{P}_{default} = d(\mathcal{P})$.

Mamba Encoder Backbone. For the backbone, we use a modified version of "Point Mamba" created by Liu et al. [13]. As shown in the bottom left of Fig. 4, it uses multiple Mamba blocks between each downsampling to effectively capture global scene information, while *also* using octree convolutions to utilise the more local information around each point.

Details for the backbone are available in the original paper [13], we make two modifications, the first is updating the Mamba blocks with the more recent Mamba-2 [5]. The second is changing the flattening process used to turn 3D data into the one directional sequence a Mamba block can be applied to. Instead of a simple three-dimensional z-order curve as used in prior 3D Mamba architectures, we used a multi step process to improve the grouping of points which belong to the same object instance.

First we sort points into 2 m square blocks along the XY place (ground plane). Blocks are sorted using a Z-order curve as usual, and within each block points are sorted by their Z-axis value. The direction of the Z-axis sorting alternates between each adjacent block in an effort to keep points belonging to the same object instance, together in the final sequence. In Fig. 3 there a wall which is spread across two XY blocks, has a continuous sequence of points.

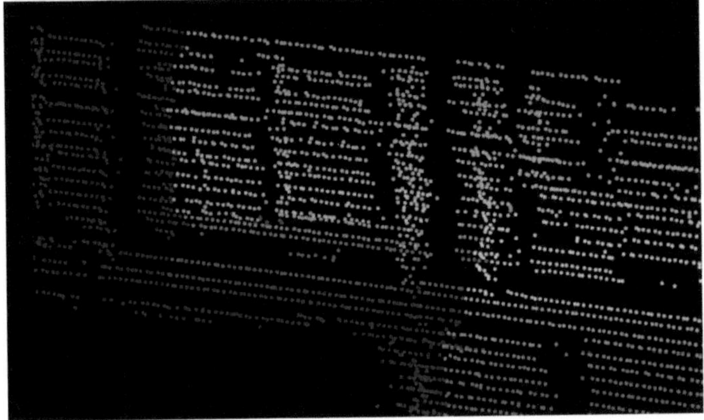

Fig. 3. A wall with points coloured according to position in flattened sequence. One XY block ascends from blue to green, and the next descends, green to red. (Color figure online)

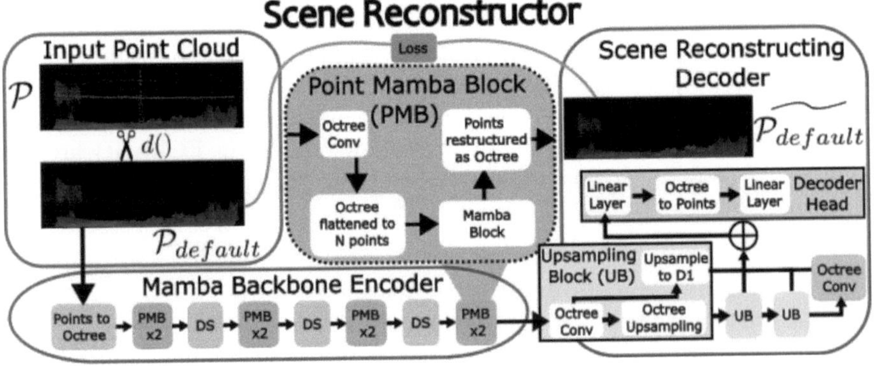

Fig. 4. Scene Reconstructor architecture for training. In this example the transmission tower and it's power lines are considered anomalous objects

3.1 Learned Scene Reconstruction

Following from successes in single-object anomaly detection, as well as a small number of scene-based open-set segmentation, we encode and decode point cloud scenes to better identify out-of-distribution anomalies. The Mamba backbone is used to encode an information-dense version of the scene $\{\mathbf{e}_i\}_{i=1}^{N_1}$. We then train a decoder to reconstruct the scene from this. The decoder uses octree convolutions between each upsampling, followed by a series of linear layers. Together, this creates the Mamba-based autoencoder shown in Fig. 4, which reconstructs a given scene $\mathcal{P}$, as $\widetilde{\mathcal{P}}$. The training loss for this reconstructor L_R is simply $L_R = CrossEntropy(\mathcal{P}, \widetilde{\mathcal{P}})$, with both point clouds masked to exclude anomalous objects.

A Scene's Default Context. We identify anomalies using both the absolute and signed difference between the original and reconstructed point clouds: $\Delta\mathcal{P} = \{\mathcal{P}-\widetilde{\mathcal{P}}, \|\mathcal{P}-\widetilde{\mathcal{P}}\|\}$. With this input, both our anomaly detection architecture and others demonstrate improved performance.

Our logic is that by learning the features of the known objects in a scene, referred to as the "default context" in the training data, the reconstructor will fail more, and by larger margins at reconstructing outlier objects (anomalies), aiding in their identification. The second half of our architecture then uses this $\Delta\mathcal{P}$ both to effectively segment the anomalous objects, identifying the needles in the haystack so to speak.

Another notable benefit from relying on the reconstructed feature difference $\Delta\mathcal{P}$ is that it abstracts the problem of anomaly detection away from the raw data values, leading to less overfitting on the known training data. For this task, the training data is often either a small selection of "known" anomalies, or synthetic anomalies, both of which can easily lead to overfitting issues when new anomalies in testing or application are completely differently in appearance.

For a problem task which revolves around robust and reliable networks which work on completely unknown data, this is a significant advantage.

Reconstructed Features. In addition to any available raw data features (RGB colour information, intensity/reflectance), we reconstruct the geometric information as well. As the point clouds can be as large in the XY plane as a 100×100 m^2, simply reconstructing the XYZ information directly is very challenging to do with accuracy. If normalised to a value from -1 to 1 for example, a slight deviation in decimals can lead to huge changes in the 100 m scene, making errors too large to be of use.

We instead reconstruct the XYZ of each point relative to it's Octree leaf node. Each point $\mathbf{p}$ will sit inside a given leaf node of the octree n, where the middle of that octree node is the co-ordinate x_n, y_n, z_n. The relative x co-ordinate x_r is a simple calculation of $x_r = x_p - x_n$ for the x-axis, and the same for y_r and z_r. By reconstructing this instead of the global position x_p, objects are still in the correct location, and errors instead present as malformed surfaces and exteriors, e.g. a flat surface no longer being flat, or a more three-dimensional object such as a bush becoming flatter, aiding in the identification of anomalies.

3.2 Mamba-Based Anomaly Detection

While Mamba has been used previously for the task of single-object anomaly detection (identifying defects) [10], we are the first to apply a Mamba backbone to the task of anomaly detection in scenes (open-set segmentation).

Using this backbone, we then have two separate decoder heads, one for the anomaly detection score $\mathcal{A}$, and one for semantic segmentation of known, in-set objects $\mathcal{C}$.

Our loss is calculated using both of these predictions and their respective groundtruth values $\mathcal{G}_C$ and $\mathcal{G}_A$, as visualised in Fig. 5. The final loss is $L = L_A + L_C$ where $L_A = BinaryCrossEntropy(\mathcal{A}, \mathcal{G}_A)$ and $L_C = CrossEntropy(\mathcal{C}, \mathcal{G}_C)$.

Anomalies "seen" during training (either synthetic, or a subset of the anomalous classes) often vary greatly from anomalies encountered in practice, making overfitting a significant issue. Known objects however, assuming reasonable training sample size, are more likely to match the training data. We therefore include skip connections in the semantic decoder head, but not the anomaly detection head where they can make the network more likely to overfit to the "training data anomalies" only.

When incorporating the reconstruction difference $\Delta\mathcal{P}$, the original point data is still extremely important for the task of open-set segmentation. While errors in the reconstruction are well-suited to anomaly detection, they provide little useful information for semantic segmentation of known classes. To this end, we add the raw data back in at each layer of the semantic segmentation decoder, as shown in Fig. 5 where P_known is repeatedly passed in to the open set segmentation model's upsampling blocks (UB) for the semantic prediction but not the anomaly detection one.

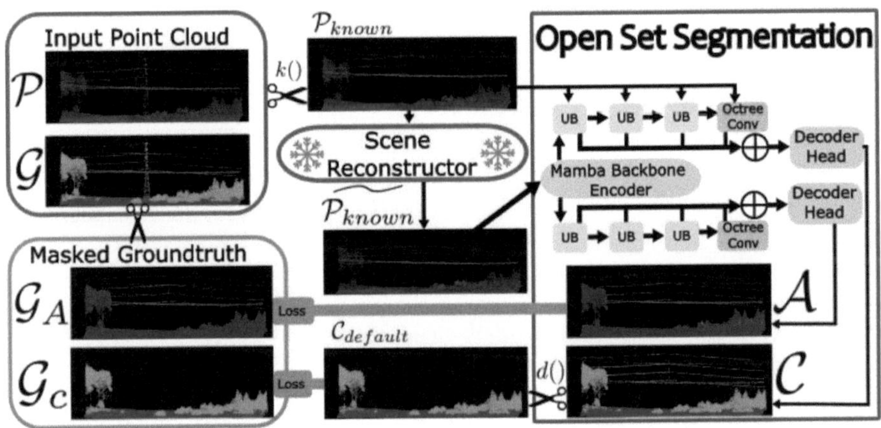

Fig. 5. Our Open Set Segmentation architecture during training.

3.3 Creating Synthetic Anomalies

As this is the task of identifying objects for which we lack training data, previous works have already explored creating synthetic data instead. We follow from Cen et al.'s REAL [3] in assuming the training data has not just semantic labels but also object instance labels for each point, to then randomly augment known objects, creating synthetic ones.

They use a scaling based method, changing the size of the object, however we are concerned that this simply leads to anomaly detection networks learning to either identify point density disparity (objects made larger are sparser than their surroundings, objects made smaller are more point-dense), or floating objects/objects which exist below the ground plane, as the object's base becomes lower or higher in the Z axis due to the overall size change.

As an alternative, we instead use an augmentation inspired by the "Rubik's Cube" toy. Each object instance is split down the middle (X, Y, Z) into eighths. Different halves of the object are then randomly rotated along their axis to create a synthetic anomalous object, which does not break the overall continuity of the scene (whether point density or the ground plane).

By only rotating each side like a Rubik's cube, as opposed to randomly flipping the individual eigths, we ensure that the corner of each eighth originally touching the object's centrepoint, continues to do so. This is to minimise the chance of e.g. accidentally creating multiple separate objects, with the assumption that few object instances are empty in their centre.

4 Experiments

We ran experiments on both the Semantic KITTI [1] and ECLAIR [15] datasets. We thoroughly test our reconstruction and anomaly detection methods both together and separately, against existing methods [3,6]. These methods were run using their preset settings, while the hyperparemeter specifics of our method are available in our code.

We will note here decisions made for the experimental setup that differ to previous works in this area:

As anomalies used for testing should not benefit the training whatsoever, we do not simply set their weighting to 0 when calculating the loss. We remove anomalous objects completely before training, referred to in our method as $k()$. This is to ensure the network cannot benefit even indirectly, such as from learning to identify the borders of objects adjacent to an anomaly, for which the loss is not ignored.

What to use as anomalous objects in training to calculate loss, is also a difficult task. One solution has been to simply group all anomalous objects as one "unknown class" and use it to train a separate loss for anomaly detection [6], however we feel this leads to difficulty in knowing whether results would be replicated on anomalous objects which are truly unseen during training. In the context of semantic kitti for example, there is only one anomalous object, "other-vehicle", available for both training and testing. A network trained using "other-vehicle" would only need to learn to identify this specific class to perform well in testing, not to identify anomalies in general.

If object instance labels are available, we agree with Cen et al. [3] that synthetic anomalies are a promising solution. In KITTI where this is available, we test both their scaling-based synthesis, and our novel rubiks-cube inspired approach.

In ECLAIR where instance labels are unavailable, we opt to use half the anomalous classes for training (referred to as "known" anomalies) and keep half exclusively for testing. This enables the performance on truly unknown anomalies to still be inferred from the experiments.

4.1 KITTI Dataset

Table 1. Semantic KITTI Results

Semantic KITTI Dataset				
Architecture	Augmentation	AUROC	AUPR	MIoU
REAL (quoted from paper)	Scale	84.9	20.8	**57.8**
REAL	Rubiks	84.6	6.3	46.8
Mamba AD	Scale	83.74	2.7	30.7
Mamba AD	Rubiks	93.3	12.2	24.8
† Using our reconstruction step trained on default scenes				
REAL †	Rubiks	83.6	2.0	24.0
Mamba AD †	Scale	82.3	3.0	22.0
Mamba AD †	Rubiks	95.6	25.4	24.4
‡ Using our reconstruction step trained on objects only				
REAL‡	Rubiks	78.0	1.4	23.5
Mamba AD ‡	Scale	85.5	3.15	23.4
Mamba AD ‡	Rubiks	**96.3**	**37.5**	25.8

Following with previous works [3,6], we use Semantic Kitti to test anomaly detection and open-set segmentation, setting "other-vehicle" as the anomalous class, with all other classes treated as "known objects". For REAL's original unaltered method (no reconstruction step, scaling based augmentation), we quote their results directly from their paper. As DOSS uses the same anomaly used for testing ("other-vehicle") to calculate it's Objectosphere Loss during training, we do not include it in these experiments.

As shown in Table 1 our Mamba AD method achieves superior performance in anomaly detection, for both the metrics of Area under the Receiver Operating Characteristic Curve (AUROC) and Area under the Precision Recall Curve (AUPR). AUPR is much more volatile and unreliable on datasets with significant imbalances between positive and negative, but we include it as well for good measure. Mean Intersection over Union (MIoU) is used to measure the semantic segmentation performance for known classes. The improved performance with our Rubiks cube based augmentation compared to Scaling, suggests that the scaling based approach does lead to problems such as the network learning to focus on point density or relation to ground plane. This perhaps enables the open-set segmentation network, having learnt a "shortcut trick", to then devote more weights to the problem of segmentation, which would explain the drop in MIoU on known objects from introducing Rubiks-cube anomalies. Finally, training the reconstruction step on objects only, more akin to the approach of single-object defect detection, shows improvement for our method, but not for REAL.

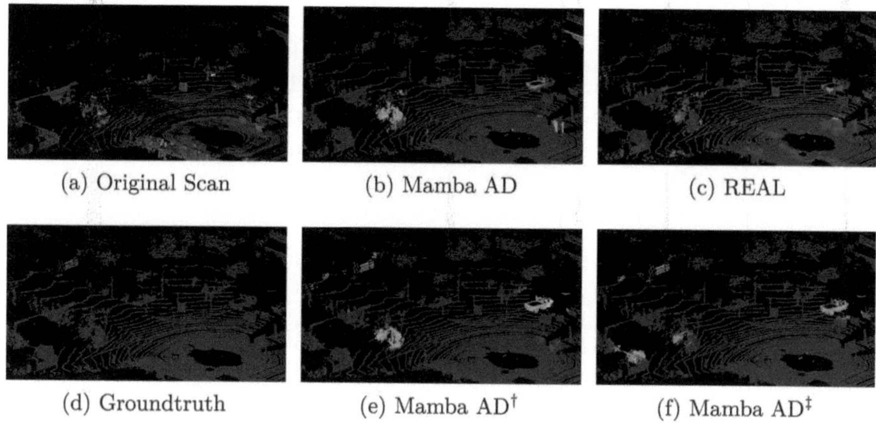

(a) Original Scan (b) Mamba AD (c) REAL

(d) Groundtruth (e) Mamba AD† (f) Mamba AD‡

Fig. 6. An anomaly detection example in KITTI. The single anomalous vehicle is extremely difficult wto identify from only a single static scan. † is using our reconstruction step trained on all known objects. ‡ is using our reconstruction step trained only on object instances.

We include an example of what this challenge looks like with a static point cloud in Fig. 6, where there is one "other-vehicle", displayed as red in the groundtruth, with the anomaly prediction score of each method shown as a heatmap.

4.2 ECLAIR Dataset

ECLAIR is a large-scale outdoor scene aerial LiDAR dataset, with each scan being a hundred square metres. We chose to test both our method, and two comparable ones (REAL, DOSS) on ECLAIR. We chose ECLAIR and not, e.g. Nuscenes as it more different from KITTI, being rural scenes instead of urban, and more importantly, large in both number of points and physical scene size, allowing the scalability of methods (e.g. Mamba vs Cylindrical Voxel Backbone Architectures) to be properly tested. We use the reccomended train, validation, and test splits provided by the dataset. For REAL we also included testing using it's "Predictive Distribution Calibration" approach which does not require any anomalies during training.

As both REAL and DOSS use Cylinder3D as a backbone, we had to modify the cylinder feature generator from a series of linear layers increasing the feature size of each point, followed by a max pooling of points, to do the max pooling when the feature size is smaller, with linear layers afterwards to reach the desired feature size. Without this modification the architectures simply could not handle large numbers of points such as is common in ECLAIR. They were otherwise kept the same. Our Mamba backbone required no changes compared to the KITTI experiments.

The “known anomalies” used for training on ECLAIR are “Trans Wires”, “Dist Wires”, “Dist Poles”, and “Vehicles”. The “unknown anomalies” for testing are “Unassigned”, “Buildings”, “Noise”, “Trans Towers”, and “Fence”. The groupings were chosen based on balancing the proportion of points in the dataset as close to 50/50 as possible, and ensuring similar objects were grouped together (Trans Wires and Dist Wires). The “default scene” used to train the reconstruction step includes neither the known nor unknown anomalies.

Table 2. Eclair Results

ECLAIR Dataset							
Architecture	Anomalies in training	AUROC (Known)	AUPR (Known)	AUROC (Unknown)	AUPR (Unknown)	MIoU
REAL	✗	77.5	1.10	76.0	0.5	69.0
REAL	✓	97.6	1.19	90.5	1.4	90.6
DOSS	✓	74.4	3.5	65.7	0.3	86.5
Mamba AD	✓	99.96	99.2	87.7	18.1	**96.9**
† Methods using our reconstruction step as preprocessing						
REAL†	✓	99.1	39.7	**91.1**	2.3	92.9
DOSS†	✓	82.0	10.7	64.7	0.4	89.2
Mamba AD†	✓	**99.97**	**99.5**	88.8	**34.6**	96.6

In Table 2 we can see the benefits of the Mamba backbones in full. Both the utilisation of long-range dependencies and scalability to large data. Our Mamba AD method outperforms on all metrics except AUROC of unknown classes, for which our reconstruction step still shows improvement for the existing method REAL. On the “Known” anomalies we achieve near perfect performance, however this near-perfection does not carry over to the unknown anomalies. We consider this an example of why it’s important that anomaly detection is tested on different *object classes* than used in training, not just different LiDAR scans. The low performance by REAL without any anomalies during training shows the importance of having some form of anomaly to calculate loss from, whether synthetic or otherwise.

In Fig. 7 we show examples of challenging point clouds where neither method perfectly identifies the anomalous objects. These highlight areas future research can explore. In Fig. 8 we show every method on the same scene for direct qualitative comparison. The scene’s left side has good RGB values, while on the right they are lacking, demonstrating the importance of method’s being able to extract geometric information from the point cloud’s co-ordinates. This is especially prevalent in REAL when trained without any synthetic anomalies, where trees on the right side are mislabeled as anomalies.

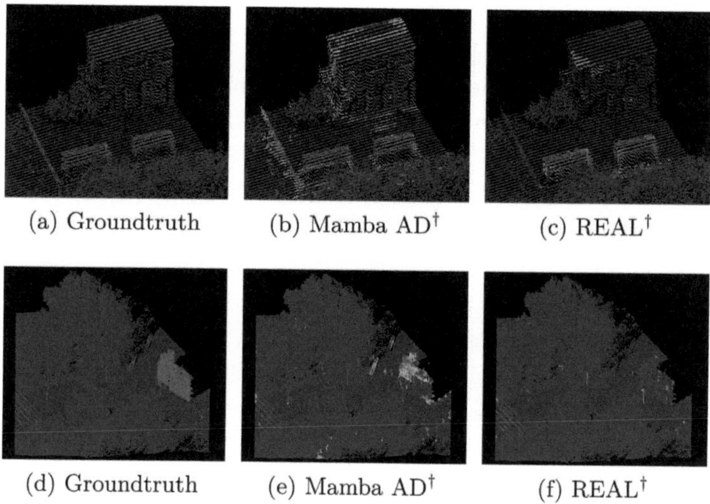

(a) Groundtruth (b) Mamba AD† (c) REAL†

(d) Groundtruth (e) Mamba AD† (f) REAL†

Fig. 7. Challenging anomaly detection examples. † Using our reconstruction step.

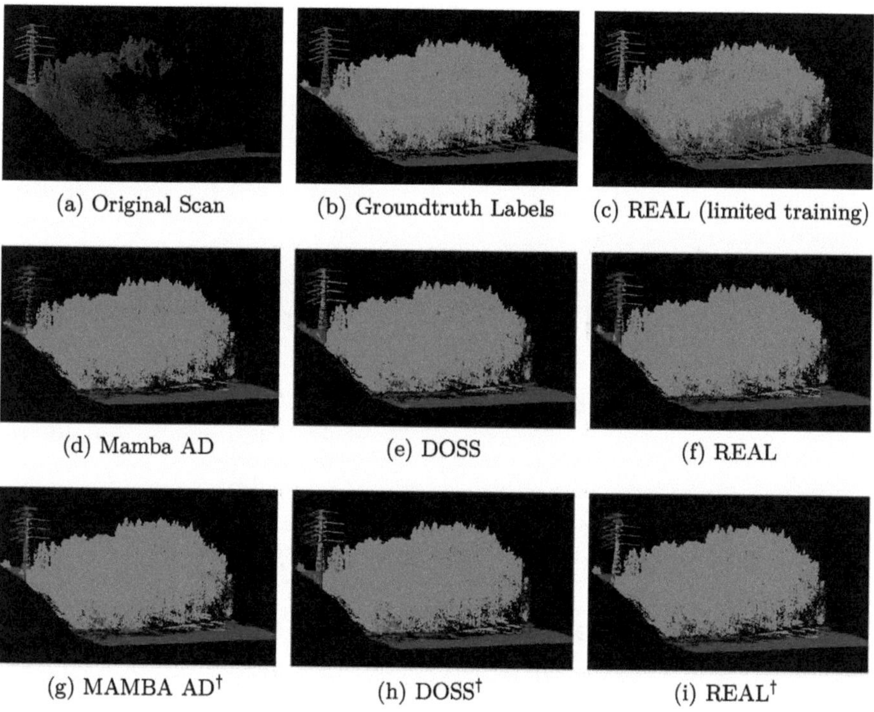

(a) Original Scan (b) Groundtruth Labels (c) REAL (limited training)

(d) Mamba AD (e) DOSS (f) REAL

(g) MAMBA AD† (h) DOSS† (i) REAL†

Fig. 8. Semantic predictions on ECLAIR dataset. Green is vegetation, brown is ground, and anomalous objects are red. † Bottom row is with our reconstruction step, middle is without. The reconstruction step assists our MambaAD network in separating the base of the anomalous object with it's neighbor. (Color figure online)

5 Conclusion

In this paper we have presented a novel application of reconstruction to large-scale point cloud scenes, as well as the first application of a Mamba backbone to the task of anomaly detection. We demonstrate consistent improvements in anomaly detection, outperforming the comparable methods by over 10% on AUROC and increasing the AUPR by 80% on KITTI. On ECLAIR only our Mamba-based anomaly detection architecture was able to achieve an AUPR of 18% on unknown anomalies, and our reconstruction step then improved it by a further 90%.

On the secondary task of segmenting known objects, there remains room for improvement, as far as our Mamba-based architecture is concerned. Our inclusion of the reconstruction step for existing methods was a direct approach, simply adding the difference $\Delta\mathcal{P}$ as extra features for each point. This method demonstrated improvement for existing methods on the ECLAIR dataset however better incorporation into existing methods could lead to superior performance.

In our ablation tests we explored whether the reconstruction step would do better trained on the scene as a whole, or only on the objects within it. The latter both being more similar to the object defect detection which inspired the method, and also allowing the reconstruction to focus more on the small objects which are more likely to resemble anomalous objects than e.g. a section of road. Our results for this specific area are inconclusive, and more research is required.

Finally, while we have shown improvement both in the scalability and performance of anomaly detection, helping the jump to real world applications be less error-prone. The task of identifying truly *unknown* anomalies remains exceedingly difficult, further improvements are still required before LiDAR based systems can reliably handle the chaos of the real world.

References

1. Behley, J., et al.: Towards 3D LiDAR-based semantic scene understanding of 3D point cloud sequences: the SemanticKITTI dataset. Int. J. Robot. Res. **40**(8–9), 959–967 (2021). https://doi.org/10.1177/02783649211006735
2. Botterman, H.L., Roussel, J., Morzadec, T., Jabbari, A., Brunel, N.: Robust PCA for anomaly detection and data imputation in seasonal time series. In: Nicosia, G., et al. (eds.) LOD, pp. 281–295. Springer, Cham (2023)
3. Cen, J., et al.: Open-world semantic segmentation for lidar point clouds. In: ECCV, pp. 318–334. Springer, Heidelberg (2022). https://doi.org/10.1007/978-3-031-19839-7_19
4. Chen, C., Ge, W.: SRMamba: Mamba for super-resolution of LiDAR point clouds (2025)
5. Dao, T., Gu, A.: Transformers are SSMs: generalized models and efficient algorithms through structured state space duality. In: ICML (2024)
6. Deng, W., Chen, X., Yu, Q., He, Y., Xiao, J., Lu, H.: A novel decomposed feature-oriented framework for open-set semantic segmentation on LiDAR data. In: ICRA (2025)

7. Dewi, A.O., Ariananda, D.D., Wibowo, S.B.: Graph signal processing for anomaly detection in cooperative power spectrum estimation. In: ICITACEE, pp. 186–191 (2024). https://doi.org/10.1109/ICITACEE62763.2024.10762809
8. Di Biase, G., Blum, H., Siegwart, R., Cadena, C.: Pixel-wise anomaly detection in complex driving scenes. In: CVPR, pp. 16913–16922 (2021). https://doi.org/10.1109/CVPR46437.2021.01664
9. Gu, A., Dao, T.: Mamba: linear-time sequence modeling with selective state spaces. arXiv preprint arXiv:2312.00752 (2023)
10. He, H., et al.: MambaAD: exploring state space models for multi-class unsupervised anomaly detection. In: Globerson, A., et al. (eds.) NeurIPS, vol. 37, pp. 71162–71187. Curran Associates, Inc. (2024)
11. Li, K., et al.: VideoMamba: state space model for efficient video understanding (2024)
12. Liang, D., et al.: PointMamba: a simple state space model for point cloud analysis. In: NeurIPS (2024)
13. Liu, J., et al.: Point Mamba: a novel point cloud backbone based on state space model with octree-based ordering strategy (2024)
14. Lu, D., Xu, L., Zhou, J., Gao, K., Gong, Z., Zhang, D.: 3D-UMamba: 3D U-Net with state space model for semantic segmentation of multi-source LiDAR point clouds. Int. J. Appl. Earth Obs. Geoinf. **136**, 104401 (2025). https://doi.org/10.1016/j.jag.2025.104401
15. Melekhov, I., Umashankar, A., Kim, H.J., Serkov, V., Argyle, D.: ECLAIR: a high-fidelity aerial LiDAR dataset for semantic segmentation. In: CVPR (2024)
16. Nunes, I., Pereira, M.B., Oliveira, H., dos Santos, J.A., Poggi, M.: Conditional reconstruction for open-set semantic segmentation. In: ICIP, pp. 946–950 (2022). https://doi.org/10.1109/ICIP46576.2022.9897407
17. Qu, S., Tao, X., Qu, Z., Gong, X., Zhang, Z., Prasad, M.: ALMRR: anomaly localization mamba on industrial textured surface with feature reconstruction and refinement (2024)
18. Zeng, K., et al.: MambaMOS: LiDAR-based 3D moving object segmentation with motion-aware state space model (2024)
19. Zhou, Q., et al.: 3DMambaIPF: a state space model for iterative point cloud filtering via differentiable rendering (2025)
20. Zhu, L., Liao, B., Zhang, Q., Wang, X., Liu, W., Wang, X.: Vision Mamba: efficient visual representation learning with bidirectional state space model (2024)
21. Zhu, X., et al.: Cylindrical and asymmetrical 3D convolution networks for LiDAR segmentation. In: CVPR, June 2021, pp. 9939–9948 (2021)

Rep2Face: Synthetic Face Generation with Identity Representation Sampling

Chao Jin[1,2], Kerui Li[1,2], Jin Liu[1,3], Junxian Duan[1,2], and Huaibo Huang[1,2](✉)

[1] MAIS & NLPR, Institute of Automation, Chinese Academy of Sciences, Beijing, China
{jinchao2024,likerui2024}@ia.ac.cn,
{junxian.duan,huaibo.huang}@cripac.ia.ac.cn

[2] School of Artificial Intelligence, University of Chinese Academy of Sciences, Beijing, China

[3] School of Information Science and Technology, ShanghaiTech University, Shanghai, China
liujin2@shanghaitech.edu.cn

Abstract. In light of escalating legal, privacy and ethical concerns surrounding real-world face datasets, synthesizing face datasets have emerged as a crucial alternative for training face recognition model. However, generating synthetic datasets presents significant challenges: it must capture essential characteristics and mitigate inherent issues present in real datasets. Existing methods predominantly focus on identity-driven image generation while overlooking the critical role of synthetic identities. As anchors, their quality directly determines the upper bound of synthetic datasets. Inspired by this, we propose a novel approach for synthetic face generation with identity representation sampling (Rep2Face). We train Identity Representation Diffusion Model (IRDM) to model the distribution of real identity representations and designs an identity sampling strategy to ensure intra-class variation, inter-class separability and racial balance in synthetic identity representations. Starting from the synthetic identities, Rep2Face generates face datasets that not only approximate real-world face distributions but also preserve the desired properties of these synthetic identities. Experimental results demonstrate that Rep2Face achieves promising performance on benchmark datasets and race-balanced datasets, and even achieves higher accuracy than real datasets of the same scale on extreme-condition datasets. The code is available at https://github.com/jinchao2001/Rep2Face.

Keywords: Face Synthesis · Face Recognition · Diffusion Model

1 Introduction

The rapid development and widespread application of face recognition [5,31,51] have been greatly facilitated by the release of large-scale face datasets. However, many of these datasets, primarily collected from the internet, raise significant

C. Wallraven et al. (Eds.): ACPR 2025, LNCS 16174, pp. 16–32, 2026.
https://doi.org/10.1007/978-981-95-4395-3_2

concerns about legality, privacy and ethics. As laws and regulations around privacy and data protection, numerous datasets [2,12,21] have been withdrawn, presenting challenges for future research. At the same time, advancements in generative models have made it feasible for synthetic datasets to replace real datasets. Previously, synthetic datasets are mainly used to assist in model generalization when real datasets are limited [17,23,49] or exhibited biases [34,50]. With the emergence of GANs and Diffusion models, however, synthetic datasets have seen significant improvements in quality, leading to growing optimism about their potential in privacy-sensitive areas, such as face recognition.

Thus, what defines a good training dataset for face recognition? Building on DCFace [32], we further identify that an ideal synthetic dataset should satisfy the three characteristics: 1) sufficient intra-class variation; 2) strong inter-class separability; and 3) the ability to overcome issues present in real datasets, such as racial bias and label noise. Therefore, synthetic face datasets can be defined as the problem of optimizing the above characteristics simultaneously.

Previous works [8,32,33,40,42,48,55] have made preliminary explorations in these three areas. Their workflow consists of two steps: face identity sampling and identity-driven generation. Early GAN-based methods [6,7,9,10,33,42] sample identities through three techniques: 1) random noise sampling, 2) perturbing the identities of real face images, and 3) generating synthetic face images using a pre-trained model and mixing the extracted identities. These identities are then used as conditional inputs to generate images. Later diffusion-based methods [8,32] follow the similar sampling paradigms but replace GANs with controllable latent diffusion models, improving the performance of synthetic datasets. However, these methods focus on the identity-driven generation while overlooking the crucial role of synthetic identities as synthetic dataset anchor. Their quality directly determines the upper bound of synthetic datasets. Recently, Arc2Face [40] and Vec2Face [55] successively achieve better performance by employing PCA-based identity sampling. This not only supports our perspective but also highlights the need for further research on identity sampling paradigms.

Specifically, previous identity sampling paradigms typically sample from real identity representations or random noise, followed by post-processing to obtain synthetic identities. This struggles to control the overall distribution of synthetic identities and suffers from inefficiency and reliance on real datasets. Moreover, while mitigating racial bias is a key advantage of synthetic datasets, apart from DCFace [32], racial balance control remains rarely explored.

To address this, we introduce Rep2Face, a method for generating synthetic face images with real identity variations. Rep2Face is composed of two components: Identity Representation Diffusion Model (IRDM) and Face Image Generation Model. For modeling real identity representations, we propose a new identity sampling paradigm. This involves training IRDM on identity representations extracted from real face dataset. The trained IRDM can iteratively samples synthetic identity representations from noise. Then face image generation model uses a fine-tuned CLIP encoder to embed both synthetic identity representation and fixed text into the cross-attention layers of U-Net, adaptively guiding face image

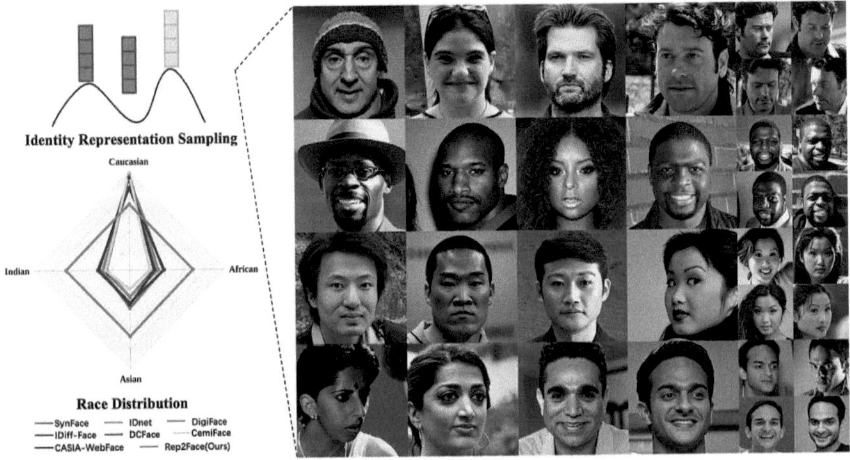

Fig. 1. The proposed **Rep2Face** performs identity representation sampling to generate high-quality face images. From top to bottom: Caucasian, African, Asian and Indian. When compared to other synthetic datasets, only ours achieves true racial balance.

generation. Additionally, to maximize the alignment of IRDM sampling with the ideal synthetic dataset standards, we design a simple yet effective sampling strategy. By incorporating loss constraints during the representation generation process, we achieve intra-class variation, inter-class separability and racial balance in the synthetic identity representations, without the need for additional training. This provides a high-quality anchor for the generative model.

We demonstrate the superior performance of Rep2Face in training face recognition model with synthetic dataset. Under the unified setting, unbiased synthetic dataset RepFace10K achieves promising performance on five benchmark datasets and a race-balanced dataset, with significant improvements on CFP-FP [45] and CPLFW [60]. On extreme-condition datasets, our method achieves the SOTA performance, even surpassing the same-scale real dataset comprehensively, demonstrating the robustness of Rep2Face in handling complex real-world scenarios. Additionally, we provide a comprehensive evaluation of existing synthetic datasets based on the characteristics of the ideal synthetic dataset. The experiments show that RepFace10K exhibits better intra-class variation and inter-class separability, making it more similar to real datasets while overcoming racial bias present in real-world data (Fig. 1).

The main contributions are summarized as follows:

- We propose Rep2Face, a framework that samples identity representations to generate synthetic face datasets with realistic identity variations.
- We train the Identity Representation Diffusion Model (IRDM) to model the distribution of real identity representations and design a sampling strategy that achieves intra-class variation, inter-class separability and racial balance without additional training.

- Our method provides RepFace10K, a 512×512 resolution racially balanced synthetic dataset for face recognition. It aligns more closely with the characteristics of the ideal synthetic dataset, achieving the promising performance on benchmark datasets and the SOTA performance on race-balanced datasets and extreme-condition datasets.

2 Related Work

2.1 Generative Models for Human Face

Recent advances in generative models [20,22,43] have significantly improved face image generation. GANs [11,27–30] are widely used for processing and editing faces by learning separable latent representations. To enhance control over face generation and 3D consistency, some methods [3,54] utilize 3D datasets like 3DMM [3] to disentangle identity from other factors. However, these approaches often require high resources and lack variability.

Diffusion models [16,39,44] have excelled in high-quality image generation, enabling tasks like text-to-image generation and inpainting [4,43]. However, when trained unsupervised, they may inherit biases, including racial biases in face image generation. Our approach addresses this by leveraging diffusion models to generate unbiased synthetic datasets through controlled identity sampling.

2.2 Synthetic Datasets for Face Recognition

As privacy and ethical concerns surrounding real face datasets become increasingly important [2,12,21], the advantages of synthetic datasets are becoming more evident. However, synthetic datasets are still limited by their quality, which cannot yet match that of real datasets. As a result, they are not widely adopted as the sole training data but are typically combined with real datasets [1,37,42].

Various generative methods [6,10,42] use pre-trained GANs like DiscoFace-GAN [15] to generate synthetic face datasets for privacy concerns. However, these models lack identity awareness, limiting performance. To address this, IDNet [33] introduces identity loss for better separability and DigiFace-1M [1] enhances intra-class diversity with 3D rendering and augmentation, though both are computationally expensive. Recently, IDiff-Face [8] uses latent diffusion models [43] for identity control, but the lack of identity awareness in VQGAN [18] reduces its sensitivity to identity. Arc2Face [40] further improves on this by fine-tuning diffusion model and leveraging ControlNet [58] to selectively control identity variations. Vec2face [55] adopts an encoder-decoder architecture that enables facial attribute control and rapid face image synthesis using only identity vectors. In contrast to previous methods that focus primarily on enhancing the image generation process, we introduce a novel controllable identity sampling paradigm. This new approach efficiently samples high-quality identity representations wtih intra-class variation, inter-class separability and racial balance.

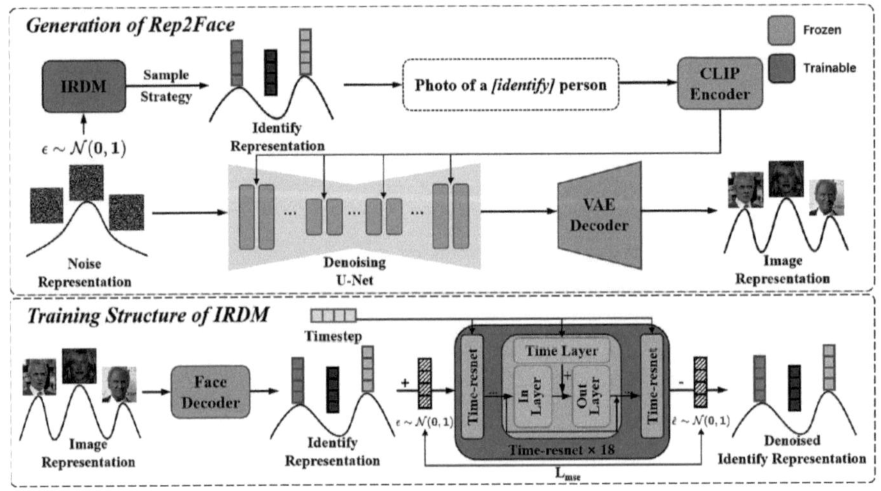

Fig. 2. The overall pipeline of the proposed Rep2Face. The Rep2Face framework consists of two stages (above). *Identity Representation Generation Stage*: IRDM employs a unique sampling strategy to generate identity representations starting from noise. *Face Image Generation Stage*: Image generator synthesizes face images conditioned on the identity representations. The training structure of IRDM (below). At each time step, gaussian noise is added to real identity representations, and the model then minimizes the noise prediction error and performs denoising.

3 Method

We propose Rep2Face, a method for generating synthetic face images with realistic identity variations. To capture the distribution of real identity representations, we train an Identity Representation Diffusion Model (IRDM) on real face datasets. The image generator then produces high-fidelity face images conditioned on identity representations sampled from IRDM. Additionally, we design a simple yet effective sampling strategy to ensure intra-class variation, inter-class separability and racial balance in the synthetic identity representations.

3.1 Preliminary

Face Identity Representation. In recent years, pre-trained face recognition networks have been widely used to assist with the optimization or generation tasks related to face recognition, typically by using features from multiple layers of the network to evaluate face identity similarity.

Specifically, given an aligned and cropped face image $X \in \mathbb{R}^{H \times W \times C}$, identity representation $w \in \mathbb{R}^d$ is defined as the output of the pre-trained face recognition model ϕ:

$$\mathbf{w} = \phi(x). \tag{1}$$

Diffusion Models. Diffusion models (DM) [22,46] synthesize images from random noise via an iterative denoising process. During training, an initial image x_0 undergoes progressive corruption by Gaussian noise at different time steps t, controlled by a predefined diffusion schedule α_t. Then a denoising U-Net ϵ_θ is trained to predict the noise $\epsilon \sim \mathcal{N}(\mathbf{0}, \mathbf{I})$ by minimizing the MSE error:

$$\mathcal{L}_{\text{DM}} = \mathbb{E}_{x_0,t,\epsilon}\left[||\epsilon - \epsilon_\theta(\sqrt{\bar{\alpha}_t}x_0 + \sqrt{1-\bar{\alpha}_t}\epsilon, t)||_2^2\right]. \tag{2}$$

Latent Diffusion Models (LDM) [43] represent a prominent variation within the diffusion modeling framework. LDMs operate by training diffusion model in the latent space of a pre-trained autoencoder [19], where the encoder maps images to latent codes, and the decoder reconstructs them. In particular, Stable Diffusion (SD) is frequently used as a strong image prior in downstream tasks.

3.2 Rep2Face

As shown in Fig. 2, Rep2Face generation paradigm consists of two primary stages: identity representation generation and face image generation. To enhance the modeling of real identity representations, we introduce a novel identity sampling paradigm. This involves training the Identity Representation Diffusion Model (IRDM) on real face dataset. The trained IRDM takes Gaussian noises as input and can iteratively sample synthetic identity representations in an unconditional manner. The sampled identity representations are projected, along with fixed text, embedded into the diffusion process via a cross-attention layer to guide the generation of face images. Additionally, by applying identity sampling strategy, we introduce an energy constraints during the identity representation sampling process. This enables IRDM to generate high-quality identity representations with intra-class variation, inter-class separability and racial balance, thus improving the quality of identity information in the final synthetic face dataset.

Identity Representation Generation. To model real identity representations, we first transform face images distribution into identity representations distribution. As described in Sect. 3.1, we use a pre-trained face recognition model [40] to extract the final layer output features of face image as the identity representation. This recognition model directly optimizes for a geodesic distance margin, yielding identity representations $w \in \mathbb{R}^d$. The resulting identity representation distribution has two key characteristics: it is low-dimensional, allowing for efficient modeling by the representation diffusion model, and it is rich in identity information, facilitating distinction among different faces. These characteristics are essential for ensuring diversity in the identities within the synthetic dataset.

Diffusion models are capable of modeling the representation space to guide image generation [36]. Thus, for the low-dimensional, rich-information identity representations, we can train an Identity Representation Diffusion Model (IRDM) to learn the distribution of these representations and unconditionally generate new ones. IRDM follows the training paradigm of DDPM [22]. During training, the identity representation w_0 extracted by face recognition model is corrupted by adding Gaussian noise $\epsilon \sim \mathcal{N}(\mathbf{0}, \mathbf{1})$ according to a predefined diffusion schedule that controls noise addition level, resulting in the distorted form $w_t = \sqrt{\bar{\alpha}_t} w_0 + \sqrt{1 - \bar{\alpha}_t} \epsilon$. The denoised identity representation $\hat{w_0}$ is obtained using $\hat{w_0} = \frac{w_t - \sqrt{1-\bar{\alpha}_t}\hat{\epsilon}}{\sqrt{\bar{\alpha}_t}}$, with $\hat{\epsilon}$ being the noise predicted by $\epsilon_\theta(w_t, t)$. Furthermore, ϵ_θ represents the denoising network of IRDM, trained to estimate the noise ϵ added to w_t, utilizing the MSE loss:

$$\mathcal{L}_{\text{IRDM}} = \mathbb{E}_{w_0,t,\epsilon} \left[||\epsilon - \epsilon_\theta(w_t, t)||_2^2 \right] . \tag{3}$$

Following the sampling strategy of DDIM [47], IRDM can generate various different identity representations from Gaussian noise. This ensures inter-class separability in the synthetic identity representations, laying the foundation for the subsequent face image generation process.

Face Image Generation. To fully leverage the strong priors in Stable Diffusion (SD), we use the pre-trained weights to enable identity-driven image generation. Here, we use the face image generation model based on stable-diffusion-v1-5, released by Papantoniou [40]. Following the SD paradigm, we project the identity representation into the text embedding space of the original model via the text encoder, creating a personalized identity text prompt, "Photo of [identity] person." This prompt is then mapped into the CLIP latent space by the fine-tuned CLIP encoder, guiding identity-specific face image generation.

Note that we do not follow IP-Adapter-FaceID [56] that generate images with fixed text prompts while directly using identity representations as additional conditions. This setup weakens identity fidelity due to the dominant influence of fixed text. Instead, we map identity representations to the text space and drive generation through a fine-tuned CLIP encoder, which reduces the impact of text embeddings and enhances identity fidelity of identity-driven generation [40].

3.3 Identity Sampling Strategy

The IRDM can generate synthetic identity representations with genuine variations in an unconditional manner, while ensuring that the distribution of synthetic identity representations closely matches the real identity distribution. However, this approach has some limitations: it leads to synthetic identity representations inheriting the long-tail data distribution and demographic biases present in real datasets, and it fails to effectively constrain the separability of identities in the synthetic identity representations. To address these issues and introduce flexible loss constraints, we propose an sampling strategy based on energy function guidance [16,57], named as Self-identity Constraint Guidance.

This strategy applies mutual constraints to the identity representations being sampled, while previous identity representations sampled from the IRDM also serve as constraints for future samples, as illustrated in Fig. 3. Specifically, for single-step conditional sampling $p(w_t|y)$, where w_t is the identity representation at the current step of the denoising process, and y represents a constraint that

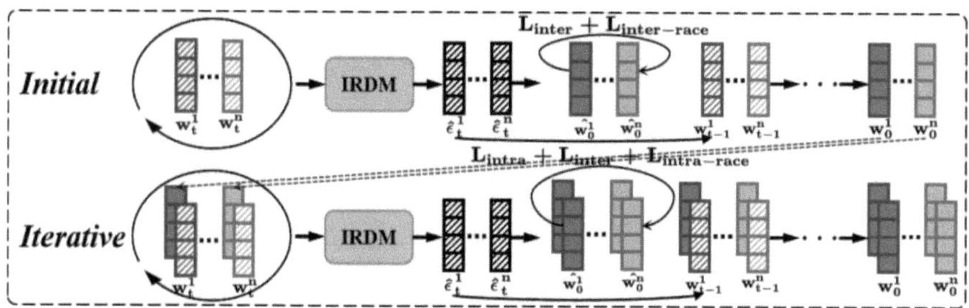

Fig. 3. The diagram of the identity sampling strategy. It consists of two stages. *Initial Stage*: n random noises are used as input $w_t^1 ... w_t^n$. Inter-class loss reduces cross-subject similarity and inter-race loss balances racial distribution, producing n distinct identities $w_0^1 ... w_0^n$. *Iterative Stage*: Identity representations are concatenated with random noises. Intra-class loss increases within-subject similarity, inter-class loss reduces cross-subject similarity and intra-race loss ensures shared racial attributes for same subject, resulting in multiple identities per subject.

the identity representation w_t must satisfy, we can rewrite the conditional score function using Bayesian formula $p(\mathbf{w}_t|\mathbf{y}) = \frac{p(\mathbf{y}|\mathbf{w}_t)p(\mathbf{w}_t)}{p(\mathbf{y})}$ as:

$$\nabla_{\mathbf{w}_t} \log p(\mathbf{w}_t|\mathbf{y}) = \nabla_{\mathbf{w}_t} \log p(\mathbf{w}_t) + \nabla_{\mathbf{w}_t} \log p(\mathbf{y}|\mathbf{w}_t), \tag{4}$$

where, the first term $\nabla_{\mathbf{w}_t} \log p(\mathbf{w}_t)$ corresponds to the trained unconditional noise estimator of IRDM $\epsilon_\theta(w_t, t)$, while the second term, $\nabla \mathbf{w}_t \log p(\mathbf{y}|\mathbf{w}_t)$, represents the conditional score term. Accurately modeling conditional score remains challenging. Following [16,57], we use an energy function to model $p(\mathbf{y}|\mathbf{w}_t)$:

$$p(\mathbf{y} \mid \mathbf{w}_t) = \frac{\exp\{-\lambda \mathcal{L}(\mathbf{y}, \mathbf{w}_t)\}}{Z}, \tag{5}$$

where, λ is the positive temperature coefficient, Z is a normalization constant and $\mathcal{L}(\mathbf{y}, \mathbf{w}_t)$ is an energy function that quantifies the relationship between $\mathbf{y}$ and $\mathbf{w}_t$. The more $\mathbf{w}_t$ satisfies the constraints of $\mathbf{y}$, the lower the energy value becomes. This allows us to use the gradient of the energy function to approximate the conditional score:

$$\nabla_{\mathbf{w}_t} \log p(\mathbf{y} \mid \mathbf{w}_t) \propto -\nabla_{\mathbf{w}_t} \mathcal{L}(\mathbf{y}, \mathbf{w}_t). \tag{6}$$

Notably, our Self-identity Constraint Guidance does not rely on an explicit constraint y. Instead, the constraint is derived from the identity representations of other samples within the same batch during the sampling process. The gradient of the self-identity constraint energy function for each identity representation is denoted as $\nabla_{\mathbf{w}_t^j} \mathcal{L}\left(\{\mathbf{w}_t^i\}_{i=1}^B, \mathbf{w}_t^j\right)$, where B is the current batch size of the sampled identity representations. In the following content, we will introduce how the specific Self-identity Constraint energy function is modeled.

Intra-class Variation Constraint. Intra-class variation includes both intra-class consistency (the similarity of identity representations for the same subject) and intra-class diversity (the diversity of multiple identity representations for the same subject). As analyzed by Kim [32], these two aspects are complementary, and when balanced, they enhance face recognition performance. The proposed IRDM works at the identity representation level for both training and inference, effectively ensuring both intra-class diversity and consistency. Specifically, we flexibly generate N identity representations $w \in \mathbb{R}^d$ per subject, ensuring intra-class diversity and utilize identity similarity constraints to control intra-class consistency. Let $d(w_i^s, w_j^s)$ denote the cosine similarity between the i-th and j-th identity representations of subject s. The intra-class constraint can be defined:

$$\mathcal{L}_{\text{intra}_j} = \begin{cases} 1 - \frac{1}{j-1}\sum_{i=1}^{j-1} d(w_i^s, w_j^s), j > 1 \\ 0, \text{otherwise.} \end{cases} \tag{7}$$

Inter-class Separability Constraint. Inter-class separability quantifies the distinctiveness among identity representations of different subjects, such that the similarity distance between identity representations of different subjects should be large. Previous synthetic face methods mainly discard identity representations with low inter-class separability through post-processing, which is inefficient and results in unusable identity representations. Therefore, we apply inter-class separability constraints during the IRDM generation process, ensuring strong separability of synthetic identity representations without requiring additional post-processing. Let $d(w_{s_i}, w_{s_j})$ represent the cosine similarity between the identity representations of subjects s_i and s_j. The inter-class constraint can be defined:

$$\mathcal{L}_{\text{inter}_j} = \begin{cases} \frac{1}{j-1}\sum_{i=1}^{j-1} d(w, w_{s_j}), j > 1 \\ 0, \text{otherwise.} \end{cases} \tag{8}$$

Racial Balance Constraint. Despite significant progress in data scale and diversity in real face datasets, they still suffer from racial bias, which synthetic face datasets should overcome. We first use the race classifier FairFace [26] to annotate real face dataset with racial labels. Then, using real identity representations and their racial labels, we train a simple race classifier β for identity representations. Finally, we apply racial constraints during IRDM generation process to maintain racial consistency within classes and achieve racial balance between classes. Let $\gamma_{balance} = \{p_i = 0.25 \mid i = 0, 1, 2, 3\}$ represent a balanced racial distribution. The racial constraint can be defined:

$$\mathcal{L}_{\text{race}} = \begin{cases} KL(\beta(w_{s_j}) || \gamma_{intra}), \text{intra-class} \\ KL(\gamma_{inter} || \gamma_{balance}), \text{inter-class} \end{cases} \tag{9}$$

where $\gamma_{intra} = \frac{1}{j-1}\sum_{i=1}^{j-1} \beta(w_{s_i})$ is the average racial distribution of the first $j-1$ identities generated by subject s and $\gamma_{inter} = \frac{1}{N}\sum_{i=1}^{N} \beta(w_{s_i})$ is the average racial distribution of the central identities of N subjects s.

Table 1. Synthetic Dataset Evaluation. Metrics for intra-class diversity, inter-class separability and racial balance are calculated on the synthetic datasets from previous methods and ours. The best result is in **bold**, and the second-best result is <u>underlined</u>.

Method	Evaluation Metrics								
	Intra-class Variation	Inter-class Separability				Racial Balance			
Name	ICV	EER ↓	FMR100 ↓	FMR1000 ↓	FDR ↑	Caucasian	African	Asian	Indian
CAISA-WebFace(Real)	0.5182	0.0565	0.0634	0.0708	7.0238	0.8665	0.0866	0.0304	0.0165
SynFace [42]	0.1833	0.3408	0.7844	0.8985	0.3976	0.9610	0.0010	0.0366	0.0014
IDnet [33]	0.3538	0.0727	0.1915	0.3911	3.3259	0.8712	0.0817	0.0301	0.0170
DigiFace [1]	0.5359	0.0350	0.0704	0.1835	6.4320	<u>0.6620</u>	<u>0.1769</u>	<u>0.1168</u>	<u>0.0443</u>
IDiff-Face [8]	0.2215	0.1200	0.3786	0.6383	2.5558	0.8077	0.0827	0.0837	0.0259
DCFace [32]	0.2845	0.0686	0.2006	0.4470	4.2253	0.8924	0.0456	0.0576	0.0044
CemiFace [48]	0.2501	0.0918	0.2846	0.5419	3.2924	0.8918	0.0443	0.0577	0.0062
Vec2Face [55]	0.4259	<u>0.0117</u>	<u>0.0135</u>	<u>0.0843</u>	<u>8.0975</u>	0.7671	0.0994	0.1014	0.0321
Rep2Face(Ours)	0.5521	**0.0071**	**0.0084**	**0.0172**	**10.3692**	**0.2500**	**0.2500**	**0.2500**	**0.2500**

Ultimately, the sampling strategy combines various constraints into a total sampling constraint energy that approximates the conditional score, thereby imposing constraints on the identity representation during the generation process. The total sampling constraint energy can be formulated as $\mathcal{L}_{\text{sampling}} = \mathcal{L}_{\text{intra}} + \mathcal{L}_{\text{inter}} + 0.5\mathcal{L}_{\text{race}}$, and the final conditional score function can be written:

$$\nabla_{\mathbf{w}_t} \log p(\mathbf{w}_t|\mathbf{y}) = \epsilon_\theta(w_t, t) - \nabla_{\mathbf{w}_t} \mathcal{L}_{\text{sampling}}. \tag{10}$$

Additionally, to impose stronger constraints, we differ from standard energy function guidance, which optimizes once per sampling step. In contrast, our approach applies multiple optimizations to the identity representation during each single-step sampling. See the Appendix for sampling details.

4 Experiments

4.1 Experimental Setup

Training Datasets. Training IRDM on larger-scale datasets allows it to learn a better distribution of identity representations. However, we train it solely on CASIA-WebFace [24] for a fair comparison with real datasets of the same scale.

Testing Datasets. To comprehensively evaluate the performance of the face recognition model, we conduct experiments on benchmark datasets, race-balanced datasets and extreme-condition datasets. Specifically, LFW [25] tests in natural scenarios, CFP-FP [45] and CPLFW [60] test pose variations, AgeDB [38] and CALFW [59] test age variations, RFW [52] tests racial balance, RMFD [53] tests extreme occlusions, Extended Yale B [35] tests extreme illumination, Oulu-CASIA [13] tests extreme facial expressions and MDF tests in makeup scenarios.

Implementation Details. IRDM is implemented with PyTorch and trained from scratch using 8 NVIDIA V100 GPUs. Specifically, we train it for 500 epochs with a batch size of 512 using AdamW optimizer with the learning rate of $1e^{-4}$. The face image generation model directly adopts pretrained weights from Arc2Face [40] and sampling steps are set to 50. For face recognition, we adopt the training scheme of [1,32,42] using IR-SE-50 [14] as backbone and AdaFace [31] as loss function. Face images are uniformly aligned to 112×112 resolution.

4.2 Synthetic Dataset Evaluation.

To assess the quality of the synthetic dataset, we measure three key metrics. We assume that ϕ is a pre-trained face recognition model, δ is a pre-trained race classifier, s is a subject, X^s is the set of synthetic face images for subject s and $d(\phi(X_i), \phi(X_j))$ is the cosine similarity between the identity representations of face images from two subjects.

Intra-class Variation. To ensure that face recognition model can identify subject under different visual variations (e.g., environment, pose, age) of the same subject, synthetic dataset should have authentic intra-class variation. This requires that synthetic images of the same subject strike a balance between intra-class consistency and diversity. To evaluate intra-class variation in synthetic dataset, we calculate the mean cosine similarity of identity representations for synthetic images within each subject, defined as follows:

$$\mathrm{ICV} = \frac{1}{S} \sum_{s=1}^{S} \frac{1}{N_s(N_s - 1)} \sum_{i=1}^{N_s} \sum_{j=i+1}^{N_s} d(\phi(X^{s_i}), \phi(X^{s_j})). \tag{11}$$

Inter-class Separability. To ensure face recognition model can distinguish subjects, synthetic dataset should exhibit strong inter-class separability, meaning that synthetic images of different subjects should be easily distinguishable. We use FMR100, FMR1000 and EER [8] to assess inter-class separability in synthetic datasets. Additionally, we report FDR [41] for a deeper analysis of the separability between genuine and impostor identities.

Racial Balance. In addition to intra-class variation and inter-class separability, synthetic dataset should also exhibit unbiased racial balance. To evaluate the racial diversity of synthetic dataset, we calculate the racial distribution of its subjects, defined as follows:

$$\mathrm{RB} = \frac{1}{S} \sum_{s=1}^{S} count(\mathrm{argmax}(\sum_{i=1}^{N_s} \delta(X^{s_i}))). \tag{12}$$

As shown in Table 1, in terms of intra-class variation, lower ICV weakens intra-class consistency, while higher ICV reduces diversity. The face recognition model performs optimally within an ideal threshold, benchmarked against real datasets. Compared to other methods, our approach achieves an ICV that closely aligns with real datasets, balancing consistency and diversity. For inter-class variation, even with race balance constraints, our method outperforms all others and real datasets, ensuring clear identity separation. In terms of racial balance, previous methods exhibit racial bias, with over 65% of the dataset consisting of Caucasian, whereas our method achieves a balanced distribution.

Table 2. Comparison with previous methods. Verification accuracy (%) of face recognition model trained on synthetic datasets on benchmark datasets and race-balanced datasets. The best accuracy is in **bold**, and the second-best accuracy is underlined.

Method Name	Dataset # Images	Verification Benchmarks							
		LFW ↑	Cross-Pose		Cross-Age		Avg ↑	Gap ↓	Balanced
			CFP-FP ↑	CPLFW ↑	AgeDB ↑	CALFW ↑			RFW ↑
CAISA-WebFace (Real)	0.49M	99.35	95.13	89.05	94.55	93.60	94.34	-	89.53
SynFace [42] (GAN)	0.5M	91.93	75.03	70.43	61.63	74.73	74.75	19.59	63.72
IDnet [33] (GAN)	0.5M	87.83	69.96	69.40	65.70	74.06	73.39	20.95	67.22
DigiFace [1] (3D)	0.5M	90.02	78.33	71.30	64.35	71.87	75.17	19.17	67.56
IDiff-Face [8] (DM)	0.5M	97.92	75.65	78.80	83.53	90.53	85.29	9.05	80.91
DCFace [32] (DM)	0.5M	98.32	81.67	82.25	89.70	91.40	88.67	5.67	82.37
CemiFace [48] (DM)	0.5M	98.50	85.26	84.22	88.47	91.30	89.55	4.79	83.50
Vec2Face [55] (GAN)	0.5M	<u>98.68</u>	<u>85.47</u>	<u>84.87</u>	**91.80**	**92.88**	<u>90.74</u>	<u>3.60</u>	<u>84.52</u>
Rep2Face (Ours, DM)	0.5M	**99.05**	**91.80**	**87.25**	<u>90.57</u>	<u>92.15</u>	**92.16**	**2.18**	**86.73**
DigiFace [1] (3D)	1.2M	92.32	81.11	73.97	67.93	75.23	78.11	16.23	69.52
DCFace [32] (DM)	1.2M	98.77	85.33	84.43	<u>91.15</u>	<u>92.47</u>	90.43	3.91	<u>85.64</u>
CemiFace [48] (DM)	1.2M	<u>98.92</u>	<u>88.11</u>	<u>86.00</u>	89.42	92.19	<u>90.93</u>	<u>3.41</u>	85.59
Rep2Face (Ours, DM)	1.2M	**99.23**	**93.78**	**89.12**	**91.98**	**93.90**	**93.60**	**0.74**	**88.95**

Table 3. More comparison with previous methods on extreme-condition datasets. The best accuracy is in **bold**, and the second-best accuracy is underlined.

Method Name	Dataset # Images	Verification Benchmarks ↑				
		RMFD	Extended Yale B	Oulu-CASIA	MDF	Avg
CASIA-WebFace (Real)	0.49M	59.50	64.30	68.03	95.44	71.82
DCFace [32]	0.5M	54.22	67.97	75.70	94.55	73.11
CemiFace [48]	0.5M	<u>57.77</u>	70.82	82.77	95.36	76.68
Vec2Face [55]	0.5M	56.78	<u>83.90</u>	<u>87.12</u>	<u>95.88</u>	<u>80.92</u>
Rep2Face (Ours)	0.5M	**63.10**	**86.92**	**89.08**	**96.03**	**83.78**

4.3 Comparison with SOTA Methods

We compare synthetic datasets with previous methods for training face recognition models using two dataset sizes: 0.5M to match CASIA-WebFace and 1.2M to assess the impact of increasing dataset size. Table 2 shows the verification accuracy across five benchmark datasets and one race-balanced dataset.

In the 0.5M setting, race-balanced synthetic dataset RepFace10k generated by our method performs only slightly lower than Vec2Face [55] on AgeDB and CALFW, while achieving the SOTA performance on all other benchmark datasets and average, further narrowing the gap between synthetic datasets and real datasets. On the race-balanced dataset RFW, RepFace10K also achieves the SOTA performance, demonstrating the advantages of racial balance. A similar trend is observed in the 1.2M setting. Despite its best performance on other benchmark datasets, RepFace10K performs slightly worse on AgeDB and CALFW, possibly due to two factors. First, benchmark datasets inherently exhibit racial bias, which can negatively impact the performance of unbiased synthetic datasets. The superior performance of RepFace10K on race-balanced dataset RFW supports this. Second, unlike other methods [40,48] trained on million-scale dataset WebFace42M, our IRDM is trained solely on CASIA-WebFace (0.5M). This limited training data may introduce distribution biases, which can affect the performance of synthetic datasets on cross-age datasets AgeDB and CALFW.

To further evaluate Rep2Face in complex real-world scenarios, we test face recognition models trained on synthetic datasets under extreme occlusion, illumination, facial expressions and makeup. As shown in Table 3, RepFace10K achieves the SOTA performance on all datasets, even surpassing the same-scale real dataset CASIA-WebFace. This demonstrates the robustness of its sampling strategy in challenging conditions, which constrains the overall distribution without precisely controlling specific attributes.

Table 4. Model Ablation. Verification accuracy (%) on benchmark datasets and race-balanced datasets for synthetic datasets generated by different sampling strategies. The best accuracy is in **bold**, and the second-best accuracy is underlined.

Training Dataset		Verification Benchmarks ↑						
Identity-Source	Sampling-Strategy	LFW	CFP-FP	CPLFW	AgeDB	CALFW	Avg	RFW
CASIA-WebFace	-	98.97	87.13	83.52	**91.45**	91.68	90.55	84.35
IDRM (Ours)	-	98.55	89.11	85.82	86.60	88.87	89.79	82.69
	Intra	98.82	90.57	86.50	88.55	90.19	90.93	83.61
	Intra+Inter	**99.10**	**91.81**	**87.68**	90.62	**92.24**	**92.29**	85.92
	Intra+Inter+Racial	99.05	91.80	87.25	90.57	92.15	92.16	**86.73**

4.4 Ablation Study

To illustrate the impact of the components proposed in Rep2Face, we conduct ablations on 1) IRDM and 2) identity sampling strategy. The scale of ablation samples generated is comparable to that of real dataset CASIA-WebFace. We show the performance on the benchmark datasets and race-balanced datasets as the evaluation metric.

IRDM. We use real identity representations from CASIA-WebFace and synthetic ones from IRDM to generate synthetic datasets through the same image generator. As shown in Table 4, face recognition model trained on unconditional IRDM samples performs only 0.76% worse on five benchmark datasets compared to real data. This demonstrates that IRDM has effectively learned the distribution of real identity representations, enabling the generation of high-quality and large-scale synthetic identity representations.

Identity Sampling Strategy. We start with unconditional sampling and progressively add constraints for intra-class variation, inter-class separability and racial balance. The synthetic identity representations are used to generate synthetic datasets through the same image generator. As shown in Table 4, adding intra-class and inter-class constraints progressively improves performance on all datasets, highlighting their effectiveness. However, performance on benchmark datasets slightly decreases due to biases in benchmark datasets may limit performance of unbiased synthetic datasets, as evidenced by the fact that the unbiased synthetic dataset performs best on race-balanced dataset RFW.

Furthermore, the workflow of synthetic dataset consists of face identity sampling and identity-driven generation. Theoretically, synthetic dataset generated by Arc2Face using real identity representations should perform close to the upper bound of Arc2Face [40]. However, synthetic datasets generated by it using synthetic identity representations from Rep2Face achieve even better performance, demonstrating the effectiveness of IRDM and identity sampling strategy.

5 Conclusion

This paper introduces a novel approach to generating synthetic datasets for face recognition, capable of efficiently producing large-scale and high-quality identity representations and face images. Rep2Face employs lightweight diffusion model to capture the distribution of real identity representations and utilizes identity sampling strategy to guide the generation process, introducing a novel identity sampling paradigm. Our method provides RepFace10K, a 512×512 resolution race-balanced synthetic dataset for face recognition. Our experiments also demonstrate that RepFace10K exhibits excellent intra-class variation, inter-class separability and racial balance, achieving superior performance across benchmark datasets, race-balanced datasets and extreme-condition datasets. In future work, we aim to explore more generalizable identity modeling and investigate alternative generation architectures for more challenging face recognition tasks.

Acknowledgements. This work was supported by the National Natural Science Foundation of China (Grant No. 62576342 and No. 62506362), Beijing Natural ScienceFoundation (4252054), Youth Innovation PromotionAssociation CAS (Grant No. 2022132) and Beijing NovaProgram (20230484276).

References

1. Bae, G., et al: DigiFace-1M: 1 million digital face images for face recognition. In: WACV (2023)
2. Bansal, A., et al: UMDFaces: an annotated face dataset for training deep networks. In: IJCB (2017)
3. Blanz, V., et al: A morphable model for the synthesis of 3D faces (2023)
4. Blattmann, A., et al: Retrieval-augmented diffusion models. In: NeurIPS (2022)
5. Boutros, F., et al: Elasticface: elastic margin loss for deep face recognition. In: CVPR (2022)
6. Boutros, F., et al: SFace: privacy-friendly and accurate face recognition using synthetic data. In: IJCB (2022)
7. Boutros, F., et al: ExFaceGAN: exploring identity directions in GAN's learned latent space for synthetic identity generation. In: IJCB (2023)
8. Boutros, F., et al: IDiff-Face: synthetic-based face recognition through fizzy identity-conditioned diffusion model. In: ICCV (2023)
9. Boutros, F., et al: Unsupervised face recognition using unlabeled synthetic data. In: FG (2023)
10. Boutros, F., et al: SFace2: synthetic-based face recognition with w-space identity-driven sampling. In: T-BIOM (2024)
11. Brock, A.: Large scale GAN training for high fidelity natural image synthesis. In: ICLR (2018)
12. Cao, Q., et al: VGGFace2: a dataset for recognising faces across pose and age. In: FG (2018)
13. Chen, J., et al: Learning mappings for face synthesis from near infrared to visual light images. In: CVPR (2009)
14. Deng, J., et al: ArcFace: additive angular margin loss for deep face recognition. In: CVPR (2019)
15. Deng, Y., et al: Disentangled and controllable face image generation via 3D imitative-contrastive learning. In: CVPR (2020)
16. Dhariwal, P., et al: Diffusion models beat GANs on image synthesis. In: NeurIPS (2021)
17. Engelsma, J.J., et al.: PrintsGAN: synthetic fingerprint generator. In: TPAMI (2022)
18. Esser, P., et al: Taming transformers for high-resolution image synthesis. In: CVPR (2021)
19. Esser, P., et al: Taming transformers for high-resolution image synthesis. In: CVPR (2021)
20. Goodfellow, I., et al: Generative adversarial nets. In: NeurIPS (2014)
21. Guo, Y., et al.: MS-Celeb-1M: a dataset and benchmark for large-scale face recognition. In: ECCV (2016)
22. Ho, J., et al: Denoising diffusion probabilistic models. In: NeurIPS (2020)
23. Hu, Y.T., et al.: SAIL-VOS 3D: a synthetic dataset and baselines for object detection and 3D mesh reconstruction from video data. In: CVPR (2021)

24. Huang, G., et al: Learning to align from scratch. In: NeurIPS (2012)
25. Huang, G.B., et al.: Labeled faces in the wild: a database for studying face recognition in unconstrained environments. In: FIR (2008)
26. Karkkainen, K., et al.: FairFace: face attribute dataset for balanced race, gender, and age for bias measurement and mitigation. In: WACV (2021)
27. Karras, T.: Progressive growing of GANs for improved quality, stability, and variation. In: NeurIPS (2017)
28. Karras, T., et al: A style-based generator architecture for generative adversarial networks. In: CVPR (2019)
29. Karras, T., et al: Analyzing and improving the image quality of StyleGAN. In: CVPR (2020)
30. Karras, T., et al.: Alias-free generative adversarial networks. In: NeurIPS (2021)
31. Kim, M., et al.: AdaFace: quality adaptive margin for face recognition. In: CVPR (2022)
32. Kim, M., et al.: DCFace: synthetic face generation with dual condition diffusion model. In: CVPR (2023)
33. Kolf, J.N., et al: Identity-driven three-player generative adversarial network for synthetic-based face recognition. In: CVPR (2023)
34. Kupas, D., et al.: Solving the problem of imbalanced dataset with synthetic image generation for cell classification using deep learning. In: EMBC (2021)
35. Lee, K.C., et al.: Acquiring linear subspaces for face recognition under variable lighting. In: TPAMI (2005)
36. Li, T., et al.: Return of unconditional generation: a self-supervised representation generation method. In: NeurIPS (2024)
37. Liu, F., et al: Controllable and guided face synthesis for unconstrained face recognition. In: ECCV (2022)
38. Moschoglou, S., et al.: AgeDB: the first manually collected, in-the-wild age database. In: CVPR (2017)
39. Nichol, A.Q., et al: Improved denoising diffusion probabilistic models. In: ICML (2021)
40. Papantoniou, F.P., et al.: Arc2Face: a foundation model of human faces. In: ECCV (2024)
41. Poh, N., et al: A study of the effects of score normalisation prior to fusion in biometric authentication tasks (2004)
42. Qiu, H., et al.: SynFace: face recognition with synthetic data. In: ICCV (2021)
43. Rombach, R., et al.: High-resolution image synthesis with latent diffusion models. In: CVPR (2022)
44. Saharia, C., et al.: Photorealistic text-to-image diffusion models with deep language understanding. In: NeurIPS (2022)
45. Sengupta, S., et al.: Frontal to profile face verification in the wild. In: WACV (2016)
46. Sohl-Dickstein, J., et al.: Deep unsupervised learning using nonequilibrium thermodynamics. In: ICML (2015)
47. Song, J., et al.: Denoising diffusion implicit models. In: ICLR (2021)
48. Sun, Z., et al.: CemiFace: center-based semi-hard synthetic face generation for face recognition. In: NeurIPS (2024)
49. Tremblay, J., et al.: Training deep networks with synthetic data: bridging the reality gap by domain randomization. In: CVPR (2018)
50. Van Breugel, B., et al.: DECAF: generating fair synthetic data using causally-aware generative networks. In: NeurIPS (2021)
51. Wang, H., et al.: CosFace: large margin cosine loss for deep face recognition. In: CVPR (2018)

52. Wang, M., et al: Racial faces in the wild: reducing racial bias by information maximization adaptation network. In: ICCV (2019)
53. Wang, Z., et al: Masked face recognition dataset and application. In: T-BIOM (2023)
54. Wood, E., et al.: Fake it till you make it: face analysis in the wild using synthetic data alone. In: ICCV (2021)
55. Wu, H., et al: Vec2Face: scaling face dataset generation with loosely constrained vectors. In: ICLR (2025)
56. Ye, H., et al.: IP-adapter: text compatible image prompt adapter for text-to-image diffusion models (2023)
57. Yu, J., et al.: Freedom: training-free energy-guided conditional diffusion model. In: ICCV (2023)
58. Zhang, L., et al.: Adding conditional control to text-to-image diffusion models. In: ICCV (2023)
59. Zheng, T., et al.: Cross-age LFW: a database for studying cross-age face recognition in unconstrained environments (2017)
60. Zheng, T., et al.: Cross-pose LFW: a database for studying cross-pose face recognition in unconstrained environments. In: CVPR (2017)

Near Real Time Explainable Detection of Small Objects in Remote Sensing

Marvin Burges(✉) and Robert Sablatnig

TU Wien, 1040 Vienna, Austria
{mburges,sab}@cvl.tuwien.ac.at
https://cvl.tuwien.ac.at

Abstract. Object detectors used in safety critical or interactive settings should make their decisions understandable. We present AttentionCAM++ (AC++), a lightweight two stage post hoc explainer for DEtection TRansformer (DETR) based detectors such as Real-Time DEtection TRansformer (RTDETR) and RoboFlow DEtection TRansformer (RFDETR). Stage one instruments the Multi-Scale Deformable Attention (MSDA) layers in the decoder with forward callbacks to record sampling locations and attention weights, which are aggregated into class evidence maps. Stage two computes integrated gradients Integrated Gradients (IG) with respect to the decoder box deltas to produce a box attribution map that explains the predicted extent. We evaluate on COCO and on four remote sensing benchmarks, CHAI, DIOR, DOTAv2 and SARDET-100K, following the Object Detection Explainable AI Evaluation Benchmark (ODExAI) protocol. We report localization, PointingGame (PG), Energy-based Pointing-Game (EBPG), faithfulness through Insertion and Deletion, as well as complexity, sparsity and runtime. AC++ delivers near real time class evidence in our setup, while the optional box attribution adds modest latency, and the method requires no changes to detector weights. Code will be released at https://github.com/mburges-cvl/ACPR-ACplusplus

Keywords: Object Detection · Explainable AI · Small Objects

1 Introduction

Object detection models continue to advance with modern deep learning methods [15,17,21,26,29]. In safety critical or user facing applications such as autonomous drones or surveillance, transparent and interpretable results are essential for user trust and for compliance with regulation, including the GDPR [7] and the EU AI Act [18]. This paper evaluates explainable object detection and studies how eXplainable AI (XAI) can be integrated into interactive or active learning pipelines, where human annotators monitor potential

This work was supported by the Austrian Research Promotion Agency (FFG) grant 880883 and the ESA Network of Resources Initiative.

C. Wallraven et al. (Eds.): ACPR 2025, LNCS 16174, pp. 33–47, 2026.
https://doi.org/10.1007/978-981-95-4395-3_3

overfitting and bias during annotation. Because rapid feedback is required, we focus on real time detectors such as RTDETR [30] and RFDETR [23].

Explanations for detection are more demanding than for image classification since a detector must justify what it predicts and where [5]. Detectors usually return many bounding boxes and often rely on Non-Maximum Suppression (NMS), which is not differentiable and limits many gradient based XAI techniques. As a result, most off the shelf methods require adaptation before they are suitable for detection tasks. Recent transformer based real time detectors ease these constraints. RTDETR shows that transformer detectors can reach You Only Look Once (YOLO) level speed without NMS [30], and RFDETR further improves accuracy [23]. Their combination of strong accuracy and low latency provides a solid foundation for interactive and explainable workflows.

Our contributions are:

1. **AttentionCAM++:** We combine class level attention attribution with integrated gradients on bounding boxes to produce sharper and query specific explanations, with particular benefits for small objects. No changes to the detector is required.
2. **Comprehensive evaluation:** Using RTDETR(v2) and RFDETR, we evaluate on COCO [13], CHAI [2], DIOR [11], DOTAv2 [27], and SarDET 100K [12]. Under the ODExAI framework [15], our method improves interpretability metrics while maintaining practical speed for interactive use.

2 Related Work

We review XAI for object detection along two directions. Post hoc methods analyze a frozen detector and return saliency or attribution maps. Intrinsic approaches build explanations into the architecture so that detections come with human readable evidence. We then summarize open challenges for remote sensing where images are large, object footprints are small, and scenes can be dense (e.g. urban) or sparse (e.g. rural).

2.1 Post Hoc Saliency and Attribution

Most vision XAI methods produce heat maps that indicate which pixels or regions support a given output. For object detection the literature divides into black box perturbation and white box feature or gradient attribution. A third line exploits attention in transformer detectors.

Region Perturbation (Black Box). These methods treat the detector as an oracle and probe it with masked versions of the input. Randomized Input Sampling for Explanation (RISE) [19] samples random binary masks and regresses an importance map from score variations. Detector Randomized Input Sampling for Explanation (DRISE) [20] adapts this idea to detection by conditioning on a chosen box. Local Interpretable Model-Agnostic Explanations (LIME) [22] explains decisions with sparse linear models over superpixels and has been used for YOLO through Surrogate Object Detection Explainer (SODEx) [24]. Hierarchical masking in Black-box Object Detection Explanation by Masking (BODEM) [14] refines coarse regions with fine masks and reports stronger explanation scores than DRISE and LIME. These approaches are model agnostic and often faithful, yet they require many queries per image and produce noisy or diffuse maps in cluttered scenes.

Feature and Gradient Attribution (White Box). Here saliency follows from internal activations or gradients with respect to a selected output. Grad-Class Attribution Maps (CAM) [25] weights a convolutional feature map by class specific gradients and projects the result to pixels. GradCAM++ [4] adjusts the weighting to favor positive evidence. ODAM [29] tunes the procedure for detection heads but still depends on the chosen layer. Gaussian Class Activation Mapping Explainer (GCAME) [16] adds Gaussian smoothing that sharpens localization yet can harm faithfulness [15]. Backpropagation rules such as Layer-wise Relevance Propagation (LRP) and DeepLIFT must be adapted such that they can handle multiple outputs or NMS. While set prediction with DETR removes NMS hurdle, mutliple outputs are an open challenge [3].

Attention Based Attribution for Transformers. Attention rollout aggregates attention weights across heads and layers to trace class evidence through the model [10]. For detection this yields query specific maps that reflect where a selected query attends in the image. In models with multi scale deformable attention the recorded sampling locations and their normalized weights provide a direct handle on query to pixel interactions. Such attention driven maps are fast and sharply localized, yet they capture classification evidence better than geometric justification and often require a second signal to explain box extent. Recent benchmarks confirm that no single method satisfies all requirements across faithfulness, localization, stability, and cost [15]. Perturbation methods tend to be faithful but also very slow. While gradient and attention based methods are faster and can have local reception field, but therefore can miss context or geometry and thus are less faithful.

2.2 Intrinsically Interpretable Detectors

Intrinsic designs embed human interpretable units into the detector. Prototype networks attach visual prototypes to Region of Interest (RoI) features so that region classification arises from similarity to a small set of learned patches [5]. The model can then justify a class by showing the most influential prototypes, for example a tire or a headlight for the class car, while keeping Mean Average Precision (mAP) close to the baseline on KITTI. Other systems add concept or attribute branches that predict factors like shape or color together with boxes and classes [8,28]. These approaches provide direct explanations but often restrict the design space, may lag in accuracy or speed compared to state of the art detectors, and require retraining.

2.3 Challenges in Remote Sensing

Remote sensing introduces additional challenges that show the limits of general purpose XAI.

- Very high resolution together with tiny targets can make heat maps unreadable unless they preserve both context and fine detail.
- Multimodal and hyperspectral inputs such as infrared or Synthetic Aperture RADAR (SAR) require channel aggregation that can bias the visualization [6].
- Large variation in spatial and spectral scale complicates attribution transfer across datasets [6].
- Crowded scenes produce many overlapping boxes. DOTAv2 often exceeds one hundred annotations per image [9]. RTDETR can predict them in under 50ms, yet DRISE needs close to 9 s **per box**, which blocks interactive use.

In summary, current methods either deliver faithfulness at high computational cost or deliver fast and sharp maps that do not justify box geometry. The gap is most visible for small objects and dense scenes. Our study targets this gap by combining classification evidence from attention with attribution that explains predicted extents, and by evaluating the trade off under the ODExAI protocol across diverse scales and sensing modalities [15].

3 Methodology

We propose AC++, a post hoc explanation module for DETR-based detectors that use deformable attention. In all experiments we use RTDETRv2 and RFDETR as base models, yet the procedure applies to any detector with a decoder utilizing MSDA layers. AC++ returns, for each prediction query, a Class Attribution Maps (CAM) and a Box Activation Map (BAM). The CAM, is obtained directly from the sampling behavior of the decoder, similar the Attention CAM (AC) proposed by Leem et al. [10], however, based on the MSDA layers [31]. The extend reasoning, which we call BAM, is obtained from the IG with respect to the unsigmoid decoder box deltas. The detector remains frozen, and we only read intermediate tensors through forward callbacks. The class component runs near real time in our setup, while BAM adds a small cost that we quantify in the experiments.

Why Both Class and Box Attributions are Needed. Decoder MSDA layers match queries to sparse image features and thus offer query specific class evidence. At the same time, box coordinates stabilize early in the decoder, while class confidence continues to refine over depth. Figure 1 illustrates this behavior for RTDETRv2 on COCO and DIOR: recall increases in the first decoder layers, whereas mAP@50 and mAP@75 continue to improve in later layers, which indicates that box extent is decided early and class labels are refined later. A similar trend holds for RFDETR. We therefore complement the CAM with a BAM such that users can see both the class specific evidence and the pixels that drive the predicted box extent.

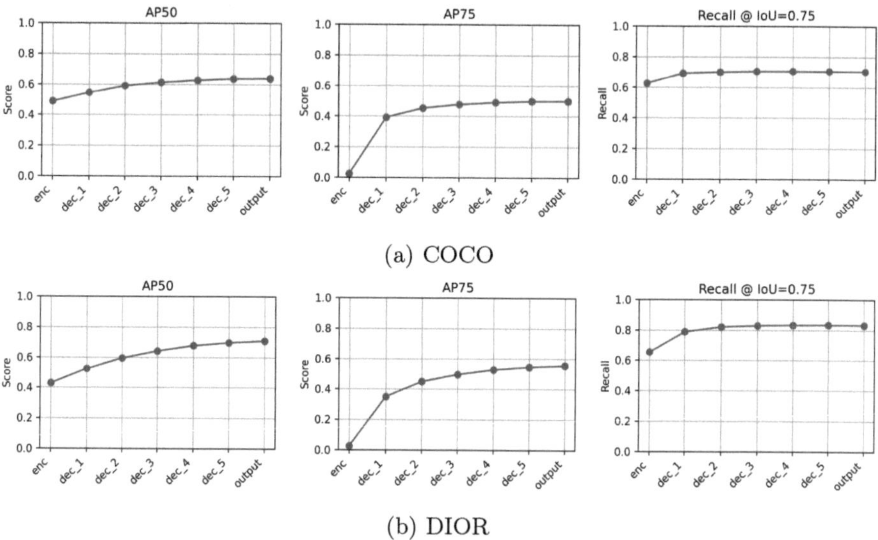

(a) COCO

(b) DIOR

Fig. 1. mAP of encoder seeds and successive decoder refinements for RTDETRv2 on COCO and DIOR. Box quality stabilizes early, while class confidence continues to improve.

Pipeline Overview. During inference we add forward callbacks to every MSDA layer in the decoder, for each query, the absolute sampling locations and their softmax normalized weights are cached. We aggregate these cached quantities across heads and layers to form the CAM via attention rollout (Subsect. 3.1). In a second, independent step we fix the anchor token of the selected prediction and compute integrated gradients of the detection logits with respect to the unsigmoid decoder box deltas to obtain BAM (Subsect. 3.2). The final saliency for a query is the mean of the class map and the box map, followed by an optional Gaussian blur for visual clarity.

3.1 Class-Level Attention Attribution

Let a decoder contain MSDA layers indexed by ℓ, with H heads, L feature levels, and P sampling points per head and level. For each query $\mathbf{q}_k$ and layer ℓ we record two tensors during the forward pass:

1. absolute sampling locations $(x^{\ell}_{h,l,p}, y^{\ell}_{h,l,p})$ obtained by adding the learned offsets to the layer reference points and rescaling to the input resolution,
2. the corresponding softmax normalized attention weights $a^{\ell}_{h,l,p}$.

Within each layer, we propagate relevance across decoder depth using attention rollout [1]. This yields per layer weights $\tilde{a}^{\ell}_{h,l,p}$ that account for upstream contributions. We then aggregate heads with a mean over h to emphasize consensus. The aggregated weights are splatted onto the image grid by in place

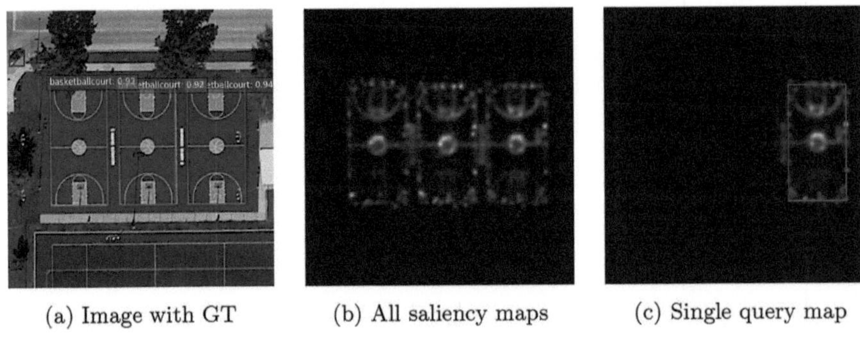

(a) Image with GT (b) All saliency maps (c) Single query map

Fig. 2. Example of AC++. Left: input image with predictions in red and ground truth in blue. Middle: mean of the three query specific maps. Right: one query specific saliency map.

accumulation at the recorded locations. Repeating this for all ℓ, l, p produces a raw class map $\mathbf{S}^{\text{cls}} \in \mathbb{R}^{H_{\text{img}} \times W_{\text{img}}}$ whose values are proportional to the attention mass assigned to each pixel by the query.

Finally, we square the accumulated scores to suppress weak responses and apply min to max normalization to $[0, 1]$. The computation uses only cached sampling locations and weights, introduces negligible memory overhead, and does not modify detector parameters. In practice, the resulting maps align well with the semantic regions that drive the classification decision of the query, as shown in Sect. 4.

3.2 Integrated Gradients-Based Box Activation Map

To justify the predicted geometric extent we derive a BAM from the IG. For a selected query we keep its anchor token fixed by tracing the memory index used by the decoder for that prediction. We then integrate the image space gradients of a scalar objective that depends on the unsigmoid decoder box deltas (Fig. 2).

Let I be the input image and I_0 a reference image. In our setting I_0 is a zero image. We also considered a strong blur of I as an alternative reference. Along the straight line from I_0 to I we sample m points

$$I_\alpha = I_0 + \alpha\,(I - I_0), \quad \alpha \in \left\{\tfrac{1}{m}, \ldots, 1\right\}. \tag{1}$$

At each α we forward I_α through the frozen detector and back propagate the scalar:

$$\mathcal{L}_{\text{box}}^{(\alpha)} = \sum_{c \in \{\Delta x, \Delta y, \Delta w, \Delta h\}} b_c^{(\alpha)}, \tag{2}$$

where b_c are the unsigmoid decoder deltas of the anchored query. We accumulate image gradients and average over the path to obtain the attribution

$$A = \frac{1}{m}\sum_{\alpha} \nabla_I \mathcal{L}_{\text{box}}^{(\alpha)}. \tag{3}$$

A single channel heat map is produced by channel wise summation of $|(I - I_0) \odot A|$ followed by normalization. Because the anchor token remains fixed for all α, the resulting BAM highlights pixels that most influence the predicted box center and scale. With $m = 50$ steps the added cost is about one second per image on a single NVIDIA RTX A5000.

Fusion. For each query we return the final map:

$$\mathbf{S}^{\text{final}} = \frac{1}{2}\left(\mathbf{S}^{\text{cls}} + \mathbf{S}^{\text{box}}\right), \tag{4}$$

where $\mathbf{S}^{\text{box}}$ is the normalized BAM. An optional Gaussian blur improves visual smoothness. We keep the detector frozen, use a single forward pass to compute the CAM, and perform $m = 50$ straight through passes for the BAM.

4 Evaluation

4.1 Explainability Metrics (ODExAI)

We follow ODExAI and assess an explainer along three independent metric: *localization*, *faithfulness*, and *complexity*. Each metric is evaluated by two quantitative measures.

Localization. **Pointing-Game (PG)** counts how often the single most salient pixel lies inside the ground truth bounding box:

$$\text{PG} = \frac{\#\text{hits}}{\#\text{hits} + \#\text{misses}}. \tag{5}$$

Energy-Based Pointing-Game (EBPG) extends PG by accumulating saliency mass inside the box:

$$\text{EBPG} = \frac{\sum_{(i,j)\in \text{bbox}} L_c(i,j)}{\sum_{(i,j)\in \text{bbox}} L_c(i,j) + \sum_{(i,j)\notin \text{bbox}} L_c(i,j)}. \tag{6}$$

Both scores approach one for perfect spatial alignment and approach zero for random localization.

Faithfulness. ODExAI measures how predictions respond to targeted perturbations. The protocol removes the top $k\,\%$ salient pixels and tracks the drop in the class score (Deletion AUC, lower is better) and inserts them into a blurred canvas and tracks the gain (Insertion AUC, higher is better). We report the **OA** defined as:

$$\text{OA} = \text{AUC}_{\text{Ins}} - \text{AUC}_{\text{Del}}, \tag{7}$$

so larger values indicate that saliency both supports the detector when present and degrades it when removed.

Complexity. Readability and runtime are captured by **Sparsity** and **Time**. Sparsity is computed on the minmax normalized saliency map as:

$$\text{Sparsity} = \frac{S_{\text{max}}}{S_{\text{mean}}}, \tag{8}$$

with higher values indicating that relevance concentrates in few pixels. Time denotes the mean wall clock required to produce one explanation, reported in seconds per image.

Together these six measures yield a seven dimensional profile, including OA, that separates where an explainer points, whether it matters for the detector, and how much effort it adds. This supports task driven choices, for example a high **PG** and low **Time** configuration for interactive use, or a high **OA** and high **Sparsity** configuration for detailed analysis.

4.2 Quantitative Results Under the ODExAI Protocol

Table 1 summarizes the results. All experiments were run on a NVIDIA RTX A5000. AC++ improves over state of the art explainers across datasets and detector variants. It yields consistently lower Deletion AUC together with higher Insertion AUC, higher OA, and higher PG. These gains indicate more accurate and more useful saliency.

AC remains faster, has higher Sparsity, and often reports higher EBPG. This follows from its design, since MSDA sampling locations tend to lie within the predicted box. AC++ trades a modest increase in Time for a better balance of faithfulness and localization by adding the IG-based Attention BAM. As shown in Sect. 4.3, this yields clearer and more interpretable maps.

Performance of DRISE and GCAME is competitive on COCO but degrades on remote sensing benchmarks. Detector-Cascading multiple Levels of Segments to Explain (DCLOSE) reaches similar scores in some settings and can surpass AC++ on individual metrics, yet it produces much denser maps with lower Sparsity and is slower by a factor of 10×, which limits interactive use. However, DCLOSE can also operate in black box scenarios, by design, without internal access, a setting that AC++ does not target.

4.3 Ablations on Class Level Attention Attribution

We study how to aggregate attention and collapse heads. We compare grad×attn (g×a), attention rollout, and head reductions by mean, max, and sum, where mean emphasizes consensus across heads, max selects the most discriminative head per location, and sum preserves total energy. Results on DIOR appear in Table 2.

AC++rollout yields the best overall performance, with the highest Ins, OA, EBPG, and PG, while maintaining low Del. Mean and sum are close in most metrics but do not match rollout. Max performs worst, which suggests that relying on a single head reduces robustness. The largest separation appears in EBPG, which is most sensitive to how attention mass is accumulated.

Table 1. The overall performance of our method compared against the state-of-the-art on 5 different dataset using RTDETRv2 and RFDETR.

Dataset	Model	Method	Del↓	Ins↑	OA↑	EBPG↑	PG↑	Sparsity↑	Time↓
CHAI	RFDETR	DCLOSE	0.02	0.80	0.78	0.02	0.38	12.00	10.31
		DRISE	0.46	0.46	0.00	0.00	0.00	3.42	12.28
		GCAME	0.40	0.40	0.01	0.03	0.12	**8440.53**	0.69
		AC	0.33	0.48	0.16	**0.58**	0.53	1288.34	**0.02**
		AC++	**0.01**	**0.93**	**0.91**	0.27	**0.64**	1387.19	0.76
	RTDETR	DCLOSE	**0.00**	**0.90**	**0.90**	0.03	**0.78**	17.67	12.41
		DRISE	0.30	0.68	0.38	0.00	0.18	6.30	10.33
		GCAME	0.60	0.61	0.02	0.00	0.00	21.07	0.82
		AC	0.00	0.88	0.88	**0.63**	0.64	**1610.69**	**0.01**
		AC++	0.01	0.89	0.89	0.26	0.73	1302.07	1.07
DIOR	RFDETR	DCLOSE	0.03	0.86	0.83	0.23	**0.85**	9.69	11.03
		DRISE	0.41	0.50	0.09	0.01	0.05	4.76	11.45
		GCAME	0.42	0.41	0.01	0.24	0.38	172.03	0.86
		AC	0.06	0.67	0.60	**0.69**	0.65	862.41	**0.01**
		AC++	**0.01**	**0.94**	**0.92**	0.45	0.66	**1435.79**	1.01
	RTDETR	DCLOSE	0.03	0.89	0.86	0.25	**0.91**	12.73	10.55
		DRISE	0.22	0.64	0.42	0.04	0.34	4.73	10.82
		GCAME	0.41	0.47	0.06	0.10	0.23	73.77	0.84
		AC	0.17	0.52	0.36	**0.74**	0.70	**797.34**	**0.01**
		AC++	**0.02**	**0.93**	**0.90**	0.64	0.85	581.02	1.04
DOTAV2	RFDETR	DCLOSE	0.02	0.84	0.82	0.05	0.58	13.97	10.47
		DRISE	0.40	0.46	0.06	0.00	0.02	5.51	11.01
		GCAME	0.31	0.46	0.15	0.16	0.33	111.68	0.85
		AC	0.01	0.72	0.71	**0.67**	0.79	**2037.78**	**0.01**
		AC++	**0.00**	**0.93**	**0.93**	0.28	**0.83**	1417.95	0.90
	RTDETR	DCLOSE	0.01	0.94	0.94	0.09	0.91	12.56	10.32
		DRISE	0.27	0.64	0.37	0.01	0.24	4.92	10.64
		GCAME	0.49	0.41	0.08	0.02	0.05	53.12	0.75
		AC	0.08	0.53	0.45	**0.80**	0.91	**845.24**	**0.01**
		AC++	**0.01**	**0.96**	**0.95**	0.50	**0.99**	564.49	1.40
SARDET-100K	RFDETR	DCLOSE	0.03	0.79	0.77	0.08	0.47	14.02	13.05
		DRISE	0.42	0.51	0.09	0.00	0.00	4.91	10.52
		GCAME	0.22	0.51	0.28	0.29	0.42	145.12	0.93
		AC	0.40	0.59	0.19	0.63	0.56	**1721.08**	**0.01**
		AC++	**0.01**	**0.80**	**0.79**	**0.39**	**0.79**	75.23	1.51
	RTDETR	DCLOSE	0.01	**0.95**	**0.94**	0.14	**0.96**	13.90	11.02
		DRISE	0.23	0.69	0.47	0.03	0.22	3.77	10.67
		GCAME	0.30	0.56	0.27	0.05	0.09	44.51	0.76
		AC	0.38	0.73	0.35	**0.69**	0.81	**1929.94**	**0.01**
		AC++	**0.01**	0.93	0.93	**0.47**	0.88	**82.33**	1.12
COCO	RFDETR	DCLOSE	0.11	0.87	0.76	0.36	**0.88**	10.33	9.25
		DRISE	0.47	0.58	0.10	0.02	0.07	6.00	12.27
		GCAME	0.52	0.51	0.01	0.43	0.59	**1612.41**	0.65
		AC	0.28	0.68	0.40	**0.77**	0.68	887.25	**0.01**
		AC++	**0.07**	**0.95**	**0.88**	0.58	0.71	469.60	0.76
	RTDETR	DCLOSE	0.11	0.93	0.82	0.37	**0.96**	13.02	12.04
		DRISE	0.40	0.69	0.28	0.09	0.30	5.44	13.45
		GCAME	0.44	0.71	0.27	0.21	0.28	1451.10	0.88
		AC	0.39	0.58	0.19	**0.84**	0.79	**846.23**	**0.01**
		AC++	**0.09**	**0.97**	**0.87**	0.55	0.85	430.90	0.79

Table 2. Ablation of class level attention on DIOR.

Model	Method	Del↓	Ins↑	OA↑	EBPG↑	PG↑
RFDETR	AC++g×a	0.03	0.89	0.86	0.44	0.49
	AC++rollout	**0.02**	**0.93**	**0.90**	**0.64**	**0.85**
	AC++mean	**0.02**	0.89	0.87	0.50	0.83
	AC++max	0.03	0.89	0.86	0.43	0.55
	AC++sum	**0.02**	0.89	0.87	0.50	0.83

4.4 Ablations on Integrated Gradients for Attention BAM

We next vary which box parameters are integrated: width and height (wh), center coordinates (xy), or all four ($xywh$). Results on DIOR are shown in Table 3.

Table 3. Ablation of integrated gradients for Attention BAM on DIOR.

Model	Method	Del↓	Ins↑	OA↑	EBPG↑	PG↑
RFDETR	AC++wh	0.02	0.82	0.72	0.41	0.61
	AC++xy	**0.01**	0.89	0.85	0.56	0.76
	AC++xywh	0.02	**0.93**	**0.90**	**0.64**	**0.85**

Integrating over all box parameters ($xywh$) delivers the strongest overall performance and the highest Ins, OA, EBPG, and PG. The xy setting achieves the lowest Del, which indicates that center coordinates are especially informative, yet the full $xywh$ version provides the best balance across metrics.

4.5 Qualitative Assessment

We visualize explanations for DRISE, GCAME, DCLOSE, the MSDA-based AC, and AC++ on five datasets using RFDETR. All methods use the same pretrained weights with an input size of 640 × 640. For DRISE and DCLOSE we sample 2000 masks per box with a grid size of 4. For GCAME we probe the final feature layer of the backbone (RTDETRv2 uses ResNet50 and RFDETR uses DINOv2). We show one target box per image for clarity. An elementwise maximum over per box maps can produce a combined map if desired.

Figure 3 first shows CHAI. DRISE, DCLOSE, AC, and AC++ all attend to the crater. AC and AC++ are sparser and less noisy. GCAME fails to focus on the selected box. We observe that GCAME depends strongly on two dimensional CNN style features and struggles when features stem from reshaped transformer maps. Early CNN backbone maps, as found in RTDETR, are also not yet informative enough.

The second row shows a stadium from DIOR. GCAME again fails to produce a useful map. DRISE and DCLOSE highlight broad regions with considerable noise. AC marks class evidence while AC++ also reveals cues that support the predicted box extent.

The third row shows an airplane from DOTAv2. As in the stadium case, state of the art baselines produce coarse maps that are less suitable for detailed interpretation. AC++ highlights fine structure, for example the open front left door.

The fourth row shows SARDET-100K. AC++ again yields the sharpest maps. DCLOSE mostly covers the predicted box region. GCAME does not localize the target. DRISE fails to produce a meaningful map in this setting.

The last row shows COCO. DRISE suggests that the detector focuses on the fabric of the chair, while DCLOSE emphasizes the seat and parts of the legs. AC++ concentrates on the frame and in particular the joints, which aligns with human intuition for object support.

Overall, the examples confirm that AC++ produces detailed yet compact maps that remain readable. AC yields even higher Sparsity due to its reliance on MSDA sampling points, but this comes at a cost in ease of interpretation.

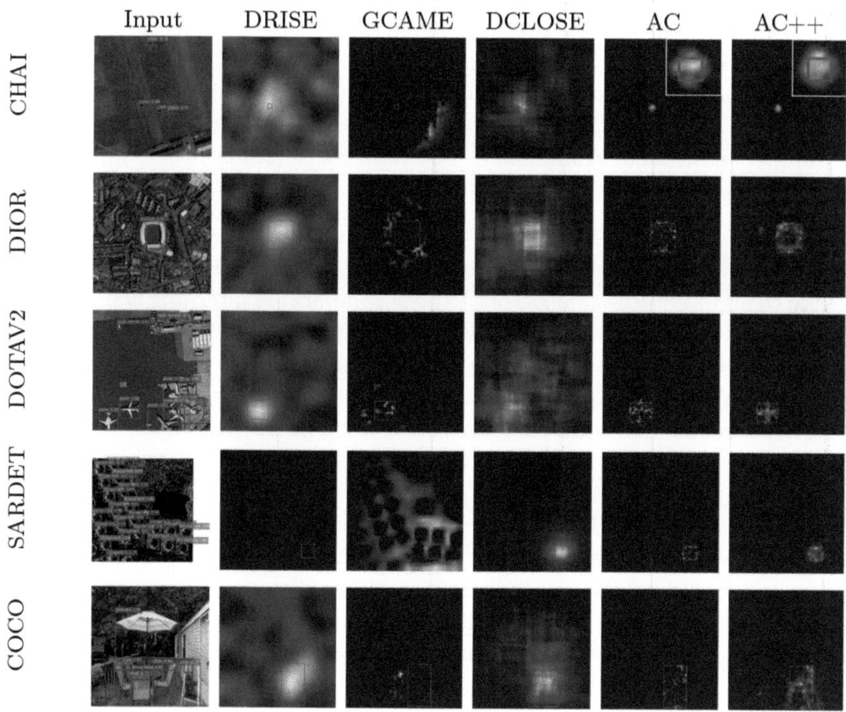

Fig. 3. Qualitative results of our method compared to the state-of-the-art on the five different datasets.

5 Discussion and Limitations

This work studies explainability for transformer-based object detectors and proposes AC++, which fuses class evidence from attention attribution with geometric justification from IG. Across natural and remote sensing benchmarks, the method outperforms the state of the art on localization and faithfulness while remaining practical. In our setup, the attention stage operates *near* real time, and the box justification stage adds a modest cost. Overall, the method reduces wall clock time by a factor between 7× and 15× when compared to common perturbation-based approaches, while producing sharper and more query-specific maps.

A central observation is the balance between efficiency and interpretability. The attention component alone, denoted AC, is very fast and yields sparse maps, yet it can miss the reasoning behind the object extent. The full AC++ pipeline augments this with IG-based box activation to recover precise support for predicted extents. This added step increases computation, but the gain in faithfulness and spatial precision is consistent over datasets and backbones in our evaluation.

The design also helps combining the traits of two families of explainers. Gradient-based methods often provide class alignment but can be diffuse on dense scenes, whereas perturbation-based methods such as DRISE tend to be robust but computationally heavy. By leveraging transformer-native sampling locations for evidence and a targeted IG path for geometry, AC++ achieves compact maps with limited additional complexity. The detector remains frozen and unmodified, which eases deployment.

Limitations. First, the approach is tailored to DETR style models with MSDA, since it relies on query-specific sampling points and weights. Extending the pipeline to architectures that do not expose comparable internals is not straightforward and would require extensive modifications. Second, the second stage depends on IG settings. The choice of the number of steps m, and the base model can influence sharpness and latency. Although we report stable defaults, sensitivity remains and may vary with data domain and resolution. Third, runtime scales with the number of active queries per image. Very dense scenes and small objects can increase cost, even when the box stage is applied only to selected queries. Finally, the current evaluation focuses on automatic metrics and our inspection. A broader user study with non-expert participants is still missing and would validate usefulness in real workflows.

Future Work. We see several directions that could broaden the impact of this study. A first step is a user study with experts in remote sensing and related domains, to assess readability, confidence calibration, and decision time in interactive analysis. A second step is multimodal attribution. Many applications combine optical, infrared, and radar signals. Producing modality-aware maps that isolate the contribution of each channel, and learning how to fuse them without losing interpretability, is an open problem. A third step is efficiency. Promising options include batched IG, early stopping based on gradient variance, query

selection that predicts which objects benefit from the box stage, and lightweight approximations that reuse intermediate Jacobians.
In summary, AC++ offers a practical path to interpretable detection by pairing attention-based class evidence with IG-based geometric support. It improves localization and faithfulness while keeping the explainer lightweight enough for interactive analysis, and it opens future research for user-centric validation, multimodal reasoning, and further gains in speed.

References

1. Abnar, S., Zuidema, W.H.: Quantifying attention flow in transformers. In: Jurafsky, D., Chai, J., Schluter, N., Tetreault, J.R. (eds.) Proceedings of the 58th Annual Meeting of the Association for Computational Linguistics, ACL 2020, Online, 5–10 July 2020, pp. 4190–4197. Association for Computational Linguistics (2020). https://doi.org/10.18653/V1/2020.ACL-MAIN.385
2. Burges, M., Zambanini, S., Pirker, P.: CHAI: craters in historical aerial images. In: IEEE/CVF Winter Conference on Applications of Computer Vision, WACV 2024, Waikoloa, HI, USA, 3–8 January 2024, pp. 8241–8250 (2024). https://doi.org/10.1109/WACV57701.2024.00807
3. Carion, N., Massa, F., Synnaeve, G., Usunier, N., Kirillov, A., Zagoruyko, S.: End-to-end object detection with transformers. In: Vedaldi, A., Bischof, H., Brox, T., Frahm, J.-M. (eds.) ECCV 2020. LNCS, vol. 12346, pp. 213–229. Springer, Cham (2020). https://doi.org/10.1007/978-3-030-58452-8_13
4. Chattopadhyay, A., Sarkar, A., Howlader, P., Balasubramanian, V.N.: Grad-CAM++: generalized gradient-based visual explanations for deep convolutional networks. In: 2018 IEEE Winter Conference on Applications of Computer Vision, WACV 2018, Lake Tahoe, NV, USA, 12–15 March 2018, pp. 839–847. IEEE Computer Society (2018). https://doi.org/10.1109/WACV.2018.00097
5. Fernandes, L., Fernandes, J.N.D., Calado, M., Pinto, J.R., Cerqueira, R., Cardoso, J.S.: Intrinsic explainability for end-to-end object detection. IEEE Access **12**, 2623–2634 (2024). https://doi.org/10.1109/ACCESS.2023.3347038
6. Höhl, A., et al.: Opening the black-box: a systematic review on explainable AI in remote sensing. CoRR abs/2402.13791 (2024). https://doi.org/10.48550/ARXIV.2402.13791
7. Hoofnagle, C.J., van der Sloot, B., Borgesius, F.Z.: The European Union general data protection regulation: what it is and what it means*. Inf. Commun. Technol. Law **28**(1), 65–98 (2019). https://doi.org/10.1080/13600834.2019.1573501
8. Khan, M.J., Zafar, A., Tumanian, V., Yue, D., Li, G.: Object detection boosting using object attributes in detect and describe framework. In: 31st IEEE International Conference on Tools with Artificial Intelligence, ICTAI 2019, Portland, OR, USA, 4–6 November 2019, pp. 886–893. IEEE (2019). https://doi.org/10.1109/ICTAI.2019.00126
9. Lee, C., et al.: Interactive multi-class tiny-object detection. In: IEEE/CVF Conference on Computer Vision and Pattern Recognition, CVPR 2022, New Orleans, LA, USA, 18–24 June 2022, pp. 14116–14125 (2022). https://doi.org/10.1109/CVPR52688.2022.01374

10. Leem, S., Seo, H.: Attention guided CAM: visual explanations of vision transformer guided by self-attention. In: Wooldridge, M.J., Dy, J.G., Natarajan, S. (eds.) Thirty-Eighth AAAI Conference on Artificial Intelligence, AAAI 2024, Thirty-Sixth Conference on Innovative Applications of Artificial Intelligence, IAAI 2024, Fourteenth Symposium on Educational Advances in Artificial Intelligence, EAAI 2014, 20–27 February 2024, Vancouver, Canada, pp. 2956–2964. AAAI Press (2024). https://doi.org/10.1609/AAAI.V38I4.28077
11. Li, K., Wan, G., Cheng, G., Meng, L., Han, J.: Object detection in optical remote sensing images: a survey and A new benchmark. CoRR abs/1909.00133 (2019)
12. Li, Y., et al.: SARDet-100K: towards open-source benchmark and toolkit for large-scale SAR object detection. CoRR abs/2403.06534 (2024). https://doi.org/10.48550/ARXIV.2403.06534
13. Lin, T.-Y., et al.: Microsoft COCO: common objects in context. In: Fleet, D., Pajdla, T., Schiele, B., Tuytelaars, T. (eds.) ECCV 2014. LNCS, vol. 8693, pp. 740–755. Springer, Cham (2014). https://doi.org/10.1007/978-3-319-10602-1_48
14. Moradi, M., Yan, K., Colwell, D., Samwald, M., Asgari, R.: Model-agnostic explainable artificial intelligence for object detection in image data. Eng. Appl. Artif. Intell. **137**, 109183 (2024). https://doi.org/10.1016/J.ENGAPPAI.2024.109183
15. Nguyen, L.P.T., Nguyen, H.T.T., Cao, H.: ODExAI: a comprehensive object detection explainable AI evaluation (2025)
16. Nguyen, Q.K., Nguyen, T.T.H., Nguyen, V.T.K., Truong, V.B., Cao, Q.H.: G-CAME: Gaussian-class activation mapping explainer for object detectors. CoRR abs/2306.03400 (2023). https://doi.org/10.48550/ARXIV.2306.03400
17. Nguyen, Q.K., Nguyen, T.T.H., Nguyen, V.T.K., Truong, V.B., Phan, T., Cao, Q.H.: Efficient and concise explanations for object detection with gaussian-class activation mapping explainer. In: Goebel, R., Zarrinkalam, F. (eds.) 37th Canadian Conference on Artificial Intelligence, Canadian AI 2024, Guelph, ON, Canada, 27–31 May 2024, Proceedings. Canadian Artificial Intelligence Association (2024)
18. European Parliament: EU AI act: first regulation on artificial intelligence (2025)
19. Petsiuk, V., Das, A., Saenko, K.: RISE: randomized input sampling for explanation of black-box models. In: British Machine Vision Conference 2018, BMVC 2018, Newcastle, UK, 3–6 September 2018, p. 151. BMVA Press (2018)
20. Petsiuk, V., et al.: Black-box explanation of object detectors via saliency maps. In: IEEE Conference on Computer Vision and Pattern Recognition, CVPR 2021, virtual, 19-25 June 2021, pp. 11443–11452. Computer Vision Foundation/IEEE (2021). https://doi.org/10.1109/CVPR46437.2021.01128
21. Rath-Manakidis, P., Strothmann, F., Glasmachers, T., Wiskott, L.: ProtoP-OD: explainable object detection with prototypical parts. CoRR abs/2402.19142 (2024). https://doi.org/10.48550/ARXIV.2402.19142
22. Ribeiro, M.T., Singh, S., Guestrin, C.: "why should I trust you?": explaining the predictions of any classifier. In: Krishnapuram, B., Shah, M., Smola, A.J., Aggarwal, C.C., Shen, D., Rastogi, R. (eds.) Proceedings of the 22nd ACM SIGKDD International Conference on Knowledge Discovery and Data Mining, San Francisco, CA, USA, 13–17 August 2016, pp. 1135–1144. ACM (2016). https://doi.org/10.1145/2939672.2939778
23. Robinson, I., Robicheaux, P., Popov, M.: RF-DETR: A SOTA real-time object detection model (2025). https://github.com/roboflow/rf-detr
24. Sejr, J.H., Schneider-Kamp, P., Ayoub, N.: Surrogate object detection explainer (SODEx) with YOLOv4 and LIME. Mach. Learn. Knowl. Extr. **3**(3), 662–671 (2021). https://doi.org/10.3390/MAKE3030033

25. Selvaraju, R.R., Cogswell, M., Das, A., Vedantam, R., Parikh, D., Batra, D.: Grad-CAM: visual explanations from deep networks via gradient-based localization. In: IEEE International Conference on Computer Vision, ICCV 2017, Venice, Italy, 22–29 October 2017, pp. 618–626. IEEE Computer Society (2017). https://doi.org/10.1109/ICCV.2017.74
26. Suciu, C., Marginean, A.: XAI-DETR: explainable AI tool for detection transformers. In: Nedevschi, S., Potolea, R., Slavescu, R.R. (eds.) 20th IEEE International Conference on Intelligent Computer Communication and Processing, ICCP 2024, Cluj-Napoca, Romania, 17–19 October 2024, pp. 1–6. IEEE (2024). https://doi.org/10.1109/ICCP63557.2024.10793046
27. Xia, G., et al.: DOTA: a large-scale dataset for object detection in aerial images. In: 2018 IEEE Conference on Computer Vision and Pattern Recognition, CVPR 2018, Salt Lake City, UT, USA, 18–22 June 2018, pp. 3974–3983 (2018). https://doi.org/10.1109/cvpr.2018.00418
28. Zafar, A., Khalid, U.: Detect-and-describe: joint learning framework for detection and description of objects. CoRR abs/2204.08828 (2022). https://doi.org/10.48550/ARXIV.2204.08828
29. Zhao, C., Chan, A.B.: ODAM: gradient-based instance-specific visual explanations for object detection. In: The Eleventh International Conference on Learning Representations, ICLR 2023, Kigali, Rwanda, 1–5 May 2023. OpenReview.net (2023)
30. Zhao, Y., et al.: DETRs beat YOLOs on real-time object detection. In: IEEE/CVF Conference on Computer Vision and Pattern Recognition, CVPR 2024, Seattle, WA, USA, 16–22 June 2024, pp. 16965–16974. IEEE (2024). https://doi.org/10.1109/CVPR52733.2024.01605
31. Zhu, X., Su, W., Lu, L., Li, B., Wang, X., Dai, J.: Deformable DETR: deformable transformers for end-to-end object detection. In: 9th International Conference on Learning Representations, ICLR 2021, Virtual Event, Austria, 3–7 May 2021. OpenReview.net (2021)

Transformer Deep Learning to Detect Microsatellite Instability Using Histopathological Slides to Guide Colorectal and Endometrial Cancer Immunotherapy

Ching-Wei Wang[1(✉)] and Tai-Kuang Chao[2,3]

[1] Graduate Institute of Biomedical Engineering, National Taiwan University of Science and Technology, Taipei, Taiwan
cweiwang@mail.ntust.edu.tw

[2] Institute of Pathology and Parasitology, National Defense Medical Center, Taipei, Taiwan
chaotai.kuang@msa.hinet.net

[3] Department of Pathology, Tri-Service General Hospital, Taipei, Taiwan

Abstract. Testing for mismatch repair deficiency (dMMR) and high-grade microsatellite instability (MSI-H) has become an integral part of the routine diagnostic workup for colorectal cancer (CRC) and endometrial cancer (EC) in clinical practice, and using MSI to predict the therapeutic response to immune checkpoint inhibitors (ICIs) has now become a hot focus. Recent reports have shown that patients with dMMR/MSI-H tumors in CRC and EC can benefit from ICIs. So far, MSI is the only widely recognized biomarker that can be used to evaluate the effectiveness of immunotherapy for CRC and EC. The humanized monoclonal anti-PD-1 antibody pembrolizumab is the first ICI to have its clinical activity investigated in patients with dMMR/MSI-H CRC and EC. Immunohistochemical testing for dMMR has recently become a standard testing item in pathology laboratories, and next-generation sequencing is also a powerful method for analyzing MSI. Although the examination of MSI is important for immunotherapy, high cost and time constraints have limited the widespread adoption of MSI testing. Here, we developed an ensemble transformer multiple instance deep learning (DL) system and evaluated the system to predict MSI status using histopathological whole slide images (WSIs) from multiple datasets of Tri-Service General Hospital and the Cancer Genome Atlas in MSI-related EC and CRC. The results demonstrate that the presented system has great potential to predict MSI status directly from H&E WSIs in EC and CRC, enabling personalized targeted immunotherapy.

Keywords: Colorectal Cancer · Endometrial Cancer · Immunotherapy · Microsatellite Instability · Deep Learning

Supported by National Science and Technology Council of Taiwan (NSTC 113-2222-E-011-003-MY3).

C. Wallraven et al. (Eds.): ACPR 2025, LNCS 16174, pp. 48–59, 2026.
https://doi.org/10.1007/978-981-95-4395-3_4

1 Introduction

Testing for dMMR/MSI-H was primarily recommended for patients with a significant family history suggestive of possible hereditary tumor predisposition syndrome, such as Lynch syndrome [6]. For sporadic CRC, somatic mutations in microsatellite loci were found in 10% to 15% of cases [15]. Subsequently, MSI has been found in various other types of malignant tumors, including EC [2,5,14,16,23]. Approximately 25%-31% of patients with EC have dMMR/MSI-H [17]. High MSI usually leads to the accumulation of somatic mutations. Among these, frameshift mutations are highly positively correlated with the frequency of neoantigens, MSI, and dMMR [18]. Due to germline mutations or acquired somatic alterations in one of the MMR genes; MutL homologue 1 (*MLH1*), MutS homologue2 (*MSH2*), MutS homologue 6 (*MSH6*), and postmeiotic segregation increased 2 (*PMS2*), cells with dMMR proteins are unable to rectify errors during DNA replication, such as base substitution mismatches, frameshift mutations, and slippage. This results in high levels of MSI, the accumulation of numerous mutations (promoting malignancies), and an increased neoantigen burden. In most cases, this leads to an increase in tumor mutation burden and immunogenic neoantigens, making dMMR/MSI-H tumors potentially sensitive to immunotherapy [4,7,12].

Precision oncology provides a diverse set of strategies for cancer treatment, which can be customized according to the unique biological characteristics of each patient's disease. This is because every patient's disease has different features that can affect treatment planning or response to treatment [1]. To facilitate and improve the effectiveness of precision oncology, DL has been applied to treatment planning and has become increasingly important in the field of precision oncology in recent years [8,9]. In this study, we developed an ensemble transformer DL-based model that can precisely and conveniently predict MSI and TP53 status as determined by the most clinically used IHC staining results using only EC histopathological whole slide images (WSIs). We validated that the model performs quite well in predicting MSI and TP53. Additionally, we used CRC histopathological WSIs from the TCGA platform and more advanced NGS-determined MSI data as the reference standard to further verify the model's predictive potential. The proposed architecture helps the model robustly capture significant pathological features and further generate accurate classification decisions. Compared to existing laboratory testing methods, the proposed system provides patients with a more convenient and rapid automated screening tool. This method has the potential to become a clinical approach for detecting the microsatellite status of CRC and EC. The model also has the potential to enhance pathological and molecular diagnostic classification.

2 Method

This study presents an Ensemble Transformer-based Multiple Instance Learning with Self-Supervised Learning Vision Transformer feature encoder (ETMIL-SSLViT), to predict pathological subtype, MSI and TP53 directly from

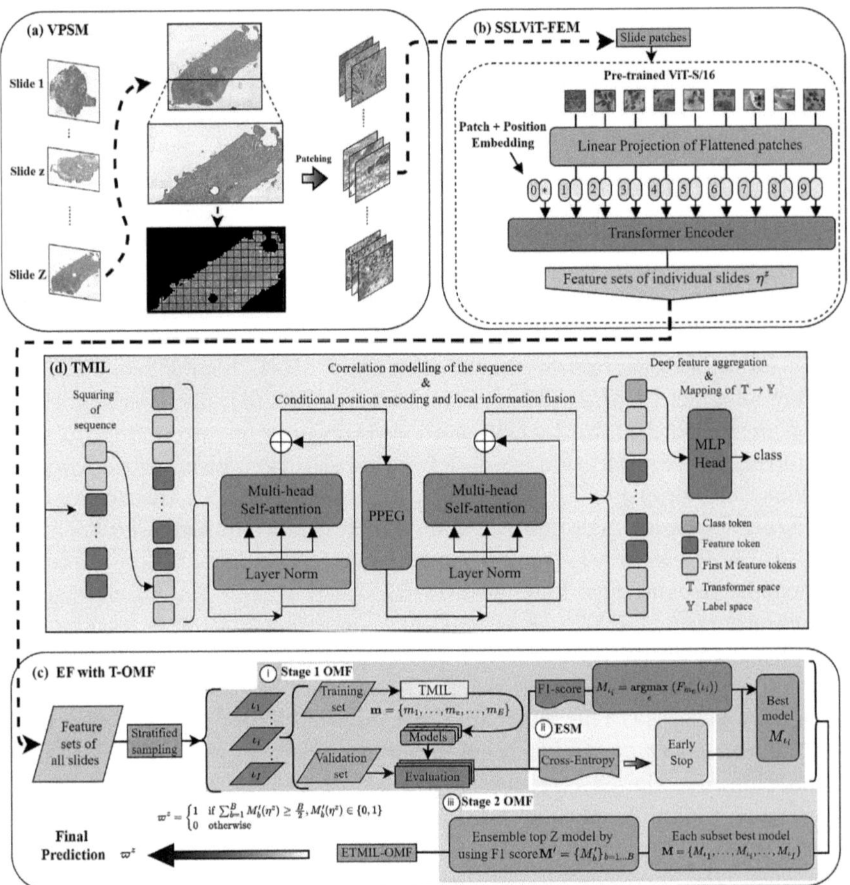

Fig. 1. Overview of the proposed Ensemble Transformer-based Multiple Instance Learning with Self-Supervised Learning Vision Transformer feature encoder (ETMIL-SSLViT): (a) a Vision Patch Segmentation Module (VPSM). (b) Self-Supervised Learning Vision Transformer Feature Encoder Module (SSLViT-FEM). (c) Ensemble Framework (EF) with Two-stage Optimal Model Finder (T-OMF). (c.i) Stage 1 OMF. (c.ii) Early Stop Mechanism (ESM). (c.iii) Stage 2 OMF. (d) Transformer-based Multiple Instance Learning (TMIL).

histopathological WSIs in CRC and EC patients. Firstly, we built a Vision Patch Segmentation Module (VPSM) to rapidly extract non-overlapping foreground patches, which helps enhance efficiency and accuracy in WSI analysis (Fig. 1(a)). Secondly, we presented a Self-Supervised Learning Vision Transformer Feature Encoder Module (SSLViT-FEM) that integrates a pre-trained ViT-S/16 with SSL techniques to extract features from WSIs (Fig. 1(b)). SSLViT-FEM captures global salient features of images to resolve long-range connections between the content of images and fully utilizes the attention mechanism to incorporate global context information into image features, enhancing the accuracy of the extracted features without significantly increasing computational cost.

Thirdly, we presented a Transformer-based Multiple Instance Learning model (TMIL), which outperforms all the latest SOTA MIL methods [3,10,11,22] in this study (Fig. 1(d)). Fourthly, an Early Stop Mechanism (ESM) was built based on the cross entropy loss to help prevent overfitting and save computational resources and time as cross entropy measures the discrepancy between the predicted probability distribution by the model and the actual label distribution, thereby directly reflecting the model's effectiveness in predicting categories (Fig. 1(c.ii)). Fifthly, we devised an Ensemble Framework (EF) using the bagging strategy with a Two-stage Optimal Model Finder method (T-OMF), respectively. The proposed ensemble improves variance reduction, predictive performance, model robustness and reduces overfitting.

3 Results

Our framework was evaluated on two different cancer cohorts, including 242 endometrial cancer (EC) tissue cores of three tissue microarrays (TMAs) from the Department of Pathology at Tri-Service General Hospital, Taipei, Taiwan and 1495 WSIs of 594 Colorectal cancer (CRC) patients from 25 tissue source sites archived in The Cancer Genome Atlas (TCGA) (see Sect. 3.1 and Fig. 2). The evaluation was conducted in three parts. Firstly, in Sect. 3.2 we compared the proposed methods with six SOTA DL methods, including ClassicMIL [3], InstanceBoostingEnsemble [20], Improved_InceptionV3_MS [21], CLAM [11], TOAD [10], and TransMIL [19]. Secondly, in Sect. 3.3 we further performed two-tailed Fisher's Exact Test to validate that the associations between the model predictions and the actual molecular or cancer subtype classification status. Thirdly, Sect. 3.4 demonstrates the interpretability of the proposed method in application to cancer subtyping in CRC samples. Our proposed models predict slides by identifying and focusing on regions of WSIs that can predict the cancer subtype (high attention score) and disregarding regions with low relevance for cancer subtyping (see Fig. 4). Importantly, our proposed weakly supervised learning models are able to differentiate cancer subtype traits using slide-level labels only without specific pixel- or patch-level annotation during training.

3.1 Datasets

Endometrial Cancer Dataset. An EC TMA cohort of patients' paraffin-embedded tissues was retrospectively retrieved from the Department of Pathology at Tri-Service General Hospital, Taipei, Taiwan. The EC TMA cohort contained 242 EC tissue cores (see Fig. 2(a)), including 127 cores of TP53 wild type and 115 cores of TP53 mutation, 138 cores of MLH1 intact and 101 cores of MLH1 loss, 151 cores of MSH2 intact and 87 cores of MSH2 loss, 182 cores of MSH6 intact and 57 cores of MSH6 loss, 119 cores of PMS2 intact and 120 cores of PMS2 loss as shown in Fig. 2(b). To generate the reference standard determined by IHC staining, the TMA sections were incubated in 3%

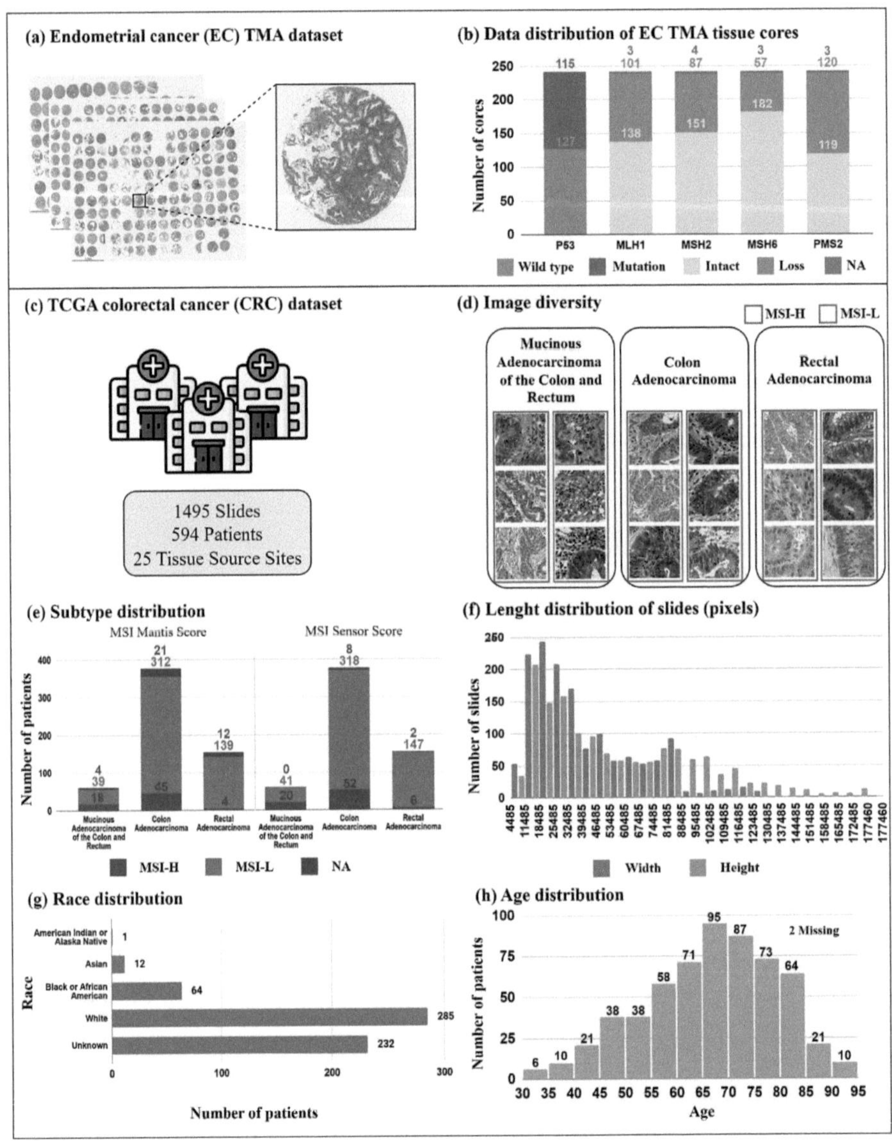

Fig. 2. Data information of EC and CRC datasets. (a) EC TMA dataset, (b) Data distribution of EC tissue cores, (c) TCGA CRC dataset, (d) Image diversity of the CRC data, (e) Subtype distribution, (f) Length distribution in pixels, (g) Race distribution and (h) Age distribution.

hydrogen peroxide for 10 min to suppress the activity of endogenous peroxidase and then incubated with anti-p53 primary antibody (ready-to-use; cat# D0-7, Roche), the antibodies anti-MSH2 (ready-to use; Cat# 760-5092, Ventana Medical Systems), anti-MSH6 (ready-to-use; Cat# 760-5093; Ventana Medical Systems), anti-PMS2 (ready-to-use; Cat# 760-5094; Ventana Medical Systems), and anti-MLH1 (ready-to-use; Cat# 760-5091; Ventana Medical Systems) for 1 h at room temperature, followed by incubation with horseradish peroxidase-labeled immunoglobulin (Dako, Carpinteria, CA, USA) for 1 h at room temperature. Peroxidase activity was visualized using a solution of diaminobenzidine (DAB) at room temperature. The WSIs were then acquired with a digital slide scanner (Leica AT Turbo) with a 20x objective lens. Abnormal p53 (mutant-type) staining is defined as either strong nuclear expression in tumor cells (>80%), the complete absence of expression in tumor cells, or unequivocal cytoplasmic expression. Wild-type p53 expression is defined as nuclear staining of variable intensity in the tumor cells [13].

Colorectal Cancer Dataset. For the TCGA CRC cohort, we collected 1495 WSIs of 594 patients from 25 tissue source sites (see Fig. 2(c)), which could be downloaded from the TCGA public repository at the National Institutes of Health https://portal.gdc.cancer.gov/ and the corresponding labels are available on https://www.cbioportal.org/study/summary?id=coadread_tcga_pan_can_atlas_2018. The CRC dataset includes H&E-stained pathological WSIs of varying image data, cancer subtype and dimension, with the width ranging from 6,000 to 177,460 pixels and the height from 4,485 to 143,104 pixels (See Fig. 2(d–f)). Our analysis encompassed images from 594 patients diagnosed with CRC, ranging from individuals aged 31 to 90 and representing over four different races, as depicted in Fig. 2 (g, h). The dataset comprises various morphological subtypes, including mucinous adenocarcinoma of the colon and rectum (n = 61), non-mucinous colon adenocarcinoma (n = 378), and non-mucinous rectal adenocarcinoma (n = 155) (see Fig. 2(e)). The reference standard of the MSI labels are generated by NGS where the first MSI label set is determined by NGS [MSI-H: MANTIS score $\geq$ 0.6 (n = 67); MSI-low: MANTIS score < 0.6 (n = 490); NA: MSI data not available (n = 37)] and the second MSI label set is determined by NGS [MSI-H: MSIsensor score $\geq$ 10 (n = 78); MSI-low: MSIsensor score < 10 (n = 506); NA: MSI data not available (n = 10)] (see Fig. 2(e)). Moreover, we excluded the eight slides due to poor morphology caused by incomplete fixation. Stratified sampling was employed to divide the cohort into independent training (2/3) and testing subsets (1/3), preserving the proportional representation of critical characteristics within each group.

3.2 Evaluation Results

Results in TP53 Prediction of EC. In evaluation of TP53 prediction (mutation-type vs wild type) of EC, the proposed ensemble transformer method achieves the best overall performance and outperforms six SOTA benchmark approaches, obtaining the highest MeanSS (81%) and accuracy (81%). These results suggest the efficacy of our proposed methods for the classification of TP53 of the EC samples (see Table 1(a)).

Table 1. Evaluation in prediction of TP53 and four MSI biomarkers of EC

Task	Method	Accu.	Sens.	Spec.	MeanSS	MeanSS Rank	Fisher Exact Test
(a) TP53 prediction (mutation-type vs wild type)	**Proposed ETMIL-SSLViT**	0.81	0.81	0.81	**0.81**	1	<0.001***
	Proposed TMIL-SSLViT	0.76	0.73	0.79	0.76	2	<0.001***
	ClassicMIL [3]	0.71	0.73	0.69	0.71	5	<0.001***
	InstanceBoostingEnsemble [20]	0.70	0.55	0.83	0.69	8	0.661
	Improved_InceptionV3_MS [21]	0.70	0.84	0.58	0.71	5	<0.001***
	CLAM [11]	0.75	0.68	0.81	0.74	3	<0.001***
	TOAD [10]	0.68	0.89	0.50	0.70	7	<0.001***
	TransMIL [19]	0.72	0.84	0.62	0.73	4	<0.001***
(b) MLH1 prediction	**Proposed ETMIL-SSLViT**	0.91	0.94	0.89	**0.92**	1	<0.001***
	Proposed TMIL-SSLViT	0.82	0.68	0.93	0.80	7	<0.001***
	ClassicMIL [3]	0.89	0.91	0.87	0.89	5	<0.001***
	InstanceBoostingEnsemble [20]	0.75	0.50	0.93	0.72	8	<0.001***
	Improved_InceptionV3_MS [21]	0.86	0.79	0.91	0.85	6	<0.001***
	CLAM [11]	0.91	0.97	0.87	0.92	1	<0.001***
	TOAD [10]	0.89	0.97	0.82	0.90	3	<0.001***
	TransMIL [19]	0.90	0.88	0.91	0.90	3	<0.001***
(c) MSH2 prediction	Proposed ETMIL-SSLViT	0.87	0.86	0.87	0.87	2	<0.001***
	Proposed TMIL-SSLViT	0.88	0.86	0.89	**0.88**	1	<0.001***
	ClassicMIL [3]	0.77	0.73	0.79	0.76	6	<0.001***
	InstanceBoostingEnsemble [20]	0.80	0.63	0.92	0.77	5	<0.001***
	Improved_InceptionV3_MS [21]	0.74	0.47	0.92	0.69	8	<0.001***
	CLAM [11]	0.74	0.78	0.72	0.75	7	<0.001***
	TOAD [10]	0.85	0.79	0.89	0.84	3	<0.001***
	TransMIL [19]	0.80	0.69	0.87	0.78	4	<0.001***
(d) MSH6 prediction	**Proposed ETMIL-SSLViT**	0.93	0.89	0.94	**0.91**	1	<0.001***
	Proposed TMIL-SSLViT	0.92	0.78	0.96	0.87	2	<0.001***
	ClassicMIL [3]	0.72	0.82	0.69	0.76	5	<0.001***
	InstanceBoostingEnsemble [20]	0.79	0.06	0.99	0.52	8	0.381
	Improved_InceptionV3_MS [21]	0.81	0.11	1.00	0.56	7	0.043*
	CLAM [11]	0.76	0.71	0.77	0.74	6	<0.001***
	TOAD [10]	0.84	0.83	0.84	0.83	3	<0.001***
	TransMIL [19]	0.76	0.94	0.72	0.83	3	<0.001***
(e) PMS2 prediction	**Proposed ETMIL-SSLViT**	0.85	0.80	0.90	**0.85**	1	<0.001***
	Proposed TMIL-SSLViT	0.84	0.87	0.83	**0.85**	1	<0.001***
	ClassicMIL [3]	0.85	0.86	0.83	0.84	3	<0.001***
	InstanceBoostingEnsemble [20]	0.79	0.86	0.70	0.78	7	<0.001***
	Improved_InceptionV3_MS [21]	0.60	0.34	0.88	0.61	8	0.023*
	CLAM [11]	0.77	0.73	0.83	0.78	6	<0.001***
	TOAD [10]	0.80	0.89	0.70	0.79	4	<0.001***
	TransMIL [19]	0.79	0.77	0.80	0.79	4	<0.001***

MeanSS: Mean of Sensitivity and Specificity; The top 1 methods are highlighted in bold; *:$p <$ 0.05, **:$p <$ 0.01 and ***:$p <$ 0.001

Results in Four MSI Biomarker Prediction of EC. In evaluation of MLH1 prediction of EC, the proposed ensemble transformer method achieves the best overall performance and outperforms six SOTA benchmark approaches, obtaining the highest MeanSS (92%) and accuracy (91%) (see Table 1(b)). Moreover, in evaluation of MSH2 prediction of EC, the proposed transformer method achieves the best overall performance and outperforms six SOTA benchmark approaches, obtaining the highest MeanSS (88%), accuracy (88%) and sensitivity (86%) (see Table 1(c)). In evaluation of MSH6 prediction of EC, the proposed ensemble

Table 2. Evaluation in Cancer Subtyping and MSI prediction of CRC.

Task	Method	Accu.	Sens.	Spec.	MeanSS	MeanSS Rank	Fisher Exact Test
(a) Subtype classification (mucinous vs non-mucinous)	**Proposed ETMIL-SSLViT**	0.86	0.75	0.87	**0.81**	1	<0.001***
	Proposed TMIL-SSLViT	0.89	0.65	0.92	0.79	2	<0.001***
	ClassicMIL [3]	0.73	0.45	0.76	0.61	7	0.056
	InstanceBoostingEnsemble [20]	0.69	0.30	0.74	0.52	8	0.429
	Improved_InceptionV3_MS [21]	0.61	0.65	0.60	0.63	6	0.344
	CLAM [11]	0.87	0.60	0.90	0.75	3	<0.001***
	TOAD [10]	0.85	0.55	0.89	0.72	4	<0.001***
	TransMIL [19]	0.90	0.44	0.95	0.70	5	<0.001***
(b) MSI prediction w.r.t. MANTIS score	**Proposed ETMIL-SSLViT**	0.89	0.68	0.91	**0.80**	1	<0.001***
	Proposed TMIL-SSLViT	0.90	0.53	0.94	0.73	2	<0.001***
	ClassicMIL [3]	0.88	0.10	0.98	0.54	4	1.000
	InstanceBoostingEnsemble [20]	0.83	0.10	0.93	0.51	5	0.626
	Improved_InceptionV3_MS [21]	0.11	0.10	0.89	0.50	7	0.698
	CLAM [11]	0.78	0.15	0.86	0.51	5	1.000
	TOAD [10]	0.89	0.25	0.97	0.61	3	0.001**
	TransMIL [19]	0.89	0.00	1.00	0.50	7	†
(c) MSI prediction w.r.t. MSIsensor score	**Proposed ETMIL-SSLViT**	0.89	0.64	0.93	**0.79**	1	<0.001***
	Proposed TMIL-SSLViT	0.85	0.72	0.87	**0.79**	1	<0.001***
	ClassicMIL [3]	0.34	0.80	0.27	0.54	3	0.627
	InstanceBoostingEnsemble [20]	0.85	0.12	0.97	0.52	4	0.084
	Improved_InceptionV3_MS [21]	0.85	0.04	0.98	0.51	6	0.512
	CLAM [11]	0.85	0.08	0.97	0.52	4	0.009**
	TOAD [10]	0.87	0.00	1.00	0.50	7	†
	TransMIL [19]	0.87	0.00	1.00	0.50	7	†

MeanSS: Mean of Sensitivity and Specificity; The top 1 methods are highlighted in bold; *:$p < 0.05$, **:$p < 0.01$ and ***:$p < 0.001$

†: No statistics are computed because the model prediction is constant

transformer method achieves the best overall performance and outperforms six SOTA benchmark approaches, obtaining the highest MeanSS (91%) and accuracy (93%) (see Table 1(d)). In evaluation of PMS2 prediction of EC, the proposed ensemble transformer method achieves the best overall performance and outperforms six SOTA benchmark approaches, obtaining the highest MeanSS (85%), specificity (90%) and accuracy (85%). The proposed transformer method also achieves the best overall performance and outperforms six SOTA benchmark approaches, obtaining the highest MeanSS (85%) (see Table 1(e)). These results show the efficacy of our proposed methods for prediction of the four MSI biomarkers directly from H&E images in EC.

Results in CRC Subtype Classification. Table 2(a) shows that in evaluation of classification of mucinous and non-mucinous CRC, the proposed ensemble transformer method (ETMIL) achieves the best overall performance and outperforms the six SOTA benchmark approaches, obtaining the highest Mean of sensitivity and specificity (MeanSS) (81%) and sensitivity (75%). These results suggest the efficacy of our proposed methods for classification of the mucinous and non-mucinous CRC even for an extremely imbalanced dataset (i.e. mucinous (10.3%) vs non-mucinous (89.7%)).

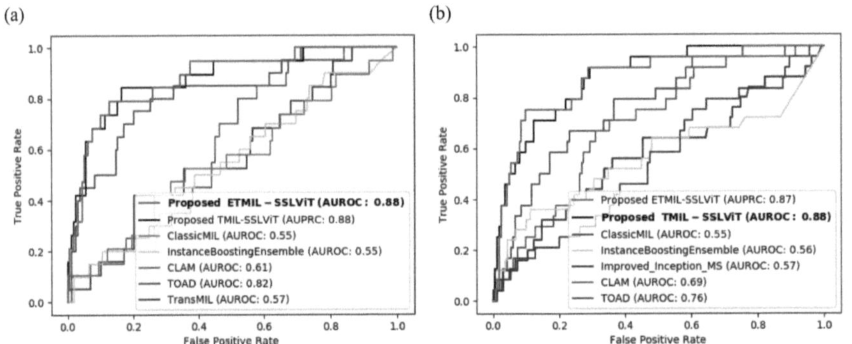

Fig. 3. Area Under the Receiver Operating Characteristic curves (AUROC curves) for MSI assessment determined by (a) NGS MSI MANTIS score (b) NGS MSIsensor score.

Results in MSI Prediction of CRC. We further evaluated the model performance in prediction of the MSI status directly from H&E WSIs of CRC samples. In evaluation with the reference labels generated by the NGS MANTIS score, the results showed that the proposed ensemble transformer method obtained superior results and outperformed all benchmark methods, obtaining the highest Mean of sensitivity and specificity (MeanSS) (80%) and area under the receiver operating characteristic curve (AUROC) of 0.88 even for an extremely imbalanced dataset (MSI-H (12.03%) vs MSI-L (87.97%)) (see Table 2(b) and Fig. 3(a)). On the other hand, in evaluation with the reference labels generated by the NGS MSIsensor score, the proposed ensemble transformer method consistently achieved the best-performing result, obtaining the highest MeanSS (79%) and accuracy (89%), and the proposed transformer method also achieved the superior performance with the highest MeanSS (79%) and AUROC of 0.88, even for an extremely imbalanced dataset (MSI-H (13.36%) vs MSI-L (86.64%)) (see Table 2(c) and Fig. 3(b)). These findings indicate the promising capability of the proposed ensemble transformer to predict MSI status directly from histopathological WSIs in CRC.

3.3 Statistical Analysis

Fisher's Exact Test in EC Dataset. According to the two-tailed Fisher's exact test, the associations between the predictions of the proposed models and the TP53 or the four MSI biomarkers are both extremely strong ($\mathbf{p} < \mathbf{0.001}$) (see Table 1). These results demonstrate the exceptional performance of our proposed methods in prediction of TP53 and the four MSI biomarkers directly from H&E samples in EC.

Fisher's Exact Test in CRC Dataset. According to the two-tailed Fisher's exact test, the associations between the predictions of the proposed models and the actual cancer subtype or MSI statuses are both extremely strong (**p < 0.001**) (see Table 2). These results convincingly show the exceptional performance of our proposed methods across three tasks: cancer subtyping, MSI prediction using MANTIS score and MSI prediction using MSIsensor score in the CRC samples. Results of some benchmark methods such as TOAD and TransMIL are poor, especially in dealing with imbalanced data, obtaining zero sensitivity in MSI prediction using MANTIS score (MSI-H [12.03%] vs MSI-L [87.97%]) and using MSIsensor score (MSI-H [13.36%] vs MSI-L [86.64%])), and hence the associated Fisher's exact test results could not be generated because of their one-sided predictions. The results show the robustness of our proposed methods to deal with extremely imbalanced data in application to cancer subtyping and MSI prediction in CRC.

3.4 Interpretability Analysis

In this section, we demonstrate that the attention maps generated by the proposed transformer DL predictive model has shown a high degree of consistency with the morphological analysis results of pathologists, and thus the attention heatmaps of the DL model could be used for artificial intelligence (AI)-assisted human-in-the-loop clinical diagnoses. The proposed model makes the slide-level prediction by first identifying and aggregating regions with high attention scores

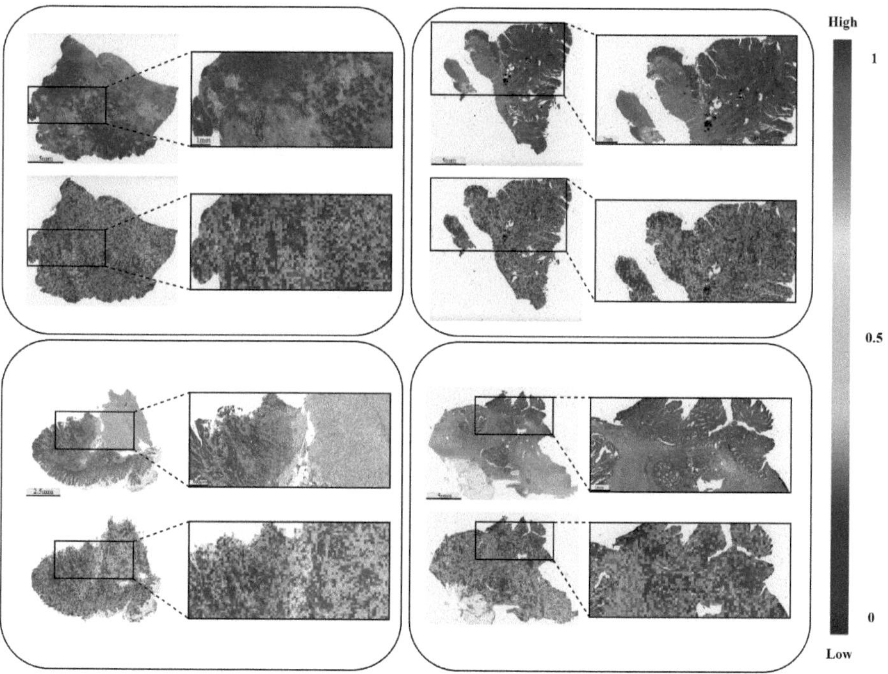

Fig. 4. Attention heatmaps generated by the proposed method in CRC subtyping.

as high diagnostically important information within WSIs while disregarding regions with low attention scores as redundant low diagnostic relevant information. To visualize and interpret the relative importance of each region in a WSI, attention heatmaps are generated by converting the attention scores of the model predictive class into percentiles and mapping the normalized scores to their corresponding spatial location in the original slide (see Fig. 4). The attention heatmaps use a color gradient where red indicates areas of high attention and blue denotes areas of low attention, effectively mapping the model's focus areas. These focus areas likely correlate with regions of high diagnostic importance as interpreted by the model. Even training without pixel-level or patch-level annotation to explicitly inform the model whether each region is tumour tissue or not, we observed that through weakly supervised learning using slide-level labels only, the proposed models highly focused on the tumour-rich regions.

4 Conclusion

In this study, we validated the proposed DL-based approach in prediction of MSI, TP53 and pathological subtype directly from histopathological images in EC and CRC, using two independent datasets from multiple tissue source sites with reference labels generated by IHC and NGS data, respectively. This may have important clinical implications for pathological diagnosis, prognosis, and drug response prediction. The proposed architecture helps the model capture specific pathological features and classify them, aiding in the development of immunotherapy plans for CRC and EC patients. Compared to existing laboratory testing methods, the proposed model provides patients with a more convenient and rapid automated screening tool.

Acknowledgments. This study is supported by the National Science and Technology Council of Taiwan (NSTC 113-2222-E-011-003-MY3, NSTC 114-2221-E-016-001), Tri-Service General Hospital, Taipei, Taiwan (TSGH-A-113012 and TSGH-A-114007) and National Taiwan University of Science and Technology- Tri-Service General Hospital (NTUST-TSGH-114-03).

References

1. Bode, A.M., Dong, Z.: Recent advances in precision oncology research. NPJ Precis. Oncol. **2**(1), 11 (2018)
2. Burks, R.T., Kessis, T.D., Cho, K.R., Hedrick, L.: Microsatellite instability in endometrial carcinoma. Oncogene **9**(4), 1163–1166 (1994)
3. Campanella, G., et al.: Clinical-grade computational pathology using weakly supervised deep learning on whole slide images. Nat. Med. **25**(8), 1301–1309 (2019)
4. Germano, G., et al.: Inactivation of DNA repair triggers neoantigen generation and impairs tumour growth. Nature **552**(7683), 116–120 (2017)
5. Gonzalez-Zulueta, M., et al.: Microsatellite instability in bladder cancer. Can. Res. **53**(23), 5620–5623 (1993)

6. Hampel, H., et al.: Feasibility of screening for lynch syndrome among patients with colorectal cancer. J. Clin. Oncol. **26**(35), 5783–5788 (2008)
7. Hou, W., Yi, C., Zhu, H.: Predictive biomarkers of colon cancer immunotherapy: present and future. Front. Immunol. **13**, 1032314 (2022)
8. Kann, B.H., Hosny, A., Aerts, H.J.: Artificial intelligence for clinical oncology. Cancer Cell **39**(7), 916–927 (2021)
9. Liñares-Blanco, J., Pazos, A., Fernandez-Lozano, C.: Machine learning analysis of TCGA cancer data. PeerJ Comput. Sci. **7**, e584 (2021)
10. Lu, M.Y., et al.: Ai-based pathology predicts origins for cancers of unknown primary. Nature **594**(7861), 106–110 (2021)
11. Lu, M.Y., Williamson, D.F., Chen, T.Y., Chen, R.J., Barbieri, M., Mahmood, F.: Data-efficient and weakly supervised computational pathology on whole-slide images. Nat. Biomed. Eng. **5**(6), 555–570 (2021)
12. Mandal, R., et al.: Genetic diversity of tumors with mismatch repair deficiency influences anti-PD-1 immunotherapy response. Science **364**(6439), 485–491 (2019)
13. Matthews, T.: The sudden infant death syndrome–a bustling ignorance! (1986)
14. Peltomäki, P., et al.: Microsatellite instability is associated with tumors that characterize the hereditary non-polyposis colorectal carcinoma syndrome. Can. Res. **53**(24), 5853–5855 (1993)
15. Pino, M.S., Chung, D.C.: Microsatellite instability in the management of colorectal cancer. Exp. Rev. Gastroenterol. Hepatol. **5**(3), 385–399 (2011)
16. Rhyu, M.G., Park, W.S., Meltzer, S.J.: Microsatellite instability occurs frequently in human gastric carcinoma. Oncogene **9**(1), 29–32 (1994)
17. Ryan, N., Glaire, M., Blake, D., Cabrera-Dandy, M., Evans, D.G., Crosbie, E.: The proportion of endometrial cancers associated with lynch syndrome: a systematic review of the literature and meta-analysis. Genet. Med. **21**(10), 2167–2180 (2019)
18. Shan, J., Han, D., Shen, C., Lei, Q., Zhang, Y.: Mechanism and strategies of immunotherapy resistance in colorectal cancer. Front. Immunol. **13**, 1016646 (2022)
19. Shao, Z., et al.: TransMIL: transformer based correlated multiple instance learning for whole slide image classification. In: Ranzato, M., Beygelzimer, A., Dauphin, Y., Liang, P., Vaughan, J.W. (eds.) Advances in Neural Information Processing Systems, vol. 34, pp. 2136–2147. Curran Associates, Inc. (2021)
20. Wang, C.W., et al.: Interpretable attention-based deep learning ensemble for personalized ovarian cancer treatment without manual annotations. Comput. Med. Imaging Graph. **107**, 102233D (2023)
21. Wang, C.W., et al.: Deep learning can predict bevacizumab therapeutic effect and microsatellite instability directly from histology in epithelial ovarian cancer. Lab. Invest. **103**(11), 100247 (2023)
22. Xiang, H., Shen, J., Yan, Q., Xu, M., Shi, X., Zhu, X.: Multi-scale representation attention based deep multiple instance learning for gigapixel whole slide image analysis. Med. Image Anal. **89**, 102890 (2023)
23. Yee, C.J., Roodi, N., Verrier, C.S., Parl, F.F.: Microsatellite instability and loss of heterozygosity in breast cancer. Can. Res. **54**(7), 1641–1644 (1994)

FGFENet: Fine-Grained Feature Enhancement Network for Brain Tumor Segmentation

Haowen Zhu[1], Shaolong Zhou[2], Minghui Chen[3], Lei Yang[4], Xin Zhao[2,6](✉), Huiqin Jiang[3](✉), and Ling Ma[5]

[1] Henan Institute of Advanced Technology, Zhengzhou University, Zhengzhou 450003, China
zhw_student@gs.zzu.edu.cn

[2] The Third Affiliated Hospital, Zhengzhou University, Zhengzhou 450052, China
{doctorzhou,zdsfyzx}@zzu.edu.cn

[3] The School of Electrical and Information Engineering, Zhengzhou University, Zhengzhou 450001, China
cmh197@gs.zzu.edu.cn, iehqjiang@zzu.edu.cn

[4] National Supercomputing Center in Zhengzhou, Zhengzhou University, Zhengzhou 450001, China
nscczzyanglei@zzu.edu.cn

[5] The School of Computer and Artificial Intelligence, Zhengzhou University, Zhengzhou 450001, China
ielma@zzu.edu.cn

[6] Tianjian Laboratory of Advanced Biomedical Sciences, Institute of Advanced Biomedical Sciences, Zhengzhou University, Zhengzhou, Henan 450000, China

Abstract. Brain tumor segmentation plays a key role in the early diagnosis and assessment of disease progression of gliomas. Magnetic resonance imaging (MRI), as one of the important means of clinical diagnosis for patients with glioma, provides an important basis for tumor segmentation. Despite the achievements of existing methods in the task of MRI brain tumor segmentation, the segmentation accuracy of fine-grained lesion boundaries is still insufficient. The lesion region has a serious foreground-background imbalance problem compared to the dominant background region, which is not adequately considered in most current segmentation methods, leading to poor performance of the model in dealing with fine-grained lesion boundaries, and making it difficult to ensure the completeness and accuracy of lesion segmentation. To address this challenge, this paper designs a fine-grained feature enhancement network, FGFENet, which aims to improve the feature characterization of fine-grained lesion regions in MRI images. The method employs a CNN-Mamba hybrid encoder for multilevel feature extraction and combines the fine-grained feature enhancement module with tiny region feature, and finally optimizes the segmentation boundary by an edge-aware decoder. On the BraTS2020 dataset, the DSC and HD95 of our method on WT,

This work was supported by Tianjian Laboratory of Advanced Biomedical Sciences and Zhengzhou collaborative innovation major special project under Grant 20XTZX11020.

C. Wallraven et al. (Eds.): ACPR 2025, LNCS 16174, pp. 60–72, 2026.
https://doi.org/10.1007/978-981-95-4395-3_5

TC, and ET are 0.9481, 0.8912, 0.9005 and 2.5037, 4.4339, and 2.1326, respectively. On the BraTS2021 dataset, the corresponding metrics are 0.9225, 0.9180, 0.8769 and 4.6175, 2.9908, and 2.3940. The performance on both datasets is better than the existing model.

Keywords: Brain tumor segmentation · Mamba · Fine-Grained Feature Enhancement

1 Introduction

Glioma is one of the most common malignant brain tumors with high incidence and low survival rate [18,19]. Achieving precise segmentation of brain tumors is important for the accurate diagnosis of gliomas, the development of treatment plans, and the assessment of prognosis. Magnetic Resonance Imaging (MRI) is a non-invasive medical imaging technique that has significant advantages over CT or X-ray scanning, especially in soft tissue imaging. MRI uses strong magnetic fields and radio waves to obtain detailed images of organs and tissues in the body, allowing doctors to clearly see the location and size of a tumour and its relationship to the surrounding tissue [17]. MRI imaging has several different modalities, T1-weighted, T2-weighted, T1-enhanced, and Flair (Fluid Attenuation Inversion Recovery), each of which provides different information about different aspects of the tumor. For example, T1-weighted images can help to distinguish the border between the tumor and normal tissue, while T2-weighted images help to assess the nature of the tumor.

CNN-based networks, such as UNet [6], have been widely used in the field of medical image segmentation. U-Net, with its encoder-decoder architecture and hopping connectivity mechanism, is able to efficiently capture and integrate image feature at different scales, and shows excellent performance in medical image segmentation tasks. Milletari [14] et al. design a volumetric fully convolutional neural network (V-Net) framework that directly processes 3D medical image volumes and optimizes a novel Dice coefficient-based objective function, thereby enhancing the accuracy and efficiency of volumetric segmentation. Oktay [16] et al. propose a novel Attention Gate (AG) model integrated into the U-Net architecture for medical image segmentation, which can automatically focus on the target structure to improve segmentation accuracy and efficiency while reducing the need for multi-stage cascaded CNN models. CNN-based networks have good local feature capabilities, but they are difficult to model long-range dependencies.

With the advent of TransFormer [21], which can model long-range dependencies, many TransFormer-based medical image segmentation methods have been proposed. Chen et al. [5] propose a medical image segmentation framework called TransUNet, which combines the strengths of Transformer and U-Net to encode global context by treating image feature as sequences and using skip connection to recover low-level details for accurate localization and segmentation. Hatamizadeh et al. [9] propose a novel Transformer architecture called UNETR for 3D medical image segmentation, which, by reformulating the 3D segmentation task as a 1D sequence-to-sequence prediction problem and utilizing a Transformer encoder to capture global multiscale information in conjunction with a Unet decoder, achieves high-precision segmentation of multiple organs and brain tumor segmentation with high accuracy. However, Transformer-based algorithms face computational bottlenecks when dealing with long sequences due to quadratic computational complexity, as well as memory bloating problems caused by caching historical tokens, thus failing to support longer context windows.

In recent research in the field of medical image segmentation, Mamba-based approaches have been introduced. Xing et al. [22] design a novel 3D medical image segmentation framework named SegMamba that leverages the Mamba state space model to capture long-range dependencies within volumetric data, thereby enhancing segmentation accuracy and efficiency compared to traditional CNN-based and transformer-based methods. Ma et al. [12] propose a novel U-Mamba framework that integrates CNNs and state space models (SSMs) to enhance long-range dependency modeling in 3D medical image segmentation, significantly improving accuracy and efficiency while maintaining linear computational complexity. Mamba [8] is based on a selective state space model that achieves linear time complexity and significantly reduces the computational overhead of long sequence processing. With selective SSM, it is able to dynamically adjust the parameters according to the input, filter irrelevant information and retain the key context. In addition, by compressing the context information into a fixed-size state, Mamba solves the memory bloat problem of the Transformer and thus supports longer context windows.

Previous methods have achieved some success in multimodal brain tumor segmentation. However, when facing fine-grained lesion boundary regions in the segmentation task, the existing methods do not take into account the small percentage of the target region relative to the background region, which results in inaccurate fine-grained lesion boundary segmentation. In addition, in the U-shape structure method, most of the methods take direct connection during skip connection or add residual blocks in skip connection to further extract the low-level feature, and do not enhance the fine-grained feature in the low-level feature. In this paper, we propose FGFENet, which aims to solve the problems of the target region occupying a relatively small area in the image, blurred boundaries, and details being easily ignored, so as to achieve more accurate segmentation of the lesion boundaries. FGFENet systematically optimizes the traditional segmentation architectures in terms of encoding, enhancement, and decoding. Firstly, we introduce a hybrid encoder based on CNN and Mamba architectures to capture both low-level local spatial feature and high-level global semantic information. CNN module is good at extracting detailed textures and edge structures, while the Mamba module can model remote dependencies and contextual information, and the combination of these two modules effectively improves the feature expression and overall sensing ability of the model. Secondly, we designed the FGFEM to further enhance the ability of the model to portray the details of the lesion area. This module significantly enhances the ability of the model to perceive tiny lesions and their border regions through multi-branch feature extraction structure, dilated convolution operation, and multi-scale information fusion mechanism, which alleviates the problem of difficult recognition of small targets. Finally, in order to enhance the ability of the model to recognize boundary regions, we introduce an edge-aware decoder. This decoder effectively directs the model to focus on the boundary transition region between the lesion and the background by explicitly modeling the edge information in the feature, thus enhancing the accuracy and contour integrity of the segmentation results.

Overall, our contributions are fourfold:

- A hybrid CNN-Mamba encoder is constructed to simultaneously extract low-level local feature and high-level global contextual representations, leveraging the strengths of both architectures for more comprehensive feature learning.
- A Fine-Grained Feature Enhancement Module (FGFEM) is introduced to enrich the representation of subtle lesion structures by incorporating multi-branch convolutions, dilated operations, and multi-scale feature fusion.
- An edge-aware decoder is designed to explicitly capture boundary information from encoded features, facilitating more accurate delineation of lesion contours in the final segmentation results.
- Compared with existing methods using the BraTS2020 and BraTS2021 datasets, FEFGNet achieves superior segmentation accuracy.

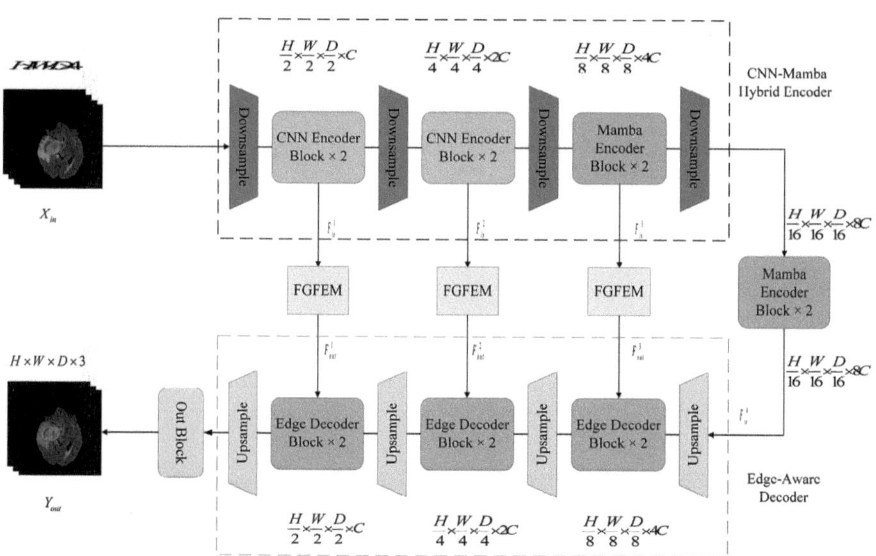

Fig. 1. Overview of the proposed FGFENet.

2 Method

In this paper, we propose FGFENet for enhancing small target feature in multimodal MRI image segmentation. Figure 1 shows an overview of the network, which consists of three main components: (1) a CNN-Mamba hybrid encoder for capturing low-level local feature and learning high-level global feature. (2) a feature enhancement module for enhancing the detail information of small target lesions. (3) an edge-aware decoder for extracting edge information from feature.

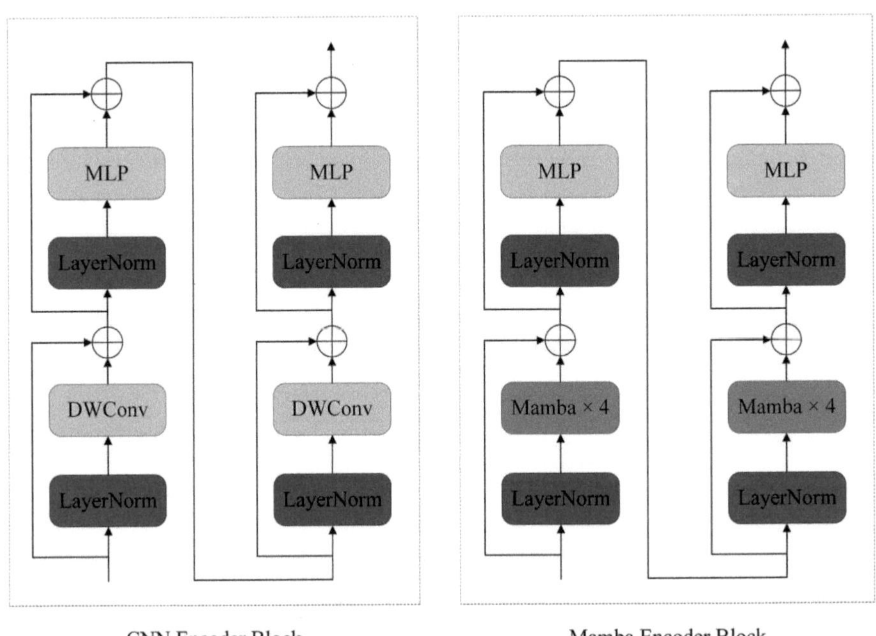

Fig. 2. The CNN Encoder Block is based on DW convolution block and the Mamba Encoder Block based on a Mamba.

2.1 CNN-Mamba Hybrid Encoder

The excellent performance achieved by Mamba in the field of long range modelling is a significant improvement for advanced global feature extraction. Hybrid CNN-Mamba structure design can extract local and global feature [3,10]. As shown in Fig. 1, the CNN-Mamba hybrid encoder has four stages, each of which goes through a downsampling module and feature extraction. In the first two stages, we use a DW(depth-wise) convolution feature extraction module to extract local feature. In the last two stages, we use a Mamba feature extraction module to model long-range dependent high-level feature in the latent space. Given an MRI image input $X_{in} \in \mathbb{R}^{C\times H\times W\times D}$, where $H \times W$ represents the spatial resolution, D denotes the depth, and C is the number of channels, we utilize an encoder to extract a context feature map F_{in}^{i}. This feature map effectively captures spatial and depth-related information across multiple modalities and scales. The process can be formulated as follows:

$$F_{in}^{1} = CNN\ Encoder\ Block(CNN\ Encoder\ Block(Down(X_{in}))) \quad (1)$$

$$F_{in}^{2} = CNN\ Encoder\ Block(CNN\ Encoder\ Block(Down(F_{in}^{1}))) \quad (2)$$

$$F_{in}^{3} = Mamba\ Encoder\ Block(Mamba\ Encoder\ Block(Down(F_{in}^{2}))) \quad (3)$$

$$F_{in}^{4} = Mamba\ Encoder\ Block(Mamba\ Encoder\ Block(Down(F_{in}^{3}))) \quad (4)$$

where $CNN\ Encoder\ Block$ is the DW convolutional feature encoder and $Mamba\ Encoder\ Block$ is the Mamba feature encoder, which are shown in Fig. 2, and $Down$ is the downsampling operation.

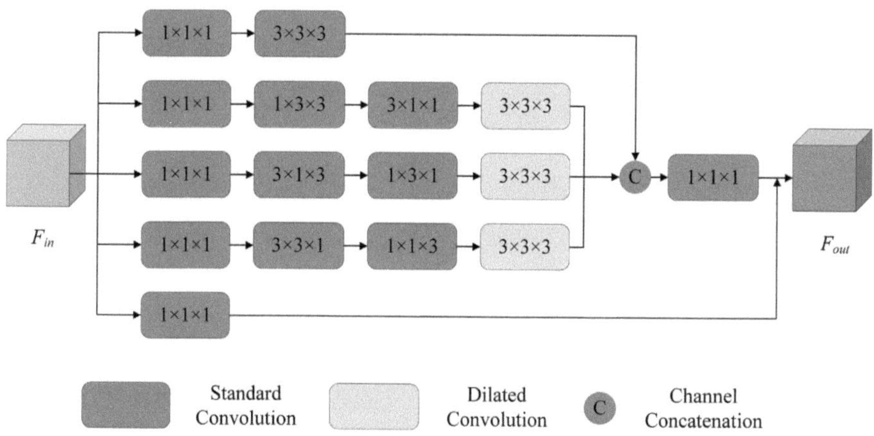

Fig. 3. Fine-Grained Feature Enhancement Module.

2.2 Fine-Grained Feature Enhancement Module

Multi-branch convolutional structure can extract multi-scale feature and enrich the feature representation through different scale convolutional kernels, while the dilated convolution maintains the feature resolution while expanding the receptive field, and both of them jointly enhance the feature representation of small targets to improve the detection ability of the model for small targets [25]. We propose a fine-grained feature enhancement module based on multi-branch convolutional structure and dilated convolution, and its structure is shown in Fig. 3. Firstly, the input feature are extracted through four parallel branches, each of which first performs a $1 \times 1 \times 1$ convolution operation on the input feature. The first branch performs the convolution of $3 \times 3 \times 3$, while the other three branches perform the convolution of $1 \times 3 \times 3$, $3 \times 1 \times 3$, $3 \times 3 \times 1$ convolution, respectively. Extra $3 \times 3 \times 3$ dilated convolution layers are added to the three middle branches. Next, the output feature of the four branches are spliced along the channel dimensions to form multi-scale fusion feature. The spliced feature are then channel transformed using the $1 \times 1 \times 1$ convolution to reduce the channel dimension and fuse the multiscale information. Finally, the input feature are channel transformed by the $1 \times 1 \times 1$ convolution and then summed with the fused feature to form the residual structure. The formula is as follow:

$$B_1^i = Conv_{3\times3\times3}(Conv_{1\times1\times1}(F_{in}^i)) \tag{5}$$

$$B_2^i = Dilated_{3\times3\times3}(Conv_{3\times1\times1}(Conv_{1\times3\times3}(Conv_{1\times1\times1}(F_{in}^i)))) \tag{6}$$

$$B_3^i = Dilated_{3\times3\times3}(Conv_{1\times3\times1}(Conv_{3\times1\times3}(Conv_{1\times1\times1}(F_{in}^i)))) \tag{7}$$

$$B_4^i = Dilated_{3\times3\times3}(Conv_{1\times1\times3}(Conv_{3\times3\times1}(Conv_{1\times1\times1}(F_{in}^i)))) \tag{8}$$

$$F_{out}^i = Conv_{1\times1\times1}(Concat(B_1^i, B_2^i, B_3^i, B_4^i)) + Conv_{1\times1\times1}(F_{in}^i) \tag{9}$$

where $Conv_{a\times b\times c}$ represents the standard convolution with a kernel size of $a \times b \times c$, $Dilated_{3\times3\times3}$ represents a dilated convolution with a kernel size of $3 \times 3 \times 3$, and $Concat$ represents the channel concatenation.

The fine-grained feature enhancement module enhances the ability of model to capture the details of the lesion region by capturing the contextual information around the lesion more effectively through multi-branch feature extraction, dilated convolution operation, multi-scale feature fusion.

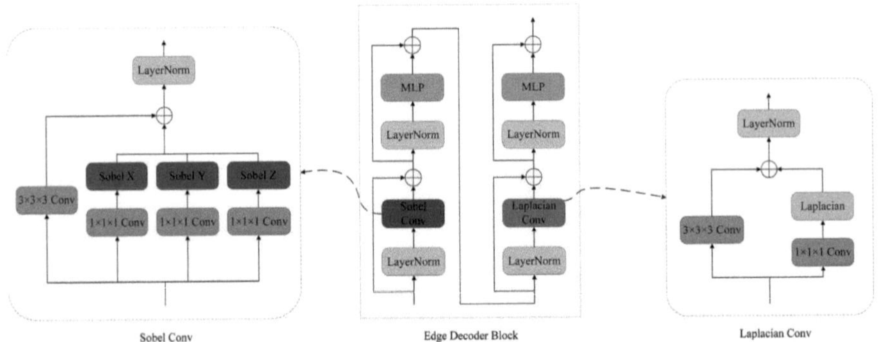

Fig. 4. Edge-aware decoder.

2.3 Edge-Aware Decoder

The Sobel operator and Laplacian operator can extract the first-order and second-order differential feature of the feature map, respectively, which significantly enhances the edge information and thus improves the accuracy and boundary prediction of brain tumor segmentation [20]. As shown in Fig. 4, we design an edge-aware decoder based on Sobel operator and Laplacian operator. The multiscale feature, F_{out}^{i}, are first entered into a Sobel operator convolution with a two-branch structure, whose first branch contains a $3 \times 3 \times 3$ convolutional layer for extracting the basic feature, and the second branch first enhances the inter-channel interactions through a $1 \times 1 \times 1$ convolutional layer followed by the extraction of the first-order differential edge information by utilizing a learnable scaling Sobel filter to extract first order differential edge information. The second order differential edge information is then extracted by a Laplacian convolution similar in structure to the Sobel operator convolution. Finally, the decoded feature information is channel transformed to obtain the segmentation result, and the process is shown below:

$$Z_1 = F_{out}^{i} + Sobel\ Conv(LayerNorm(F_{out}^{i})) \tag{10}$$

$$Z_2 = Sobel\ Decoder(F_{out}^{i}) = Z_1 + MLP(LayerNorm(Z_1)) \tag{11}$$

$$Z_3 = Z_2 + Laplacian\ Conv(LayerNorm(Z_2)) \tag{12}$$

$$Laplacian\ Decoder(F_{out}^{i}) = Z_3 + MLP(LayerNorm(Z_3)) \tag{13}$$

$$Edge\ Decoder(F_{out}^{i}) = Laplacian\ Decoder(Sobel\ Decoder(F_{out}^{i})) \tag{14}$$

3 Experiment

3.1 Dataset and Evaluation Metric

To validate the performance of the proposed FGFENet, we conduct experiments on two datasets (i.e., BraTS2020 and BraTS2021 [1,2,13]) of the Multimodal Brain Tumor Segmentation Challenge (BraTS). BraTS2020 has a total of 369 cases, each of which contains four modalities, T2, T1ce, T1, and Flair, with segmentation goals of WT (Whole Tumor), TC (Tumor Core) and ET (Enhancing Tumor). TC and ET are small target area in segmentation lesions. BraTS2021 has 1251 cases and the rest of the information is consistent with BraTS2020. According to the recent works [20,23], BraTS2020 is divided into training set, validation set and test set according to 315/17/37 respectively. The division of training set/validation set/test set for BraTS2021 is 1001/125/125.

DSC (Dice similarity coefficient) [7] can measure the similarity between two sets, and can evaluate the overlap between the predicted segmentation results and the ground truth, and its value is between 0 and 1, the closer to 1 means that the higher the overlap between the prediction and the ground truth, which indicates that the segmentation effect of model is better. HD95 (95% Hausdorff Distance) [24] is a metric used to evaluate the distance between two geometric shapes or sets of points in image segmentation to assess the quality of the boundary of the segmentation result, with a value between 0 and infinity, with a value closer to 0 representing a higher degree of overlap between the predicted and ground truth.

3.2 Implementation Details

Our model is implemented in PyTorch 2.5.1 and MONAI 1.2.0 on a NVIDIA GeForce RTX 3090 GPU. The model is trained with the AdamW optimizer [11] with a weight decay of 1×10^{-5} for 300 epochs. The initial learning rate is 2×10^{-4}. The loss function is a combination of dice loss and cross-entropy loss [4]. Data augmentation during training included flipping, identity scaling, croping and shifting.

3.3 Results

We compare FGFENet with four baseline models on BraTS2020 and BraTS2021, including CNN-based methods (3DUNet [6], SegResNet [15]), Transformer-based method (EoFormer [20]), and Mamba-based method (SegMamba [22]). The results are shown in Table 1 and Table 2. Figure 5 represents the visualization of the segmentation results on the BraTS 2020 dataset.

Table 1 shows the performance of FGFENet on BraTS 2020 dataset compared with other methods. The DSC of WT and ET on FGFENet are 0.9481 and 0.9005, which are better than the four baseline models. TC achieves 0.8912, surpassing 3DUNet, EoFormer and SegMamba. In addition, FGFENet attains the best HD95 scores on WT, TC, and ET. Table 2 illustrates the performance comparison between FGFENet and other methods on BraTS2021. DSC and HD95 on ET have the best results compared to other methods.

Table 1. Quantitative comparison with the state-of-the-art models on the BraTS2020 dataset.

Method	DSC			HD95		
	WT	TC	ET	WT	TC	ET
3DUNet [6]	0.9227	0.8393	0.8333	6.8971	9.2564	3.4284
SegResNet [15]	0.9431	**0.9004**	0.8762	3.4615	3.8629	2.8794
EoFormer [20]	0.9469	0.8685	0.8697	2.9393	5.0807	3.1350
SegMamba [22]	0.9361	0.8785	0.8805	6.2709	7.9702	5.0351
Ours	**0.9481**	0.8912	**0.9005**	**2.5037**	**4.4339**	**2.1326**

3.4 Ablation

We conduct ablation experiments on BraTS 2020 to investigate the effectiveness of our proposed FGFENet. In Table 3, FGFEM represents the fine-grained feature enhancement module and Number of Mamba layer represents the number of mamba layers in *Mamba Encoder Block*. The FGFEM module improves the DSC of ET by 0.01 and reduces HD95 by 0.2, respectively. This demonstrates that FGFEM effectively captures the detailed information in the lesion

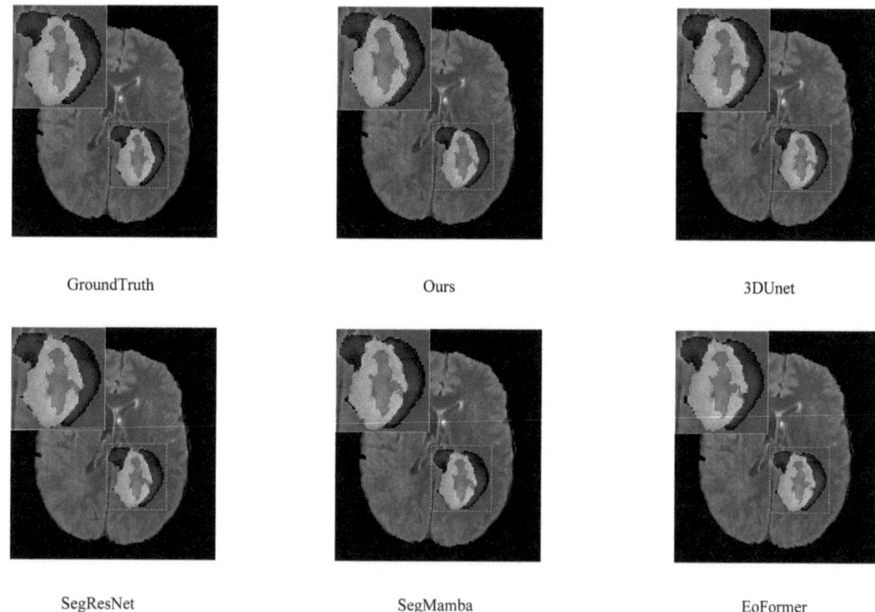

Fig. 5. The visual comparison results on BraTS2020 dataset. The green region denotes WT, the red represents TC and the yellow means ET. (Color figure online)

Table 2. Quantitative comparison with the state-of-art models on BraTS2021 dataset.

Method	DSC			HD95		
	WT	TC	ET	WT	TC	ET
3DUNet [6]	0.9242	0.9072	0.8661	4.6285	3.9301	2.7793
SegResNet [15]	**0.9252**	0.9175	0.8665	5.2536	3.2724	3.1025
EoFormer [20]	0.9219	0.9161	0.8732	6.5111	**2.9639**	2.9087
SegMamba [22]	0.9238	0.9117	0.8737	4.6826	3.3554	2.7252
Ours	0.9225	**0.9180**	**0.8769**	**4.6175**	2.9908	**2.3940**

and improves the accuracy of small target area segmentation. In addition, we also investigate the effect of different number of Mamba layers on the network, when Mamba layer = 2, the model performance is better, while more layers of Mamba will make the model performance degraded, which shows that more Mamba layers are not better.

Table 3. Validate the influence of FGFEM and the number of Mamba layer on the proposed model on BraTS2020 dataset.

FGFEM	Number of Mamba Layer	DSC			HD95		
		WT	TC	ET	WT	TC	ET
✓	1	0.9450	**0.9034**	0.8948	2.4584	4.9894	2.2019
✓	2	**0.9481**	0.8912	**0.9005**	2.5037	**4.4339**	**2.1326**
✓	4	0.9464	0.8830	0.8906	**2.3939**	5.0479	2.1458
✓	8	0.9356	0.8407	0.8529	3.0695	6.3654	3.8973
×	2	0.9428	0.8918	0.8943	2.9209	4.8476	2.3664

4 Conclusion

In this work, we propose a novel MRI image segmentation method, FGFENet. The method mainly consists of a hybrid encoder of CNN and Mamba architectures, a fine-grained feature enhancement module, and an edge-aware decoder. The hybrid encoder fully combines the ability of CNN in extracting local feature and the advantage of Mamba in modeling global dependencies, which enables the network to capture both low-level local feature and high-level semantic information in the image, and improves the overall feature expression capability. The fine-grained feature enhancement module is used to further improve the segmentation accuracy of the model for the lesion region. By introducing a multi-branch feature extraction structure and a dilated convolution operation, the module effectively enhances the ability of the model to perceive the edges of the lesion and its surrounding contextual information, which significantly improves the detailed portrayal of complex lesion structures. The edge-aware decoder is able to optimize the edge part of the segmentation result. Our FGFENet outperforms other state-of-the-art methods on both BraTS 2020 and BraTS 2021.

References

1. Bakas, S., et al.: Advancing the cancer genome atlas glioma MRI collections with expert segmentation labels and radiomic features. Sci. Data **4**(1), 1–13 (2017)
2. Bakas, S., et al.: Identifying the best machine learning algorithms for brain tumor segmentation, progression assessment, and overall survival prediction in the brats challenge. arXiv preprint arXiv:1811.02629 (2018)
3. Chang, A., Zeng, J., Huang, R., Ni, D.: EM-net: efficient channel and frequency learning with mamba for 3d medical image segmentation. In: Linguraru, M.G., et al. (eds.) MICCAI 2024. LNCS, vol. 15009, pp. 266–275. Springer, Cham (2024). https://doi.org/10.1007/978-3-031-72114-4_26
4. Chen, C., Dou, Q., Jin, Y., Chen, H., Qin, J., Heng, P.-A.: Robust multimodal brain tumor segmentation via feature disentanglement and gated fusion. In: Shen, D., et al. (eds.) MICCAI 2019. LNCS, vol. 11766, pp. 447–456. Springer, Cham (2019). https://doi.org/10.1007/978-3-030-32248-9_50

5. Chen, J., et al.: Transunet: transformers make strong encoders for medical image segmentation. arXiv preprint arXiv:2102.04306 (2021)
6. Çiçek, Ö., Abdulkadir, A., Lienkamp, S.S., Brox, T., Ronneberger, O.: 3D U-net: learning dense volumetric segmentation from sparse annotation. In: Ourselin, S., Joskowicz, L., Sabuncu, M.R., Unal, G., Wells, W. (eds.) MICCAI 2016. LNCS, vol. 9901, pp. 424–432. Springer, Cham (2016). https://doi.org/10.1007/978-3-319-46723-8_49
7. Dice, L.R.: Measures of the amount of ecologic association between species. Ecology **26**(3), 297–302 (1945)
8. Gu, A., Dao, T.: Mamba: linear-time sequence modeling with selective state spaces. arXiv preprint arXiv:2312.00752 (2023)
9. Hatamizadeh, A., et al.: Unetr: transformers for 3d medical image segmentation. In: Proceedings of the IEEE/CVF Winter Conference on Applications of Computer Vision, pp. 574–584 (2022)
10. Liu, A., et al.: LM-Unet: whole-body PET-CT lesion segmentation with dual-modality-based annotations driven by latent mamba U-net. In: Linguraru, M.G., et al. (eds.) MICCAI 2024. LNCS, vol. 15009, pp. 405–414. Springer, Cham (2024). https://doi.org/10.1007/978-3-031-72114-4_39
11. Loshchilov, I., Hutter, F.: Decoupled weight decay regularization. arXiv preprint arXiv:1711.05101 (2017)
12. Ma, J., Li, F., Wang, B.: U-mamba: enhancing long-range dependency for biomedical image segmentation. arXiv preprint arXiv:2401.04722 (2024)
13. Menze, B.H., et al.: The multimodal brain tumor image segmentation benchmark (BRATS). IEEE Trans. Med. Imaging **34**(10), 1993–2024 (2014)
14. Milletari, F., Navab, N., Ahmadi, S.A.: V-net: fully convolutional neural networks for volumetric medical image segmentation. In: 2016 Fourth International Conference on 3D Vision (3DV), pp. 565–571. IEEE (2016)
15. Myronenko, A.: 3D MRI brain tumor segmentation using autoencoder regularization. In: Crimi, A., Bakas, S., Kuijf, H., Keyvan, F., Reyes, M., van Walsum, T. (eds.) BrainLes 2018. LNCS, vol. 11384, pp. 311–320. Springer, Cham (2019). https://doi.org/10.1007/978-3-030-11726-9_28
16. Oktay, O., et al.: Attention U-net: learning where to look for the pancreas. arXiv preprint arXiv:1804.03999 (2018)
17. Ranjbarzadeh, R., Caputo, A., Tirkolaee, E.B., Ghoushchi, S.J., Bendechache, M.: Brain tumor segmentation of MRI images: a comprehensive review on the application of artificial intelligence tools. Comput. Biol. Med. **152**, 106405 (2023)
18. Rodríguez-Camacho, A., et al.: Glioblastoma treatment: state-of-the-art and future perspectives. Int. J. Mol. Sci. **23**(13), 7207 (2022)
19. Schaff, L.R., Mellinghoff, I.K.: Glioblastoma and other primary brain malignancies in adults: a review. JAMA **329**(7), 574–587 (2023)
20. She, D., Zhang, Y., Zhang, Z., Li, H., Yan, Z., Sun, X.: EoFormer: edge-oriented transformer for brain tumor segmentation. In: Greenspan, H., et al. (eds.) MICCAI 2023. LNCS, vol. 14223, pp. 333–343. Springer, Cham (2023). https://doi.org/10.1007/978-3-031-43901-8_32
21. Vaswani, A., et al.: Attention is all you need. In: Advances in Neural Information Processing Systems, vol. 30 (2017)
22. Xing, Z., Ye, T., Yang, Y., Liu, G., Zhu, L.: SegMamba: long-range sequential modeling mamba for 3d medical image segmentation. In: Linguraru, M.G., et al. (eds.) MICCAI 2024. LNCS, vol. 15008, pp. 578–588. Springer, Cham (2024). https://doi.org/10.1007/978-3-031-72111-3_54

23. Xing, Z., Yu, L., Wan, L., Han, T., Zhu, L.: Nestedformer: nested modality-aware transformer for brain tumor segmentation. In: Wang, L., Dou, Q., Fletcher, P.T., Speidel, S., Li, S. (eds.) MICCAI 2022. LNCS, vol. 13435, pp. 140–150. Springer, Cham (2022). https://doi.org/10.1007/978-3-031-16443-9_14
24. Yang, J., et al.: Autosegmentation for thoracic radiation treatment planning: a grand challenge at AAPM 2017. Med. Phys. **45**(10), 4568–4581 (2018)
25. Zhang, Y., Ye, M., Zhu, G., Liu, Y., Guo, P., Yan, J.: FFCA-yolo for small object detection in remote sensing images. IEEE Trans. Geosci. Remote Sens. **62**, 1–15 (2024)

Facial Image Aging Simulation and Domain Transformation Using Generative AI

Takeshi Nagata[1,2](✉), Yuna Kawamoto[1], Takumi Enari[1], Hiroshi Endo[1], Syuhei Ozawa[1], Hina Kawasaki[1], Chie Nyui[1], Aiko Ishihara[1], Natsumi Nishiyama[1], Tamami Sanbongi[2], Chandra Louis[2], and kiyoshi Hizukuri[3]

[1] Meiji Gakuin University, 518 Kamikurata-Cho Totsuka-Ku Yokohama-Shi, Kanagawa, Japan
takeshi.nagata@mi.meijigakuin.ac.jp

[2] University of Tsukuba, 1-1-1 Tennodai, Tsukuba 305-8577, Ibaraki, Japan

[3] Yokohama City University, 22-2 Seto, Kanazawa-Ku, Yokohama, Japan

Abstract. Conventional aging simulations require the collection of facial images by age group; thus, a lack of training data poses an issue. As a result, generative AI that learns from big data has attracted attention. However, generative AI has the characteristic of generating plausible results but not necessarily accurate and has the drawback of lacking objectivity. This research aims to perform an objective aging simulation while leveraging the diverse facial expression generation capabilities of generative AI trained on big data to compensate for the lack of training data. When compared with aging simulations that utilizes prompt instructions with generative AI, the results tended to be uniform aging simulations for all individuals. However, the proposed method results in an aging simulation that reflects individual characteristics, and it was confirmed that an objective simulation can be realized while taking advantage of generative AI's ability to generate plausible images.

Keywords: Generative AI · Domain Transformation · Aging Simulation · Face Transformation

1 Introduction

Generative AI can sometimes produce plausible falsehoods, which is a problem. For example, when using generative AI to perform aging simulations, the input image is converted into an old person's face by prompting with instructions such as "old man with gray hair." However, this generates merely a plausible image of an elderly person, and it remains uncertain whether the target person will age in that way [1, 2].

However, conventional aging simulations also have problems. There are limitations to the collection of image data by age group, and machine learning is performed using limited training data [3–13], which raises concerns about accuracy and generalizability.

This research compensates for the lack of training data, a drawback of conventional aging simulation research, with the diverse facial expression generation capabilities

C. Wallraven et al. (Eds.): ACPR 2025, LNCS 16174, pp. 73–85, 2026.
https://doi.org/10.1007/978-981-95-4395-3_6

of generative AI trained on big data, and performs objective aging simulation while generating plausible images, which is the strength of generative AI.

In the generative AI StyleGAN2 [16], its mapping network is designed to improve linearity in the latent variable space, enabling advanced image processing through linear operations. This makes it well-known for high-precision facial image synthesis. In particular, this high degree of linearity enables accurate learning even with limited training data, making it particularly suitable for high-quality domain transformation.

We collected Japanese facial images of various age groups and propose an aging simulation (domain transformation) that takes into account the probability distribution for each age group (domain). For example, we calculate the probability distribution of face length (aspect ratio) for children and adults. We assume that if a person's face length is in the top Q% among children, there is a high probability that they will grow to be in the top Q% among adults. Although "face length" is used as a sample transformation axis, in this study, these transformation axes are determined in a data-driven manner. With the proposed method, adaptive transformation is possible for each face. If the assumptions hold, objective aging simulation results can be achieved. In this presentation, we will report on the overview of the proposed method and the verification results of the aging simulation (domain transformation).

2 Related Research

Facial aging simulation began with simulating the texture of the face surface simula, such as age spots and wrinkles, and has evolved to incorporate changes in shape, such as changes in bone structure and fleshiness [3–7]. Initially, face images were frequency-analyzed, changes in frequency components due to age were reflected, and aging parts such as age spots and wrinkles were supplemented to create plausible aging images.

Also, since the aging phenomenon involves changes in three-dimensional shape, three-dimensional face images have also been explored [8]. In this case, an objective aging simulation is realized by integrating aging simulations of the texture of the face surface and aging simulations of the shape.

In recent years, aging simulations using generative AI based on deep learning have become popular. Initially, aging simulations using GANs were attempted [9–13], but recently, aging simulations using large-scale language image models that have learned a larger number of images have gained popularity [1, 2, 14, 15]. This is because CLIP, which calculates the similarity between natural language and images, has made it easy to achieve high-quality aging simulations that are different from conventional methods by prompt instructions.

However, there are problems with aging simulations that use generative AI. This is because generative AI can produce plausible falsehoods. It generates results that seem plausible, but the basis for this is unclear, and even if they look plausible, their accuracy in predicting real aging is uncertain.

Therefore, in this study, we propose an aging simulation that uses generative AI and is based on objective evidence.

3 Image Acquisition

Images of Japanese faces were collected through internet searches. Ages were divided into five categories: 9–12 years, 15 years, 20–25 years, 40–45 years, and 100 years. Ideally, we would need people in their 60s and 80s, and we plan to expand the data in the future (Table 1).

Table 1. Number of images collected by age group.

	9–12	15	20–25	40–45	100
Female	397	204	616	383	100
male	299	202	394	336	76

4 Method

4.1 Transformation to StyleGAN2 Latent Variables

The collected images were converted into latent variables (18 × 512) using the Restyle Encoder (e4e) [17], which is characterized by its ability to reproduce the original image while being editable, and the celebA model [16], which was trained using image data of various foreign celebrities.

The mean face obtained by using the method shown in Fig. 1 (averaging the latent variables and decoding them with StyleGAN2) is shown Fig. 2. Unlike the average face found from an image base, the latent variables average various facial features themselves, so details are reproduced without blurring. In this way, the latent variable space of StyleGAN2 combines linearity (editability) and reproducibility, making advanced image editing possible with simple operations.

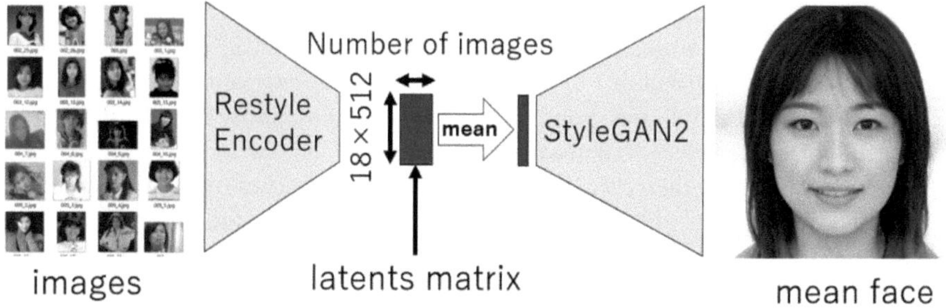

Fig. 1. Mean face creation flow

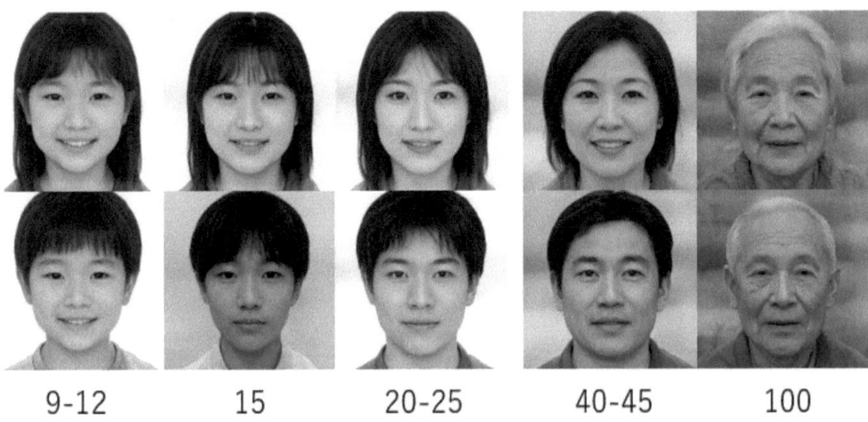

Fig. 2. Mean face of each age

4.2 Domain Transformation

StyleGAN2 is designed to exhibit high linearity in the latent variable space. This inherent high linearity enables that highly accurate learning with a relatively small amount of data, such as a few hundred images.

In this study, we reduce the dimensionality of the latent variables through linear processing and execute domain transformation based on linear transformation.

Generally, PCA (principal component analysis) is used for dimensionality compression, but because PCA finds principal component axes with large covariance, it is not always possible to obtain principal component axes that are convenient for domain transformation. For example, when PCA is performed on face images, variations in lighting conditions frequently manifest as dominant principal components, but differences in lighting conditions are entirely independent of actual aging changes and are therefore not appropriate for aging simulation. Therefore, in this study, we execute domain transformation by finding the principal component axis to be transformed using Partial Least Squares (PLS) [18], which is a method for finding principal components that are highly correlated with the objective variable.

For example, in the case of a simulation of aging from teens to twenties, the objective variable is age and a transformation axis is found using PLS, and the probability distribution (normal distribution) of teens and twenties is estimated along axis using maximum likelihood estimation. Subsequently, faces that are in the top Q% of the normal distribution of teenagers on that axis are transformed into the top Q% of the normal distribution of people in their 20s (Fig. 3). This research focuses on aging simulation, but the proposed domain transformation methodology is not limited to aging simulations and can also be used for gender transformation and transformation from ordinary people to idols. In that case, PLS can be applied by assigning the objective variable of the domain data before transformation to 0 and the objective variable of the domain data after transformation to 1.

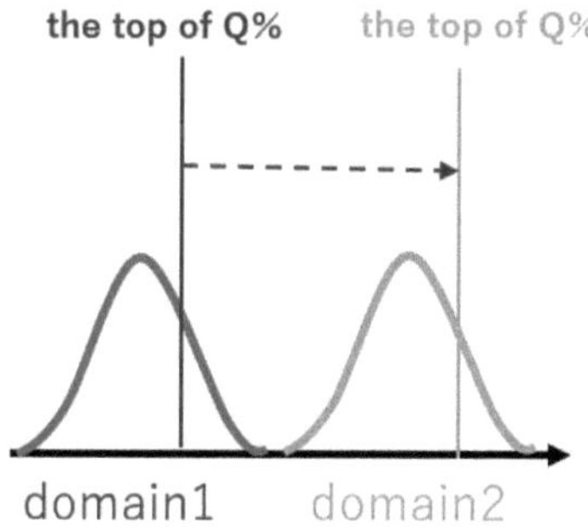

Fig. 3. Domain transformation on the transformation axis

The learning flow for domain transformation between two domains is shown in Fig. 4. PLS is performed on the latent variables of the two domains to find the transformation axis.

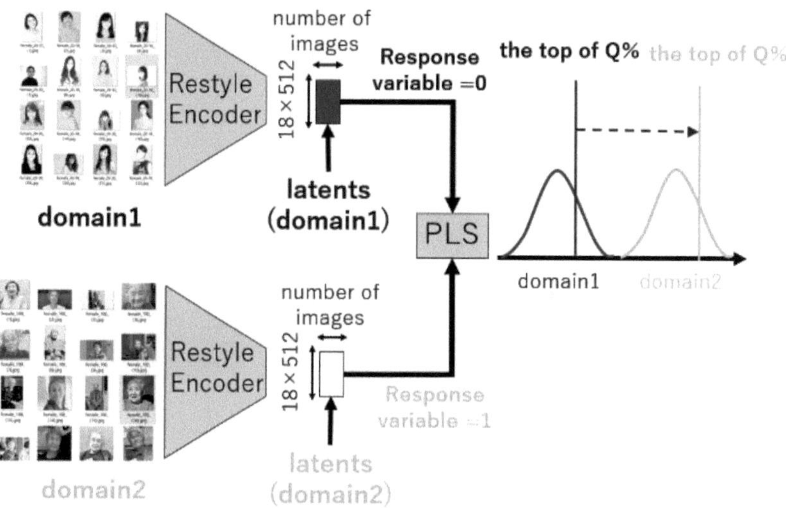

Fig. 4. Learning Domain Transformation

The flow of domain transformation is shown in Fig. 6. The input image is converted to a latent variable. This latent variable is then encoded into a PLS score, and the domain transformation is performed along the PLS principal component axis. Following this, the result is decoded back into a latent variable, which is then finally decoded into an image using StyleGAN2. The number of principal components used for conversion was set to 200 (Fig. 5).

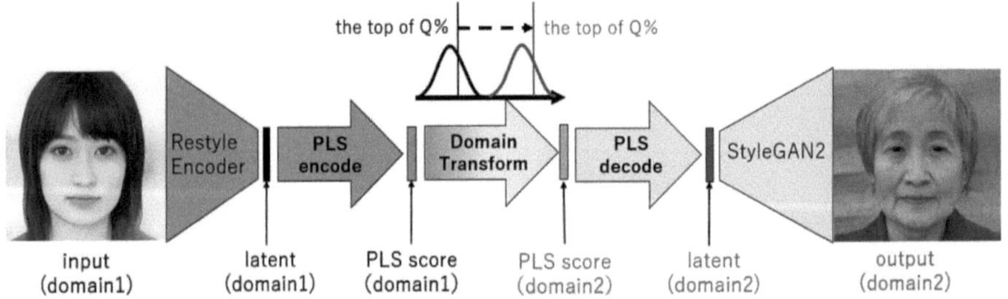

Fig. 5. Domain Transformation

5 Verification

We performed principal component analysis on the latent variables of collected images of ordinary people (20–25 years old), randomly assigned principal component scores on the principal component axis, and artificially generated images of Japanese people (20–25 years old). We then conducted an aging simulation on the generated images (Fig. 6, Fig. 7). The simulation of aging to 60 and 80 years of age uses a model that converts from 40 to 100 years of age, calculates the amount of change dl in the latent variable from 40 to 100 years of age. It adds 1/3 dl to the latent variable for 40 years of age to obtain the latent variable for 60 years of age, and adds 2/3 dl to the latent variable for 40 years of age to obtain the latent variable for 80 years of age.

For comparison, we performed similar simulations using StyleCLIP [1], and Qwen-image-edit[2]. StyleCLIP is based on StyleGAN2 [16] and generates images with high similarity to text using CLIP. Qwen-image-edit [2] which is the state-of-the-art image generation AI understands the semantics of images and can generate consistent images. In this verification, we generated an aging simulation by giving the following prompts (Table 2, Table 3).

Figure 6, Fig. 7 show that the prompted aging methods (StyleCLIP and Qwen-image-edit) tend to produce uniform changes that fail to reflect individual characteristics. In contrast, the proposed method demonstrates the ability to preserve and reflect individual characteristics in the aged images.

Table 4 and Table 5 show the subjective evaluations (on a 5-point scale) of the results of the aging simulation (Fig. 6, Fig. 7) by eight research participants. A statistically significant difference was observed between the average subjective evaluations of Prompted aging methods (StyleCLIP and Qwen-image-edit) and the proposed method. The proposed method achieving an average evaluation value of 3.9 or higher, with the exception of a few participants (15-year-old male), whereas StyleCLIP had an average of 2.1 or lower, particularly for participants aged 30 and over. Comparing Qwen-image-edit with the proposed method, the average score for those under 15 is almost 3 or more, but this is not as good as the proposed method, and for those over 30, the average score is less than 3, which is far below the proposed method, which is almost 4 or more. This subjective evaluation demonstrates that the proposed method is statistically significantly superior to the large-scale language image models.

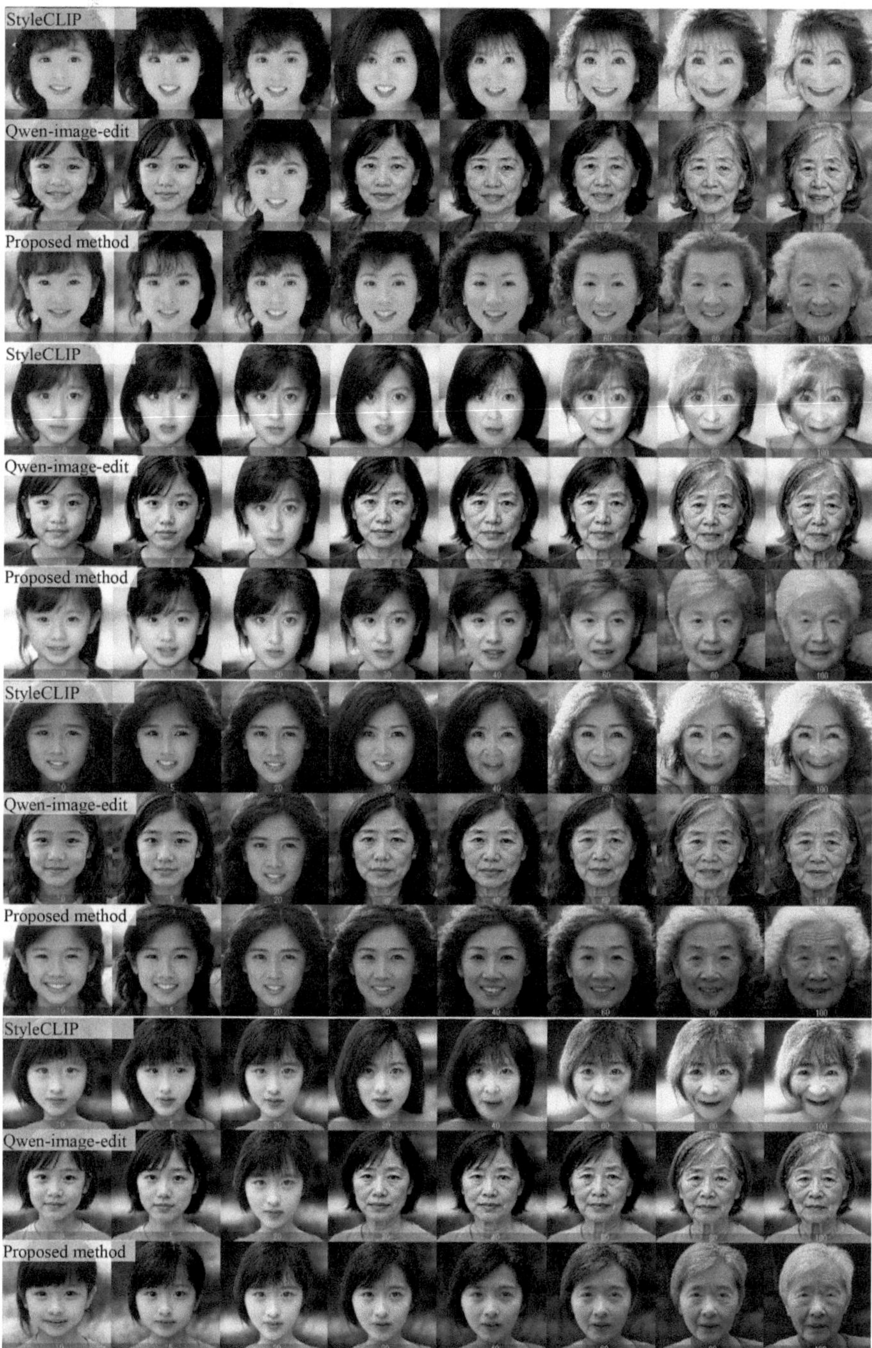

Fig.6. Result of aging simulation (Female)

Fig.6. (*continued*)

The top row shows the results of StyleCLIP with prompt, the middle row shows the results of Qwen-image-edit, and the bottom row shows the proposed method.

From the left, the results of 10 years, the results of 15 years, input of 20 years, the results of 30 years, the results of 40 years, the results of 60 years, the results of 80 years, the results of 100 years.

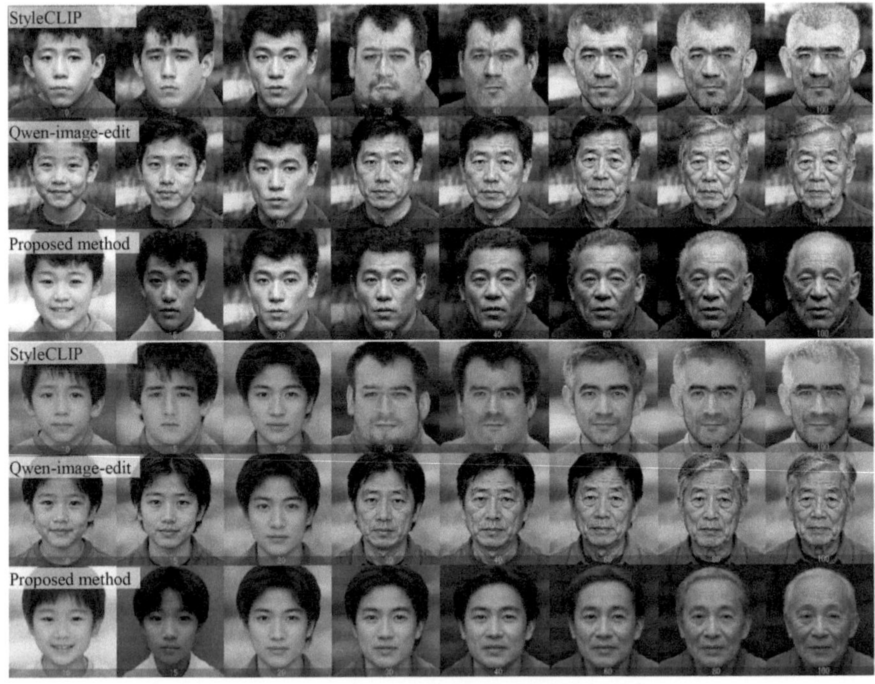

Fig. 7. Result of aging simulation (Male)

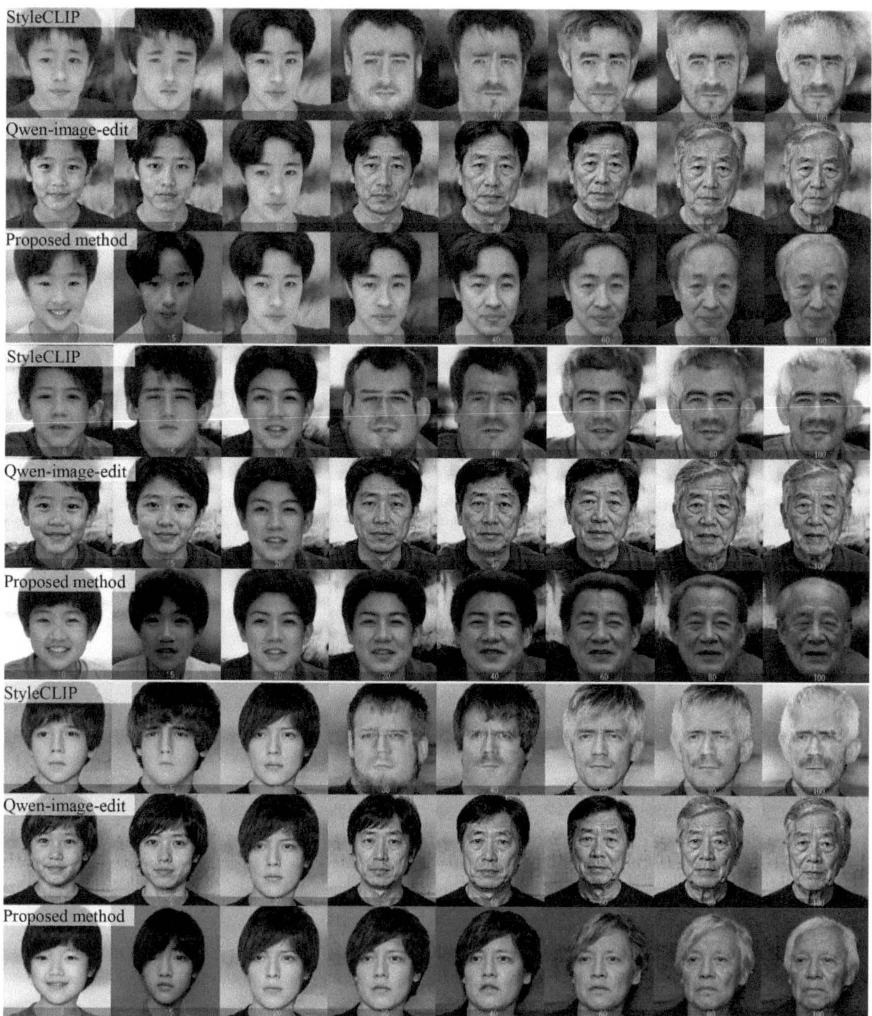

Fig. 7. (*continued*)

The top row shows the results of StyleCLIP with prompt, the middle row shows the results of Qwen-image-edit, and the bottom row shows the proposed method.

From the left, the results of 10 years, the results of 15 years, input of 20 years, the results of 30 years, the results of 40 years, the results of 60 years, the results of 80 years, the results of 100 years.

Table 2. Aging simulation prompt entered into StyleCLIP[1].

Sex	Age	Prompt
Female	10	A 10 year old elementary school girl
Female	15	A 15 year old high school girl
Female	30	A 30 year old adult woman
Female	40	A 40 year old middle-aged woman
Female	60	A 60 year old elderly wrinkled woman with grey hair
Female	80	A 80 year old elderly wrinkled woman with grey hair
Female	100	A 100 year old elderly wrinkled woman with grey hair
male	10	A 10 year old elementary school boy
male	15	A 15 year old high school boy
male	30	A 30 year old adult man
male	40	A 40 year old middle-aged man
male	60	A 60 year old elderly wrinkled man with grey hair
male	80	A 80 year old elderly wrinkled man with grey hair
male	100	A 100 year old elderly wrinkled man with grey hair

Table 3. Aging simulation prompt entered into Qwen-image-edit [2].

Sex	Age	Prompt
Female	10	A 10 year old elementary school girl. Generate an image with the changed age while retaining the characteristics of the input image as much as possible.
Female	15	A 15 year old high school girl. Generate an image with the changed age while retaining the characteristics of the input image as much as possible.
Female	30	A 30 year old woman. Generate an image with the changed age while retaining the characteristics of the input image as much as possible.
Female	40	A 40 year old woman. Generate an image with the changed age while retaining the characteristics of the input image as much as possible.
Female	60	A 60 year old woman. Generate an image with the changed age while retaining the characteristics of the input image as much as possible.
Female	80	A 80 year old woman with grey hair. Generate an image with the changed age while retaining the characteristics of the input image as much as possible.
Female	100	A 100 year old woman with grey hair. Generate an image with the changed age while retaining the characteristics of the input image as much as possible.
male	10	A 10 year old elementary school boy. Generate an image with the changed age while retaining the characteristics of the input image as much as possible.
male	15	A 15 year old high school boy. Generate an image with the changed age while retaining the characteristics of the input image as much as possible.

(*continued*)

Table 3. (*continued*)

Sex	Age	Prompt
male	30	A 30 year old man. Generate an image with the changed age while retaining the characteristics of the input image as much as possible.
male	40	A 40 year old man. Generate an image with the changed age while retaining the characteristics of the input image as much as possible.
male	60	A 60 year old man. Generate an image with the changed age while retaining the characteristics of the input image as much as possible.
male	80	A 80 year old man with grey hair. Generate an image with the changed age while retaining the characteristics of the input image as much as possible.
male	100	A 100 year old man with grey hair. Generate an image with the changed age while retaining the characteristics of the input image as much as possible.

Table 4. Average of subjective evaluations (On a 5-point scale, Female)

Age	10	15	30	40	60	80	100
①StyleCLIP	3.20 ($\sigma =$ 1.18)	2.48 ($\sigma =$ 0.99)	2.20 ($\sigma =$ 0.72)	1.43 ($\sigma =$ 0.68)	1.95 ($\sigma =$ 0.88)	1.57 ($\sigma =$ 0.81)	1.10 ($\sigma =$ 0.30)
②Qwen-image-edit	3.13 ($\sigma =$ 1.20)	3.20 ($\sigma =$ 1.10)	2.03 ($\sigma =$ 1.10)	2.30 ($\sigma =$ 1.15)	2.67 ($\sigma =$ 1.12)	2.93 ($\sigma =$ 1.20)	2.70 ($\sigma =$ 1.21)
③Proposed Method	4.62 ($\sigma =$ 0.59)	3.90 ($\sigma =$ 0.90)	3.90 ($\sigma =$ 0.84)	4.03 ($\sigma =$ 0.62)	3.92 ($\sigma =$ 0.73)	4.22 ($\sigma =$ 0.83)	4.22 ($\sigma =$ 0.77)
P-value (①vs③)	1.6e-09	2.4e-09	5.0e-15	2.1e-29	1.9e-17	1.1e-23	1.1e-37
P-value (②vs③)	2.4e-09	4.6e-03	1.7e-11	1.6e-11	3.2e-07	1.3e-06	1.4e-08

The subjective evaluation of the aging results (Fig. 6) by the eight study participants.

Table 5. Average of subjective evaluations (On a 5-point scale, Male)

Age	10	15	30	40	60	80	100
①StyleCLIP	3.33 ($\sigma =$ 1.05)	1.20 ($\sigma =$ 0.41)	1.00 ($\sigma =$ 0.00)	1.02 ($\sigma =$ 0.16)	2.10 ($\sigma =$ 1.08)	1.48 ($\sigma =$ 0.55)	1.20 ($\sigma =$ 0.46)
②Qwen-image-edit	3.10 ($\sigma =$ 1.03)	2.87 ($\sigma =$ 0.97)	2.10 ($\sigma =$ 0.96)	2.03 ($\sigma =$ 0.93)	2.53 ($\sigma =$ 1.22)	2.57 ($\sigma =$ 1.19)	2.67 ($\sigma =$ 1.35)

(*continued*)

Table 5. (*continued*)

Age	10	15	30	40	60	80	100
③Proposed Method	3.85 ($\sigma =$ 1.12)	3.05 ($\sigma =$ 1.22)	4.15 ($\sigma =$ 0.66)	4.05 ($\sigma =$ 0.90)	3.92 ($\sigma =$ 0.69)	4.05 ($\sigma =$ 0.71)	4.15 ($\sigma =$ 0.74)
P-value (①vs③)	3.3e-02	6.5e-14	1.1e-44	1.3e-33	1.2e-13	1.6e-29	1.9e-34
P-value (②vs③)	5.5e-03	5.0e-01	5.3e-16	2.0e-13	7.8e-08	1.3e-08	1.3e-07

The subjective evaluation of the aging results (Fig. 7) by the eight study participants.

6 Consideration

We leveraged the linearity of StyleGAN2's latent variables to propose a domain conversion using a deformation transformation using PLS, and verified its effectiveness by collecting Japanese facial images of various age groups. We confirmed that the proposed method solves the problem that the large-scale language image models causes uniform aging changes and does not reflect the characteristics of each person.

When utilizing generative AI, images that are subjectively very plausible are generated, but the problem is that objectivity is not guaranteed.

In the past, learning from a large number of images was necessary to ensure objectivity, but this research has shown that highly accurate domain conversion is possible with just a few hundred images. We believe this breakthrough paves the way for new applications of generative AI that combine both plausibility and objectivity.

In the future, we aim to apply this methodology to a wider range of data and explore its expansion to large-scale language-image models, such as diffusion models.

References

1. Patashnik, Or, et al.: Styleclip: Text-driven manipulation of stylegan imagery. In: Proceedings of the IEEE/CVF International Conference on Computer Vision (2021)
2. Qwen team, Qwen-Image Technical Report. https://arxiv.org/pdf/2508.02324
3. Lanitis, A., Taylor, C.J., Cootes, T.F.: Toward automatic simulation of aging effects on face images. IEEE Trans. Pattern Anal. Mach. Intell. **24**(4), 442–455 (2002)
4. Suo, J., et al.: A multi-resolution dynamic model for face aging simulation. In: 2007 IEEE Conference on Computer Vision and Pattern Recognition. IEEE (2007)
5. Suo, J., et al.: A compositional and dynamic model for face aging. IEEE Trans. Pattern Anal. Mach. Intell. **32**(3), 385–401 (2009)
6. Yang, H., et al.: Face aging effect simulation using hidden factor analysis joint sparse representation. IEEE Trans. Image Process. **25**(6), 2493–2507 (2016)
7. Park, U., Tong, Y., Jain, A.K.: Face recognition with temporal invariance: a 3d aging model. In: 2008 8th IEEE International Conference on Automatic Face & Gesture Recognition. IEEE (2008)

8. Nagata, T., Matsuzaki, K., Taniguchi, K., Ogawa, Y., Imaizumi, K.: Development of facial aging simulation system combined with three-dimensional shape prediction from facial photographs. In The International Conference on Quality Control by Artificial Vision 2017, pp. 103380G–103380G. International Society for Optics and Photonics, March 2017
9. Antipov, G., Baccouche, M., Dugelay, J.-L.: Face aging with conditional generative adversarial networks. In: 2017 IEEE international conference on image processing (ICIP). IEEE (2017)
10. Nagata, S., Sase, S.: Simulation of aging from child to adult. ViEW2020
11. Huang, Z., et al.: PFA-GAN: progressive face aging with generative adversarial network. IEEE Trans. Inf. Forens. Secur. **16**, 2031–2045 (2020)
12. Fang, H., et al.: Triple-GAN: progressive face aging with triple translation loss. In: Proceedings of the IEEE/CVF Conference on Computer Vision and Pattern Recognition Workshops (2020)
13. Ning, X., et al.: Conditional generative adversarial networks based on the principle of homology continuity for face aging. Concurrency Comput. Practice Exp. **34**(12), e5792 (2022)
14. Banerjee, S., et al.: Identity-preserving aging of face images via latent diffusion models. In: 2023 IEEE International Joint Conference on Biometrics (IJCB). IEEE (2023)
15. Chen, X., Lathuilière, S.: Face aging via diffusion-based editing. arXiv preprint arXiv:2309. 11321 (2023)
16. Karras, T., et al.: Analyzing and improving the image quality of stylegan. In: CVPR 2020
17. Alaluf, Y., et al.: Restyle: a residual-based stylegan encoder via iterative refinement. In: ICCV 2021 (2021)
18. Geladi, P., Kowalski, B.R.: Partial least-squares regression: a tutorial. Anal. Chim. Acta **185**, 1–17 (1986)

Do End-to-End TTS Systems Exploit Patterns in Speech?

Parth Khadse(✉) and Sunil Kumar Kopparapu(✉)

TCS Research, Tata Consultancy Services Limited, Mumbai, India
{parth.khadse,sunilkumar.kopparapu}@tcs.com
http://www.tcs.com, http://www.tcs.com

Abstract. An end-to-end (e2e) text-to-speech (TTS) system is a deep architecture that learns to associate a text string with acoustic speech patterns from a dataset. It is expected that all aspects associated with speech production, such as phone duration, speaker characteristics, and intonation among other things are captured in the trained TTS model. Human speech is complex, involving *smooth* transitions between articulatory configurations (ACs). Due to anatomical constraints, some ACs are challenging to mimic or transition between. In this paper, we pose the question "Do e2e-TTS systems benefit by the constraints imposed by human anatomy?". To answer this, we build systems using reverse text and reverse speech. Experiments demonstrate that e2e TTS systems are purely data-driven. Interestingly, the generated speech by *reverse* systems exhibits better fidelity, better perceptual intelligibility, and better naturalness.

Keywords: TTS · reverse speech · end to end models · tokenization

1 Introduction

Articulation is the process of producing speech sounds by manipulating the airstream from the lungs using the articulatory organs. The specific movements of the articulatory organs, called articulatory configuration (AC) determine the different speech sounds that humans produce. One could look at a sequence of ACs smoothly transitioning from one AC to another resulting in spoken speech. Visible Speech (VS) symbols [2], introduced in 1867, provided visual representation of the position of the speech organs needed to articulate an individual sound. The concept of VS was used effectively to identify words that are difficult to articulate based on the degree of change in the position of articulators that is required to speak a word [18]. While appreciating the fact that speech production is much more complex, namely, the next word or phrase that we produce is dependent on *what* has been spoken prior not only linguistically but also in terms of *how* we emote it in the form of intonation, there is also an aspect of breath cycle, pauses, filler words, stress on certain words, language grammar and much more. Aware of this, we hypothesize that the language we speak has

C. Wallraven et al. (Eds.): ACPR 2025, LNCS 16174, pp. 86–99, 2026.
https://doi.org/10.1007/978-981-95-4395-3_7

evolved over a period of time and the sounds that we produce are such that they are *optimal* in terms of the amount of energy required to change the position of the articulators or transition from one AC to another when we speak a sentence. We refer to the speech produced under these constraints, to consist of *natural patterns* in spoken speech. It is possible, humans have refined and adapted the language structure, syntax, etc. to make it suitable, comfortable and easy for them to use.

With the growing need for voice user interfaces, there is a dire need for generating speech from text, also called text to speech (TTS). The area of TTS has evolved significantly from the rudimentary Klatt synthesizer [8] to current day end-to-end TTS (e2e-TTS) models like Tacotron-2 [17], FastSpeech [14], Glow-TTS [6], F5-TTS [3], and VITS [7]. The e2e-TTS systems are traditionally sequence to sequence (seq2seq) architectures that learn to map a text sequence and the corresponding audio. These e2e-TTS are trained on a large amount of training text-speech corpora. In this paper, we ask if these e2e-TTS models benefit from (a) the constraints imposed by the articulatory anatomy where only certain transitions of AC's are possible or (b) some implicit patterns in the syntactic structure of the language and speech. We further assume that these patterns or AC transition constraints do not exist in a reverse audio. For clarity, if $s(t)$ is the spoken speech of duration T, namely, $0 \leq t \leq T$ then $s(T-t) = \bar{s}(t)$ is the reverse speech. In this paper, we would like to study and understand if an e2e-TTS architecture can be trained on *unnatural (to human) patterns* or in other words does the constraints on possible AC imposed by the articulatory anatomy or the smooth transition from one AC to another help the conventionally trained e2e-TTS system.

The rest of the paper is organized as follows. In Sect. 2 we describe the approach that we adopted and in Sect. 3 we analyze the experiments that we conducted and conclude in Sect. 4.

2 The Setup

Tacotron-2 [17] is an e2e-TTS deep learning architecture that consists of two main components. As seen in Fig. 1, the first component is a recurrent sequence-to-sequence (seq2seq) model with an attention mechanism, and a WaveGlow-based vocoder. The seq2seq model takes in a sequence of characters (text) and outputs a sequence of mel-spectrogram features. These output mel-spectrogram features pass through a pre-trained WaveGlow vocoder to generate the audio waveform (speech).

Specifically, the text to mel-spectrogram seq2seq model consists of an encoder and a decoder, implemented as recurrent neural networks (RNNs). The encoder takes in the input text and encodes it into a sequence of high-level representations, which are then passed to the decoder. The decoder uses an attention mechanism to focus on different parts of the input sequence at each time step, allowing it to generate a sequence of mel-spectrogram features that represent the input text. On the other hand, the WaveGlow [11] vocoder is a deep generative flow-based model trained on a large corpus of speech data, allowing it to generate highly realistic and natural-sounding speech. The two stage architecture of seq2seq followed by vocoder (see Fig. 1) allows generation of high-quality and natural-sounding speech from input text.

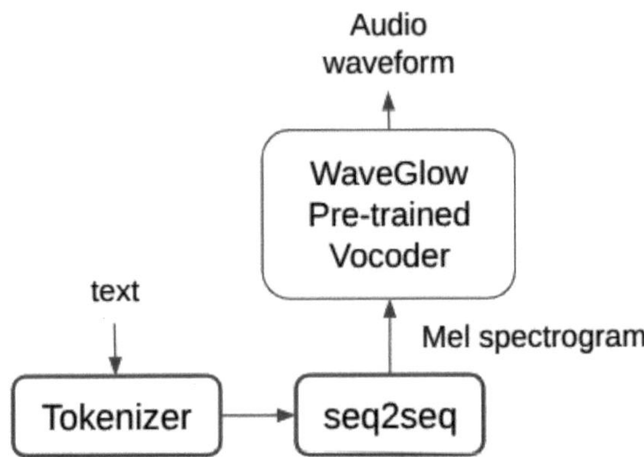

Fig. 1. High level block diagram of e2e-TTS (Tacotron-2) architecture. We train the seq2seq block while using a pre-trained vocoder. The tokenizer is a standard character tokenizer.

While using a pre-trained vocoder [4] we built four e2e-TTS systems by training four different seq2seq models as shown in Fig. 1. The first seq2seq model was trained using the standard text, denoted by w and mel-spectrogram extracted from $s(t)$ for the system denoted by e2e-TTS. Namely,

$$w \longrightarrow \boxed{\text{e2e-TTS}} \longrightarrow s(t)$$

The second system, called, r-e2e-TTS while using the same pre-trained vocoder, used the reverse text[1] denoted by $\bar{w}$ and mel-spectrogram extracted from reverse speech denoted by $\bar{s}(t)$ to train the seq2seq model. The trained r-e2e-TTS is denoted by

$$\bar{w} \longrightarrow \boxed{\text{r-e2e-TTS}} \longrightarrow \bar{s}(t)$$

Note that $\bar{s}(t)$ has to be reversed for any further analysis, namely $\bar{\bar{s}}(t)$ (reverse of $\bar{s}(t)$). In both the cases we use the same standard seq2seq architecture to train for the text to its corresponding mel-spectrogram, while using a pre-trained WaveGlow model.

[1] "dlrow olleh" is the reverse text corresponding to "hello world".

3 Experimental Details

The Tacotron-2 [17] model is trained on the text-speech paired data of English male speaker, released as part of the LIMMITS'25 grand challenge [5]. The dataset consists of approximately 40 hours of speech data spoken by a single speaker recorded at 48 kHz sampling rate.

The following data prepossessing was done on the dataset to train the seq2seq model. The speech was down-sampled to 22.05 kHz using `sox` utility and mel-spectrogram was extracted from the speech with window length of 1024 samples, hop length of 256 samples and 80 mel channels. The text was converted to lower case, followed by normalization (numerical converted to words, for example "10" was converted to "ten", etc.). We followed the same pre-processing for training the seq2seq model for e2e-TTS, r-e2e-TTS, BPE-e2e-TTS, and r-BPE-e2e-TTS.

Comparing e2e-TTS and r-e2e-TTS, both seq2seq models were trained under identical conditions, namely, on the same machine, using a batch size of 16 and a learning rate of $2.5 * 10^{-4}$. All the models were trained for 50000 iterations.

Figure 2 shows the alignment plots between encoder and decoder steps generated during the training process at 45000th iteration. It can be observed that there are no *observable* differences in the alignment plots demonstrating that both the trained models e2e-TTS (r-e2e-TTS) effectively learned to convert text sequence, w ($\bar{w}$) into audio $s(t)$ ($\bar{s}(t)$).

We selected 2500 text samples, not used during seq2seq training, at random, from Librispeech-960 [10] corpus. We discarded all the sentences that had less than 5 words or greater that 40 words which resulted in a total of 1715 sentences. We generated audio, using the trained e2e-TTS and r-e2e-TTS models separately for these 1715 sentences. A well documented problem in seq2seq model is its inability to identify the End-of-Sentence (EoS). A total of 14 generated audios (see Table 1) by either e2e-TTS (10) or r-e2e-TTS (4) resulted in an extended duration (limited by the maximum duration of the audio chosen as the hyper-parameter) audio because they resulted in the seq2seq model not being able to identify EoS. We discarded these 14 audio files during our analysis. All the analysis is based on the remaining 1701 generated audios, common to both e2e-TTS and r-e2e-TTS.

Table 1. Synthesized audio seq2seq EoS problem.

Model	Generated (#)	EoS issues (#)
e2e-TTS	1715	10
r-e2e-TTS	1715	4

We evaluated the audio generated by e2e-TTS and r-e2e-TTS in two different ways. In the first set of evaluation, we transcribed the generated audio using OpenAI's Whisper `small.en` and WhisperX `small` model [13]. Note that while

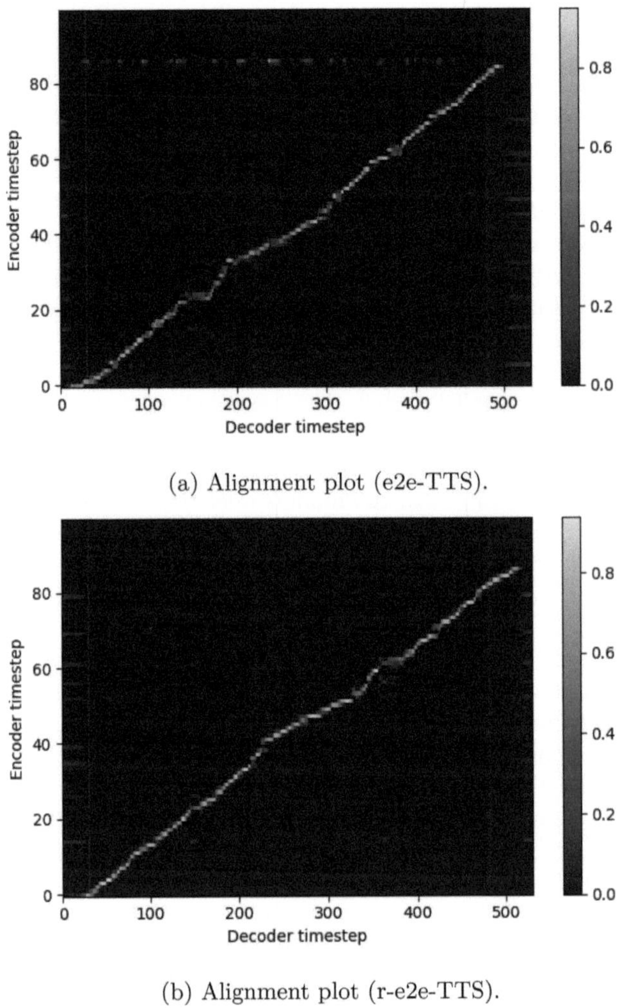

(a) Alignment plot (e2e-TTS).

(b) Alignment plot (r-e2e-TTS).

Fig. 2. Alignment plots for both e2e-TTS and r-e2e-TTS show no observable differences.

we passed $s(t)$ generated by e2e-TTS directly, we reversed the output of r-e2e-TTS namely used $\bar{\bar{s}}(t)$ for transcription. As an objective evaluation metric, we computed the Word Error Rate (WER) and Character Error Rate (CER), by finding the edit distance between the transcribed text and the original text used for generating the audio. Table 2 captures the fidelity of the audio generated by e2e-TTS and r-e2e-TTS, in terms of WER and CER as a proxy measure. Note that smaller values of WER and CER are better and suggest that the generated audio is more reliably transcribed by the speech recognition engine.

Clearly, the speech synthesized by r-e2e-TTS is better recognised by the ASR (both Whisper and WhisperX) than the conventional e2e-TTS generated audio.

It can be observed that the r-e2e-TTS performance is 6.5% (5.6%) better than e2e-TTS in absolute terms and 37.58% (34.36%) in relative terms for Whisper (WhisperX). It can also be observed that WhisperX, the more recent model performs, as expected, better than Whisper.

Table 2. WER and CER (lower values better) calculated on 1701 text samples.

		Tacotron-2	
	Model	WER (%)	CER (%)
Whisper (`small.en`)	e2e-TTS	17.3	7.5
	r-e2e-TTS	**10.8**	**4.0**
WhisperX (`small`)	e2e-TTS	16.3	6.9
	r-e2e-TTS	**10.7**	**3.9**

These observations indicate that r-e2e-TTS is not only capable of learning the seq2seq mapping between the reverse text sequence and the corresponding mel-spectrogram of the reverse audio, but also generates speech that is *better* transcribed by the automatic speech recognition engine; both Whisper [12] and WhisperX [1].

The second set of evaluations are based on human perception, in terms of mean opinion scores (MOS). We asked 5 subjects (3 male, 2 female) to listen to a total of 16 generated audio waveforms (8 each generated using e2e-TTS and r-e2e-TTS) and give a score between 1 and 5 for both naturalness and intelligibility. The subjects were provided the information mentioned in Table 3 as reference.

Table 3. Reference provided to subjects to mark naturalness and intelligibility.

Score	Naturalness	Intelligibility
1	awkward, robotic	cannot understand speech
2	strange/ not smooth	understandable; mostly unclear
3	like human voice	understandable; hard to follow
4	smooth and natural	easy to understand
5	sounds very natural	completely understandable

Note that the subjects were not aware of which audio was generated by which system. Table 4 shows the results of this perceptual evaluation in terms of MOS. While the MOS for both e2e-TTS and r-e2e-TTS are close to each other, the audio generated by r-e2e-TTS gets a higher MOS for both naturalness (3.75 in comparison to 3.4) and intelligibility (3.58 compared to 3.38). Again demonstrating the superior performance of r-e2e-TTS over e2e-TTS.

Table 4. Mean Opinion Scores (Naturalness and Intelligibility).

	e2e-TTS	r-e2e-TTS
Naturalness	3.40 ± 0.11	$\mathbf{3.75 \pm 0.22}$
Intelligibility	3.38 ± 0.27	$\mathbf{3.58 \pm 0.60}$

In another perceptual evaluation test, the same 5 subjects were presented with 5 pairs of audio samples, generated using the same text (w for e2e-TTS and $\bar{w}$ for r-e2e-TTS), while one was generated using e2e-TTS the other paired audio was generated using r-e2e-TTS. These audio waveform were presented in random order, meaning in some instances the first audio waveform in the pair was from e2e-TTS while in some instances the first waveform was from r-e2e-TTS. The subjects were then asked to mark the audio sample which they felt was comparatively better of the two. Note that no specific instruction was communicated to the subjects in terms of what they should look for in the audio. In all, we got 5 responses from each of the 5 subjects, totaling 25 responses as shown in Table 5. It can be observed that 92% of the time (23/25) the subjects felt that the audio generated by r-e2e-TTS was better than the corresponding audio generated by e2e-TTS and only in 2 instances did the subjects choose the audio generated by e2e-TTS over r-e2e-TTS (see Table 5).

Table 5. Paired audio perceptual test. 1 represents the instance when r-e2e-TTS generated audio was chosen as being better.

	Sub# 1	Sub# 2	Sub# 3	Sub# 4	Sub# 5
Pair# 1	0	1	1	1	1
Pair# 2	1	1	1	1	1
Pair# 3	1	0	1	1	1
Pair# 4	1	1	1	1	1
Pair# 5	1	1	1	1	1

Clearly, the perceptual evaluation, though by a small set of 5 independent subjects, demonstrates the trend towards their preference for audio generated by r-e2e-TTS.

Further, it was observed that the total duration of the 1701 audio generated by r-e2e-TTS was 1.85% shorter (14786.21 seconds compared to 15064.73 seconds by e2e-TTS) than that generated by e2e-TTS. On an average for the same w ($\bar{w}$ for r-e2e-TTS) the e2e-TTS generated $s(t)$ was of longer duration (8.85 s) compared to the duration of $\bar{s}(t)$ (8.69 s). Figure 3 captures the scatter plot of the duration of the audio produced by e2e-TTS and r-e2e-TTS for the same text. It can be observed that the number of points below the red diagonal far exceed the number of points above the diagonal.

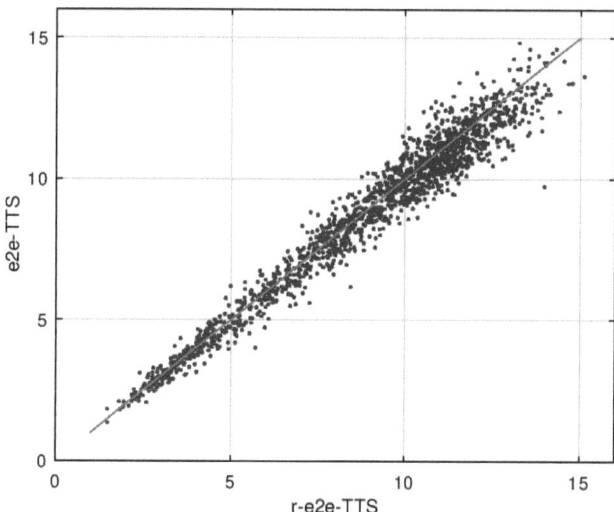

Fig. 3. Scatter plot of duration of the audio for the same text produced by e2e-TTS (y-axis) and r-e2e-TTS (x-axis). The duration of audio generated by e2e-TTS is overall longer than the audio generated by r-e2e-TTS.

3.1 Effect of Text Tokenization

Motivated by [16], in addition to e2e-TTS and r-e2e-TTS we also trained a set of models where the input text was encoded using byte pair encoding (BPE) [15] instead of directly using the characters in the text (see Fig. 1). For the same text input, generally BPE encoding results in lesser number of tokens, compared to character tokenization. As seen in Table 6 BPE results in 21 tokens compared to 34 character tokens for the example text `‘‘The stars twinkle and shine bright’’`.

Table 6. Tokenization for the sentence `‘‘The stars twinkle and shine bright’’`. We use character tokenizer for e2e-TTS and r-e2e-TTS while we use BPE for BPE-e2e-TTS and r-BPE-e2e-TTS.

Tokenizer (# of tokens)	Tokens
character (34)	`t h e _ s t a r s _ t w i n k l e _ a n d _ s h i n e _ b r i g h t`
Byte Pair Encoding (21)	`the, _, st, ar, s, _t, w, in, k, le, _, and, _s, h, in, e, _b, ri, g, h, t`

Tokenization algorithms, broadly work on the principle of iteratively merging frequently occurring pairs of characters or tokens to create a vocabulary of tokens that can represent the language's vocabulary efficiently. This as we will observe later, results in better machine transcription of the generated audio. We call these TTS systems,

$$w \longrightarrow \overbrace{\boxed{\text{BPE}} \longrightarrow \boxed{\text{e2e-TTS}}}^{\text{BPE-e2e-TTS}} \longrightarrow s(t)$$

and

$$\bar{w} \longrightarrow \overbrace{\boxed{\text{BPE}} \longrightarrow \boxed{\text{r-e2e-TTS}}}^{\text{r-BPE-e2e-TTS}} \longrightarrow \bar{s}(t)$$

As mentioned earlier, the BPE models were trained on w for BPE-e2e-TTS while it was trained with $\bar{w}$ for r-BPE-e2e-TTS. Figure 4 shows the alignment plots between the encoder and decoder steps. From the plots it can seen clearly that the trained BPE models BPE-e2e-TTS (r-BPE-e2e-TTS) are able to effectively convert the BPE sequence to speech. As earlier identical training condition was enabled for training both BPE-e2e-TTS and r-BPE-e2e-TTS. We trained the SentencePiece [9], with BPE (–vocab_size=n, –model_type=`bpe`, –split_by_whitespace=False). We use $n = 50$ and impose a constraint on the token length to be 2.

These BPE models were also evaluated on the same set of 1715 sentences. We generated separate audio files for all the 1715 files for both the models. A total of 7 (see Table 7) generated audio files suffered from EoS problem, while BPE-e2e-TTS resulted in 4, r-BPE-e2e-TTS resulted in 3 instances of EoS. So during the evaluation these 7 files were discarded and the evaluation process was performed on the remaining 1708 files.

Table 7. Synthesized audio seq2seq EoS problem using BPE-e2e-TTS and r-BPE-e2e-TTS.

Model	Generated (#)	EoS issues (#)
BPE-e2e-TTS	1715	4
r-BPE-e2e-TTS	1715	3

Along earlier lines, we computed the WER and CER of the audio files generated using BPE models. For transcribing we used OpenAI's Whisper `small` and WhisperX `small` models. Table 8 shows that though r-BPE-e2e-TTS (9.4%) performs better than BPE-e2e-TTS (9.6%), the improvement, 0.2% (0.4%) in absolute terms and 2.1% (4.2%) relative terms for Whisper (WhisperX) is significantly dwarfed compared to using text without tokenization, namely, e2e-TTS and r-e2e-TTS. Further, it can be observed that audio produced by BPE models (both BPE-e2e-TTS and r-BPE-e2e-TTS; Table 8) result in better WER (9.6%) than the best (10.7%; Table 2) when BPE is not used for encoding input text.

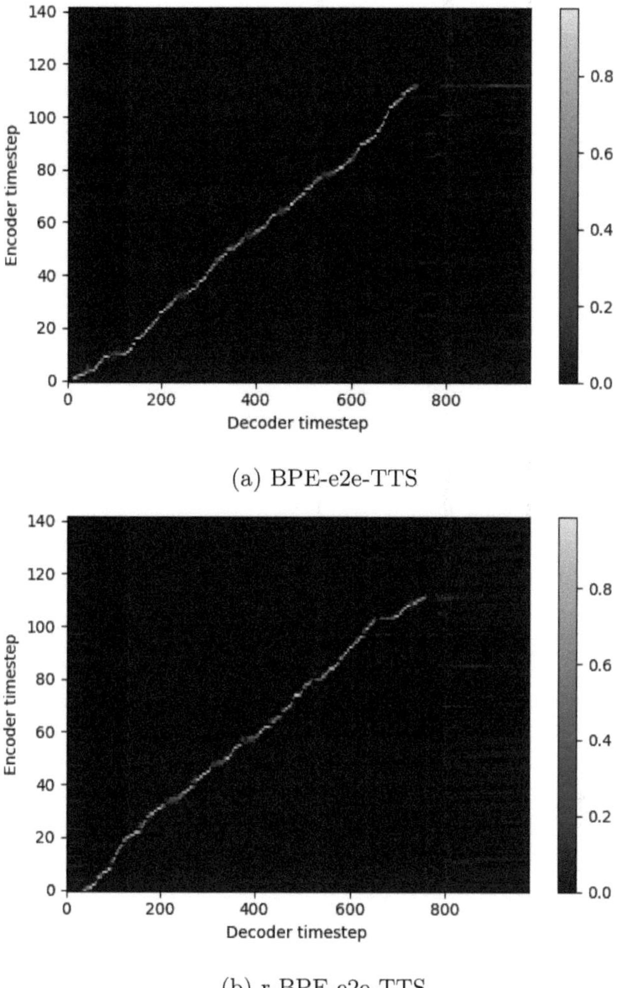

(a) BPE-e2e-TTS

(b) r-BPE-e2e-TTS

Fig. 4. Alignment plots for both BPE-e2e-TTS and r-BPE-e2e-TTS show no observable differences.

Table 8. WER and CER (lower values better) calculated on 1708 text samples on audio generated by BPE-e2e-TTS and r-BPE-e2e-TTS.

	Model	WER (%)	CER (%)
Whisper (`small.en`)	BPE-e2e-TTS	9.6	3.4
	r-BPE-e2e-TTS	**9.4**	**3.3**
WhisperX (`small`)	BPE-e2e-TTS	9.5	3.4
	r-BPE-e2e-TTS	**9.1**	**3.2**

Table 9. Comparison between Tacotron-2 and VITS models

Aspect	Tacotron-2 (2018)	VITS (2021)
Architecture Type	Two-stage	Single-stage
	Autoregressive pipeline	Non-autoregressive pipeline
Component Structure	Encoder-decoder with attention (text to spectrogram)	Integrated prior encoder, posterior encoder, decoder
	WaveGlow vocoder for raw audio from spectrogram	Duration predictor + discriminator
Speed and Efficiency	Slower	Faster
	(frame-wise generation)	(parallel generation)
Alignment Mechanism	Location-sensitive attention	Monotonic Alignment Search
	–	Normalizing flow framework

3.2 Tacotron-2 Dependency

To validate if the performance of r-e2e-TTS being better than e2e-TTS was dependent in Tacotron-2 architecture, we experimented with VITS (Variational Inference Text-to-Speech) [7] a non-autoregressive TTS architecture. Table 9 captures the salient differences between the Tacotron-2 model and VITS model.

Table 10. WER and CER (lower values better) calculated on 1715 text samples.

		VITS	
	Model	WER (%)	CER (%)
Whisper (`small.en`)	e2e-TTS	12.36	6.37
	r-e2e-TTS	**11.80**	**5.90**
WhisperX (`small`)	e2e-TTS	12.11	6.18
	r-e2e-TTS	**11.69**	**5.80**

Table 10 shows the objective evaluation results of the VITS model. The speech synthesized by r-e2e-TTS version of VITS (trained using $\bar{w}$ and $\bar{s}(t)$) is better transcribed by both Whisper and WhisperX ASR compared to the e2e-TTS version (VITS trained using w and $s(t)$). As seen in Table 10 the performance of re2e-TTS is 0.56% (0.47%) better than e2e-TTS in absolute terms for Whisper (WhisperX). It can be observed that the performance of the r-e2e-TTS is better that the performance of e2e-TTS *irrespective* of the TTS architecture, as seen in Table 2 for Tacotron-2 and Table 10 for VITS.

Additionally, on an average for the same text w ($\bar{w}$ for r-e2e-TTS) the duration of the generated audio was 8.62 s for e2e-TTS compared to a duration of 8.54 s for the r-e2e-TTS system (shorter by 0.93%). A trend similar to that observed using the Tacotron-2 architecture.

4 Conclusion

We hypothesized that there might be hidden *natural* properties in the speech produced by human because of the constraints imposed by the anatomy of the human articulatory mechanism and asked ourselves if these properties, if any, influenced the training of an e2e-TTS system. Our experiments, based on Tacotron-2 and VITS architecture suggest that e2e deep learning systems execute as a *brute-force* and *blind* data-mapping exercise, seq2seq learning the text sequence and the corresponding mel-spectrogram of the audio as seen in Fig. 2 and Fig. 4. Thus, negating our initial hypothesis that e2e TTS systems might be exploiting *hidden* patterns due to constraints imposed by anatomy of articulators.

All our experiments used read speech (it is common to use read speech in TTS literature), however, it remains to be seen if the articulatory transition constraints are more visible if spontaneous speech was used to train an e2e TTS system. In normal communication, humans speak spontaneously, which introduces pauses and variations in word arrangement within sentences randomly. It remains to be explored whether e2e systems exploit these properties.

We enumerate some of our observations, many of which, in our opinion, require further exploration for deeper analysis and better understanding.

1. End to end (e2e) TTS systems seem to primarily adopt a blind data-mapping exercise and train well for both forward and reverse e2e TTS systems.
   (a) All the models namely, e2e-TTS, r-e2e-TTS (both Tacotron-2 and VITS), BPE-e2e-TTS and r-BPE-e2e-TTS are able to train and produce natural and intelligible speech.
   (b) It is not clear why the performance, in terms of speech recognition by ASR and speech perception by humans, is better for audio generated using r-e2e-TTS and r-BPE-e2e-TTS. We plan to study this in future.
2. The audio generated by r-BPE-e2e-TTS and r-e2e-TTS are transcribed more accurately than the audio generated by e2e-TTS by the state of the art ASR engines, Whisper and WhisperX. We are in the process of investigating this in future.
3. The use of BPE results in lower (better) WER, demonstrating that the use of a text encoder to represent input text to train the seq2seq model seems to better capture the text-speech mapping. It is probably because longer length tokens can capture *contextual information* embedded in the speech better than character based tokens.
   (a) However, using longer size tokens ($\geq$3) when using Tacotron-2 architecture resulted in poor quality audio generation in terms of both naturalness and intelligibility. This requires further investigation.

4. While there are no challenges in training an r-e2e-TTS (r-BPE-e2e-TTS), the appropriateness of the data used to train requires attention.
   (a) The $\bar{s}(t)$ (reverse audio) used for training is "artificial" and synthetically generating reverse speech is not really equivalent to a human speaking in reverse (whatever that means!).
   (b) Our attempt to get a few subjects to speak a sentence in reverse showed that it was not only impossible to utter the sentence (all of them) without unusual pauses, but also when the recorded sentence was played in reverse, it sounded gibberish.

References

1. Bain, M., Huh, J., Han, T., Zisserman, A.: WhisperX: time-accurate speech transcription of long-form audio (2023). https://arxiv.org/abs/2303.00747
2. Bell, A.M.: Visible Speech: The Science of Universal Alphabetics. Internet Archive (1867). https://archive.org/details/b21782520. Accessed 29 May 2025
3. Chen, Y., et al.: F5-TTS: a fairytaler that fakes fluent and faithful speech with flow matching (2025). https://arxiv.org/abs/2410.06885
4. NVIDIA Corporation: WaveGlow: a flow-based generative network for speech synthesis. https://github.com/NVIDIA/waveglow. Accessed 21 Mar 2023
5. IISc: LIMMITS25 multi-speaker, multi-lingual INDIC TTS with voice cloning grand challenge. https://sites.google.com/view/limmits25. Accessed 22 Mar 2023
6. Kim, J., Kim, S., Kong, J., Yoon, S.: Glow-TTS: a generative flow for text-to-speech via monotonic alignment search. In: Proceedings of the 34th International Conference on Neural Information Processing Systems, NIPS 2020. Curran Associates Inc., Red Hook, NY, USA (2020)
7. Kim, J., Kong, J., Son, J.: Conditional variational autoencoder with adversarial learning for end-to-end text-to-speech. In: International Conference on Machine Learning, pp. 5530–5540. PMLR (2021)
8. Klatt, D.H.: Software for a casette-based speech synthesis system. Technical report. HLR-80-06, Haskins Laboratories, New Haven, CT, August 1980. http://www.haskins.yale.edu/pubs/pubs.html
9. Kudo, T., Richardson, J.: SentencePiece: a simple and language independent subword tokenizer and detokenizer for neural text processing, November 2018. https://doi.org/10.18653/v1/D18-2012, https://aclanthology.org/D18-2012
10. Panayotov, V., Chen, G., Povey, D., Khudanpur, S.: Librispeech: an ASR corpus based on public domain audio books. In: 2015 IEEE International Conference on Acoustics, Speech and Signal Processing (ICASSP), pp. 5206–5210. IEEE (2015)
11. Prenger, R., Valle, R., Catanzaro, B.: WaveGlow: a flow-based generative network for speech synthesis. In: ICASSP 2019-2019 IEEE International Conference on Acoustics, Speech and Signal Processing (ICASSP), pp. 3617–3621. IEEE (2019)
12. Radford, A., et al.: Whisper: automatic Speech Recognition with Open AI. https://openai.com/index/whisper/. Accessed 22 Mar 2023
13. Radford, A., Kim, J.W., Xu, T., Brockman, G., McLeavey, C., Sutskever, I.: Robust speech recognition via large-scale weak supervision. In: International Conference on Machine Learning, pp. 28492–28518. PMLR (2023)

14. Ren, Y., et al.: FastSpeech: fast, robust and controllable text to speech. In: Wallach, H., Larochelle, H., Beygelzimer, A., d'Alché-Buc, F., Fox, E., Garnett, R. (eds.) Advances in Neural Information Processing Systems, vol. 32. Curran Associates, Inc. (2019)
15. Sennrich, R., Haddow, B., Birch, A.: Neural machine translation of rare words with subword units. In: Erk, K., Smith, N.A. (eds.) Proceedings of the 54th Annual Meeting of the Association for Computational Linguistics (Volume 1: Long Papers), August 2016, pp. 1715–1725. Association for Computational Linguistics, Berlin, Germany (2016). https://doi.org/10.18653/v1/P16-1162. https://aclanthology.org/P16-1162
16. Shah, N., Khadse, P., Karande, S., Kopparapu, S.K.: Hamaraawaz: advancing low-latency streaming tts for multilingual speech in Indian languages. In: 2025 IEEE International Conference on Acoustics, Speech and Signal Processing (ICASSP), ICASSP 2025, pp. 1–2. IEEE (2025)
17. Shen, J., et al.: Natural TTS synthesis by conditioning WaveNet on MEL spectrogram predictions. In: 2018 IEEE International Conference on Acoustics, Speech and Signal Processing (ICASSP), pp. 4779–4783. IEEE (2018)
18. Tripathi, A., Bhosale, S., Kopparapu, S.K.: Automatic speaker independent dysarthric speech intelligibility assessment system. Comput. Speech Lang. **69**, 101213 (2021). https://doi.org/10.1016/j.csl.2021.101213. https://www.sciencedirect.com/science/article/pii/S0885230821000206

Few-Shot Connectivity-Aware Text Line Segmentation in Historical Documents

Rafael Sterzinger(✉), Tingyu Lin, and Robert Sablatnig

Computer Vision Lab, TU Wien, Vienna, Austria
{Rafael.Sterzinger,Tingyu.Lin,Robert.Sablatnig}@tuwien.ac.at

Abstract. A foundational task for the digital analysis of documents is text line segmentation. However, automating this process with deep learning models is challenging because it requires large, annotated datasets that are often unavailable for historical documents. Additionally, the annotation process is a labor- and cost-intensive task that requires expert knowledge, which makes few-shot learning a promising direction for reducing data requirements. In this work, we demonstrate that small and simple architectures, coupled with a topology-aware loss function, are more accurate and data-efficient than more complex alternatives. We pair a lightweight UNet++ with a connectivity-aware loss, initially developed for neuron morphology, which explicitly penalizes structural errors like line fragmentation and unintended line merges. To increase our limited data, we train on small patches extracted from a mere three annotated pages per manuscript. Our methodology significantly improves upon the current state-of-the-art on the U-DIADS-TL dataset, with a 200% increase in Recognition Accuracy and a 75% increase in Line Intersection over Union. Our method also achieves an F-Measure score on par with or even exceeding that of the competition winner of the DIVA-HisDB baseline detection task, all while requiring only three annotated pages, exemplifying the efficacy of our approach. Our implementation is publicly available at: https://github.com/RafaelSterzinger/acpr_few_shot_hist.

Keywords: Few-Shot Learning · Text Line Segmentation · Historical Document Analysis

1 Introduction

In historical documents, text line segmentation is a foundational task of computational document analysis. Approaches to early layout analysis relied on heuristics, such as projection profiles and clustering of connected components [14,18,21]. While effective on clean documents, these rule-based pipelines often fail when faced with the complexities inherent in historical manuscripts, such as bleed-through, elaborate ornamentation, or degraded scripts [15]. As a consequence of these challenges, a shift towards data-driven approaches occurred

C. Wallraven et al. (Eds.): ACPR 2025, LNCS 16174, pp. 100–114, 2026.
https://doi.org/10.1007/978-981-95-4395-3_8

using deep neural networks such as CNNs, which re-framed the task as an end-to-end learning problem [16]. However, the performance of deep learning models depends on the availability of large, pixel-precise annotated datasets. In the context of historical documents, the required annotated datasets are either prohibitively expensive and time-consuming to create, or the data itself is simply unavailable.

Given this data scarcity, much research has focused on few-shot learning, where models are trained using only a handful of annotated examples. The challenge of this low-data regime is evident in research where powerful architectures, such as DeepLabV3+ [4], achieve poor results when trained on just three pages per manuscript [31]. In response to these challenges, some have employed increasingly complex models, such as transformer-based hybrids [25].

Our approach, however, illustrates the principle of *Occam's Razor*: when a simpler method outperforms more complex ones, additional complexity is not only unnecessary but can be counterproductive, as an increased number of parameters raises the risk of overfitting and reduces generalization. In this work, we make the following contributions:

- We demonstrate that a simple and lightweight architecture is sufficient to significantly outperform more complex models [31] in a few-shot setting. In addition, we incorporate an established patch-level training strategy, which efficiently handles high-resolution imagery and has proven effective in data-scarce domains [6,23] to increase data.
- We propose the usage of a connectivity-aware loss function, originally proposed for neuron morphology reconstruction [12], to the task of text line segmentation, to address the critical importance of structural integrity in text lines: standard pixel-level losses often fail to prevent fragmentation or unintended merging, which severely impact line-level evaluation metrics.
- We perform a thorough evaluation of our methodology on two public competition datasets, U-DIADS-TL [2,31] and DIVA-HisDB [22], under a strict few-shot constraint of only three annotated training pages. Our results establish a new SOTA for the former and demonstrate the approach's generalizability on the latter.

Our final model sets a new baseline on the U-DIADS-TL dataset, achieving relative gains of over 75% in Line Intersection over Union (IoU) and nearly 200% in Recognition Accuracy (RA) compared to the baseline reported by Zottin et al. [31]. Furthermore, on the DIVA-HisDB baseline detection task, our few-shot approach achieves performance competitive or even superior to top-ranked systems from the ICDAR 2017 competition [22], despite using three instead of 20 annotated pages, i.e., 85% less training data.

2 Related Work

In the following, we provide an overview of relevant literature on text line segmentation as well as few-shot learning with an emphasis on its application within historical documents.

(a) Latin 14396 (b) Latin 2 (c) Syriaque 341

(d) CB55 (e) CSG18 (f) CSG863

Fig. 1. Our few-shot method improves SOTA on U-DIADS-TL (Top) by 200% in RA and 75% in Line IoU, and matches or surpasses DIVA-HisDB (Bottom) top scores using just three annotated pages.

Learning-Based Text Line Segmentation. Introducing Fully Convolutional Networks (FCNs) shifted research toward an end-to-end, data-driven formulation [16]. UNet [19], an encoder-decoder architecture with skip connections, demonstrated that precise pixel-level predictions can be learned. In the context of historical documents, Barakat et al. [3] trained an FCN able to cope with irregular inter-line gaps in medieval Hebrew scrolls. In contrast, Fizaine et al. [10] evaluated a Mask-RCNN against UNet on four public archives and found that instance-aware models handle intertwining marginalia more effectively. More recent transformer hybrids such as SeamFormer [25] employ scribble-conditioned refinement to link diacritics and resolve touching ascenders, achieving SOTA precision on dense palm-leaf manuscripts. Alberti et al. [1] further combined semantic pixel labeling with polygon extraction in a labelingcutting-grouping pipeline.

To preserve global structure, recent work augments standard segmentation losses with connectivity-aware terms. For instance, such losses have been used for road extraction [17], for class-imbalance mitigation [20], or have evolved into supervoxel connectivity losses that maintain object continuity with linear complexity and minimal overhead [12].

Few-Shot Learning Approaches. With the shortage of richly annotated datasets, research shifted to text line segmentation under extreme data scarcity. Zottin et al. [31] explored FCNs, the PSPNet [27], and DeepLabV3+ [4] with only three labeled pages per manuscript. In a similar context, De Nardin et al. [6] proposed an efficient framework that converts a handful of high-resolution manuscript pages into several thousand training patches via dynamic instance generation and refines coarse masks with Sauvola thresholding, achieving fully supervised quality on DIVA-HisDB with only two annotated pages per manuscript for layout analysis. An extension replaced Sauvola with adaptive local thresholding while retaining the same pixel-level F-score under a stricter evaluation [7]. Follow-up work demonstrated that a single labeled page per Arabic manuscript can suffice when combined with lightweight augmentation and class-balanced losses [8].

3 Methodology

In the following section, we describe our methodology to enable efficient few-shot learning capabilities for text line segmentation and baseline detection of ancient manuscripts.

3.1 Model Architecture

We adopt UNet++ [28], derived from the original UNet [19], paired with a ResNet34 [13] encoder. Despite its simplicity, the UNet++ consistently outperforms more complex architectures, such as the commonly used DeepLabV3+ architecture [6,31]. We attribute this to better generalization, reduced overfitting, and suitability to the data-scarce nature of historical document segmentation.

In comparison to [31], we opt for training on patch-level as opposed to the whole image, as this has been an established practice in domains where data is scarce, such as in the case of historical documents [6,23]. With accompanying benefits such as better capturing fine-grained text line structures or reducing memory usage, we apply our model to random crops extracted from high-resolution input images during training and overlapping patches during validation and testing. In detail, we extract patches of size 448×448 pixels and perform random rotations between -5 and +5° and a random shear transformation between -3 and $+3°$. We incorporate these augmentations to include non-horizontally aligned text lines.

To obtain a prediction for a whole page, overlapping patches are first processed independently, and predictions are stitched back together to form the full-size image. To avoid visual artifacts at border regions, each patch is scaled by a 2D Gaussian function, emphasizing its central region, which ensures smooth and seamless blending across overlapping areas.

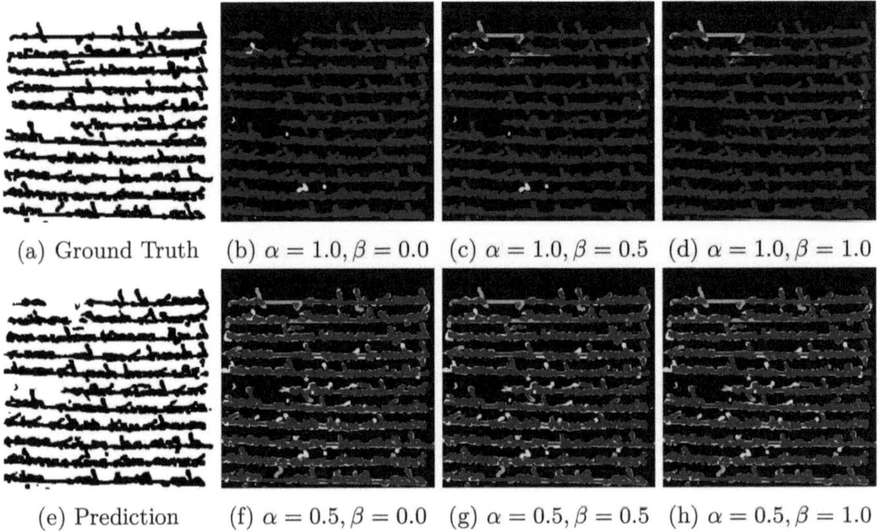

Fig. 2. An illustration of the parameters α and β and their effect on the loss using a sample patch of Syriaque 341: they control the trade-off between pixel- and structure-level errors, and between split and merge penalties, respectively [12].

3.2 Connectivity-Preserving Loss

As text lines, by their very nature, are continuous, curvilinear structures (cf. Fig. 2a), and maintaining their integrity – avoiding fragmentation or unintended merging – is crucial for accurate text line segmentation and detection. Concerning commonly used evaluation metrics for text line segmentation, minor errors at a pixel level, lead to significant drops in performance at the line-level.

We therefore propose the integration and adaptation of a novel connectivity-aware loss function, initially introduced by Grim et al. [12] for neuron morphology reconstruction. In detail, this loss also penalizes topological errors at a global component level rather than solely at the pixel level.

Formally, the loss function is expressed as:

$$\mathcal{L}(y, \hat{y}) = (1 - \alpha)\mathcal{L}_0(y, \hat{y}) + \alpha\Big((1 - \beta) \sum_{C \in \mathcal{N}(\hat{y}_-)} \mathcal{L}_0(y_C, \hat{y}_C) \tag{1}$$

$$+ \beta \sum_{C \in \mathcal{P}(\hat{y}_+)} \mathcal{L}_0(y_C, \hat{y}_C)\Big). \tag{2}$$

Here, y represents the ground truth text line segmentation and $\hat{y}$ is the network's prediction. Furthermore, the sets $\mathcal{N}(\hat{y}_-)$ and $\mathcal{P}(\hat{y}_+)$ identify components that would alter the number of connected components in the predicted text lines. It is important to note that in our implementation, we use an *inverted ground truth* representation. Consequently, $\mathcal{P}(\hat{y}_+)$ captures false negative regions that cause a text line to appear fragmented (a false split), while $\mathcal{N}(\hat{y}_-)$ captures false positive regions that bridge two distinct ground truth lines (a false merge). Moreover, $\mathcal{L}_0$ refers to a standard pixel-level objective, such as, e.g., the binary cross-entropy loss. In our methodology, we adapted the loss by adding the Dice loss [24] and weighing the two terms to be of the same magnitude:

$$1 - \frac{2\sum_i^N y_i \hat{y}_i}{\sum_i^N y_i + \sum_i^N \hat{y}_i} + \frac{10}{N}\sum_i^N \mathcal{L}(y_i, \hat{y}_i). \quad (3)$$

Finally, the hyperparameters α and β provide crucial control over the connectivity: $\alpha \in [0, 1]$ balances the influence of the conventional pixel-level loss against the topological penalties, with higher values prioritizing the correction of connectivity errors. As this is vital for maintaining the precise structure of text lines in ancient manuscripts prone to fragmentation or merging, we select $\alpha = 1$. Concurrently, $\beta \in [0, 1]$ allows for differential weighting between false merge and false split errors in text line segmentation; a $\beta < 0.5$ prioritizes penalizing merged lines, while a $\beta > 0.5$ emphasizes correcting fragmented lines, enabling tailored error correction based on the specific challenges of the segmentation task. Interestingly, for both our selected datasets, we found that focusing exclusively on penalizing false merged lines yielded the best performance, and thus we chose $\beta = 0$. To better illustrate the impact of these hyperparameters, Fig. 2 shows the penalized error in yellow overlaid on the prediction.

Due to the high computational cost of calculating the connected components and matching them, we utilize the structure-aware loss solely to fine-tune a model that has been pretrained with only the Dice loss. For similar reasons, we do not employ the structure-aware loss for model selection during the fine-tuning stage. Instead, we utilize the mean IoU as a proxy function to evaluate performance during validation.

4 Datasets

Our experiments are grounded in publicly available datasets from recent academic competitions focused on advancing text line segmentation for historical documents. These benchmarks, including the ICDAR 2017 HisDoc-Layout-Comp [22] and the ICDAR 2025 FEST track [30], emphasize challenges such as complex layouts, document degradation, and the latter, critically, few-shot learning constraints where only a handful of annotated examples are available for training. We use two such datasets: U-DIADS-TL [2,31] and DIVA-HisDB [22], a widely-used dataset for historical layout analysis. While our primary development targets the proposed few-shot paradigm of U-DIADS-TL, we also adapt and evaluate DIVA-HisDB in a few-shot setting to test the generalization of our method.

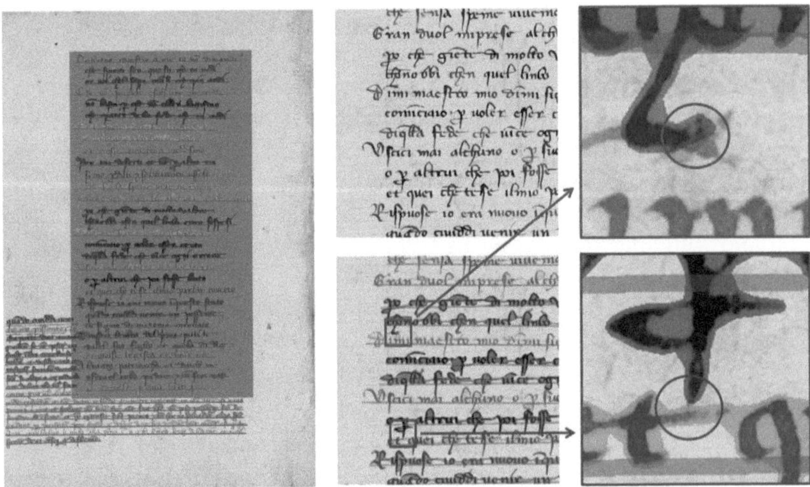

Fig. 3. Example excerpts of the CB55 manuscript in DIVA-HisDB illustrating the issue of overlapping text line segments.

4.1 U-DIADS-TL

The U-DIADS-TL dataset is the official benchmark for the FEST 2025 competition and is explicitly designed for few-shot text line segmentation [31]. It is a subset of the larger U-DIADS-Bib [29] collection, which provides a rich resource for multi-class layout analysis.

Technical Details. The dataset contains 105 high-resolution color images from three distinct medieval manuscripts: Latin 2, Latin 14396, and Syriaque 341. These sources feature diverse scripts, two- and three-column layouts, interlinear glosses, and significant degradation. For each manuscript, the data is strictly partitioned into 3 pages for training, 10 for validation, and 22 for testing, thus requiring effective methods to handle such low data regimes. The ground truth consists of pixel-precise binary masks that distinguish text lines from the background, with no overlap between line instances. Our methodology is designed to adhere to the official evaluation protocol described in [2,31].

4.2 DIVA-HisDB

The DIVA-HisDB dataset was introduced for the ICDAR 2017 HisDoc-Layout-Comp [22] competition. It is recognized for its complex page layouts, which include marginalia, decorated initials, and interlinear glosses.

Technical Details. The DIVA-HisDB consists of 150 pages from three manuscripts (CB55, CSG18, CSG863), provided as 600 dpi RGB scans with ground truth in PAGE XML format. For our experiments, we downsample all images by a factor of three to make the image dimensions between the two datasets coherent. The dataset supports multiple layout analysis tasks, including full text line segmentation (Task 3), equal to the FEST 2025 competition. However, the polygon annotations in PAGE XML format for this task feature overlapping regions between adjacent lines, as illustrated in Fig. 3. This characteristic is incompatible with models designed to produce a single, non-overlapping binary segmentation mask, making a pixel-level evaluation ambiguous.

To address this, we opt for the task of baseline detection (Task 2), which requires the prediction of start and end-points of baselines instead of full polygons, providing a suitable proxy for text line localization without the issue of overlapping regions. To maintain consistency with the few-shot evaluation setting of U-DIADS-TL, we do not use the full training partition of 20 pages per manuscript, but instead, for each experiment, we randomly sample three pages for training, allowing us to assess our model's few-shot generalization.

5 Evaluation

In the following section, we evaluate our proposed methodology. We begin by introducing the relevant evaluation metrics and experimental setup, followed by an ablation study of each component using our primary dataset, U-DIADS-TL. Finally, we assess the full approach on both benchmark datasets to underscore its effectiveness and generalizability.

5.1 Metrics

For the U-DIADS-TL dataset, we report Pixel IoU and Line IoU as well as Detection Rate (DR), Recognition Accuracy (RA), and F-Measure (FM) from matched line segments as proposed by Zottin et al. [2,31]. Pixel IoU and Line IoU are metrics based on the IoU, which is defined as:

$$\text{IoU} = \frac{TP}{TP + FP + FN}, \tag{4}$$

where TP is the number of true positives, FP false positives, and FN false negatives of the predicted binary mask. Subsequently, Pixel IoU evaluates segmentation quality at the pixel level, whereas Line IoU evaluates detection accuracy at the line level, where connected components are matched if pixel-level precision and recall exceed a threshold of 75%.

Concerning DR, RA, and FM, these metrics are based on a matching score, MatchScore. For predicted line R_i and ground-truth line G_j, the MatchScore is defined as:

$$\text{MatchScore}(i, j) = \frac{T(G_j \cap R_i)}{T(G_j \cup R_i)}, \tag{5}$$

where a pair (i, j) is considered a one-to-one match if $\text{MatchScore}(i, j) \geq 0.75$. Let M be the number of such matches, N_1 the number of ground-truth lines, and N_2 the number of detected lines, then the match-based metrics are defined as follows:

$$\mathrm{DR} = \frac{M}{N_1}, \ \mathrm{RA} = \frac{M}{N_2}, \ \mathrm{FM} = \frac{2 \cdot \mathrm{DR} \cdot \mathrm{RA}}{\mathrm{DR} + \mathrm{RA}}. \tag{6}$$

Based on overlapping text line annotations and resulting problems when evaluating text line segmentation on pixel-level (cf. Fig. 3), for the DIVA-HisDB dataset, we opt for the simplified task of text baseline detection. With this comes the necessity of employing suitable evaluation metrics for which we follow closely the evaluation protocol denoted in the work by Simistira et al. [22], which is based on the cBAD competition [9]. Here, an F-Measure metric is employed, which assesses baseline extraction by calculating recall and precision for polygonal chains representing baselines [9].

5.2 Evaluation Protocol

For model training, an AdamW optimizer is employed with a learning rate of $3e-4$, and models are trained or fine-tuned for 100 epochs using a batch size of eight. An early stopping criterion is implemented to prevent overfitting, halting training after 10 iterations and fine-tuning after 30 iterations without improvement in validation performance. Model selection for final evaluation is based on the highest validation mean IoU achieved during each run.

Regarding evaluation across datasets, we report the average performance obtained from training with at least three random seeds for U-DIADS-TL. Conversely, for the DIVA-HisDB dataset, performance is reported from the model that achieves the highest validation performance, consistent with its competition setting. Furthermore, specific to the DIVA-HisDB dataset, a post-processing pipeline is applied to facilitate comparison with ICDAR competition results from 2017 [22], which include filtering out segments shorter than 50 pixels and subsequently merging lines that are both geometrically close (within a 50-pixel distance threshold) and similarly oriented (within a 15-degree angle threshold).

5.3 Ablation

In the following section, we will ground our proposed method by conducting an ablation study on the individual components. Each component yields significant

Table 1. Ablation Study of the Proposed Method.

Name	Pixel IoU	Line IoU	DR	RA	FM
Baseline [31]	49.0	44.3	29.1	17.7	21.7
DeepLabV3+	52.44	51.90	48.32	30.00	36.44
+ UNet++	64.50	70.06	66.97	41.83	50.77
+ Lighter Encoder	65.29	71.24	68.30	42.39	51.94
+ Connectivity Loss	67.83	75.17	72.07	46.36	55.66
Final Model (Tuned)	**70.64**	**77.38**	**73.90**	**52.96**	**61.40**

performance improvements, which are denoted in Table 1, which summarizes the results of the performed study.

Model Architectures. First, we ablate different model architectures. For architecture selection, we considered the same as Zottin et al. [31] plus a transformer-based one; however, this time, training on patches instead of the whole image this time. Inspecting the results in Table 2, we observe that simpler architectures, e.g., the UNet [19] or derived variants, i.e., the UNet++ [28], yield drastically better performance over all metrics. In line with the theory that less bias reduces the risk of overfitting [11], we select the UNet++ given our context of data-scarce training regimes in the few-shot setting.

Table 2. Ablating Architectures.

Name	Pixel IoU	Line IoU	DR	RA	FM
PSPNet [27]	42.22	44.08	37.31	33.33	34.18
SegFormer [26]	50.10	49.27	46.42	29.66	35.50
UNet++ [28]	64.50	70.06	66.97	41.83	50.77
DeepLabV3+ [4]	52.44	51.90	48.32	30.00	36.44
UNet [19]	64.34	69.56	66.71	39.92	49.31

Encoder Parameter Size. Continuing with the previous made insight, we ablate encoder depth, evaluating ResNets [13] pre-trained on ImageNet [5] with varying amounts of network layers. We illustrate our findings in Fig. 4, which indicates a similar trend: performance tends to increase with decreasing depth. However, this trend is not stable as there is some fluctuation. For instance, a ResNet with a depth of 18 performs clearly worse than one with 34 layers, while being better than larger variants with up to 152 layers.

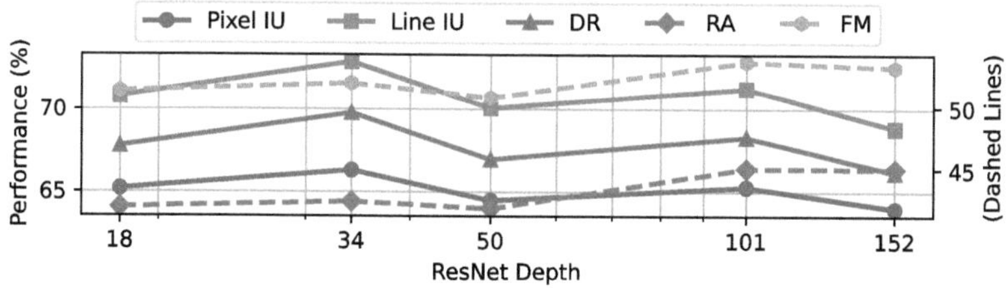

Fig. 4. Ablation on Network Depth.

Connectivity Loss. An essential component of our proposed methodology for few-shot text line segmentation is the tuned connectivity-aware loss function proposed by Grim et al. [12] and leveraged within our methodology. As the hyperparameters α and β influence the trade-off between pixel-level and topological loss and between penalizing false merge and false split errors, we perform an ablation study on these parameters to select them optimally.

We illustrate our findings in Fig. 5 and observe in Fig. 5a that performance is best when considering only the topology of the mask (i.e., $\alpha = 1$), neglecting pixel-level performance, which is expected due to our additional incorporation of the Dice loss. In contrast to initial assumptions that both false merges and false splits play a crucial role in performance, results of Fig. 5b show that only false merges are problematic (i.e., $\beta = 0$). Given these results, we performed the same ablation for the DIVA-HisDB baseline detection task and found $\beta = 0$ to also work best.

5.4 Results

Our comprehensive evaluation on two distinct historical document datasets, DIVA-HisDB and U-DIADS-TL, unequivocally demonstrates the competitive performance and generalizability of our proposed few-shot methodology in extremely scarce data settings of only three available annotated pages. Summarized in Tables 3 and 4, our results highlight the impact of the connectivity-aware loss, which we propose for text line segmentation and baseline detection,

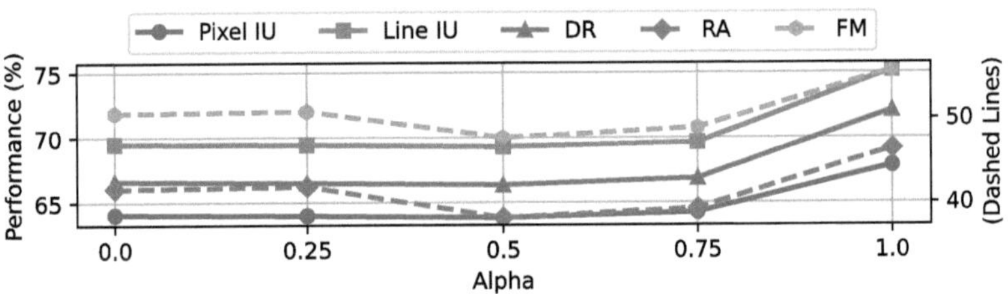

(a) Varying α, while keeping β constant at 0.5.

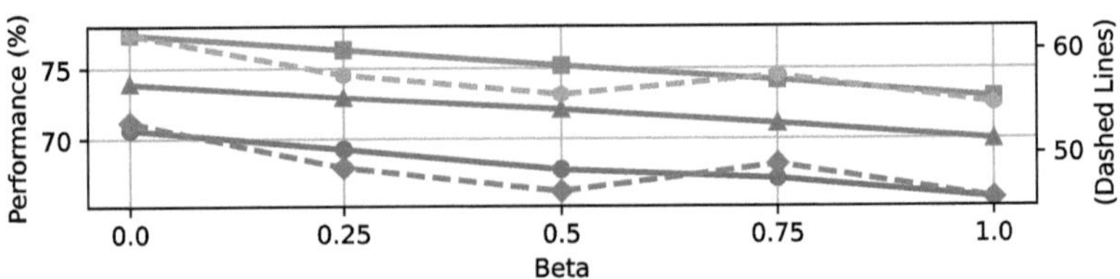

(b) Varying β, while keeping α constant at 1.

Fig. 5. Ablating the Hyper-Parameters of the Connectivity Loss.

in addition to our use of smaller and simpler architectures compared to previous SOTA methods.

Table 3. Final Results DIVA-HisDB.

Name	Samples	CB55	CSG18	CSG863	Avg. F1
System-8 [22]	20	98.96	98.53	97.16	**98.22**
System-2 [22]		95.97	**98.79**	**98.30**	97.68
UNet++		**99.66**	94.31	92.24	95.40
UNet++	3	93.17	83.17	86.62	87.65
+Connectivity Loss		96.07	87.27	86.02	89.79
+Post-Processing		99.00	94.13	93.62	95.58

In more detail, on the DIVA-HisDB dataset with the task of baseline detection (Table 3), our suggested lightweight UNet-based methodology, trained on patches with only three annotated pages, achieves an average F1 score of 95.58%. In comparison to the UNet++ baseline trained on a significantly larger dataset (20 samples versus 3, 95.40% F1) and approaching or even outperforming the F1 scores of top competition systems (System-8: 98.22%, System-2: 97.68%) that leveraged considerably more training data, the efficacy of our methodology in the few-shot setting is underscored.

Table 4. Final Results U-DIADS-TL.

Metric	Latin 14396	Latin 2	Syriaque 341	Avg. Ours	Avg. [31]	Rel. Gain to [31]
Pixel IoU	73.71	77.83	60.36	70.64	49.0	+44.16
Line IoU	79.78	86.28	66.09	77.38	44.3	+74.67
DR	79.45	84.37	57.89	73.90	29.1	+153.95
RA	51.20	65.40	42.27	52.96	17.7	+199.21
F-Measure	61.96	73.43	48.83	61.40	21.7	+182.95

On the more challenging task of text line segmentation of the U-DIADS-TL dataset (Table 4), the impact of our methodology is further exemplified, where our final, tuned model sets a new SOTA for few-shot text line segmentation. Across all metrics, our approach achieves relative gains ranging from 75% to 200%. Specifically, we observe a nearly 200% gain in RA and an approximate 185% gain in FM. Complementary improvements include a plus of around 75% in Line IoU (reaching 77.38%), an over 150% relative gain in DR (attaining 73.90%), and a nearly 45% relative improvement in Pixel IoU, with an absolute performance of 70.64%. An excerpt of qualitative results is depicted in Fig. 1.

6 Conclusion

In this work, we challenged the prevailing trend of increasing model complexity for few-shot text line segmentation in historical documents. We demonstrated that a simpler, lightweight UNet++ architecture, when paired with a connectivity-aware loss function, yielded superior performance in a low-data regime. Our approach directly addressed the critical issue of maintaining topological correctness by penalizing common structural errors such as line fragmentation and inadvertent merges.

Our experimental results substantiated the effectiveness of this methodology. On the U-DIADS-TL benchmark, our model established a new state-of-the-art, improving the Line IoU by over 75% and the RA by nearly 200% relative to the baseline. Furthermore, it showed strong generalization capabilities on the DIVA-HisDB dataset, producing results competitive with top-performing systems while utilizing 85% less training data. These findings confirmed our central hypothesis: architectural simplicity, when combined with a topologically informed loss function, provides a more potent and efficient solution for few-shot segmentation than more complex, data-hungry models.

References

1. Alberti, M., Vögtlin, L., Pondenkandath, V., Seuret, M., Ingold, R., Liwicki, M.: Labeling, cutting, grouping: an efficient text line segmentation method for medieval manuscripts. In: 2019 International Conference on Document Analysis and Recognition (ICDAR), pp. 1200–1206. IEEE (2019)
2. AVML Lab Fest Organizers: FEST @ ICDAR 2025: Competition on few-shot text line segmentation of ancient handwritten documents (2025)
3. Barakat, B., Droby, A., Kassis, M., El-Sana, J.: Text line segmentation for challenging handwritten document images using fully convolutional network. In: 2018 16th International Conference on Frontiers in Handwriting Recognition (ICFHR), pp. 374–379. IEEE (2018)
4. Chen, L.C., Papandreou, G., Kokkinos, I., Murphy, K., Yuille, A.L.: DeepLab: semantic image segmentation with deep convolutional nets, atrous convolution, and fully connected CRFs. IEEE Trans. Pattern Anal. Mach. Intell. **40**(4), 834–848 (2018). https://doi.org/10.1109/tpami.2017.2699184
5. De Nardin, A., Zottin, S., Colombi, E., Piciarelli, C., Foresti, G.L.: Is ImageNet always the best option? An overview on transfer learning strategies for document layout analysis. In: International Conference on Image Analysis and Processing, pp. 489–499. Springer (2023)
6. De Nardin, A., Zottin, S., Paier, M., Foresti, G.L., Colombi, E., Piciarelli, C.: Efficient few-shot learning for pixel-precise handwritten document layout analysis. In: 2023 IEEE/CVF Winter Conference on Applications of Computer Vision (WACV). IEEE (2023)
7. De Nardin, A., Zottin, S., Piciarelli, C., Colombi, E., Foresti, G.L.: Few-shot pixel-precise document layout segmentation via dynamic instance generation and local thresholding. Int. J. Neural Syst. **33**(10) (2023)

8. De Nardin, A., Zottin, S., Piciarelli, C., Colombi, E., Foresti, G.L.: A one-shot learning approach to document layout segmentation of ancient Arabic manuscripts. In: 2024 IEEE/CVF Winter Conference on Applications of Computer Vision (WACV). IEEE (2024)
9. Diem, M., Kleber, F., Fiel, S., Gruning, T., Gatos, B.: cBAD: ICDAR2017 competition on baseline detection. In: 2017 14th IAPR International Conference on Document Analysis and Recognition (ICDAR), pp. 1355–1360. IEEE (2017). https://doi.org/10.1109/icdar.2017.222
10. Fizaine, F.C., et al.: Historical text line segmentation using deep learning algorithms: Mask-RCNN against U-Net networks. J. Imag. **10**(3), 65 (2024)
11. Goodfellow, I., Bengio, Y., Courville, A.: Deep Learning. MIT Press (2016)
12. Grim, A., Chandrashekar, J., Sümbül, U.: Efficient connectivity-preserving instance segmentation with super voxel-based loss function. In: Proceedings of the AAAI Conference on Artificial Intelligence, vol. 39, no. 3, pp. 3167–3175 (2025). https://doi.org/10.1609/aaai.v39i3.32326
13. He, K., Zhang, X., Ren, S., Sun, J.: Deep residual learning for image recognition. In: 2016 IEEE Conference on Computer Vision and Pattern Recognition (CVPR), pp. 770–778. IEEE (2016)
14. Likforman-Sulem, L., Hanimyan, A., Faure, C.: A Hough-based algorithm for extracting text lines in handwritten documents. In: Proceedings of 3rd International Conference on Document Analysis and Recognition, vol. 2, pp. 774–777. IEEE (1995)
15. Likforman-Sulem, L., Zahour, A., Taconet, B.: Text line segmentation of historical documents: a survey. IJDAR **9**, 123–138 (2007)
16. Long, J., Shelhamer, E., Darrell, T.: Fully convolutional networks for semantic segmentation. In: Proceedings of the IEEE Conference on Computer Vision and Pattern Recognition, pp. 3431–3440 (2015)
17. Mosinska, A., Marquez-Neila, P., Koziński, M., Fua, P.: Beyond the pixel-wise loss for topology-aware delineation. In: Proceedings of the IEEE Conference on Computer Vision and Pattern Recognition, pp. 3136–3145 (2018)
18. O'Gorman, L.: The document spectrum for page layout analysis. IEEE Trans. Pattern Anal. Mach. Intell. **15**(11), 1162–1173 (1993)
19. Ronneberger, O., Fischer, P., Brox, T.: U-Net: convolutional networks for biomedical image segmentation. In: Navab, N., Hornegger, J., Wells, W.M., Frangi, A.F. (eds.) MICCAI 2015. LNCS, vol. 9351, pp. 234–241. Springer, Cham (2015). https://doi.org/10.1007/978-3-319-24574-4_28
20. Salehi, S.S.M., Erdogmus, D., Gholipour, A.: Tversky loss function for image segmentation using 3D fully convolutional deep networks. In: International Workshop on Machine Learning in Medical Imaging, pp. 379–387. Springer (2017)
21. Shapiro, V., Gluhchev, G., Sgurev, V.: Handwritten document image segmentation and analysis. Pattern Recogn. Lett. **14**(1), 71–78 (1993)
22. Simistira, F., et al.: ICDAR2017 competition on layout analysis for challenging medieval manuscripts. In: 2017 14th IAPR International Conference on Document Analysis and Recognition (ICDAR), vol. 01, pp. 1361–1370 (2017). https://doi.org/10.1109/ICDAR.2017.223
23. Sterzinger, R., Brenner, S., Sablatnig, R.: Drawing the line: deep segmentation for extracting art from ancient Etruscan mirrors. In: ICDAR 2024, pp. 39–56. Springer, Cham (2024). https://doi.org/10.1007/978-3-031-70543-4_3
24. Sudre, C.H., Li, W., Vercauteren, T., Ourselin, S., Jorge Cardoso, M.: Generalised dice overlap as a deep learning loss function for highly unbalanced segmentations.

In: Cardoso, M.J., et al. (eds.) DLMIA/ML-CDS -2017. LNCS, vol. 10553, pp. 240–248. Springer, Cham (2017). https://doi.org/10.1007/978-3-319-67558-9_28
25. Vadlamudi, N., Krishna, R., Sarvadevabhatla, R.K.: SeamFormer: high precision text line segmentation for handwritten documents. In: International Conference on Document Analysis and Recognition, pp. 313–331. Springer (2023)
26. Xie, E., Wang, W., Yu, Z., Anandkumar, A., Alvarez, J.M., Luo, P.: SegFormer: simple and efficient design for semantic segmentation with transformers. In: Ranzato, M., Beygelzimer, A., Dauphin, Y., Liang, P., Vaughan, J.W. (eds.) Advances in Neural Information Processing Systems, vol. 34, pp. 12077–12090. Curran Associates, Inc. (2021)
27. Zhao, H., Shi, J., Qi, X., Wang, X., Jia, J.: Pyramid scene parsing network. In: 2017 IEEE Conference on Computer Vision and Pattern Recognition (CVPR). IEEE (2017). https://doi.org/10.1109/cvpr.2017.660
28. Zhou, Z., Siddiquee, M.M.R., Tajbakhsh, N., Liang, J.: UNet++: a nested U-Net architecture for medical image segmentation. In: Deep Learning in Medical Image Analysis and Multimodal Learning for Clinical Decision Support, pp. 3–11. Springer (2018)
29. Zottin, S., De Nardin, A., Colombi, E., Piciarelli, C., Pavan, F., Foresti, G.L.: U-DIADS-Bib: a full and few-shot pixel-precise dataset for document layout analysis of ancient manuscripts. Neural Comput. Appl. **36**(20), 11777–11789 (2024). https://doi.org/10.1007/s00521-023-09356-5
30. Zottin, S., De Nardin, A., Foresti, G.L., Colombi, E., Piciarelli, C.: ICDAR 2024 competition on few-shot and many-shot layout segmentation of ancient manuscripts (SAM). In: International Conference on Document Analysis and Recognition, pp. 315–331. Springer (2024)
31. Zottin, S., et al.: Exploring few-shot text line segmentation approaches in challenging ancient manuscripts. In: Cornia, M., et al. (eds.) Proceedings of the 21st Conference on Information and Research science Connecting to Digital and Library Science, Udine, Italy, February 20–21, 2025. CEUR Workshop Proceedings, vol. 3937. CEUR-WS.org (2025)

From Coarse to Fine, Easy to Hard: Dual-Progressive 3D Hand Mesh Reconstruction

Yuqing Lu, Zhengrong Zuo, and Nong Sang(✉)

Key Laboratory of Image Processing and Intelligent Control, School of Artificial Intelligence and Automation, Huazhong University of Science and Technology, Wuhan, China
{luyuqing0920,zhrzuo,nsang}@hust.edu.com

Abstract. Despite notable progress in hand mesh reconstruction, many existing methods still face two common limitations: (1) early-stage prediction errors tend to propagate through refinement stages, and (2) training with randomly sampled data ignores the various difficulty levels of samples. To address these issues, we propose a **D**ual-**P**rogressive **F**ramework (DPF), consisting of Progressive Structural Regression (PSR) and Progressive Curriculum Learning (PCL). Specifically, the former adopts a coarse-to-fine refinement that progressively regresses hand representations from semantic features to joint features and finally to mesh vertices. It leverages spatial confidence maps and stacked-GCN to mitigate early-stage errors and enhance hand topological awareness. Meanwhile, the latter schedules samples from easy to hard through a Self-Paced Learning strategy, based on Unified Difficulty derived from both data-level and model-level. It helps promote more stable and effective model convergence. Furthermore, we propose Dual-Factor Dynamic Loss (DFDL) that adaptively adjusts the model's supervisory emphasis according to PSR and PCL, enabling a coherent interaction. Experiments on the FreiHAND dataset demonstrate that our method outperforms existing approaches.

Keywords: Hand Mesh Reconstruction · Coarse-to-Fine · Curriculum Learning

1 Introduction

Hand Mesh Reconstruction (HMR) aims to recover hand mesh vertices from a single RGB image. It has attracted widespread attention due to its broad applications in motion capture and human-computer interaction. Despite this, HMR still faces two common limitations: the propagation of early-stage prediction errors during refinement, and the lack of mechanisms for accommodating the various difficulty levels of training samples.

Many methods [5,6,14,17,18] adopt a coarse-to-fine pipeline, where global features are used to predict coarse representations before regressing dense mesh

C. Wallraven et al. (Eds.): ACPR 2025, LNCS 16174, pp. 115–129, 2026.
https://doi.org/10.1007/978-981-95-4395-3_9

vertices. However, as shown in Fig. 1, it is hard to rectify early-stage errors, because models tend to emphasize fine-grained details in later stages, which will further amplify initial inaccuracy. Meanwhile, to enhance the generalization of HMR, recent methods [23,24] increasingly adopt merged multi-source training datasets, driven by the rapid expansion of hand pose datasets [2,11,13,20,38,39]. However, as illustrated in Fig. 2, differences in imaging conditions and visual characteristics among datasets introduce challenges and potential instability in the training process. Although much attention has been given to training across multiple datasets, the impact of training sample order within a single dataset, which significantly affects model convergence and performance [1,34,36], remains underexplored.

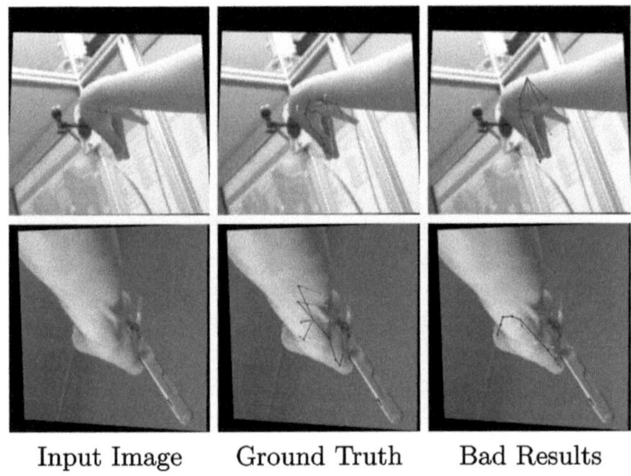

Fig. 1. Imprecise 2D keypoint localization in early-stage will cause notable degradation in mesh reconstruction accuracy.

Motivated by these observations, we propose a novel **D**ual-**P**rogressive **F**rame-work (DPF) for hand mesh reconstruction, which integrates Progressive Structural Regression (PSR) and Progressive Curriculum Learning (PCL). Specifically, PSR includes two components that collaboratively implement a coarse-to-fine refinement: Semantic-to-Joint and Joint-to-Mesh (See § 3.1). In Semantic-to-Joint, spatial confidence maps and stacked-GCN [27] are applied to mitigate early-stage errors and enhance hand topological awareness, while a hierarchical decoder in Joint-to-Mesh is used to recover detailed meshes. In parallel, PCL schedules training samples from easy to hard through a Self-Paced Learning strategy (See Sect. 3.2). It is guided by Unified Difficulty, which is derived from both data-level and model-level. We further propose Dual-Factor Dynamic Loss (DFDL) to adaptively adjust the model's supervisory emphasis, encouraging more supervision on shallow layers for easy samples, and more on deeper layers for harder ones (See Sect. 3.3).

Our main contributions can be summarized as:

Fig. 2. Illustration of different hand pose datasets, showing variations in appearance, lighting, and realism. FreiHAND [39], DexYCB [2], HO3D v3 [13], and ARCTIC [11] are real-world datasets, while RHD [38] and InterHand2.6M [20] are synthetic datasets rendered from 3D models.

- We propose a novel **D**ual-**P**rogressive **F**rame-work (DPF) that integrates Progressive Structural Regression (PSR) with Progressive Curriculum Learning (PSL). The former implements a coarse-to-fine refinement, and the latter schedules training samples from easy to hard.
- We introduce Dual-Factor Dynamic Loss (DFDL) that adjust the model's supervisory emphasis based on the dual progressive processes.
- Extensive experiments on the FreiHAND dataset [39] demonstrate the effectiveness of our method, achieving good performance across multiple metrics.

2 Related Work

In this section, we briefly review existing hand mesh estimation methods, with a focus on coarse-to-fine refinement strategies. We also introduce curriculum learning and discuss its application in the field of hand mesh reconstruction.

2.1 Hand Mesh Estimation

As it is challenging to regress dense hand meshes directly from images, many methods [5–7,10,14,17,18,18,23,26,27,29] adopt a coarse-to-fine pipeline. These methods can be broadly categorized into three refinement aspects: dimensional elevation, quantity expansion, and accuracy enhancement.

Dimensional Elevation: From 2D to 3D. To obtain accurate hand meshes, existing methods [5,6,14] often use 2D representations as an intermediate step before lifting to 3D features or coordinates, which can be seen as a type of coarse-to-fine refinement. Chen et al. [5] extract 2D pose via heatmap encoding before predicting the 3D mesh. Kim et al. [14] leverage 2D heatmaps to guide local feature sampling, bridging the gap between image and mesh representations.

Quantity Expansion: From Sparse to Dense. Other approaches [17,18] often begin with sparse keypoints (e.g., 21 joints) and progressively refine them into dense meshes. Lin et al. [18] predict a 431-vertex submesh and expand it to 6K vertices for human mesh reconstruction.

Accuracy Enhancement: From Inaccurate to Precise. Accuracy enhancement aims to refine initial predictions using dedicated modules. Potamias et al. [23] iteratively update MANO [26] parameters and camera poses using ViT-based [10] predictions and multi-scale features. Cho et al. [7] and Lin et al. [18] refine inaccurate tokens via Transformer [29] and GNN [27] to obtain precise hand mesh.

2.2 Curriculum Learning

Curriculum Learning (CL), first proposed by Bengio et al. [1], simulates the human cognitive process by presenting easier samples first and gradually introducing more complex ones. It has been widely applied in natural language processing [30] and computer vision tasks [31], especially in scenarios with imbalanced data. Generally, CL involves two key components: Difficulty Measurement and Sample Scheduling.

Difficulty Measurement. Difficulty measurement is fundamental in curriculum learning, because it determines the order in which samples are fed to the model. Early studies manually define difficulty using task-specific cues such as object count and occlusion. However, these handcrafted metrics are often dataset-dependent and may not align with the model's actual learning challenges. To overcome this limitation, automated difficulty estimation methods have been developed [12,32]. For example, Wei et al. [32] use a strong pre-trained model as a teacher to evaluate sample difficulty based on its performance. Platanios et al. [22] propose dynamical difficulty measurement according to the current model's training loss.

Sample Scheduling. Sample scheduling determines when to present harder samples during training. Static strategies like Babystep [1] follow a predefined easy-to-hard order. In contrast, dynamic approaches such as Self-Paced Learning (SPL) [16] allow the model to select samples based on current loss, reducing instability from early exposure to difficult examples. More advanced methods [4, 25] use reinforcement learning to adaptively select samples in response to model feedback.

In 3D pose estimation, curriculum learning has been increasingly adopted. Dai et al. [8] propose DMH-CL, a training strategy for complex multi-person pose estimation, which focuses on easy examples early and harder ones later. However, in hand mesh estimation, the integration of coarse-to-fine refinement with easy-to-hard sample scheduling remains underexplored.

3 Method

In this section, we introduce the overall architecture of our proposed **D**ual-**P**rogressive **F**ramework (DPF) and provide its main components: Progressive Structural Regression (PSR) and Progressive Curriculum Learning (PCL). PSR includes Semantic to Joint and Joint to Mesh, while PCL incorporates Unified Difficulty and Self-Paced Learning strategy. Dual-Factor Dynamic Loss is introduced later.

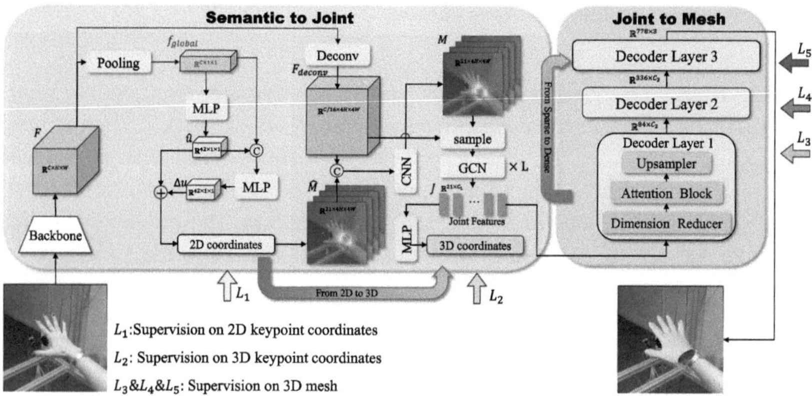

Fig. 3. The overall architecture of the proposed DPF. The input image is processed by Semantic to Joint (yellow region) and then Joint to Mesh (blue region) to generate the final 3D mesh output. For the hierarchical decoder, only the components of the Decoder Layer 1 are shown in detail for clarity, as the subsequent blocks share the same architecture. Hollow arrows indicate supervisions applied to different layers of the model, while color intensity reflects the depth of each layer. (Color figure online)

3.1 Progressive Structural Regression: From Coarse to Fine

Semantic to Joint. Given an input image, our model utilizes a backbone to extract image features $F \in \mathbb{R}^{C\times H\times W}$. After global average pooling, the global vector $f_{\text{global}} \in \mathbb{R}^{C\times 1\times 1}$ is passed through a multilayer perceptron to estimate the initial 2D joint locations $\hat{u}$. We further introduce a residual regression module that refines the coarse predictions by learning coordinate offsets. Specifically, the initial predictions are concatenated with the global vector to estimate residuals, which help correct potential early-stage errors.

Many methods [23,37] use bilinear sampling to sample joint features, which tend to amplify initial estimation errors. To mitigate this, we first upsample the feature map F to get $F_{\text{deconv}} \in \mathbb{R}^{C/16\times 4H\times 4W}$, enabling more precise localization. We then generate Gaussian heatmaps $\hat{M}_i \in \mathbb{R}^{4H\times 4W}$ centered at the refined uv coordinates and concatenate them with F_{deconv} to jointly get spatial confidence maps M_i, which are then used to sample from F and generate joint features, as follows:

$$J_i = \sum_{x,y} M_i(x, y) \cdot F_{\text{deconv}}(x, y), \tag{1}$$

where x,y represent the 2D coordinates in the feature maps and i denotes the index of joints.

A stacked-GCN is then employed to enhance joint features, where each layer enables interaction with one-hop, two-hop, and three-hop neighbors, respectively. This allows the model to progressively incorporate broader structural context and enhance hand topological awareness.

Joint to Mesh. To reconstruct dense hand mesh vertices from sparse joint features, we adopt a hierarchical decoder inspired by prior work [37] that progressively expands joint-level features into mesh-level representations. At each layer, Attention Block captures keypoint dependencies while the Upsampler increases resolution and the Dimension Reducer reduces the feature dimension. Positional embeddings are added to maintain structural alignment. Finally, a linear head regresses 3D coordinates of all mesh vertices. We follow the layer dimensions used in [37], i.e. [84, 336, 778], and additionally introduce linear regression heads at the first two layers to support further intermediate supervision (See Sect. 3.3).

3.2 Progressive Curriculum Learning: From Easy to Hard

To address the overlooked impact of training sample scheduling, we propose a curriculum learning strategy that progressively arranges training samples from easy to hard. It comprises two components: Unified Difficulty, which quantifies the difficulty level, and Self-Paced Learning, which governs the data scheduling.

Unified Difficulty. To establish Unified Difficulty (UD) as a comprehensive metric for quantifying sample difficulty, we consider both data-level and model-level perspectives, aiming to capture the geometric complexity as well as model performance (Fig. 4).

Data-level Difficulty (DD) is motivated by the observation that geometric factors, e.g. self-occlusion and extreme viewpoints, have a significant impact on hand pose estimation accuracy. For each sample I, we design two statistical metrics that explicitly quantify the geometric complexity of each sample.

- Orientation Ambiguity (OA): Severe self-occlusion often occurs when the palm plane is close to perpendicular to the camera view, making it difficult to observe key structures. As the palm plane is formed by the wrist, index base, and little finger base, orientation ambiguity is then measured as:

$$OA_I = \sin\theta_I = \sqrt{1 - \left(\frac{\mathbf{n}_I \cdot \mathbf{n}}{|\mathbf{n}_I||\mathbf{n}|}\right)^2}, \tag{2}$$

(a) easy samples with simple poses

(b) hard samples with occlusion or extreme articulation

Fig. 4. Examples of Data-level Difficulty.

where $\mathbf{n}_I$ and $\mathbf{n}$ are unit vectors of the palm orientation and camera viewing direction, respectively.

- Structural Dispersion (SD): SD characterizes the spatial distribution of hand joints relative to the root joint. A larger dispersion reflects a more open hand configuration with reduced self-occlusion, which typically facilitates more accurate pose estimation. SD is defined as the average distance between joints and the wrist(root), normalized by the length of the middle finger bone L_{middle} as:

$$SD_I = \frac{1}{J} \sum_{j=1}^{J} \frac{\|p_j - p_{\text{root}}\|_2}{L_{\text{middle}}}, \tag{3}$$

where J is the total number of joints, p_j and p_{root} are the 3D coordinates of joint j and the root joint respectively. SD is further normalized as $1 - SD_I / \max(SD)$, to align with OA and ensure that samples with more compact joint distributions are considered harder.

The overall Data-level Difficulty is defined as a weighted combination of the two metrics, as follows:

$$DD_I = \alpha \cdot OA_I + (1 - \alpha) \cdot SD_I, \tag{4}$$

where $\alpha \in [0, 1]$ is a weighting factor balancing the importance of OA and SD.

Moreover, *Model-level Difficulty (MD)* originates from the model's perspective, complementing data-level difficulty by capturing factors such as background ambiguity. Specifically, the training set $D = \{(I, Y_I)\}_{I=1}^{N}$ is randomly and evenly partitioned into L subsets $\{D_i\}_{i=1}^{L}$. We then train L independent teacher models, where each model P_{θ_i} is trained exclusively on its corresponding subset, as follows:

$$\theta_i = \arg\min_{\theta} \sum_{I \in D_i} \mathcal{L}(P(I; \theta), Y_I). \tag{5}$$

For any image $I_j \in D_k$, predictions are made using the remaining $L-1$ teacher models excluding k, producing evaluation scores s_j according to the reconstruction performance, which are then averaged to MD_I.

Unified Difficulty (UD) then integrates both aspects to produce a global difficulty score:

$$UD_I = \beta \cdot DD_I + (1-\beta) \cdot MD_I, \tag{6}$$

where $\beta \in [0,1]$ is a weighting factor that controls the trade-off between geometric complexity and model feedback.

Self-paced Learning. Based on the UD score of each sample, we adopt a Self-Paced Learning strategy to mitigate the negative impact of difficult samples in early training and facilitate more stable and effective convergence. It dynamically filters samples according to their difficulty, allowing the model to progressively learn from easier to more challenging examples, thereby facilitating more stable convergence.

At training iteration t, a difficulty threshold function $\lambda(t)$ controls the subset of samples visible for training:

$$D_t = \{(I, Y_I) \in D \mid S_i \leq \lambda(t)\}, \tag{7}$$

where $\lambda(t) \in [0,1]$ is a monotonically increasing function over the training process, regulating the pace at which more difficult samples are introduced.

Since the model's capacity typically grows steadily during training, a linear schedule offers a simple yet effective way to progressively increase sample difficulty in alignment with the model's learning pace.

$$\lambda(t) = \min\left(\lambda_{\text{max}}, \lambda_{\text{min}} + \frac{t}{T}(\lambda_{\text{max}} - \lambda_{\text{min}})\right), \tag{8}$$

where λ_{min} denotes the initial allowed difficulty and λ_{max} denotes the final maximum difficulty allowed; T is the total number of training epochs.

3.3 Dual-Factor Dynamic Loss

To seek the trade-off between sample difficulty and structural granularity, we propose Dual-Factor Dynamic Loss. The loss function enables the model to gradually adapt supervision emphasis through the coarse-to-fine process, promoting effective learning across samples of various complexity.

Specifically, in the process of PSR, we assign independent supervision to the output of each layer, as illustrated in Fig. 3, e.g. uv coordinates, 3D joint coordinates, and mesh vertices. The total loss is defined as:

$$L_{\text{total}} = \sum_{k=0}^{K} \lambda_k \cdot L_k, \tag{9}$$

where L_k denotes the supervision loss for the k-th layer, λ_k is its corresponding loss weight, and K is the total number of decoder layers.

For each sample I with difficulty score $UD_I \in [0, 1]$, the weight for the k-th layer is computed as:

$$\lambda_I^k = \alpha^k \cdot (1 - UD_I) + \beta^k \cdot UD_I, \tag{10}$$

where $\alpha^k = 1 - \frac{k}{K}$ and $\beta^k = \frac{k+1}{K}$.

This formulation ensures that for easy samples, supervision is focused on shallower layers (α^k-dominated), assigning stronger guidance; for hard samples, supervision is focused more on deeper layers (β^k-dominated).

Table 1. Comparison of different methods on the PA-MPJPE, PA-MPVPE, F@05, F@15 metrics.

Method	PA-MPJPE ↓	PA-MPVPE ↓	F@05 ↑	F@15 ↑
I2L-MeshNet [19]	7.4	7.6	0.681	0.973
CMR [6]	6.9	7.0	0.715	0.977
I2UV [3]	7.2	7.4	0.682	0.973
MobRecon [5]	6.9	7.2	0.694	0.979
METRO [35]	6.7	6.8	0.717	0.981
MeshGraphormer [18]	6.3	6.5	0.738	0.983
FastMETRO [7]	6.5	7.1	0.687	0.983
Deformr [33]	6.2	6.4	0.743	0.984
PointHMR [14]	6.1	6.6	0.720	0.984
FastViT [28]	6.6	6.7	0.722	0.981
Wilor [23]	5.8	6.1	**0.793**	**0.990**
Ours	**5.7**	**6.0**	0.772	**0.990**

4 Experiments

In this section, we evaluate the proposed **D**ual-**P**rogressive **F**ramework (DPF) on the FreiHAND [39] dataset.We first compare DPF with several state-of-the-art hand mesh reconstruction methods both quantitatively and qualitatively. Then, through ablation studies, we validate the effectiveness of the key components.

4.1 Experiments Settings

Implementation Details. We adopt FastVit-MA36 [28] as our backbone, initialized with weights pre-trained on ImageNet [9]. Our network is implemented using PyTorch [21]. Training is conducted for 200 epochs using the AdamW optimizer [15] with a learning rate of 2e-4. Experiments run on four RTX 4090 GPUs, with a batch size of 32 per GPU. In Unified Difficulty, α is set to 0.5 and β is set to 0.4. In SPL, $\lambda_{\min}$ and $\lambda_{\max}$ are set to 0.4 and 1.0, respectively.

Dataset. We train and evaluate our model on the FreiHAND [39] dataset, which includes 130,240 training and 3,960 testing samples annotated with 3D joint positions and MANO mesh labels. The dataset features a diverse range of hand poses and viewpoints, offering challenging scenarios for robust model assessment.

Evaluation Metrics. We evaluate 3D hand mesh reconstruction accuracy using Procrustes Aligned Mean Per Joint Position Error (PA-MPJPE) and Procrustes Aligned Mean Per Vertex Position Error (PA-MPVPE). Both metrics align the predicted mesh to the ground truth via Procrustes analysis to remove global rotation and scale effects. Additionally, we report the F-score at thresholds of 5mm and 15mm (F@5, F@15), indicating the proportion of accurately reconstructed poses within these error margins.

4.2 Results

We compare DPF with a comprehensive set of representative methods on the FreiHAND dataset [39], including both Transformer- and CNN-based architectures. As shown in Table 1, experimental results demonstrate that our method achieves superior performance. Specifically, we achieve the lowest PA-MPJPE (5.7 mm) and PA-MPVPE (6.0 mm), indicating superior accuracy in joint and vertex estimation. Although Wilor [23] slightly surpasses our method on the F@5 metric (0.793 vs. 0.772), our approach attains the highest F@15 score (0.990), demonstrating more robust mesh reconstruction at a relaxed threshold. Compared to both Transformer-based [29] methods like METRO [35] and FastMETRO [7] and CNN-based models such as I2L-MeshNet [19] and MobRecon [5], our framework consistently delivers improved precision, validating the effectiveness of our DPF.

The qualitative comparison results are shown in Fig. 5. Our method accurately estimates hand meshes that better match the ground truth in both global hand pose and fine-grained details. When other methods struggle to reconstruct overlapping fingers, our approach successfully preserves the original pose.

Table 2. Ablation study on Progressive Structural Regression.

Model Variant	PA-MPJPE ↓	PA-MPVPE ↓	F@5 ↑	F@15 ↑
Full Model	**5.7**	**6.0**	**0.772**	**0.990**
w/o confidence map	5.9	6.0	0.743	0.984
w/o stacked-GCN	5.8	6.1	0.733	0.983
w/o hierarchical decoder	7.8	7.7	0.660	0.922

Table 3. Ablation study on Progressive Curriculum Learning.

Method Variant	PA-MPJPE ↓	PA-MPVPE ↓
Full Method	**5.7**	**6.0**
w/o Data-Level Difficulty	5.9	6.1
w/o Model-Level Difficulty	6.3	6.4
w/o SPL	5.8	6.1
w Babystep	6.7	6.5

Table 4. Ablation study on DFDL.

Model Variant	PA-MPJPE ↓	PA-MPVPE ↓
Full Model	**5.7**	**6.0**
w/o DFDL	5.9	6.0

4.3 Ablation Study

To validate the effectiveness of each component, we conduct ablation studies on the FreiHAND dataset [39]. The results of these experiments, detailed in Tables 2, 3 and 4, show that each module contributes positively towards enhancing overall performance.

Progressive Structural Regression. We sequentially ablate them from the full model: removing the heatmap generation and refinement, omitting the GCN-based joint feature enhancement, and replacing the hierarchical decoder with a stack of MLP layers of the same depth for direct vertex regression.

Progressive Curriculum Learning. To evaluate Progressive Curriculum Learning, we conduct ablation studies from three aspects: (1) removing data-level difficulty, (2) removing model-level difficulty, and (3) using random sampling instead of SPL (Self-Paced Learning) or replacing it with Babystep. Model performance generally declines when our proposed method is removed. Notably, Babystep experiences a significant drop due to overfitting on simpler data.

Dual-Factor Dynamic Loss. To demonstrate the benefits of integrating structural refinement with difficulty-aware sample scheduling, we replace DFDL with fixed weights assigned to specific layers only.

Limits and Failure Cases. Despite the overall strong performance, our model shows noticeable accuracy drops on rare, unseen hand poses and in cases of heavy occlusion, as shown in Fig. 6. These challenges suggest the need for future work to enhance generalization to unusual poses and improve robustness against occlusions.

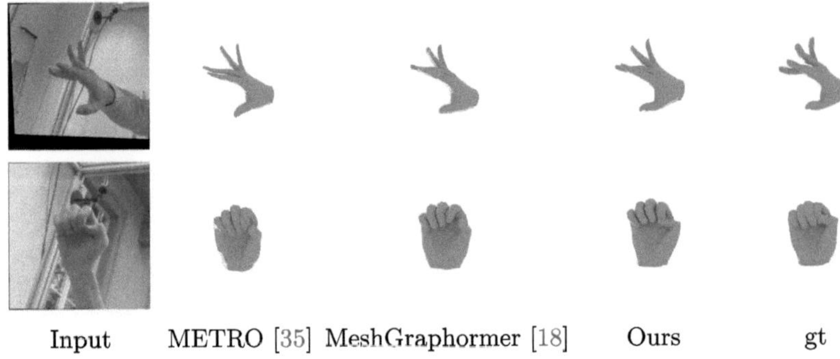

Fig. 5. Qualitative comparison between our method and other approaches.

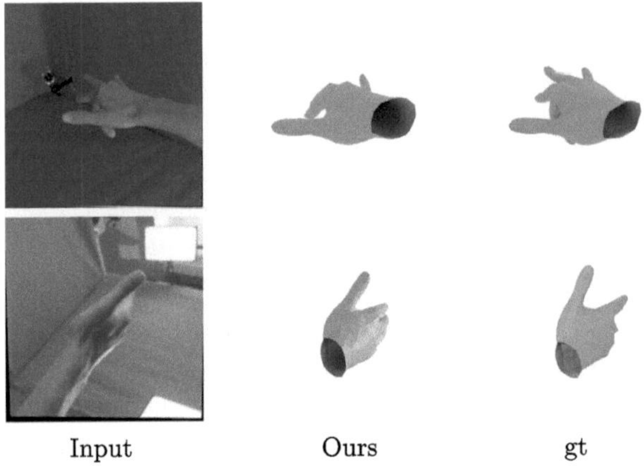

Fig. 6. Typical Failure Cases. Failure cases are concentrated in scenes with self-occlusion.

5 Conclusion

In this paper, we propose a Dual-Progressive Framework (DPF) to tackle two issues in hand mesh reconstruction: the early-stage error accumulation and the neglect of sample difficulty during training. Our framework consists of two synergistic components. One is Progressive Structural Regression, which performs coarse-to-fine refinement using spatial confidence maps and stacked-GCN; another is Progressive Curriculum Learning, which schedules training samples through a Self-Paced Learning strategy, based on Unified Difficulty derived from both data- and model-level. We further introduce Dual-Factor Dynamic Loss (DFDL) to enable effective interaction between the two progressive processes. Quantitative and qualitative experiments on the FreiHAND dataset show our method's effectiveness. In future work, we aim to extend this framework to real-time scenarios as well as improve its adaptability to occluded and rare hand poses.

References

1. Bengio, Y., Louradour, J., Collobert, R., Weston, J.: Curriculum learning. In: Proceedings of the 26th Annual International Conference on Machine Learning, pp. 41–48 (2009)
2. Chao, Y.W., et al.: DexYCB: a benchmark for capturing hand grasping of objects. In: Proceedings of the IEEE/CVF Conference on Computer Vision and Pattern Recognition, pp. 9044–9053 (2021)
3. Chen, P., et al.: I2UV-HandNet: image-to-UV prediction network for accurate and high-fidelity 3D hand mesh modeling. In: Proceedings of the IEEE/CVF International Conference on Computer Vision, pp. 12929–12938 (2021)
4. Chen, X., et al.: Sample balancing for deep learning-based visual recognition. IEEE Trans. Neural Netw. Learn. Syst. **31**(10), 3962–3976 (2019)
5. Chen, X., et al.: MobRecon: mobile-friendly hand mesh reconstruction from monocular image. In: Proceedings of the IEEE/CVF Conference on Computer Vision and Pattern Recognition, pp. 20544–20554 (2022)
6. Chen, X., et al.: Camera-space hand mesh recovery via semantic aggregation and adaptive 2D–1D registration. In: Proceedings of the IEEE/CVF Conference on Computer Vision and Pattern Recognition, pp. 13274–13283 (2021)
7. Cho, J., Youwang, K., Oh, T.H.: Cross-attention of disentangled modalities for 3D human mesh recovery with transformers. In: European Conference on Computer Vision, pp. 342–359. Springer (2022)
8. Dai, Y., Chen, B., Gao, L., Song, J., Shen, H.T.: DMH-CL: dynamic model hardness based curriculum learning for complex pose estimation. IEEE Trans. Multimedia **26**, 3180–3193 (2023)
9. Deng, J., Dong, W., Socher, R., Li, L.J., Li, K., Fei-Fei, L.: ImageNet: a large-scale hierarchical image database. In: 2009 IEEE Conference on Computer Vision and Pattern Recognition, pp. 248–255. IEEE (2009)
10. Dosovitskiy, A., et al.: An image is worth 16x16 words: transformers for image recognition at scale. arXiv preprint arXiv:2010.11929 (2020)
11. Fan, Z., et al.: Arctic: a dataset for dexterous bimanual hand-object manipulation. In: Proceedings of the IEEE/CVF Conference on Computer Vision and Pattern Recognition, pp. 12943–12954 (2023)
12. Hacohen, G., Weinshall, D.: On the power of curriculum learning in training deep networks. In: International Conference on Machine Learning, pp. 2535–2544. PMLR (2019)
13. Hampali, S., Sarkar, S.D., Lepetit, V.: HO-3D_v3: improving the accuracy of hand-object annotations of the HO-3D dataset. arXiv preprint arXiv:2107.00887 (2021)
14. Kim, J., Gwon, M.G., Park, H., Kwon, H., Um, G.M., Kim, W.: Sampling is matter: point-guided 3D human mesh reconstruction. In: Proceedings of the IEEE/CVF Conference on Computer Vision and Pattern Recognition, pp. 12880–12889 (2023)
15. Kingma, D.P.: Adam: a method for stochastic optimization. arXiv preprint arXiv:1412.6980 (2014)
16. Kumar, M., Packer, B., Koller, D.: Self-paced learning for latent variable models. Adv. Neural Inf. Process. Syst. **23** (2010)
17. Li, H., Chen, P.P., Zhou, Y.: 3D hand mesh recovery from monocular RGB in camera space. arXiv preprint arXiv:2405.07167 (2024)
18. Lin, K., Wang, L., Liu, Z.: Mesh Graphormer. In: Proceedings of the IEEE/CVF International Conference on Computer Vision, pp. 12939–12948 (2021)

19. Moon, G., Lee, K.M.: I2L-MeshNet: image-to-lixel prediction network for accurate 3D human pose and mesh estimation from a single RGB image. In: Vedaldi, A., Bischof, H., Brox, T., Frahm, J.-M. (eds.) ECCV 2020. LNCS, vol. 12352, pp. 752–768. Springer, Cham (2020). https://doi.org/10.1007/978-3-030-58571-6_44
20. Moon, G., Yu, S.I., Wen, H., Shiratori, T., Lee, K.M.: InterHand2.6M: a dataset and baseline for 3D interacting hand pose estimation from a single RGB image. In: Computer Vision–ECCV 2020: 16th European Conference, Glasgow, UK, August 23–28, 2020, Proceedings, Part XX 16, pp. 548–564. Springer (2020)
21. Paszke, A., et al.: Automatic differentiation in PyTorch (2017)
22. Platanios, E.A., Stretcu, O., Neubig, G., Poczos, B., Mitchell, T.M.: Competence-based curriculum learning for neural machine translation. arXiv preprint arXiv:1903.09848 (2019)
23. Potamias, R.A., Zhang, J., Deng, J., Zafeiriou, S.: Wilor: End-to-end 3d hand localization and reconstruction in-the-wild. arXiv preprint arXiv:2409.12259 (2024)
24. Prakash, A., Tu, R., Chang, M., Gupta, S.: 3D hand pose estimation in everyday egocentric images. In: European Conference on Computer Vision, pp. 183–202. Springer (2024)
25. Ren, M., Zeng, W., Yang, B., Urtasun, R.: Learning to reweight examples for robust deep learning. In: International Conference on Machine Learning, pp. 4334–4343. PMLR (2018)
26. Romero, J., Tzionas, D., Black, M.J.: Embodied hands: modeling and capturing hands and bodies together. arXiv preprint arXiv:2201.02610 (2022)
27. Scarselli, F., Gori, M., Tsoi, A.C., Hagenbuchner, M., Monfardini, G.: The graph neural network model. IEEE Trans. Neural Netw. **20**(1), 61–80 (2008)
28. Vasu, P.K.A., Gabriel, J., Zhu, J., Tuzel, O., Ranjan, A.: FastViT: a fast hybrid vision transformer using structural reparameterization. In: Proceedings of the IEEE/CVF International Conference on Computer Vision, pp. 5785–5795 (2023)
29. Vaswani, A., et al.: Attention is all you need. Adv. Neural Inf. Process. Syst. **30** (2017)
30. Wang, X., Zhou, Y., Chen, H., Zhu, W.: Curriculum learning: theories, approaches, applications, tools, and future directions in the era of large language models. In: Companion Proceedings of the ACM Web Conference 2024, pp. 1306–1310 (2024)
31. Wang, Y., et al.: EfficientTrain: exploring generalized curriculum learning for training visual backbones. In: Proceedings of the IEEE/CVF International Conference on Computer Vision, pp. 5852–5864 (2023)
32. Wei, Y., et al.: STC: a simple to complex framework for weakly-supervised semantic segmentation. IEEE Trans. Pattern Anal. Mach. Intell. **39**(11), 2314–2320 (2016)
33. Yoshiyasu, Y.: Deformable mesh transformer for 3D human mesh recovery. In: Proceedings of the IEEE/CVF Conference on Computer Vision and Pattern Recognition, pp. 17006–17015 (2023)
34. Zhang, J., Song, J., Gao, L., Shen, H.: Free-lunch for cross-domain few-shot learning: style-aware episodic training with robust contrastive learning. In: Proceedings of the 30th ACM International Conference on Multimedia, pp. 2586–2594 (2022)
35. Zhang, X., Li, Q., Mo, H., Zhang, W., Zheng, W.: End-to-end hand mesh recovery from a monocular RGB image. In: Proceedings of the IEEE/CVF International Conference on Computer Vision, pp. 2354–2364 (2019)
36. Zhou, T., Wang, S., Bilmes, J.: Curriculum learning by dynamic instance hardness. Adv. Neural. Inf. Process. Syst. **33**, 8602–8613 (2020)
37. Zhou, Z., Zhou, S., Lv, Z., Zou, M., Tang, Y., Liang, J.: A simple baseline for efficient hand mesh reconstruction. In: Proceedings of the IEEE/CVF Conference on Computer Vision and Pattern Recognition, pp. 1367–1376 (2024)

38. Zimmermann, C., Brox, T.: Learning to estimate 3D hand pose from single RGB images. In: Proceedings of the IEEE International Conference on Computer Vision, pp. 4903–4911 (2017)
39. Zimmermann, C., Ceylan, D., Yang, J., Russell, B., Argus, M., Brox, T.: FreiHAND: a dataset for Markerless capture of hand pose and shape from single RGB images. In: Proceedings of the IEEE/CVF International Conference on Computer Vision, pp. 813–822 (2019)

DExNet: Combining Observations of Domain Adapted Critics for Leaf Disease Classification with Limited Data

Sabbir Ahmed[1(✉)], Md. Bakhtiar Hasan[1], Tasnim Ahmed[1,2], and Md. Hasanul Kabir[1]

[1] Department of CSE, Islamic University of Technology, Gazipur, Bangladesh
{sabbirahmed,bakhtiarhasan,tasnimahmed,hasanul}@iut-dhaka.edu, tasnim.ahmed@queensu.ca

[2] School of Computing, Queen's University, Ontario, Canada

Abstract. While deep learning-based architectures have been widely used for correctly detecting and classifying plant diseases, they require large-scale datasets to learn generalized features and achieve state-of-the-art performance. This poses a challenge for such models to obtain satisfactory performance in classifying leaf diseases with limited samples. This work proposes a few-shot learning framework, Domain-adapted Expert Network (DExNet), for plant disease classification that compensates for the lack of sufficient training data by combining observations of a number of expert critics. It starts with extracting the feature embeddings as 'observations' from nine 'critics' that are state-of-the-art pre-trained CNN-based architectures. These critics are 'domain adapted' using a publicly available leaf disease dataset having no overlapping classes with the specific downstream task of interest. The observations are then passed to the 'Feature Fusion Block' and finally to a classifier network consisting of Bi-LSTM layers. The proposed pipeline is evaluated on the 10 classes of tomato leaf images from the PlantVillage dataset, achieving promising accuracies of 89.06%, 92.46%, and 94.07%, respectively, for 5-shot, 10-shot, and 15-shot classification. Furthermore, an accuracy of $98.09 \pm 0.7\%$ has been achieved in 80-shot classification, which is only 1.2% less than state-of-the-art, allowing a 94.5% reduction in the training data requirement. The proposed pipeline also outperforms existing works on leaf disease classification with limited data in both laboratory and real-life conditions in single-domain, mixed-domain, and cross-domain scenarios.

Keywords: Few-Shot Learning · Domain adaptation · CNN Feature Fusion · Plant Disease Classification · Plantvillage

1 Introduction

The decline in agricultural production due to diseases is a major threat to food security worldwide, causing severe losses for all stakeholders [34]. Traditional

C. Wallraven et al. (Eds.): ACPR 2025, LNCS 16174, pp. 130–146, 2026.
https://doi.org/10.1007/978-981-95-4395-3_10

disease detection methods are limited due to their low detection efficiency and poor reliability [10]. This is compounded by the lack of professional knowledge of farmers and the scarcity of agricultural experts in remote locations. As a result, the need for developing smart systems that can enable early detection and classification of diseases using tools and technologies available to the farmers can be pivotal [26].

Recent advancements in Deep Learning (DL) approaches using Convolutional Neural Networks (CNN) have become a powerful tool for several downstream classification tasks [6,8,23,36,48]. In particular, the utilization of transfer learning techniques using pre-trained architectures has provided numerous solutions in plant disease detection [1,9,12,28,29]. However, most of these solutions propose deep and complex networks focusing on increasing detection accuracy, requiring a huge number of training images. Moreover, the challenge is exacerbated by the absence of substantial public datasets for categorizing rare plant diseases [47]. Thus, developing effective algorithms that can accurately detect diseases with limited data is crucial to improve the situation. One promising approach is Few-Shot Learning (FSL), which aims to enable models to generalize effectively from only a small number of labeled examples [2,40]. Although some FSL-based solutions for classifying leaf diseases have been suggested in the literature [7,27,33,46], most of them have not demonstrated satisfactory performance and have proven ineffective in applications outside their original domain.

To this end, we utilize nine different state-of-the-art CNN-based feature extractors that are adapted to extract generalized features in the agriculture domain. These extracted features are then combined and passed through a classification block for effective disease prediction. Given the limited number of samples per class, we adopt an ensemble strategy leveraging multiple CNN-based feature extractors to obtain diverse and complementary representations of the input data. Each model contributes distinct feature perspectives, and their integration enhances the overall discriminative capacity of the system. This approach enables improved prediction performance despite the scarcity of labeled samples. Our contributions can be summarized as follows:

1. We introduced domain-specific knowledge into pre-trained Deep CNN-based feature extractors in order to adapt them to the agriculture domain to compensate for target domain data scarcity.
2. We incorporated a feature fusion block to combine extracted features from the critics to provide multi-faceted observation from limited samples.
3. We utilized a Bi-LSTM architecture to capture the dependencies among the combined features to effectively classify leaf diseases.
4. We outperformed the existing state-of-the-art FSL-based implementations in both laboratory and real-life conditions in single, multi, and cross-domain tasks.

2 Related Work

The progressive integration of Deep Learning in agriculture requires a large amount of data to achieve reliable generalization, high classification accuracy, and resilience to variability in environmental conditions, crop types, and disease manifestations [5,18]. However, collecting and annotating such large-scale agricultural datasets is often labor-intensive, time-consuming, and infeasible for many real-world applications, particularly in regions with limited technical resources [35]. However, few-shot learning (FSL) algorithms have shown promise in addressing this limitation by mimicking the human capacity to learn quickly with just a few labeled examples [50]. Different branches of FSL algorithms include metric-learning-based methods, parameter optimization, and data augmentation [3].

In few-shot leaf image classification, a small labeled support set provides reference samples for each disease class, while an unlabeled query set is classified by comparing its images to the support set using distance metrics that are critical for accurate prediction under limited data scenarios [43]. Metric-learning-based approaches utilize distance functions to measure the similarity and dissimilarity between leaf samples in the support set and the query set [49]. The model produces an embedding vector from the input image, which is compared with the embeddings of other classes to predict the disease.

Metric-based FSL approaches, such as Siamese Networks [24], Prototypical Networks [39], MatchingNet [44], etc., have shown superior performance over conventional CNN-based methods when dealing with limited data. Argüeso *et al.*[7] employed an InceptionV3 backbone [41] trained on 32 leaf disease classes to extract features for a Siamese Network using triplet loss, achieving competitive results with up to 90% less training data. Similarly, Wang *et al.*[45] utilized a Siamese architecture with shared weights to extract features from image pairs, learning a similarity metric optimized via a contrastive loss, followed by K-NN classification. However, the high inter-class variation in their dataset reduced task complexity. To address more challenging scenarios, Egusquiza *et al.*[14] curated a real-world dataset of 5 crops and 17 diseases captured under varied and complex conditions, demonstrating that metric-based models outperform traditional CNNs even with fewer than 200 samples per class. Li *et al.*[27] proposed a task-adaptive meta-learning framework for crop and pest classification, evaluating it under single-domain, mixed-domain, and cross-domain settings. Although their dataset aggregated samples from multiple public sources, its relatively low intra-class similarity simplified classification; nonetheless, performance degraded notably in cross-domain scenarios.

Parameter optimization-based techniques in FSL entail learning how to tune the parameters of a DL network using optimizers. Finn *et al.*[15] proposed Model Agnostic Meta-learning (MAML), which solves few-shot tasks by learning an initialization parameter θ. Once learned, new tasks can be solved with a few gradient updates. MAML is independent of the meta-learner algorithm used, making it ideal for machine learning algorithms that require quick adaptation. Other improvements on MAML include TAML [22], Reptile [31], etc. In this regard, Wang *et al.*[46] exploited the MAML approaches with soft-center loss function and PReLU activation function for leaf disease classification. The proposed method outperformed other FSL approaches and achieved 63.8%, 91.35%, and 96.0% accuracy for 1-shot, 15-shot, and 80-shot classification, respectively. However, the approach requires a large number of tasks and consumes high computational resources, and further optimization is needed to increase speed and reduce computational overhead.

Expanding the number of samples via data augmentation can solve the lack of labeled samples to some extent. Hu *et al.*[19] proposed an FSL method for tea leaf disease identification that uses SVM for feature extraction and C-DCGAN for data augmentation. The augmented samples were used to train the VGG16 architecture [38], achieving an accuracy of up to 90% on a self-curated dataset of three tea leaf diseases. In another work, Nesteruk *et al.*[30] claimed that the use of such augmentation techniques can improve the performance of other downstream tasks involving leaf diseases, such as object detection, segmentation, contouring, denoising, etc. However, the authenticity of the augmented samples in reflecting real-world data distributions remains uncertain.

Recent studies have demonstrated that transfer learning with pre-trained architectures can effectively generate generalizable feature representations for few-shot learning tasks. Chen *et al.*[11] proposed a simple transfer learning-based approach using pre-trained CNN and linear classifiers that outperforms traditional FSL methods. Kolesnikov *et al.*[25] suggested that a high-quality feature extractor is the best way to solve FSL tasks and proposed an approach to train a large model on a large dataset to learn the feature space. Yonglong *et al.*[42] also demonstrated that a simple transfer-based approach can outperform advanced meta-learners. Dvornik *et al.*[13] introduced diversity in feature extraction by using a set of feature extractors trained on different datasets. They used ensembling to train multiple deep CNNs during the meta-training phase and encouraged diversity in the learned representations.

In the domain of agriculture, Nuthalapati *et al.*[33] proposed a method for FSL that utilizes a ResNet18-based feature extractor pre-trained on ImageNet. A transformer block is used to further enhance the feature embeddings of all support set samples. During classification, similarity between the query image embedding and the class prototypes is computed using the Mahalanobis distance. The effectiveness of the model was shown using mixed-domain and cross-domain experiments using the Plant and Pest [27] and the Tomato leaf subset of the Plantvillage dataset [21]; where the proposed model achieved up to 14% and 24% performance gain compared to the earlier works. Moreover, to validate the performance of the model in real-world images, the authors curated the 'Plants in Wild' dataset and provided a baseline.

While transfer learning-based approaches have gained traction in the FSL domain, their performance remains constrained, particularly in real-world scenarios, due to restricted feature diversity from relying on a single pre-trained model. To address these challenges, we integrate multiple pre-trained feature extractors adapted with domain-specific knowledge, followed by feature fusion and classification modules. This enables robust and generalizable leaf disease classification under limited data conditions, achieving state-of-the-art performance.

3 Task Formulation

Few-shot learning (FSL) experiments have two phases: meta-training and meta-testing. The datasets used in these two phases have non-overlapping classes. Each of them is divided into Support sets (S) and Query sets (Q), similar to the train-test splits of the traditional DL experiments.

The meta-training set is used to train feature extractors that learn to generate discriminative embeddings from limited samples, with no restriction on the number of classes or examples, provided there is no overlap with the meta-testing set. The meta-testing set contains N classes, each represented using k labeled examples extracted from the Support set (i.e., k-shot). After training the classifier using these few samples, performance is evaluated on Q unseen examples per class drawn from the Query set. To ensure statistical robustness, models are evaluated across multiple tasks, each defined by randomly sampled Support and Query sets.

To comprehensively assess the FSL pipeline, single-domain, mixed-domain, and cross-domain experiments are conducted. In single-domain settings, the meta-training and meta-testing datasets originate from similar domains with disjoint classes. Cross-domain experiments involve meta-training and meta-testing datasets drawn from distinct domains, presenting increased difficulty due to significant domain distribution discrepancies. Mixed-domain experiments include classes from multiple domains in both meta-training and meta-testing phases.

For the single-domain experiments, we have used the PlantVillage Dataset [21], the largest open-access repository of expertly curated samples for leaf disease classification tasks, consisting of 38 classes. Out of these classes, we have picked the 10 classes of tomato leaf images for the meta-testing phase and used the rest of the 28 classes for domain adaptation. In the meta-training phase, the 28 classes have been used to fine-tune the feature extractors to enhance their capabilities for leaf disease identification. On the other hand, the 10 classes of tomato leaf samples have been divided into Support and Query sets with an $80:20$ ratio following the work of Ahmed *et al.*[4] Hence, out of the 18160 samples of tomato leaf images, 3629 samples have been considered as the available samples as the Query set, and the remaining images have been used as the Support set. For each task, k Support samples and Q query samples per class are randomly picked from the available images. To remove biases, this process has been repeated 100 tasks, and the average performance has been reported.

For the Mixed-domain and Cross-domain experiments, we have utilized the 'Plants & Pest' dataset proposed by Li *et al.*[27]. The dataset consists of 20 classes in total, out of which 10 classes belong to different kinds of plants, such as apple, blueberry, cherry, grape, etc. The other 10 classes contain images of different kinds of pests, such as cydia-pomonella, fruit-fly, gryllotalpa, snail, etc. Each of the classes contains 300 images. We have followed the recommended splits by the original authors for the mixed and cross-domain experiments [27]. In the mixed-domain tasks, we have taken 5 plants and 5 pest classes for meta-training and the rest of the classes for meta-testing. For the Cross-domain experiments, we have conducted two kinds of experiments. In the first one, the meta-training set consists of the 10 pest classes, and in another cross-domain scenario, we have considered all 10 plant classes for meta-training and the remaining classes for meta-testing.

Furthermore, to evaluate the efficacy of the proposed pipeline in real-world field images, we conducted experiments on two publicly available datasets, 'Potato Leaf Disease Classification'[1] [37] and 'Cotton Leaf Disease'[2] [32], consisting of diversified samples collected from the field. All these experiments ensure that our proposed pipeline has been validated under diverse and challenging conditions, demonstrating its robustness, adaptability, and generalization capabilities across single-domain, mixed-domain, cross-domain, and real-world field scenarios.

4 DExNet

The Domain-adapted Expert Network (DExNet) pipeline addresses the challenge of limited labeled samples per class by aggregating insights from multiple specialized expert models, or "critics." These critics are exposed to a broad distribution of leaf images during domain adaptation, enabling them to learn generalizable features of diseased leaves. Although they are not trained on the target classes, their learned representations remain descriptive and informative, allowing the model to perform effectively even with very few target samples.

DExNet comprises three main components: the Domain Adaptation Block (DAB), the Feature Fusion Block (FFB), and the Classifier Block (CB). In the DAB, we fine-tune nine pre-trained deep CNN models (referred to as *critics*) using a diverse set of publicly available leaf images. This domain adaptation process enables the critics to specialize in extracting disease-relevant features, effectively transforming them into *experts*. In the FFB, feature representations (termed *observations*) are extracted by passing target-class samples through each of the domain-adapted experts. The resulting nine feature vectors are then concatenated to form a unified representation. Finally, the CB employs a Bi-LSTM layer with 1024 nodes followed by a fully-connected layer to perform the final classification. Figure 1 illustrates the proposed pipeline DExNet.

4.1 CNN-Based Feature Extractor

While conventional DL methods rely on large amounts of data to achieve satisfactory performance, such data requirements are impractical in FSL scenarios. To address this limitation, we combine the extracted features from several

[1] https://github.com/rizqiamaliatuss/PotatoLeafDiseaseClassification.

[2] https://www.kaggle.com/datasets/seroshkarim/cotton-leaf-disease-dataset.

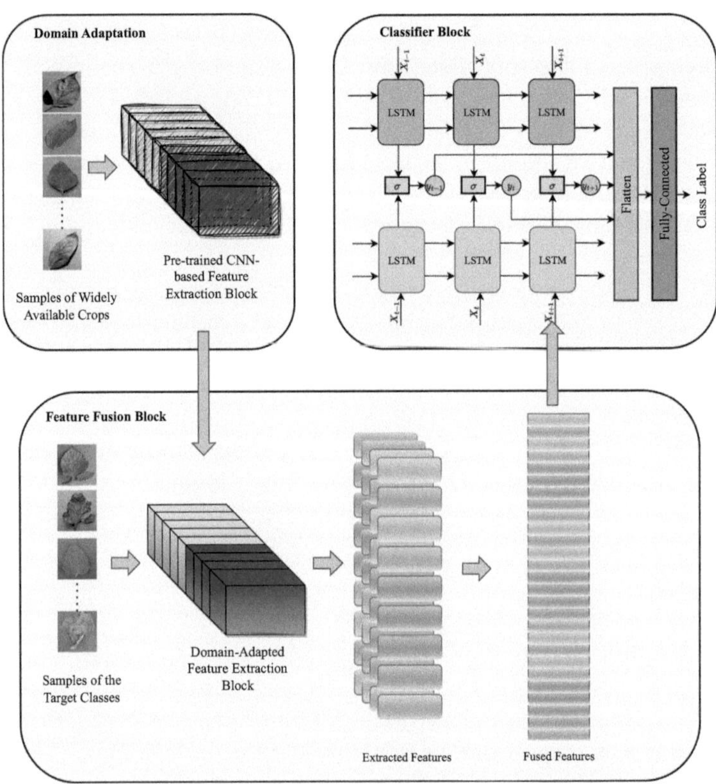

Fig. 1. Overview of the Proposed Pipeline DExNet

Deep CNN architectures, each with its unique method of feature extraction, to generate multiple observations. We hypothesize that showing a few samples to multiple critics and deciding the result based on their aggregated observations can provide a better understanding of the samples. Here, the feature extractor is compared to a *critic*, and the features produced are the *observations* of the leaf images. This approach enables using spatial information in the image to generate feature vectors for training an FSL pipeline.

Our CNN-based Feature Extraction Block consists of state-of-the-art pre-trained residual and dense CNN architectures. The Residual Networks (ResNets) [17] offer significant improvements over previous architectures to facilitate the training of many stacked layers by introducing residual connections between layers, allowing information to flow from shallow layers to deeper layers and gradients to flow back, skipping a few layers. We incorporated five pre-trained variants of ResNets in our domain-adapted expert feature extractor block, namely ResNet-18, ResNet-34, ResNet-50, ResNet-101, and ResNet-152. Expanding on this idea, Dense Convolutional Network (DenseNet) [20] connects all layers with matching feature-map sizes directly with each other. Here, each layer receives input from all the previous layers and sends its output to all the subsequent layers via concatenation. Creating a dense connection between all the layers ensures the maximum flow of information and gradient between layers. Four variants of the DenseNet architecture were chosen based on the number of layers and their computational complexity: DenseNet-121, DenseNet-161, DenseNet-169, and DenseNet-201. Each of the models is pre-trained on the ILSVRC2012 dataset, and the final prediction layers were removed from the feature extractors to retain the feature embeddings.

4.2 Domain Adaptation

The feature extraction architectures are capable of extracting highly sophisticated features that can be utilized for any classification problem. When these networks are used for any classification task, a common practice is to fine-tune the architectures based on the available training images. However, in the FSL problems, it is not possible to fine-tune such deep models due to the limited number of samples in the Support set. An alternative solution to this problem is to provide knowledge of a similar domain so that, despite the model having never directly seen the target classes, it can have some idea about their general characteristics— a process we term as *Domain Adaptation.*

To apply domain adaptation in the proposed pipeline, we have trained the CNN-based architectures with a substantial amount of leaf images containing healthy and diseased samples. For this, we used the 28 classes of the PlantVillage dataset except for the samples of the tomato leaves. We hypothesize that since the models were already capable of extracting useful features, this knowledge base can be further enriched by fine-tuning them using a lot of leaf samples. After fine-tuning, even though the model has never seen any 'tomato leaf samples', it knows what a healthy or diseased leaf looks like, what features to look for in a leaf image, and how to differentiate the classes of diseases, etc., turning it into an *expert* model. Thus, when limited samples are provided, the expert models can extract even better features compared to their earlier states.

4.3 Feature Fusion Block (FFB)

We leverage nine domain-adapted expert models for feature extraction, resulting in nine distinct feature vectors for each input image. These feature vectors (referred to as *observations*) reflect the individual perspectives of the experts, with each model capturing unique characteristics of the input. To enhance the representational power, we concatenate all nine observations into a single 13, 984-dimensional feature vector per sample. This fusion approach preserves the distinct information captured by each expert, enabling the model to learn complex interactions among the features and facilitating the extraction of more informative and comprehensive representations.

4.4 Classifier Block (CB)

The Classifier Block processes the concatenated feature vector from FFB using a Bi-LSTM layer with 1024 units [16], followed by a fully connected layer to produce the final classification output. The main purpose of this block is to effectively combine the diverse observations from the expert models and capture intricate relationships within the high-dimensional feature vector. The Bi-LSTM layer consists of two LSTM networks running in parallel, processing the inputs in opposite directions. This structure allows the model to capture both local dependencies between adjacent elements and the broader contextual information of the entire sequence, enhancing the model's ability to learn complex interactions. Upon empirical evaluation with varying dimensions (e.g., 256, 512, 1024, 2048), we found that 1024 units provided the best performance.

5 Results and Discussions

5.1 Single vs Ensemble Feature Extractor

The performance of each of the feature extractors was thoroughly analyzed for different choices of k shots. Along with finding the performance of the individual networks, we also considered an ensemble of ResNets, an ensemble of DenseNets, and finally, the ensemble of all nine architectures. Since the focus was on finding the best combination of feature extractors, we only added a Dense layer of 1024 hidden units after the flattened feature vector from the pretrained extractors, followed by a softmax layer. We experimented with four combinations of $k = 1, 5, 10, \&15$. For the test samples, $Q = 50$ images per class were taken at random. To remove any bias, this random sampling was repeated for 100 separate trials, and the average value was reported. The findings of this experiment are shown in Table 1.

The objective was to find the feature extractor that works best with the provided 'few-shots'. Since the performance of the individual networks was close to each other, we hypothesized that ensembling them could provide better results because each of them has unique strengths in extracting certain types of features useful for detecting specific types of diseases. By ensembling similar types of networks, we achieved better performance than the individual ones. The best performance was achieved by combining all nine feature extractors.

5.2 Combination of the Extracted Features

The features extracted from the domain-adapted feature extraction blocks are subsequently combined and passed to the classifier block for both training and evaluation phases. To identify an effective feature integration strategy, we consider two approaches: 'Parallel Observation' and 'Concatenated Observation'. In the Parallel Observation approach, each of the nine feature vectors, one from each feature extractor, is treated as an independent input to the classifier. This can be viewed as nine distinct observers offering complementary perspectives on

Table 1. Performance of Single vs Ensemble Feature Extractors

Feature Extractor	$k = 1$	$k = 5$	$k = 10$	$k = 15$
ResNet18	34.36 ± 0.82	55.42 ± 0.77	62.56 ± 0.67	66.76 ± 0.62
ResNet34	29.65 ± 0.91	49.93 ± 0.81	57.93 ± 0.56	63.69 ± 0.54
ResNet50	30.62 ± 0.88	54.24 ± 0.92	61.79 ± 0.65	65.99 ± 0.64
ResNet101	29.64 ± 0.93	52.73 ± 0.79	61.61 ± 0.74	65.79 ± 0.68
ResNet152	29.75 ± 0.84	52.61 ± 0.86	61.39 ± 0.74	66.44 ± 0.68
DenseNet121	32.48 ± 0.99	54.93 ± 0.89	64.09 ± 0.72	68.21 ± 0.56
DenseNet161	32.29 ± 1.07	56.58 ± 0.88	65.59 ± 0.71	70.56 ± 0.66
DenseNet169	32.89 ± 0.97	55.39 ± 0.78	64.09 ± 0.72	69.39 ± 0.7
DenseNet201	33.51 ± 0.94	57.21 ± 0.87	65.71 ± 0.86	70.77 ± 0.73
Ensemble of ResNets	36.34 ± 1.01	60.04 ± 0.91	68.74 ± 0.71	73.84 ± 0.68
Ensemble of DenseNets	35.94 ± 1.03	61.47 ± 0.96	70.26 ± 0.79	75.42 ± 0.65
Ensemble of Nine Extractors	$\mathbf{37.89 \pm 0.99}$	$\mathbf{62.07 \pm 0.98}$	$\mathbf{72.33 \pm 0.81}$	$\mathbf{76.93 \pm 0.66}$

the same image. In contrast, the Concatenated Observation approach merges all nine extracted features into a single high-dimensional representation by concatenation, resulting in a 13,985-dimensional vector per sample. This unified representation enables the classifier to learn cross-feature dependencies and integrate multi-perspective cues into a single, discriminative embedding. In both cases, given the architectural heterogeneity of the feature extractors, each vector encodes unique complementary information, which enhances the classifier's ability to generalize by implicitly increasing the diversity of the input space.

For each approach, two types of classifiers have been used: Dense Classifier with 1024 nodes, and Bi-LSTM classifier with 1024 units. We have also considered the impact of domain adaptation for each of the combinations. For this experiment, we have considered the values of k as 1, 5, 10&15 and $Q = 50$ applied for 100 tasks. The findings are mentioned in Table 2. For each combination, the domain-adapted feature extractors have provided $5-10\%$ performance improvement compared to the pre-trained ones. The Dense classifier is a better fit for the parallel observation approach, whereas the Bi-LSTM classifier is more suitable for the feature concatenation approach. Out of all the experiments, the Domain Adapted Concatenated feature extraction approach with Bi-LSTM classifier is the best performing one, having an accuracy as high as 90.97% and 94.02% respectively for 10-shot and 15-shot classification.

5.3 Selection of Classifier Network

The performance of Dense, LSTM, GRU, Bi-GRU, and Bi-LSTM classifiers was evaluated to determine the most effective classifier network. Each of the classifiers consisted of 1024 nodes followed by a softmax layer of 10 nodes, representing the 10 classes of the target samples. Experiments have been conducted on the base

Table 2. Performance of Various Combinations of Features in Different FSL Scenarios

Observation Type	Classifier	Domain Adopt	$k = 1$	$k = 5$	$k = 10$	$k = 15$
Parallel	Dense	×	40.2 ± 1.46	72.95 ± 0.97	82.6 ± 0.97	85.71 ± 0.78
Parallel	Dense	✓	50.38 ± 1.68	83.78 ± 1.16	89.07 ± 0.91	92.79 ± 0.69
Parallel	Bi-LSTM	×	39.84 ± 1.65	48.27 ± 2.20	52.66 ± 1.75	63.42 ± 1.78
Parallel	Bi-LSTM	✓	53.4 ± 1.74	74.75 ± 1.68	79.3 ± 1.90	81.99 ± 1.81
Concatenated	Dense	×	37.89 ± 0.99	62.07 ± 0.98	72.33 ± 0.81	76.93 ± 0.66
Concatenated	Dense	✓	46.56 ± 1.07	72.17 ± 1.04	81.18 ± 0.68	85.12 ± 1.02
Concatenated	Bi-LSTM	×	42.53 ± 1.25	81.9 ± 1.37	87.80 ± 1.23	89.06 ± 1.22
Concatenated	Bi-LSTM	✓	$\mathbf{51.36 \pm 1.54}$	$\mathbf{89.19 \pm 1.20}$	$\mathbf{90.75 \pm 1.09}$	$\mathbf{94.02 \pm 0.86}$

feature extractors without applying domain adaptation, with $k = 1, 5, 10, and\ 15$. For this analysis, we considered the entire test set, comprising a total of 3629 images ($Q = Full$). The findings have been reported in Table 3.

Table 3. Performance of Different Classifier Networks

Classifier	$k = 1$	$k = 10$	$k = 15$	$k = 80$
Dense Layer	37.73 ± 0.49	61.08 ± 0.88	73.54 ± 0.72	75.79 ± 0.81
LSTM	43.24 ± 1.72	69.16 ± 1.75	74.15 ± 1.52	72.84 ± 1.02
GRU	40.21 ± 1.55	68.15 ± 1.54	78.97 ± 1.54	81.08 ± 1.56
Bi-GRU	43.03 ± 0.51	72.69 ± 1.28	85.53 ± 1.26	90.94 ± 1.03
Bi-LSTM	$\mathbf{48.02 \pm 1.63}$	$\mathbf{84.36 \pm 1.62}$	$\mathbf{88.97 \pm 1.80}$	$\mathbf{91.22 \pm 1.67}$

RNN-based classifiers are typically better suited for tasks that involve sequential data, as they can capture long-term dependencies and relationships between elements in a sequence. However, dense classifiers provide higher importance to each feature separately, but they are unable to capture spatial relationships among them. In our case, capturing the spatial relationships among the concatenated features can provide a better understanding of the leaf samples from which they were extracted. Since RNN-based architectures are better suited for capturing important information from the observations of the expert critics, their performances are significantly better than Dense classifiers.

Among RNN variants, Bi-LSTM offers additional benefits by processing the input in both forward and backward directions, which is particularly useful in our context where the disease class may depend on interactions across the entire feature sequence. Furthermore, Bi-LSTM demonstrates improved performance when handling long input vectors, as is the case with our high-dimensional concatenated features, outperforming both unidirectional LSTM and GRU classifiers. We also explored attention-based classifier variants but observed degraded performance, likely due to the limited size of the training data. As a result, we adopted Bi-LSTM as the classifier of choice.

5.4 Impact of Domain Adaptation

The baseline CNN-based feature extractors are pre-trained on large-scale ImageNet datasets with the capability of extracting useful features from any input samples. However, to make them even more specialized in finding appropriate leaf features, we applied domain adaptation, which significantly improved the overall performance of the pipeline. We have used the Bi-LSTM classifier since it is most useful on the feature concatenation approach. The experimental findings are available in Table 4.

Table 4. Impact of Domain Adaptation

k-shot	Domain Adaptation	$Q = Full$
$k = 1$	×	48.02 ± 1.63
	✓	56.19 ± 1.72
$k = 5$	×	84.36 ± 1.62
	✓	89.06 ± 1.30
$k = 10$	×	88.97 ± 1.80
	✓	92.46 ± 1.75
$k = 15$	×	91.22 ± 1.67
	✓	94.07 ± 1.40
$k = 20$	×	92.66 ± 1.87
	✓	95.68 ± 1.20
$k = 40$	×	93.7 ± 1.66
	✓	97.04 ± 0.98
$k = 80$	×	97.38 ± 1.48
	✓	98.09 ± 0.77

In this experiment, we have also considered larger values of k such as 20, 40, and 80, along with considering the entire test set containing 3629 images. The trained models have been tested using all the samples from the meta-testing set. After domain adaptation, the models were already capable of distinguishing different types of leaf disease. Hence, even though it never saw any tomato leaf samples, it could achieve high accuracy like 89.06%, 92.46%, 94.07% respectively, for the 5-shot, 10-shot, and 15-shot classification tasks. The results were even more promising as the number of samples increased. We achieved 98.09% accuracy with 20× fewer data compared to the existing works. One obvious observation was that, as the value of k goes higher, the significance of Domain adaptation becomes lower. Our conclusion from this experiment is that domain adaptation is an effective approach that enables the model to use 20× fewer data, compromising only 1.22% accuracy.

5.5 Performance Comparison with Related Works

To evaluate the robustness of our proposed pipeline in different circumstances, we conducted experiments in single-domain and cross-domain environments. In the first experiment, we used the dataset of the few-shot task proposed by Argueso *et al.*[7]. In this task, the target classes contained 6 leaf diseases of apple, blueberry, and cherry plants. The experiments were conducted on $Q = 50$ for 20 randomly sampled tasks. We applied the model under similar experimental setups, and it significantly outperformed the state-of-the-art. The results are mentioned in Table 5.

Table 5. Performance Comparison with Related works on PlantVillage Dataset

Approach	$k = 1$	$k = 10$	$k = 15$	$k = 80$
Argüeso *et al.*[7]	55.5	77.0	80.0	90.0
Wang *et al.*[46]	63.8	×	91.3	96.0
Ours	$\mathbf{74.7 \pm 3.12}$	$\mathbf{99.73 \pm 0.24}$	$\mathbf{99.92 \pm 0.09}$	$\mathbf{99.9 \pm 0.07}$

Table 6. Single-Domain and Cross-Domain Experiments

k-shots	Approach	Single-Mixed Domain	Cross-Domain 1	Cross-Domain 2
$K = 1$	Li *et al.*[27]	81.1	72.1	44.1
	Nuthalapati *et al.*[33]	84.1	79.2	52
	Ours	$\mathbf{95.56 \pm 0.91}$	$\mathbf{90.29 \pm 0.91}$	$\mathbf{90.05 \pm 1.06}$
$K = 5$	Li *et al.*[27]	87	84.9	53.1
	Nuthalapati *et al.*[33]	91.2	93.7	66.5
	Ours	$\mathbf{99.97 \pm 0.03}$	$\mathbf{99.8 \pm 0.1}$	$\mathbf{99.51 \pm 0.14}$
$K = 10$	Li *et al.*[27]	90.4	87.1	55.8
	Nuthalapati *et al.*[33]	92.9	95.5	71.6
	Ours	$\mathbf{99.97 \pm 0.03}$	$\mathbf{99.89 \pm 0.05}$	$\mathbf{99.41 \pm 0.28}$

Afterward, the robustness of the pipeline was shown with the single-domain and cross-domain tasks as proposed in [27]. For this task, the 'Plants & Pest' dataset has been utilized. Following the authors [27], this experiment has been conducted keeping three tasks in mind, named as, single-mixed domain, cross-domain1, and cross-domain2 (results in Table 6). In the single-mixed domain experiment, the source class contained samples of both leaves and pests. Although the target classes contained different types of leaves or pests, the classification task was simpler. In the cross-domain 1 experiment, the pest classes were chosen as the source class and the plant classes as the target class. The cross-domain 2 experiment was the other way around. The merit of these experiments is that, if the model can learn leaves after only being trained on pest samples, it signifies that it has learned very good feature representation. Regardless of the single or cross-domain tasks, the pipeline has outperformed the works of [27,46] by a good margin. This shows the generalizing ability of the model under different circumstances.

The existing literature used samples that were mostly taken in laboratory conditions. Hence, to further investigate the robustness of the pipeline in different field conditions, we tested the performance on two more datasets, namely the 'Potato Leaf Disease' [37] and 'Cotton Leaf Disease' [32]. To the best of our knowledge, this is the first few-shot benchmark for these two datasets. We took the results for $k = 1, 5, 10, \&15$, considered all the remaining images as Query samples, and repeated the evaluation for 100 tasks. The findings presented in Table 7 shows that the proposed pipeline has achieved satisfactory performance even with the samples taken under real-world field conditions with diversified backgrounds.

Table 7. Performance comparison on Field Conditions

k-shot	Potato Disease Dataset	Cotton Disease Dataset
$k = 1$	48.61 ± 3.68	63.88 ± 2.54
$k = 5$	76.96 ± 1.84	97.58 ± 0.45
$k = 10$	89.61 ± 2.03	99.40 ± 0.49
$k = 15$	92.95 ± 2.07	99.28 ± 0.56

6 Conclusion

The limited availability of large-scale, diverse leaf disease datasets has motivated the development of models capable of achieving high accuracy with a minimal amount of samples. In this work, we proposed DExNet, an FSL pipeline for leaf disease classification under data-scarce conditions. Our approach leverages a CNN-based feature extraction block composed of nine state-of-the-art architectures, each contributing a distinct representation of the input. These multi-perspective features are fused and processed by a Bi-LSTM-based classifier for final prediction. To enhance generalization to unseen classes, we incorporate domain adaptation, enabling feature extractors to capture domain-specific cues. The proposed method achieves competitive accuracy substantially outperforming baseline FSL approaches. The strength of DExNet is further demonstrated through solid performance on mixed-domain and cross-domain tasks. This work offers a scalable and data-efficient solution for plant disease diagnosis, with potential applications in real-world agricultural settings. Future work could extend the framework to few-shot segmentation or detection and explore lightweight feature extractors for deployment on edge devices.

References

1. Abbas, A., Jain, S., Gour, M., Vankudothu, S.: Tomato plant disease detection using transfer learning with C-GAN synthetic images. Comput. Electron. Agric. **187**, 106279 (2021)
2. Ahamed, M., Kabir, R.B., Dipto, T.T., Al Mushabbir, M., Ahmed, S., Kabir, M.H.: Performance analysis of few-shot learning approaches for Bangla handwritten character and digit recognition. In: 2024 6th International Conference on Sustainable Technologies for Industry 5.0 (STI), pp. 1–6 (2024)
3. Ahmed, S.: Classification of plant disease from leaf images using few-shot learning, M.Sc. thesis, Department of Computer Science and Engineering (CSE), Islamic University of Technology (2022)
4. Ahmed, S., Hasan, M.B., Ahmed, T., Sony, M.R.K., Kabir, M.H.: Less is more: lighter and faster deep neural architecture for tomato leaf disease classification. IEEE Access **10**, 68868–68884 (2022)
5. Ahmed, T., Hasan, M.B., Ahmed, S., Kabir, M.H.: ExE-Net: explainable ensemble network for potato leaf disease classification. In: 2024 IEEE Canadian Conference on Electrical and Computer Engineering (CCECE), pp. 335–339 (2024)
6. Alanezi, M.A., Shahriar, M.S., Hasan, M.B., Ahmed, S., Sha'aban, Y.A., Bouchekara, H.R.E.H.: Livestock management with unmanned aerial vehicles: a review. IEEE Access **10**, 45001–45028 (2022)
7. Argüeso, D., et al.: Few-shot learning approach for plant disease classification using images taken in the field. Comput. Electron. Agric. **175**, 105542 (2020)
8. Rahman, A., et al.: Two decades of Bengali handwritten digit recognition: a survey. IEEE Access **10**, 92597–92632 (2022)
9. Ashmafee, M.H., Ahmed, T., Ahmed, S., Hasan, M.B., Jahan, M.N., Ashikur Rahman, A.: An efficient transfer learning-based approach for apple leaf disease classification. In: International Conference on Electrical, Computer and Communication Engineering (ECCE), pp. 1–6 (2023)
10. Buja, I., et al.: Advances in plant disease detection and monitoring: from traditional assays to in-field diagnostics. Sensors **21**(6) (2021)
11. Chen, W., Liu, Y., Kira, Z., Wang, Y.F., Huang, J.: A closer look at few-shot classification. arXiv preprint arXiv:1904.04232 (2019)
12. Chowdhury, R.H., Ahmed, S.: MangoLeafViT: leveraging lightweight vision transformer with runtime augmentation for efficient mango leaf disease classification. In: 2024 27th International Conference on Computer and Information Technology (ICCIT), pp. 699–704 (2024). https://doi.org/10.1109/ICCIT64611.2024.11022482
13. Dvornik, N., Schmid, C., Mairal, J.: Selecting relevant features from a multi-domain representation for few-shot classification. In: Vedaldi, A., Bischof, H., Brox, T., Frahm, J.-M. (eds.) ECCV 2020. LNCS, vol. 12355, pp. 769–786. Springer, Cham (2020). https://doi.org/10.1007/978-3-030-58607-2_45
14. Egusquiza, I., et al.: Analysis of few-shot techniques for fungal plant disease classification and evaluation of clustering capabilities over real datasets. Front. Plant Sci. **13** (2022)
15. Finn, C., Abbeel, P., Levine, S.: Model-agnostic meta-learning for fast adaptation of deep networks. In: Proceedings of the 34th International Conference on Machine Learning, 06–11 Aug, vol. 70, pp. 1126–1135. PMLR (2017)

16. Graves, A., Schmidhuber, J.: Framewise phoneme classification with bidirectional LSTM and other neural network architectures. Neural Netw. **18**(5–6), 602–610 (2005)
17. He, K., Zhang, X., Ren, S., Sun, J.: Deep residual learning for image recognition. In: IEEE Conference on Computer Vision and Pattern Recognition (CVPR), pp. 770–778 (2016)
18. Herok, A., Ahmed, S.: Cotton leaf disease identification using transfer learning. In: 2023 International Conference on Information and Communication Technology for Sustainable Development (ICICT4SD), pp. 158–162 (2023)
19. Hu, G., Wu, H., Zhang, Y., Wan, M.: A low shot learning method for tea leaf's disease identification. Comput. Electron. Agric. **163**, 104852 (2019)
20. Huang, G., Liu, Z., Van Der Maaten, L., Weinberger, K.Q.: Densely connected convolutional networks. In: IEEE Conference on Computer Vision and Pattern Recognition (CVPR), pp. 2261–2269 (2017)
21. Hughes, D.P., Salathé, M.: An open access repository of images on plant health to enable the development of mobile disease diagnostics through machine learning and crowdsourcing. arXiv preprint. Computing Research Repository (2015)
22. Jamal, M.A., Qi, G.J.: Task agnostic meta-learning for few-shot learning. In: Proceedings of the IEEE/CVF Conference on Computer Vision and Pattern Recognition (CVPR) (2019)
23. Khan, A.M., Ashrafee, A., Sayera, R., Ivan, S., Ahmed, S.: Rethinking cooking state recognition with vision transformers. In: 25th International Conference on Computer and Information Technology (ICCIT), pp. 170–175 (2022)
24. Koch, G., Zemel, R., Salakhutdinov, R.: Siamese neural networks for one-shot image recognition. In: Proceedings of the 32nd International Conference on Machine Learning. JMLR (2015)
25. Kolesnikov, A., et al.: Big transfer (BiT): general visual representation learning. In: Vedaldi, A., Bischof, H., Brox, T., Frahm, J.-M. (eds.) ECCV 2020. LNCS, vol. 12350, pp. 491–507. Springer, Cham (2020). https://doi.org/10.1007/978-3-030-58558-7_29
26. Li, L., Zhang, S., Wang, B.: Plant disease detection and classification by deep learning-a review. IEEE Access **9**, 56683–56698 (2021)
27. Li, Y., Yang, J.: Meta-learning baselines and database for few-shot classification in agriculture. Comput. Electron. Agric. **182**, 106055 (2021)
28. Maeda-Gutierrez, V., et al.: Comparison of convolutional neural network architectures for classification of tomato plant diseases. Appl. Sci. **10**(4) (2020)
29. Morshed, M.S., Ahmed, S., Ahmed, T., Islam, M.U., Ashikur Rahman, A.: Fruit quality assessment with densely connected convolutional neural network. In: 2022 12th International Conference on Electrical and Computer Engineering (ICECE), pp. 1–4 (2022)
30. Nesteruk, S., Shadrin, D., Pukalchik, M.: Image augmentation for multitask few-shot learning: agricultural domain use-case. arXiv preprint arXiv:2102.12295 (2021)
31. Nichol, A., Achiam, J., Schulman, J.: On first-order meta-learning algorithms. arXiv preprint arXiv:1803.02999 (2018)
32. Noon, S.K., Amjad, M., Ali Qureshi, M., Mannan, A.: Computationally light deep learning framework to recognize cotton leaf diseases. J. Intell. Fuzzy Syst. **40**(12383–12398), 6 (2021)
33. Nuthalapati, S.V., Tunga, A.: Multi-domain few-shot learning and dataset for agricultural applications. In: Proceedings of the IEEE/CVF International Conference on Computer Vision (ICCV) Workshops, pp. 1399–1408. arXiv:2109.09952 (2021)

34. Panno, S., et al.: A review of the most common and economically important diseases that undermine the cultivation of tomato crop in the Mediterranean basin. Agronomy **11**(11), 2188 (2021)
35. Rafi, M.H., Ratul Mahjabin, M., Rahman, M.S., Hasanul Kabir, M., Ahmed, S.: A critical analysis of deep learning applications in crop pest classification: promising pathways and limitations. In: 2023 26th International Conference on Computer and Information Technology (ICCIT), pp. 1–6 (2023)
36. Raiyan, S.R., Amio, Z.Z., Ahmed, S.: HaSPeR: an image repository for hand shadow puppet recognition. In: ICCV 2025 Workshop on Cultural Continuity of Artists (2025)
37. Sholihati, R.A., Sulistijono, I.A., Risnumawan, A., Kusumawati, E.: Potato leaf disease classification using deep learning approach. In: International Electronics Symposium (IES), pp. 392–397 (2020)
38. Simonyan, K., Zisserman, A.: Very deep convolutional networks for large-scale image recognition. arXiv preprint arXiv:1409.1556 (2014)
39. Snell, J., Swersky, K., Zemel, R.: Prototypical networks for few-shot learning. In: Advances in Neural Information Processing Systems, vol. 30. Curran Associates, Inc. (2017)
40. Sun, J., Cao, W., Fu, X., Ochi, S., Yamanaka, T.: Few-shot learning for plant disease recognition: a review. Agron. J. **116**(3), 1204–1216 (2024)
41. Szegedy, C., Vanhoucke, V., Ioffe, S., Shlens, J., Wojna, Z.: Rethinking the inception architecture for computer vision. In: IEEE Conference on Computer Vision and Pattern Recognition (CVPR), pp. 2818–2826 (2016)
42. Tian, Y., Wang, Y., Krishnan, D., Tenenbaum, J.B., Isola, P.: Rethinking few-shot image classification: a good embedding is all you need? In: Vedaldi, A., Bischof, H., Brox, T., Frahm, J.-M. (eds.) ECCV 2020. LNCS, vol. 12359, pp. 266–282. Springer, Cham (2020). https://doi.org/10.1007/978-3-030-58568-6_16
43. Uskaner Hepsağ, P.: Efficient plant disease identification using few-shot learning: a transfer learning approach. Multimedia Tools Appl. **83**(20), 58293–58308 (2024)
44. Vinyals, O., Blundell, C., Lillicrap, T., Kavukcuoglu, K., Wierstra, D.: Matching networks for one shot learning. In: Advances in Neural Information Processing Systems, vol. 29. Curran Associates, Inc. (2016)
45. Wang, B., Wang, D.: Plant leaves classification: a few-shot learning method based on Siamese network. IEEE Access **7**, 151754–151763 (2019)
46. Wang, Y., Wang, S.: IMAL: an improved meta-learning approach for few-shot classification of plant diseases. In: IEEE 21st International Conference on Bioinformatics and Bioengineering (BIBE), pp. 1–7 (2021)
47. Xu, M., et al.: Embracing limited and imperfect training datasets: opportunities and challenges in plant disease recognition using deep learning. Front. Plant Sci. **14**, 1225409 (2023)
48. Yasmeen, A., Rahman, F.I., Ahmed, S., Kabir, M.H.: CSVC-Net: code-switched voice command classification using deep CNN-LSTM network. In: 2021 Joint 10th International Conference on Informatics, Electronics & Vision (ICIEV) and 2021 5th International Conference on Imaging, Vision & Pattern Recognition (icIVPR), pp. 1–8 (2021)
49. Zabihzadeh, D., Masoudifar, M.: ZS-DML: zero-shot deep metric learning approach for plant leaf disease classification. Multimedia Tools Appl. **83**(18), 54147–54164 (2024)
50. Zhao, J., Kong, L., Lv, J.: An overview of deep neural networks for few-shot learning. Big Data Min. Anal. **8**(1), 145–188 (2025)

Robust Gait-Based Disease Estimation Against Occlusion and Distortion via Deep Mutual Learning

Saito Takase[1(✉)], Shiori Furukawa[1], Yu Moriguchi[2], and Noriko Takemura[1]

[1] Kyushu Institute of Technology, 680-4 Kawazu, Iizuka, Fukuoka 820-8502, Japan
takase.saito696@mail.kyutech.jp, takemura@ai.kyutech.ac.jp

[2] The University of Osaka, Osaka, Japan

Abstract. With the progression of an aging society, the number of patients with gait disorders is increasing. Representative conditions causing such disorders include lumbar spinal canal stenosis and cervical spondylotic myelopathy. This study aims to estimate these diseases from gait videos recorded from a lateral view of the patient. However, capturing gait videos typically requires a large space, and when recorded in a limited environment, the videos may suffer from occlusion and distortion, potentially degrading estimation accuracy. To address this issue, we propose a robust disease estimation method using Deep Mutual Learning (DML), where multiple models learn while sharing knowledge with each other. In the proposed framework, two deep learning models with shared parameters are used: one receives complete gait data and the other receives incomplete gait data. The models are trained to extract similar features from both types of input, enabling reliable disease estimation even from degraded videos. We demonstrate the effectiveness of the proposed method through evaluation experiments using gait videos of patients with gait disorders and healthy individuals.

Keywords: Gait · Disease Estimation · Occlusion and Distortion Robustness

1 Introduction

With the progression of the aging society, the number of patients suffering from diseases that impair walking is increasing. Representative diseases include lumbar canal stenosis (LCS), cervical spondylotic myelopathy (CSM), Parkinson's disease, peripheral artery disease, and cerebrovascular disease. In particular, LCS and CSM are highly prevalent; it has been reported that there are approximately 5.8 million patients with LCS and 14.7 million with CSM in Japan. Despite this large patient population, there are currently no simple screening methods such as biomarkers for these gait disorders. It has also been reported that approximately 43% of patients with CSM are misdiagnosed at their first visit, and on average, they consult 5.2 physicians before receiving an appropriate diagnosis

C. Wallraven et al. (Eds.): ACPR 2025, LNCS 16174, pp. 147–158, 2026.
https://doi.org/10.1007/978-981-95-4395-3_11

[9]. Gait disorders not only reduce mobility but also adversely affect physical and mental health, leading to an increased burden of caregiving. Therefore, the development of technologies to support early detection and accurate diagnosis of such diseases is an urgent issue.

In recent years, many studies have been conducted on gait-based personal identification [8] and attribute estimation (such as gender and age) [10,11], demonstrating that gait contains a wealth of features reflecting individual and physical conditions. It is considered possible to utilize these features for disease estimation, and indeed, research using gait video for disease estimation has been reported [1,4,6]. Estimation methods based on gait video can be performed without specialized equipment or medical personnel, making them well-suited for screening purposes.

In this study, we investigate a disease estimation method using gait videos taken from the side with a monocular camera. Lateral-view videos can clearly capture features such as the curvature of the neck and waist and the movement of limbs. On the other hand, previous studies have assumed that the entire body of the walker is always within the camera's field of view and that the camera angle does not change. Although the use of treadmills has been tried to relax spatial constraints, this is not realistic for patients with gait disorders due to safety concerns such as the risk of falling. Therefore, gait video recording needs to be conducted while maintaining sufficient distance between the walker and the camera. For example, in the study by Furukawa et al. [1], a 10-meter walking path and a 4-meter distance between the camera and the walker were set as conditions, requiring at least a $4\,\mathrm{m}\times 10\mathrm{m}$ space. However, such large spaces can only be secured at large-scale hospitals or hospitals equipped with rehabilitation facilities, whereas, for disease estimation aimed at early detection and screening, introduction in smaller clinics is more desirable. Therefore, gait videos must be captured in narrower spaces, but this leads to issues such as the person moving out of the camera frame or, if filmed with a wide-angle lens to avoid this, distortion occurring at the edges of the video. These factors can lead to the loss of features necessary for disease estimation, significantly reducing accuracy.

To address this issue, this study proposes a robust disease estimation method for gait videos with occlusion or distortion using Deep Mutual Learning (DML) [13], a type of knowledge distillation. DML is a method in which multiple models simultaneously learn while referencing each other's outputs. Compared to conventional distillation methods, which require a pre-trained teacher model, DML has the advantage of achieving high accuracy without pre-training. DML has demonstrated performance improvements in various fields, such as image classification, person re-identification, and medical image diagnosis [7,12]. In this study, we build two deep learning models that share parameters: one receives complete gait data, and the other receives incomplete gait data with occlusion or distortion. By training these models to extract equivalent features from both types of data, high-accuracy disease estimation can be achieved even from incomplete videos. We verify the effectiveness of the proposed method by conducting evaluation experiments using gait videos of patients with gait disorders and healthy individuals.

2 Proposed Method

In this study, we use the Gait Energy Image (GEI) [3], which is generated from gait videos, as input, and conduct learning using the Deep Mutual Learning (DML) framework. The training framework of the proposed method is shown in Fig. 1. As illustrated in Fig. 1, one of the two models receives a complete GEI as input, while the other receives an incomplete GEI that includes occlusion or distortion; each model is trained in a mutually collaborative manner. The details of the proposed method are described below.

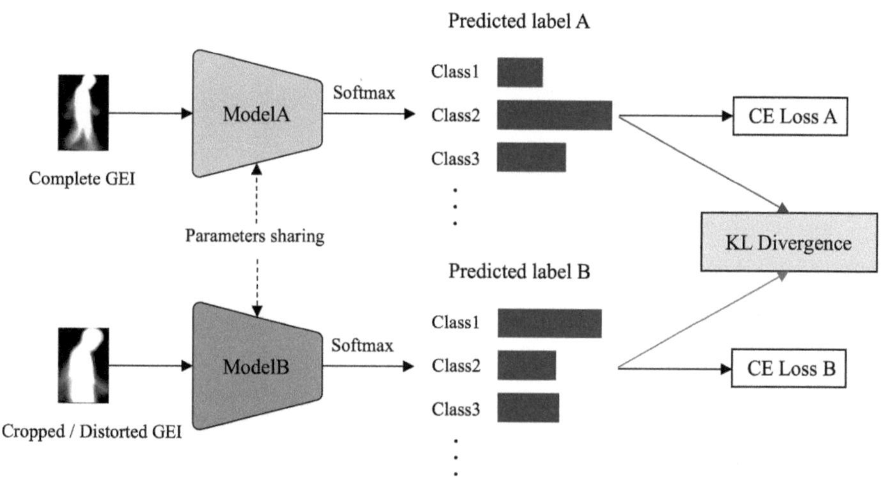

Fig. 1. Framework of proposed method. The Model A receives complete GEIs, while Model B receives occluded or distorted GEIs. Both models are trained in a Deep Mutual Learning framework, encouraging Model B to learn robust features by leveraging the knowledge from Model A.

2.1 Generation of GEI

In this method, a Gait Energy Image (GEI) is generated from gait videos (sequences of RGB images) and used as the input to the proposed method. While the proposed method is compatible with various data types, such as skeleton graph data and silhouette image sequences, the primary aim of this study is to demonstrate the utility of the DML-based framework. Therefore, we use the GEI—which is convenient to handle and can integrally represent both static and dynamic gait features in a single image—as the input data for performance evaluation.

The procedure for generating GEIs is shown in Fig. 2. First, a person region segmentation method based on graph transfer learning [2] is applied to the gait videos (RGB image sequences) recorded by a camera to create a sequence of silhouette images. Next, height normalization is performed on the silhouette sequence to generate normalized silhouette images (of size 128 × 88 pixels). Finally, a single GEI (also 128×88 pixels) is generated by averaging the pixel values over 40 normalized silhouette images. Normally, GEI is created using images covering one gait cycle, but since the patients targeted in this study may have unstable gait, making it difficult to accurately estimate the gait cycle, we experimentally use a sequence of 40 frames to generate GEIs in this study. Furthermore, instead of using gait videos that actually contain occlusion or distortion, we artificially process normal gait data to simulate occlusion and distortion for the experiments.

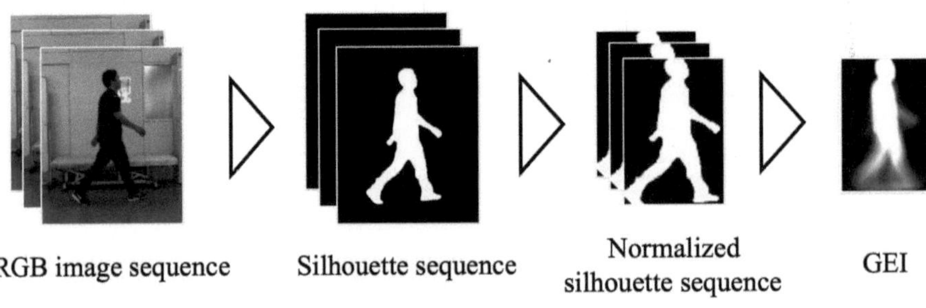

Fig. 2. Generation procedure of GEI

Generation of Occluded GEI. Figure 3 shows the process of generating an occluded GEI. In this study, we simulated occluded GEIs by first randomly cropping the top and bottom portions of the silhouette image sequence by a certain ratio before generating the GEI. The cropping ratio was randomly set between 40% and 70% of the original image height, thereby simulating the loss of information in the vertical direction.

Fig. 3. Generation procedure of occluded GEI

Generation of Distorted GEI. Figure 4 shows the process of generating a distorted GEI. In this study, we assume non-linear distortion—specifically, "barrel distortion," which is commonly observed when using wide-angle lenses and causes the image to bulge outward from the center. First, the barrel distortion transformation used in the study by Li et al. [5] is applied to the silhouette image sequence to generate a distorted silhouette sequence. Then, a GEI is generated from the distorted image sequence, thereby reproducing a GEI with distortion. Since the strength of distortion varies depending on the camera environment, the distortion parameters are randomly set for each subject to introduce individual variation in the degree of distortion.

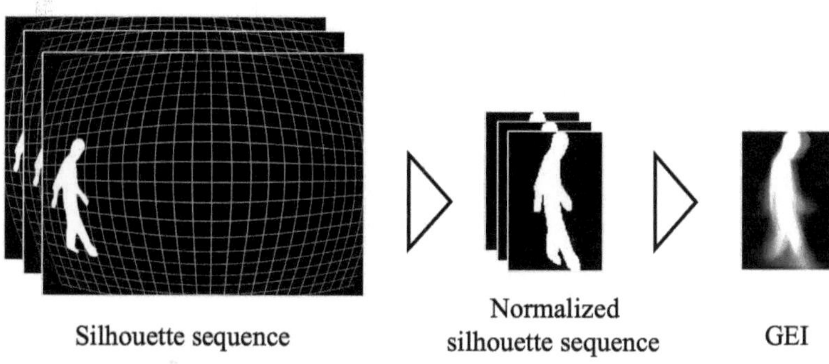

Fig. 4. Generation procedure of distorted GEI

2.2 Disease Estimation Model

Deep Mutual Learning. Deep Mutual Learning (DML) is a method in which multiple models are typically provided with the same input data, and each model independently estimates a class probability distribution while referencing each other's outputs during the learning process. The main objective of this mutual knowledge distillation is to suppress the variance in outputs between models, thereby stabilizing predictions and improving generalization performance. Notably, DML enables the acquisition of robust representations that are difficult to obtain with a single model, thus contributing to accuracy improvement.

While conventional DML is based on the assumption that the same input data is fed to all models, in this study, we intentionally relax this assumption and propose a new framework that utilizes input data of different properties. Specifically, a complete gait video without occlusion or distortion and an incomplete gait video containing such imperfections are fed into separate models, and training is performed so as to minimize the KL divergence between the output class probability distributions. In this way, the goal is for the model to extract features from incomplete videos that are similar to those extracted from complete videos, thereby achieving comparable prediction results.

Thus, this study extends the traditional DML framework of "mutual learning with identical data" and introduces the novelty of enhancing the stability and reliability of disease estimation by sharing knowledge between heterogeneous input data, thereby compensating for common imperfections observed in real gait videos. The following sections provide detailed explanations regarding the design of the loss functions and the training procedures necessary to implement this framework.

Loss Function. In the proposed method, learning is performed using a model that receives a complete GEI as input (Model A, upper in Fig. 1) and a model that receives an incomplete GEI as input (Model B, upper in Fig. 1). For each model, loss functions based on Cross Entropy Loss (hereafter, CE loss) and Kullback-Leibler Divergence (hereafter, KLD) are defined, and mutual learning is conducted between the two models. Denote the CE losses for Model A and Model B as $L_{CE,A}$ and $L_{CE,B}$, the output probability distributions as P_A and P_B, and the KLDs for mimicking the output distributions of the counterpart models as $D_{\mathrm{KL}}(P_B||P_A)$ and $D_{\mathrm{KL}}(P_A||P_B)$, respectively. Then, the total losses for each model, L_A and L_B, are defined as shown in Eq. 1.

$$\begin{aligned} L_{\mathrm{A}} &= L_{CE,A} + D_{\mathrm{KL}}(P_B||P_A) \\ L_{\mathrm{B}} &= L_{CE,B} + D_{\mathrm{KL}}(P_A||P_B) \end{aligned} \tag{1}$$

By introducing KLD, the knowledge of Model A, which receives complete GEIs as input, can be transferred to Model B, which receives incomplete GEIs, enabling robust learning even for data with occlusion or distortion. Furthermore, to appropriately balance the contributions of both models' losses, the final loss function L_{total} is defined as shown in Eq. 2. Here, the losses for each model are weighted using the hyperparameter α.

$$L_{\mathrm{total}} = \alpha L_{\mathrm{A}} + (1-\alpha) L_{\mathrm{B}} \tag{2}$$

α is a parameter that controls the contribution of each model's loss and is set in advance within the range $0 \leq \alpha \leq 1$. By optimizing this loss function, it is expected that both models will enhance their classification performance on their respective input data while leveraging each other's knowledge.

Learning Procedure. In the proposed method, both Model A and Model B in Fig. 1 employ ResNet50. One of the two ResNet50 models receives a complete GEI as input, while the other receives an incomplete GEI as input. For each model, Cross Entropy (CE) loss is calculated based on the predicted and ground-truth labels for the input image, and Kullback-Leibler Divergence (KLD) is further calculated between the output distribution of the other model (as shown in Eq. 1). The KLD is computed using the class probability distributions P_A and P_B, which are obtained by applying the Softmax function to the output logits of each model. The value of α in the loss function shown in Eq. 2 is set in advance. Based on these calculations, training proceeds to optimize the loss function.

In standard DML, model diversity can be achieved by not sharing parameters and learning from different perspectives. However, in our method, the parameters of the two ResNet50 are shared to ensure that both models follow the same learning path. This design allows the model to be trained to extract equivalent disease-related features from incomplete GEIs as it would from complete GEIs. Ultimately, the disease estimation is performed using the trained shared-parameter model (Model A/B). During inference, either a complete or incomplete GEI is provided as input, and disease class is determined based on the model's output. For evaluation, we compared the cases where occluded GEIs and distorted GEIs were input as incomplete GEIs, as well as the case where a complete GEI was input. Disease estimation performance was verified under each condition.

3 Evaluation

Gait videos of patients with gait disorders and healthy subjects were collected, and evaluation experiments were conducted.

3.1 Dataset

To verify the effectiveness of the proposed method, we conducted evaluation experiments using gait videos collected by our research group. During video recording, each subject was filmed from the side while walking straight for 10 m on flat ground. In order to capture steady-state gait, the camera was positioned so that the first and last 3 m of each walk were excluded from the recording range, and only the middle 4 m of the walk were recorded. The camera was placed at the 5-meter point on the walking path and at a distance of 4 m from the subject.

In this study, GEIs generated from gait videos of patients with lumbar canal stenosis (LCS, including those with comorbidities), patients with other diseases, and healthy individuals were used. The number of data samples for each group is shown in Table 1. The gait image dataset used consisted of approximately 114,000 GEIs generated from a total of 1,301 gait videos of 512 individuals, with each individual contributing 1 to 4 gait sequences.

All participants gave prior informed consent for the use of their data for research purposes. In addition to the gait data, information was provided regarding whether each subject had been diagnosed by a physician as having a disease

Table 1. The number of samples

	#subject	#GEI
LCS	165	54,105
Other Diseases	77	21,124
Healthy	134	18,214

(LCS or other), which was used for performance evaluation. Since the number of GEIs varied among subjects, the number of GEIs used per gait video in the experiment was limited to 200.

3.2 Evaluation Method

In this study, evaluation experiments were conducted using two classifiers: an LCS estimator that predicts whether a subject has lumbar canal stenosis (LCS) or not, and a Disease estimator that predicts whether a subject is a patient with any disease or a healthy individual. To validate the machine learning models of the proposed method and comparative approaches, we employed 5-fold cross-validation.

For 5-fold cross-validation, the dataset was first divided into five groups based on participants. In each iteration, one group was used as the validation data, another as the test data, and the remaining three as the training data; this process was repeated five times, shifting the groups each time. In the training data, undersampling was performed after splitting to ensure that the number of samples for each label was balanced and to avoid class imbalance. The model was evaluated on the validation data at each epoch, and the model from the epoch with the highest macro-F1 score was saved; this best model was then evaluated on the test data. Normally, when the dataset is not sufficiently large, the results may be biased depending on the choice of test data; however, by averaging the results over the five splits in 5-fold cross-validation, more generalizable results can be obtained.

The evaluation metrics used were the macro-F1 score, area under the ROC curve (AUC), sensitivity, and specificity, with the mean values over the five folds reported. AUC measures the discriminatory performance for each class as the area under the ROC curve and allows for the evaluation of overall model performance independent of decision thresholds. Sensitivity represents the true positive rate and specificity represents the true negative rate; both are important for understanding trends in missed detections and false positives, respectively. The macro-F1 score is the arithmetic mean of the F1 scores for each class, giving equal weight to all classes, and is calculated by first computing the F1 score for each class and then averaging them.

In this study, because the number of samples varied among classes, the macro-F1 score was used as the main evaluation metric to fairly assess the classification performance for each class. This approach avoids underestimating the performance on minority classes and allows for the selection of a balanced classification model overall.

In the experiments, the batch size was set to 512, the initial learning rate was set to 0.0001, and training was conducted for 100 epochs. The optimizer used was Adam (Adaptive Moment Estimation) with a weight decay of 0.0001. In addition, for the proposed method, the loss function weight α introduced in Sect. 2.2 was set to 0.4. Hyperparameters were tuned based on the results of validation data in the first fold, and those values were then used for training in the subsequent folds.

3.3 Result

The results of the evaluation experiments for the LCS estimator and the Disease estimator are shown in Tables 2 and 3, respectively. In these experiments, as comparative approaches, we used a single ResNet50 with the same architecture as that used in the proposed method (with the loss function being only the CE loss), trained either on complete GEIs, incomplete GEIs, or both.

Table 2. The result of LCS estimator. Bold is the best

method	train data			test data			F1-score	AUC	Sensitivity	Specificity
	Complete	Occlusion	Distortion	Complete	Occlusion	Distortion				
ResNet50	✓			✓			**0.625**	0.673	**0.792**	0.474
DML(**Ours**)	✓	✓		✓			0.581	0.641	0.765	0.406
DML(**Ours**)	✓		✓	✓			0.606	**0.689**	0.765	**0.490**
ResNet50	✓				✓		0.477	0.497	0.668	0.330
ResNet50		✓			✓		0.584	0.627	0.719	0.462
ResNet50	✓	✓			✓		0.582	0.629	0.705	**0.473**
DML(**Ours**)	✓	✓			✓		**0.588**	**0.643**	**0.746**	0.440
ResNet50	✓					✓	0.539	0.615	0.787	0.339
ResNet50			✓			✓	0.591	0.642	0.726	**0.472**
ResNet50	✓		✓			✓	0.587	0.643	0.758	0.436
DML(**Ours**)	✓		✓			✓	**0.611**	**0.667**	**0.844**	0.376

Table 3. The result of Disease estimator. Bold is the best

method	train data			test data			F1-score	AUC	Sensitivity	Specificity
	Complete	Occlusion	Distortion	Complete	Occlusion	Distortion				
ResNet50	✓			✓			0.752	0.872	0.907	0.598
DML(**Ours**)	✓	✓		✓			0.757	0.885	**0.909**	0.589
DML(**Ours**)	✓		✓	✓			**0.804**	**0.897**	**0.909**	**0.722**
ResNet50	✓				✓		0.484	0.619	0.490	**0.664**
ResNet50		✓			✓		0.738	0.829	**0.900**	0.579
ResNet50	✓	✓			✓		0.729	0.820	0.871	0.620
DML(**Ours**)	✓	✓			✓		**0.743**	**0.847**	0.889	0.623
ResNet50	✓					✓	0.705	0.817	0.914	0.483
ResNet50			✓			✓	0.807	0.890	0.908	**0.721**
ResNet50	✓		✓			✓	0.803	0.890	0.913	0.693
DML(**Ours**)	✓		✓			✓	**0.811**	**0.901**	**0.926**	0.693

When using complete GEIs as test data, for the LCS estimator, the ResNet50 trained solely on complete GEIs achieved the highest F1 score. On the other hand, in terms of AUC and specificity, the proposed method—which was trained on both complete and distorted GEIs—demonstrated superior performance. For the Disease estimator, the proposed method achieved the highest performance across all evaluation metrics, outperforming the ResNet50 trained only on complete GEIs.

When using occluded GEIs as test data, for the LCS estimator, the proposed method—trained on both complete and occluded GEIs—achieved the highest sensitivity, F1 score, and AUC. This advantage was consistent when compared with other ResNet50 models trained on only complete GEIs, only occluded GEIs, or both. Similarly, for the Disease estimator, the proposed method achieved the highest values for F1 score and AUC, and also demonstrated a good balance between sensitivity and specificity.

The same trend was observed when using distorted GEIs as test data. For both the LCS estimator and the Disease estimator, the proposed method—which was trained on both complete and distorted GEIs—showed the best performance in terms of sensitivity, F1 score, and AUC.

These results indicate that DML-based training, which combines complete and incomplete GEIs, is an effective approach for robust disease estimation even when the input is incomplete. Of particular note is that the proposed method often outperformed models trained only on complete data, even when the test input was a complete GEI. This suggests that mutual learning with incomplete data enabled the model to gain better generalization ability, resulting in improved accuracy even with complete inputs.

On the other hand, the specificity of the LCS estimator tended to be generally lower than that of the Disease estimator. Figure 5 shows a confusion matrix obtained by the proposed method, indicating that most subjects labeled as "not LCS" but misclassified as "LCS" were patients with other diseases rather than

Actual		Predicted: LCS	Predicted: Others
LCS		6708	2176
Others	Healthy	109	526
	Other diseases	4321	1573

(a) test data:Complete

Actual		Predicted: LCS	Predicted: Others
LCS		10164	1399
Others	Healthy	168	701
	Other diseases	3694	1403

(b) test data:Complete

Actual		Predicted: LCS	Predicted: Others
LCS		9941	2692
Others	Healthy	549	1333
	Other diseases	1278	575

(c) test data:Occlusion

Actual		Predicted: LCS	Predicted: Others
LCS		7850	1034
Others	Healthy	99	536
	Other diseases	4637	1257

(d) test data:Distortion

Fig. 5. Confusion matrix in proposed method. The numbers in the confusion matrix represent the amount of data.

healthy individuals. This suggests that there is similarity in gait between LCS and other disease groups, making discrimination between the two difficult for the model. This confusion is likely a factor contributing to the lower specificity of the LCS estimator. On the other hand, as shown in Table 1 and Fig. 5, classification between disease presence (disease vs. healthy controls) was generally performed with high accuracy.

4 Conclusion

In this study, we proposed a robust disease estimation method for incomplete gait data containing occlusions or distortions, based on Deep Mutual Learning. Although sufficient space is generally required for recording gait videos, in real clinical settings, shooting environments are often restricted, which can result in videos with occlusion or distortion. To maintain high prediction accuracy even for such incomplete data, our method employs two deep learning models with shared parameters, where one model is provided with complete gait data and the other with incomplete gait data, and mutual learning is conducted between them.

The results of the evaluation experiments showed that the proposed method generally achieved higher accuracy than conventional methods, and demonstrated stable disease estimation even for incomplete inputs. Furthermore, in many cases, the proposed method also outperformed conventional methods when tested with complete input data, suggesting that mutual learning enhanced the representational capacity of the model.

In the future, we plan to expand the scope of target diseases beyond LCS, and to introduce more refined feature representations that can accurately capture subtle differences between LCS and other diseases. In addition, we aim to further evaluate the reliability of the proposed method for practical applications by validating it with real data that actually contains occlusion and distortion.

References

1. Furukawa, S., Takemura, N.: Disease estimation based on gait images by separating individual features using variational autoencoder. AROB-ISBC-SWARM (2024)
2. Gong, K., Gao, Y., Liang, X., Shen, X., Wang, M., Lin, L.: Graphonomy: universal human parsing via graph transfer learning. In: Proceedings of the IEEE/CVF Conference on Computer Vision and Pattern Recognition, pp. 7450–7459 (2019)
3. Han, J., Bhanu, B.: Individual recognition using gait energy image. IEEE Trans. Pattern Anal. Mach. Intell. **28**(2), 316–322 (2005)
4. Kidziński, Ł, Yang, B., Hicks, J.L., Rajagopal, A., Delp, S.L., Schwartz, M.H.: Deep neural networks enable quantitative movement analysis using single-camera videos. Nat. Commun. **11**(1), 4054 (2020)
5. Li, X., Zhang, B., Sander, P.V., Liao, J.: Blind geometric distortion correction on images through deep learning. In: 2019 IEEE/CVF Conference on Computer Vision and Pattern Recognition (CVPR), pp. 4850–4859 (2019). https://doi.org/10.1109/CVPR.2019.00499

6. Liao, R., Moriwaki, K., Makihara, Y., Muramatsu, D., Takemura, N., Yagi, Y.: Health indicator estimation by video-based gait analysis. IEICE Trans. Inf. Syst. **E104.D**(10), 1678–1690 (2021). https://doi.org/10.1587/transinf.2020ZDP7502
7. Liu, X., Qu, L., Xie, Z., Shi, Y., Song, Z.: Deep mutual learning among partially labeled datasets for multi-organ segmentation. arXiv preprint arXiv:2407.12611 (2024)
8. Wang, L., Tan, T., Ning, H., Hu, W.: Silhouette analysis-based gait recognition for human identification. IEEE Trans. Pattern Anal. Mach. Intell. **25**(12), 1505–1518 (2003)
9. Wu, J.C., et al.: Epidemiology of cervical spondylotic myelopathy and its risk of causing spinal cord injury: a national cohort study. Neurosurg. Focus **35**(1), E10 (2013)
10. Xu, C., et al.: Real-time gait-based age estimation and gender classification from a single image. In: 2021 IEEE Winter Conference on Applications of Computer Vision (WACV), pp. 3459–3469 (2021). https://doi.org/10.1109/WACV48630.2021.00350
11. Xu, C., et al.: Uncertainty-aware gait-based age estimation and its applications. IEEE Trans. Biometrics Behav. Identity Sci. **3**(4), 479–494 (2021)
12. Zhang, H., et al.: DCML: deep contrastive mutual learning for COVID-19 recognition. Biomed. Sig. Process. Control **77**, 103770 (2022). https://doi.org/10.1016/j.bspc.2022.103770
13. Zhang, Y., Xiang, T., Hospedales, T.M., Lu, H.: Deep mutual learning. In: 2018 IEEE/CVF Conference on Computer Vision and Pattern Recognition, pp. 4320–4328 (2018). https://doi.org/10.1109/CVPR.2018.00454

Estimating Learners' Position and Work Time for Teaching Reflection in Agricultural Training

Koshi Saito[1(✉)], Tsubasa Minematsu[2], and Atsushi Shimada[1]

[1] Kyushu University, Fukuoka, Japan
saito.koshi.005@s.kyushu-u.ac.jp, atsushi@ait.kyushu-u.ac.jp
[2] Kyushu Institute of Technology, Fukuoka, Japan
minematsu@ai.kyutech.ac.jp

Abstract. Due to the shortage of agricultural labor, agricultural education has become increasingly important. It consists of both classroom lectures and practical training. However, teacher observations during agricultural training are often subjective and lack objective evaluation criteria. To support teachers' reflection, we aim to objectively record learner behaviors. In order to explore the educational applicability of this recording approach, we developed a vision-based system to estimate and visualize learners' positions and work time during agricultural training. Learners' positions are estimated from a 360° video using pose estimation, multi-object tracking, and person re-identification, while their work states are classified using features extracted from egocentric videos. To evaluate what kind of information and granularity are useful, four prototypes of visualizations were created. We collected data from actual training sessions and applied our system to the recordings. We then interviewed teachers to explore how they utilize the visualizations to reflect on and improve their agricultural training practice. In preliminary quantitative evaluations, both position estimation and work activity recognition achieved over 70% accuracy across several of our own datasets. Interview results indicated that the visualizations were generally consistent with the teachers' observations and were regarded as useful for objectively assessing learners' farm work.

Keywords: Teaching Reflection · Agricultural Education · Visualization

1 Introduction

In Japan, the shortage of agricultural labor has become an especially serious issue, increasing the importance of agricultural education for cultivating future agricultural workers. Agricultural education requires not only classroom-based lectures for learning theoretical knowledge but also practical training sessions [9,10]. During the practical training sessions, learners perform farm work

C. Wallraven et al. (Eds.): ACPR 2025, LNCS 16174, pp. 159–174, 2026.
https://doi.org/10.1007/978-981-95-4395-3_12

while teachers observe their work activities and provide appropriate guidance and feedback.

However, teacher-led qualitative evaluations tend to be subjective. Subjective assessments may vary between teachers, potentially leading to unfairness. This poses a challenge to objectively evaluating and comparing learners. Furthermore, with a limited number of teachers, it is challenging to monitor all learners simultaneously and provide thorough evaluations.

To address these challenges, there is a need for a method that can objectively and quantitatively capture learner behaviors during practical training to support instructional activities. In nursing [3,8] and early childhood education [14], multimodal learning analytics (MMLA) [1] has been explored to analyze learner behavior in practical settings, demonstrating educational effectiveness.

However, the required type and granularity of information vary depending on the specific field and content of training. In the agricultural domain, although various studies have focused on quantifying agricultural activities [4,7,16,17], there has been limited discussion on how such findings can be utilized to support agricultural education. Therefore, to support agricultural training effectively, a system is required that can flexibly and objectively capture the appropriate granularity and content of farm work data.

In this study, we developed a vision-based system to estimate the "time", "position", and "work activity" of learners during agricultural training, as a step toward evaluating the educational usefulness of quantifying agricultural tasks for educational support. We adopted this approach to make the system more suitable for real educational settings by reducing costs, minimizing intrusion, and lowering the burden on learners and the training environment. As a preliminary evaluation to determine whether the estimation accuracy is sufficient for use in educational settings, we quantitatively assessed the system's performance. To explore the educational applicability of the results, we created four prototypes of visualizations that varied in the information used and their level of granularity, and conducted interviews with teachers to assess the consistency between the visualizations and their perceptions. By visualizing fundamental activities, this system supports teaching reflection before and after training sessions and enables more objective evidence-based assessment and feedback on learners' farm work.

2 Related Work

Multimodal Learning Analytics (MMLA) is a research approach that aims to better understand learning processes by collecting and analyzing data from multiple modalities [1]. Relying solely on digital log data, which has been the primary focus of traditional Learning Analytics, risks producing a "streetlight effect," where analysis centers on easily accessible traces rather than those most relevant to the learning construct [11]. MMLA addresses this limitation by integrating diverse and context-rich sources of evidence, allowing for a more comprehensive understanding of complex learning activities such as face-to-face interactions and physical tasks.

For spatial behavior analysis, Echeverria et al. [3] proposed a system to collect and analyze learner position and audio data from sensors, supporting feedback in nursing simulation classes. Similarly, Xinyu Li et al. [8] estimated learner positions using multi-object tracking from videos recorded during nursing simulations, enabling comparisons between high-performing and low-performing teams. Likewise, Saquib et al. [14] developed a system to track children's positions and interactions with teaching materials, assisting observation in early childhood education. These studies demonstrate the potential for data-driven support, but their findings are inherently domain-specific. Consequently, the type and granularity of information considered useful in one context may not apply to another and require careful re-evaluation.

In the agricultural domain, some studies utilized RFID tags to identify agricultural tasks [4], while others used accelerometers in beacons or smartwatches to analyze tomato harvesting performance [7]. Some studies have directly addressed the classification of farm work types from video data using deep learning models [17], while others have explored combining pose estimation and object detection for more detailed recognition [16]. Although advanced methods such as a Vision Transformer based model for pose estimation [18] and person re-identification techniques that utilize keypoints and prompt-based features [15] have achieved high accuracy, they may be unnecessarily complex for practical applications such as agricultural work estimation.

To the best of our knowledge, no previous research has focused on learners during agricultural training to estimate both their position and work activity using computer vision techniques and to evaluate the educational value of the combined analysis through teacher feedback. Our approach integrates the domains of agriculture, computer vision, and education, presenting a novel approach for supporting agricultural training and education. Rather than pursuing state-of-the-art model performance, we focus on building an integrated system that achieves sufficient accuracy required in educational settings and is feasible for deployment in real-world practice.

3 Vision-Based Approach for Estimating Farm Work

Figure 1 provides an overview of our developed system. We adopted a vision-based approach rather than relying on high-cost positioning systems or invasive sensors. By using only cameras, we simplify data integration and reduce the burden on learners and the training environment, making the system more suitable for real-world educational settings. We use two types of cameras: a 360° camera[1] mounted on a fixed tripod in the training field, which enables non-intrusive, wide-area monitoring with minimal installation effort; and a neck-worn wearable camera[2], which captures detailed hand movements from an egocentric perspective without interfering with the learners' farm work. This setup offers

[1] Insta360 X4 https://www.insta360.com/product/insta360-x4.
[2] THINKLET https://mimi.fairydevices.jp/technology/device/thinklet/en/.

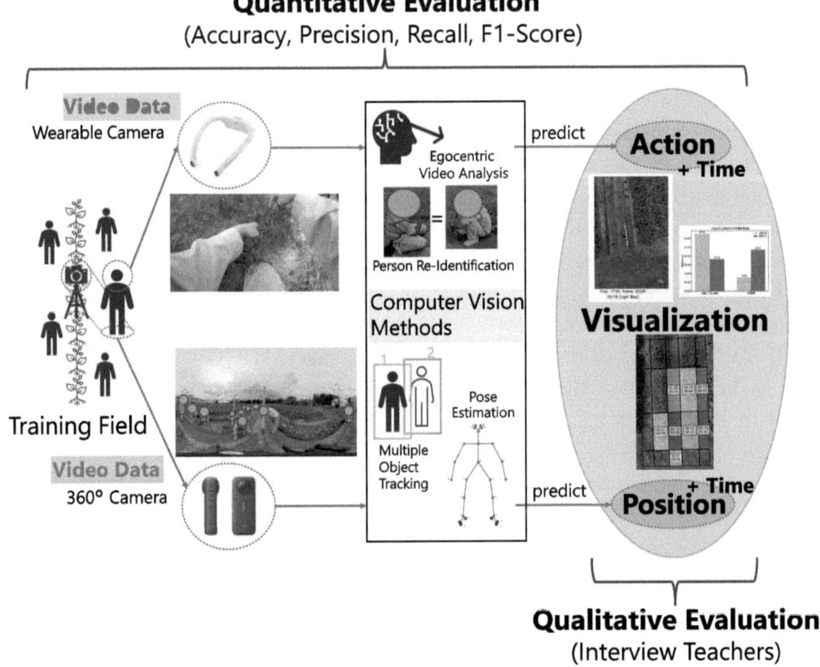

Fig. 1. Overview of the developed system for estimating and visualizing learners' position and working time using wearable and 360° cameras.

a cost-effective and practical solution for collecting multimodal learning data in authentic agricultural training scenarios.

3.1 Position Estimation Method

Figure 2 provides an overview of our position estimation method. In this study, each learner's position is estimated as the average foot position viewed from above, using six foot-related keypoints detected by OpenPose [2]. This assumption is justified because the training field is almost flat, and the learners' vertical movement during the tasks is minimal. To support person re-identification, learners are asked to wear clothing in distinguishable colors. The use of colorful bibs, commonly adopted in physical education classes in Japanese schools, makes this practical and economical.

First, the distorted equirectangular video captured by the 360° camera is converted into multiple perspective videos by varying the pan angles while setting parameters such as FOV, tilt angle, and output resolution to cover all directions. These parameters are determined according to the camera height from the ground, the resolution of the original video, and the performance of the computer used. Pose estimation is then applied to each view, and the coordinates of six keypoints related to the feet are averaged to define the foot position. For

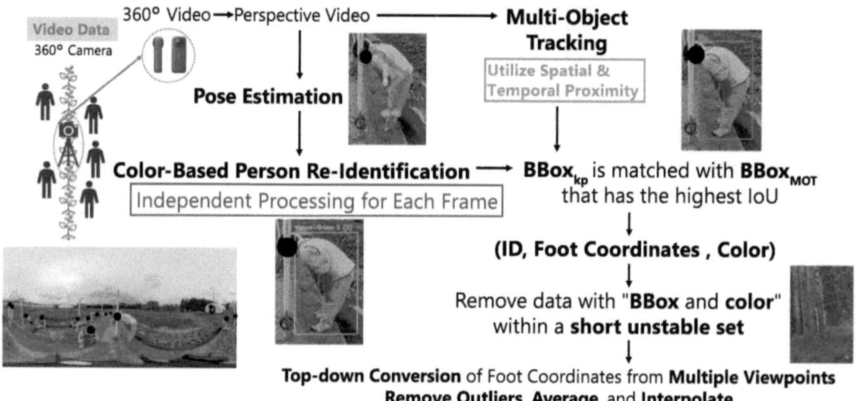

Fig. 2. Overview of the position estimation method.

each person detected in a frame, a bounding box ($\mathrm{BBox_{kp}}$) is calculated from their keypoints, and a cropped body image is extracted for further processing.

After extracting foot positions in each frame, we perform color-based person re-identification to associate them across frames. Clothing color ranges in HSV format are defined by extracting over ten sample points from each individual's clothing in cropped images at the start of the video. In each frame, we calculate the number of pixels within the defined HSV color range for each person. Then, based on the most frequently matching pixels, a color is assigned to only one individual, thereby enabling person re-identification. Note that while more advanced deep learning based re-identification methods exist, we adopted a simple color-based approach under the reasonable condition that each learner wore distinguishable clothing colors, which could be replaced with a more robust technique if necessary.

However, relying on only color information does not take into account the spatial and temporal proximity of $\mathrm{BBox_{kp}}$ across consecutive frames. Therefore, we utilize multi-object tracking using MOTIP [5] with $\mathrm{BBox_{MOT}}$ and assigned unique IDs to each individual to remove outliers such as sudden false detections in single frames. To reduce issues like ID switch or reassignment of new IDs when a person reappears after being out of frame, we divide the entire video into short frame segments of about one second. In this step, each $\mathrm{BBox_{kp}}$ is matched with the $\mathrm{BBox_{MOT}}$ that has the highest IoU in the same frame. When multiple $\mathrm{BBox_{kp}}$ are associated with a single $\mathrm{BBox_{MOT}}$, the one with the highest average keypoint confidence is selected, enabling a one-to-one mapping of foot positions and IDs.

Subsequently, for each short frame segment of about one second, we group the data by ID, where each ID corresponds to an individual tracked by MOT. Within each segment, only those data satisfying both of the following thresholds are retained: the number of detection frames and the number of frames in which the most frequent color appears. In other words, we regard data as "reliable"

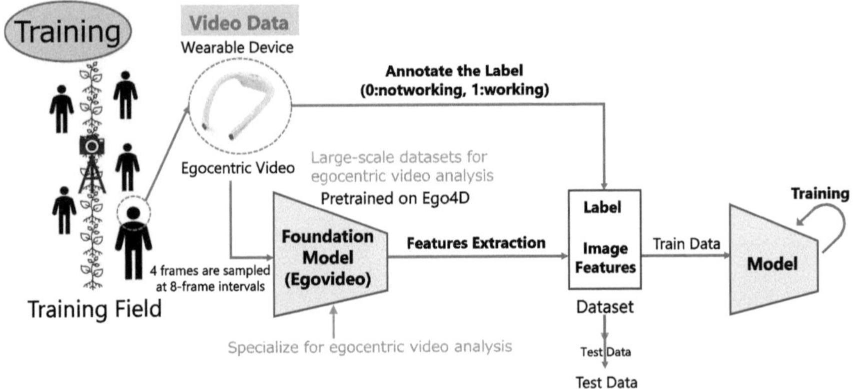

Fig. 3. Overview of the work activity recognition method.

when a person is detected in most of the frames within a segment and the detected color remains largely consistent across those detections.

Finally, the foot coordinates obtained from multiple perspectives are transformed into a bird's eye view. Frames with outliers are removed based on coordinate distance thresholds between views. The remaining coordinates are averaged to estimate each learner's foot position at each time point. When any frames are missing, linear interpolation is applied by using the estimated coordinates immediately before and after in the time series.

3.2 Work Activity Recognition Method

Figure 3 provides an overview of our work activity recognition method. We construct a binary classifier to recognize whether a learner is "0: not working" or "1: working" from video input, enabling time-series quantification of work activity. We use EgoVideo [13], a foundation model pretrained on the large-scale dataset Ego4D [6]. Four frames are sampled every 8 frames from the 30 fps video, and one image feature vector is extracted every 32 frames.

Using the extracted features, we implement a binary classifier with a multi-layer perceptron that classifies each 32-frame video segment as either "0: not working" or "1: working". Specifically, the 512-dimensional feature vector is passed through hidden layers to an output layer. A sigmoid output indicates the probability of working, with a threshold of 0.5 for classification. Cross-entropy is used as the loss function. To create training data, the collected video is annotated throughout the entire video, dividing it into segments labeled as either "0: not working" or "1: working".

4 Experiments

We recorded three agricultural training sessions involving 10–11 third-year students and two teachers. Recordings followed the normal class setup to unobtru-

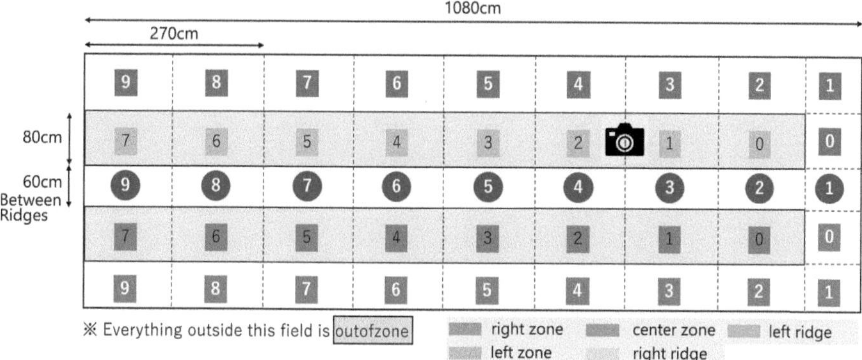

Fig. 4. Simplified diagram of the training field divided into defined zones. From the top, the rows correspond to right zone, right ridge, center zone, left ridge, and left zone.

sively capture natural student behavior. The training field had two 1080×80 cm ridges, spaced 60 cm apart and divided into eight zones with different crops as shown in Fig. 4. One or two students were assigned per zone and worked individually. The teachers observed the students' activities and provided guidance or assistance as needed. Each student wore a fixed bib color. A 360° camera was used to record the entire duration of each session from start to finish. Prior to data collection, informed consent was obtained from all participating students and the teachers. Additionally, two students wore a neck-worn wearable camera each day: (e.g., Yellow Green & Light Blue on Session 1; Red & Light Blue on Session 2; Gold & Blue on Session 3). In Session 1, the wearable camera malfunctioned and recorded only the first 27 minutes of the class. In Session 2, the class included a break, so the recording was split into a first half and a second half.

For the position estimation method, we generated perspective-view videos with a fixed FOV of 140, tilt angle of −30°, and an output resolution of 2160×3840. We used six viewpoints with pan angles of 0°, 50°, 130°, 180°, 210°, and 310°. To annotate work activity, we consulted with agricultural high school teachers to align on the criteria for determining whether a student was working, especially in cases where this distinction was ambiguous.

4.1 Evaluation of Position Estimation

In this study, we evaluated the reliability of our position estimation method as a zone-level classification problem. In the context of agricultural training, it is sufficient to roughly understand where on a ridge a student is working, and centimeter-level precision is not required. Therefore, we assessed whether the estimated foot position fell within the correct predefined zone.

The evaluation focused on the students who wore the wearable cameras. The field was divided into several zones. Each ridge (270×80 cm) and inter-ridge

Table 1. Accuracy of position estimation at different region expanded distances. Values in parentheses are calculated using only "reliable" frames before interpolation.

		Expanded Distance				
Session	**Student**	**0px**	**5px**	**10px**	**Between Ridges(60cm)**	**Interpolated**
1	Light Blue	**0.788**(**0.802**)	0.845(0.862)	0.870(0.882)	0.983(0.995)	24.0%
1	Yellow Green	**0.867**(**0.861**)	0.950(0.953)	0.967(0.970)	0.992(0.996)	29.3%
2 (1st Half)	Light Blue	0.512(0.601)	0.552(0.649)	0.583(0.679)	**0.823**(**0.955**)	41.6%
2 (1st Half)	Red	**0.742**(**0.753**)	0.817(0.825)	0.864(0.872)	0.980(0.987)	10.6%
2 (2nd Half)	Light Blue	0.652(**0.807**)	**0.728**(0.915)	0.800(0.942)	0.883(0.970)	**73.2%**
2 (2nd Half)	Red	0.546(0.583)	0.650(0.697)	**0.764**(**0.821**)	0.883(0.924)	41.4%
3	Gold	0.382(0.341)	0.501(0.514)	0.586(0.631)	0.698(**0.783**)	**64.6%**
3	Blue	0.580(0.610)	0.689(**0.719**)	**0.781**(0.801)	0.962(0.964)	54.3%
Average		0.634(0.670)	0.717(0.767)	0.777(0.825)	0.900(0.947)	42.4%

space (270×60 cm) was further split in half as shown in Fig. 4. Ground truth was created by annotating each student's location over time using the 360-degree videos. To ensure the evaluation reflected actual lesson time, we limited the evaluation period to the segment between the first and last occurrence of a label other than "outofzone" in the time series.

We formulated a classification problem by checking whether the foot coordinates estimated at each frame fell within the ground truth zone. Specifically, we calculated the accuracy as the ratio of the number of frames where the estimated foot coordinates matched the ground truth zone to the total number of frames in the evaluation period. To analyze the impact of linear interpolation, we also computed the accuracy using only "reliable" frames.

However, zone-level evaluation may be sensitive to small deviations near the boundaries of adjacent zones. For instance, even a slight shift in the estimated coordinates could cause a point near the boundary to be classified as incorrect, despite being practically acceptable to grasp approximate students' position. To account for this boundary ambiguity, zones were extended to overlap with adjacent zones. We examined how accuracy changed with varying expansion widths. Each edge of the zones was extended in pixel units, and at the vertices, circular arcs were drawn with the extension length as the radius, connecting adjacent edges. Note that the bird eye view was converted from 360° view, pixel-to-ground distance increases with distance from the camera. Focusing on zones closer to the camera as shown in Fig. 4, we expanded the zones until the extended width approximately matched the distance between ridges, which is 60 cm. Note that in Session 1, the distance between ridges was 44 pixels, so 1 pixel corresponded to approximately 1.36 cm. Similarly, the values calculated for Session 2 and Session 3 were approximately 0.6 cm and 0.58 cm. These differences arose from variations in the camera height above the ground in each session.

As shown in Table 1, three samples–Light Blue (Session 1), Yellow Green (Session 1), and Red (1st half, Session 2)–achieved over 70% accuracy even without zone expansion. These three also exceeded 70% accuracy when using only reliable frames, suggesting that their estimations were more stable compared to others. Their stability corresponds to a low interpolation rate (under 30%), indicating a high proportion of reliable frames.

For Light Blue (2nd half, Session 2), the overall accuracy was 0.652, but achieved 0.807 when using only reliable frames. The 15.5% accuracy drop, likely due to a high interpolation rate 73.2%, suggests the need for more advanced interpolation methods.

The samples Light Blue (1st half, Session 2), Red (2nd half, Session 2), and Blue (Session 3) initially had 50–60% accuracy, but Red and Blue improved to nearly 80% with 10-pixel zone expansion. These improvements are likely due to their prolonged presence in zones near the camera. In contrast, Light Blue remained for about 3 minutes in a distant zone (left zone 7) that was rarely estimated correctly, with minimal time spent in neighboring zones, limiting the benefit of expansion.

In our method, for each individual, we computed the number of pixels within their bounding box that matched the defined color range, and associated the most frequent color with their foot coordinates. When multiple individuals shared the same most frequent color, the person with the higher pixel count was given priority, which gave an advantage to students closer to the camera. Indeed, when the Light Blue student was in left zone 7, their color was frequently misidentified as belonging to a foreground student or the background.

For the sample Gold (Session 3), the classification accuracy without zone expansion fell below 40%. One major factor was that 64.6% of the frames were interpolated. In addition, the gold bib was visually similar to the color of the soil in the field, leading to frequent misidentification–individuals not wearing the gold bib were often mistakenly recognized as Gold.

In conclusion, our position estimation method achieved an average accuracy of over 70% with a 5 pixel zone expansion. Although some samples showed performance degradation due to color-based person re-identification and simple interpolation, this result indicates that the method provides sufficient accuracy for estimating students' positions. While improvements of person re-identification may enhance performance, using color-coded bibs remains effective, especially in Japanese agricultural high schools where students wear similar uniforms.

4.2 Evaluation of Work Activity Recognition

The collected data spanned 17,014 s (4h 44 m 34 s) with 55.67% labeled as "0: not working" and 44.33% as "1: working". Auxiliary labels included 1.73% "ambiguous", 8.64% "hidden", and 4.67% "other-people-working".

First, five-fold cross-validation was performed using data from all six learners. The maximum number of training iterations was set to 2000. Samples were randomly shuffled to mitigate ordering bias, and label distributions were preserved in each fold. To determine the optimal hyperparameters, we conducted a grid search using accuracy as the evaluation metric. We searched over hidden layer sizes (50, 100, (50, 50), (100, 50)), activation functions (ReLU, Tanh, Logistic), and L2 regularization strengths (0.0001, 0.001, 0.01).

Table 2. Evaluation metrics for work activity recognition on each dataset.

Session	Student	Accuracy	Precision	Recall	F1-Score
1	Light Blue	0.756	0.637	0.785	0.697
1	Yellow Green	0.744	0.842	0.787	0.814
2	Light Blue	0.860	0.722	0.612	0.662
2	Red	0.824	0.784	0.891	0.834
3	Gold	0.767	0.888	0.563	0.689
3	Blue	0.706	0.930	0.514	0.662
Average		0.776	0.801	0.692	0.726

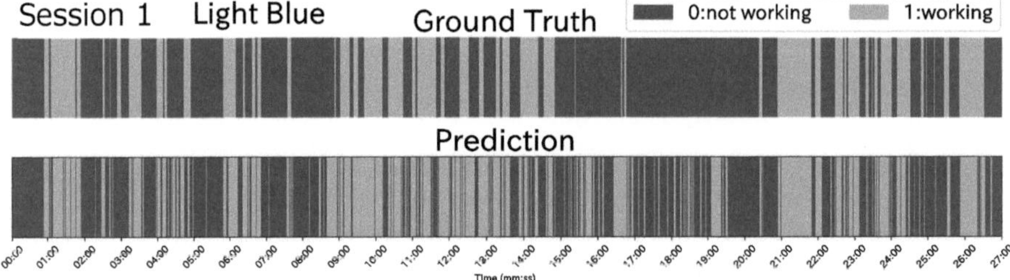

Fig. 5. Time-series comparison of predicted and actual work activity labels (Light Blue on Session 1). (Color figure online)

As a result of this grid search, the best-performing model used a hidden layer size of 50, ReLU as the activation function, and an L2 regularization coefficient of 0.01. In the five-fold cross-validation using all data, the classification model achieved an accuracy of 0.886 ± 0.005, precision of 0.898 ± 0.005, recall of 0.876 ± 0.012, and F1-score of 0.897 ± 0.012. These consistently high scores indicate the method's effectiveness for work activity classification.

Next, we evaluated the model using a leave-one-day-out approach: training on data from two of the three days and testing on the remaining day, rotating through all combinations. This setup simulated real-world deployment by separating training and testing data by date, and allowed us to assess generalizability to variations in task content and field conditions. The experimental settings, including hyperparameters, were kept consistent with the full-data evaluation.

As shown in Table 2, the performance metrics for each data segment were generally lower than those obtained when using all the data. Although there were differences among the datasets, all achieved accuracy above 0.70 and the average F1-score exceeded 0.70. Focusing on precision, only the data for Light Blue on Session 1 fell below 0.70. Therefore, we visualized the predicted labels and ground truth over time for further analysis as shown in Fig. 5. Between 17:00 and 19:30, the model frequently predicted "1: working" when the ground truth was "0: not working". Reviewing the original video revealed that the student

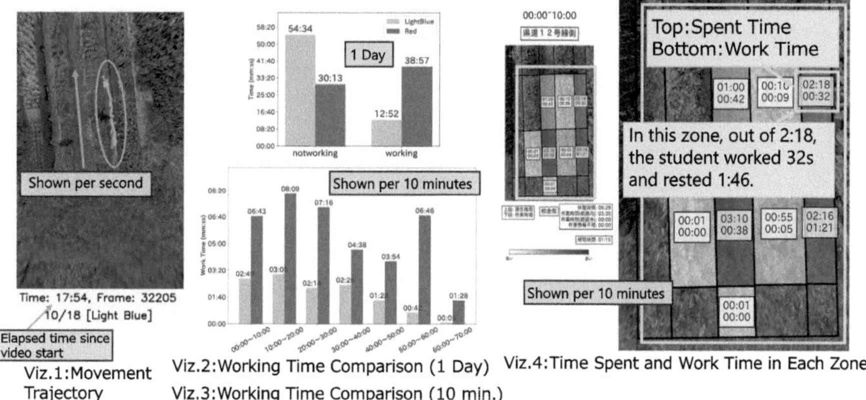

Fig. 6. Examples of visualizations shown to teachers during interviews.

was using a tool to touch the soil, but was merely digging meaningless holes. The model likely misclassified these actions as "1: working" because it placed emphasis on hand movements or the use of tools. As humans easily identified these as non-working, improving the recognition of such ambiguous cases remains a challenge.

The comparison between predicted and ground truth proportions showed that for four samples from Session 1 and 2, the difference in the proportion of "working" labels remained within 3–10%, indicating that the estimated work duration was reasonably accurate on a daily basis. In contrast, the two samples from Session 3 underestimated the actual work duration by more than 15%. These samples also showed high precision but low recall, likely due to the imbalance in the training data, where "not working" labels were predominant. To investigate the cause of the underestimation, we analyzed the videos in detail. We found that approximately 15% of the Gold sample segments involved cases where the hands were not visible or were occluded by clothing, and about 6% of the Blue sample segments involved scenes in which other people's work appeared. These factors likely contributed to misclassification. Improving robustness to such ambiguous conditions remains a challenge.

4.3 Visualizations and Interviews with Teachers

Figure 6 shows four prototypes of visualizations that were generated based on the estimated "time", "position", and "work activity", varying the type and levels of granularity of information used as shown in Table 3. For example, Viz.1 represents point-level position data at one-second intervals, but it does not include work activity data. Viz.2 and Viz.3 both display the work duration of two individuals who worked on the same day. Viz.2 shows the total work duration throughout the session, whereas Viz.3 breaks it down into 10-minute intervals. Viz.4

Table 3. Comparison of data granularity in the visualizations and average scores from the two teachers on the 14 questionnaire items.

Viz.	Data Granularity			Average Score
	When	Where	Work Duration	
1	Fine(1-sec intervals)	Fine(Point-level)	N/A	3.89
2	N/A	N/A	Coarse(Daily total)	4.68
3	Medium(10-min intervals)	N/A	Medium(10-min intervals)	4.43
4	Medium(10-min intervals)	Medium(Zone-level)	Medium(10-min intervals)	4.25

Table 4. Average scores of each visualization for different evaluation factors (n=2).

Viz.	Visual Attraction	Understanding	Perceived Usefulness	Behavioral Changes
	Q1-Q4	Q5-Q8	Q9-Q11	Q12-Q14
1	4.00	3.88	3.17	4.50
2	4.50	4.63	4.67	5.00
3	4.25	4.38	4.17	5.00
4	3.38	4.63	4.17	5.00

integrates all three types of information by displaying both the time spent and the work duration for each predefined field region at 10-minute intervals.

We conducted a 14-item questionnaire using a 5-point Likert scale for each visualization, where 1 represents strongly disagree and 5 represents strongly agree. The questionnaire was designed to evaluate visual attraction, understanding, perceived usefulness, and behavioral changes, based on the evaluation factors originally proposed for dashboard assessment [12].

The questionnaire was intended both to help participants compare the four visualizations and to lead naturally into the interviews. We then conducted semi-structured interviews with two agricultural high school teachers involved in the training. The aim was to evaluate the consistency between the visualizations and their intuitive observations, and to determine the types and granularity of information required to effectively understand student activity during training.

In the interviews, follow-up questions were flexibly added based on responses to the prepared questions, aiming to gather specific reasons for educational usefulness and suggestions for improvement. As shown in Table 3, Viz.2 received the highest score. This suggests that "work activity" is a highly useful piece of information. Furthermore, as shown in the Understanding column of Table 4, Viz.4 received the same high score of 4.63 as Viz.2, indicating that combining "time", "position", and "work activity" in a visualization is educationally beneficial.

The interviews revealed that teacher perceptions closely matched the content of Viz.2 and Viz.4. They also found it useful to represent position as discrete zones, as done in Viz.4. On the other hand, the lower accuracy of Viz.1 was noted, and high-resolution time-position data was considered unnecessary for supporting practical training. Teachers also expressed that the types of information they wanted varied depending on the lesson content. Rather than arbitrarily dividing time into 10-minute blocks as in Viz.3 and Viz.4, they preferred time segmentation aligned with the actual instructional phases. Teachers also mentioned that, rather than simply knowing the duration of work, information about the specific content of farm work, the progress of the task, the procedures followed, and the learner's intention behind the action would be more helpful for instructional support in agricultural training.

Regarding the potential use of these visualizations, teachers mentioned they would be useful for reflecting before and after lessons and for sharing information with other teachers who did not attend the training. Despite remaining issues in accuracy, the visualizations were also seen as having potential to support grading. Finally, it was suggested that visualizations independent of field size or the number of participating students would be valuable in future applications.

5 Limitations and Future Work

5.1 Technical Limitations and Future Directions

The position estimation relied on color-based person re-identification using bibs. While practical and easy to implement, this approach was prone to misidentification and was sensitive to environmental factors such as changes in lighting conditions, similarity of bib colors with soil or background elements, similarity with the clothing colors of nearby learners, occlusions when learners overlapped, and the presence of dirt or stains. In this study, multi-object tracking (MOT) was incorporated in order to utilize spatial and temporal information, mainly to retain only those data segments in which color-based person re-identification was performed stably. However, MOT was used merely as a post-processing step after color-based re-identification, and relying solely on bib color for re-identification remained prone to errors and instability. Missing frames that resulted from the removal of unstable segments by MOT were addressed using linear interpolation, but excessive use often reduced accuracy.

Moreover, relying solely on foot keypoints for position estimation raises concerns about reduced accuracy under occlusion or on uneven terrain. Although the experimental environment featured relatively few occlusions and level ground, and the use of a 360° camera helped minimize blind spots, such factors cannot be completely avoided, indicating that the robustness of this approach is limited.

While computational cost and the practical constraints of agricultural training environments, including limitations in available equipment and infrastructure, must be taken into account, several directions are promising for improving position estimation. Incorporating deep learning-based re-identification can leverage features beyond color, providing more robust identification under varying environmental conditions. In addition, utilizing multiple keypoints or integrating supplementary sensor information such as GPS would help compensate for occlusion and further enhance robustness.

For work activity recognition, ambiguous movements such as fidgeting or idle tool handling reduced classification performance. Occluded hands and the presence of others in the field of view also lowered recall. While these issues impacted performance, the current binary classification achieved accuracy sufficient for practical use. However, more sophisticated approaches will be necessary for future work involving detailed classification of task content. For example, augmenting training data with background classes such as ambiguous movements or the presence of other learners could improve accuracy. In addition, focusing on hand movements and handobject interactions in egocentric views may allow ambiguous movements to be explicitly filtered out. Furthermore, since the current method classifies every 32 frames independently, incorporating temporal information across frames would likely improve robustness against ambiguous movements.

In addition, as the method was tested on a relatively small dataset with a limited number of learners in a fixed-size field, the robustness of the current approach to larger-scale situations remains unclear. When applied to broader fields with more participants or under varying environmental conditions, such as variations in weather and lighting, further evaluation experiments will be required to assess whether the proposed method remains effective.

5.2 Educational and Practical Limitations and Future Directions

Interviews with teachers revealed two key limitations. First, the use of 10-minute time-based visualizations did not align with the actual instructional phases, and teachers reported that such arbitrary segmentation made it unclear how the information could be used for reflective practice. Second, knowing only the total duration of work was insufficient to capture learners' activities. Agricultural training involves various tasks, each with distinct procedures and progress, which highlights the need for visualizing task sequences and progress rather than only total work time. Furthermore, teachers pointed out that understanding how learners think and make decisions during tasks is also important for educational purposes. Therefore, effective teaching requires not only tracking procedures and progress but also grasping the intent behind each action.

Addressing these limitations will require moving beyond binary classification toward more detailed recognition of work activities. For example, multi-class classification could be used to identify specific task types (e.g., weeding and watering), hierarchical models could capture task procedures and progress, and tool detection could provide additional cues for activity recognition. Furthermore, incorporating multimodal data such as audio or sensor information may enable the estimation of learners' intentions and reasoning, which are difficult to infer from video alone. Such semantic understanding can better support instruction and feedback.

Moreover, agricultural training in real-world settings varies greatly in terms of field layouts, crop types, number of participants, weather, and lighting conditions. Future work should therefore include evaluations in such diverse environments and larger-scale training sessions to validate the system's practical applicability in authentic educational contexts.

6 Conclusion

In this study, we developed a system for estimating learners' "time", "position", and "work activity" during agricultural training using computer vision on 360° and egocentric video. The position estimation achieved an average accuracy over 70% as shown in the 5px column of Table 1. The work activity recognition reached over 70% accuracy across all datasets as shown in Table 2. Interviews with agricultural high school teachers confirmed that the visualizations aligned with their observations and that combining time, position, and work activity was useful for objectively assessing learners' farm work. These results suggest that our approach can support reflection and instructional decisions in agricultural training. For future work, we aim to improve estimation accuracy, recognize specific types of farm tasks, and develop visualizations that incorporate instructional content and context.

Acknowledgments. This work was supported by JST CREST Grant Number JPMJCR22D1, JSPS KAKENHI Grant Number JP22H00551, and MEXT "Innovation Platform for Society 5.0" Program Grant Number JPMXP0518071489, Japan. We also thank Itoshima Agricultural High School in Fukuoka for their cooperation in the experiments.

Competing Interests. The authors have no competing interests to declare that are relevant to the content of this article.

References

1. Blikstein, P.: Multimodal learning analytics. In: Suthers, D., Verbert, K. (eds.) Proceedings of the Third International Conference on Learning Analytics and Knowledge, pp. 102–106. ACM (2013)
2. Cao, Z., Hidalgo Martinez, G., Simon, T., Wei, S., Sheikh, Y.A.: Openpose: realtime multi-person 2D pose estimation using part affinity fields. IEEE Trans. Pattern Anal. Mach. Intell. **43**(1), 172–186 (2019). https://doi.org/10.1109/tpami.2019.2929257
3. Echeverria, V., et al.: Teamslides: a multimodal teamwork analytics dashboard for teacher-guided reflection in a physical learning space. In: Proceedings of the 14th Learning Analytics and Knowledge Conference, pp. 112–122. ACM (2024)
4. Fukatsu, T., Nanseki, T.: Farm operation monitoring system with wearable sensor devices including RFID. In: Deploying RFID-Challenges, Solutions, and Open Issues, pp. 141–158 (2011). https://doi.org/10.5772/17390
5. Gao, R., Qi, J., Wang, L.: Multiple object tracking as ID prediction. In: Proceedings of the Computer Vision and Pattern Recognition Conference (CVPR), pp. 27883–27893 (2025)
6. Grauman, K., et al.: Ego4D: around the world in 3,000 hours of egocentric video. In: Proceedings of the IEEE/CVF Conference on Computer Vision and Pattern Recognition, pp. 18995–19012. IEEE (2022). https://doi.org/10.1109/cvpr52688.2022.01842
7. Hashimoto, Y., et al.: Measurement and visualization of farm work information, pp. 1–7 (2016)

8. Li, X., Yan, L., Zhao, L., Martinez-Maldonado, R., Gasevic, D.: CVPE: a computer vision approach for scalable and privacy-preserving socio-spatial, multimodal learning analytics. In: LAK23: 13th International Learning Analytics and Knowledge Conference, pp. 175–185. ACM (2023)
9. Ministry of Education, Culture, Sports, Science and Technology in Japan: Course of study for upper secondary school: agriculture [in Japanese] (2018). https://www.mext.go.jp/content/20230120-mxt_kyoiku02-100002604_03.pdf
10. Ministry of Education, Culture, Sports, Science and Technology in Japan: Manual for the 2018 course of study in upper secondary schools: agriculture [in Japanese] (2018). https://www.mext.go.jp/content/1407073_13_1_1_2.pdf
11. Ochoa, X., Lang, C., Siemens, G., Wise, A., Gasevic, D., Merceron, A.: Multimodal learning analytics-rationale, process, examples, and direction. In: The Handbook of Learning Analytics, pp. 54–65 (2022). https://doi.org/10.18608/hla22.006
12. Park, Y., Jo, I.-H.: Factors that affect the success of learning analytics dashboards. Educ. Tech. Res. Dev. **67**, 1–25 (2019). https://doi.org/10.1007/s11423-019-09693-0
13. Pei, B., et al.: EgoVideo: exploring egocentric foundation model and downstream adaptation. arXiv preprint arXiv:2406.18070 (2024)
14. Saquib, N., Bose, A., George, D., Kamvar, S.: Sensei: sensing educational interaction. In: Proceedings of the ACM on Interactive, Mobile, Wearable and Ubiquitous Technologies, vol. 1, no. 4, pp. 1–27 (2018)
15. Somers, V., Alahi, A., Vleeschouwer, C.D.: Keypoint promptable re-identification. In: Leonardis, A., Ricci, E., Roth, S., Russakovsky, O., Sattler, T., Varol, G. (eds.) European Conference on Computer Vision, vol. 15137, pp. 216–233. Springer, Springer Science+Business Media (2024). https://doi.org/10.1007/978-3-031-72986-7_13
16. Vasconez, J.P., Admoni, H., Cheein, F.A.: A methodology for semantic action recognition based on pose and human-object interaction in avocado harvesting processes. Comput. Electron. Agricult. **184**, 106057 (2021). https://doi.org/10.1016/j.compag.2021.106057
17. Wei, C., Hu, X., Ye, H., Li, X.: Recognition of plantation farming behavior based on deep learning. In: Proceeding of the 2024 5th International Conference on Computer Science and Management Technology, pp. 257–264. ACM (2024)
18. Xu, Y., Zhang, J., Zhang, Q., Tao, D.: ViTPose: simple vision transformer baselines for human pose estimation. Adv. Neural Inf. Process. Syst. **35**, 38571–38584 (2022). https://doi.org/10.48550/arxiv.2204.12484

Zero-Shot Estimation of Compound Emotional Expressions from Facial Images Using Only Basic Emotional Expression Features

Riku Yamamoto[1](✉) and Noriko Takemura[2]

[1] Kyushu Institute of Technology, 680-4 Kawazu, Iizuka 820-8502, Japan
yamamoto.riku878@mail.kyutech.jp
[2] Kyushu Institute of Technology, 680-4 Kawazu, Iizuka 820-8502, Japan
takemura@ai.kyutech.ac.jp

Abstract. Facial Expression Recognition (FER) technology can be applied to various systems targeting humans. However, conventional research is biased toward basic emotional expressions such as "Happiness" and "sadness," which limits its application in real environments where there are many ambiguous and complex emotional expression. In particular, data collection and annotation are difficult, making database construction a bottleneck and a barrier to achieving highly accurate recognition. Based on the theory that complex emotional expressions are formed by combining basic emotional expressions, we propose a zero-shot method for estimating complex emotional expressions from basic emotional expression features. First, a continuous feature space reflecting the relationships among emotions is learned using facial images corresponding to six basic emotional expressions. Next, the middle point of the basic emotional expression is defined as the representative vector of the complex emotional expression in the space, and estimation is performed based on the similarity with the input image. This makes it possible to construct that feature space without using any data on complex emotional expressions, thereby overcoming the problem of insufficient data. The method outperforms supervised methods despite the fact that it does not use any supervised data on complex emotional expressions. Furthermore, despite using only facial expression data, the accuracy of the method is comparable to that of conventional multimodal methods.

Keywords: Facial Expression Recognition · Complex Emotional Expression · Zero-Shot Learning · Basic Emotional Expression · CutMix

1 Introduction

Facial expressions are an important means of conveying human emotions, and it is said that approximately 55% of emotional communication takes place through

C. Wallraven et al. (Eds.): ACPR 2025, LNCS 16174, pp. 175–189, 2026.
https://doi.org/10.1007/978-981-95-4395-3_13

facial expressions [2]. Since they can be captured using ordinary cameras, the installation cost is relatively low. For this reason, facial expression recognition (FER) plays a crucial role in building flexible systems that can respond to the emotions and needs of individuals. Consequently, FER has been applied in various fields such as education [15,18], medicine [21], and security [13,17]. Many previous studies have focused on facial expressions related to the Ekman's basic emotions: surprise, fear, disgust, happiness, and anger [7]. These facial expressions are simple and well-defined, making them relatively easy to analyze; however, human emotional expressions are not limited to basic emotions and often involve more subtle and complex feelings. Therefore, in order to apply emotion recognition to real-world systems, it is important to estimate such complex expressions.

A major challenge in building models for estimating complex expressions is the creation of appropriate datasets. While data for facial expressions related to basic emotions can be intentionally produced through acted expressions, complex expressions naturally emerge in daily life, making them difficult to generate artificially. Moreover, complex expressions are often ambiguous and subject to varying interpretations among individuals, making annotation difficult [1]. In addition, a sufficient amount of data is required for each of the many diverse emotional categories. These challenges in dataset construction have become a major bottleneck in the recognition of complex expressions. To address this issue, few-shot and zero-shot learning methods have been proposed, enabling expression recognition from only a small amount of data. However, these approaches often require multimodal information, such as Action Units (AUs) [7], audio, and scene context, rather than relying solely on facial images. As a result, the problem of high annotation cost still remains.

On the other hand Du et al. deficed 21 type of compound facial expressions composed of combinations of basic emotions, and showed that each of them reflected the AU (Action Unit) pattern of basic emotion they were composed of [5,6]. AU refers to the movements of facial muscles involved in generating expressions. For example, AUs related to surprise include movements such as "raising the eyebrows significantly" and "widening the eyes." Emotions are expressed through combinations of such AUs. Basic emotions are generally emotion categories that are widely shared and easily understood by people. By using them as a foundation to explain more complex expressions, interpretability can be significantly improved, allowing for a more detailed representation of the subtle nuances in human emotional experiences.

In this study, we propose a zero-shot recognition method for compound expressions using only facial expression features related to basic emotions (basic expressions). Specifically, we first use a basic expression dataset to train a feature extractor for basic expressions, and representative vectors that express the center of each basic expression. By introducing metric learning at this time, we can obtain separated features for each expression. Furthermore, in metric learning, we use cosine similarity, i.e., angle-base distance, instead of Euclidean distance. This allows us to ignore the magnitude of feature vectors and become robust to noise information such as occlusion and gender. Moreover, in order to make the distribution of features relevant to compound expression fall between the representative vectors of the basic expressions that compose them, we train so that the features extracted from the pseudo compound expression images, which are constructed by CutMix of basic expression images, approach the vector linearly combined at the same ratio of the corresponding basic expression representative vectors. By designing the feature space so that it can continuously transition between two basic expressions, it becomes possible to represent the features of compound expressions within the same feature space. When recognizing compound expressions, a representative vector for each compound expression is calculated as a linear combination of the representative vectors of its constituent basic expressions. Then, the recognized expression is determined as the one whose representative vector has the highest cosine similarity with the feature vector related to basic expressions, extracted by the feature extractor described above.

The contributions of this study are as follows.

Compound Expression Recognition Using Basic Expression In compound expression datasets, it is often difficult to secure a sufficient number of samples for each expression, and such data imbalance may degrade recognition accuracy. Since the proposed method uses only basic expression data, it avoids this problem.

Recognition of a Wide Variety of Facial Expressions In the proposed method, it is not necessary to predefine the set of compound expressions to be estimated–they can be flexibly specified on the fly. Moreover, since even undefined expressions can be quantitatively represented as weighted combinations of basic expressions, this approach is expected to contribute to advances in the understanding of complex expressions in the field of psychology.

Improved Interpretability of Recognition Results In the proposed method, recognition results are expressed as combinations of basic expressions, making them easier to interpret. Furthermore, by analyzing the positional relationships of basic expressions within the feature space, it is also possible to assess the reliability of the expression results.

No Need for Auxiliary Labels Many recent studies rely on auxiliary labels such as AUs, audio signals, or scene captions. However, these labels not only require significant effort to obtain, but also carry the risk of being inaccurately annotated. In contrast, the proposed method uses only facial image data, eliminating the need for such auxiliary labels.

2 Related Work

This section describes related work on basic expression recognition and compound expression recognition.

2.1 Basic Expression Recognition from Facial Images

Ekman's basic emotions (surprise, fear, disgust, happiness, sadness, and anger) are considered fundamental components of human emotional expression and the facial expressions expressed from these emotions are believed to be universally shared across different cultures and societies [7]. Recognizing these facial expressions plays an essential role in understanding human affect. Thus, research on basic emotional facial expression (basic expression) recognition has been actively conducted for many years. Numerous studies have proposed methods based on deep learning, particularly using Convolutional Neural Networks (CNNs) and Vision Transformers (ViTs) [4], which have significantly improved recognition accuracy.

The DDAMFN (Dual-Direction Attention Mixed Feature Network) [23] proposed by Zhuan et al. captures feature dependencies by extracting features using convolutional kernels of different sizes and generating feature maps through a dual-direction attention mechanism. This architecture allows the model to effectively learn both local and global relationships within facial expressions, leading to improved accuracy in basic emotion recognition. POSTER++ [16] proposed by Mao et al. enhances expression features by capturing the interactions between facial landmarks and image features through a cross-attention mechanism. This approach allows the model to effectively integrate structural facial information with visual features, improving emotion recognition performance. By doing so, it enables a comprehensive understanding of facial expressions. These studies improve the accuracy of basic expression recognition by leveraging advanced attention mechanisms to identify which regions of the face are important and how these regions interact with one another. This approach is crucial for understanding facial expressions and is also considered effective for capturing more complex expressions.

2.2 Compound Expression Recognition

To address the issue of data scarcity in complex expression recognition, recent studies have proposed learning approaches such as few-shot and zero-shot learning. These methods aim to estimate facial expressions with only a small amount of labeled data or even without any labeled samples for the target emotion category, thereby alleviating the need for large, well-balanced datasets. C-EXPR-NET [10] adopts a multi-task learning approach that simultaneously performs Action Unit (AU) detection alongside complex expression recognition. By leveraging the interactions between these tasks, the model can efficiently learn from a small amount of complex facial expression data. This multi-task setting enables the network to extract more informative and generalizable features, improving performance under data-scarce conditions. EmoClip [8] is a Vision-Language Model (VLM) that learns expression features by combining videos with their caption texts, and uses these features to perform zero-shot complex expression recognition. While such models can achieve higher performance in complex expression estimation compared to conventional classification tasks, they rely on

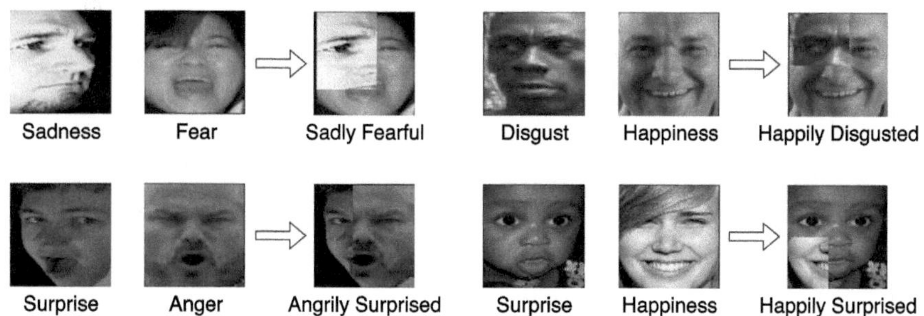

Fig. 1. Example of a CutMix Image. A new image is created by replacing a part of a basic expression image with a region from another image.

multimodal information such as Action Units (AUs) and scene captions. These modalities, however, require high annotation costs, posing a significant challenge for practical deployment.

2.3 CutMix

CutMix method [22] is a data augmentation technique that combines two images by replacing a rectangular region of one image with a corresponding region from another. Specifically, the method prepares image A and image B along with their corresponding labelsy_a and y_b. The area ratio λ of the rectangle is determined based on a Beta distribution, and the center of the rectangular region is randomly selected. A square region centered on the selected point, with an area equal to $1 - \lambda$ times the total image area, is designated as the replacement region, and this region is extracted from image B. Finally, the extracted region is pasted onto the corresponding area of image A. The new label is then computed using the following formula:

$$y_c = \lambda y_A + (1 - \lambda) y_B$$

An example of an image generated using this method is shown in Fig. 1. In this study, we propose a different way of using the CutMix.

3 Proposed Method

In this study, we propose a novel method for recognizing compound expressions using only basic expression data. First, the model is trained on six classes of basic expressions to obtain a feature extractor that can extract the features related to basic facial expressions, as well as to obtain representative vectors for each basic expression in the feature space. Here, a representative vector refers to the centroid of each emotion class in the feature space. To enable the compound expression within the same feature space, the model is also trained using synthetic images generated by CutMix, allowing it to learn intermediate expression states. Next, representative vectors for compound expressions are calculated as linear combinations of the trained basic expression vectors. Compound expression recognition is then performed by computing the similarity between the feature vector of an input facial image–extracted by the trained feature extractor–and the representative vectors of compound expressions. In this method, only the feature training for basic expressions is performed, and no additional training is conducted for compound expressions. As a result, labeled data for compound emotions is not required, which significantly reduces the cost of dataset collection. The following sections provide a detailed explanation of each step in the proposed approach.

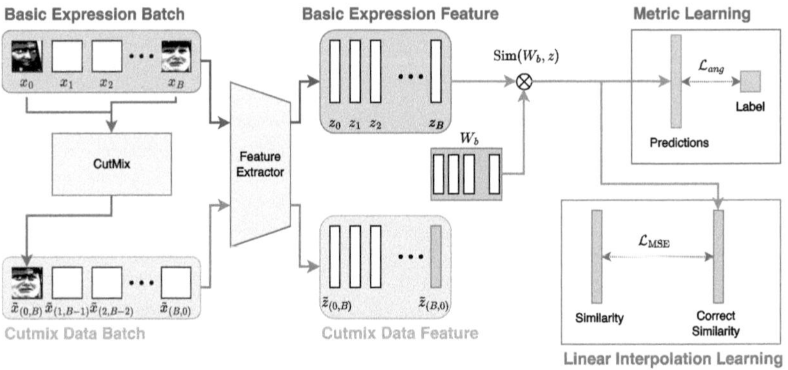

Fig. 2. Overview of the Basic Expression Feature Learning Method. The proposed method learns basic expression features using two loss functions. (a) Metric Learning: Basic expression data is input, and the model is trained so that the resulting feature vectors are distributed near the corresponding representative vectors of the basic expressions. (b) Linear Interpolation Learning: Pseudo-intermediate expression images are generated using CutMix applied to basic expression data, and the model is trained so that the feature vectors of these images are distributed between the representative vectors of the basic expressions involved. Through these two learning processes, the feature extractor and the representative vectors of the basic expressions are jointly learned.

3.1 Learning Basic Expression Features

An overview of this step is shown in Fig. 2. First, the model acquires knowledge of basic expressions using basic expression data. In this process, our method performs two types of learning simultaneously. Each of these is described in detail below.

Angle-Based Metric Learning. Through metric learning focused on basic expressions, the model learns both a feature extractor and representative vectors corresponding to each basic expression. Unlike standard classification tasks, this approach explicitly learns a vector that represents the center of each expression class in the feature space. These representative vectors are later used to define the representative vectors for compound expressions during the recognition phase.

Cosine similarity is used as the distance measure, which allows the model to ignore the magnitude of the feature vectors. As a result, it helps eliminate noise specific to facial images, such as variations in head orientation, lighting conditions, and individual differences [3,14,19].

The specific training procedure is as follows. First, a basic expression image $x \in \mathbb{R}^{C\times H\times W}$ is input into the feature extractor, and a feature vector $z \in \mathbb{R}^{N_z}$ is obtained.

$$z = FE(x)$$

Here, $FE(\cdot)$ denotes the feature extractor, C is the number of channels in the input image, H and W are the height and width, respectively, and N_z is the dimensionality of the feature vector. The feature extractor FE contains learnable parameters. After obtaining the feature vector z, the angle-based loss function $\mathcal{L}_{\text{ang}}$ is computed using z and the basic expression representative vector matrix $W_b = [w_{b0}, w_{b1}, \cdots w_{bN_b}] \in \mathbb{R}^{N_z\times N_b}$.

$$\mathcal{L}_{\text{ang}} = -\frac{1}{B}\sum_{i=0}^{B}\log\frac{e^{\|z_i\|\cos(w_{bi},z_i)}}{\sum_j^{N_b} e^{\|z_i\|\cos(w_{bj},z_i)}} \tag{1}$$

Here, B denotes the batch size, and N_b is the number of basic expression classes. The representative vector matrix W_b consists of learnable parameters. In this loss function, the model is trained so that the cosine similarity between the feature vector z_{bi} and the correct expression vector w_{bi} is maximized, while the cosine similarities with the other expression vectors are minimized.

Learning Intermediate Expressions via Linear Interpolation. The previously described feature extractor transforms all input images into feature vectors that are distributed near one of the basic expression representative vectors. However, compound expression images are expected to be distributed between the representative vectors of the basic expressions in the feature space. To achieve this, our method simultaneously trains the feature extractor that introduce diversity in the distribution of the resulting feature vectors. Specifically, we generate pseudo-intermediate expression images by mixing basic expression images using CutMix. Since compound expressions can be represented as combinations of Action Units corresponding to basic expressions, we assume that CutMix-based data synthesis can approximate this property. The generated pseudo-intermediate expression image is then input into the feature extractor, and training is conducted so that the resulting feature vector is distributed between the representative vectors of the involved basic expressions.

Specifically, given two basic expression images $x_a, x_b \in \mathbb{R}^{C\times H\times W}$, a pseudo-intermediate expression image $\tilde{x}_{(a,b)} \in \mathbb{R}^{C\times H\times W}$ is generated using CutMix:

$$\tilde{x}_{(a,b)}, \lambda = CutMix(x_a, x_b, \alpha) \tag{2}$$

Here, λ is the mixing ratio, and α is the parameter of the Beta distribution that determines λ.

Next, the pseudo-intermediate image $\tilde{x}_{(a,b)}$ is passed through the feature extractor to obtain a feature vector $\tilde{z}_{(a,b)} \in \mathbb{R}^{N_z}$. Then, the cosine similarity between $\tilde{z}_{(a,b)}$ and the basic expression representative vectors is computed.

$$C(\tilde{z}_{(a,b)}, W_b) = \begin{bmatrix} \cos\left(\tilde{z}_{(a,b)}, w_{b0}\right) \\ \cos\left(\tilde{z}_{(a,b)}, w_{b1}\right) \\ \vdots \\ \cos\left(\tilde{z}_{(a,b)}, w_{bn}\right) \end{bmatrix} \tag{3}$$

Similarly, the original data x_a and x_b are converted into feature vectors z_a and z_b, and the cosine similarities with the representative vectors, $C(z_a, W_b)$ and $C(z_b, W_b)$, are computed. Using these similarities and the mixing ratio λ, the ideal similarity vector for the CutMix image, $\hat{C}(\tilde{z}_{(a,b)}, W_b)$, is calculated.

$$\hat{C}(\tilde{z}_{(a,b)}, W_b) = \lambda C(z_a, W_b) + (1 - \lambda) C(z_b, W_b) \tag{4}$$

Then, the distance between the similarity vector of the CutMix data and the ideal similarity vector is calculated as the loss function $\mathcal{L}_{\text{MSE}}$. This loss function is used to train the model so that the distance between $C(\tilde{z}_{(a,b)}, W_b)$ and $\hat{C}(\tilde{z}_{(a,b)}, W_b)$ is minimized.

$$\mathcal{L}_{\text{MSE}} = \frac{1}{B} \sum_{i=0}^{B} \| C(\tilde{z}_{(i,B-i)}, W_b) - \hat{C}(\tilde{z}_{(i,B-i)}, W_b) \|^2 \tag{5}$$

Integration of Loss Functions. The final loss function is a combination of the angle-based metric learning loss for basic expressions, $\mathcal{L}_{\text{ang}}$, and the distance-based loss for intermediate expressions, $\mathcal{L}_{\text{MSE}}$.

$$\mathcal{L}_{\text{total}} = \mathcal{L}_{\text{ang}} + r \mathcal{L}_{\text{MSE}} \tag{6}$$

Here, r is the weight for the loss function related to intermediate expressions. Using this combined loss function, the model is trained solely on basic expression data.

3.2 Compound Expression Recognition

Compound expression recognition follows the same inference process as in the pretraining stage with basic expressions: the predicted expression is determined as the one whose representative vector has the highest cosine similarity with the extracted feature vector. To do this, it is necessary to define representative vectors for compound expressions. In this study, the representative vector of a compound expression is defined as a one-to-one linear combination of the representative vectors of the corresponding basic expressions, as shown in the following equation.

$$W_c = W_b \Lambda \tag{7}$$

Here, $W_c \in \mathbb{R}^{N_z \times N_c}$ is the matrix of representative vectors for compound expressions, $W_b \in \mathbb{R}^{N_z \times N_b}$ is the matrix of representative vectors for basic expressions, N_c is the number of compound expression classes, and $\Lambda \in \mathbb{R}^{N_b \times N_c}$ is the weight matrix indicating the contribution of each basic expression to the corresponding compound expression. Each element of Λ is set to 1 if the basic expression is part of the compound expression, and 0 otherwise. For example, the representative vector for *Happily Surprise* is calculated as follows:

Table 1. Comparison Between the Proposed Method and SOTA Models.

Method	Modality	Dataset	N-shot	UAR	WAR
ResNet50 [9]	Image	RAF(compound)	Supervised	0.239	0.398
DAN [20]				0.383	0.568
DDAMFN [23]				0.481	**0.648**
POSTER++ [16]				0.496	0.610
C-EXPR-NET [10]	Image, Text	C-EXPR-DB*	Zero-shot	0.517	-
- (Transfer Learning)		+RAF(compound)	Transfer	**0.601**	-
CDNet [24]	Image	5 basic datasets**	1-shot	-	0.461
			5-shot	-	0.630
Proposed Method	Image	RAF(basic)	Zero-shot	**0.579**	0.608
w/o $\mathcal{L}_{\text{ang}}$				0.515	0.562
w/o CutMix				0.537	0.608
- (Transfer Learning)				0.561	**0.694**

* C-EXPR-DB is a dataset that includes basic expression multi-labels and Action Unit (AU) annotations.
** CK+, MMI, Oulu-CASIA, RAF-DB(Basic), SFEW

$$w_{\text{hap sur}} = 1.0 * w_{\text{happy}} + 1.0 * w_{\text{surprised}} \tag{8}$$

Next, we provide a detailed explanation of the recognition process. The representative vectors for compound expression are computed using Equation (7). Then, given a compound expression image, its feature vector $z_c \in \mathbb{R}^{N_z}$ is extracted. The cosine similarities between z_c and each of the compound expression representative vectors $W_c = [w_{c0}, w_{c1}, \cdots, w_{cN_c}]$ are computed, and the compound expression with the highest similarity is taken as the predicted label $\hat{y}$.

$$\hat{y} = \underset{i \in N_c}{\operatorname{argmax}} \cos(z_c, w_{ci}) \tag{9}$$

4 Experiments and Results

4.1 Experimental Setup

Dataset. In this study, we use the RAF-DB dataset [11,12] as the source of both basic and compound expression data. This dataset consists of natural facial images (224 × 224 pixels) collected from the internet, including a wide variety of attributes such as age, gender, and occlusion. It contains two types of annotations: one labeled with seven basic expressions including Neutral, and another labeled with 11 compound expressions composed of combinations of two basic expressions. All labels were assigned by 40 annotators via crowdsourcing.

Since Neutral represents the absence of emotion and is considered to have limited relevance for compound expression recognition, we exclude it and use only the remaining six basic expressions in this study. The dataset contains 12,135 basic expression images and 3,954 compound expression images across training, validation, and test sets. Although the dataset provides predefined training and test splits, we randomly allocate 20% of the training data as validation data for model selection. Due to the small number of samples in some classes, we apply data augmentation to the training data using random horizontal flipping and random rotation.

Hyperparameters. In our experiments, we use a batch size of 128 and set the initial learning rate to 0.001. The CutMix parameter α is set to 1.0, and the weight of the loss $\mathcal{L}_{\mathrm{MSE}}$ is set to $r = 0.5$. We use Stochastic Gradient Descent (SGD) as the optimizer. To improve training efficiency, we apply early stopping with a patience of 10 epochs. Therefore, the number of training epochs may vary depending on the model. During testing, we use the model from the epoch where the validation loss was minimized.

Evaluation Metrics. To evaluate the accuracy of compound emotion estimation, we use Unweighted Average Recall (UAR) and Weighted Average Recall (WAR). UAR is the average of the True Positive Rates (TPR) across all classes, while WAR is the average of the TPRs weighted by the number of samples in each class, and is equivalent to overall accuracy. UAR treats each class equally, making it a suitable metric for comparing performance across datasets with imbalanced class distributions. On the other hand, WAR emphasizes performance on classes with more samples, giving higher scores to models that perform well on majority classes.

Feature Extractor

The proposed method allows for various backbones to be used as the feature extractor; however, in the comparative experiments, we adopt the backbone of DDAMFN [23].

4.2 Comparison with SOTA Models

We compare the proposed method with ResNet50 [9], DAN [20], DDAMFN [23], and POSTER++ [16]. Table 1 shows the results of compound expression recognition using each of these models. ResNet50, DAN, DDAMFN, and POSTER++

are trained on datasets that include compound expression labels, treating the task as a standard classification problem. In contrast, the proposed method achieves the highest UAR despite not using any compound expression labels during training. Figure 3 shows the confusion matrices of the proposed method and DDAMFN. In the case of DDAMFN, classes with a large number of training samples are correctly predicted, while the accuracy for classes with fewer samples is lower. As a result, the WAR is relatively high, but the UAR is low. This reflects the challenge that compound expression data is difficult to collect and is often highly imbalanced across classes, significantly affecting the model's performance. On the other hand, since the proposed method does not rely on compound expression data at all, it achieves high UAR, indicating that it evaluates all classes more evenly and fairly.

Furthermore, the bottom of Table 1 shows the results when the feature extractor from the proposed method is used for transfer learning. In this setting, a fully connected layer and batch normalization are added after the feature extractor, and only these newly added layers are trained using compound expression data. The fully connected layer transforms the feature vector into probabilities over compound emotion classes. As a result, this approach achieves the highest WAR among all methods, but the UAR is lower than that of the proposed method. This indicates that while the model performs well on frequently occurring classes (contributing to higher WAR), its ability to generalize across all classes remains inferior to the original proposed method.

Next, we compare the proposed method with compound emotion recognition approaches that utilize N-shot learning. The middle section of Table 1 shows the results of C-EXPR-NET [10] and CDNet [24].

C-EXPR-NET performs multitask learning using both AU (Action Unit) detection and compound emotion classification to improve recognition accuracy. CDNet, on the other hand, uses multiple basic expression datasets such as CK+ and MMI simultaneously and employs meta-learning to recognize compound expressions.

When comparing the proposed method with C-EXPR-NET, the transfer learning setup favors the baseline, which achieves a higher score. However, in the zero-shot setting, the proposed method outperforms it. Furthermore, when compared with CDNet, the proposed method achieves higher accuracy than the one-shot version of CDNet and performs comparably to its five-shot version.

These results demonstrate that despite using only basic expression datasets, the proposed method achieves high accuracy in zero-shot compound expression recognition, highlighting its effectiveness.

4.3 Discussion

In the proposed method, we introduce angle-based metric learning and intermediate expression learning via CutMix to train basic expression features. To investigate the impact of these techniques on the proposed method, bottom section of Table 1 shows the results when each method is excluded.

Effectiveness of Angle Loss. To verify the effectiveness of the angle loss, we compare the results with and without the angle loss. When excluding the angle-based metric learning, we use the following loss function, which evaluates the distance between the representative vectors using Euclidean distance instead of angle-based distance:

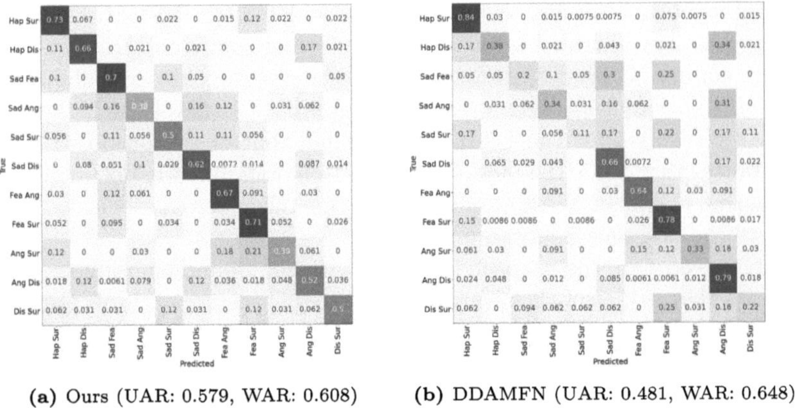

(a) Ours (UAR: 0.579, WAR: 0.608) (b) DDAMFN (UAR: 0.481, WAR: 0.648)

Fig. 3. Confusion matrices of the proposed method and DDAMFN. While DDAMFN achieves a high WAR, its UAR is low, which results in smaller values along the diagonal of the confusion matrix, indicating lower accuracy across less frequent classes.

$$\mathcal{L}_s = -\frac{1}{B}\sum_{i=0}^{B} \log \frac{e^{w_{bi}^T z_i}}{\sum_j^{N_b} e^{w_{bj}^T z_i}}$$

This loss function is a Softmax function without the bias term, where z_i represents the feature vector, and w_{bi} represents the representative vector. The results show that when the angle-based metric learning is excluded, the UAR decreases by 0.064. This indicates that the angle-based metric learning is effective in improving the proposed method's performance.

Effectiveness of CutMix. Next, we examine the effectiveness of intermediate image generation using CutMix by comparing results with and without its use. As shown in result, introducing CutMix improves the UAR by 0.042. To further demonstrate the similarity between the features of CutMix-generated images and those of real compound expression images, we plot the cosine similarities between feature vectors and the representative vectors of basic expressions in Fig. 4. In this example, the horizontal axis represents the cosine similarity with the representative vector of *Surprise*, while the vertical axis represents the similarity with *Fear*. Data points with *Surprise* and *Fear* labels, as well as CutMix-generated images labeled as *Fear+Surprise*, are plotted as circles. The centroids (i.e., the mean positions) of each data group are plotted as crosses. By comparing the centroid positions of the CutMix and real compound emotion images, we observe that the centroid of the CutMix data lies close to that of the actual compound emotion images. Additionally, Table 2 presents the

Table 2. Cosine similarity between the centroids of the data distributions of CutMix-generated images and compound emotion images.

Hap Sur	Hap Dis	Sad Fea	Sad Ang	Sad Sur	Sad Dis	Fea Ang
0.997	0.960	0.899	0.892	0.826	0.925	0.956
Fea Sur	Ang Sur	Ang Dis	Dis Sur			
0.996	0.976	0.932	0.774			

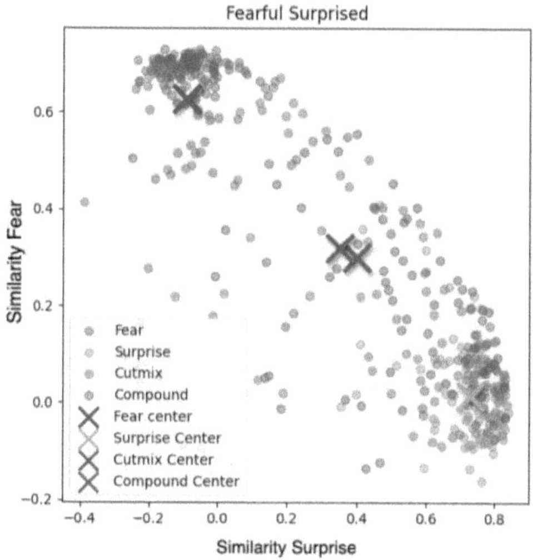

Fig. 4. Similarity Plot with Basic Emotion Representative Vectors. Data labeled as *Fear*, *Surprise*, *Fearfully Surprised*, and CutMix-generated *Fear+Surprise* (equal in number) are plotted as circles, with centroids shown as crosses. The horizontal and vertical axes represent cosine similarities with *Surprise* and *Fear* representative vectors. The results show that CutMix-generated features closely resemble those of real compound expression images.

cosine similarities between the centroids of the CutMix and compound emotion data distributions, further supporting the similarity between the two.

5 Conclusion

In this study, we proposed a novel method for compound expression recognition using only basic expression features. The most significant advantage of this method is that it does not require any compound expression data or metadata for recognition. Since complex expressions are difficult to annotate and collect, making it challenging to construct large-scale datasets, our method offers a promising solution to this problem. Furthermore, experiments demonstrated that even when using only basic expression features, the recognition accuracy of compound expressions improved. In addition, the proposed method achieved high accuracy compared to other approaches that use metadata beyond expression labels.

Future work includes addressing the influence of the dataset used for training basic expression features. It is necessary to reduce the impact of basic expression recognition performance on the overall system, or to further improve feature separability. Another issue is the performance degradation in UAR (Unweighted Average Recall) after applying transfer learning. A drop in UAR suggests that, like general classification methods, the model is affected by bias in the training data. Therefore, mitigating these biases will be essential for improving UAR in future studies.

References

1. Bryant, D., Deng, S., Sephus, N., Xia, W., Perona, P.: Multi-dimensional, nuanced and subjective—measuring the perception of facial expressions. In: 2022 IEEE/CVF Conference on Computer Vision and Pattern Recognition (CVPR), pp. 20900–20909 (2022). https://doi.org/10.1109/CVPR52688.2022.02026
2. Darwin, C.: The Expression of Emotions in Man and Animals. Oxford University Press (1872)
3. Deng, J., Guo, J., Xue, N., Zafeiriou, S.: ArcFace: additive angular margin loss for deep face recognition. In: Proceedings of the IEEE/CVF Conference on Computer Vision and Pattern Recognition (CVPR) (2019)
4. Dosovitskiy, A., et al.: An image is worth 16x16 words: transformers for image recognition at scale. In: International Conference on Learning Representations (2021). https://openreview.net/forum?id=YicbFdNTTy
5. Du, S., Martinez, A.M.: Compound facial expressions of emotion: from basic research to clinical applications. Dialogues Clin. Neurosci. **17**(4), 443–455 (2015). https://doi.org/10.31887/dcns.2015.17.4/sdu https://doi.org/10.31887/dcns.2015.17.4/sdu
6. Du, S., Tao, Y., Martinez, A.M.: Compound facial expressions of emotion. Proc. Natl. Acad. Sci. **111**(15), E1454–E1462 (2014). https://doi.org/10.1073/pnas.1322355111
7. Ekman, P., Friesen, W.V.: Facial action coding system. Environ. Psychol. Nonverbal Behav. (1978)

8. Foteinopoulou, N.M., Patras, I.: EmoCLIP: a vision-language method for zero-shot video facial expression recognition. In: 2024 IEEE 18th International Conference on Automatic Face and Gesture Recognition (FG) (2024)
9. He, K., Zhang, X., Ren, S., Sun, J.: Deep residual learning for image recognition. In: 2016 IEEE Conference on Computer Vision and Pattern Recognition (CVPR), pp. 770–778 (2016). https://doi.org/10.1109/CVPR.2016.90
10. Kollias, D.: Multi-label compound expression recognition: C-EXPR database & network. In: Proceedings of the IEEE/CVF Conference on Computer Vision and Pattern Recognition (CVPR), pp. 5589–5598 (2023)
11. Li, S., Deng, W.: Reliable crowdsourcing and deep locality-preserving learning for unconstrained facial expression recognition. IEEE Trans. Image Process. **28**(1), 356–370 (2019)
12. Li, S., Deng, W., Du, J.: Reliable crowdsourcing and deep locality-preserving learning for expression recognition in the wild. In: 2017 IEEE Conference on Computer Vision and Pattern Recognition (CVPR), pp. 2584–2593. IEEE (2017)
13. Li, Z., Zhang, T., Jing, X., Wang, Y.: Facial expression-based analysis on emotion correlations, hotspots, and potential occurrence of urban crimes. Alex. Eng. J. **60**(1), 1411–1420 (2021)
14. Liu, W., Wen, Y., Yu, Z., Li, M., Raj, B., Song, L.: SphereFace: deep hypersphere embedding for face recognition. In: Proceedings of the IEEE Conference on Computer Vision and Pattern Recognition (CVPR) (2017)
15. Mannepalli, K., Sastry, P.N., Suman, M.: A novel adaptive fractional deep belief networks for speaker emotion recognition. Alex. Eng. J. **56**(4), 485–497 (2017). https://doi.org/10.1016/j.aej.2016.09.002
16. Mao, J., Xu, R., Yin, X., Chang, Y., Nie, B., Huang, A.: Poster v2: a simpler and stronger facial expression recognition network. arXiv preprint arXiv:2301.12149 (2023)
17. Nan, Y., Ju, J., Hua, Q., Zhang, H., Wang, B.: A-MobileNet: an approach of facial expression recognition. Alex. Eng. J. **61**(6), 4435–4444 (2022)
18. Tonguç, G., Ozaydn Ozkara, B.: Automatic recognition of student emotions from facial expressions during a lecture. Comput. Educ. **148**, 103797 (2020). https://doi.org/10.1016/j.compedu.2019.103797
19. Wang, H., Wang, Y., Zhou, Z., Ji, X., Gong, Li, Z., Liu, W.: CosFace: large margin cosine loss for deep face recognition. In: Proceedings of the IEEE Conference on Computer Vision and Pattern Recognition (CVPR) (2018)
20. Wen, Z., Lin, W., Wang, T., Xu, G.: Distract your attention: multi-head cross attention network for facial expression recognition. Biomimetics **8**(2) (2023). https://doi.org/10.3390/biomimetics8020199
21. Yun, S.S., Choi, J., Park, S.K.: Bong: Social skills training for children with autism spectrum disorder using a robotic behavioral intervention system. Autism Res. **10**(7), 1306–1323 (2017). https://doi.org/10.1002/aur.1778
22. Yun, S., Han, D., Oh, S.J., Chun, S., Choe, J., Yoo, Y.: CutMix: regularization strategy to train strong classifiers with localizable features. In: International Conference on Computer Vision (ICCV) (2019)
23. Zhang, S., Zhang, Y., Zhang, Y., Wang, Y., Song, Z.: A dual-direction attention mixed feature network for facial expression recognition. Electronics **12**(17) (2023). https://doi.org/10.3390/electronics12173595
24. Zou, X., Yan, Y., Xue, J.H., Chen, S., Wang, H.: When facial expression recognition meets few-shot learning: A joint and alternate learning framework. In: Proceedings of the AAAI Conference on Artificial Intelligence, vol. 36, no. 5, pp. 5367–5375 (2022). https://doi.org/10.1609/aaai.v36i5.20474

Rank-Aware Sports Scoring: A Learning-to-Rank Approach for Judged Sports

Tatsuma Furuya(✉) and Noriko Takemura

Kyushu Institute of Technology, 680-4 Kawazu, Iizuka 820-8502, Japan
furuya.tatsuma704@mail.kyutech.jp, takemura@ai.kyutech.ac.jp

Abstract. Ensuring fairness in scoring is a critical challenge in judged sports. While automated scoring systems that predict scores from performance data have emerged as a promising solution, the annotated scores used for training such models often reflect subjective biases among individual judges, leading to inconsistencies in the dataset. To address this issue, we propose a learning framework that incorporates relative ranking information between performance samples—relationships that are typically more stable across different judges. By focusing on ranking-based learning rather than direct score regression, our method aims to reduce the influence of individual scoring biases and improve model consistency. We conduct comprehensive experiments on three judged sports datasets, including a newly constructed figure skating dataset. The results show that our ranking-based learning framework significantly improves the prediction accuracy of automated scoring models compared to conventional regression-based methods.

Keywords: Sports Applications · Ranking-based Learning · Relative Learning · Artistic Sports

1 Introduction

In judged sports such as figure skating and rhythmic gymnastics, it is essential to ensure fairness by suppressing variations in subjective scoring and establishing a unified evaluation standard. Traditional scoring methods heavily rely on the judges' subjective opinions, which can lead to inconsistencies in evaluations even for the same performance. To address this issue, research on automated scoring systems has been actively conducted. In recent years, score prediction using machine learning models based on monocular camera footage has become mainstream.

For example, in the field of figure skating, research on machine learning network architectures that effectively learn from performance videos has been actively conducted, such as MIT-Skate [5] and Skating-Mixer [6]. In addition, datasets such as Fis-V [7] and FS1000 [6] have been constructed. Research on

C. Wallraven et al. (Eds.): ACPR 2025, LNCS 16174, pp. 190–205, 2026.
https://doi.org/10.1007/978-981-95-4395-3_14

automatic scoring using monocular videos has also progressed not only in figure skating, but also in other sports such as rhythmic gymnastics, trampoline, and diving [4,5].

However, existing research on automatic scoring faces the challenge of insufficiently considering the unique data characteristics of judged sports. In judged sports, the panel of judges differs for each competition, leading to variability in scoring standards and a tendency for score data to lack consistency. As a result, the same performance may receive different scores depending on the competition. On the other hand, relative ranking information—such as the superiority or inferiority of performances between athletes—tends to be relatively consistent even when the judges change, and is therefore considered more reliable. Ignoring such data characteristics limits the potential for improving the reliability and fairness of automatic scoring systems.

In this study, we focus on the relative nature of score data in judged sports and propose a novel automatic scoring method that leverages learning-to-rank by reformulating the traditional score regression problem as a ranking problem. While many existing methods aim to improve ranking performance indirectly by enhancing the accuracy of absolute score prediction, considering the unique characteristics of judged sports—such as score variability and differing standards among judges—it is more reasonable to directly utilize relative ranking information.

This study aims to simultaneously optimize the two key performance aspects required in automatic scoring systems: the accuracy of absolute score prediction, which is essential for providing feedback during training, and the accuracy of ranking prediction, which is crucial for ensuring fairness in competition evaluations. By doing so, we establish a novel learning framework that leverages the bidirectional learning effect, where score prediction and ranking prediction complement and enhance each other.

In this study, we validate our proposed method using datasets from figure skating and rhythmic gymnastics. In particular, for figure skating, existing datasets often mix data from pair skating, ice dance, and single skating, resulting in a data distribution that differs from actual scoring environments. To address this issue, we constructed a new dataset called the SoloFS dataset—the largest scoring dataset to date specialized for single figure skating. This allows for model evaluation that better reflects real-world competition settings.

2 Methodology

In this section, we provide a detailed explanation of our approach to reformulating the automatic scoring task in judged sports as a ranking problem and incorporating learning-to-rank techniques.

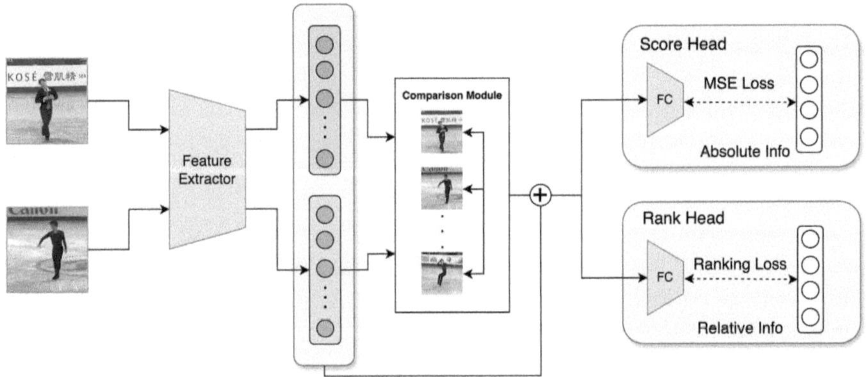

Fig. 1. Overview of the Network Architecture and Training Process for Scoring Sports with Ranking-Based Learning.

2.1 Formulation

To incorporate a learning-to-rank approach that considers relative information between input data in the automatic scoring task, we first reformulate the task.

Conventional Formulation. The automatic scoring task in judged sports is formulated as a regression problem where the score y is directly predicted. Given an input performance data x, the goal is to learn a function $f : \mathcal{X} \to \mathbb{R}$ that estimates the score y_i for each input x_i. Here, i represents the index of a sample in the dataset, and if the dataset consists of N samples, then each input data x_i and its corresponding ground-truth score y_i are given for $i = 1, 2, \ldots, N$.

The predicted score $\hat{y}_i$ is defined as the model output and can be expressed as follows:

$$\hat{y}_i = f(x_i) \tag{1}$$

where $\hat{y}_i$ is the predicted score obtained by the model f when given x_i as input.

If the batch size used during training is B, a subset of the training dataset is prepared as follows:

$$\mathcal{D} = \{(x_i, y_i)\}_{i=1}^{B} \tag{2}$$

The objective is to optimize the function f so that the predicted score $\hat{y}_i$ aligns as closely as possible with the true score y_i.

In this study, we incorporate the Pairwise approach [2], which extracts relative relationships between paired data, and the Listwise approach [3], which captures relative relationships based on ranking probabilities among multiple data samples.

Formulation of the Pairwise Approach. In the method employed in this study, relative information between input data is considered by imposing a constraint that ensures if the corresponding scores satisfy $y_i > y_j$ for a given pair of samples x_i, x_j, then the predicted values must also satisfy $f(x_i) > f(x_j)$.

This relationship can be explicitly expressed as follows:

$$y_i > y_j \quad \Rightarrow \quad f(x_i) > f(x_j) \tag{3}$$

By incorporating this constraint, the learning task is extended from a conventional regression problem to one that accounts for ranking. More generally, the objective is to learn a function $f(x)$ that satisfies the following constraint for all sample pairs (i, j):

$$\forall (i, j) \in \mathcal{D}, \quad y_i > y_j \quad \Rightarrow \quad f(x_i) > f(x_j) \tag{4}$$

Formulation of the Listwise Approach. In the Listwise approach, a batch of samples selected from the entire training dataset is treated as a single list, and learning is performed while considering the ranking relationships within the entire list.

Let $X = \{x_1, x_2, \ldots, x_B\}$ be a list containing B samples, which is a subset of the training dataset, and let the corresponding ground-truth scores be $Y = \{y_1, y_2, \ldots, y_B\}$, where B denotes the batch size. The model f predicts a score for each sample x_i, and the predicted scores for the entire batch are expressed as $f(X) = (f(x_1), f(x_2), \ldots, f(x_B))$. The objective is to train the model such that the predicted ranking of the scores aligns as closely as possible with the ranking determined by the ground-truth scores.

To define the ground-truth ranking, we consider an operation that sorts Y in descending order. Let π_* be the permutation that arranges the indices of Y in descending order, where $\pi_*(i)$ represents the index of the i-th largest score in Y. That is, π_* is determined such that

$$y_{\pi_*(1)} \geq y_{\pi_*(2)} \geq \cdots \geq y_{\pi_*(B)} \tag{5}$$

This permutation π_* represents the ground-truth ranking of the data.

On the other hand, based on the predicted scores $f(X)$, the samples can be rearranged in descending order of their predicted values, yielding a new permutation π_f. This permutation represents the ranking predicted by the model and is defined such that

$$f(x_{\pi_{f(1)}}) \geq f(x_{\pi_{f(2)}}) \geq \cdots \geq f(x_{\pi_{f(B)}}) \tag{6}$$

The objective of the model is to make the predicted ranking π_f as close as possible to the ground-truth ranking π_*.

Thus, the Listwise approach focuses on optimizing the consistency between the predicted and true rankings, considering the entire list rather than individual samples.

2.2 Loss Function

Mean Squared Error Loss. To enhance the absolute score prediction performance in the automatic scoring system, we employ the mean squared error (MSE) loss as the objective function. The MSE loss is defined as follows:

$$L_{MSE} = \frac{1}{B}\sum_{i=1}^{B}(\hat{y}_i - y_i)^2 \tag{7}$$

where y_i represents the score predicted by the model and B denotes the number of samples in a batch. In this study, we set $B = 16$. By minimizing the mean squared difference between the predicted and actual scores, this loss function contributes to improving the accuracy of score prediction as a regression problem.

Pairwise Loss. In this approach, the probability that sample i ranks higher than sample j is estimated using the difference between the predicted scores $\hat{y}_i$ and $\hat{y}_j$. Specifically, this probability P_{ij} is computed by applying the sigmoid function σ as follows:

$$P_{ij} = \sigma(\hat{y}_i - \hat{y}_j) = \frac{1}{1 + \exp(-(\hat{y}_i - \hat{y}_j))} \tag{8}$$

Additionally, based on the actual scores y_i and y_j, the ground-truth pairwise label Y_{ij} is defined as:

$$Y_{ij} = \begin{cases} 1, & (y_i > y_j) \\ 0, & (y_i < y_j) \\ 0.5, & (y_i = y_j) \end{cases} \tag{9}$$

In this study, we set the batch size for ranking learning to $B = 16$ and compute the loss for all possible pairs within a batch, i.e., $\{(i, j) \mid 1 \leq i < j \leq B\}$. The loss function is defined using Binary Cross Entropy (BCE) between the predicted probability P_{ij} and the ground-truth label Y_{ij}. The final loss is obtained by averaging over all valid pairs where $y_i \neq y_j$, and it is formulated as follows:

$$L_{\text{rank, pair}} = \frac{1}{N_P}\sum_{i,j}\text{BCE}(P_{ij}, Y_{ij}) \tag{10}$$

where N_P denotes the total number of valid pairs satisfying $y_i \neq y_j$.

By employing this method, the model learns relative ranking relationships, enabling it to appropriately capture the ordering of scores.

Listwise Loss. The listwise loss is defined by first applying the softmax function to both the ground-truth scores y_i and the predicted scores $\hat{y}_i$, resulting in the following probability distributions:

$$\hat{Y}_i = \frac{\exp(\hat{y}_i)}{\sum_{j=1}^{B}\exp(\hat{y}_j)}, Y_i = \frac{\exp(y_i)}{\sum_{j=1}^{B}\exp(y_j)}, \tag{11}$$

Next, the discrepancy between the predicted distribution $\hat{Y}_i$ and the ground-truth distribution Y_i is evaluated using the cross-entropy loss. The loss function is defined as follows:

$$L_{\text{rank,list}} = -\sum_{i=1}^{B} Y_i \log(\hat{Y}_i + \epsilon) \tag{12}$$

where ϵ is a small constant introduced to prevent numerical instability. In this study, we set $\epsilon = 1e - 10$.

2.3 Network

As shown in Fig. 1, the network used in this study consists of the following three main components. First, the feature extractor generates feature vectors by integrating temporal and modality information from the performance data. Next, the Comparison Module explicitly compares the relative relationships between the generated feature vectors. Finally, the Rank Head/Score Head is responsible for learning both the ranking and score regression tasks. By combining these components, the model achieves integrated learning from both relative information and absolute scores.

Feature Extractor. For feature extraction from performance data, we adopt Skating-Mixer [6]. This module integrates visual and auditory modalities while processing temporal information, and ultimately outputs a 516-dimensional feature vector for each sample. When training on data that does not include auditory information, the modality integration is skipped, and visual information alone is processed using Skating-Mixer to obtain a 516-dimensional vector in the same manner.

Comparison Module. The Comparison Module is a multi-head attention mechanism that takes as input the 516-dimensional feature vectors generated by the feature extractor and enhances the relative relationships among samples. First, the feature vectors of all samples are treated as a set and passed through the attention layer, which aggregates the relationships between samples using learned weights. A linear transformation is then applied element-wise to the attention output, projecting it back into the 516-dimensional space to produce feature representations enriched with relative information that are suitable for subsequent heads.

This process enables the intermediate layers to effectively capture fine-grained relationships among data that simple fully connected layers may miss, thereby improving the quality of input features for ranking learning. In this study, the resulting feature representations with embedded relative information are used in training based on the Pairwise loss. By doing so, we aim to construct a novel training strategy that integrates the local comparison capability of the Pairwise approach—capable of clearly distinguishing between superior and inferior samples—with the global consistency of the Listwise approach, which considers the overall ranking structure.

Rank Head/Score Head. The Rank Head consists of a single fully connected layer. Its primary purpose is not to directly maximize the accuracy of the final ranking prediction, but rather to guide the feature extractor to learn representations that reflect relative relationships between data. If the Rank Head were overly complex, the learning of ranking information could become confined within the head itself, potentially hindering the feature extractor from fulfilling its intended role in representation learning. Therefore, a simple structure is adopted to ensure that relative ranking information is effectively propagated back to the feature extractor through backpropagation.

On the other hand, the Score Head employs a deeper architecture consisting of two fully connected layers combined with a ReLU activation function. This design improves the accuracy of absolute score prediction and enables the model to capture fine-grained differences in scores. The purpose of this structure is to enhance non-linearity and expressive power in score regression.

Loss Integration. During training, we compute the ranking loss L_{rank} (either pairwise or listwise) based on the ranking scores from the Rank Head, and the mean squared error loss L_{MSE} based on the regression output from the Score Head. These two losses are then integrated as a weighted sum:

$$L = \alpha L_{\text{rank}} + (1 - \alpha) L_{\text{MSE}} \tag{13}$$

The entire model is optimized jointly using this combined loss. In this way, the framework achieves a balance between relative learning and absolute score prediction, aiming for high-accuracy ranking and score regression.

The proposed methods in this study are summarized in Table 1. First, PW-Rank is a model that uses only the pairwise loss, learning based on relative ranking relationships between performances. On the other hand, LW-Rank uses only the listwise loss, performing ranking learning by simultaneously considering multiple performances. Finally, PW-LW-Rank combines the pairwise loss with the Comparison Module, resulting in a model that incorporates the strengths of both the pairwise and listwise approaches.

Table 1. Characteristics of Each Proposed Method

	Pairwise Loss	Listwise Loss	Comparison Module
PW-Rank	○	×	×
LW-Rank	×	○	×
PW-LW-Rank	○	×	○

3 Dataset

In this study, we constructed a new figure skating scoring dataset, SoloFS, to enable high-quality evaluation using figure skating data. Previously proposed datasets for judged sports have faced the issue of limited scale. For example, the FisV dataset [7], a scoring dataset for figure skating, contains only about 500 samples. Similarly, the Rhythmic Gymnastics dataset [8] includes only 250 video samples per category, which is insufficient for training machine learning models.

On the other hand, FS1000 [6] contains over 1,000 figure skating performance videos and is large in scale. However, it mixes data from pair skating, ice dance, and single skating—disciplines with different judging criteria—resulting in a dataset that diverges from real-world scoring environments.

In this study, to enable method validation through large-scale machine learning that better reflects real-world scoring conditions, we constructed a dataset called SoloFS, specifically designed for the task of predicting program component scores that evaluate the artistic quality of single skating performances.

SoloFS is built using videos from the Junior Grand Prix Series, an international-level competition, and is designed for predicting the artistic scores in single skating. In collecting the data, we sourced videos from junior-level international competitions, which include skaters of diverse skill levels, to ensure a wide range of performance quality could be utilized for machine learning. To construct a more consistent dataset, only single skating performance videos were used—data from ice dance and pair skating were excluded. The collected videos were annotated with program component scores based on the detailed scoring information publicly released after each competition.

As part of the data preprocessing, non-scoring segments such as name announcements and waiting scenes in the Kiss and Cry area were manually trimmed from the videos, and only the footage from the start to the end of each performance was extracted.

In figure skating, program component scores consist of five elements: Skating Skills, Transitions, Performance, Composition, and Interpretation of Music. The SoloFS dataset is annotated with all five of these component scores.

The SoloFS dataset contains a total of 2,998 figure skating videos, making it the largest dataset among those proposed so far for judged sports.

Table 2. Comparison of Figure Skating Datasets Proposed in Previous Studies and the SoloFS Dataset. "A" and "V" denote Audio and Video modalities, respectively.

Dataset	Number of Videos	Modality	Category Mix	Component Scores
FisV	500	V	No	No
FS1000	1,604	A+V	Yes	Yes
SoloFS (ours)	2,998	A+V	No	Yes

For validation data, we used 221 samples from the 2015 Junior Grand Prix Riga Cup and the 2016 Junior Grand Prix Tallinn Cup. For test data, we used 113 samples from the 2015 Junior Grand Prix Linz competition (Table 2).

Table 3. Setting of α Values for Pairwise and Listwise Losses

Dataset	PW-Rank	LW-Rank	PW-LW-Rank
FS1000	0.8	0.2	0.5
Rhythmic Gymnastics			
Ball	0.7	0.4	0.5
Clubs	0.7	0.4	0.2
Hoop	0.5	0.5	0.4
Ribbon	0.4	0.1	0.4
Mixed	0.7	0.1	0.1

4 Experiment

4.1 Experimental Setup

In this section, we present the experimental results using datasets from figure skating and rhythmic gymnastics. Specifically, we evaluate the learning performance of the automatic scoring models using the FS1000 dataset for figure skating, the independently constructed SoloFS dataset, and the Rhythmic Gymnastics dataset.

- Mean Squared Error (MSE): A metric that measures the absolute error between the predicted scores and the actual scores.
- Spearman's Rank Correlation Coefficient: A metric that evaluates the agreement between the predicted and actual score rankings.

In particular, Spearman's rank correlation coefficient indicates how well the predicted rankings align with the ground-truth rankings, and is used to evaluate the model's ranking performance.

The following three proposed models are used for evaluation. The first is PW-Rank, which incorporates a Rank Head and is trained using the pairwise loss. The second is LW-Rank, which uses the same network architecture but is trained with the listwise loss. The third is PW-LW-Rank, which adds a Comparison Module and uses the pairwise loss to integrate both pairwise and listwise approaches.

As a baseline for ranking-based learning, we use the conventional Skating-Mixer [6]. This method consists only of a Score Head as the output layer and serves as a simple score regression model that uses mean squared error (MSE) as its loss function. The model is trained to minimize the MSE between the predicted scores from the Score Head and the ground-truth scores.

In the experiments using the SoloFS dataset, the learning rate is fixed at 0.0001. To investigate the effect of the ranking loss weight α, we conduct experiments by varying α from 0.1 to 0.9 in increments of 0.1.

For the experiments using FS1000 and Rhythmic Gymnastics, we adjust only the learning rate for the baseline Skating-Mixer. For the ranking-based models, both the learning rate and α are tuned. Parameter tuning is performed using Optuna [1] with Bayesian optimization over 30 trials on the validation data.

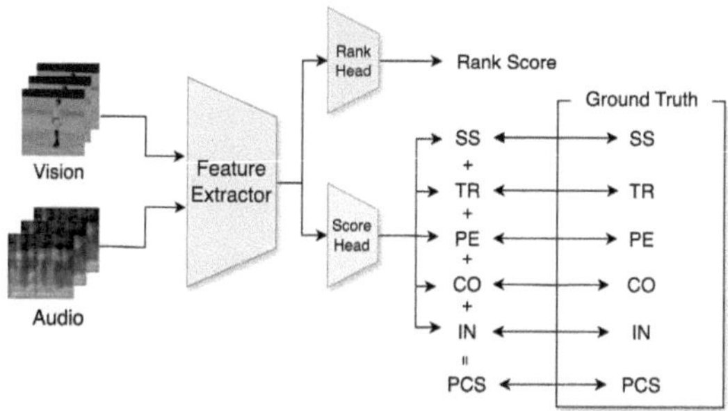

Fig. 2. Training framework for the figure skating scoring model

4.2 Figure Skating

Here, we present the experimental results using the FS1000 [6] and SoloFS figure skating datasets.

FS1000 is a dataset that contains over 1,000 video samples across eight competition categories (men's and women's singles, pairs, and ice dance—each with short program and free program segments). Each performance in the dataset is annotated with both technical scores and program component scores for each category. Since annotation information for the test set is not publicly available in FS1000, we randomly select 18 samples from the 265 publicly available validation samples to use as the test set for this experiment.

This experiment focuses specifically on the estimation of program component scores, which are more susceptible to subjectivity from judges.

An overview of the figure skating scoring model used in this study is shown in Fig. 2. This study proposes a scoring model for the program components in figure skating, where the Score Head outputs individual scores for five criteria: Skating Skills, Transition, Performance, Composition, and Interpretation of Music. Each of these scores is trained to minimize the absolute error with respect to its corresponding ground-truth value. In addition, the total score, calculated as the sum of the five components, is also optimized to match the actual total score.

While previous studies have commonly employed single-task learning to predict only the total score, such approaches obscure the breakdown of individual

Table 4. Comparison of Mean Square Error and Spearman Correlation across datasets and methods. The best-performing values in each column are highlighted in bold.

Datasets	Methods	Mean Square Error (↓)						Spearman Correlation (↑)					
		PCS	SS	TR	PE	CO	IN	PCS	SS	TR	PE	CO	IN
SoloFS(Ours)	Skating-Mixer	20.78	0.92	0.84	0.82	0.83	0.87	0.49	0.53	0.49	0.49	0.51	0.49
	PW-Rank(Ours)	20.41	0.87	**0.80**	0.82	**0.81**	0.85	0.57	0.57	0.58	0.59	0.57	0.57
	LW-Rank(Ours)	20.22	**0.84**	0.83	0.80	**0.81**	0.84	0.56	0.53	0.56	0.59	0.55	0.57
	PW-LW-Rank(Ours)	**19.90**	0.86	**0.80**	**0.78**	**0.81**	**0.81**	**0.59**	**0.59**	**0.59**	**0.62**	**0.59**	**0.61**
FS1000	Skating-Mixer	10.29	**0.38**	0.41	0.45	0.42	0.44	0.65	0.70	0.64	0.65	0.65	0.65
	PW-Rank(Ours)	10.29	0.39	**0.40**	0.45	0.41	0.45	0.72	**0.76**	0.76	0.68	0.72	**0.72**
	LW-Rank(Ours)	12.52	0.49	0.50	0.53	0.50	0.54	0.61	0.62	0.65	0.63	0.61	0.61
	PW-LW-Rank(Ours)	**10.01**	0.41	0.41	**0.42**	**0.39**	**0.42**	**0.74**	0.71	**0.80**	**0.74**	**0.74**	**0.72**

component scores, resulting in reduced interpretability. In practical settings, it is essential that judges and athletes can understand and be convinced by the scores assigned to each criterion. Therefore, this study adopts a multi-task learning approach to explicitly predict each component score, aiming to enhance the model's explainability.

In actual competitions, the final program component score is computed by applying a coefficient k to the sum of the five component scores. This coefficient k differs depending on the competition category and reflects category-specific weightings defined by the official rules. However, if the model is trained to predict this adjusted score directly, it may implicitly learn to identify the competition category, leading to biased learning that deviates from the goal of evaluating artistic expression itself.

To avoid this issue, our approach does not incorporate the coefficient k during training. Instead, we use the unweighted sum of the five component scores as the target, thereby promoting fair and category-independent evaluation of artistic quality.

Results on SoloFS. The evaluation results using the SoloFS dataset are shown in Table 4. Note that the results in this table are based on models trained with parameter tuning performed only on the validation data. Specifically, the results correspond to settings where $\alpha = 0.3$ for PW-Rank, $\alpha = 0.8$ for LW-Rank, and $\alpha = 0.9$ for PW-LW-Rank. In the SoloFS evaluation, the effectiveness of ranking-based learning methods is confirmed in both score prediction and ranking performance, compared to the baseline Skating-Mixer, which learns only from absolute score information. In particular, PW-LW-Rank, which employs the most robust ranking learning strategy among the tested methods, achieves the highest performance, underscoring the importance of incorporating ranking-based learning. These results suggest that, especially in environments with consistent scoring criteria—such as single skating—ranking-based methods can effectively learn relative information between data samples and serve as a promising approach to improving model prediction accuracy.

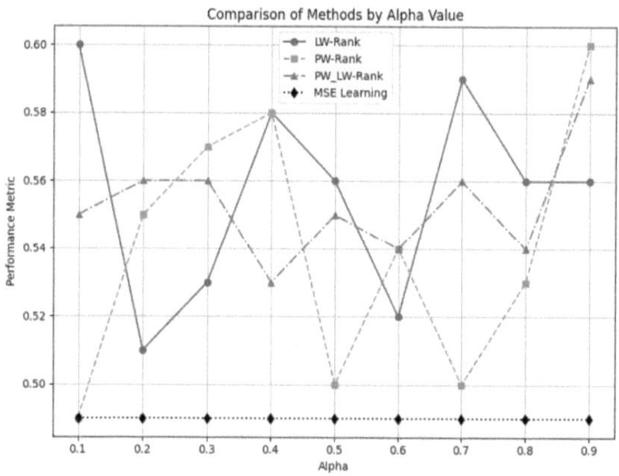

Fig. 3. Effect of Alpha on Learning Performance

Next, we investigate the effect of varying the ranking loss weight α on model performance using the SoloFS dataset. The results are shown in Fig. 3. This experiment confirms that the introduction of ranking-based learning is beneficial for all models—LW-Rank, PW-Rank, and PW-LW-Rank—across all tested values of α from 0.1 to 0.9. However, it also reveals that model performance is highly sensitive to the value of α. This indicates that the strength of ranking-based learning significantly affects the training process and highlights the necessity of proper parameter tuning for α.

Results on FS1000. In the experiments using FS1000, we applied the α values shown in Table 3 based on parameter tuning results. The experimental results showed that both PW-Rank and PW-LW-Rank, which incorporate pairwise loss, consistently achieved higher Spearman rank correlation coefficients compared to the conventional Skating-Mixer model that uses only mean squared error (MSE). This demonstrates that pairwise loss effectively captures the relative ranking information between samples and remains effective even in environments with mixed judging criteria and diverse score distributions.

Furthermore, PW-LW-Rank not only exhibited strong ranking performance but also achieved excellent results in terms of MSE, which evaluates the accuracy of absolute score prediction. This method preserves local ranking consistency through pairwise loss while also incorporating relative relationships among features via the Comparison Module. As a result, it enables bias adjustment across the overall score space, thereby achieving a good balance between ranking correlation and regression accuracy.

On the other hand, LW-Rank, which uses listwise loss, showed decreased performance in both ranking correlation and regression accuracy despite the listwise learning property of jointly optimizing all samples within a batch. This suggests that in datasets with multiple judging standards and diverse score distributions, global ranking optimization is more susceptible to noise. It is difficult for listwise loss alone to robustly handle such complex score spaces. This trend is also consistent with the results observed in the rhythmic gymnastics dataset discussed later.

In summary, PW-Rank and PW-LW-Rank, which utilize pairwise loss, demonstrated strong performance in both relative ranking learning and absolute score prediction, even with heterogeneous datasets such as FS1000. In particular, PW-LW-Rank excels in simultaneously achieving local ranking consistency and global bias correction, making it a promising and robust approach for handling heterogeneous data. In contrast, methods using listwise loss, such as LW-Rank, were found to be sensitive to noise and less reliable when used alone.

Table 5. Results of Spearman's Rank Correlation Coefficient and Mean Square Error on the Rhythmic Gymnastics dataset. The best-performing values in each column are highlighted in bold.

Method	Ball		Clubs		Hoop		Ribbon		Mixed	
	MSE(↓)	Spearman(↑)	MSE(↓)	Spearman(↑)	MSE(↓)	Spearman(↑)	MSE(↓)	Spearman(↑)	MSE(↓)	Spearman(↑)
Skating-Mixer	12.07	0.057	10.05	0.405	12.58	**0.406**	14.62	0.249	12.38	0.311
PW-Rank (Ours)	**11.89**	0.091	9.71	**0.445**	12.35	0.301	14.48	0.282	12.88	**0.321**
LW-Rank (Ours)	11.92	0.090	**9.37**	0.436	**11.21**	0.258	**14.14**	**0.289**	**12.26**	0.302
PW-LW-Rank (Ours)	11.91	**0.277**	14.72	0.445	18.81	0.207	15.11	0.156	17.32	0.223

Table 6. Penalty Impact and Score Distribution Analysis

Category	Variance (Penalty=0)	Variance (Penalty>0)
Ball	9.21	12.62
Clubs	11.75	13.21
Hoop	10.23	17.27
Ribbon	9.57	9.37

Rhythmic Gymnastics. This section presents the experimental results using the Rhythmic Gymnastics scoring dataset [8].

As with previous experiments, the α values used in this study are set based on parameter tuning results, as shown in Table 3.

The Rhythmic Gymnastics dataset contains a total of 1,000 videos—250 for each of the four apparatus categories: ball, clubs, hoop, and ribbon. Each performance is annotated with three types of scores given by judges: difficulty score, execution score, and total score. In this experiment, we evaluate learning methods based on the regression task of predicting the total score.

Since the dataset is relatively small, data augmentation is applied during training. Specifically, for each epoch, a randomly selected 83-second segment is

Table 7. Comparison of Spearman's Rank Correlation Coefficients with and without Penalty during Training on the Rhythmic Gymnastics Hoop Data.

Method	Hoop	
	Penalty	No Penalty
MSE Learning	**0.446**	0.415
PW-Rank (ours)	0.340	**0.347**
LW-Rank (ours)	0.301	**0.327**
PW-LW-Rank (ours)	0.143	**0.299**

extracted from a random start point in the video. Only one sample is used per video per epoch for training.

As shown in Table 5, the experimental results for each category—Ball, Clubs, and Ribbon—show that the proposed methods, PW-Rank and LW-Rank, were effective in both absolute score prediction and ranking performance. However, in the case of PW-LW-Rank, no clear improvement was observed in either metric.

This is likely due to the limited size of the datasets for each category. PW-LW-Rank incorporates a Comparison Module with multi-head attention to model relative relationships between features, significantly increasing the number of parameters in the network. As a result, training becomes less stable and prone to overfitting, especially in data-scarce environments.

In the "Mixed" setting, where data from all categories are combined for training, PW-Rank showed improvement only in ranking prediction performance, while no improvements were observed in absolute score prediction or other evaluation metrics. As noted in Sect. 4.2, this reflects a structural issue: the presence of multiple categories with different judging criteria makes it difficult for ranking-based learning to function effectively.

In particular, for LW-Rank, which uses listwise loss, absolute score prediction performance improved, but ranking performance declined. This may be because listwise loss optimizes all samples within a batch simultaneously, and when label information is inconsistent—as in a heterogeneous dataset—the learning signals become noisy and ambiguous.

Additionally, in the Hoop dataset, while the effectiveness of the proposed methods was confirmed in terms of MSE, a drop in performance was observed for Spearman's rank correlation coefficient compared to the conventional MSE-based method. This outcome is attributed to the unique score distribution characteristics of the Hoop data.

In Hoop scoring, penalties have a particularly strong influence on total scores compared to other apparatuses. In fact, the score variance of penalized samples is approximately 1.7 times higher than that of non-penalized samples (see Table 6), indicating that penalties amplify inconsistencies in judgment among different judges. That is, in the presence of penalties, personal interpretations of their weight and impact can vary, reducing score consistency.

Under such conditions, the assumption of "stable relative ranking between samples" foundational to ranking-based models becomes fragile. Even when the quality of performances is similar, variations in penalty judgments can significantly affect scores, making it difficult for the model to learn stable rankings. As a result, Spearman's rank correlation coefficient may drop, and ranking predictions may become unstable.

Indeed, a comparison of Spearman's rank correlation coefficient by penalty presence in the Hoop category (Table 7) shows that conventional MSE-based methods achieve relatively high ranking performance in the presence of penalties, whereas the proposed ranking-based methods show more stable and higher correlation scores in the non-penalized group. This suggests that the presence of penalties introduces noise that undermines the robustness of ranking-based learning.

Nevertheless, for training data where the impact of penalties is not excessively large, all ranking-based methods demonstrate effectiveness. This supports the importance of modeling relative relationships between input samples in automatic scoring systems for judged sports.

5 Conclusion

In this study, we introduced a learning-to-rank approach that considers relative information between input data for the automatic scoring task in judged sports and evaluated its effectiveness. The experimental results confirmed that this method positively impacts both absolute score prediction and ranking performance.

We also discussed the conditions under which ranking-based learning is effective. The findings indicate that this approach performs particularly well when learning from consistent data, whereas challenges arise in sports where a single error can cause significant ranking fluctuations.

This study suggests that by properly leveraging a previously overlooked characteristic of judged sports data—namely, the inherent variation in ground-truth scores across different competitions—it is possible to improve the performance of traditional scoring models. Moreover, the proposed approach is easily applicable to various existing methods, and as feature extraction techniques for sports videos continue to advance, combining them with our method is expected to further enhance the development of high-performance automatic scoring systems.

References

1. Akiba, T., Sano, S., Yanase, T., Ohta, T., Koyama, M.: Optuna: a next-generation hyperparameter optimization framework. In: Proceedings of the 25th ACM SIGKDD International Conference on Knowledge Discovery & Data Mining, pp. 2623–2631 (2019)
2. Burges, C., et al.: Learning to rank using gradient descent. In: Proceedings of the 22nd International Conference on Machine Learning, pp. 89–96 (2005)

3. Cao, Z., Qin, T., Liu, T.Y., Tsai, M.F., Li, H.: Learning to rank: from pairwise approach to listwise approach. In: Proceedings of the 24th International Conference on Machine Learning, pp. 129–136 (2007)
4. Parmar, P., Morris, B.T.: What and how well you performed? A multitask learning approach to action quality assessment. In: Proceedings of the IEEE/CVF Conference on Computer Vision and Pattern Recognition, pp. 304–313 (2019)
5. Pirsiavash, H., Vondrick, C., Torralba, A.: Assessing the quality of actions. In: Fleet, D., Pajdla, T., Schiele, B., Tuytelaars, T. (eds.) ECCV 2014. LNCS, vol. 8694, pp. 556–571. Springer, Cham (2014). https://doi.org/10.1007/978-3-319-10599-4_36
6. Xia, J., et al.: Skating-mixer: Long-term sport audio-visual modeling with MLPs. In: Proceedings of the AAAI Conference on Artificial Intelligence, vol. 37, pp. 2901–2909 (2023)
7. Xu, C., Fu, Y., Zhang, B., Chen, Z., Jiang, Y.G., Xue, X.: Learning to score figure skating sport videos. IEEE Trans. Cir. Syst. Video Technol. **30**(12), 4578–4590 (2019)
8. Zeng, L.A., et al.: Hybrid dynamic-static context-aware attention network for action assessment in long videos. In: Proceedings of the 28th ACM International Conference on Multimedia, pp. 2526–2534 (2020)

Newborn Fingerprint Recognition Using Fingerprint Classification

Koichi Ito[1(✉)], Daiki Kimura[1], Yoshinori Koda[2,3], Takafumi Aoki[1], Satoshi Kaneko[3], and Samson Muuo Nzou[4]

[1] Graduate School of Information Sciences, Tohoku University, Sendai, Japan
ito@aoki.ecei.tohoku.ac.jp, daiki.kimura.s3@alumni.tohoku.ac.jp, aoki@ecei.tohoku.ac.jp

[2] Biometrics Research Laboratories, NEC Corporation, Tokyo, Japan
y_koda@nec.com

[3] Institute of Tropical Medicine, Nagasaki University, Nagasaki, Japan
skaneko@nagasaki-u.ac.jp

[4] Center for Microbiology Research, Kenya Medical Research Institute, Nairobi, Kenya

Abstract. Fingerprint images of newborns differ significantly from those of adults due to strong deformation, large pores, and thin valleys. As a result, minutiae, which are key features used in traditional fingerprint recognition, cannot be reliably detected in newborn fingerprint images. However, ridge patterns in newborn fingerprints remain observable and resemble those of adult fingerprints. We propose a novel newborn fingerprint recognition method based on fingerprint classification. The proposed method integrates an attention branch network and FingerNet to effectively process these challenging fingerprint images. Through a set of experiments using newborn fingerprint images captured between 2 and 24 h after birth, we demonstrate the effectiveness of the proposed method.

Keywords: fingerprint recognition · fingerprint classification · newborn fingerprint · biometrics

1 Introduction

Fingerprint recognition is used in a wide range of applications, including the national ID system, because of its reliability and convenience in personal identification [9]. The existing fingerprint scanners are optimized mainly for adults, and it is difficult to capture clear fingerprint images from newborns. The main challenges for newborns are the small size of their fingers, which are soft and easily deformed, and the narrow intervals between ridges. For this reason, fingerprint registration of newborns has not been generally conducted, for example, in Aadhaar, India[1], where it is limited to citizens aged five years or older. On the

[1] https://uidai.gov.in/en/.

C. Wallraven et al. (Eds.): ACPR 2025, LNCS 16174, pp. 206–220, 2026.
https://doi.org/10.1007/978-981-95-4395-3_15

other hand, the use of fingerprint recognition to support the legal identification of newborns has been attracting international attention. If newborn fingerprint recognition can be established, birth registration-based identification will be possible throughout life, contributing to human rights guarantees and the achievement of the SDGs, especially in developing countries. The above backgrounds call for the technological development of newborn fingerprint recognition.

To realize fingerprint recognition for newborns, Koda et al. developed a high-resolution newborn fingerprint scanner with 2,674 dpi and succeeded in collecting fingerprint images from newborns two hours after birth [8]. As shown in Fig. 1, newborn fingerprint images are different from adult fingerprints in that the ridges are thicker and the valley lines are collapsed, making minutia matching, which is commonly used in fingerprint recognition, ineffective. The newborn fingers are soft due to their high water content, and elastic deformation during image capture causes deformation and wrinkling. In addition, immediately after birth, there is adhesion of fetal fat, which reduces the contrast of fingerprints and makes it difficult to trace ridges. For this reason, as shown in Fig. 1, it has been confirmed that VeriFinger SDK[2], a commercial fingerprint matching software, cannot correctly extract the minutiae from a newborn fingerprint image. As described above, conventional minutia matching is difficult to apply to newborn fingerprints, whereas the global pattern of ridges can be identified. Taking advantage of this characteristic, a fingerprint recognition method based on fingerprint image classification has been proposed [7]. As shown in Fig. 2, newborn fingerprints can be classified into the five types of "Arch", "Left loop", "Right loop", "Double loop", and "Whorl", as well as adult fingerprints. By combining the classification results for multiple fingerprints, it is possible to identify individuals even from newborn fingerprints. In general, fingerprint classification is based on ridge orientation maps, since fingerprint classes are defined by ridge patterns [9]. On the other hand, as mentioned above, newborn fingerprints do not always provide highly accurate orientation maps because of the unclear ridges. Therefore, only a simple method using ResNet-18 [4] has been proposed [7], which does not achieve sufficient recognition accuracy at this point, and further research is needed to support the effectiveness of fingerprint classification.

In this paper, we propose a newborn fingerprint recognition method that combines four key components: network architecture, preprocessing, data augmentation, and loss function, to improve the classification accuracy of newborn fingerprint images. A feature extractor based on Attention Branch Network (ABN) [3] is used to focus on the global pattern of ridges, which is important in fingerprint classification. To take advantage of orientation maps commonly used in fingerprint classification, a feature extractor based on Orientation Map Encoder (OME), which is a feature extractor of FingerNet [15], is used in combination, and the accuracy is improved by integrating these features. Image enhancement using the frequency spectrum [17] is applied to deal with blurred ridges, and data augmentation is applied to emulate the inherent variability of newborn fingerprints. In addition, MagFace [10], a deep metric learning method based on image

[2] https://www.neurotechnology.com/verifinger.html.

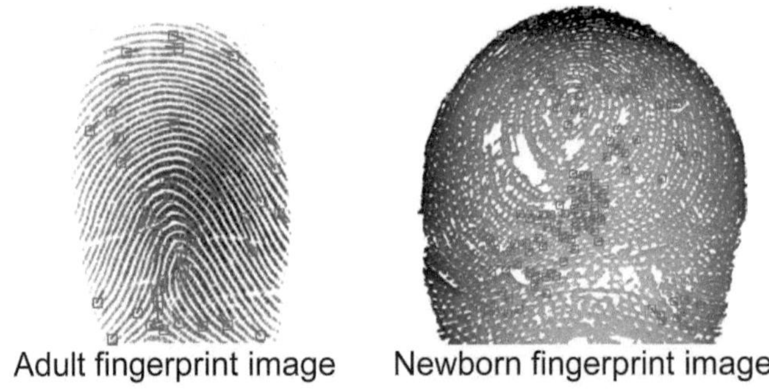

Fig. 1. Adult and newborn fingerprint images with minutiae detected by VeriFinger[6].

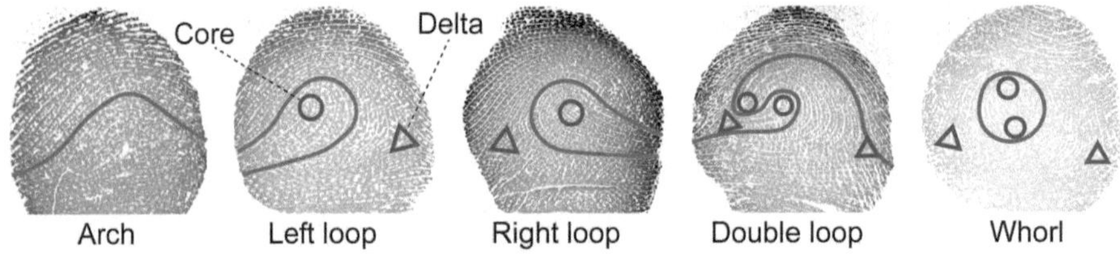

Fig. 2. Fingerprint types used in fingerprint classification.

quality, is used as a loss function. To evaluate the effectiveness of the proposed method, we conduct performance evaluation experiments using the newborn fingerprint dataset [7,8] collected in Kenya, and demonstrate the effectiveness of the proposed method by comparing it with the conventional method.

2 Newborn Fingerprint Recognition Using Fingerprint Classification

In this section, we describe the newborn fingerprint recognition method proposed in this paper. Figure 3 shows the overview of the proposed method. First, an image enhancement method based on the frequency spectrum [17] is applied to the input image. During training, data augmentation is then applied with a probability of 50%. Next, the pre-processed image is input to the newborn fingerprint recognition network, which consists ABN and OME. The ABN-based architecture is based on ABN [3] and extracts 512-dimensional feature vectors from the input fingerprint images. The OME-based architecture uses OME of FingerNet [15] to extract features related to the orientation map and obtain a 512-dimensional feature vector in the same way. These two feature vectors are combined to form a 1,024-dimensional vector, which is then input to the fully-connected layer. Then, a softmax function is applied to the output to obtain classification results. For the computation of the loss functions during training, we prepare a fully-connected layer corresponding to the 512-dimensional feature

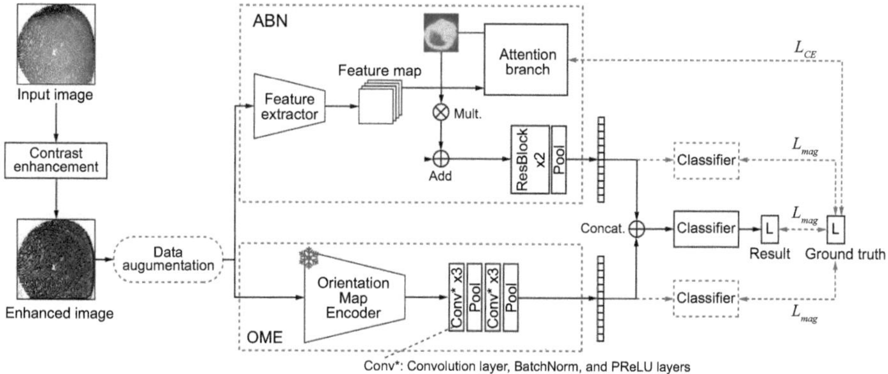

Fig. 3. Overview of the proposed method of newborn fingerprint recognition using fingerprint classification. The weights for OME is fixed in training of the proposed method.

vectors of each of ABN and OME, and apply a deep metric learning, MagFace [10], to each of the prediction score. In addition, for the prediction scores output by the attention branch of ABN, we also compute the cross entropy loss. We describe each process in detail below.

2.1 ABN-Based Architecture

The proposed method utilizes an ABN-based network to focus on global patterns in newborn fingerprint images. ABN [3] is a method for focusing on regions of importance in classification by incorporating an attention mechanism, i.e., an attention branch in ABN, into general deep learning models such as ResNet [4]. In ABN-based Architecture, a feature map is extracted from an input image using ResNet-18 as well as ABN [3]. The attention branch generates an attention map based on the class activation map [20] using that feature map, and assigns weights to regions of interest in the feature map using this attention map. The weighted feature map is added to the original feature map to obtain a new feature map that focuses on the regions of interest while preventing the loss of important information. Thus, we expect that ABN will improve classification accuracy by focusing on global patterns that are effective for classification even in newborn fingerprint images.

2.2 OME-Based Architecture

The proposed method utilizes an OME-based network to exploit the ridge flow, i.e., orientation map information, in fingerprint images. The OME-based architecture utilizes the structure of the orientation map generation network designed as a preliminary step for minutia extraction in FingerNet [15]. FingerNet is a deep learning method specialized for minutia extraction and has the ability to

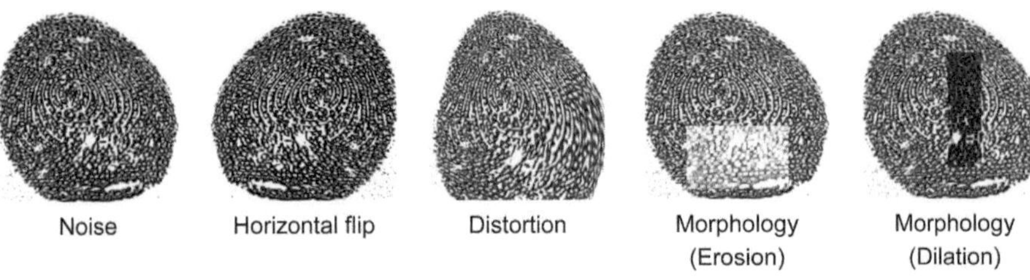

Fig. 4. Newborn fingerprint images after data augmentation used in this paper.

estimate the direction, spacing, and confidence level of ridges from fingerprint images. The proposed method utilizes the OME part, which generates orientation maps, to extract useful features from fingerprint images. The OME-based architecture consists of OME followed by a posterior part that consists of convolution blocks and pooling layers. In the proposed method, the convolution block consists of a convolution layer, batch normalization, and PReLU. After passing through the convolution block, pooling is applied, and this configuration is repeated twice to extract features related to the orientation map while compressing them. While the ABN-based architecture focuses on the region of interest from the entire image, the OME-based architecture focuses on the geometrical information of ridge flow. The integration of both architectures is designed to efficiently extract features useful for classification even from unclear newborn fingerprint images.

2.3 Data Augmentation

We apply data augmentation to improve the diversity of training data to enhance the classification performance for newborn fingerprint images. The proposed method employs four methods that have been reported to be effective in fingerprint recognition [11,14]: RandomNoise, RandomHorizontalFlip, RandomDistortion, and RandomMorphology. RandomNoise adds random noise to the entire image, while RandomHorizontalFlip flips left and right to increase robustness to geometric changes in the fingerprint image. RandomDistortion and RandomMorphology are introduced to emulate the variations inherent in fingerprint images. RandomDistortion reproduces the distortion [1] caused by the softness of the finger during image acquisition, and gradually adds distortion from the center of the image to the outside. The strength of this distortion is changed randomly for each image. RandomMorphology is a process that applies morphology operations locally to the ridge structure, applying erosion to half of the images and dilation to the other half. Erosion can emulate dry fingers, and dilation can emulate wet fingers. Each of these data augmentation processes is applied to the training data with a probability of 50%. Figure 4 shows examples of a fingerprint image after applying data augmentation.

2.4 Loss Functions

The proposed method uses two types of loss functions, MagFace [10] and cross entropy loss, in training the network. MagFace [10] is one of the deep metric learning methods such as ArcFace [2] and AdaCos [18], and aims to improve the discriminability of the feature space in classification tasks. MagFace [10] improves the discriminability between classes by keeping the angles of feature vectors between the same class small and increasing the angles between different classes, and also introduces image quality-dependent constraints on the amplitude of feature vectors. The amplitude of vectors corresponding to images with small angles between feature vectors, i.e., high image quality, is trained to be larger, and the amplitude of vectors corresponding to low image quality with large angles is trained to be smaller. This is expected to result in robust feature representation for low quality newborn fingerprint images. In addition, the cross entropy loss is applied as an auxiliary loss to the prediction score output from the attention branch in the ABN-based architecture to improve classification accuracy. The total loss function is the sum of the deep metric learning loss by MagFace and the cross entropy loss, and aims to achieve both recognition performance and robustness.

2.5 OME Pre-training

The proposed method uses a pre-trained OME module, which is responsible for extracting orientation information of fingerprint ridges, and incorporates the trained model into the classification network. As mentioned above, OME is a module designed as part of FingerNet [15] and is responsible for extracting orientation maps from fingerprint images. Although the ground truth of orientation map, segmentation mask, and minutiae are required for training FingerNet [15], it is difficult to obtain these ground truth values for newborn fingerprint images because of the extremely low contrast of the ridges. Therefore, in this paper, we apply data augmentation to adult fingerprint images with clear structure to emulate low-quality newborn fingerprint images, train FingerNet [15] using these images, and use the resulting OME as a pre-trained module.

We use the NIST Special Database 4 (NIST SD4)[3] provided by the National Institute of Standards and Technology (NIST) for training FingerNet. NIST SD4 is widely used in fingerprint recognition and contains fingerprint images of diverse patterns and qualities. In this paper, we use 4,000 adult fingerprint images in NIST SD4 for training. We apply data augmentation to the fingerprint images, such as distortion and contrast changes described in Sect. 2.3, to emulate the characteristics of newborn fingerprints. In addition, RandomErasing [19] is introduced to mask a portion of the fingerprint region with a rectangular region of random size and position to reproduce defects caused by fetal finger surface. For training FingerNet, Adam [6] is used as the optimizer, the learning rate is set to 1.0×10^{-4}, the batch size to 16, and the number of training epochs to 200.

[3] https://www.nist.gov/srd/nist-special-database-4.

The ground-truth minutiae are extracted using VeriFinger SDK[6], which is a commercial fingerprint recognition software. The ground-truth orientation map is obtained by applying a Sobel filter to the input image $I(x, y)$ to compute the horizontal and vertical gradient components G_x and G_y, respectively, and then computing the gradient direction $\theta(x, y)$ for each local block by

$$\theta(x,y) = \frac{1}{2}\arctan\left(\frac{2\sum G_x G_y}{\sum G_x^2 - \sum G_y^2 + \epsilon}\right), \tag{1}$$

where ϵ is a small constant to prevent zero division in the denominator. A window of 17×17 pixels is used for this gradient aggregation, which is applied to the entire image in strides of 8-pixel intervals to obtain a smooth angle map for each local region. In creating the ground-truth segmentation mask, the image $I(x, y)$ is first normalized based on the mean and standard deviation to obtain a normalized image $I'(x, y)$. A Sobel filter is then applied to $I'(x, y)$ to obtain the gradient components G'_x and G'_y. Using them, the magnitude of the gradient $G'(x, y)$ is calculated by

$$G'(x,y) = \sqrt{{G'_x}^2 + {G'_y}^2}. \tag{2}$$

This gradient $G'(x, y)$ is divided into 17×17 pixel windows and scanned in 8-pixel strides. Within each block, the variance of $G'(x, y)$ is calculated, and the ground-truth segmentation mask $S(x, y)$ is obtained by assigning 1 to the block if the variance exceeds a threshold, and 0 to the other blocks as the background. In addition, the morphological operation, i.e., dilation, is applied to interpolate noise and small gaps that exist on the mask to improve the smoothness and continuity between regions.

FingerNet [15] is trained with the orientation map, segmentation mask, and minutiae obtained by the above process as the ground truth, and the OME module responsible for orientation map generation is obtained from the trained FingerNet. The trained OME is incorporated into the network of the proposed method with fixed weights. Thus, robust feature extraction with respect to the global ridge orientation can be achieved even for the blurred newborn fingerprint images.

2.6 Newborn Fingerprint Recognition Using Fingerprint Classification

In the proposed method, newborn fingerprint images are classified, and person authentication is performed based on the classification results. The proposed method employs four fingers, including the thumbs and index fingers of both hands, since the recognition accuracy is not sufficient with only one finger. Fingerprint image classification is performed on each finger using the proposed method, and the class with the highest score is used as the classification result for that finger. The finger is identified when the classification results for all four fingers completely match. The number of combination patterns that can theoretically be distinguished varies depending on the number of fingerprint types used for classification. For example, there are $4^5 = 1,024$ patterns when 5 types are used, and $4^4 = 256$ patterns when 4 types are used, however, this number of combinations is not sufficient for large-scale newborn authentication. In actual operation, therefore, mother-child authentication is achieved by connecting the biometric information of the mother and the newborn to increase the accuracy and reliability of identification. In an environment where the matching target is limited, such as birth registration and personal identification in a hospital unit, the combination of classification results using this method is sufficient, and identification of twins is also possible. In a field study in Kenya, we have confirmed that there is no problem in applying the method in such an operational setting.

3 Experiments and Discussion

In this section, we describe the dataset and experimental conditions, and conduct fundamental studies of OME, an ablation study of the proposed method, and a performance comparison with the conventional method to verify the effectiveness of the proposed method.

3.1 Newborn Fingerprint Image Dataset

The experiments in this paper employs a fingerprint image dataset collected from newborns between 2 and 24 h after birth, as part of an empirical study conducted in Kenya [7,8]. This dataset comprises fingerprint images from 82 newborns, captured four times from each of the thumbs and index fingers on both hands. Each image is manually annotated by experts with one of five fingerprint pattern labels: "Arch", "Double loop", "Left loop", "Right loop", or "Whorl". The dataset is divided into three subsets: the training set consists of 1,357 images (Arch: 229, Double: 120, Left: 319, Right: 343, Whorl: 346); the validation set consists of 166 images (Arch: 44, Double: 26, Left: 33, Right: 30, Whorl: 33); and the test set consists of 1,172 images (Arch: 96, Double: 118, Left: 304, Right: 281, Whorl: 373).

3.2 Experimental Condition

In training of the proposed method, RMSprop [16] is used as the optimizer, the weight decay factor is set to 4.0×10^{-5}, the learning rate is set to 1.0×10^{-4}, and the batch size is 16, and training is executed for 200 epochs. The hyperparameters of MagFace are set as scaling factor $s = 2$, weight factor $\lambda = 110$, magnitude range of feature vectors as $[l_m, u_m] = [0.04, 0.08]$, and angle margin range as $[l_a, u_a] = [10, 110]$. Since we have found that "Double loop" and "Whorl" tend to be confused with each other in newborn fingerprint images through our empirical study, we merge them and use four classes of Arch (A), Left loop (L), Right loop (R), and Double/Whorl (D/W) in the experiments. The performance of methods is evaluated using the accuracy (Acc.), which indicates the rate of correct classification for fingerprint image classification, and True Accept Rate (TAR), which is the acceptance rate for personal authentication.

Table 1. Experimental results of angular resolution for creating orientation maps. Bold type indicates the best results.

Angular resolution	Acc. [%]↑					TAR [%]↑
	A	L	R	D/W	All	
2°	71.88	95.72	**94.37**	97.02	94.02	85.37
6°	79.17	96.71	93.66	96.62	94.52	**87.80**
10°	**81.25**	96.71	92.25	95.63	93.93	80.49
20°	71.88	96.38	92.61	**97.22**	93.85	**87.80**
30°	**81.25**	96.38	92.96	95.03	93.77	82.93
45°	79.17	**98.03**	93.66	96.42	**94.78**	85.37

3.3 Fundamental Studies on OME

We investigate fundamental studies on OME by conducting two experiments. The first is to verify the effect of angular resolution on classification accuracy in orientation maps. Angle resolution is a measure of how many degrees the ridge direction is discretized and represented as an orientation map, where the default value in FingerNet is 2°. Since FingerNet is designed for adult fingerprint images, the same resolution may not be optimal for newborn fingerprint images. Therefore, we verify the appropriate angular resolution by setting multiple resolutions, evaluating their performance, and comparing the classification accuracy of each. The second is to investigate the effect of the network architecture consisting of OME on the classification performance. The original configuration of FingerNet is based on VGG-D (VGG-16) [13], which uses only the first three of the five convolutional blocks and removes the fully-connected layer. This configuration is not necessarily optimal for newborn fingerprint images. Therefore, we compare several configurations with different encoder architectures and evaluate their impact on classification performance.

(i) Angular Resolution for Orientation Maps—In creating orientation maps, the angular resolution was set to 2°, 6°, 10°, 20°, 30°, and 45°, and the accuracy of fingerprint image classification was evaluated under each condition. Table 1 shows the experimental results. When the angular resolution was set to 45°, the accuracy and TAR were 94.78% and 85.37%, respectively. On the other hand, finer resolution improved classification accuracy for some fingerprint types, while overall classification performance decreased. This is consistent with the objective of this paper, which is to classify fingerprint images based on global ridge patterns rather than minutia detection. Fine angular resolution is not required, and the coarse angular resolution suppresses the effect of noise, likely highlighting the major directional structures that contribute to classification. The coarse angular resolution is also more practical given the limitation of fine orientation estimation due to the ridge blurring inherent in newborn fingerprint images. Based on the above, in the following experiments, the angular resolution is set to 45° in the creation of orientation maps.

Table 2. Experimental results of encoder architectures used for OME. Bold type indicates the best results.

Encoder	Acc. [%]↑					TAR [%]↑
	A	L	R	D/W	All	
VGG-A [13]	**81.25**	95.39	92.61	96.22	93.93	85.37
VGG-B [13]	73.96	95.72	92.25	95.63	93.09	84.15
VGG-C [13]	73.96	97.37	**94.37**	95.63	94.02	86.59
VGG-D [13]	79.17	**98.03**	93.66	96.42	**94.78**	85.37
VGG-E [13]	72.92	97.70	92.61	**96.82**	94.10	85.37
ResNet-18 [4]	79.17	95.39	91.20	96.02	93.34	82.93
ResNet-34 [4]	71.88	96.38	92.25	96.62	93.51	84.15
SE-ResNet-18 [5]	76.04	95.39	91.90	94.63	92.67	82.93
SE-ResNet-34 [5]	**81.25**	96.38	93.31	96.22	94.36	**87.80**

(ii) Encoder Architecture for OME—We investigated the impact of encoder architectures used in OME on the performance of fingerprint image classification. In this experiment, we compared five architectures based on VGG [13], two ResNets [4], and two SE-ResNets, which integrate ResNet and Squeeze-and-Excitation (SE) module [5]. VGG is a model that extracts hierarchical features by stacking 3×3 small convolution kernels, where configurations A-E correspond to VGG-11, VGG-13, improved VGG-13, VGG-16, and VGG-19, respectively, as in [13]. ResNet [4] is a model that suppresses gradient loss during deepening by using residual connections and enables efficient training. SE-ResNet introduces a Squeeze-and-Excitation (SE) module [5] that dynamically trains the relationship between channels, and selectively emphasizes important features to improve the representation performance. Table 2 shows the experimental results. SE-ResNet-34 achieved the highest TAR, while VGG-D (VGG-16) achieved the highest classification accuracy, especially for the Arch and Double/Whorl classes. These results indicate that VGG-D, which was originally used as an encoder for OME in FingerNet [15], has high performance for the newborn fingerprint classification task. Focusing on the high accuracy of fingerprint image classification, we use VGG-D (VGG-16) as the encoder for OME in the following experiments.

3.4 Ablation Study of Image Enhancement and Data Augmentation

We conducted an ablation study to examine the effectiveness of image enhancement and data augmentation in the proposed method. The five target components are image enhancement (En), RandomNoise (No), RandomHorizontalFlip (HF), RandomDistortion (Di), and RandomMorphology (Mo). For each of these components, we evaluated their impact on the accuracy of fingerprint image classification by comparing the condition in which one of them was removed with the condition in which all of them were applied. Table 3 shows the experimental results. The highest classification accuracy and second highest TAR were

Table 3. Experimental results of ablation study for the proposed method (En: Image enhancement, No: RnadomNoise, HF: RandomHorizontalFlip, Di: RandomDistortion, and Mo: RandomMorphology). Bold type indicates the best results.

Component					Acc. [%]↑					TAR [%]↑
En	No	HF	Di	Mo	A	L	R	D/W	All	
✓	✓	✓	✓	✓	79.17	**98.03**	**93.66**	**96.42**	**94.78**	85.37
	✓	✓	✓	✓	73.96	94.74	90.85	94.43	92.00	82.93
✓		✓	✓	✓	76.04	94.74	91.55	95.03	92.59	84.15
✓	✓		✓	✓	67.71	95.39	92.96	93.44	91.74	78.05
✓	✓	✓		✓	71.88	96.71	92.96	96.02	93.51	**86.59**
✓	✓	✓	✓		**82.29**	96.05	92.96	95.63	94.02	85.37

Table 4. Experimental results of loss function used in the proposed method. Bold type indicates the best results.

Loss function	Acc. [%]↑					TAR [%]↑
	A	L	R	D/W	All	
CE Loss	70.83	**98.35**	93.30	**96.82**	94.27	**86.59**
ArcFace [2]	77.08	94.08	91.20	95.83	92.75	81.71
AdaCos [18]	77.08	96.38	**94.37**	95.03	93.77	82.93
MagFace [10]	**79.17**	98.03	93.66	96.42	**94.78**	85.37

achieved when all components were applied. On the other hand, overall accuracy and performance degradation in some classes were observed when any one component was removed. Image enhancement improved contrast for newborn fingerprint images with unclear ridges and contributed to the enhancement of directional structure. RandomNoise and RandomHorizontalFlip improved generalization performance by introducing diversity for a limited number of datasets. RandomDistortion and RandomMorphology emulated image deformations inherent to newborns and improved robustness to low-quality images. From the above results, the introduction of image enhancement and all data augmentation in the proposed method is effective in improving the classification performance for newborn fingerprint images. In the following experiments, we use image enhancement and all data augmentation in the proposed method.

3.5 Comparison of Loss Function

We conducted experiments on the effect of different loss functions on the performance of fingerprint image classification. The loss functions used in this experiment are the Cross entropy loss (CE Loss), ArcFace [2], AdaCos [18], and MagFace [10]. CE Loss is the most fundamental classification loss function and minimizes the cross-entropy with the ground-truth label. ArcFace [2] is a method

Table 5. Experimental results of network architectures used in the proposed method. Bold type indicates the best results.

Architecture	Acc. [%]↑					TAR [%]↑
	A	L	R	D/W	All	
ABN	76.04	96.71	**94.01**	95.63	93.93	84.15
OME	52.08	89.47	90.85	90.66	87.28	71.95
ABN+OME	**79.17**	**98.03**	93.66	**96.42**	**94.78**	**85.37**

Table 6. Comparison of the conventional method and the proposed method. Bold type indicates the best results.

Method	Acc. [%]↑					TAR [%]↑
	A	L	R	D/W	All	
Koda et al. [7]	69.79	88.82	89.79	91.05	88.46	71.95
Proposed	**79.17**	**98.03**	**93.66**	**96.42**	**94.78**	**85.37**

that improves discriminability between classes by introducing an angular margin at the classification boundary. AdaCos [18] aims at efficient normalization-based learning by automatically adjusting scaling factors in the feature space during training. MagFace [10] uses the same angular distance-based loss as ArcFace [2] and AdaCos [18], and furthermore, by using the magnitude information of the feature vectors, it enables learning based on the image difficulty and quality. Table 4 shows the experimental results. MagFace achieved the highest overall classification accuracy and the second highest TAR. CE Loss also achieved the highest accuracy, although the classification accuracy of "Arch" was significantly lower than that of the other loss functions. These results indicate that for newborn fingerprint images, which are difficult to classify due to unclear ridge structures, the loss calculation depending on the image quality as MagFace works effectively and contributes to improving the overall classification performance and identification accuracy.

3.6 Comparison of Network Architecture

We conducted experiments to demonstrate the effectiveness of the combination of ABN and OME architectures used in the proposed method by comparing the results with those obtained when ABN and OME are used individually. Table 5 shows the experimental results. ABN exhibited high classification performance by focusing on important regions on the image, while OME, which complements the structural information in the image, did not exhibit satisfactory performance. ABN+OME exhibited the highest classification performance due to the effective combination of local attention mechanisms and global structural information. The results indicate that the combination of ABN and OME can provide robust

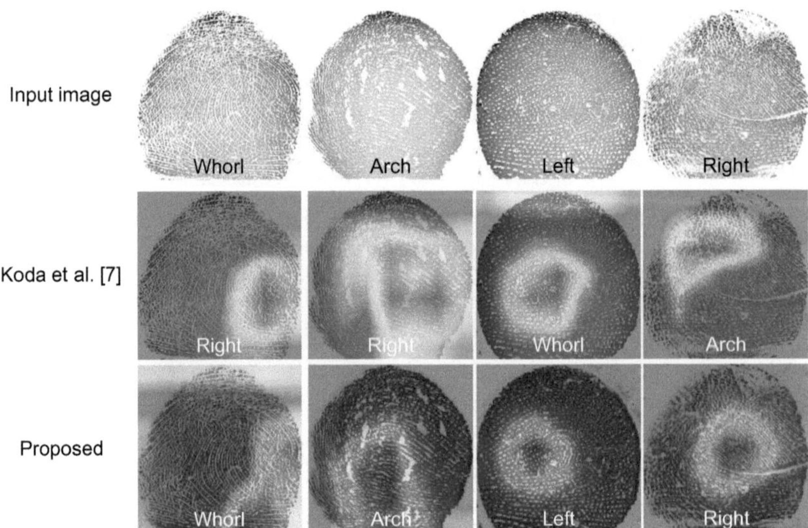

Fig. 5. Visualization results of the regions of attention using Grad-CAM [12] and classification results for the conventional and proposed methods.

feature extraction and stable classification even for low-quality newborn fingerprint images.

3.7 Comparison of Conventional Method

We conducted the experiment to verify the effectiveness of the proposed method by comparing it with a conventional method [7]. Table 6 shows the experimental results. The proposed method outperformed the accuracy of the conventional method [7] in all evaluations. This is due to the introduction of a combined ABN and OME architecture, image enhancement, data augmentation, and an image quality-aware loss function, taking into account the characteristics of the newborn fingerprint images. We also attempted fingerprint classification and matching using VeriFinger (see Footnote 2), however, we could not obtain valid results since the ridges in the newborn fingerprint images were unclear and minutiae could not be detected. We also visualized the regions of attention using Grad-CAM [12] to compare the classification evidence of the conventional and the proposed methods. Figure 5 shows the visualization results and the corresponding classification results. The conventional method fails to accurately focus on the cores and deltas, often leading to misclassification, whereas the proposed method correctly classifies the newborn fingerprint images since the cores and deltas can be accurately focused on. These results indicate that the proposed method properly focuses on the characteristic regions of each class and achieves stable classification decisions.

4 Conclusion

We proposed a newborn fingerprint recognition method based on fingerprint classification. The proposed method integrates attention-based and orientation-aware feature extraction, image enhancement, data augmentation, and an image quality-aware loss to address the challenges of newborn fingerprint classification. Experimental evaluations on a real-world dataset collected in Kenya demonstrated that the proposed method outperformed conventional method in both classification and recognition accuracy. These results highlight the potential of the proposed method for reliable newborn recognition in practical settings

Acknowledgment. Authors hereby declare that the parents or guardians of babies who join this research were requested correctly to sign a consent form as permission for their participation in this research. Before data collection, this research is appropriately approved by SERU of KEMRI. The authors disclose the receipt of the extraordinary on-site assistance for the research of this article from supporters in Kenya. We hereby express our gratitude to the Kwale County government, Kenya, the NUITM-KEMRI project office in Kenya of Nagasaki University Institute of Tropical Medicine, The Center for Microbiology Research, KEMRI, and the Director General, KEMRI. This work was supported in part by JSPS KAKENHI 23H00463 and 25K03131.

References

1. Cappelli, R., Maio, D., Maltoni, D.: Modelling plastic distortion in fingerprint images. In: Proceedings of the International Conference on Advances in Pattern Recognition, pp. 371–378 (2001)
2. Deng, J., Guo, J., Zafeiriou, S.: ArcFace: additive angular margin loss for deep face recognition. In: Proceedings of the IEEE/CVF Conference on Computer Vision and Pattern Recognition, pp. 4685–4694 (2019)
3. Fukui, H., Hirakawa, T., Yamashita, T., Fujiyoshi, H.: Attention branch network: learning of attention mechanism for visual explanation. In: Proceedings of the IEEE/CVF Conference on Computer Vision and Pattern Recognition, pp. 10705–10714 (2019)
4. He, K., Zhang, X., Ren, S., Sun, J.: Deep residual learning for image recognition. In: Proceedings of the IEEE/CVF Conference on Computer Vision and Pattern Recognition, pp. 770–778 (2016)
5. Hu, J., Shen, L., Sun, G.: Squeeze-and-excitation networks. In: Proceedings of the IEEE/CVF Conference on Computer Vision and Pattern Recognition, pp. 7132–7141 (2018)
6. Kingma, D.P., Ba, J.: Adam: a method for stochastic optimization. arXiv preprint arXiv:1412.6980 (2017)
7. Koda, Y., et al.: Fundamental study of neonate fingerprint recognition using fingerprint classification. In: Proceedings of the International Conference on Biometrics Special Interest Group, pp. 162–172 (2022)
8. Koda, Y., Takahashi, A., Ito, K., Aoki, T., Kaneko, S., Nzou, S.M.: Development of 2,400PPI fingerprint sensor for capturing neonate fingerprint within 24 hours after birth. In: Proceedings of the International Conference on Biometrics Special Interest Group, pp. 95–106 (2019)

9. Maltoni, D., Maio, D., Jain, A.K., Feng, J.: Handbook of Fingerprint Recognition. Springer (2022)
10. Qiang, M., Shichao, Z., Zhida, H., Feng, Z.: MagFace: a universal representation for face recognition and quality assessment. In: Proceedings of the IEEE/CVF Conference on Computer Vision and Pattern Recognition, pp. 14225–14234 (2021)
11. Sasuga, N., Ito, K., Aoki, T.: Fingerprint feature extraction using CNN with multiple attention mechanisms. In: Proceedings of the International Conference on Biometrics, pp. 1–8 (2022)
12. Selvaraju, R., Cogswell, M., Das, A., Vedantam, R., Parikh, D., Batra, D.: Grad-CAM: visual explanations from deep networks via gradient-based localization. In: Proceedings of the IEEE International Conference on Computer Vision, pp. 618–626 (2017)
13. Simonyan, K., Zisserman, A.: Very deep convolutional networks for large-scale image recognition. arXiv preprint arXiv:1409.1556 (2015)
14. Takahashi, A., Koda, Y., Ito, K., Aoki, T.: Fingerprint feature extraction by combining texture, minutiae, and frequency spectrum using multi-task CNN. In: Proceedings of the International Joint Conference on Biometrics, pp. 1–8 (2020)
15. Tang, Y., Gao, F., Feng, J., Liu, Y.: FingerNet: an unified deep network for fingerprint minutiae extraction. In: Proceedings of the IEEE International Conference on Biometrics, pp. 108–116 (2017)
16. Tieleman, T., Hinton, G.: Lecture 6.5-RMSprop: neural networks for machine learning. COURSERA: Neural Netw. Mach. Learn. **4**(2), 26–31 (2012)
17. Watson, C., Candela, G., Grother, P.: Comparison of FFT fingerprint filtering methods for neural network classification. NISTIR **5493**, 1–30 (1994)
18. Xiao, Z., Rui, Z., Yu, Q., Xiaogang, W., Hongsheng, L.: AdaCos: adaptively scaling cosine logits for effectively learning deep face representations. In: Proceedings of the IEEE/CVF International Conference on Computer Vision and Pattern Recognition, pp. 10823–10832 (2019)
19. Zhong, Z., Zheng, L., Kang, G., Li, S., Yang, Y.: Random erasing data augmentation. Proc. AAAI Conf. Artif. Intell. **34**(7), 13001–13008 (2020)
20. Zhou, B., Khosla, A., Lapedriza, A., Oliva, A., Torralba, A.: Learning deep features for discriminative localization. In: Proceedings of the IEEE/CVF International Conference on Computer Vision and Pattern Recognition, pp. 2921–2929 (2016)

SCReedSolo: A Secure and Robust LSB Image Steganography Framework with Randomized Symmetric Encryption and ReedSolomon Coding

Syed Rifat Raiyan[1] and Md. Hasanul Kabir[2(✉)]

[1] Systems and Software Lab (SSL), Department of Computer Science and Engineering, Islamic University of Technology, Dhaka, Bangladesh
rifatraiyan@iut-dhaka.edu

[2] Computer Vision Lab (CVLab), Department of Computer Science and Engineering, Islamic University of Technology, Dhaka, Bangladesh
hasanul@iut-dhaka.edu

Abstract. Image steganography is an information-hiding technique that involves the surreptitious concealment of covert informational content within digital images. In this paper, we introduce SCReedSolo, a novel framework for concealing arbitrary binary data within images. Our approach synergistically leverages Random Shuffling, Fernet Symmetric Encryption, and ReedSolomon Error Correction Codes to encode the secret payload, which is then discretely embedded into the carrier image using LSB (Least Significant Bit) Steganography. The combination of these methods addresses the vulnerability vectors of both security and resilience against bit-level corruption in the resultant stego-images. We show that our framework achieves a data payload of 3 bits per pixel for an RGB image, and mathematically assess the probability of successful transmission for the amalgamated n message bits and k error correction bits. Additionally, we find that SCReedSolo yields good results upon being evaluated with multiple performance metrics, successfully eludes detection by various passive steganalysis tools, and is immune to simple active steganalysis attacks. Our code and data are available at https://github.com/Starscream-11813/SCReedSolo-Steganography

Keywords: Cryptography · Error Correction · Fernet · Reed–Solomon Coding · Steganography · Symmetric Cipher

1 Introduction

The fundamental aim of image steganography is to embed a confidential message within an image with such precision and subtlety that its presence remains wholly indiscernible to both scrutiny and suspicion. Unlike cryptographic techniques, which mainly focus on rendering messages unintelligible to unauthorized

C. Wallraven et al. (Eds.): ACPR 2025, LNCS 16174, pp. 221–237, 2026.
https://doi.org/10.1007/978-981-95-4395-3_16

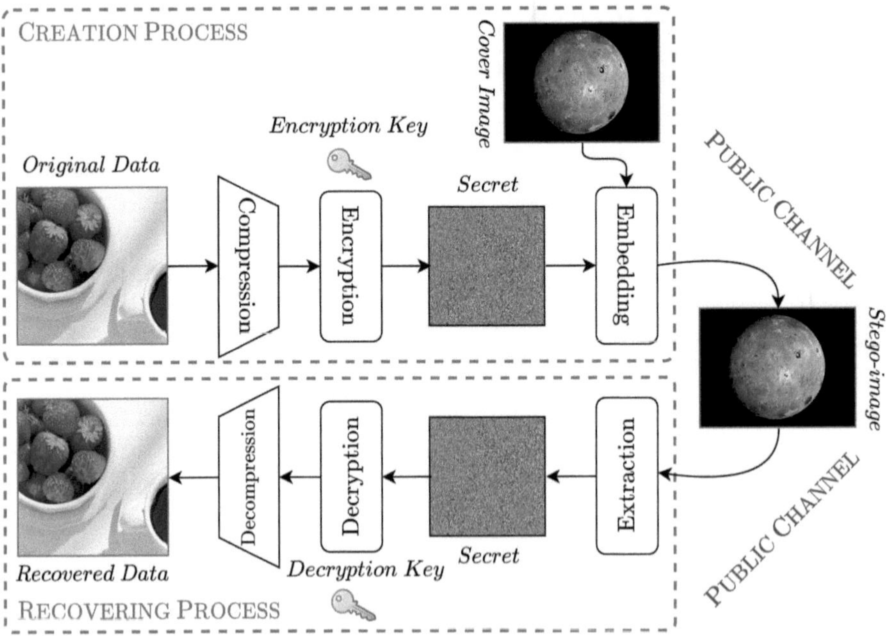

Fig. 1. General pipeline of a secure image steganography algorithm

interlocutors, steganography adopts an orthogonal objective: to veil the message's very presence and perceptual detectability [17]. In a typical use case, a sender embeds the hidden message utilizing a cover image as a substrate, which is then dispatched to the recipient through a communication channel, ostensibly indistinguishable from its unaltered counterpart to unauthorized observers. The recipient, in order to retrieve the latent message, invokes an extraction protocol—often predicated on shared cryptographic primitives or stego-key synchronization, thereby ensuring that any intercepting party remains oblivious of the message's existence [10]. The general pipeline of image steganography is as portrayed in Fig. 1. Steganography has been practiced for centuries, with one of its most widely recognized forms being invisible writing, often achieved through the use of invisible ink. This technique gained particular prominence during World War II [7].

Conventional image steganographic methodologies are constrained by an empirically established payload threshold of approximately 0.4 bits per pixel [13]. Exceeding this critical threshold invariably induces quantifiable distortions, such as deviations in histogram distributions or localized pixel correlation anomalies, which manifest as statistical anomalies detectable by adversarial steganalysis tools and, in severe cases, perceptible to the human eye. However, a new wave of image steganography techniques has emerged with the rapid development of deep learning technologies over the past decade [1,4,21]. These modern methods adopt a bifurcated strategy: either by assimilating neural network architectures to refine established algorithmic frameworks—such as leveraging deep learning to discern optimal loci for data concealment—or function as end-to-end image processing pipelines that integrate a carrier image and secret payload into a steganographic construct. Contemporary deep learning-based methods, however, exhibit certain limitations when juxtaposed with traditional techniques. For instance, they often impose dimension-specific constraints, *e.g.* the requirement for 32×32 pixel cover images in the method proposed by [4]. Moreover, these methods primarily focus on embedding images within other images, instead of arbitrary messages or binary data streams, while not fully probing into security, noise immunity, and finding the upper bounds of quantifiable information that can be effectively concealed. To avoid the temporal overhead of such resource-hungry approaches [20], in this paper, we resort to a rudimentary approach, which is LSB Steganography [3]. We also introduce the idea of amalgamating cryptography, more specifically Fernet Symmetric Encryption [2], with image steganography to fortify the confidentiality and integrity of the secret message as it traverses the communication channel between the originating and receiving entities. This channel, however, may be susceptible to bit-corruption attacks, which is why we also include the Reed–Solomon error correction codes [14] of the secret message as a portion of the payload. The harmonious integration of the aforementioned methods culminates in our proposed novel framework SCREEDSOLO, a secure and robust image steganography method where the secret message is Randomly **S**huffled, encrypted using the Fernet Symmetric **C**ipher, and safeguarded using **Reed**–**Solo**mon codes. The primary contributions of this paper are:

1. We propose SCREEDSOLO, a novel and robust steganographic framework. Our approach uniquely combines Random Shuffling for obscurity, Fernet Symmetric Encryption for confidentiality, and Reed–Solomon Error Correction Codes for data integrity, all within a traditional LSB embedding scheme.
2. We address two critical vectors of vulnerability in data transmission—security and resilience. The cryptographic layer ensures that the hidden payload remains unintelligible even if detected, while the error correction layer guarantees message recovery in the presence of channel noise or simple active attacks.
3. We achieve a high data payload of 3 bits per pixel for an RGB carrier image, a significant capacity that pushes the boundaries of LSB-based methods without introducing statistically significant artifacts.
4. We conduct a thorough validation of SCREEDSOLO, presenting a mathematical assessment of its error correction capabilities and demonstrating its effectiveness through extensive evaluation with multiple performance metrics and its ability to elude various passive steganalysis tools.

2 Literature Review

The dawn of research on steganography can be traced back to ancient Greece and Rome [18]. Since then, numerous steganographic techniques have emerged, and they can be categorized across a multitude of classes.

2.1 Traditional Approaches

Among the standard algorithms in the domain of image steganography, the Highly Undetectable steGO^{TM} (HUGO) stands out as a paragon of cost function-based approaches. This sophisticated algorithm employs meticulously crafted features to quantify the distortion introduced by pixel value modifications at specific loci within the image. When tasked with the embedding of N bits, HUGO leverages its distortion function to identify the optimal N pixels for modification, thereby minimizing the aggregate distortion across the entire image [13].

In contrast, the JSTEG algorithm represents a specialized approach tailored explicitly for JPEG image formats. To appreciate the nuances of JSTEG, one must first understand the underlying mechanics of JPEG compression. This process entails the transformation of the image into the frequency domain via the Discrete Cosine Transform (DCT), followed by the selective elimination of high-frequency components, culminating in a reduction of the image file size. JSTEG ingeniously co-opts this frequency domain transformation, but diverges in its methodology by manipulating the least significant bits of the frequency coefficients [9].

2.2 Deep Learning-Based Approaches

The application of deep learning methodologies to the domain of image steganography has recently garnered significant attention within the research community, yielding a spectrum of promising outcomes. The extant corpus of proposals in this burgeoning field exhibits a remarkable diversity, spanning a continuum of approaches that synergistically integrate neural networks with traditional steganographic techniques.

At one end of this spectrum, we observe efforts to augment and refine conventional steganographic methods through the judicious application of neural network architectures [16]. This approach seeks to leverage the pattern recognition and feature extraction capabilities of deep learning to enhance the efficacy and robustness of established steganographic algorithms. In contrast, at the frontier of this field, we find more prudent propositions that advocate for the implementation of end-to-end convolutional neural networks. These advanced systems harness the power of adversarial training paradigms to generate steganographic images of unprecedented convincingness and undetectability [4,21]. Such approaches represent a paradigm shift in steganographic methodology, moving away from hand-crafted features and heuristics towards learned representations that can adapt to the nuances of diverse image types and potential attacks.

The nascent field of deep learning-based steganography witnessed its inaugural contributions in the seminal works of [1,19]. These pioneering studies converged on a specific paradigm: the embedding of a secret image within a cover image. While groundbreaking, this approach represents a distinct departure from the conventional steganographic objective of embedding arbitrary data. The fundamental divergence in these methodologies presents a significant challenge when attempting to draw comparative analyses between these novel techniques and traditional steganographic algorithms, particularly in terms of relative payload capacity. The crux of this disparity lies in the inherent properties of natural images, which were the focus of both [1,19]. Such images invariably exhibit strong spatial correlations, a characteristic that convolutional neural networks, when trained for image-in-image hiding, are inherently predisposed to exploit. This exploitation of image-specific properties, while advantageous for the task at hand, introduces a critical limitation: the resultant models, finely tuned to leverage these spatial correlations, lack the versatility required for the embedding of arbitrary data. The specialization that grants these models their efficacy in image-based steganography simultaneously constrains their applicability to more generalized data-hiding scenarios. The subsequent evolution in deep learning-based image steganography is exemplified by the works of [4,21], which ingeniously incorporate adversarial training techniques. These approaches represent a significant departure from our methodology, with key differentiations manifesting in the loss functions employed for model training, the architectural design of the neural networks, and the manner in which data is presented to these networks. The framework proposed by the authors of [4] is particularly noteworthy for its constraints and unique approach. Their method is predicated on operating exclusively with images of a fixed dimensionality, a limitation that bears significant implications for its practical applicability. The process they delineate involves a series of transformations: initially flattening the image into a vector representation, subsequently concatenating this with the data vector, and finally applying a sequence of feedforward, reshaping, and convolutional layers. In terms of the optimization criteria, their approach utilizes a tripartite loss function strategy. The encoder component is optimized using mean squared error, while the discriminator employs cross-entropy loss. Concurrently, the decoder's performance is again evaluated and optimized through mean squared error. This multi-faceted loss function approach aims to balance the competing demands of data embedding and image fidelity preservation. However, a notable limitation of their method emerges when attempting to increase the data payload beyond a certain threshold. Specifically, they report a significant degradation in image quality when endeavoring to embed more than 0.4 bits per pixel. This constraint underscores the delicate balance between steganographic capacity and the preservation of image integrity, a fundamental challenge in the field of image steganography.

3 Methodology

The purpose of image steganography is to conceal a secret object that can be either an image $f(x, y)$, or an audio signal $f(t)$, or a piece of text S, implicitly within a cover image $g(x, y)$. After the image steganography process is completed, the cover image $g(x, y)$ is called a stego-image $g'(x, y)$, which is then transmitted to the receiver side. If the stego-image reaches the receiver side in its unaltered and uncorrupted form, then the receiver can perform the exact reverse operations to extract the payload secret object from the stego-image

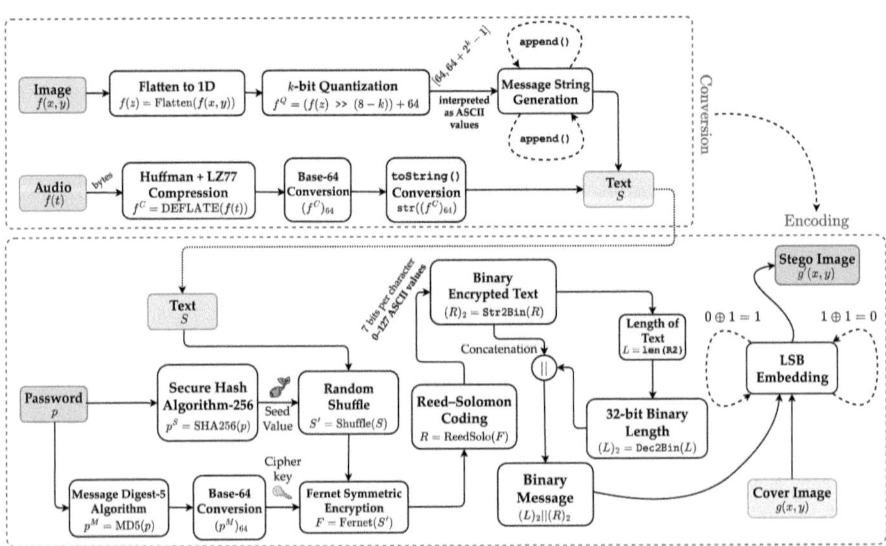

Fig. 2. Overview of our proposed framework SCREEDSOLO. The workflow's upper part converts the image and audio to text, and the part beneath portrays SCREEDSOLO's encoding process.

11101101 11101110 11111000 11110111 01111111 00111111

$R: 62$, $G: 182$, $B: 237$ | $R: 62$, $G: 182$, $B: 238$ | $R: 248$, $G: 127$, $B: 250$ | $R: 247$, $G: 127$, $B: 250$ | $R: 144$, $G: 127$, $B: 250$ | $R: 144$, $G: 63$, $B: 250$

+1, elicits little to no perceptible change.
–1, elicits little to no perceptible change.
–64, elicits significant discoloration.

Fig. 3. Imperceptibility of LSB substitution

$g'(x, y)$. The undergirding idea beneath steganography is the exploitation of the fact that the eyes of human beings cannot perceive minuscule changes in color luminance (see Fig. 3). Figure 2 shows an overview of our proposed framework.

3.1 Signal-to-Text Conversion

For image signals, the first step is to flatten the $c \times M \times N$ image to a 1D array of cMN pixel values. If the cover image doesn't have the necessary capacity to harbor the secret payload, then we can opt to perform k-bit quantization on the pixel values of the secret image. The stipulation here is that the k least significant bits of the pixel values may be worth sacrificing if those bits don't contain useful spatial information. For the flattened image f, we perform the quantization as follows,

$$f^Q = (f >> (8-k)) + 64 \tag{1}$$

It is to be noted that we add a constant value of 64 so that the resultant values can be interpreted as ASCII values (*i.e.* for k-bit quantization, we end up with values from 64 to $64 + 2^k - 1$). Once this quantization is done, the secret image cannot be extracted in its original form, since quantization is irreversible. After the optional k-bit quantization step, we take the ASCII characters and append them to a single text string S.

Due to the repetitive nature of audio signals, it is a salient approach to apply signal compression techniques to reduce the number of bits that we have to eventually embed in the cover image. In SCREEDSOLO we use the proprietary DEFLATE algorithm [11] of the `zlib`[1] package. It is a combination of two lossless compression techniques, namely Huffman coding [5] and LZ77 coding [22].

$$f^C = \text{DEFLATE}(f(t)) \tag{2}$$

Then we convert the compressed byte stream to its corresponding base-64 positional notation, denoted using $(f^C)_{64}$. Since the symbols used in the base-64 notation constitute alphanumeric characters, we can simply typecast it as a string.

$$S = \texttt{str}((f^C)_{64}) \tag{3}$$

3.2 SCREEDSOLO Text Encoding

The sender and receiver sides must share a password p that they use to encode and decode the secret message, respectively.

Pseudo-Random Shuffling. In the encoding process, at first, we take the message string S and randomly shuffle it. The caveat here is that the shuffling is not absolutely random, but based on a pseudo-random permutation of the string indices. The permutation is uniform, *i.e.*, each of the $|S|!$ possible permutations is equally likely. The seed value p^s that we use for generating the pseudo-random permutation is the hash value of p that is yielded by using the Secure Hash Algorithm-256 [12], colloquially known as SHA-256.

$$p^s = \text{SHA256}(p) \tag{4}$$

$$S' = \text{Shuffle}(S, p^s) \tag{5}$$

Fernet Symmetric Encryption. We generate the cipher key $(p^m)_{64}$ by applying the Message Digest-5 hashing algorithm, also known as the MD-5 algorithm; then the numerical hash-value is converted to its corresponding base-64 notation.

$$p^m = \text{MD5}(p) \tag{6}$$

$$F = \text{Fernet}(S', (p^m)_{64}) \tag{7}$$

[1] https://docs.python.org/3/library/zlib.html.

In symmetric encryption algorithms, the same key is used for both encryption and decryption. Fernet is a cryptographic technique that offers a straightforward method for both authentication and encryption. It utilizes HMAC (Hash-based Message Authentication Code) with SHA-256 for authentication and employs symmetric AES-128 (Advanced Encryption Standard-128) encryption in Cipher Block Chaining (CBC) mode, with PKCS7 (Public Key Cryptography Standards #7) padding.

Reed–Solomon Coding. Reed–Solomon error-correcting codes belong to the family of linear block codes based on the working principle: for an input message of length k, the encoding procedure produces an output codeword of length n where $n \geq k$, guaranteeing the correction of up to $\lfloor \frac{n-k}{2} \rfloor$ errors [14]. This error-resilience property emerges from the codes' mathematical structure, which leverages the benefit of Theorem 1, by treating message symbols as coefficients in a polynomial equation.

Theorem 1 (Polynomial Uniqueness). *A polynomial $P_d(x) = a_0 + a_1x + a_2x^2 + \cdots + a_dx^d$ of degree $d \leq n$ that passes through a given set of $n+1$ data points $(x_0, y_0), \ldots, (x_n, y_n)$ is unique.*

By sampling this polynomial at multiple points to generate redundant symbols, ReedSolomon encoding creates a system where the original polynomial—and thus the original message—can be reconstructed even when some sample points become corrupted. Therefore, given a steganography algorithm which, on average, returns an incorrect bit with probability p, it is desirable that,

$$\mathbb{E}[X] = p \times n \leq \frac{n-k}{2} \tag{8}$$

where X denotes the number of corrupted bits. The effective information throughput, signified by the ratio $\frac{k}{n}$, quantifies the average number of *'real'* data bits conveyed per *'message'* data bit. The main pitfall of resorting to Reed–Solomon coding in our framework is the aforementioned additional data overhead of the error-correction codes, *i.e.*, the size of the encoded message R will be higher than the size of the Fernet encrypted message F. The advantage, however, is of course, the ability of the framework to withstand the bit-corruption of at most $\lfloor \frac{n-k}{2} \rfloor$ bits.

$$R = \text{ReedSolo}(F) \tag{9}$$

Forming the Binary Message. R consists of characters that have ASCII values $\in [0, 127]$, and each of these characters take at most 7 bits to be expressed in the binary notation. We replace the characters of R with their corresponding base-2 values, thus forming $(R)_2$. For the decoding process at the receiver side, it is necessary to know the length of this entire binary message. So we pretend this length L using a bitset of 32 bits (*i.e.*, $(L)_2$) at the anterior part of the binary message.

$$(R)_2 = \texttt{String2Binary}(R) \tag{10}$$

$$L = \text{Length}((R)_2) \tag{11}$$

$$(L)_2 = \texttt{Decimal2Binary}(L) \tag{12}$$

$$M = (L)_2 \Big|\Big| (R)_2 \tag{13}$$

We posit that the final binary message M is the concatenated binary string $(L)_2\|(R)_2$.

LSB Steganography. LSB (Least Significant Bit) Steganography is a technique in which secret information is embedded into the least significant bits of pixels in a digital image. By modifying only the last few bits of each pixel value, LSB steganography exploits the fact that such small changes are imperceptible to the human eye (as evident in Fig. 3), allowing the secret message to remain hidden while preserving the appearance of the image. In a typical n-bit image, each pixel's color value can be represented as an n-bit binary number, and the least significant bit of each pixel can be used to encode the secret data.

$$g'(x,y) = \begin{cases} g(x,y) \oplus 1; & \text{if pixel's LSB} \neq \text{message's bit} \\ g(x,y); & \text{otherwise} \end{cases} \tag{14}$$

The capacity of LSB steganography depends on the number of bits available in the cover image. In an 8-bit grayscale image, each pixel can store 1 bit of the message. Thus, for an image with $M \times N$ pixels, the total message capacity is $M \times N$ bits. For a 24-bit color image, each pixel can store 3 bits (one in each of the 3 channels), allowing a higher embedding capacity of $3 \times M \times N$ bits. As per Eq. 14, we simply alter the LSB of the cover image $g(x,y)$ if the pixel in question has an LSB that is different from the bit that we are trying to embed. Otherwise, we keep the pixel unaltered. The resultant image $g'(x,y)$ is referred to as the stego-image.

4 Experiment

We experiment with multiple modalities of secret objects (*e.g.* text, audio, and image) and embed them in cover images of different resolutions. The metrics that we use to evaluate the performance of SCREEDSOLO are Cover Image Loss, Cosine Similarity (CSim), Mean Square Error (MSE), Peak Signal-to-Noise Ratio (PSNR), Structural Similarity Index Measure (SSIM), Variation of Information (VI) Hausdorff Distance (HDist), and Normalized Root Mean Square Error (NRMSE).

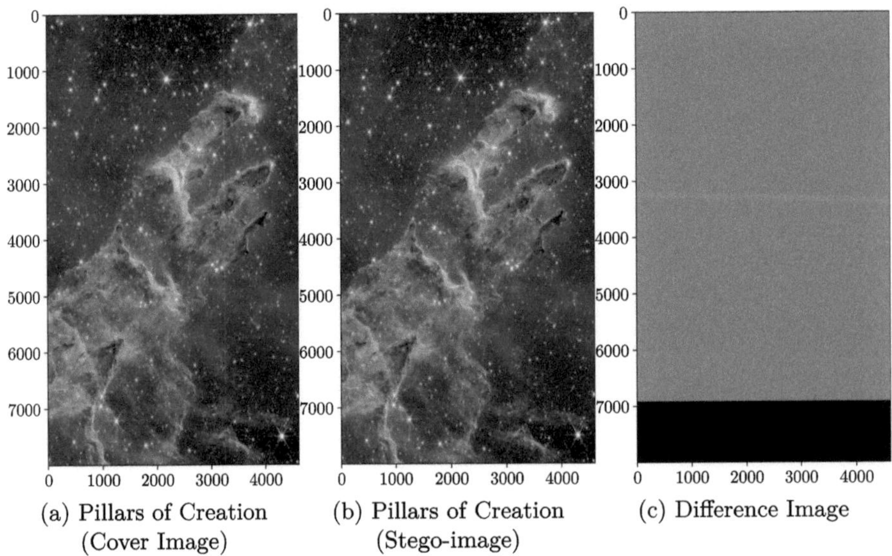

(a) Pillars of Creation (Cover Image) (b) Pillars of Creation (Stego-image) (c) Difference Image

Fig. 4. Hiding *The Complete Works of Shakespeare* inside the *Pillars of Creation*

Table 1. Quantitative evaluation results for Fig. 4

Loss	CSim	MSE	PSNR	SSIM	VI	HDist	NRMSE
86.422	0.999	1.296	51.774	0.996	$\langle 0.982, 0.982 \rangle$	3.464	0.007

4.1 Text Hiding

Text Corpus. In order to test out the secret text embedding process, we consider the classical literature corpus called *The Complete Works of Shakespeare* [15] obtained from Project Gutenberg.[2] *The Complete Works of William Shakespeare* is the standard name given to any volume containing all the plays and poems of William Shakespeare. The entire text body has a length of 5,458,195 characters. After compression, the size shrinks down to 2,680,939 characters. After the encryption process, the length becomes 11,972,988. After conversion to binary notation, the total bits to embed becomes 95,783,904.

Cover Image. The cover image that we consider for hiding this payload is a Near-Infrared Camera (NIRCam) image taken by the James Webb Space Telescope in 2022 (see Fig. 4a). The resolution of the image is $14589 \times 8423 \times 3$.

[2] https://www.gutenberg.org/ebooks/100.

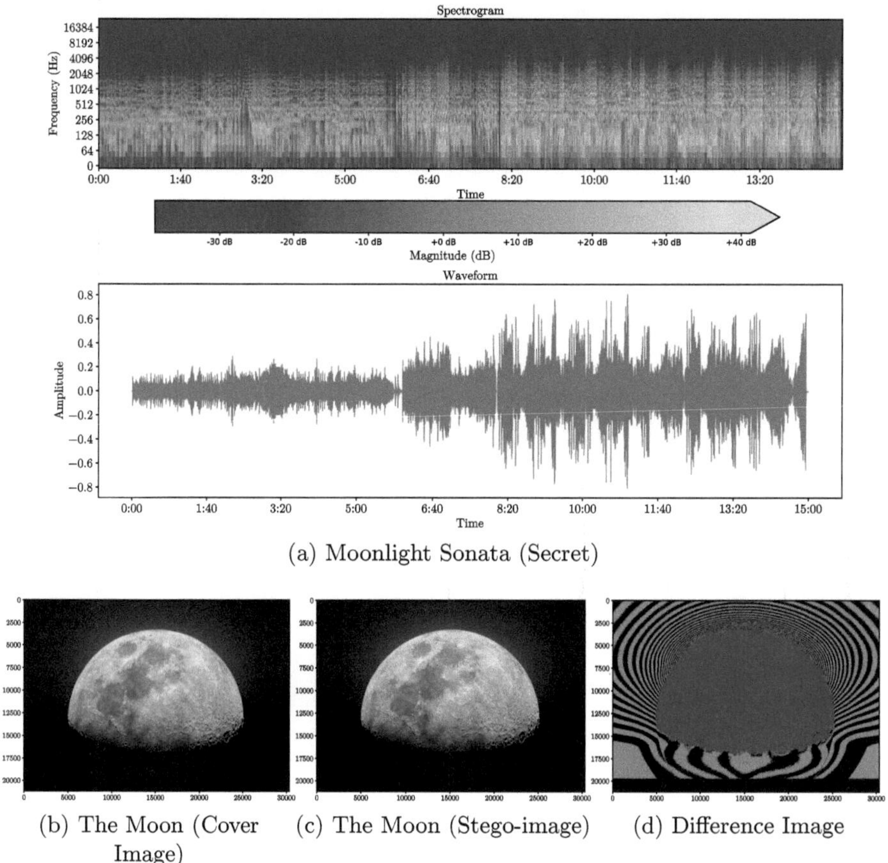

(a) Moonlight Sonata (Secret)

(b) The Moon (Cover Image)

(c) The Moon (Stego-image)

(d) Difference Image

Fig. 5. Hiding the *Moonlight Sonata* inside the *Moon*

4.2 Audio Hiding

Audio Signal. In order to test out the secret audio embedding process, we consider the classical music score called *Moonlight Sonata.* The Piano Sonata No. 14 in C-sharp minor, marked *Quasi una fantasia*, Op. 27, No. 2, is a piano sonata by Ludwig van Beethoven [6]. The duration of the score is 15 min, and due to the repetitive nature of the score, we compress it using DEFLATE. In its original state, the audio file has a length of 61,777,387 bytes. After compression, it becomes 35,999,084 bytes in length. We convert the audio to text by maintaining the pipeline outlined in Fig. 2. The encrypted text has a length of 2,23,727,460 and the binary message is of length 1,789,819,680 bits.

Table 2. Quantitative evaluation results for Fig. 5

Loss	CSim	MSE	PSNR	SSIM	VI	HDist	NRMSE
92.844	0.999	1.412	57.653	0.936	$\langle 0.902, 0.828 \rangle$	2.0	0.007

Cover Image. The cover image that we consider for hiding this payload is a detailed image of the Moon captured by astrophotographer Andrew McCarthy (see Fig. 5b). The resolution of the image is $21188 \times 30328 \times 3$.

4.3 Image Hiding

Image Payload. We use the Chalk image shown in Fig. 6b as our secret image. We use $k = 5$ while performing the optional k-bit quantization. As a pragmatic pursuit, we downsample the image to the resolution $100 \times 100 \times 3$, so the total number of pixel values that we encode is 30,000.

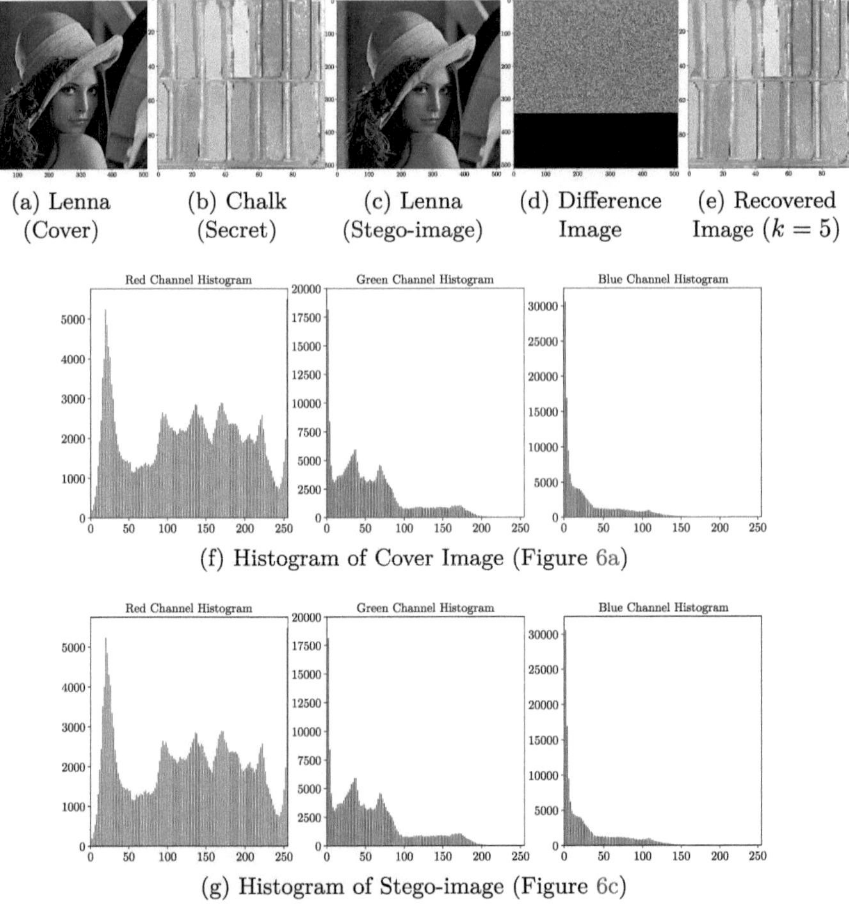

(a) Lenna (Cover) (b) Chalk (Secret) (c) Lenna (Stego-image) (d) Difference Image (e) Recovered Image ($k = 5$)

(f) Histogram of Cover Image (Figure 6a)

(g) Histogram of Stego-image (Figure 6c)

Fig. 6. Hiding the *Chalk* image inside the *Lenna* image

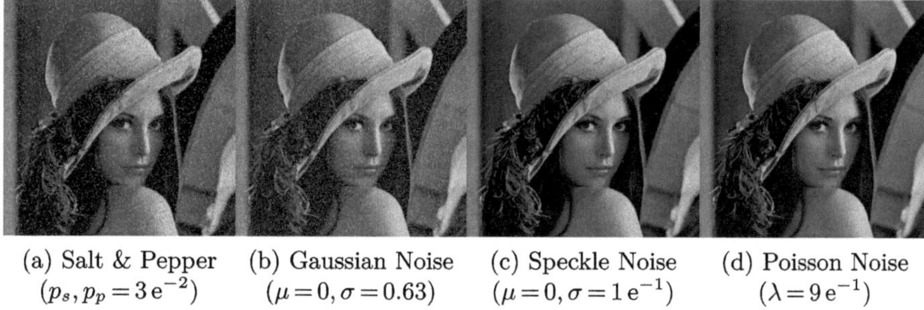

(a) Salt & Pepper ($p_s, p_p = 3\,\mathrm{e}^{-2}$) (b) Gaussian Noise ($\mu = 0, \sigma = 0.63$) (c) Speckle Noise ($\mu = 0, \sigma = 1\,\mathrm{e}^{-1}$) (d) Poisson Noise ($\lambda = 9\,\mathrm{e}^{-1}$)

Fig. 7. Applying different types of noise on the stego-image

Cover Image. We use the Lenna image shown in Fig. 6a as our cover image. The image's resolution is 512 × 512.

Table 3. Quantitative evaluation results for Fig. 6

Loss	CSim	MSE	PSNR	SSIM	VI	HDist	NRMSE
67.142	0.999	1.003	52.888	0.996	$\langle 0.914, 0.878\rangle$	2.0	0.006

Steganalysis Attacks—Noise and Bit-Corruption. The incorporation of Reed–Solomon error-correction codes enables the stego-image to withstand corruption and noise contingent on the fact that the noise must not alter more than half of the number of error-correction bits. We test this proposition with 4 types of noise (see Fig. 7). In tandem, Table 4 shows SCREEDSOLO's resilience against visual/spatial perturbations, which are as follows:

$$\text{Salt-and-Pepper Noise:} f'(x,y) = \begin{cases} f(x,y); & p = 1 - p_s - p_p \\ 0 \text{ (black)}; & p = p_p \\ 1 \text{ (white)}; & p = p_s \end{cases} \tag{15}$$

$$\text{Gaussian Noise: } f'(x,y) = f(x,y) + n; \text{ where} n \sim \mathcal{N}(\mu, \sigma^2) \tag{16}$$

$$\text{Speckle Noise: } f'(x,y) = f(x,y) \cdot n; \text{ where} n \sim \mathcal{N}(\mu = 1, \sigma^2) \tag{17}$$

$$\text{Poisson Noise: } f'(x,y) \sim \text{Pois}(f(x,y)) \tag{18}$$

As long as the noise doesn't affect $\geq \lfloor \frac{n-k}{2} \rfloor$ bits of the error-correction codes as delineated in Eq. 8, the effect of the noise is nullified, and the receiver can recover the secret payload in its entirety.

Table 4. Effect of noise on the stego-image (Fig. 6c)

Noise	CSim	MSE	PSNR	SSIM	VI	HDist	NRMSE
Fig. 7a	0.976	1349.961	21.598	0.665	0.315	2.0	0.221
Fig. 7b	0.979	1188.227	22.153	0.725	0.317	2.0	0.207
Fig. 7c	0.999	1.340	51.628	0.995	1.855	2.0	0.006
Fig. 7d	0.999	0.026	68.604	0.999	0.143	2.0	0.0009

Proposition 1 (Parity Consistency). For a given $3 \times M \times N$ LSB stego-image $f(x, y)$ harboring k message bits and $(n-k)$ ReedSolomon error correction bits, and steganalysis transformation T, if S is the set of surviving embedded positions, which is defined as follows,

$$S = \{\forall x, \forall y, \langle x, y\rangle \in \{\langle x, y\rangle \mid T(f(x, y)) \wedge 1 = f(x, y) \wedge 1\}\}$$

then a necessary but not sufficient condition for a successful transmission is

$$|S| \geq \lceil \frac{n+k}{2} \rceil$$

Justification. For an input message of length k, the Reed–Solomon encoding procedure produces an output codeword of length n, which can correct up to $\lfloor \frac{n-k}{2} \rfloor$ substitution errors. Equivalently, at least $n - \lfloor \frac{n-k}{2} \rfloor = \lceil \frac{n+k}{2} \rceil$ symbols must be correct. Under our bit-level model (one symbol per embedded LSB), each position in S is a correct symbol. Hence $|S| \geq \lceil \frac{n+k}{2} \rceil$ is required.

Owing to this insufficiency, we mathematically analyze the noise immunity likelihood for SCReedSolo's stego-images.

Theorem 2 (Survival Probability). *If the random variable X denotes the number of uncorrupted least significant bits for a given steganalysis transformation T on a $3 \times M \times N$ stego-image $f(x, y)$ harboring k message bits and $(n-k)$ ReedSolomon error correction bits such that $n \leq 3MN$, then the probability of successful payload transmission is*

$$\mathbb{P}\left(X \geq \lceil \frac{n+k}{2} \rceil | f, T\right) = \sum_{i=\lceil \frac{n+k}{2} \rceil}^{n} \binom{n}{i} \times \frac{\binom{3MN}{n}}{2^n}$$

Proof. Each channel of each pixel constitutes only 1 bit (LSB) of information related to the secret message. So, for m-bit pixel channels, the probability $\mathbb{P}(\text{LSB remains unchanged}) = \frac{2^{m-1}}{2^m} = \frac{1}{2}$. This implies that X follows the binomial distribution, *i.e.*, $X \sim \text{Binomial}(n, p = 0.5)$. So, following Eq. 8, the cumulative distribution function $F\left(\lceil \frac{n+k}{2} \rceil; n, p\right)$ can be obtained as follows

$$\mathbb{P}\left(X \geq \lceil\frac{n+k}{2}\rceil\right) = \underbrace{\left[\frac{\binom{n}{\lceil\frac{n+k}{2}\rceil}}{2^n} + \frac{\binom{n}{\lceil\frac{n+k}{2}\rceil+1}}{2^n} + \cdots + \frac{\binom{n}{n}}{2^n}\right]}_{\text{Upper tail of the Binomial CDF}} \times \binom{3MN}{n}$$

$$= \sum_{i=\lceil\frac{n+k}{2}\rceil}^{n} \binom{n}{i} \times \frac{\binom{3MN}{n}}{2^n} \quad \square \text{ Q.E.D.}$$

Steganalysis Tools. We use the `aletheia` toolbox[3] developed by [8]. The framework performs well across multiple passive steganalysis methods.

4.4 Result Discussion

The quantitative evaluations of the steganographic outputs, as presented in Tables 1, 2, and 3 demonstrate the efficacy of the proposed methodology in achieving nigh-imperceptible data embedding across different cover images. The cover image loss, of course, is proportional to the size of the secret message payload and can be pictorially visualized from the difference images in Figs. 4c, 5d, and 6d. We also observe high visual fidelity between the original cover images and their corresponding stego-images, as is evidenced by the histogram comparison (Figs. 6f–6g) and values for the other image similarity and quality metrics in the aforementioned tables.

5 Conclusion and Future Work

In this paper, we present SCReedSolo, a novel framework for image steganography that offers a secure and corruption-resilient method for embedding arbitrary binary data into images, achieving a high payload capacity of 3 bits per pixel with minimal spatial perturbations and stochastically effective obfuscated transmission. There are several avenues for future work to potentiate this framework. First, further optimizations could be applied to improve the embedding capacity, particularly for applications requiring higher payloads without sacrificing security. Additionally, although the framework proves resistant to simple active steganalysis attacks, more advanced and adversarial steganalysis methods could be explored to ensure its defense against increasingly sophisticated attacks.

6 Limitations

While the proposed SCReedSolo framework demonstrates significant improvements in terms of security and robustness, there are certain limitations that warrant further attention. First, the robustness of the stego image is contingent on

[3] https://github.com/daniellerch/aletheia.

the integrity of the error-correction bits; specifically, the image remains resistant to corruption only if more than half of the Reed–Solomon error-correction bits remain intact (as shown in Eq. 8). If a larger portion of these bits is compromised, the hidden message may not be recoverable. Additionally, the resolution of the cover image must be considerably high to embed larger secret objects effectively. Embedding substantial amounts of data in lower-resolution images can lead to visible artifacts, undermining the goal of imperceptibility. Another limitation arises from the use of the DEFLATE compression algorithm, which, in some cases, can lead to data expansion instead of compression [11]. This poses a challenge when optimizing the payload size, as it may inadvertently increase the data to be embedded, requiring additional capacity from the carrier image. Finally, the use of k-bit quantization in our framework (although it is optional and circumstantial) imposes constraints on the precision of the secret data. This quantization process can result in a loss of fidelity, making it impossible to recover the secret object in its exact original form, particularly when embedding images or high-precision data.

Acknowledgments. We convey our heartfelt gratitude to the anonymous reviewers for their constructive criticisms and insightful feedback, which were conducive to the improvement of the research work outlined in this paper. We also appreciate the Islamic University of Technology (IUT) for funding our research, and the Systems and Software Lab (SSL) of IUT for the generous provision of computing resources during the course of this project. Syed Rifat Raiyan, in particular, wants to thank his parents, Syed Sirajul Islam and Kazi Shahana Begum, for everything.

Disclosure of Interests. The authors have no competing interests to declare that are relevant to the content of this article.

References

1. Baluja, S.: Hiding images in plain sight: deep steganography. Adv. NeurIPS **30** (2017)
2. Delfs, H., Knebl, H., Delfs, H., Knebl, H.: Symmetric-key encryption. In: Introduction to Cryptography: Principles and Applications, pp. 11–31 (2007)
3. Deshpande, N., Kamalapur, S., Jacobs, D.: Implementation of LSB steganography and its evaluation for various bits. In: Proceedings of the 1st International Conference on Digital Information Management (ICDIM 2006), pp. 173–178. IEEE, Bangalore, India (2006). https://doi.org/10.1109/ICDIM.2007.369349
4. Hayes, J., Danezis, G.: Generating steganographic images via adversarial training. Adv. Neural Inf. Process. Syst. **30** (2017)
5. Huffman, D.A.: A method for the construction of minimum-redundancy codes. Proc. Inst. Radio Eng. **40**(9), 1098–1101 (1952). https://doi.org/10.1109/JRPROC.1952.273898
6. Jones, T.: Beethoven: The 'Moonlight' and Other Sonatas, op. 27 and op. 31. Cambridge University Press (1999)
7. Kumar, A., Pooja, K.: Steganography—a data hiding technique. Int. J. Comput. Appl. **9**(7), 19–23 (2010). https://www.ijcaonline.org/archives/volume9/number7/1398-1887/

8. Lerch-Hostalot, D., Megas, D.: Aletheia: an open-source toolbox for steganalysis. J. Open Source Softw. **9**(93), 5982 (2024). https://doi.org/10.21105/joss.05982 https://doi.org/10.21105/joss.05982 https://doi.org/10.21105/joss.05982
9. Li, B., He, J., Huang, J., Shi, Y.Q.: A survey on image steganography and steganalysis. J. Inf. Hiding Multim. Sig. Process. **2**, 142–172 (2011). https://api.semanticscholar.org/CorpusID:41329625
10. Lou, D.C., Liu, J.L.: Steganographic method for secure communications. Comput. Secur. **21**(5), 449–460 (2002). https://doi.org/10.1016/S0167-4048(02)00515-1
11. Oswal, S., Singh, A., Kumari, K.: Deflate compression algorithm. Int. J. Eng. Res. General Sci. **4**(1) (2016)
12. Penard, W., Van Werkhoven, T.: On the secure hash algorithm family. Cryptography in Context (2008)
13. Pevnỳ, T., Filler, T., Bas, P.: Using high-dimensional image models to perform highly undetectable steganography. In: Information Hiding: 12th International Conference, pp. 161–177. Springer (2010). https://doi.org/10.1007/978-3-642-16435-4_13
14. Reed, I.S., Solomon, G.: Polynomial codes over certain finite fields. J. Soc. Ind. Appl. Math. **8**(2), 300–304 (1960). https://doi.org/10.1137/0108018
15. Shakespeare, W.: The Complete Works of William Shakespeare, vol. 10. Harper (1907)
16. Tang, W., Tan, S., Li, B., Huang, J.: Automatic steganographic distortion learning using a generative adversarial network. IEEE Sig. Process. Lett. **24**(10), 1547–1551 (2017)
17. Wang, H., Wang, S.: Cyber warfare: steganography vs. steganalysis. Commun. ACM **47**(10), 76–82 (2004). https://doi.org/10.1145/1022594.1022597
18. Watkins, J.: Steganography-messages hidden in bits. Multimedia Systems Coursework, Dept of Electronics and CS, University of Southampton, SO17 1BJ, UK (2001)
19. Wu, P., Yang, Y., Li, X.: StegNet: mega image steganography capacity with deep convolutional network. Future Internet **10**(6), 54 (2018)
20. Zhang, K.A., Cuesta-Infante, A., Xu, L., Veeramachaneni, K.: SteganoGAN: high capacity image steganography with GANs. arXiv preprint arXiv:1901.03892 (2019)
21. Zhu, J., Kaplan, R., Johnson, J., Fei-Fei, L.: Hidden: hiding data with deep networks. In: Computer Vision – ECCV 2018. LNCS, vol. 11219, pp. 682–697. Springer, Cham (2018). https://doi.org/10.1007/978-3-030-01267-0_40
22. Ziv, J., Lempel, A.: A universal algorithm for sequential data compression. IEEE Trans. Inf. Theory **23**(3), 337–343 (1977). https://doi.org/10.1109/TIT.1977.1055714

VeriChain: Reinforced Document Image Forgery Verification via Self-revealing Reasoning Chain

Hao Sun[1,2], Yanbo Wang[1,2], Junxian Duan[1,2(✉)], and Ran He[1,2]

[1] School of Artificial Intelligence, University of Chinese Academy of Sciences, Beijing 100049, China
{hao.sun,junxian.duan}@cripac.ia.ac.cn, wangyanbo2023@ia.ac.cn
[2] MAIS & NLPR, Institute of Automation, Chinese Academy of Sciences, Beijing 100190, China
rhe@nlpr.ia.ac.cn

Abstract. Current multimodal forgery detection methods often struggle with generalizing across unseen manipulation types and lack transparent decision processes. To tackle these challenges, we introduces VeriChain–a novel reinforcement learning framework designed for explainable and generalizable document image forgery verification. Unlike traditional supervised fine-tuning approaches, VeriChain adopts a decoupled architecture that combines a Cognitive Reasoning Module with a Spatial Anomaly Segmentation Module. The Reasoning Module autonomously generates a self-revealing chain of forensic thoughts, highlighting multimodal inconsistencies and extracting spatially-grounded cues. These cues guide the Segmentation Module to precisely delineate pixel-level manipulation footprints. Trained exclusively via autoregressive policy optimization with a sophisticated dual-reward mechanism–enforcing structural coherence and forensic fidelity, VeriChain achieves emergent reasoning capabilities without explicit forensic reasoning data. This paradigm fosters robust zero-shot generalization across diverse and unseen manipulation techniques while delivering unprecedented interpretability through its self-derived reasoning chains. Comprehensive experiments on our proposed DocTruth benchmark, comprising over 126,000 diverse document images, demonstrate VeriChain's state-of-the-art performance, achieving 90.8% detection accuracy, 78.3% localization IoU, and significantly superior explanation quality compared to existing methods. VeriChain establishes a new paradigm for trustworthy and adaptive document image integrity verification.

Keywords: Document Forgery Detection · Generalization Robustness · Multimodal Localization

1 Introduction

With the rapid growth of AI-generated content(AIGC) [2,3], document manipulation that targets both text and images is becoming increasingly common

C. Wallraven et al. (Eds.): ACPR 2025, LNCS 16174, pp. 238–249, 2026.
https://doi.org/10.1007/978-981-95-4395-3_17

and sophisticated on social platforms. Traditional text forgery detection methods struggle in several ways. They rely heavily on supervised fine-tuning with labeled data, which makes them prone to forgetting previously learned patterns and unable to adapt to new types of tampering. These methods also often lack the ability to explain why a document is suspicious and usually require tedious pixel-level annotations. Recent advances in multimodal large models have improved the understanding of both visual and linguistic information. However, these models still depend on massive datasets and rigid architectures, making it hard to adapt to the diverse and changing nature of real-world forgeries. Existing reinforcement learning methods are also limited, as they rarely consider the unique challenges of text-based manipulation, such as the need to jointly analyze spatial, semantic, and linguistic features. To address these challenges, we introduce VeriChain, an innovative framework based on reinforcement learning that brings together forgery detection, localization, and interpretable reasoning. VeriChain uses a decoupled architecture with two main modules. The Cognitive Reasoning Module analyzes the document and generates a step-by-step forensic reasoning chain that highlights suspicious areas and provides explanations. This information is then passed to the Spatial Anomaly Segmentation Module, which accurately identifies and marks the tampered regions at the pixel level. Our training strategy moves beyond conventional supervised learning by using Group Relative Policy Optimization(GRPO) [10]. We requires only a small amount of initial training data and guides the model with a dual reward system. The rewards encourage the model to maintain structural consistency, achieve high accuracy in pinpointing manipulated characters, and ensure that its explanations make sense in the context of the document. We evaluate our method on the DocTruth benchmark, a large and diverse dataset of over 120,000 document images with detailed pixel-level annotations. The results show that VeriChain not only achieves higher accuracy and better localization of tampered regions compared to existing methods, but also provides clear and trustworthy explanations. This demonstrates strong generalization across different types of manipulations and real-world scenarios. The contributions of our work can be summarized as follows:

- We introduce VeriChain, the first reinforcement learning framework enabling simultaneous document forgery detection, pixel-level localization, and human-interpretable reasoning through self-revealing multimodal chain-of-thought generation.
- We devise a hierarchical dual-reward mechanism that orchestrates semantic coherence constraints, character-level tamper segmentation accuracy, and reasoning-guided cross-modal consistency to refine forensic reasoning credibility.
- We establish the DocTruth benchmark, comprising 126,017 rigorously annotated document samples, and demonstrate state-of-the-art performance with significant improvements in generalization capability and robustness under real-world degradations.

2 Related Work

Recent advancements in multimodal reasoning have increasingly unified visual perception and linguistic interpretation for holistic content analysis. Pioneering frameworks such as Seg-Zero [1] utilize structured reasoning chains to generate human-readable justifications while localizing visual elements, capitalizing on pretrained vision-language encoders like Qwen2.5-VL [4] to model cross-modal dependencies. These systems deduce spatial relationships through contextual inference rather than template matching. Nevertheless, their reliance on deterministic feature extractors or heuristic artifact detection fundamentally constrains adaptability to semantically coherent forgeries, particularly manipulations involving contextual incoherence or content substitution [5–7].

Concurrently, reinforcement learning paradigms–especially Group Relative Policy Optimization (GRPO) [10] have enabled dynamic refinement of vision-language architectures through reward-guided behavior shaping. Systems including Visual-RFT [8] and VLM-R1 [9] exemplify how iterative policy calibration harmonizes localization precision with explanatory transparency. For instance, SAM-R1 [88] innovatively leverages segmentation foundations as differentiable reward generators, providing pixel-accurate feedback to align reasoning trajectories with spatial outputs. Similarly, Seg-Zero [1] enforces dual optimization objectives: structural output integrity (JSON-formatted coordinates) and geometric fidelity metrics. Despite these innovations, prevailing RL methods exhibit limited robustness under domain shift, faltering in annotation-scarce regimes or semantically ambiguous scenarios–critical gaps in real-world forensic applications [11–13].

3 Method

This section introduces our end-to-end framework for text forgery detection and localization, which incorporates multimodal chain-of-thought generation, reinforcement learning optimization, and task-specific reward mechanisms. The architecture adopts a decoupled design of semantic analysis and visual segmentation, and introduces linguistic consistency metrics to ensure high-level reasoning capability as well as accurate detection of character-level manipulations. During training, we employ GRPO and multi-dimensional reward functions to dynamically balance structural coherence, character-level localization accuracy, and semantic consistency. The following sections will provide a detailed description of the model architecture, training strategy, and reward mechanisms.

3.1 Dataset Construction

To construct a comprehensive benchmark for text tampering detection, we designed the DocTruth dataset that integrates multiple sources and annotation strategies to ensure diversity, realism, and interpretability. DocTruth is built from three main sources: the DocTamper dataset, real-world internet documents, and synthetic documents generated by GPT4o. At the core of DocTruth are 120,000 tampered document images sourced from DocTamper, covering a wide range of document types such as legal contracts, financial invoices, academic certificates, and ID papers. Each image is carefully annotated to reflect different tampering techniques, ensuring the dataset captures the complexity of real-world forgery scenarios. To provide reliable reference samples, we also collected 4,017 authentic documents from the internet, including social platforms, professional sharing communities, and academic databases. All these documents have undergone rigorous expert validation and forensic analysis to guarantee that they are free from any manipulation, making them trustworthy examples of real, untampered documents. In addition, DocTruth addresses the growing challenge of synthetic forgery by including 2,000 fully synthetic tampered documents generated using GPT4o. These samples simulate advanced scenarios, such as forged payment terms in financial reports or fake signatures on academic diplomas. The generation process is continuously refined to ensure that these documents closely resemble real ones in font, layout, and structure. All images in DocTruth are standardized to a resolution of 512×512 pixels and are further processed using JPEG compression, noise injection, and geometric transformations, such as rotation and perspective distortion. These steps mimic the imperfections commonly found in images captured by mobile devices or scanners, making the dataset more representative of real-world conditions. Beyond providing annotated tampered regions, DocTruth emphasizes the importance of interpretability. Each sample is accompanied by expert reasoning chains that explain the evidence and logic behind the tampering judgment, such as inconsistencies in paragraph alignment or unusual ink patterns in signatures. This approach not only helps train models to identify visual and textual anomalies but also guides them to understand and explain the reasoning process behind their decisions. Through this integrated and multi-dimensional construction, DocTruth serves as a robust benchmark for evaluating both the detection of low-level visual artifacts and the understanding of high-level semantic inconsistencies in a wide range of real and synthetic forgery scenarios.

3.2 Architecture Overview

We employ a dual-module architecture, as illustrated in Fig. 1, where a reasoning module and a segmentation module operate sequentially on the input. The multimodal reasoning model $\mathcal{F}\text{reason}$ processes the input image $\mathbf{I}$ and textual instruction $\mathbf{T}$, generating structured output $\mathbf{C} = \mathcal{F}\text{reason}(\mathbf{I}, \mathbf{T})$. This output $\mathbf{C}$ encapsulates analytical reasoning sequences within $\langle$think$\rangle$ tags and bounding box coordinates $\mathbf{B} = [x_1, y_1, x_2, y_2]$ formatted within JSON $\langle$answer$\rangle$ tags. The segmentation model $\mathcal{F}\text{seg}$ then utilizes these coordinates to produce pixel-level masks $\mathbf{M} = \mathcal{F}\text{seg}(\mathbf{I}, \mathbf{B}; \Theta_{\text{fix}})$, with its parameters Θ_{fix} frozen during reinforcement learning. The reasoning module detects tampering artifacts at the textual semantic level–identifying anomalies like abrupt font inconsistencies or contextual contradictions–while the segmentation module precisely delineates the spa-

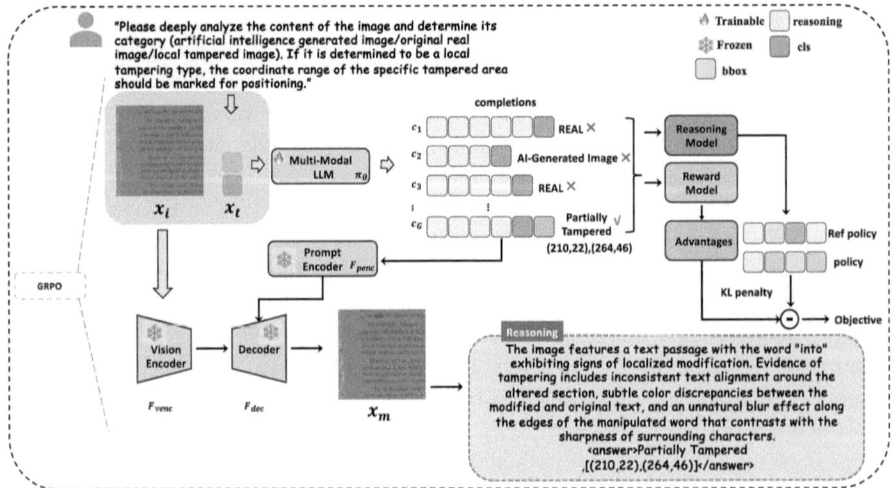

Fig. 1. Architecture of the proposed VeriChain. The Cognitive Reasoning Module processes multimodal inputs to generate forensic reasoning chains and spatial cues. Subsequently, the Segmentation Module delineates manipulation footprints using these cues while reward optimization aligns reasoning with pixel-level outputs.

tial boundaries of manipulated text regions within the image. Crucially, during cold-start training, backpropagated gradients derived from semantic consistency assessments establish a direct connection between visual localization outcomes and textual authenticity verification.

3.3 Training Strategy and GRPO Optimization

Training progresses through two distinct phases designed to balance efficiency with reasoning capability emergence, beginning with supervised foundation building, followed by reward-driven refinement. The cold-start phase initializes $\mathcal{F}_{\text{reason}}$ using limited annotated samples by minimizing the cross-entropy loss:

$$\mathcal{L}_{\text{SFT}} = -\frac{1}{N}\sum_{i=1}^{N}\sum_{t=1}^{L}\log P\left(w_t^{(i)} \mid \mathbf{I}^{(i)}, \mathbf{T}^{(i)}, w_{<t}^{(i)}\right) \tag{1}$$

where w_t represents sequential reasoning tokens conditioned on multimodal inputs. This establishes baseline proficiency in text manipulation pattern recognition. Subsequent reinforcement learning employs Group Relative Policy Optimization (GRPO) where for each input query $\mathbf{q} = (\mathbf{I}, \mathbf{T})$, the system samples G candidate responses $\{\mathbf{C}_i\}_{i=1}^{G}$ from the current policy $\pi_{\theta_{\text{old}}}$ Rewards $R_{\text{total}}^{(i)}$ are computed through a composite function detailed in the next section and converted to normalized advantages via $A_i = \frac{R_{\text{total}}^{(i)} - \mu_R}{\sigma_R}$ with $\mu_R = \frac{1}{G}\sum_{j=1}^{G} R_{\text{total}}^{(j)}$ and $\sigma_R = \sqrt{\frac{1}{G}\sum_{j=1}^{G}(R_{\text{total}}^{(j)} - \mu_R)^2}$. Policy optimization then occurs through the objective function:

$$\mathcal{J}(\theta) = \mathbb{E}\left[\frac{1}{G}\sum_{i=1}^{G} \min\left(r_i A_i, \text{clip}(r_i, 1-\epsilon_l, 1+\epsilon_h)A_i\right) - \beta D_{\text{KL}}(\pi_\theta \parallel \pi_{\text{ref}})\right] \quad (2)$$

where $r_i = \pi_\theta(\mathbf{C}_i)/\pi_{\theta_{\text{old}}}(\mathbf{C}_i)$ and asymmetric clipping thresholds $\epsilon_l = 0.2, \epsilon_h = 0.3$ promote exploration of high-reward text forgery hypotheses while maintaining training stability. Throughout GRPO fine-tuning, the segmentation parameters remain frozen, ensuring reward consistency while gradients flow exclusively through the reasoning module to align chain-of-thought generation with localization outcomes. This optimization strategy effectively balances the discovery of novel text manipulation patterns with the preservation of linguistic constraints inherent in authentic content.

3.4 Reward Mechanism and Generalization

A multifaceted reward function orchestrates model behavior across four critical dimensions of text forgery detection, with each component dynamically weighted to address specific challenges. Format rewards enforce structural integrity through $R_{\text{fmt}} = \mathbb{I}[\text{ValidXML}(\mathbf{C}) \wedge \text{ValidJSON}(\mathbf{B})]$ requiring proper XML tagging and JSON coordinate formatting. Detection accuracy rewards implement tiered scoring based on character-level overlap.

$$R_{\text{det}} = \begin{cases} 3 & \text{if IoU}_{\text{char}} > 0.75 \wedge \text{correct} \\ 2 & \text{if } 0.5 < \text{IoU}_{\text{char}} \leq 0.75 \wedge \text{correct} \\ 0 & \text{otherwise} \end{cases} \quad (3)$$

where IoU_{char} measures glyph alignment rather than generic bounding boxes. Localization precision rewards combine spatial metrics $R_{\text{loc}}\mathbb{I}[\text{IoU}(\mathbf{B}, \mathbf{B}_{\text{gt}}) > 0.5] + \mathbb{I}[\|\mathbf{B} - \mathbf{B}_{\text{gt}}\|_1 < 10]$ ensuring both region coverage and coordinate accuracy. The novel semantic consistency reward constitutes our key innovation, integrating OCR verification with logical rule adherence:

$$R_{\text{sem}} = \text{ROUGE} - \text{L}(\mathcal{G}_{\text{OCR}}(\mathbf{M}), \mathcal{G}_{\text{OCR}}(\mathbf{M}_{\text{gt}})) \times \exp\left(-|\text{BLEU}(\mathbf{C}_{\text{reason}}, \mathbf{Y}_{\text{rule}}) - \tau|\right) \quad (4)$$

where Y_{rule} encodes domain heuristics such as "font size discrepancies imply tampering" and T controls sensitivity to explanation coherence. These rewards collectively drive the model toward discovering intrinsic manipulation patterns without explicit supervision. For generalization, we implement stochastic augmentations during cold-start training, including synthetic font corruption, background interference, and perspective distortions while GRPO's group-relative advantage computation inherently promotes robustness to distribution shifts. Reward weights $\lambda_{\text{fmt}}, \lambda_{\text{det}}, \lambda_{\text{loc}}, \lambda_{\text{sem}}$ undergo dynamic adjustment during training, progressively emphasizing semantic consistency in later stages to refine linguistic reasoning capabilities against sophisticated forgeries. The complete reward composition is formalized as $R_{\text{total}} = \lambda_{\text{fmt}} R_{\text{fmt}} + \lambda_{\text{det}} R_{\text{det}} + \lambda_{\text{loc}} R_{\text{loc}} + \lambda_{\text{sem}} R_{\text{sem}}$ creating a balanced optimization landscape that addresses both visual and textual facets of manipulation.

4 Experiments

We conduct comprehensive experiments to evaluate the effectiveness of VeriChain on the DocTruth dataset. The experiments focus on three core tasks: text tampering detection, localization of manipulated regions, and generation of interpretable explanations. We compare VeriChain with state-of-the-art methods across multiple benchmarks and analyze its performance under realistic perturbations.

4.1 Setup

Implementation Details. We use Qwen2.5VL-7B [4] as our base model and SAM2-Large [15] as the segmentation model. All experiments are conducted on 8×A100 GPUs. During training, we sample 8 responses per question, set $\varepsilon_{\text{high}} = 0.3$, and use a learning rate of 1.0×10^{-6}. To ensure the model's robustness across different domains, we resize all images to 512×512 before feeding them into the MLLM during both training and evaluation.

Datasets. VeriChain was trained through a two-phase pipeline. First, cold-start training was performed on 8,500 document images curated from DocTruth, leveraging forensic rationale annotations to establish foundational detection capabilities. Subsequently, GRPO fine-tuning was applied to this same subset to enhance explanatory depth, tamper classification accuracy, and localized manipulation detection. To rigorously evaluate cross-domain robustness, models were tested on DocTruth's dedicated benchmark comprising synthetically generated document forgeries excluded from the training distribution.

Metrics. We use image-level accuracy and F1 scores to evaluate classification correctness. Intersection over Union and region-based F1 metrics assess localization precision. For explanatory explainability, Cosine Semantic Similarity and ROUGE-L measures compute semantic space and lexical overlap respectively, between predicted and reference rationales. All benchmark explanations are generated by Claude 3.7 Sonnet [16].

4.2 Comparison Results on DocTruth

We comprehensively evaluate VeriChain against state-of-the-art methods on the DocTruth benchmark. As shown in Table 1, VeriChain demonstrates leading performance across all three forensic tasks. For detection, VeriChain achieves 90.8% accuracy and 90.7% F1 score, showing competitive capability compared to specialized detection methods like Diffforensics. In localization, VeriChain significantly outperforms existing approaches with 82.5% F1 and 78.3% IoU, surpassing the best comparison method by 29.9% in F1 and 27.9% in IoU. For explanation quality, VeriChain reaches a ROUGE-L score of 0.512 and CSS of 0.882, exceeding the best LLM baseline (InternVL-8B) by 0.16 in ROUGE-L

Table 1. Comparison of VeriChain with other methods in detection accuracy, F1 score, localization IoU, and interpretation quality on DocTruth.

Method	Year	Type	Detection		Localization		Explanation	
			Acc	F1	F1	IOU	ROUGE-L	CSS
Diffforensics [17]	2023	Detection	**91.7**	**91.4**	-	-	-	-
HIFI-Net [18]	2023	Detection	83.5	79.1	-	-	-	-
Trufor [19]	2023	Detection	-	-	52.6	50.4	-	-
Yi-VL-6B [20]	2024	LLM	-	-	-	-	0.281	0.856
LLaVA-1.5-13B [21]	2024	LLM	-	-	-	-	0.2645	0.839
Qwen2.5-VL-7B [4]	2024	LLM	-	-	-	-	0.290	0.871
GPT4o [22]	2024	LLM	-	-	-	-	0.338	0.885
InternVL3-8B [23]	2024	LLM	-	-	-	-	0.352	0.902
SIDA [5]	2024	LLM	-	-	-	-	0.294	**0.916**
Ours	2025	LLM	90.8	90.7	**82.5**	**78.3**	**0.512**	0.882

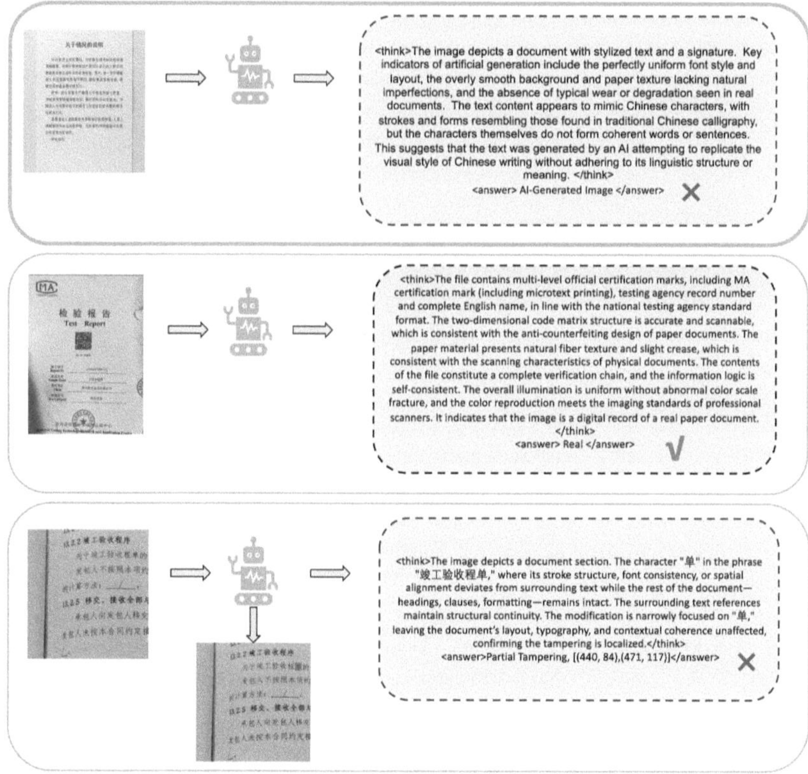

Fig. 2. VeriChain Qualitative results. The detection and interpretable results of three types of AI-generated Image, Real and partial tampering are shown respectively.

Table 2. Performance comparison on DocTruth with zero-shot settings.

Method	Detection		Localization		Explanation	
	Acc	F1	F1	IOU	ROUGE-L	CSS
Univer [24] (2023)	32.1	30.7	37.4	32.2	-	-
DIRE [25] (2023)	32.0	30.5	35.7	31.5	-	-
LGrad [26] (2023)	31.8	29.7	38.6	33.8	-	-
Yi-VL-6B [20] (2024)	23.3	21.7	29.1	26.3	-	-
GPT4o [22] (2024)	30.6	28.9	36.1	30.4	-	-
Llama-3.1-8B-Instruct [27] (2024)	32.2	29.2	52.6	50.4	0.2645	0.839
SIDA [5] (2024)	-	-	-	-	0.290	0.871
InternVL3-8B [23] (2025)	-	-	-	-	0.352	0.902
Qwen2.5-VL-7B [4] (2025)	-	-	-	-	0.294	0.916
Ours	**68.5**	**67.9**	**58.2**	**52.7**	**0.412**	0.864

while maintaining competitive semantic similarity. This comprehensive evaluation highlights VeriChain's ability to simultaneously excel in detection precision, localization accuracy, and explanation quality.

We further assess VeriChain's generalization capability under zero-shot settings in Table 2 VeriChain demonstrates remarkable robustness, achieving 68.5% detection accuracy and 67.9% F1 score - more than doubling the performance of the strongest baseline (Llama-3.1-13B at 32.2% accuracy). In localization, VeriChain attains 58.2% F1 and 52.7% IoU, outperforming all comparable methods by significant margins. For explanation, VeriChain achieves 0.412 ROUGE-L, substantially exceeding specialized LLMs like InternVL-8B while maintaining a competitive CSS of 0.864. These results validate VeriChain's strong generalization to unseen data distributions without task-specific fine-tuning.

4.3 Robustness Evaluation

To evaluate VeriChain's practical robustness, we rigorously test it under diverse document-specific degradations, including compression artifacts, watermarks, color distortions, and sensor noise. As demonstrated in Table 3, VeriChain maintains strong performance across all forensic tasks even with significant image quality deterioration. Under aggressive JPEG compression (QF=80), the system achieves 88.6% detection accuracy and 74.8% localization IoU, only 2.2% and 3.5% below pristine conditions. When confronted with center-positioned watermarks (a common real-world distortion), VeriChain retains 86.4% detection accuracy and 72.1% localization IoU, outperforming leading methods by over 5% in localization metrics. Most notably, under severe color jitter (50% intensity), VeriChain maintains 85.7% detection accuracy and 0.849 CSS, demonstrating only 5.6% and 3.7% degradation from optimal performance. These results validate VeriChain's exceptional resilience to practical document degradation scenarios.

Table 3. Demonstrate the performance of VeriChain under common image degradations

	Detection		Localization		Explanation	
Perturbation	ACC	F1	F1	IOU	ROUGE-L	CSS
JPEG 80	88.6	88.3	78.9	74.8	0.485	0.865
JPEG 90	89.2	88.9	79.4	75.2	0.492	0.869
Watermark (Center)	86.4	86.1	76.2	72.1	0.476	0.858
Watermark (Corner)	88.1	87.8	77.8	73.6	0.483	0.862
Color Jitter (30%)	87.3	86.9	76.8	72.5	0.478	0.856
Color Jitter (50%)	85.7	85.2	75.1	70.8	0.469	0.849
Gaussian Noise (σ=5)	88.9	88.6	79.1	74.9	0.489	0.866
Gaussian Noise (σ=10)	87.5	87.1	77.3	73.1	0.480	0.859
Original	**90.8**	**90.7**	**82.5**	**78.3**	**0.512**	**0.882**

4.4 Ablation Studies

We conduct ablation studies to evaluate the contributions of core components in VeriChain's training framework. As shown in Table 4, the results demonstrate that both supervised fine-tuning (SFT) and gradient-based policy optimization (GRPO) play critical yet distinct roles. When using only SFT, the model achieves 61.4% detection accuracy, establishing essential baseline capabilities. The GRPO component alone significantly boosts performance to 85.7% accuracy, a 24.3% point improvement, highlighting its importance for precision learning. However, the full integration of SFT and GRPO yields optimal performance at 90.8% accuracy, outperforming the GRPO-only configuration by 5.1% points. This synergistic effect confirms that SFT provides necessary foundational knowledge while GRPO enables advanced refinement, with their combination delivering state-of-the-art detection capability.

Table 4. Ablation study on training strategy.

SFT	GRPO	Detection Acc.
✓		61.4
	✓	85.7
✓	✓	**90.8**

4.5 Qualitative Results

We show the qualitative analysis results of VeriChain on diverse document image tampering types (including real, partial tampering, and AI-generated) through

Fig. 2, highlighting its accurate detection of tampered regions, pixel-wise localization of abnormal content, and generation of human-understandable semantic explanations. This synchronous output mechanism of detection and explanation provides a logically coherent inference chain for each prediction, which significantly improves the confidence and traceability of the results.

5 Conclusion

In this work, we establish VeriChain, a reinforcement learning framework for explainable document integrity verification, alongside the DocTruth benchmark encompassing 126K+ diverse legal, financial, and academic documents with pixel-level tamper annotations. VeriChain's novel dual-reward mechanism–integrating structural coherence enforcement and OCR-guided semantic consistency–enables autonomous derivation of forensic reasoning chains without manual supervision. Experiments confirm its efficacy in detecting and localizing text forgeries while generating human-aligned explanations, significantly outperforming existing methods in both in-domain and cross-domain scenarios. The framework offers a robust approach for addressing unseen manipulation techniques and real-world degradations, providing the document forensics community with a versatile solution for advancing trustworthy authentication methodologies.

Acknowledgements. This work was supported by the National Natural Science Foundation of China (Grant No. 62506362).

References

1. Liu, Y., Peng, B., Zhong, Z., et al.: Seg-Zero: reasoning-chain guided segmentation via cognitive reinforcement. arXiv preprint arXiv:2503.06520 (2025)
2. Shuai, X., Ding, H., Ma, X., et al.: A survey of multimodal-guided image editing with text-to-image diffusion models. arXiv preprint arXiv:2406.14555 (2024)
3. Han, K., Guo, J., Tang, Y., et al.: Free Video-LLM: prompt-guided visual perception for efficient training-free video LLMs. arXiv preprint arXiv:2410.10441 (2024)
4. Bai, S., Chen, K., Liu, X., et al.: Qwen2. 5-VL technical report. arXiv preprint arXiv:2502.13923 (2025)
5. Huang, Z., Hu, J., Li, X., et al.: SIDA: social media image deepfake detection, localization and explanation with large multimodal model. In: Proceedings of the Computer Vision and Pattern Recognition Conference, pp. 28831–28841 (2025)
6. Xu, Z., Zhang, X., Li, R., et al.: FakeShield: explainable image forgery detection and localization via multi-modal large language models. arXiv preprint arXiv:2410.02761 (2024)
7. Li, Y., Tian, Y., Huang, Y., et al.: FakeScope: large multimodal expert model for transparent ai-generated image forensics. arXiv preprint arXiv:2503.24267 (2025)
8. Liu, Z., Sun, Z., Zang, Y., et al.: Visual-RFT: visual reinforcement fine-tuning. arXiv preprint arXiv:2503.01785 (2025)

9. Shen, H., Liu, P., Li, J., et al.: VLM-R1: a stable and generalizable R1-style large vision-language model. arXiv preprint arXiv:2504.07615 (2025)
10. Guo, D., Yang, D., Zhang, H., et al.: DeepSeek-R1: incentivizing reasoning capability in LLMs via reinforcement learning. arXiv preprint arXiv:2501.12948 (2025)
11. Guo, X., Liu, X., Masi, I., et al.: Language-guided hierarchical fine-grained image forgery detection and localization. Int. J. Comput. Vis. **133**(5), 2670–2691 (2025)
12. Guillaro, F., Cozzolino, D., Sud, A., et al.: TruFor: leveraging all-round clues for trustworthy image forgery detection and localization. In: Proceedings of the IEEE/CVF Conference on Computer Vision and Pattern Recognition, pp. 20606–20615 (2023)
13. Ojha, U., Li, Y., Lee, Y.J.: Towards universal fake image detectors that generalize across generative models. In: Proceedings of the IEEE/CVF Conference on Computer Vision and Pattern Recognition, pp. 24480–24489 (2023)
14. Qu, C., Liu, C., Liu, Y., et al.: Towards robust tampered text detection in document image: new dataset and new solution. In: Proceedings of the IEEE/CVF Conference on Computer Vision and Pattern Recognition, 5937–5946 (2023)
15. Ravi, N., Gabeur, V., Hu, Y.T., et al.: SAM 2: segment anything in images and videos. arXiv preprint arXiv:2408.00714 (2024)
16. Light logo. Claude. **7**, 13 (2024). https://claude.ai/
17. Yu, Z., Ni, J., Lin, Y., et al.: DiffForensics: leveraging diffusion prior to image forgery detection and localization. In: Proceedings of the IEEE/CVF Conference on Computer Vision and Pattern Recognition, pp. 12765–12774 (2024)
18. Guo, X., Liu, X., Masi, I., et al.: Language-guided hierarchical fine-grained image forgery detection and localization. Int. J. Comput. Vis. **133**(5), 2670–2691 (2025)
19. Guillaro, F., Cozzolino, D., Sud, A., et al.: TruFor: leveraging all-round clues for trustworthy image forgery detection and localization. In: Proceedings of the IEEE/CVF Conference on Computer Vision and Pattern Recognition, pp. 20606–20615 (2023)
20. Young, A., Chen, B., Li, C., et al.: Yi: open foundation models by 01. AI. arXiv preprint arXiv:2403.04652 (2024)
21. Liu, H., Li, C., Wu, Q., et al.: Visual instruction tuning. Adv. Neural. Inf. Process. Syst. **36**, 34892–34916 (2023)
22. https://openai.com/
23. Zhu, J., Wang, W., Chen, Z., et al.: InternVL3: exploring advanced training and test-time recipes for open-source multimodal models. arXiv preprint arXiv:2504.10479 (2025)
24. Ojha, U., Li, Y., Lee, Y.J.: Towards universal fake image detectors that generalize across generative models. In: Proceedings of the IEEE/CVF Conference on Computer Vision and Pattern Recognition, pp. 24480–24489 (2023)
25. Wang, Z., et al.: DIRE for diffusion-generated image detection. In: ICCV, vol. 8, p. 14 (2023)
26. Wang, Z., Bao, J., Zhou, W., et al.: Dire for diffusion-generated image detection. In: Proceedings of the IEEE/CVF International Conference on Computer Vision, pp. 22445–22455 (2023)
27. Touvron, H., Lavril, T., Izacard, G., et al.: LLaMA: open and efficient foundation language models. arXiv preprint arXiv:2302.13971 (2023)

A Transformer Based Handwriting Recognition System Jointly Using Online and Offline Features

Ayush Lodh[1], Ritabrata Chakraborty[1,2], Shivakumara Palaiahnakote[3(✉)], and Umapada Pal[1]

[1] Indian Statistical Institute, Kolkata, India
umapada@isical.ac.in
[2] Manipal University Jaipur, Jaipur, India
[3] University of Salford, Salford, UK
s.palaiahnakote@salford.ac.uk

Abstract. We posit that handwriting recognition benefits from complementary cues carried by the rasterized complex glyph and the pen's trajectory, yet most systems exploit only one modality. We introduce an end-to-end network that performs early fusion of offline images and online stroke data within a shared latent space. A patch encoder converts the grayscale crop into fixed-length visual tokens, while a lightweight transformer embeds the (x, y, pen) sequence. Learnable latent queries attend jointly to both token streams, yielding context-enhanced stroke embeddings that are pooled and decoded under a cross-entropy loss objective. Because integration occurs before any high-level classification, temporal cues reinforce each other during representation learning, producing stronger writer independence. Comprehensive experiments on IAMOn-DB, and VNOn-DB demonstrate that our approach achieves state-of-the-art accuracy, exceeding previous bests by up to 1%. Our study also shows adaptation of this pipeline with gesturification on the ISI-Air dataset. Our code can be found here: https://github.com/AZTECLUPR/HATChar-Classifier

Keywords: Handwritten text recognition · Transformer · Online–offline fusion

1 Introduction

Handwritten Text Recognition (HTR) is a foundational task in the broader domain of handwriting analysis [1], with widespread applications in document digitization, education technology, and human-computer interaction. While many advances have been made in recognizing isolated characters using deep learning, most existing models are trained on datasets such as UNIPEN [14],

A. Lodh and R. Chakraborty—Contributed equally to this work.
R. Chakraborty—Work done during internship at Indian Statistical Institute.

C. Wallraven et al. (Eds.): ACPR 2025, LNCS 16174, pp. 250–264, 2026.
https://doi.org/10.1007/978-981-95-4395-3_18

comprising neatly segmented, individual characters written in isolation. However, this is far removed from real-world scenarios, where characters look different when embedded within a word, influenced by neighboring characters, and written in a variety of natural handwriting styles.

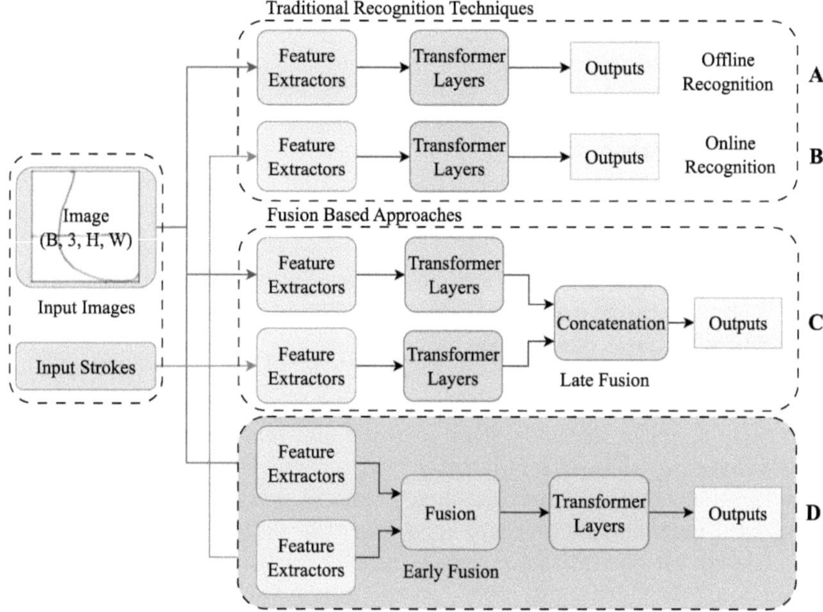

Fig. 1. An overview of input modalities and their architectures for handwritten text recognition. A: Image-only input, B: Stroke-only input, C: Late Fusion based dual input, D: Early Fusion based dual input (Ours).

Early handwritten-character recognition systems were designed around a single modality. Offline pipelines (Fig. 1-A) treat a scanned glyph as an image and rely on convolutional or transformer backbones to map pixels to character sequences [24]. Conversely, online pipelines (Fig. 1-B) discard appearance altogether, interpreting only the pen-tip trajectory captured by the digitiser [31]. Each view is incomplete as images lose temporal order, while stroke traces omit shading, pen pressure, and context such as ligatures or serifs. To mitigate this limitation, bimodal fusion emerged in a multiscale network [37] that concatenates high-level image and stroke embeddings before classification (late fusion; Fig. 1-C). Such strategies boost robustness, yet they still process both streams independently until the penultimate layer. As a result, misaligned timelines, redundant features, and modality-specific noise remain unaddressed, and the network cannot learn shared primitives—e.g., a cusp that appears as both a sharp curvature in trajectory space and a dark pixel cluster in image space.

We posit that early fusion (Fig. 1-D) unlocks deeper complementarity. **By projecting raw visual patches and stroke tokens into a shared latent**

space and allowing cross-attention before any task-specific transformer layers, the model can utilise the interaction between how a character looks in pixel space and how it is traced through the pen vectors. We utilize IAMOn-DB [27] and VNOn-DB [30] datasets adapted for character-level recognition to deisgn our experimental study for this hypothesis. We also display recognition results on the ISI-Air [33] dataset, showing strong results to air-writing data.

i. We explore a novel direction in the field of handwritten text recognition, leveraging the relationship of character images and the pen stroke vectors used in tracing them.
ii. We propose HATCharClassifier, a first of its kind handwritten text recognizer that provides robust character recognition results through early fusion of multiple inputs (image + stroke).
iii. We benchmark our model as state-of-the-art for multiple multimodal handwritten text datasets such as IAMOn-DB [27] and VNOn-DB [30], along with air writing datasets like ISI-Air [33].

The rest of the paper is structured as follows: Sect. 2 explores related literature on early classical methods, deep learning and transformer based methods, and fusion based models for handwritten text recognition. Section 3 explores our proposed framework HATCharClassifier. Section 4 describes experiment design, datasets used and metrics we employ to show the performance of our method. Section 5 delves into quantitative and qualitative results for the proposed framework. Section 6 provides a discussion on the importance of such a method with regards to current research and its caveats, and finally, Sect. 7 concludes the paper.

2 Related Work

2.1 Early Methods for Handwriting Recognition

Statistical and classical machine learning approaches have played a pivotal role in advancing handwritten text recognition in the early years of the field. Hidden Markov Models (HMMs) emerged as the dominant framework for modeling sequential handwriting, particularly excelling in cursive script recognition due to their ability to perform implicit segmentation and probabilistic modeling of character sequences [5,7,29,32]. Support Vector Machines (SVMs) gained traction for isolated character recognition by leveraging margin-based classification and kernel methods, with adaptations such as dynamic time warping kernels enabling their application to online handwriting sequences [3]. To capture richer dependencies, discriminative models like Conditional Random Fields (CRFs) were also explored, for example, [10] showed that CRFs can outperform HMMs on whole-word recognition tasks. These classical methods typically operate on carefully engineered features. For instance, Bai and Huo [4] extract 8-directional histogram features from pen trajectories for online Chinese character recognition. Likewise, many systems convert raw strokes into offline images or other local descriptors to feed into the sequence model. Alongside these, k-Nearest Neighbors (k-NN) and shallow neural networks like multilayer perceptrons served as competitive baselines for digit and character recognition, especially on benchmarks such as UNIPEN [14] and CEDAR [16]. These classifiers were highly reliant on carefully engineered features such as zoning, projection histograms, contour profiles, and geometric descriptors—extracted from normalized and preprocessed handwriting samples [18,32]. Together, these classical methods laid the algorithmic foundation for contemporary handwritten text recognition systems.

2.2 Deep Learning Based Methods

With the advent of deep learning [22], end-to-end neural models became standard for HTR. [34] introduced the CRNN architecture, combining CNN feature extraction with bidirectional RNN sequence modeling. Bi-directional LSTM (BiLSTM) networks [17] or gated RNNs then capture long-range context in the stroke/image sequence. [12] demonstrate that a BLSTM trained with Connectionist Temporal Classification (CTC) loss [11] can significantly outperform traditional HMM baselines on unconstrained handwriting recognition. Encoder–decoder models with attention have also been applied for lexicon-free transcription. More recently, fully Transformer-based OCR models have appeared. For example, [23] propose TrOCR, which uses a pre-trained Vision Transformer encoder and text Transformer decoder, yielding state-of-the-art results on handwritten text recognition benchmarks. These works paved the way towards performance-maximising models suitable for multilingual and multidomain use-cases.

2.3 Recent Attention-Based Methods

With the advent of attention mechanisms [36], transformer architectures have begun to be applied to handwriting recognition. [24] adapted the Vision Transformer (ViT) [9] for line-level text recognition. Their HTR-VT model uses a CNN for feature extraction and employs sharpness-aware minimization, achieving competitive accuracy on standard HTR datasets like IAMOn-DB [27]. [20] introduce Character Queries, a transformer decoder where each character is represented by a learned query vector; this approach excels at segmenting on-line strokes into characters given a known transcription. C-TST [8], a two-stream model using a 1D convolution + Transformer branch for temporal stroke features and a Vision Transformer for spatial image features; fusing both streams yields high accuracy on Chinese benchmarks. [25] utilized the Swin Transformer as the encoder to extract image features, focusing on Chinese character characteristics. These Transformer-based methods complement and often improve upon earlier RNN and CNN-based systems.

2.4 Bimodal Fusion Methods

Multimodal (image + stroke) fusion has been widely studied to improve robustness. Most recent methods employ late-fusion multi-stream architectures: separate encoders process pen trajectories and images, and their outputs are merged. For example, [37] propose a multi-scale bimodal fusion network that combines features from both streams using Transformers, achieving state-of-the-art accuracy on IAMOn-DB (e.g. 4.7% CER). Similarly, Bhunia et al. [6] fuse online trajectory features with rendered images for Indic script recognition. While these late-fusion models yield high accuracy, they incur extra complexity due to separate image rendering and fusion modules. We identify this as a **domain gap**: training stroke and image encoders independently can limit joint feature learning. To address this, we introduce an *early fusion* strategy that jointly embeds stroke and image information from the outset.

3 Methodology

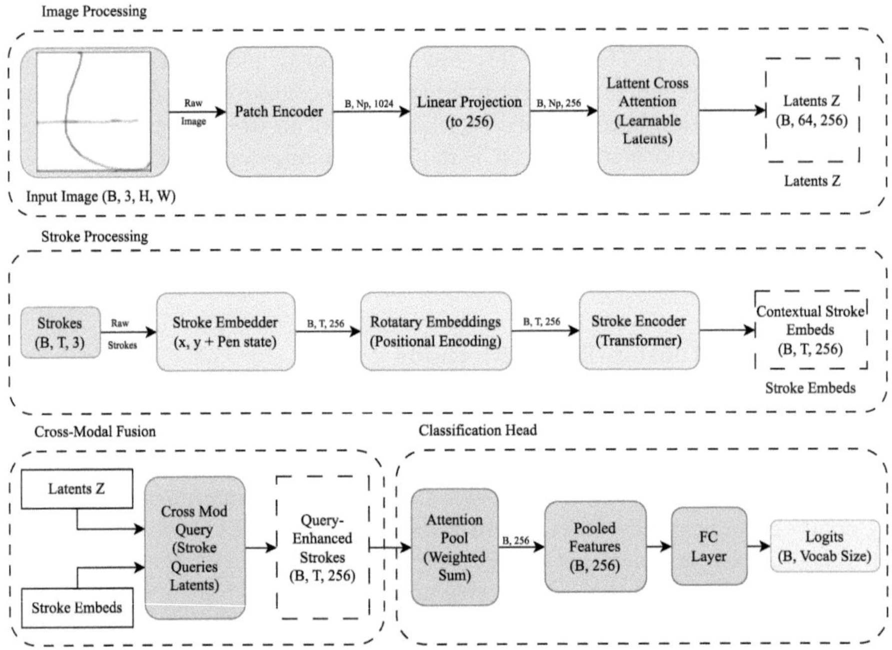

Fig. 2. Our proposed pipeline.

Notation. Let $\mathcal{D} = \{(\mathbf{I}_i, \mathbf{S}_i, y_i)\}_{i=1}^{M}$ with $\mathbf{I}_i \in \mathbb{R}^{H\times W\times C}$ (gray or RGB image), $\mathbf{S}_i = [(x_t, y_t, p_t)]_{t=1}^{T_i} \in \mathbb{R}^{T_i\times 3}$ (online stroke sequence, $p_t \in \{0, 1\}$ pen state), and $y_i \in \{1, \ldots, V\}$. HAT converts either modality—or both—into a common d-dimensional token space and classifies with a linear head (Fig. 2).

Image Patch Encoder. We first (bi-linearly) resize $\mathbf{I}$ to 224×224 and, when necessary, replicate its single channel to obtain $C = 3$. A pretrained Swin-B [26] backbone outputs the last-stage feature map $\mathbf{F} \in \mathbb{R}^{7\times7\times1024}$. Flattening the spatial axes and projecting with $\mathbf{W}_p \in \mathbb{R}^{1024\times d}$ gives

$$\mathbf{E}_p = \text{reshape}(\mathbf{F})\,\mathbf{W}_p \in \mathbb{R}^{N\times d}, \qquad N = 7\times 7. \tag{1}$$

Latent Cross-Attention. Following Perceiver-IO [19], we introduce L learnable *latent tokens* $\mathbf{Z}^{(0)} \in \mathbb{R}^{L\times d}$. For layers $\ell = 0,\dots,L_{\text{img}} - 1$

$$\tilde{\mathbf{Z}}^{(\ell)} = \text{MHA}(\mathbf{Q} = \mathbf{Z}^{(\ell)}, \mathbf{K} = \mathbf{E}_p, \mathbf{V} = \mathbf{E}_p), \tag{2a}$$

$$\mathbf{Z}^{(\ell+1)} = \text{TransformerLayer}\big(\mathbf{Z}^{(\ell)} + \tilde{\mathbf{Z}}^{(\ell)}\big). \tag{2b}$$

Layer-norm on the final state yields $\mathbf{Z} = \text{LN}(\mathbf{Z}^{(L_{\text{img}})})$.

Stroke Encoder. Each point (x_t, y_t, p_t) is embedded by concatenating raw coordinates with a pen-state lookup $\mathbf{E}_{\text{pen}} \in \mathbb{R}^{2\times d/8}$:

$$\mathbf{s}_t = [x_t, y_t, \mathbf{E}_{\text{pen}}[p_t]] \in \mathbb{R}^{2+d/8}. \tag{3}$$

After a point-wise projection, BatchNorm, and Dropout we obtain

$$\mathbf{E}_s = \big[\mathbf{s}_t\big]_{t=1}^{T} \mathbf{W}_s \in \mathbb{R}^{T\times d}, \qquad \mathbf{W}_s \in \mathbb{R}^{(2+d/8)\times d}. \tag{4}$$

Rotary Positional Encoding. Splitting every token into even/odd parts and rotating with angle $\phi_t = t\boldsymbol{\Theta}$ (see [35]) gives $\hat{\mathbf{E}}_s \in \mathbb{R}^{T\times d}$.

Temporal Transformer. An N_{stk}-layer Transformer processes the sequence

$$\mathbf{H} = \text{TransformerEncoder}(\hat{\mathbf{E}}_s) \in \mathbb{R}^{T\times d}, \tag{5}$$

which is refined via a residual 2-layer MLP:

$$\mathbf{E}_{\text{stroke}} = \mathbf{H} + \text{MLP}\big(\text{LN}(\mathbf{H})\big). \tag{6}$$

Cross-Modal Querying. With both modalities present, stroke tokens query the latent image tokens:

$$\tilde{\mathbf{E}}_{\text{stk}} = \text{MHA}(\mathbf{Q} = \mathbf{E}_{\text{stroke}}, \mathbf{K} = \mathbf{Z}, \mathbf{V} = \mathbf{Z}), \tag{7a}$$

$$\mathbf{E}_{\text{cross}} = \text{TransformerLayer}\big(\mathbf{E}_{\text{stroke}} + \tilde{\mathbf{E}}_{\text{stk}}\big). \tag{7b}$$

If images (resp. strokes) are missing we set $\mathbf{T} = \mathbf{Z}$ (resp. $\mathbf{T} = \mathbf{E}_{\text{stroke}}$).

Attention Pooling and Classification. Given token matrix $\mathbf{T} \in \mathbb{R}^{N_t\times d}$ ($N_t = L$ or T), scalar importances

$$\alpha_i = \frac{\exp\big(\mathbf{w}_2^{\top}\tanh(\mathbf{W}_1\mathbf{t}_i)\big)}{\sum_{j=1}^{N_t}\exp\big(\mathbf{w}_2^{\top}\tanh(\mathbf{W}_1\mathbf{t}_j)\big)}, \qquad \mathbf{g} = \sum_{i=1}^{N_t}\alpha_i\mathbf{t}_i, \tag{8}$$

are computed with $\mathbf{W}_1 \in \mathbb{R}^{d\times d}$, $\mathbf{w}_2 \in \mathbb{R}^d$. The classifier is

$$\mathbf{o} = \mathbf{W}_c\mathbf{g} + \mathbf{b}_c \in \mathbb{R}^V, \tag{9}$$

and we minimise cross-entropy

$$\mathcal{L} = -\frac{1}{M}\sum_{i=1}^{M} \log \frac{\exp(o_{i,y_i})}{\sum_{v=1}^{V} \exp(o_{i,v})}. \tag{10}$$

Algorithm 1. HAT (refer to Eq. (1)–(10)as aforementioned)

Require: mini-batch $\{(\mathbf{I}_i, \mathbf{S}_i, y_i)\}_{i=1}^{B}$, mode $m \in \{\textsc{Image}, \textsc{Stroke}, \textsc{Both}\}$

for $i \leftarrow 1$ **to** B **do**
  if $m \neq \textsc{Stroke}$ **then** ▷ image branch
    $\mathbf{E}_p \leftarrow \textsc{ImagePatchEncoder}(\mathbf{I}_i)$ ▷ Eq. (1)
    $\mathbf{Z} \leftarrow \textsc{LatentCrossAttn}(\mathbf{E}_p)$ ▷ Eqs. (2a)–(2b)
  end if
  if $m \neq \textsc{Image}$ **then** ▷ stroke branch: Sec. 3
    $\mathbf{E}_{\text{stk}} \leftarrow \textsc{StrokeEncoder}(\mathbf{S}_i)$ ▷ Eqs. (4)–(6)
  end if
  Select T
  • m=$\textsc{Image} \rightarrow \mathbf{T} = \mathbf{Z}$
  • m=$\textsc{Stroke} \rightarrow \mathbf{T} = \mathbf{E}_{\text{stk}}$
  if $m = \textsc{Both}$ **then** ▷ hybrid: Sec. 3
    $\mathbf{T} \leftarrow \textsc{CrossModalQuery}(\mathbf{E}_{\text{stk}}, \mathbf{Z})$ ▷ Eq. (7b)
  end if
  $\mathbf{g} \leftarrow \textsc{AttentionPool}(\mathbf{T})$ ▷ Eq. (8)
  $\mathbf{o}_i \leftarrow \mathbf{W}_c\mathbf{g} + \mathbf{b}_c$ ▷ Eq. (9)
end for
$\mathcal{L} \leftarrow \textsc{CrossEntropy}(\{\mathbf{o}_i\}, \{y_i\})$ ▷ Eq. (10)
Back-propagate $\nabla\mathcal{L}$; update parameters

In summary, HAT maps images (via a frozen Swin$_B$) and online strokes (via a rotary-encoded transformer) to a shared d-dimensional token space. Stroke tokens optionally query image tokens through a single cross-modal attention layer, after which attentional pooling yields a global vector for linear classification with cross-entropy. The same lightweight architecture handles image-only, stroke-only, and hybrid inputs without altering parameters.

4 Experiments

4.1 Datasets

Table 1. Dataset statistics after pre-processing.

Dataset	Train Set	Val. Set	Test Set	# Cls.
IAMOn-DB [27]	72,508	18,954	21,455	84
VNOn-DB [30]	197,140	57,763	77,389	145
ISI-Air [33]	10,000	2,000	-	10

We evaluate on three on-line handwriting corpora, each trained and tested in isolation. Qualitative examples are given in Figs. 3, 4, 5, while Table 1(left) reports the final number of character instances per split together with the number of target classes.

The **IAMOn-DB** [27] dataset is a widely used benchmark for online handwriting recognition, particularly focused on English cursive script. It contains handwritten text samples collected from 221 writers using a stylus on a tablet, capturing the temporal sequence of pen strokes along with their spatial coordinates. IAMOn-DB supports writer-independent and writer-dependent evaluation protocols and is frequently used for training and evaluating sequence models like HMMs and RNNs. Its high-quality online handwriting data has made it a standard in evaluating temporal modeling capabilities in handwriting recognition systems.

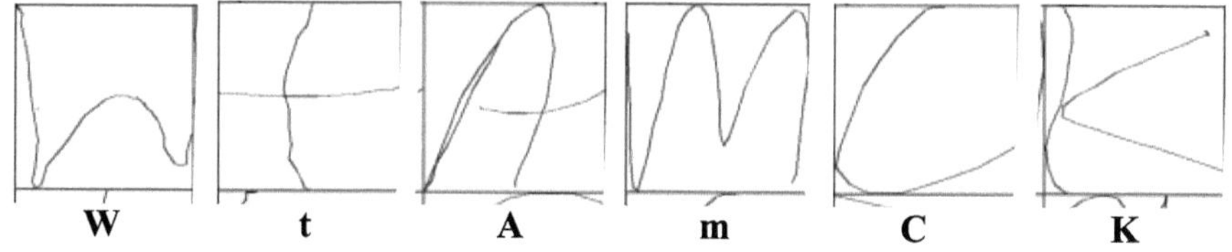

Fig. 3. Some examples from IAMOn-DB dataset.

The VNOn-DB (Vietnamese Online Handwriting Database) [30] is a large-scale dataset designed to support research in Vietnamese online handwriting recognition. It comprises pen trajectory data collected from over 200 writers, covering all 134 Vietnamese characters including diacritics. Each character is annotated with stroke order and pen-up/pen-down events, providing rich temporal and spatial information. VNOn-DB presents challenges specific to the Vietnamese language, such as compound characters and tonal marks, making it a valuable resource for evaluating script-specific handwriting models.

The ISI-AIR dataset [33] is a publicly available corpus designed for research in mid-air handwriting recognition using motion capture. Collected at the Indian Statistical Institute (ISI), the dataset comprises 3D hand trajectory recordings of English digits captured using a webcam. Unlike traditional handwriting, ISI-AIR features freehand air gestures without physical contact, introducing challenges such as higher spatial variance, motion blur, and absence of surface constraints.

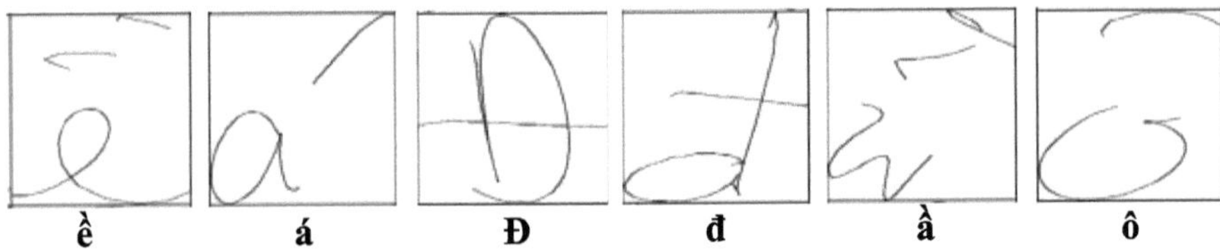

Fig. 4. Some examples from VNOn-DB dataset.

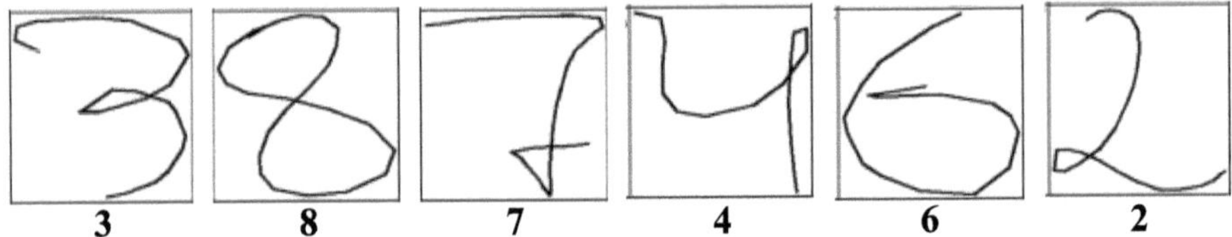

Fig. 5. Some examples from ISI-Air dataset.

4.2 Implementation Details

All experiments are conducted on a single NVIDIA RTX A5000 (24 GB) GPU using the PyTorch [2] framework. Training proceeds with the AdamW [28] optimizer (initial learning rate 1×10^{-4}, $\beta_1 = 0.9$, $\beta_2 = 0.999$, weight-decay 0.01). The learning rate follows a cosine-annealing schedule that decays to zero, and gradients are clipped to an ℓ_2-norm of 1.0. Classification uses cross-entropy with label-smoothing 0.1, while dropout ($p = 0.1$) and batch-normalization regularize the stroke pathway. We evaluate with overall accuracy and the class-balanced macro variants of precision, recall and F_1. The pre-segmented characters for the datasets [27,30] follows the procedures described in [20].

5 Results

Table 2 displays the performance of comparable models in literature against our proposed recognizer. For the **IAMOn-DB** dataset, we note a mean 1.5% improvement in acurracy across all modes (image-only, stroke-only and dual input). OLHTR [37] exceeds for dual input marginally (<1%) in precision, recall and F-1 score. We observe an interesting 3.8% gain in accuracy for image-only mode, highlighting the robustness and utility of our framework even when both inputs are not available. For **VNOn-DB** and we provide their first dual-input benchmarking results. For VNOn-DB, we note an accuracy of 95.8% for dual input, as opposed to 72.1% on stroke-only mode. This further reinforces our claim, because although we assume the per-character stroke richness and vocabulary size (145) of the dataset would be much higher than IAMOn-DB, simply relying on stroke information leads to confusion in predictions. Combining image inputs and correlating offline characteristics with the strokes leads to robust identification. We notice a similar trend in accuracy for the **ISI-Air** dataset, with our

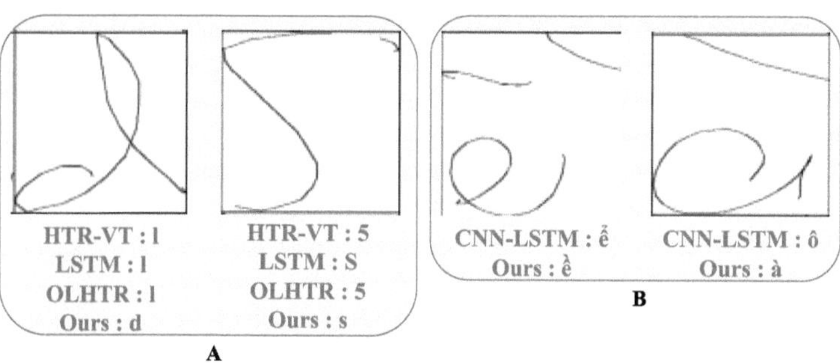

Fig. 6. Qualitative results (A): IAM-OnDB, (B): VN-OnDB. Red denotes incorrect recognition, our methods show correctly recognized class in green for all cases shown here. (Color figure online)

Table 2. Comparison across datasets. Highest values per metric are highlighted. I: Image, S: Stroke, D: Dual

Architecture	Mode	Acc. (%)	Precision (%)	Recall (%)	F1 (%)
IAM Dataset [27]					
HTR-VT [24]	I	**95.3**	**94.9**	**94.7**	**94.8**
HAT	I	91.5	90.8	88.0	89.4
LSTM [13]	S	**90.7**	89.3	**90.0**	**88.6**
HAT	S	89.5	**90.2**	85.0	87.5
OLHTR [37]	D	95.3	**95.1**	**94.6**	**93.8**
HAT	D	**96.4**	94.0	92.5	93.7
VNOn-DB Dataset [30]					
CNN-LSTM [21]	I	**95.3**	**95.0**	**94.2**	**94.6**
HAT	I	92.6	91.5	90.7	91.1
HAT	S	72.1	71.0	68.5	69.7
HAT	D	**95.8**	**95.5**	**95.0**	**95.2**
ISI-Air Dataset [33]					
HAT	I	99.5	98.7	99.1	98.4
HAT	S	98.1	97.3	97.4	98.0
RNN-LSTM [33]	D	98.7	98.6	98.5	98.6
HAT	D	**99.8**	**99.5**	**98.2**	**98.7**

dual-input model achieving a 1.7% increase from stroke-only input mode, and an overall 1.1% increase compared to the traditional RNN-LSTM architecture previously reported in literature [33].

We display some qualitative recognition results in Fig. 6. It is interesting to note that even though character isolation removes the context of the word it is taken from, our model provides correct results for slightly varying characters even when other paradigms fail.

5.1 Ablations

We provide insights into various settings of feature extraction by swapping out the patch encoder backbone shown in Table 4. Swin-B 224 [26] displays the best accuracy when used in training; by using frozen weights, the accuracy drops notably by 10%. At its lightest setting (ResNet-18) [15] we get an accuracy of 79.13% highlighting the impact of our chosen Swin-B [26] backbone. Training cost is considerably alleviated since our model converges at the 4th epoch itself for the chosen setting.

Table 3. Comparison of convergence with other models on IAMOn-DB [27]. "#Params" denotes total model parameters; "–" = not reported in the paper.

Models	Acc. (%)	#Params (M)	Conv. Epochs
LSTM [13]	90.07	–	150
HAT (Strokes)	89.50	4.3	46
HTR-VT [24]	95.30	53.5	1 165
HAT (Images)	91.50	88.6	4
OLHTR [37]	95.30	–	–
HAT (Fusion)	96.42	94.4	3

We benchmark the proposed HAT variants against representative on-line/off-line recognisers. We observe LSTM and recent transformer-based systems require hundreds to thousands of epochs. In contrast, the efficient-fusion HAT converges in just **three** epochs while retaining competitive accuracy (see Table 3).

Table 4. Ablation study with different image feature extractors.

Feature Extractor	Status	Acc. (%)	#Params (M)	Conv. Epochs
ResNet-18 [15]	❄	79.13	–	15th
ResNet-18 [15]	🔥	82.95	25.04	8th
ResNet-34 [15]	❄	76.31	–	16th
ResNet-34 [15]	🔥	80.23	35.14	9th
ViT (Base) [9]	❄	82.42	–	9th
ViT (Base) [9]	🔥	86.14	93.47	4th
Swin-B 224 [26]	❄	82.33	–	22nd
Swin-B 224 [26]	🔥	**92.42**	94.48	4th

All results are measured on the IAMOn-DB for dual inputs. #Params refers to the parameters of the complete model, including both the stroke and the image branch. ❄ denotes frozen and 🔥 denotes trainable parameters

Table 5. Fusion-level comparison of our models on IAMOn-DB [27]. "Acc." = accuracy.

Model Variant	Fusion	Acc. (%)
HAT	Early	**96.40**
HAT	Middle	92.10
OLHTR [37]	Late	95.30

Table 6. Robustness of the dual-trained model to modality dropout (IAMOn-DB). Δ is the absolute accuracy drop relative to the full-input baseline.

Train → Test	Acc. (%)	Δ (%)
Dual → Dual	92.4	0.0
Dual → Image-only	88.1	-4.3
Dual → Stroke-only	85.7	-6.7

We benchmark two fusion strategies for our HAT architecture on IAMOn-DB. Early and mid-level fusions are contrasted with the transformer-based OLHTR baseline. Numerical results are summarised in Table 5 (Table 6).

We train a single model with dual modalities and then evaluate it under three conditions: (i) the full input, (ii) image stream only and (iii) stroke stream only. The network gracefully degrades when a modality is absent at test time. A modest drop of 4–7% shows the model remains fairly robust to real-world sensor failure.

6 Discussion

Convergence. Rapid 3–4 epoch convergence is plausible here because most representational burden is carried by a strong pre-trained visual backbone and a shallow, low-capacity fusion/head stack, trained with AdamW, cosine annealing, label smoothing, and gradient clipping on an easy-to-adapt, character-level task—so validation metrics plateau quickly despite a large total parameter count that is largely reused rather than learned from scratch.

Limitations. The current system recognises isolated glyphs, assumes pre segmented inputs, and depends on a training visual backbone of 90 M parameters. Performance has not been audited across writer demographics or fine-grained stroke disorders, and segmentation errors in IAM0n-DB and VNOn-DB introduce small but uncorrected label noise. We also notice some failure cases for our model in Fig. 7.

Future Work. Future work lies in curation of a large level multilingual word level and line level dataset to extend the usage of this framework to real applications. There is also potential in providing for manually segmented character information that might help in better benchmarking results.

Ethical Considerations. Pen trajectories may act as a biometric, enabling unintended writer-identification. Some security concerns might stem from learned correlations between motor patterns through stroke and subsequent formed character images, which warrants careful auditing of software that uses this framework.

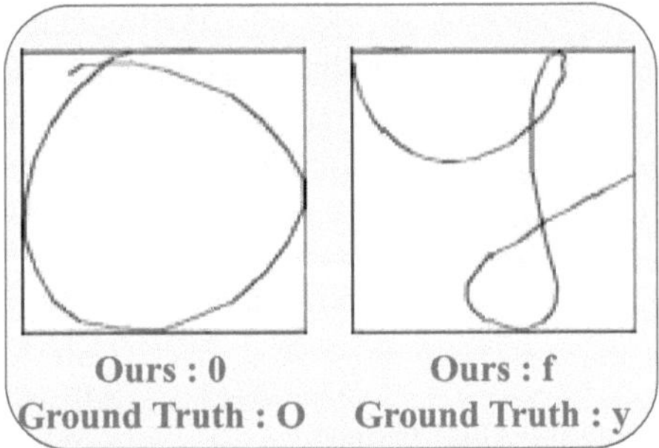

Fig. 7. Failure cases for our model.

7 Conclusion

We propose HATCharClassifier, a novel framework that utilises early fusion utilising online and offline input modalities for handwritten text recognition. Our method displays the utility of capturing the correlation between the two modalities using cross-modal querying, leading to more robust recognition across multiple datasets as discussed above. Our approach opens a new direction in this field, motivating future work for word-level and line-level air-writing dataset collection and benchmarking. We notice some limitations as discussed above which leaves potential for future work.

References

1. AlKendi, W., Gechter, F., Heyberger, L., Guyeux, C.: Advancements and challenges in handwritten text recognition: a comprehensive survey. J. Imaging **10**(1) (2024). https://doi.org/10.3390/jimaging10010018. https://www.mdpi.com/2313-433X/10/1/18
2. Ansel, J., et al.: PyTorch 2: faster machine learning through dynamic Python bytecode transformation and graph compilation. In: Proceedings of the 29th ACM International Conference on Architectural Support for Programming Languages and Operating Systems, Volume 2, ASPLOS 2024, April 2024. Association for Computing Machinery (2024). https://doi.org/10.1145/3620665.3640366. https://docs.pytorch.org/assets/pytorch2-2.pdf
3. Bahlmann, C., Haasdonk, B., Burkhardt, H.: Online handwriting recognition with support vector machines-a kernel approach. In: Proceedings Eighth International Workshop on Frontiers in Handwriting Recognition, pp. 49–54. IEEE (2002)
4. Bai, Z.L., Huo, Q.: A study on the use of 8-directional features for online handwritten Chinese character recognition. In: Eighth International Conference on Document Analysis and Recognition, ICDAR'05, pp. 262–266. IEEE (2005)
5. Bengio, Y., LeCun, Y., Nohl, C., Burges, C.: LeRec: a NN/HMM hybrid for on-line handwriting recognition. Neural Comput. **7**(6), 1289–1303 (1995)
6. Bhunia, A.K., Mukherjee, S., Sain, A., Bhunia, A.K., Roy, P.P., Pal, U.: Indic handwritten script identification using offline-online multi-modal deep network. Inf. Fus. **57**, 1–14 (2020)

7. Bozinovic, R.M., Srihari, S.N.: Off-line cursive script word recognition. IEEE Trans. Pattern Anal. Mach. Intell. **11**(1), 68–83 (1989)
8. Chen, Y., Zheng, H., Li, Y., Ouyang, W., Zhu, J.: Online handwritten Chinese character recognition based on 1-d convolution and two-streams transformers. IEEE Trans. Multimedia **26**, 5769–5781 (2023)
9. Dosovitskiy, A., et al.: An image is worth 16x16 words: transformers for image recognition at scale. arXiv preprint arXiv:2010.11929 (2020)
10. Feng, S., Manmatha, R., McCallum, A.: Exploring the use of conditional random field models and HMMs for historical handwritten document recognition. In: Second International Conference on Document Image Analysis for Libraries, DIAL'06, p. 8 IEEE (2006)
11. Graves, A., Fernández, S., Gomez, F., Schmidhuber, J.: Connectionist temporal classification: labelling unsegmented sequence data with recurrent neural networks. In: Proceedings of the 23rd International Conference on Machine Learning, pp. 369–376 (2006)
12. Graves, A., Liwicki, M., Fernández, S., Bertolami, R., Bunke, H., Schmidhuber, J.: A novel connectionist system for unconstrained handwriting recognition. IEEE Trans. Pattern Anal. Mach. Intell. **31**(5), 855–868 (2008)
13. Greff, K., Srivastava, R.K., Koutník, J., Steunebrink, B.R., Schmidhuber, J.: LSTM: a search space odyssey. IEEE Trans. Neural Netw. Learn. Syst. **28**(10), 2222–2232 (2016)
14. Guyon, I., Schomaker, L., Plamondon, R., Liberman, M., Janet, S.: UNIPEN project of on-line data exchange and recognizer benchmarks. In: Proceedings of the 12th IAPR International Conference on Pattern Recognition, vol. 3-Conference C: Signal Processing (Cat. No. 94CH3440-5), vol. 2, pp. 29–33. IEEE (1994)
15. He, K., Zhang, X., Ren, S., Sun, J.: Deep residual learning for image recognition. In: Proceedings of the IEEE Conference on Computer Vision and Pattern Recognition, pp. 770–778 (2016)
16. www.cedar.buffalo.edu/ilt/research.html
17. Huang, Z., Xu, W., Yu, K.: Bidirectional LSTM-CRF models for sequence tagging. arXiv preprint arXiv:1508.01991 (2015)
18. Impedovo, D., Pirlo, G.: Zoning methods for handwritten character recognition: a survey. Pattern Recogn. **47**(3), 969–981 (2014)
19. Jaegle, A., et al.: Perceiver IO: a general architecture for structured inputs & outputs. arXiv preprint arXiv:2107.14795 (2021)
20. Jungo, M., Wolf, B., Maksai, A., Musat, C., Fischer, A.: Character queries: a transformer-based approach to on-line handwritten character segmentation. In: International Conference on Document Analysis and Recognition, pp. 98–114. Springer (2023)
21. Le, A.D., Nguyen, H.T., Nakagawa, M.: An end-to-end recognition system for unconstrained Vietnamese handwriting. SN Comput. Sci. **1**(1), 7 (2020)
22. LeCun, Y., Bengio, Y., Hinton, G.: Deep learning. nature **521**(7553), 436–444 (2015)
23. Li, M., et al.: TrOCR: transformer-based optical character recognition with pre-trained models. In: Proceedings of the AAAI Conference on Artificial Intelligence, vol. 37, pp. 13094–13102 (2023)
24. Li, Y., Chen, D., Tang, T., Shen, X.: HTR-VT: handwritten text recognition with vision transformer. Pattern Recogn. **158**, 110967 (2025)
25. Li, Z., Zhao, H., Nishizaki, H., Leow, C.S., Shen, X.: Chinese character recognition based on Swin transformer-encoder. Digit. Sig. Process. **161**, 105080 (2025)

26. Liu, Z., et al.: Swin transformer: hierarchical vision transformer using shifted windows. In: Proceedings of the IEEE/CVF International Conference on Computer Vision, pp. 10012–10022 (2021)
27. Liwicki, M., Bunke, H.: IAM-OnDB-an on-line English sentence database acquired from handwritten text on a whiteboard. In: Eighth International Conference on Document Analysis and Recognition (ICDAR'05), pp. 956–961. IEEE (2005)
28. Loshchilov, I., Hutter, F.: Decoupled weight decay regularization. In: International Conference on Learning Representations (2019). https://openreview.net/forum?id=Bkg6RiCqY7
29. Marti, U.V., Bunke, H.: The IAM-database: an English sentence database for offline handwriting recognition. Int. J. Doc. Anal. Recogn. **5**, 39–46 (2002)
30. Nguyen, H.T., Nguyen, C.T., Nakagawa, M.: ICFHR 2018–competition on Vietnamese online handwritten text recognition using HANDS-VNOnDB (VOHTR2018). In: 2018 16th International Conference on Frontiers in Handwriting Recognition (ICFHR), pp. 494–499. IEEE (2018)
31. Ott, F., Rügamer, D., Heublein, L., Bischl, B., Mutschler, C.: Auxiliary cross-modal representation learning with triplet loss functions for online handwriting recognition. IEEE Access **11**, 94148–94172 (2023). https://doi.org/10.1109/ACCESS.2023.3310819
32. Plamondon, R., Srihari, S.N.: Online and off-line handwriting recognition: a comprehensive survey. IEEE Trans. Pattern Anal. Mach. Intell. **22**(1), 63–84 (2000)
33. Rahman, A., Roy, P., Pal, U.: Air writing: Recognizing multi-digit numeral string traced in air using RNN-LSTM architecture. SN Comput. Sci. **2**(1), 20 (2021)
34. Shi, B., Bai, X., Yao, C.: An end-to-end trainable neural network for image-based sequence recognition and its application to scene text recognition. IEEE Trans. Pattern Anal. Mach. Intell. **39**(11), 2298–2304 (2016)
35. Su, J., Ahmed, M., Lu, Y., Pan, S., Bo, W., Liu, Y.: Roformer: enhanced transformer with rotary position embedding. Neurocomputing **568**, 127063 (2024)
36. Vaswani, A., et al.: Attention is all you need. Adv. Neural Inf. Process. Syst. **30** (2017)
37. Xu, Z., et al.: A multi-scale bimodal fusion network for robust and accurate online handwriting recognition. In: 2024 IEEE International Conference on Acoustics, Speech and Signal Processing (ICASSP), ICASSP 2024, pp. 6460–6464. IEEE (2024)

XMamba: Fully Enhanced Mamba for X-Ray Prohibited Items Detection

Litao Li[1,2], Hongxia Gao[2(✉)], and Tian Qi[1]

[1] School of Automation Science and Engineering, South China University of Technology, Guangzhou 510641, China
202320116452@mail.scut.edu.cn, auqt@scut.edu.cn

[2] School of Cyber Science and Engineering, Xi'an Jiaotong University, Xi'an 710049, China
hxgao@xjtu.edu.cn

Abstract. Prohibited items detection is crucial for maintaining security in public areas like airports and train stations. Despite progress in target detection and semantic segmentation algorithms that aid in identifying contraband, X-ray imaging presents unique difficulties due to the severe distortion of pixel information caused by object stacking and density variations. Many existing detection methods fail to account for the complex interplay between foreground and background pixels, resulting in subpar performance. We introduce XMamba, a specialized architecture derived from the VMamba model, designed specifically for detecting prohibited items in X-ray images. XMamba incorporates an Equalization Perception Module (EPM) and a Foreground Channel Decoupling (FCD) method to tackle the challenges of weak features, internal pseudo-contours, and perspective interferences. By leveraging state-space modeling (SSM) to reduce self-attention complexity, XMamba effectively captures global information and minimizes distortion caused by these challenges. Our approach strikes a balance between parameter count, GFLOPs, and accuracy, outperforming both CNN-based and transformer-based detectors. Experimental results demonstrate that our proposed XMamba detector, when combined with cascaded Mask R-CNN, comprehensively surpasses all state-of-the-art methods.

Keywords: Prohibited Items Detection · X-ray images · State-Space Modeling

1 Introduction

Prohibited items detection is vital to ensuring the safety of public places such as airports and stations as it identifies potential hazards. Staff use X-ray imaging and manual or automated detection methods to identify these items. While researchers have developed detection algorithms based on target recognition

L. Li and H. Gao—Contributed equally to this study.

C. Wallraven et al. (Eds.): ACPR 2025, LNCS 16174, pp. 265–279, 2026.
https://doi.org/10.1007/978-981-95-4395-3_19

and semantic segmentation, X-ray images of prohibited items present unique challenges: because X-ray image pixel values are correlated with the density of the object medium, ultra-low density objects can have feature representations that can be very close to the background, and inside the object, density imbalances can lead to the creation of internal pseudo-contours, which can affect detector judgment. In addition, object stacking can produce perspective interference, affecting pixel information and leading to distortion of information in the occluded region, as shown in Fig. 1. Conventional general detectors cannot accomplish this task effectively.

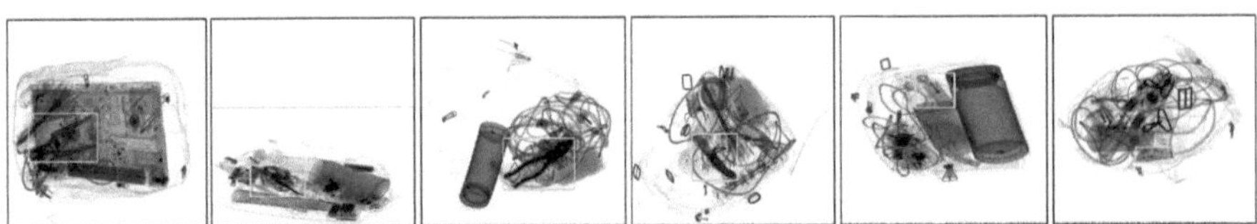

Fig. 1. Examples of the hidden category in the PIDray [36] dataset, The yellow bounding boxes are the area where the prohibited items are located. (Color figure online)

Researchers have devised targeting strategies to enhance the precision of general detectors for X-ray detection of banned items. The primary approaches encompass feature integration and foreground-background separation. Foreground-background separation methods, such as LAcls, LAreg [38], and IAA [18], primarily focus on label assignment strategies. However, these methods neglect the complex interplay between pixels in the foreground and background, leading to an overemphasis on the contour information of prohibited items, thereby compromising the effectiveness of these approaches.

Among the feature fusion methods, DOAM, SDANet, and LIM proposed by OPIXray [32], PIDray [36], and HiXray [30] all similarly adopt the dense connection of feature pyramids to further optimize the feature maps extracted from the backbone network, and use the universally adopted attentional mechanism alignment for feature selection. This approach is limited by the accuracy of the feature maps extracted by the backbone network and is prone to overfitting.

Some methods have introduced DETR [2] and its variants, like AO-DETR [17], into X-ray prohibited item detection to address CNNs' limitations in capturing global information. However, self-attention mechanism leads to high time complexity and large parameter size, reducing inference speed. The Mamba architecture [11] mitigates this by reducing self-attention to linear complexity using the State Space Model (SSM), improving efficiency while retaining global information capture. VMamba [23], derived from Mamba, shows great potential for visual tasks.

In light of this, we construct a dedicated Mamba-based backbone network, named XMamba, in the field of X-ray prohibited items detection. Specifically, XMamba still follows the design concept of the VMamba [23] family, and designs Equalization Perception Module (EPM) and Foreground Channel Decoupling Method (FCD) for the specific nature of X-ray images in HSV color space and the coupling relationship between the front and background pixels. The input patch is sensed by the front EPM and fed into the VSS Block [23] for feature extraction, and then decoupled and modulated at each level of the feature map using the FCD and finally fed into the neck section for feature fusion. Our proposed method not only maintains the advantage of VMamba in capturing global information, but also effectively mitigates the perspective interference and internal pseudo-profile problem in X-ray images, and achieves the current optimal balance in terms of the number of parameters, GFLOPs, and model performance.

The main contributions of our work are as follows:

- We propose the XMamba based on the VMamba, which to the best of our knowledge is the first time a Mamba model has been applied to the field of X-ray prohibited items detection, and experimentally demonstrates that the XMamba-based detector outperforms the generalized detector and state-of-the-art methods based on CNN and Transformer.
- We introduce the Equalization Perception Module (EPM) and Foreground Channel Decoupling (FCD) to improve X-ray image analysis. EPM adjusts HSV channel weights to enhance detection of prohibited items. FCD transfers channel information to focus on foreground regions and reduce perspective interference effects.
- Extensive experiments have shown that XMamba achieves excellent performance in X-ray prohibited items detection, providing a new baseline for X-ray prohibited items detection.

2 Related Work

2.1 Object Detection

General object detectors are typically categorized into single-stage, two-stage, and DETR-style detectors. Single-stage detectors like YOLOv7 [31], SSD [22], and ATSS [37] are CNN-based and offer fast inference and easy deployment, but often lag in accuracy. Two-stage detectors such as Faster R-CNN [26], Mask R-CNN [12], Cascade R-CNN [1], and FCOS [8] employ more complex feature fusion and region refinement, achieving higher accuracy at the cost of speed and model complexity. Recently, Transformer-based detectors have emerged, with DETR [2] combining CNNs and Transformers to leverage global modeling and inductive bias. To address DETRs slow convergence, Deformable DETR [39] introduces deformable attention, Sparse DETR [27] suppresses background tokens, and DINO [35] improves matching via denoising and hybrid queries.

2.2 X-Ray Prohibited Items Detection

From the perspective of foreground separation and feature fusion, several methods have advanced X-ray object detection through improved label assignment and feature enhancement. CLCXray [38] introduces LAcls and LAreg to refine label assignment. GADet [18] leverages physical diagonal length constraints and IoU-aware assignment to better localize prohibited items using their physical characteristics. Xdet [3] adopts hard-negative sample selection to balance training samples and simplify optimization. AO-DETR [17] proposes a foreground instability score and category-specific one-to-one assignment to improve anchor selection and labeling. For feature fusion, OPIXray [32] enhances spatial perception with a de-occlusion attention module focusing on edges and regions, PIDray [36] employs a densely connected network to integrate multi-scale features, and HIXray [30] reduces background interference using lateral inhibition and boundary activation mechanisms.

2.3 Mamba in Vision Tasks

Recent studies have explored Mamba in vision tasks. VMamba [23] extends the State Space Model to 2D for global context modeling, while LocalMamba [15] captures local dependencies through window-based selective scanning. Mamba has shown promise in medical segmentation with VM-UNet [28] and remote sensing with RSMamba [6]. Yet its potential in object detection remains largely unexplored.

3 Methods

3.1 Preliminaries

2D-Selective-Scan. Since the visual data is not temporal and there exists spatial location information and edge texture information, Selective Scan Mechanism (SSM) [11] in temporal task becomes no longer applicable, VMamba proposes a 2D-Selective-Scan (SS2D) optimized SSM method for visual data. Specifically, SS2D resets the image from four different directions into patches and performs SSM. SSM still follows the State Space Models (SSMs) approach [23], and the linear ordinary differential equations for continuous time SSMs are shown below:

$$\mathrm{h}'(t) = \mathrm{Ah}(t) + \mathrm{B}u(t), y(t) = \mathrm{Ch}(t) + Du(t), \tag{1}$$

where $\mathbf{h}(t) \in \mathbb{R}^N$ is the hidden state, $\mathbf{u}(t) \in \mathbb{R}$ is the input stimulation and $\mathbf{y}(t) \in \mathbb{R}$ is the output response. $\mathbf{A} \in \mathbb{R}^{N\times N}$, $\mathbf{B} \in \mathbb{R}^{N\times 1}$, $\mathbf{C} \in \mathbb{R}^{1\times N}$, and $\mathbf{D} \in \mathbb{R}^1$ belong to the state transfer matrix. As shown in Fig. 5, the patches after SSM are re-fused in the original direction by Cross Merge to get the output response of the image.

Perspective Interference. In X-ray prohibited items detection, low-density objects are often obscured by high-density objects due to the see-through effect, causing perspective interference. This interference distorts the target's color and contour, leading to absorbance bias in the stacked portions. The pixel value of the color image for any material unit area is given by Eq. 2.

$$I = A\varphi_0 e^j + B, j = -\mu d \tag{2}$$

where A, B, φ_0 are the imaging parameters, j is the X-ray attenuation rate, μ, d are the density and thickness of the material. When there is a perspective interference, the pixel value of the overlapping region is shown in Eq. 3:

$$I = A\varphi_0 e^{-(j_1+\ldots+j_n)} + B \tag{3}$$

where n is the number of different substances. Perspective interference transforms the pixels from Eq. 2 to Eq. 3. In practical applications, we cannot obtain all the substance density and thickness information. Additionally, the pixels of perspective interference do not follow a simple stacking relationship. Therefore, we assume an implicit coupling relationship between the stacked pixels in the channel, which persists during feature extraction.

Internal Pseudo-Contour. Another challenge arises when the substance inside an object differs in density from the external material, as illustrated by the liquid bottle in Fig. 2(b). In this scenario, the contrasting densities of the bottle and the liquid can create target pseudo-contours, leading to incorrect modeling of contour information. This phenomenon is referred to as **Internal Pseudo-Contour**.

3.2 Equalization Perception Module

Objects in X-ray images are better represented in the HSV color space, especially in terms of local homogeneity in the S and V channels. As shown in Fig. 2, even bottles with different internal densities exhibit homogeneity in the S channel, which helps reduce contour confusion. However, this effect is weaker for low-density materials compared to high-density ones. Traditional spatial attention mechanisms, which highlight target regions using channel dimensions, often result in lower scores for low-density objects and hinder effective feature perception. To address this, we introduce the **Equalization Perception Module (EPM)**. It leverages the advantages of the HSV space to enhance perception of low-density objects by reducing internal pseudo-contours, while maintaining a low parameter count. The architecture of EPM is shown in Fig. 3.

We transform the image into HSV space and denote the channels as X_h, X_s, and X_v. The EPM reconstructs these into X_R. To reduce color sensitivity, we focus on the S and V channels, using two color-encoders to filter them and suppress the background. The color encoder consists of two convolutional layers connected by residuals, where the size of the convolutional kernel is chosen to be 5×5 to obtain a suitable receptive field. We introduce a modulation parameter γ to adjust the attention maps, forming the final result.

$$\begin{aligned} X_s^r &= Softmax(CE(X_s)) \\ X_v^r &= Softmax(CE(X_v)) \end{aligned} \tag{4}$$

$$X_R = \gamma X_s^r + (1-\gamma) X_v^r \tag{5}$$

where X_s^r, X_v^r, CE denote the reconstructed S, V channels and the color-encoder, we consider the information provided by both channels to be equally important, so the parameter γ is set to 0.5.

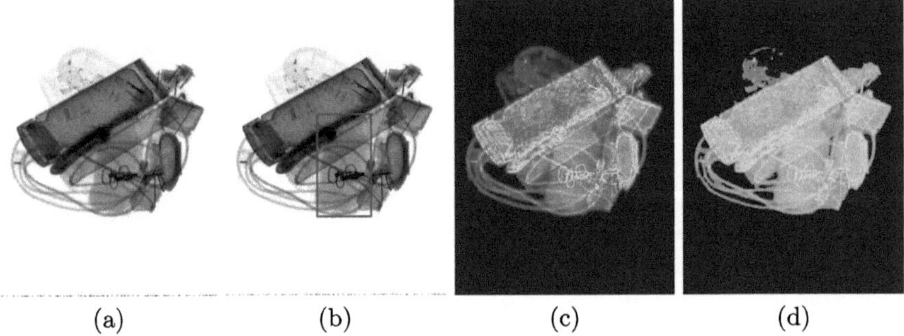

(a) (b) (c) (d)

Fig. 2. (a) The original image (b) Inner and outer densities with different liquid locations are indicated by red bounding boxes (c) S-channel of the original image (d) EPM reconstruction map (Color figure online)

3.3 Foreground Channel Decoupling

The EPM utilizes the HSV channel to address issues caused by perspective interference. However, there remains a coupling relationship between the occluded object feature maps at different stages of the hierarchy, which distorts the original pixel information of the occluded object. To mitigate this, we propose an information decoupling method called **Foreground Channel Decoupling (FCD)**. FCD consists of two phases: **Channel Decoupling (CD) and Foreground Select (FS)**. The framework of FCD is depicted in Fig. 4.

CD employs MLP as decouplers to separate channels at each level. The decoupled channel information is then used to modulate the channel information of the subsequent level through dense connections. This process continues, with each level using the modulated information to inform the next, until the channel information at the previous level integrates both shallow and deep features. Compared to simple channel attention mechanisms like SE-Block [14], CD also synthesizes spatial location information by leveraging multi-scale features. The CD modulation process is detailed in Eq. 6.

$$C_i^D = \alpha_i Up(MLP(C_{i-1}^D), C_D = \sum_{i=1}^{4} C_i^D \tag{6}$$

where C_i^D is the channel information of the ith layer feature map, $Up(\cdot)$ is the up-sampling operation, the up-sampling coefficient is determined by the proportion of the channel transformations between the backbone networks, and α_i is the modulation coefficient, which ranges from 0 to 1, and is a learnable parameter. C_D is a weighted sum of C_i^D.

Suppose backbone outputs a collection of feature maps:

$$F = \{F_1, F_2, F_3, F_4\} \tag{7}$$

FS is applied to the feature map at the final level, where the CD-modulated channel scores are used to rank and select the top 50% foreground channels.

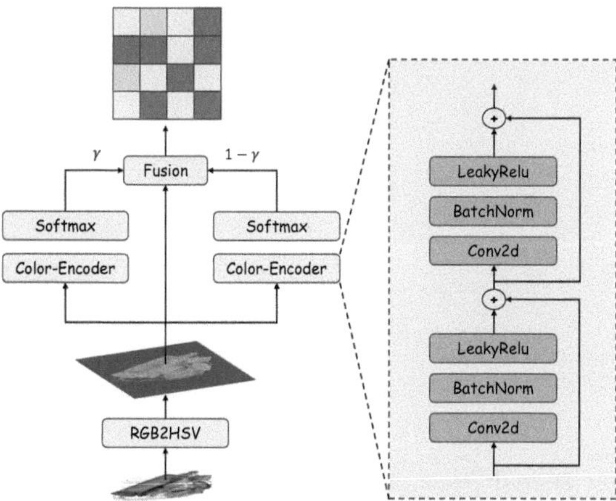

Fig. 3. The overall architecture of the Equalization Perception Module (EPM), which performs average parameter modulation via Fusion and thus obtains the perceptual attention matrix.

The channel count is then reset to the original number to enhance foreground informativeness. This approach avoids over-reliance on IoU loss [34] for learning foreground information and speeds up model convergence. The calculation process of FS is shown in Eq. (8):

$$C_R = Select(Conv(C_D)), F_4^R = C_R \odot F_4 \tag{8}$$

where $Select(\cdot)$ is sorted and takes the top 50% scored channels, $Conv(\cdot)$ is a convolution with a kernel size of 1 in order to expand to the original number of channels. F_4^R is F_4 after decoupling, and the final backbone outputs a collection of feature maps as:

$$F = \{F_1, F_2, F_3, F_4^R\} \tag{9}$$

3.4 Overall Architecture of XMamba

We built XMamba by integrating EPM, FCD, and VMamba [23]. The architecture of XMamba is shown in Fig. 5. The EPM is located after the input to improve the HSV channel sensing after the patch operation. We fuse the CD operation in the FCD into the VSS Block to constitute the CDSS Block. The FCD aggregates channel information from the CDSS Block feature maps and feeds the enhanced feature maps into the detector neck for feature fusion through the decoupler and modulator.

We preserve the VSS Block structure from VMamba [23] for reliable feature extraction and develop XMamba in two configurations: XMamba-tiny and XMamba-Small. XMamba-tiny is a downsized version of XMamba-Small. The design of XMamba incorporates EPM and FCD, bolstering its robustness against

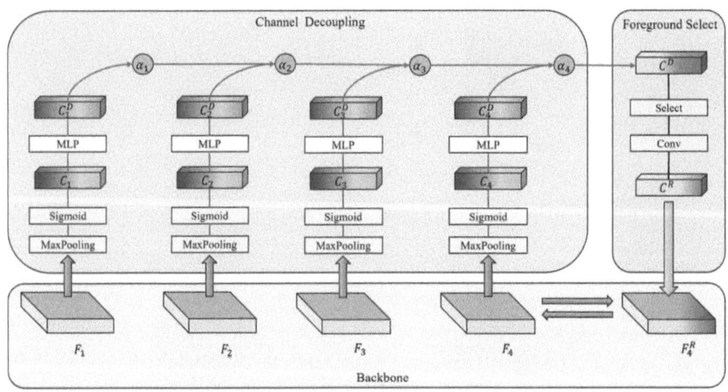

Fig. 4. Foreground Channel Decoupling. We perform adaptive channel selection on the feature maps of each layer, and use learnable parameters to aggregate the outputs from all feature layers to modulate the final feature map.

perspective interference and internal pseudo-contouring, and facilitating easy integration into various detection frameworks.

4 Experiments

4.1 Experimental Setup

Datasets and Evaluation Metrics: The test set of PIDray is categorized into three occlusion cases, easy, hard, and hidden, and PIDray provides bounding boxes as well as segmentation labels. We mainly use the mean accuracy (mAP) from COCO [21] Metric to evaluate the performance of each class of models on the detection and segmentation tasks under the three occlusion cases of PIDray. mAP represents to some extent the accuracy and recall of the detector.

For OPIXray, we used the VOC [9] evaluation metric and performed a categorical evaluation. mAP was calculated from the area under the Precision-Recall curve for one category with an IoU threshold of 0.5. The mAP is then calculated as the average of the APs of all categories.

Model Training Setup: We use the MMDetection 3.3.0 framework [5] with consistent training settings for fair comparison. CNN-based models are optimized with SGD using a base learning rate of 0.01, momentum of 0.9, and weight decay of 0.1. Transformer-based and Mamba-based models use AdamW with a learning rate of 0.0001 and weight decay of 0.0001. All backbones are initialized with ImageNet pre-trained weights [7]. Transformer-based detectors typically converge by the 12th epoch, so we train all models for 12 epochs to ensure a uniform evaluation standard. Experiments are conducted on 4 NVIDIA GeForce RTX 3090 GPUs running Ubuntu 20.04 with PyTorch 2.1.2.

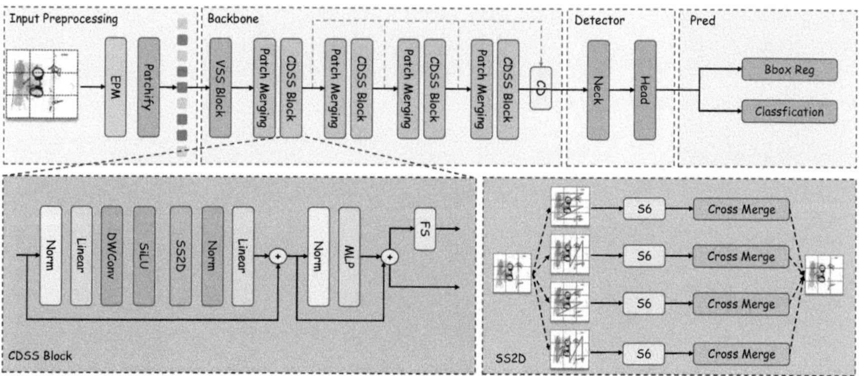

Fig. 5. Architecture of XMamba, where the CDSS Block is a combination of the native VSS Block and Foreground Select (FS), where we fused all the layers of features of the backbone through FS and modulated them through Channel Decoupling (CD) to form the final features to be input to the detector. FS and CD are described in Sect. 3.3.

4.2 Comparison Experiments

In order to validate the excellent performance of our proposed XMamba in the field of X-ray Prohibited Items detection, we test the detection and segmentation performance on PIDray using Mask R-CNN, Cascade Mask R-CNN combined with XMamba. For OPIXray, we use Faster R-CNN combined with XMamba detector for the test.

PIDray:
Table 1 demonstrates that XMamba, when combined with Mask R-CNN and Cascade Mask R-CNN, outperforms both general detectors and the latest X-ray prohibited items detector across all PIDray occlusion scenarios. It achieves the highest detection mAP of **79.8%, 72.7%, and 58.3%** in easy-obscurity, hard-obscurity, and occlusion scenarios, respectively, and the highest segmentation mAP of 68.7%, 61.4%, and 45.0% for easy, difficult, and hidden cases. Compared to ForkNet [19], which is the previous best X-ray prohibited items detector, XMamba improves the detection mAP by **3.4%**. Notably, XMamba not only exceeds ResNet-101 [13] and Swin-L [24] in parameter count and computational efficiency but also holds a superior performance position overall. In addition, although XMamba-t and XMamba-s perform worse than ForkNet in the HIDDEN scenario, ForkNet's design follows a dual-branch backbone network and significantly surpasses XMamba in terms of number and FLOPs. In terms of overall detection performance and efficiency balance, XMamba's design is superior.

Moreover, compared to other state-of-the-art methods such as Cascade Mask R-CNN + SDANet [36], our proposed XMamba consistently outperforms this approach across all variants. Notably, although SDANet improves the baseline model's detection accuracy in the Easy and Hidden scenarios, the improvement

Table 1. Performance Comparison with General Detectors and State-Of-The-Art Prohibited Items Detectors(with *) on PIDray [36]. Params, GFLOPs denote the number of Parameters and Giga Floating Point Operations. "-" means that the detector does not support segmentation tasks.

Method	Backbone	Detection AP				Segmentation AP				Params	GFLOPs	Reference
		Easy	Hard	Hidden	Overall	Easy	Hard	Hidden	Overall			
SSD512 [22]	VGG16	68.1	58.9	45.7	57.6	-	-	-	-	26.01M	89.09	ECCV16
FCOS [8]	ResNet-101-FPN	61.8	51.7	37.5	50.3	-	-	-	-	51.13M	59.78	ICCV19
Faster R-CNN [26]	ResNet-101-FPN	63.3	57.2	42.1	54.2	-	-	-	-	60.75M	220.0	TPAMI17
Mask R-CNN [12]	ResNet-101-FPN	64.7	59.0	43.8	55.8	57.6	50.2	35.2	47.7	63.02M	123.0	ICCV17
Cascade Mask R-CNN [4]	ResNet-101-FPN	72.4	66.9	50.9	63.4	60.8	53.1	37.1	50.3	96.06M	1648	CVPR18
EfficientDet-D0 [29]	EfficientNet	58.1	48.9	37.9	48.3	-	-	-	-	3.92M	2.11	CVPR20
Deformable DETR [39]	ResNet-50(Box-Refine)	48.6	36.6	21.3	35.5	-	-	-	-	41.09M	41.97	ICLR21
DINO [35]	Swin-L	62.5	56.4	37.5	52.1	-	-	-	-	218.0M	166.0	ICLR23
YOLOv7-tiny [31]	CSPNet	67.4	56.3	40.9	54.9	-	-	-	-	6.18M	13.26	CVPR23
SDANet* [36]	ResNet-101-FPN	72.3	64.2	49.5	62.0	59.9	52.0	37.4	49.8	72.34M	65.31	IJCV23
Cascade Mask R-CNN+SDANet* [36]	ResNet-101-FPN	72.5	64.9	51.3	62.9	61.1	52.0	38.7	50.6	114.5M	1678	IJCV23
DAMN* [19]	ResNet-101-FPN	72.7	66.6	52.1	63.8	64.0	58.6	41.4	54.7	-	-	Electronics
ForkNet* [16]	R101&R18	75.0	66.9	**58.6**	66.8	-	-	-	-	190.6M	2130	TIM24
SAM2 [25]	Hiera Base	-	-	-	-	62.0	52.1	32.0	48.7	160.6M	1011	Arxiv24
Mask R-CNN [12]	XMamba-t (ours)	72.8	66.3	53.9	64.3	63.6	56.8	42.1	54.2	49.85M	109.0	-
	XMamba-s (ours)	74.7	67.4	54.2	65.4	64.9	57.8	42.6	55.1	69.29M	125.0	
Cascade Mask R-CNN [4]	XMamba-t (ours)	76.6	70.4	55.7	67.6	65.8	58.6	42.9	55.8	84.75M	1635	-
	XMamba-s (ours)	**77.7**	**72.2**	56.6	**68.8**	**66.4**	**60.3**	**43.5**	**56.7**	104.0M	1650	

is limited, and its performance even degrades in the Hard scenario. This further highlights the limitations of SDANet and underscores the superiority of XMamba.

OPIXay: As shown in Table 2, our proposed XMamba in the Faster R-CNN [26] framework also outperforms the current General Detectors on OPIXray [32] as well as the State-Of-The-Art Prohibited Item Detectors, achieving a mAP of **90.7%** in the case of XMamba-s only, outperforming the AO-DETR [17] by **1.7%**, and maintaining a high accuracy in all categories of mAP.

4.3 Ablation Study

As shown in Table 3, we have carried out extensive ablation studies on our proposed EPM and FCD using PIDray with VMamba-t and VMamba-s [23] as baselines, respectively. These experiments are performed within the overall framework of Cascade Mask R-CNN [4] to assess the impact of EPM and FCD on the baseline's detection performance. VMamba-t benefits from EPM and FCD, which improve the detection mAP by **1.8% and 0.9%**, and the segmentation mAP by **1.7% and 1.1%**, respectively. For VMamba-s, both EPM and FCD enhance the detection mAP by **0.6%** and the segmentation mAP by **0.7% and 0.6%**, respectively.

When both EPM and FCD are added, VMamba-t achieves the highest detection mAP of **67.6%** and segmentation mAP of **55.9%**, with improvements of **2.3% and 2.5%** over the baseline, respectively. Similarly, VMamba-s reaches optimal performance with detection and segmentation mAPs of **68.8% and 56.7%**, respectively, showing a **1.2% and 1.3%** improvement over the base-

Table 2. Performance Comparison with General Detectors and State-Of-The-Art Prohibited Items Detectors(with *) on OPIXray [32]. FO, ST, SC, UT, and MU represent Folding Knife, Straight Knife, Scissor, Utility Knife, and Multi-toll Knife.

Method	Backbone	mAP	FO	ST	SC	UT	MU	Reference
Faster R-CNN [26]	ResNeXt-101-32x4d	73.4	80.6	45.4	89.1	69.1	83.1	TPAMI17
Mask R-CNN [12]	ResNeXt-101-32x4d	77.2	83.6	55.9	89.8	71.5	85.2	ICCV17
Cascade R-CNN [4]	ResNeXt-101-32x4d	88.0	89.1	78.2	95.8	87.1	90.0	CVPR18
ATSS [37]	ResNet-101	86.6	92.3	86.6	96.6	80.4	91.7	CVPR20
EfficientDet-D0 [29]	EfficientNet	59.2	69.3	36.9	70.8	59.4	59.6	CVPR20
YOLOv7-tiny [31]	CSPNet	71.5	77.2	54.1	81.1	68.0	77.3	CVPR23
Deformable DETR [39]	ResNet-50	63.4	70.1	29.0	86.0	55.7	76.4	ICLR21
DINO [35]	Swin-L	80.0	84.2	61.1	89.0	78.9	86.6	ICLR23
DOAM* [32]	ResNet-50	82.3	86.2	68.8	90.0	78.5	87.9	ACM MM20
ATSS+LAreg* [38]	ResNet-50	87.4	92.8	71.2	96.6	83.3	92.9	TIFS22
ATSS+LAcls* [38]	ResNet-50	88.3	90.0	75.0	97.6	85.7	**93.0**	TIFS22
FAPID* [20]	VGG16	88.4	89.8	**84.3**	90.3	88.0	89.6	ICIP23
GADet-X* [18]	Modified CSP v5	78.1	83.1	56.3	89.8	75.7	85.5	JSEN24
ForkNet* [16]	R101&R18	87.9	89.1	79.2	96.0	86.5	88.7	TIM24
AO-DETR* [17]	Swin-L	89.0	89.4	80.4	**97.8**	87.4	90.0	TNNLS24
Faster R-CNN [26]	XMamba-t (ours)	90.6	92.9	80.0	**97.8**	90.1	92.4	-
	XMamba-s (ours)	**90.7**	**94.0**	78.0	**97.8**	**91.3**	92.7	-

Table 3. Ablation results of the proposed EPM and FCD on the PIDray [36] dataset.

Methond	Backbone	EPM	FCD	Detection AP				Segmentation AP				Params	GFLOPs
				Easy	Hard	Hidden	Overall	Easy	Hard	Hidden	Overall		
Cascade Mask R-CNN	VMamba-t	✗	✗	74.1	67.5	54.4	65.3	63.2	56.0	41.1	53.4	82.88M	1634
		✓	✗	76.2	69.9	55.3	67.1	65.4	57.9	42.0	55.1	82.88M	1634
		✗	✓	75.3	68.7	54.6	66.2	64.3	57.6	41.7	54.5	84.75M	1635
		✓	✓	**76.6**	**70.4**	**55.7**	**67.6**	**65.8**	**58.6**	**42.9**	**55.8**	84.75M	1635
	VMamba-s	✗	✗	77.5	70.3	54.9	67.6	66.3	58.2	41.7	55.4	102.0M	1650
		✓	✗	77.4	71.0	56.3	68.2	66.1	59.1	43.0	56.1	102.0M	1650
		✗	✓	77.3	71.4	55.8	68.2	66.0	59.6	42.3	56.0	104.0M	1650
		✓	✓	**77.7**	**72.2**	**56.6**	**68.8**	**66.4**	**60.3**	**43.5**	**56.7**	104.0M	1650

line. These results indicate that our proposed EPM and FCD are complementary, and the combined use of both methods yields the best optimization for the performance of XMamba.

Furthermore, we have compared the additional parameters introduced by EPM and FCD to the model. EPM does not significantly increase the number of parameters or computational load, whereas FCD adds only 1.87M parameters to the model. To assess the effectiveness of EPM, we conducted ablation studies using SE [14], CBAM [33], and DA [10] as baselines. The results, presented in Table 4, demonstrate that the detector's performance with EPM significantly

Table 4. Comparison of EPM with various attention methods.

Models	Easy mAP	Hidden mAP	Hard mAP	Overall mAP
VMamba-t	74.1	67.5	54.4	65.3
+SE	73.9	66.5	53.9	64.8
+CBAM	74.1	67.3	54.2	65.2
+DA	74.6	67.8	54.8	65.7
+EPM	**76.2**	**69.9**	**55.3**	**67.1**

surpasses that of the aforementioned attention mechanisms. This outcome validates the relevance and efficacy of our proposed EPM for enhancing the detection of prohibited items in X-ray images.

4.4 Visualization Analysis

We evaluate XMamba's feature extraction capability for X-ray contraband detection by visualizing its feature maps as heatmaps. As shown in Fig. 6, the original image contains pincers in an unobscured state and a hammer with significant occlusion. XMamba accurately identifies the location and contour of the contraband items in the initial feature maps, even under heavy occlusion. In deeper feature maps, XMamba focuses on regions that introduce perspective interference.

We compared the detection and segmentation performance of various X-ray prohibited items detectors, including general and specialized models, against Cascade Mask R-CNN combined with XMamba-s on the challenging PIDray dataset. Results in Fig. 7 show that Cascade Mask R-CNN (XMamba-s) outperforms other detectors, especially in identifying ultra-low-density contraband regions and achieving higher segmentation accuracy than SDANet and ResNet-101.

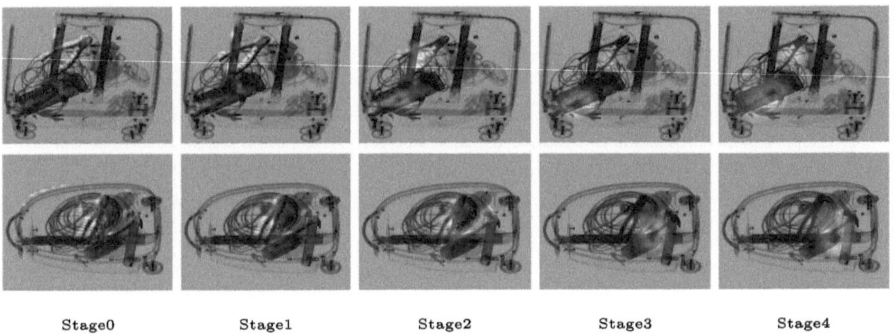

Fig. 6. XMamba-s individual stage output feature maps.

In the **hidden** case, Faster R-CNN and DINO fail to detect the obscured portion of the hammer, while Cascade Mask R-CNN (ResNet-101) incorrectly segments the background. Although Cascade Mask R-CNN (SDANet) provides a detection effect similar to Cascade Mask R-CNN (XMamba-s), it produces significantly more incorrect segmentation regions than the latter.

In addition to this, in the last row of Fig. 7, for the extreme Hidden case, although SDANet is able to detect a portion of the contraband region, it generates an excessive number of erroneous bounding boxes, whereas XMamba-s generates only a single erroneous bounding box, which further proves the robustness of XMmaba.

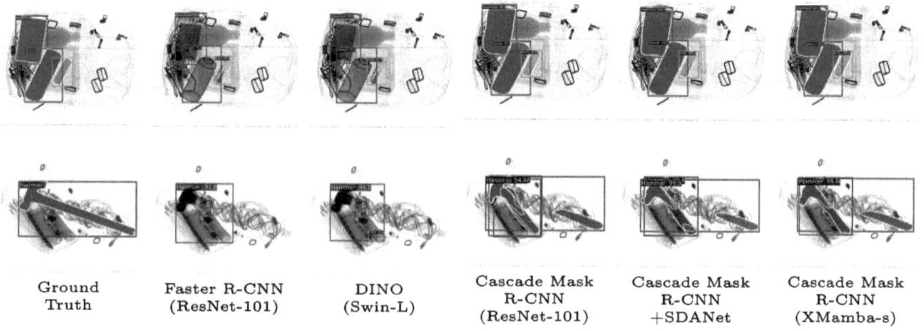

Fig. 7. Comparison of the detection results of different detectors, the leftmost column shows the ground truth.

Acknowledgement. This work was funded by the Fundamental Research Funds for the Central Universities of Xi'an Jiaotong University (xxj042025001).

References

1. Cai, Z., Vasconcelos, N.: Cascade R-CNN: delving into high quality object detection. In: Proceedings of the IEEE Conference on Computer Vision and Pattern Recognition, pp. 6154–6162 (2018)
2. Carion, N., Massa, F., Synnaeve, G., Usunier, N., Kirillov, A., Zagoruyko, S.: End-to-end object detection with transformers. In: European Conference on Computer Vision, pp. 213–229. Springer (2020)
3. Chang, A., Zhang, Y., Zhang, S., Zhong, L., Zhang, L.: Detecting prohibited objects with physical size constraint from cluttered X-ray baggage images. Knowl.-Based Syst. **237**, 107916 (2022)
4. Chen, K., et al.: Hybrid task cascade for instance segmentation. In: Proceedings of the IEEE/CVF Conference on Computer Vision and Pattern Recognition, pp. 4974–4983 (2019)

5. Chen, K., et al.: MMDetection: open MMLab detection toolbox and benchmark. arXiv preprint arXiv:1906.07155 (2019)
6. Chen, K., Chen, B., Liu, C., Li, W., Zou, Z., Shi, Z.: RSMamba: remote sensing image classification with state space model. IEEE Geosci. Remote Sens. Lett. (2024)
7. Deng, J., Dong, W., Socher, R., Li, L.J., Li, K., Fei-Fei, L.: ImageNet: a large-scale hierarchical image database. In: 2009 IEEE Conference on Computer Vision and Pattern Recognition, pp. 248–255. IEEE (2009)
8. Detector, A.F.O.: FCOS: a simple and strong anchor-free object detector. IEEE Trans. Pattern Anal. Mach. Intell. **44**(4) (2022)
9. Everingham, M., Van Gool, L., Williams, C.K., Winn, J., Zisserman, A.: The pascal visual object classes (VOC) challenge. Int. J. Comput. Vis. **88**, 303–338 (2010)
10. Fu, J., et al.: Dual attention network for scene segmentation. In: Proceedings of the IEEE/CVF Conference on Computer Vision and Pattern Recognition, pp. 3146–3154 (2019)
11. Gu, A., Dao, T.: Mamba: linear-time sequence modeling with selective state spaces. arXiv preprint arXiv:2312.00752 (2023)
12. He, K., Gkioxari, G., Dollár, P., Girshick, R.: Mask R-CNN. In: Proceedings of the IEEE International Conference on Computer Vision, pp. 2961–2969 (2017)
13. He, K., Zhang, X., Ren, S., Sun, J.: Deep residual learning for image recognition. In: Proceedings of the IEEE Conference on Computer Vision and Pattern Recognition, pp. 770–778 (2016)
14. Hu, J., Shen, L., Sun, G.: Squeeze-and-excitation networks. In: Proceedings of the IEEE Conference on Computer Vision and Pattern Recognition, pp. 7132–7141 (2018)
15. Huang, T., Pei, X., You, S., Wang, F., Qian, C., Xu, C.: LocalMamba: visual state space model with windowed selective scan. arXiv preprint arXiv:2403.09338 (2024)
16. Jia, T., Ma, B., Wang, H., Li, M., Lin, S., Chen, D.: ForkNet: overlapping image disentanglement for accurate prohibited item detection. IEEE Trans. Instrum. Meas. (2024)
17. Li, M., et al.: AO-DETR: anti-overlapping DETR for x-ray prohibited items detection. IEEE Trans. Neural Netw. Learn. Syst. (2024). https://doi.org/10.1109/TNNLS.2024.3487833
18. Li, M., Ma, B., Wang, H., Chen, D., Jia, T.: GADet: a geometry-aware X-ray prohibited items detector. IEEE Sens. J. (2023)
19. Li, Y., Zhang, C., Sun, S., Yang, G.: X-ray detection of prohibited item method based on dual attention mechanism. Electronics **12**(18), 3934 (2023)
20. Liao, H., Huang, B., Gao, H.: Feature-aware prohibited items detection for X-ray images. In: 2023 IEEE International Conference on Image Processing (ICIP), pp. 1040–1044. IEEE (2023)
21. Lin, T.-Y., et al.: Microsoft COCO: common objects in context. In: Fleet, D., Pajdla, T., Schiele, B., Tuytelaars, T. (eds.) ECCV 2014. LNCS, vol. 8693, pp. 740–755. Springer, Cham (2014). https://doi.org/10.1007/978-3-319-10602-1_48
22. Liu, W., et al.: SSD: single shot multibox detector. In: Leibe, B., Matas, J., Sebe, N., Welling, M. (eds.) ECCV 2016. LNCS, vol. 9905, pp. 21–37. Springer, Cham (2016). https://doi.org/10.1007/978-3-319-46448-0_2
23. Liu, Y., et al.: VMamba: visual state space model. arXiv preprint arXiv:2401.10166 (2024)
24. Liu, Z., et al.: Swin transformer: hierarchical vision transformer using shifted windows. In: Proceedings of the IEEE/CVF International Conference on Computer Vision, pp. 10012–10022 (2021)

25. Ravi, N., et al.: SAM 2: segment anything in images and videos. arXiv preprint arXiv:2408.00714 (2024)
26. Ren, S., He, K., Girshick, R., Sun, J.: Faster R-CNN: towards real-time object detection with region proposal networks. In: Advances in Neural Information Processing Systems, vol. 28 (2015)
27. Roh, B., Shin, J., Shin, W., Kim, S.: Sparse DETR: efficient end-to-end object detection with learnable sparsity. arXiv preprint arXiv:2111.14330 (2021)
28. Ruan, J., Xiang, S.: VM-UNet: vision mamba UNet for medical image segmentation. arXiv preprint arXiv:2402.02491 (2024)
29. Tan, M., Pang, R., Le, Q.V.: EfficientDet: scalable and efficient object detection. In: Proceedings of the IEEE/CVF Conference on Computer Vision and Pattern Recognition, pp. 10781–10790 (2020)
30. Tao, R., et al.: Towards real-world X-ray security inspection: a high-quality benchmark and lateral inhibition module for prohibited items detection. In: Proceedings of the IEEE/CVF International Conference on Computer Vision, pp. 10923–10932 (2021)
31. Wang, C.Y., Bochkovskiy, A., Liao, H.Y.M.: YOLOv7: trainable bag-of-freebies sets new state-of-the-art for real-time object detectors. In: Proceedings of the IEEE/CVF Conference on Computer Vision and Pattern Recognition, pp. 7464–7475 (2023)
32. Wei, Y., Tao, R., Wu, Z., Ma, Y., Zhang, L., Liu, X.: Occluded prohibited items detection: an X-ray security inspection benchmark and de-occlusion attention module. In: Proceedings of the 28th ACM International Conference on Multimedia, pp. 138–146 (2020)
33. Woo, S., Park, J., Lee, J.Y., Kweon, I.S.: CBAM: convolutional block attention module. In: Proceedings of the European Conference on Computer Vision (ECCV), pp. 3–19 (2018)
34. Yu, J., Jiang, Y., Wang, Z., Cao, Z., Huang, T.: UnitBox: an advanced object detection network. In: Proceedings of the 24th ACM International Conference on Multimedia, pp. 516–520 (2016)
35. Zhang, H., et al.: Dino: DETR with improved denoising anchor boxes for end-to-end object detection. arXiv preprint arXiv:2203.03605 (2022)
36. Zhang, L., Jiang, L., Ji, R., Fan, H.: PIDray: a large-scale x-ray benchmark for real-world prohibited item detection. Int. J. Comput. Vis. **131**(12), 3170–3192 (2023)
37. Zhang, S., Chi, C., Yao, Y., Lei, Z., Li, S.Z.: Bridging the gap between anchor-based and anchor-free detection via adaptive training sample selection. In: Proceedings of the IEEE/CVF Conference on Computer Vision and Pattern Recognition, pp. 9759–9768 (2020)
38. Zhao, C., Zhu, L., Dou, S., Deng, W., Wang, L.: Detecting overlapped objects in X-ray security imagery by a label-aware mechanism. IEEE Trans. Inf. Forensics Secur. **17**, 998–1009 (2022)
39. Zhu, X., Su, W., Lu, L., Li, B., Wang, X., Dai, J.: Deformable DETR: deformable transformers for end-to-end object detection. arXiv preprint arXiv:2010.04159 (2020)

Optimal Transport Regularization for Speech Text Alignment in Spoken Language Models

Wenze Xu[1,2], Chun Wang[1(✉)], Jiazhen Yu[3], Sheng Chen[1], Liang Gao[1], and Weihong Deng[1]

[1] Mashang Consumer Finance Co., Ltd., Chongqing, China
lukewang25@live.cn, {sheng.chen02,liang.gao01,weihong.deng}@msxf.com

[2] The University of Sydney, Sydney, Australia
wexu0327@uni.sydney.edu.au

[3] Macau University of Science and Technology, Macau SAR, China
1210030170@student.must.edu.mo

Abstract. Spoken Language Models (SLMs), which extend Large Language Models (LLMs) to perceive speech inputs, have gained increasing attention for their potential to advance speech understanding tasks. However, despite recent progress, studies show that SLMs often struggle to generalize across datasets, even for trained languages and tasks, raising concerns about whether they process speech in a text-like manner as intended. A key challenge underlying this limitation is the modality gap between speech and text representations. The high variability in speech embeddings may allow SLMs to achieve strong in-domain performance by exploiting unintended speech variations, ultimately hindering generalization. To mitigate this modality gap, we introduce Optimal Transport Regularization (OTReg), a method that formulates speech-text alignment as an optimal transport problem and derives a regularization loss to improve SLM training. In each training iteration, OTReg first establishes a structured correspondence between speech and transcript embeddings by determining the optimal transport plan, then incorporates the regularization loss based on this transport plan to optimize SLMs in generating speech embeddings that align more effectively with transcript embeddings. OTReg is lightweight, requiring no additional labels or learnable parameters, and integrates seamlessly into existing SLM training procedures. Extensive multilingual ASR experiments demonstrate that OTReg enhances speech-text alignment, mitigates the modality gap, and consequently improves SLM generalization across diverse datasets.

Keywords: Spoken language model · Optimal transport · Modality gap

---

Work done when Wenze Xu interned at Mashang Consumer Finance Co., Ltd.
W. Xu and C. Wang—Contributed equally to this work.

C. Wallraven et al. (Eds.): ACPR 2025, LNCS 16174, pp. 280–294, 2026.
https://doi.org/10.1007/978-981-95-4395-3_20

1 Introduction

Large Language Models (LLMs) [6,18] have significantly advanced text-based language understanding and generation. Their success has driven progress in speech understanding research, leading to efforts to extend LLMs into Spoken Language Models (SLMs) [2,20], which can directly process speech input–an essential and natural aspect of language representation.

One practical approach to building SLMs involves integrating a pretrained speech encoder with an LLM through an adapter module [1]. The adapter functions as a bridge, transforming speech embeddings into a representation compatible with the LLM's input space, thereby enabling direct speech input processing. This method leverages the strengths of existing components, allowing the SLM to process speech inputs while preserving the LLM's advanced language understanding capabilities. Previous studies have shown that SLMs employing this approach achieve competitive performance in major speech understanding tasks, such as automatic speech recognition (ASR) [14] and speech-to-text translation [24], validating the effectiveness of adapter-based integration in SLM development.

Despite advancements in in-domain datasets, recent studies [7,12] indicate that SLMs experience significant performance degradation across datasets, even when the spoken languages and tasks were included in training. These findings raise concerns that SLMs may not truly comprehend speech in a text-like manner as intended. Instead, their strong performance on in-domain data may partially result from exploiting unintended speech variations, suggesting overfitting [12]. Addressing these limitations is crucial for enhancing generalization and unlocking the full potential of SLMs in diverse speech applications.

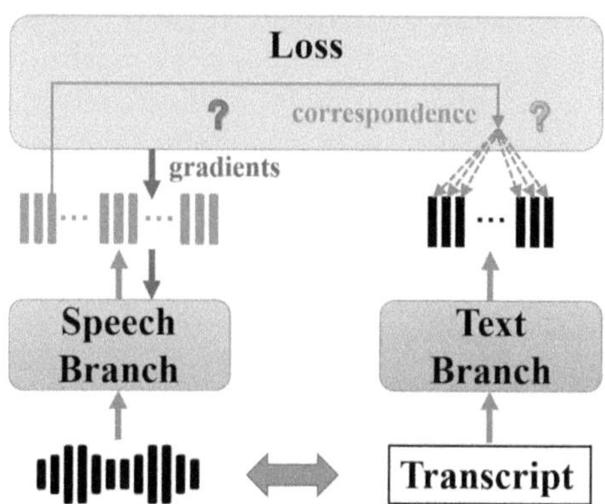

Fig. 1. Challenges in speech-text alignment.

Recent studies [7,13,22] suggest that the modality gap between speech and text is a key factor in this challenge. Because of high frame rates, speech embeddings are often substantially longer than their corresponding transcript embeddings. Furthermore, unlike transcript embeddings, which primarily encode linguistic content, speech embeddings also incorporate paralinguistic features such as pauses and variations in speech rate, adding complexity to their representation. These differences make speech more dynamic than text, increasing the likelihood that SLMs will capture irrelevant variations in speech rather than focusing solely on linguistic content. Addressing these issues requires precise speech-text alignment to reduce the modality gap, thereby enhancing SLM generalization.

Achieving precise speech-text alignment during SLM training presents two key challenges. As illustrated in Fig. 1, the first challenge is that while pairing speech with its transcript is straightforward, defining and establishing meaningful pointwise correspondences between heterogeneous speech and transcript embeddings remains difficult. The second challenge is designing a differentiable and robust loss function that optimizes the speech model to generate speech embeddings aligned with transcript embeddings based on the established pointwise correspondences. This is particularly challenging because dynamically established correspondences are often noisy and tend to change during training.

In this paper, to tackle these challenges, we introduce Optimal Transport Regularization (OTReg) as a novel approach to bridging the modality gap in SLMs. We formulate speech-text alignment as an optimal transport (OT) problem [21], treating speech embeddings as the source and transcript embeddings as the target. In this framework, pointwise correspondences between the source and target are represented by a transport plan. Given a predefined cost matrix, OT determines the optimal transport plan by solving an optimization problem that minimizes the total transport cost. To encourage correspondences between similar embeddings, we define the transport cost based on cross-modal embedding similarity, ensuring that lower transport costs occur when embeddings exhibit higher similarity. Furthermore, to train SLMs to generate speech embeddings that better align with transcript embeddings, we derive a regularization loss from the optimal transport plan and incorporate it into the SLM training process. Each training iteration consists of two steps: first, estimating the optimal transport plan based on speech embeddings generated using the current SLM parameters; second, computing a regularization loss derived from the estimated transport plan and integrating it with the primary loss, jointly optimizing the SLM through backpropagation.

The proposed OTReg directly employs transcript embeddings as alignment targets, requires no additional annotated labels, and introduces no extra learnable parameters, ensuring seamless integration into the SLM training framework. Experimental results on multilingual ASR tasks demonstrate that OTReg effectively enhances speech-text alignment, reduces the modality gap, and consequently improves the generalization of SLMs across diverse datasets.

The remainder of this paper is structured as follows: Sect. 2 covers preliminaries, then Sect. 3 reviews related work. The proposed method is detailed in Sect. 4. Then, Sect. 5 and Sect. 6 present the experimental setup and results, respectively. Finally, Sect. 7 concludes the paper.

2 Preliminaries

In this section, we provide a concise recap of CTC and Optimal Transport to facilitate understanding of related work and this study.

2.1 Connectionist Temporal Classification

Connectionist Temporal Classification (CTC) loss [10] is widely used in speech processing tasks to align speech embeddings with textual labels when annotated pointwise correspondence is unavailable. Instead of relying on predetermined alignments, CTC formulates the alignment problem by predicting a probability distribution over all possible label sequences derived from speech embeddings. The training objective is to maximize the cumulative probability of all sequences that, when appropriately collapsed, match the ground truth label sequences. To handle non-informative segments such as silence or pauses in speech, CTC introduces a special "blank" label (denoted as "-"), allowing the model to accommodate timing and duration variability.

CTC-based compression [9] extends CTC to reduce redundancy in speech embeddings while preserving essential linguistic information. It leverages CTC predictions to merge consecutive embeddings corresponding to the same label and discard non-informative embeddings associated with the blank label. This approach enhances speech-to-text alignment and boosts computational efficiency by reducing the number of processed embeddings.

Although generally effective, CTC may be suboptimal for SLMs. The classifier used in CTC has a large number of parameters, making it prone to overfitting itself. Additionally, CTC relies on textual labels as intermediate targets, providing only indirect supervision. As a result, the generated speech embeddings may not align well with the LLM's transcript embeddings in the metric space, creating a gap between the supervision signal and the ultimate goal of speech-text alignment in SLMs.

2.2 Optimal Transport

Optimal Transport (OT) [21] provides a mathematical framework for discovering meaningful relationships between probability distributions by optimally transferring mass while preserving structural properties. It achieves this by solving a constrained optimization problem that minimizes a predefined cost function. The transport plan, which is the mathematical solution to this problem, specifies how mass is redistributed from the source to the target while minimizing transport cost, establishing meaningful correspondences between distributions.

A significant challenge in applying OT is its computational complexity, particularly in high-dimensional settings. To address this, techniques such as entropic regularization–exemplified by the Sinkhorn algorithm [5]–have been developed. These methods introduce a regularization term that smooths the optimization landscape, enabling efficient computations through iterative scaling while preserving solution accuracy.

3 Related Work

3.1 Spoken Language Models

Prior studies on SLMs generally follow two main paradigms. One approach focuses on developing unified speech-text foundation models that natively process spoken language by jointly learning from both audio and text modalities. However, this approach typically requires extensive multimodal data and substantial computational resources, which limit its feasibility [1,11].

An alternative and increasingly popular approach enhances text-based LLMs with speech understanding capabilities. In this framework, a dedicated speech encoder is integrated with an LLM via an adapter module, aligning speech embeddings with the model's textual representation space. Recent studies have adopted this strategy to develop SLMs for specific tasks–such as ASR [14] and speech-to-text translation [24]–as well as for general-purpose applications, exemplified by Qwen2-Audio [2] and SALMONN [20]. These models have demonstrated competitive performance across multiple tasks. Our work builds upon this approach, further refining speech and text alignment to enhance the generalization of SLMs.

3.2 Speech-Text Cross-Modality Alignment

Precise speech-text alignment is essential for bridging the modality gap between spoken and written language. Prior studies have explored explicit alignment methods to bring speech representations closer to text representations. Chuang et al. [3] apply pretrained word embeddings as intermediate supervision, aligning speech embeddings by minimizing cosine distance. WACO [15] employs contrastive learning to enhance representation similarity between corresponding speech and text words while pushing apart non-corresponding representations in the embedding space. However, these methods struggle to accommodate unstable and noisy pointwise cross-modality correspondences during training. In scenarios where precise pointwise annotations are unavailable, Connectionist Temporal Classification (CTC) [9,24] has emerged as the most widely used approach (see [1] for further details). However, it relies on textual labels as intermediate targets, which are not well aligned with the ultimate goal of speech-text alignment in embedding space. More recently, Optimal Transport (OT) has been applied to establish correspondences. To accommodate the temporal nature of speech, CMOT [25] integrates a window strategy into OT to enforce monotonicity and locality when aligning speech sequences to text sequences, while Le et al. [13] introduces positional encoding to ensure that correspondences between the two sequences remain monotonic. However, due to inherent dynamics in speech–such as variations in speech rate and silence segments–these position-based constraints are difficult to determine. Therefore, in this work, we choose to use unique transcript embeddings as alignment targets rather than pursuing monotonicity.

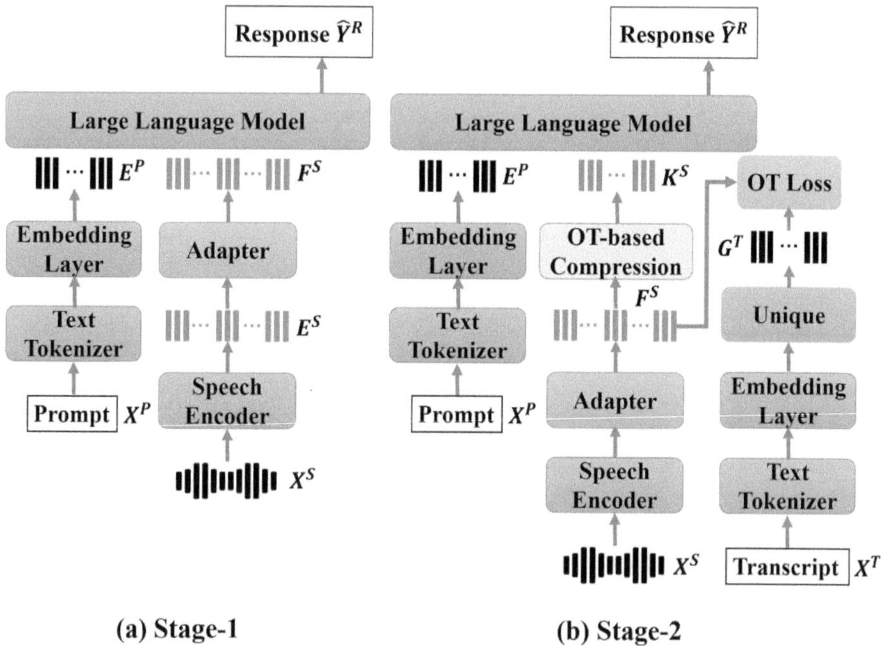

Fig. 2. Overview of SLM training across Stage 1 and Stage 2. During training, blue modules remain frozen, orange modules are learnable, and green modules function without trainable parameters. (Color figure online)

4 Method

This section begins with an overview of the SLM architecture, followed by a detailed explanation of the proposed Optimal Transport Regularization (OTReg). Finally, we integrate OTReg into the existing SLM training framework and present a two-stage training approach.

4.1 Model Architecture

As illustrated in Fig. 2(a), an SLM extends a text-based LLM by incorporating speech understanding capabilities and consists of three core components: a speech encoder, an adapter, and a text-based LLM, with its tokenizer and embedding layer exposed.

Unlike conventional LLMs that process only text, SLMs accept multimodal inputs, including a text prompt, $\mathbf{X^P}$, and a speech signal, $\mathbf{X^S}$. These inputs are encoded separately into distinct embeddings.

The text prompt, $\mathbf{X^P}$, is processed using the LLM's tokenizer and embedding layer to generate the prompt embeddings, $\mathbf{E^P} \in \mathbb{R}^{n_p \times d_l}$:

$$\mathbf{E^P} = \text{EmbedLayer}(\text{Tokenizer}(\mathbf{X^P})), \tag{1}$$

where n_p denotes the sequence length, and d_l represents the LLM's embedding dimension.

Similarly, the speech signal, $\mathbf{X^S}$, is processed through the speech encoder to produce the raw speech embeddings, $\mathbf{E^S} \in \mathbb{R}^{n_s \times d_s}$:

$$\mathbf{E^S} = \text{SpeechEncoder}(\mathbf{X^S}), \tag{2}$$

where n_s and d_s denote the sequence length and embedding dimension of the speech embeddings, respectively.

Next, the adapter transforms the raw speech embeddings, $\mathbf{E^S}$, into transformed speech embeddings, $\mathbf{F^S} \in \mathbb{R}^{n_a \times d_l}$, ensuring compatibility with the LLM's embedding space. Here, n_a represents the sequence length of the transformed speech embeddings.

Several adapter designs have been proposed in the literature [1]. Without loss of generality, we follow the approach presented in [14] and implement the adapter using two linear layers with an intermediate ReLU activation function. The adapter has a hidden layer dimension, d_h, and is formulated as:

$$\mathbf{F^S} = \text{Linear}(\text{ReLU}(\text{Linear}(\mathbf{H^S}))). \tag{3}$$

The intermediate representation, $\mathbf{H^S} \in \mathbb{R}^{(n_s//k)\times(d_s \cdot k)}$, is a compact reformulation of $\mathbf{E^S}$, where every k consecutive embeddings, $\mathbf{e}_i^{\mathbf{S}}, \mathbf{e}_{i+1}^{\mathbf{S}}, \ldots, \mathbf{e}_{i+k-1}^{\mathbf{S}}$, are concatenated into a single compact embedding, $\mathbf{h}_j^{\mathbf{S}}$.

Finally, the model integrates multimodal information and passes it into the LLM to generate a text response, $\hat{\mathbf{Y}}^{\mathbf{R}}$:

$$\text{Template}(\mathbf{E^P}, \mathbf{F^S}) \rightarrow \text{LLM} \rightarrow \hat{\mathbf{Y}}^{\mathbf{R}}, \tag{4}$$

where Template refers to the instruction template used by the underlying LLM.

During supervised fine-tuning (SFT), the SLM is optimized by minimizing a cross-entropy (CE) loss function, L_{CE}, computed between the generated $\hat{\mathbf{Y}}^{\mathbf{R}}$ and the ground truth, $\mathbf{Y^R}$. A common fine-tuning strategy involves updating only the adapter while keeping the speech encoder and LLM components frozen, thereby preserving their pre-trained capabilities.

4.2 Optimal Transport Regularization

In the absence of annotated pointwise correspondences, we formulate the speech-text alignment problem as an OT problem. In our formulation, as illustrated in Fig. 3(a), the transformed speech embeddings, $\mathbf{F^S}$, serve as the source. For the target, transcripts often contain repeated patterns–such as "banana"–which can introduce ambiguity into the transport process. To address this issue, we derive unique transcript embeddings, $\mathbf{G^T}$, from the speech transcript, $\mathbf{X^T}$, using a dedicated processing procedure, as follows.

First, the transcript, $\mathbf{X^T}$, is processed using the LLM's tokenizer and embedding layer to produce transcript embeddings, $\mathbf{E^T} \in \mathbb{R}^{n_t \times d_l}$:

$$\mathbf{E^T} = \text{EmbedLayer}(\text{Tokenizer}(\mathbf{X^T})), \tag{5}$$

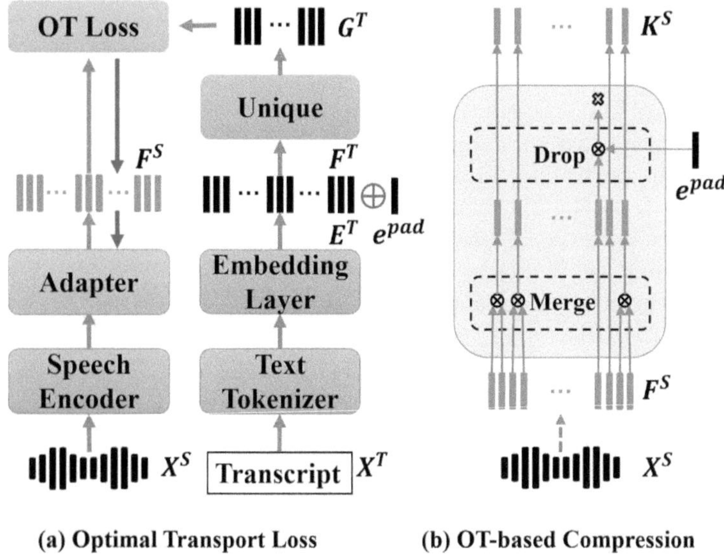

Fig. 3. Illustration of OT loss and OT-based compression.

where n_t denotes the sequence length.

Second, to accommodate blank embeddings, $\mathbf{E^T}$ is concatenated with the LLM's pad token embedding, $\mathbf{e}^{\text{pad}}$, to obtain the augmented transcript embeddings, $\mathbf{F^T}$:

$$\mathbf{F^T} = \text{Concat}([\mathbf{E^T}; \mathbf{e}^{\text{pad}}]). \tag{6}$$

Third, we generate the set of unique embeddings, $\mathcal{S}^{\mathbf{T}}$, by extracting unique embeddings from $\mathbf{F^T}$. Uniqueness is determined by comparing cosine similarities to filter out semantically equivalent embeddings. Since speech embeddings should align only with those present in the transcript, $\mathcal{S}^{\mathbf{T}}$–which encompasses all distinct transcript embeddings–serves as a robust target for the OT-based alignment process. To enhance usability, we concatenate the embeddings in $\mathcal{S}^{\mathbf{T}}$ into the unique transcript embeddings, $\mathbf{G^T} \in \mathbb{R}^{n_g \times d_l}$, where n_g represents the number of unique embeddings. Note that the order of unique embeddings in $\mathbf{G^T}$ does not affect alignment, as OT is invariant to temporal order.

Another key component of the OT framework is the cost function, which quantifies the transport cost between embeddings from the source and target sequences. For each source embedding, $\mathbf{f}_i \in \mathbf{F^S}$, and each target embedding, $\mathbf{g}_j \in \mathbf{G^T}$, the cost is defined as:

$$\mathbf{C}_{ij} = 1 - \text{CosineSimilarity}\left(\frac{\mathbf{f}_i}{\|\mathbf{f}_i\|_2}, \frac{\mathbf{g}_j}{\|\mathbf{g}_j\|2}\right), \tag{7}$$

where CosineSimilarity returns values in the range $[-1, 1]$, ensuring similarity is computed using unit vectors. Consequently, $\mathbf{C}_{ij}$ falls within the range $[0, 2]$, with lower cost values occurring when transport happens between source and target embeddings of higher similarity, aligning with the objective of effective cross-modal alignment.

In a standard OT problem, the primary objective is to determine a transport plan, $\gamma \in \mathbb{R}^{n_a \times n_g}$, that minimizes the total transport cost while satisfying the given marginal constraints. In our approach, we further need to derive a regularization loss from the obtained transport plan to optimize the SLM, making differentiability essential. To achieve this, we employ entropic-regularized OT and solve it using the Sinkhorn algorithm [5].

Formally, the entropic-regularized OT problem is defined as:

$$\begin{aligned} \min_{\gamma} \quad & \sum_{i=0}^{n_a-1}\sum_{j=0}^{n_g-1} \gamma_{ij}\mathbf{C}_{ij} - \epsilon H(\gamma) \\ \text{subject to} \quad & \gamma_{ij} \geq 0, \quad \forall 0 \leq i < n_a,\ 0 \leq j < n_g, \\ & \sum_{j=0}^{n_g-1} \gamma_{ij} = 1/n_a, \quad \forall 0 \leq i < n_a, \\ & \sum_{i=0}^{n_a-1} \gamma_{ij} = 1/n_g, \quad \forall 0 \leq j < n_g. \end{aligned} \tag{8}$$

where $\epsilon > 0$ is a weight controlling the entropy term, and the Shannon entropy is defined as:

$$H(\gamma) = -\sum_{i=0}^{n_a-1}\sum_{j=0}^{n_g-1} \gamma_{ij}\log\gamma_{ij}. \tag{9}$$

The optimal transport plan, $\hat{\gamma}$, which minimizes (8), can be efficiently computed using the Sinkhorn algorithm.

Given the optimal transport plan, $\hat{\gamma}$, we further derive a regularization loss consisting of two terms. The first term, the total transport cost, L_{cost}, quantifies the overall alignment quality via the total transport cost and is computed as

$$L_{\text{cost}}(\hat{\gamma}) = \sum_{i=0}^{n_a-1}\sum_{j=0}^{n_g-1} \hat{\gamma}_{ij}\mathbf{C}_{ij}. \tag{10}$$

For the second term, we introduce a sparsity constraint, L_{spr}, to encourage a focused point-to-point transport plan, ensuring that each source speech embedding aligns primarily with a single transcript embedding. We compute this task-specific constraint using the L2 norm of each row in the row-normalized optimal transport plan, $\hat{\gamma}^{\text{row}}$, defined as

$$L_{\text{spr}}(\hat{\gamma}) = \frac{1}{n_a}\sum_{i=0}^{n_a-1}\left(1 - L_2(\hat{\gamma}_{i:}^{\text{row}})\right). \tag{11}$$

Each row, $\hat{\gamma}_{i:}^{\text{row}} = \frac{\hat{\gamma}_{i:}}{\sum_{j=0}^{n_g-1}\hat{\gamma}_{ij}}$, forms a valid probability distribution over transcript embeddings. The term, $1 - L_2(\hat{\gamma}_{i:}^{\text{row}}) \in [0, 1]$, is minimized when the probability distribution is highly concentrated (i.e., nearly one-hot), and the correspondence is nearly one-to-one. Consequently, minimizing this sparsity cost promotes a clear and distinct alignment between speech and transcript embeddings.

Finally, given the optimal transport plan, $\hat{\gamma}$, the derived regularization loss, L_{OT}, is defined as

$$L_{\mathrm{OT}}(\hat{\gamma}) = L_{\mathrm{cost}}(\hat{\gamma}) + \lambda_{\mathrm{spr}} L_{\mathrm{spr}}(\hat{\gamma}^{row}), \tag{12}$$

where $\lambda_{\mathrm{spr}} > 0$ is the weighting coefficient.

4.3 OT-Based Compression

To reduce redundancy in the speech embeddings, $\mathbf{F}^{\mathbf{S}}$, the proposed OTReg introduces a content-aware compression method. The OT-based compression merges consecutive repetitive embeddings and removes non-informative embeddings while preserving essential content. Unlike CTC-based compression, which relies on classifier predictions to identify consecutive repeats and blanks, OT-based compression operates in a similarity-based manner, leveraging the fact that embeddings are trained using cosine similarity.

Specifically, as illustrated in Fig. 3(b), the OT-based compression consists of two steps. In the merge step, speech embeddings are grouped into adjacent pairs (e.g., 0 and 1, 2 and 3, etc.) and merged when their similarity exceeds a predefined threshold, as they are considered semantically identical. Otherwise, the embeddings remain unchanged. Notably, merging is performed only on adjacent pairs to prevent excessive compression, which could distort sequences; for example, converting "hheellllоо" into "helo" is excessive. Furthermore, in the drop step, any speech embedding highly similar to the LLM's pad token embedding, $\mathbf{e}^{\mathrm{pad}}$, is regarded as non-informative and removed. This OT-based compression procedure is fully differentiable and introduces no additional learnable parameters.

The resulting condensed speech embeddings

$$\mathbf{K}^{\mathbf{S}} = \mathrm{OTCompression}(\mathbf{F}^{\mathbf{S}}) \tag{13}$$

can then be combined with the prompt embeddings and passed into the LLM to generate a text response, as follows:

$$\mathrm{Template}(\mathbf{E}^{\mathbf{P}}, \mathbf{K}^{\mathbf{S}}) \rightarrow \mathrm{LLM} \rightarrow \hat{\mathbf{Y}}^{\mathbf{R}}. \tag{14}$$

4.4 Two-Stage Training of the SLM

In this section, we integrate OTReg into the SLM training procedure and train the SLM using a two-stage process. As illustrated in Fig. 2(a), the first stage follows the standard supervised fine-tuning (SFT) approach. The SLM generates responses using (4) and is optimized for the next-token prediction task with the cross-entropy loss, L_{CE}, while only the adapter module is trainable.

Notably, OTReg, including OT-based compression, is not applied during the first stage, as its effectiveness depends on similarity measures that require a well-initialized model. Upon completing this stage, the adapter can produce transformed speech embeddings that are approximately compatible with the LLM's embedding space.

In stage two, as shown in Fig. 2(b), fine-tuning continues with the integration of the proposed OTReg, including OT-based compression. During each fine-tuning iteration, in addition to the SFT steps, the model also determines the transport plan and calculates the regularization loss, as follows:

1. Obtain transformed speech embeddings ($\mathbf{F^S}$) using (3), based on the current SLM parameters.
2. Generate condensed speech embeddings ($\mathbf{K^S}$) using (13).
3. Generate the model output ($\hat{\mathbf{Y}}^{\mathbf{R}}$) using (14).
4. Evaluate performance by computing the cross-entropy loss (L_{CE}).
5. Compute the optimal transport plan ($\hat{\gamma}$) by solving (8).
6. Calculate the regularization loss ($L_{\text{OT}}(\hat{\gamma})$) according to (12).
7. Update the SLM parameters via backpropagation using the total loss:

$$L_{\text{total}} = L_{\text{CE}} + \lambda_{OT} L_{\text{OT}}, \tag{15}$$

where $\lambda_{OT} > 0$ is the weighting coefficient.

This two-stage approach improves speech-text alignment, reduces the modality gap, and thereby enhances generalization.

Compared to CTC, which provides a framework suitable for broader scenarios, our proposed OTReg is specifically designed for SLMs. OTReg establishes direct and dense supervision by leveraging unique transcript embeddings as concrete alignment targets, enabling similarity-based cross-modal comparison. In contrast, CTC relies on textual labels as intermediate targets, providing only indirect supervision. Consequently, the generated speech embeddings may not align well with the transcript embeddings of the LLM in the metric space, leaving a gap between the supervision signal and the ultimate goal of speech-text alignment in SLMs.

5 Experiments

5.1 Datasets

To evaluate the effectiveness of our proposed OTReg on SLMs, we consider the multilingual ASR task–a primary challenge in speech understanding–and assess our method using multiple benchmark datasets. For in-domain training and evaluation, we utilize the English data of the LibriSpeech (LR960) dataset [16] along with the French and Spanish subsets of the Multilingual LibriSpeech (MLS) dataset [17]. For cross-domain evaluation, we leverage the English, French, and Spanish datasets from CoVoST-2 [23] as well as the FLEURS dataset [4]. All datasets are used with their official splits.

5.2 Model Implementation

In this work, we utilize Whisper-large-v3 [19] as the speech encoder and Qwen2.5-7B-Instruction [18] as the LLM. Following [14], the adapter is designed with a hidden layer dimension of $d_h = 2048$ and a downsampling rate of $k = 5$, resulting in transformed speech embeddings, $\mathbf{F^S}$, at a frequency of 10 Hz. For compression, we apply a cosine similarity threshold of 0.9. The prompt, $\mathbf{X^P}$, is set to "Write down the user's content word for word in {language}, without incorporating any other details.", where {language} acts as a placeholder whose value is determined by the input sample language. Throughout the paper, we set $\lambda_{\text{spr}} = 0.1$ for the loss function while ablating the value of λ_{OT}.

5.3 Training Details

All experiments were conducted using four A800-80GB GPUs with a batch size of 48. Optimization was performed using the AdamW optimizer with a peak learning rate of 1e-4. A cosine decay learning rate scheduler was applied, gradually reducing the learning rate to a minimum of 1e-6. For all experiments, Stage-1 training was run for 2 epochs, followed by Stage-2 training for an additional 3 epochs. Model checkpoints were selected based on the lowest validation loss.

6 Results

In this section, we first evaluate our method on the English ASR task, comparing it with recent SLMs. Next, we assess its performance on the multilingual ASR task to demonstrate its effectiveness across different languages. For both tasks, we use the Whisper normalizer [19] to preprocess transcripts and evaluate performance using the standard Word Error Rate (WER) metric.

Table 1. English ASR results.

Model	In domain (WER↓)		Cross domain (WER↓)	
	LS960 (clean)	LS960 (other)	CoVoST-2 (test)	FLEURS (test)
SLAM-ASR [14]	2.43	**4.91**	28.66	8.88
SALMONN [20]	4.20	7.18	**12.78**	**6.20**
Base	**2.09**	*4.96*	16.06	7.63
Base+CTC	2.44	5.00	18.16	7.71
Base+OTReg(λ_{OT}=0.1)	2.28	5.19	15.59	8.23
Base+OTReg(λ_{OT}=0.3)	*2.19*	5.24	*13.12*	*6.90*
Base+OTReg(λ_{OT}=0.5)	2.20	5.24	13.67	7.10
Base+OTReg(λ_{OT}=0.7)	2.28	5.31	13.38	7.10
Base+OTReg(λ_{OT}=1.0)	2.21	5.37	13.17	7.12

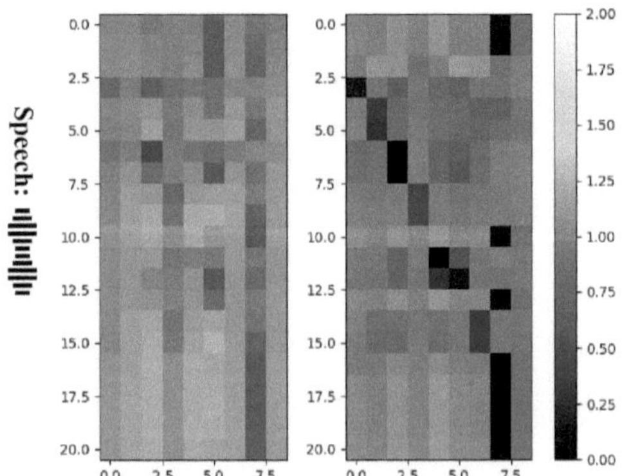

Fig. 4. Distance between speech and transcript embeddings: lower values correspond to higher similarity.

Table 2. Multilingual ASR results.

Model	In Domain (WER↓)				Cross Domain (WER↓)					
	LS960		MLS		CoVoST-2			FLEURS		
	En(clean)	En(other)	Es	Fr	En	Es	Fr	En	Es	Fr
Base	**2.17**	**4.97**	4.79	**5.67**	16.21	12.42	19.33	8.30	7.78	**10.76**
Base+CTC	2.18	5.30	**4.63**	5.71	15.45	12.72	18.57	7.44	**7.77**	11.30
Base+OTReg	2.35	5.26	5.03	6.46	**13.03**	**9.54**	**15.61**	**6.92**	7.86	11.13

Table 1 summarizes the results of the English ASR task, revealing several key findings. First, we evaluate two recent SLMs. SLAM-ASR[1] [14], trained on LS960, suffers a significant performance drop across different datasets. In contrast, SALMONN[2], a generic SLM trained on massive data and tasks, achieves considerably better results on CoVoST-2 and FLEURS but performs poorly on LS960. These results confirm the generalization issue of SLMs [12] and indicate that it cannot be eliminated simply by training with more data and tasks.

Second, we develop our SLM, which retains the architectural foundation of SLAM-ASR but integrates more advanced components, including Whisper-large-v3 and Qwen2.5-7B-Instruction. We train multiple SLM variants using the proposed two-stage approach, applying either CTC or OTReg in the second stage, while Base is trained solely with CE loss. Results indicate that both CTC and OTReg achieve balanced performance across domains, performing comparably to SLAM-ASR on in-domain datasets while approaching SALMONN's results in cross-domain evaluations. Furthermore, OTReg demonstrates robustness to loss

[1] https://github.com/X-LANCE/SLAM-LLM/tree/main/examples/asr_librispeech; choose wavlm_large_linear_vicuna_7b.

[2] https://huggingface.co/tsinghua-ee/SALMONN-7B.

weighting, yielding consistent results, with the best cross-domain performance observed at $\lambda_{OT} = 0.3$.

Following [8,12], we further illustrate the pairwise distance between speech embeddings, $\mathbf{F^S}$, and their corresponding transcript embeddings, $\mathbf{E^T}$. A test-set sample is shown in Fig. 4, where Base-SLM (left) generates misaligned speech embeddings, suggesting that it may achieve good in-domain performance by leveraging speech variations. In contrast, with OTReg (right), the SLM produces speech embeddings that are well-aligned with transcript embeddings, mapping non-informative segments to the final pad embedding. This effectively reduces the modality gap, enabling the SLM to interpret speech in a text-like manner as intended while enhancing its ability to generalize across domains.

The results of the Multilingual ASR task are summarized in Tab. 2. Similar to the English ASR cases, while Base-SLM has already demonstrated strong performance across datasets, the proposed OTReg ($\lambda_{OT} = 0.3$) further enhances SLM performance, particularly on cross-domain datasets for all three languages, reinforcing OTReg's effectiveness in improving SLM's generalization across diverse linguistic scenarios.

7 Conclusion

In this work, we address the challenge of cross-dataset generalization in SLMs by bridging the gap between speech and text modalities. We introduce Optimal Transport Regularization (OTReg), an efficient parameter-free method that seamlessly integrates into SLM training, refining speech-text alignment and enhancing SLMs' generalization across datasets. Looking ahead, extending OTReg to broader speech understanding applications, such as zero-shot language settings, presents a promising direction for future research.

References

1. Arora, S., et al.: On the landscape of spoken language models: a comprehensive survey. arXiv:2504.08528 (2025)
2. Chu, Y., et al.: Qwen2-audio technical report. arXiv:2407.10759 (2024)
3. Chuang, S.P., Sung, T.W., Liu, A.H., Lee, H.Y.: Worse WER, but better BLEU? Leveraging word embedding as intermediate in multitask end-to-end speech translation. In: Proceedings of the 58th Annual Meeting of the Association for Computational Linguistics, pp. 5998–6003 (Jul 2020)
4. Conneau, A., et al.: FLEURS: few-shot learning evaluation of universal representations of speech. In: 2022 IEEE Spoken Language Technology Workshop (SLT), pp. 798–805 (2023)
5. Cuturi, M.: Sinkhorn distances: lightspeed computation of optimal transport. In: Proceedings of the 27th International Conference on Neural Information Processing Systems, vol. 2, pp. 2292–2300. NIPS'13 (2013)
6. Dubey, A., et al.: The llama 3 herd of models. arXiv:2407.21783 (2024)
7. Fan, R., et al.: AlignFormer: modality matching can achieve better zero-shot instruction-following speech-LLM. arXiv:2412.01145 (2024)

8. Fathullah, Y., et al.: AudioChatLlama: towards general-purpose speech abilities for LLMs. In: Proceedings of the 2024 Conference of the North American Chapter of the Association for Computational Linguistics: Human Language Technologies (Volume 1: Long Papers), pp. 5522–5532. Mexico City, Mexico (2024)
9. Gaido, M., et al.: CTC-based compression for direct speech translation. In: Proceedings of the 16th Conference of the European Chapter of the Association for Computational Linguistics: Main Volume, pp. 690–696 (2021)
10. Graves, A., Fernández, S., Gomez, F., Schmidhuber, J.: Connectionist temporal classification: labelling unsegmented sequence data with recurrent neural networks. In: Proceedings of the 23rd International Conference on Machine Learning, pp. 369–376. ICML '06 (2006)
11. Ji, S., et al.: WavChat: a survey of spoken dialogue models. arXiv:2411.13577 (2024)
12. Kumar, S., et al.: Performance evaluation of SLAM-ASR: the good, the bad, the ugly, and the way forward. In: 2025 IEEE International Conference on Acoustics, Speech, and Signal Processing Workshops (ICASSPW), pp. 1–5 (2025)
13. Le, P.H., Gong, H., Wang, C., Pino, J., Lecouteux, B., Schwab, D.: Pre-training for speech translation: CTC meets optimal transport. In: Proceedings of the 40th International Conference on Machine Learning. Proceedings of Machine Learning Research, vol. 202, pp. 18667–18685 (2023)
14. Ma, Z., et al.: Speech recognition meets large language model: benchmarking, models, and exploration. Proc. AAAI Conf. Artif. Intell. **23**, 24840–24848 (2025)
15. Ouyang, S., Ye, R., Li, L.: WACO: word-aligned contrastive learning for speech translation. In: Proceedings of the 61st Annual Meeting of the Association for Computational Linguistics (Volume 1: Long Papers), pp. 3891–3907 (Jul 2023)
16. Panayotov, V., Chen, G., Povey, D., Khudanpur, S.: LibriSpeech: an ASR corpus based on public domain audio books. In: 2015 IEEE International Conference on Acoustics, Speech and Signal Processing (ICASSP), pp. 5206–5210 (2015)
17. Pratap, V., Xu, Q., Sriram, A., Synnaeve, G., Collobert, R.: MLS: a large-scale multilingual dataset for speech research. In: Interspeech 2020, pp. 2757–2761 (2020)
18. Qwen Team: Qwen2.5: a party of foundation models (2024)
19. Radford, A., Kim, J.W., Xu, T., Brockman, G., Mcleavey, C., Sutskever, I.: Robust speech recognition via large-scale weak supervision. In: Proceedings of the 40th International Conference on Machine Learning. Proceedings of Machine Learning Research, vol. 202, pp. 28492–28518 (2023)
20. Tang, C., et al.: SALMONN: towards generic hearing abilities for large language models. In: The Twelfth International Conference on Learning Representations (2024)
21. Torres, L.C., Pereira, L.M., Amini, M.H.: A survey on optimal transport for machine learning: theory and applications. arXiv:2106.01963 (2021)
22. Tsiamas, I., Gállego, G.I., Fonollosa, J.A.R., Costa-jussà, M.R.: Pushing the limits of zero-shot end-to-end speech translation. In: Findings of the Association for Computational Linguistics: ACL 2024, pp. 14245–14267 (2024)
23. Wang, C., Wu, A., Pino, J.: CoVoST 2 and massively multilingual speech-to-text translation. arXiv:2007.10310 (2020)
24. Wu, J., et al.: On decoder-only architecture for speech-to-text and large language model integration. In: 2023 IEEE Automatic Speech Recognition and Understanding Workshop (ASRU), pp. 1–8 (2023)
25. Zhou, Y., Fang, Q., Feng, Y.: CMOT: cross-modal mixup via optimal transport for speech translation. In: Proceedings of the 61st Annual Meeting of the Association for Computational Linguistics (Volume 1: Long Papers), pp. 7873–7887 (2023)

DiffS-NOCS: 3D Point Cloud Reconstruction Through Coloring Sketches to NOCS Maps Using Diffusion Models

Di Kong[1,2,3] and Qianhui Wan[4(✉)]

[1] Beijing University of Posts and Telecommunications, Beijing, China
[2] Tsinghua University, Beijing, China
[3] Zhongguancun Academy, Beijing, China
[4] Beijing Normal University, Beijing, China
dikong@bupt.edu.cn, wan_qianhui@163.com

Abstract. Reconstructing a 3D point cloud from a given conditional sketch is challenging. Existing methods often work directly in 3D space, but domain variability and difficulty in reconstructing accurate 3D structures from 2D sketches remain significant obstacles. Moreover, ideal models should also accept prompts for control, in addition with the sparse sketch, posing challenges in multi-modal fusion. We propose DiffS-NOCS (Diffusion-based Sketch-to-NOCS Map), which leverages ControlNet with a modified multi-view decoder to generate NOCS maps with embedded 3D structure and position information in 2D space from sketches. The 3D point cloud is reconstructed by combining multiple NOCS maps from different views. To enhance sketch understanding, we integrate a viewpoint encoder for extracting viewpoint features. Additionally, we design a feature-level multi-view aggregation network as the denoising module, facilitating cross-view information exchange and improving 3D consistency in NOCS map generation. Experiments on ShapeNet demonstrate that DiffS-NOCS achieves controllable and fine-grained point cloud reconstruction aligned with sketches.

Keywords: Sketch-to-Point Cloud · Normalized Object Coordinate Space · Diffusion Model · Cross-Modal Reconstruction

1 Introduction

Sketches, as abstract and efficient expressions, simplify complex ideas into simple lines and have long been used in 3D modeling. However, their geometric distortions and lack of texture, shading, and color make 3D reconstruction challenging, driving research to replicate this human capability in intelligent machines. Existing 3D generation and reconstruction methods [1–3] achieve great stability by incorporating real 3D object data, benefiting from strong 3D priors. However, this comes at a high computational cost, particularly for high-resolution and

C. Wallraven et al. (Eds.): ACPR 2025, LNCS 16174, pp. 295–307, 2026.
https://doi.org/10.1007/978-981-95-4395-3_21

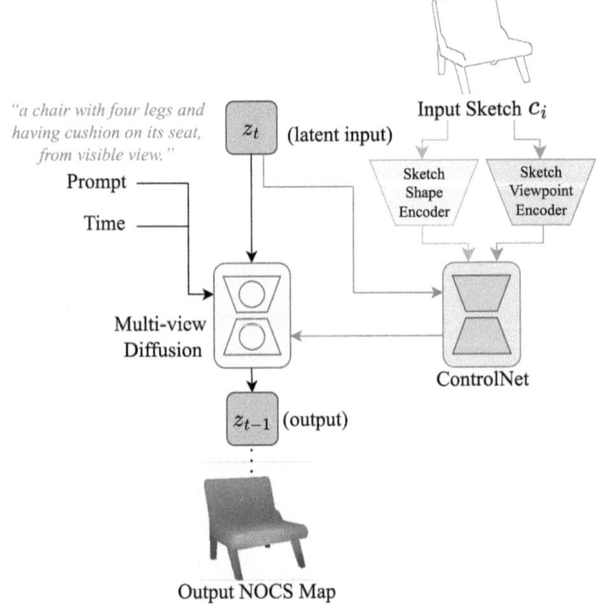

Fig. 1. One-step denoising process for our DiffS-NOCS model.

fine-grained tasks, where training and inference times, as well as resource consumption, increase significantly. Meanwhile, 2D image-based approaches often rely on depth maps [4] or normal maps [5], which poorly represent the positional information of 3D point clouds and are primarily used as auxiliary supervision (Fig. 1).

Can 3D objects be accurately reconstructed using only 2D training and inference, without real 3D priors? To bridge the gap between 2D images and 3D objects, we use Normalized Object Coordinate Space (NOCS) map [6], which predicts 3D point cloud positions directly from 2D images. A deep learning model extracts features from the 2D input and maps them to a NOCS representation for 3D reconstruction. In this work, we aim to generate NOCS maps from sketches, leveraging both front-view NOCS (Visible NOCS) and back-view NOCS (Occluded NOCS, X-NOCS) [7]. The inclusion of X-NOCS addresses spatial ambiguity by incorporating shape and positional information from the backside of the object, enhancing reconstruction accuracy.

In recent years, diffusion models [8–10] have surpassed Generative Adversarial Networks (GANs) [11,12] in many generative tasks [13–15], demonstrating exceptional ability to capture high-dimensional data structures in various dimensional spaces. In previous studies, the work of completing 2D image generation based on diffusion models is more mature than that of completing 3D generation. Inspired by their strong reasoning capabilities, we propose a conditional generative model for coloring sketches into NOCS maps using a modified ControlNet

[15]. However, generating corresponding NOCS maps from multi-view sketches poses two key challenges: (i) Sketch-based diffusion models often rely only on text prompts and shape features extracted from one input sketch, but our multi-view reconstruction task needs viewpoint information extracted from multiple sketches. (ii) Multi-view inputs share overlapping information across viewpoints. How to use this information and maintain consistency during the generation process is the key to multi-view reconstruction task. To address these, we train a viewpoint encoder to extract viewpoint information from sketches. This encoder is combined with the encoder of Stable Diffusion (SD) for contour extraction and feeds into a feature-level multi-view aggregation network, namely the multi-view decoder which is fine-tuned on the vanilla decoder of SD as a denoising network that facilitates cross-view information exchange and dynamically aggregates features to generate consistent outputs across varying input views. Such multi-view decoder, compared to the vanilla decoder in SD, is trained on multi-view NOCS maps and guarantees 3D consistency in the model's outputs, since more 3D priors are inherited.

Our contributions. We are the first to explore reconstructing 3D point clouds from multi-view sketches in 2D space using diffusion models. Our main contributions are: (i) We establish a novel connection between multi-view sketches and fine-grained 3D point cloud reconstruction via NOCS representation, enabling efficient 3D reconstruction in 2D space. (ii) We introduce a viewpoint encoder and a multi-view denoising network, ensuring controllable and consistent point cloud reconstruction for arbitrary viewpoint inputs. (iii) Experiments on synthetic and hand-drawn sketch datasets demonstrate that our model achieves excellent performance in 3D point cloud reconstruction from sketches.

2 Related Works

2.1 Generative Diffusion Models

Diffusion models [8–10] are a powerful class of generative models that have shown remarkable performance across diverse tasks, including high-resolution image generation [16,17], biomedical image super-resolution [18], text-to-image generation [13,19,20], video generation [21,22] and 3D data generation [1–3,23]. Compared to GANs [11] and Variational Autoencoders (VAEs) [24], diffusion models offer superior sample quality, stable training, and the ability to compute accurate likelihoods. Among these, Stable Diffusion [14] has gained prominence for its ability to generate high-quality images from text prompts. ControlNet [15] extends Stable Diffusion by incorporating additional control inputs, allowing for more precise guidance during generation.

2.2 Sketch-To-3D Generation and Reconstruction

Research on sketch-based 3D generation and reconstruction can be categorized into single-view and multi-view approaches.

Single-View. A single-view sketch is drawn from a specific angle. Several approaches aim to generate 3D contents using single-view reconstruction. For example, Sketch2Mesh [25] leverages an encoder-decoder framework to create a latent representation of the input sketch, which is then refined by aligning the reconstructed 3D mesh's contours with the sketch during sampling. A diffusion model-based approach [1], LAS-Diffusion, uses 2D image block features to guide 3D voxel feature learning through a novel view-aware local attention mechanism, which greatly improves local controllability and generalization ability. Sketch2Model [26], with single view sketch input but varying angles, explores the importance of viewpoint specification to overcome the reconstruction ambiguity problem and proposes a novel single view-aware generation method.

Multi-view. Multi-view sketches are drawn from multiple different angles. Theoretically, 3D reconstruction based on multi-view sketches can obtain a more accurate 3D model, but almost no one has conducted research in this direction. The 3D-R2N2 [27] method is inspired by the progress of LSTM networks, along with single-view 3D reconstruction. And it proposes a new architecture that accepts one or more object instance images from different viewpoints and outputs 3D reconstruction results. It is important to note that 3D-R2N2 is not tailored for sketches, but for general images. Its performance decreases significantly when the input is sketch.

3 Method

In this section, we first briefly review the NOCS map, latent diffusion models and ControlNet. Then, we introduce the DiffS-NOCS model, highlighting the design of multi-modal content fusion and multi-view diffusion.

3.1 Preliminary

NOCS Map. We choose NOCS map as the 3D encoded representation, because it can capture the dense shapes of objects observed from any given viewpoint, while offering computationally efficient signal processing (such as 2D convolution). As shown in Fig. 2, NOCS map is a two-dimensional projection of the instance three-dimensional NOCS point seen from a specific perspective. It contains 3 channels whose values are within $[0, 1]$, representing the coordinates in the canonical space. In other words, each pixel in the NOCS map represents the three-dimensional position of the object point in NOCS (encoded by RGB). By reading out the pixel values, they can be easily converted to point clouds. The point clouds read out from different NOCS maps of the same object can also be directly combined together because they are all in the same canonical space.

Latent Diffusion Models (LDM). To deal with resources consuming problem in Denoising Diffusion Probabilistic Model [9], the LDM was proposed, which introduced a VAE to compress and encode the original object x_0 first, and then apply the encoded vector (the low-dimensional representation z_0 of the image)

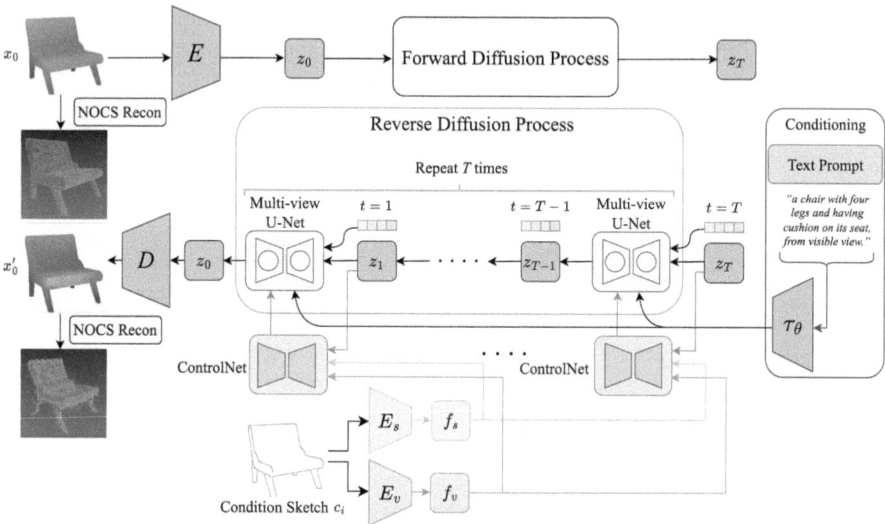

Fig. 2. Overview of our proposed DiffS-NOCS model.

to the diffusion model. By adding the Attention mechanism to U-Net, the conditional variable y is processed. The objective function of conditional LDM is:

$$\begin{aligned} z_0 &= E(x_0), \\ z_t &= \sqrt{\bar{\alpha}_t} z_0 + \sqrt{1 - \bar{\alpha}_t} \epsilon, \ \epsilon \sim \mathcal{N}(0, \mathbf{I}) \\ \mathcal{L}_{\text{LDM}} &= \mathbb{E}_{t, z_0, \epsilon, y} \left[\|\epsilon - \epsilon_\theta(z_t, t, \tau_\theta(y))\|_2^2 \right]. \end{aligned} \tag{1}$$

Here, y is the conditional data, and τ_θ is responsible for processing y into a feature vector. In this work, y is a text prompt describing the object to be generated, and τ_θ is the text encoder in the pre-trained CLIP model.

ControlNet. ControlNet is a neural network that controls a pre-trained latent diffusion model (e.g. Stable Diffusion). It allows input of conditioned images, which are then used to guide image generation. In a pre-trained model, ControlNet incorporates an additional fully connected mapped condition c. This condition is introduced to the layer input, processed by a duplicate network mirroring the original layer's structure, and then re-mapped before being added back to the layer's output.

3.2 Multi-modal Content Fusion

To reconstruct multi-view images, we first train a sketch viewpoint perception network to extract multi-view information from the input sketch. The network uses an encoder-decoder architecture based on a convolutional neural network (CNN) to predict the object's viewpoint category. We employ a pre-trained

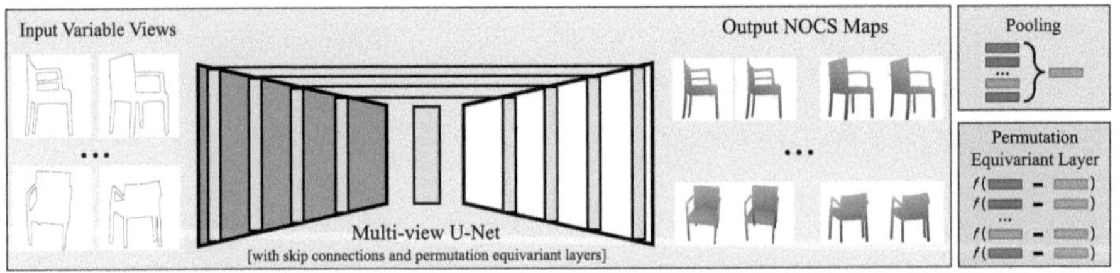

Fig. 3. Feature level multi-view aggregation denoising U-Net.

ResNet-50 [28] (denoted E_v) as the encoder, and a simple fully connected network as the decoder to predict the viewpoint of the object. The encoder's weights are initialized with ResNet-50's pre-trained values and updated during training based on the sketch image and viewpoint label. The resulting Sketch Viewpoint Encoder encodes the input sketch c_i into the viewpoint feature $f_v = E_v(c_i)$. This viewpoint feature f_v is then concatenated with the shape feature $f_s = E_s(c_i)$ to form $c_f = F_{con}(f_v, f_s)$, where F_{con} aggregates these two vectors. Finally, c_f is passed to the NOCS map multi-view decoder D_{MV} (in Sect. 3.3), providing it with both viewpoint and shape information for effective decoding. The addition of information and its placement are also crucial. While it may seem intuitive to integrate cross-modal information at the Encoder stage of U-Net for guiding the Decoder, we adopt a different approach. Instead of adding modules solely at key points, such as the Cross-Attention layer, we perform information fusion at the end of each layer, treating all added information equally.

3.3 Multi-view Diffusion

We now move to the design of the multi-view diffusion model to conduct multi-view NOCS map prediction from input sketches. Multi-view images of objects contain significant overlapping information, and effectively utilizing this overlap is crucial for multi-view reconstruction. To enhance information exchange between different views and support varying numbers of input views, we design a feature-level multi-view aggregation denoising U-Net as the multi-view decoder D_{MV} to replace the vanilla decoder in Stable Diffusion. Specifically, we propose using permutation equivariant layers that are independent of the view order.

The multi-view decoder D_{MV} is illustrated in Fig. 3. It mirrors the original decoder (vanilla D_{LDM}) except for the inclusion of several permutation equivariant layers (orange bars). A layer is considered envelope-equivariant if the diagonal elements of the learned weight matrix are equal to the diagonal elements. This is achieved by pooling the features from different views, subtracting the pooled features from each individual feature map, and then applying a nonlinear function. Namely, the permutation equivariant layer consists of mean subtraction followed by a convolutional nonlinearity. Multiple permutation equivariant layers (vertical orange bars) are applied after each downsampling and upsampling operation in the encoder-decoder of U-Net. Both average and maximum pooling can be used, but experimental results show that average pooling yields the best performance.

Loss Function. The DiffS-NOCS model we propose follows the ControlNet design. We jointly train the multi-view decoder and ControlNet to generate NOCS maps from multi-view sketches. To incorporate viewpoint information, we replace the vanilla decoder in Stable Diffusion with a multi-view decoder, which includes permutation equivariant layers while retaining the pretrained weights from Stable Diffusion 2.1. The overall training objective consists of two components: (1) a denoising loss for multi-view decoder to learn an effective view-aware latent representation, and (2) a ControlNet-specific loss to ensure the generated NOCS maps align with the input sketches. The overall loss function is:

$$\mathcal{L} = \lambda_{\text{MV-LDM}} \mathcal{L}_{\text{MV-LDM}} + \mathcal{L}_{\text{ControlNet}} \tag{2}$$

where $\mathcal{L}_{\text{MV-LDM}}$ is the updated LDM denoising loss defined in Eq. 1:

$$\mathcal{L}_{\text{MV-LDM}} = \mathbb{E}_{t,z_0,\epsilon,y,c_f}\left[\|\epsilon - \epsilon_\theta(z_t, t, \tau_\theta(y), c_f)\|_2^2\right] \tag{3}$$

And the ControlNet loss consists of an L1 loss for pixel-wise supervision and a perceptual loss to preserve structural integrity:

$$\mathcal{L}_{\text{ControlNet}} = \lambda_1 \mathcal{L}_{L1} + \lambda_2 \mathcal{L}_{\text{perc}} \tag{4}$$

where $\mathcal{L}_{L1} = \mathbb{E}_{\mathbf{x_0},\hat{\mathbf{x_0}}}\left[\|\mathbf{x_0} - \hat{\mathbf{x_0}}\|_1\right]$ ensures direct alignment with the ground truth NOCS map $\mathbf{x_0}$, and $\mathcal{L}_{\text{perc}}$ minimizes the feature space difference using a pre-trained VGG network:

$$\mathcal{L}_{\text{perc}} = \sum_i \|\phi_i(\mathbf{x_0}) - \phi_i(\hat{\mathbf{x_0}})\|_2^2 \tag{5}$$

where ϕ_i denotes the activation of the ith layer in the VGG network. We adopt a two-stage training strategy: (1) we first train ControlNet while freezing multi-view decoder to ensure effective conditioning, and (2) we jointly fine-tune both networks to optimize the overall generation quality. This approach ensures that ControlNet learns to modulate multi-view decoder effectively while allowing multi-view decoder to adapt to viewpoint-aware NOCS map reconstruction. $\lambda_{\text{MV-LDM}}$, λ_1 and λ_2 are the coefficients that balance each loss.

During training, we randomly replaced 50% of the text prompts y with empty strings to help DiffS-NOCS better interpret the input conditional sketch. This forces the model to rely more on the information of sketch, enhancing the DiffS-NOCS's ability to understand its semantic content. By leveraging the ControlNet architecture with the pre-trained Stable Diffusion model, the DiffS-NOCS model gains improved control over the NOCS map generation process, resulting in more accurate and well-aligned NOCS maps.

4 Experiments

4.1 Experimental Setup

Datasets. To our knowledge, no dataset exists for sketch-NOCS map pairing. Therefore, we render the ShapeNet [29] dataset to generate NOCS map images

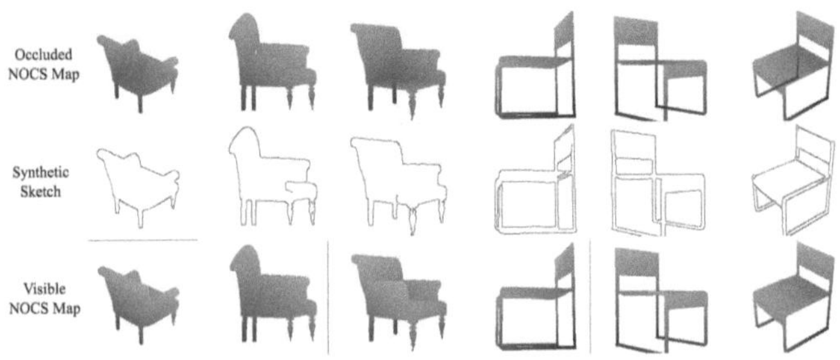

Fig. 4. Composition of the *S2N-ShapeNet* dataset.

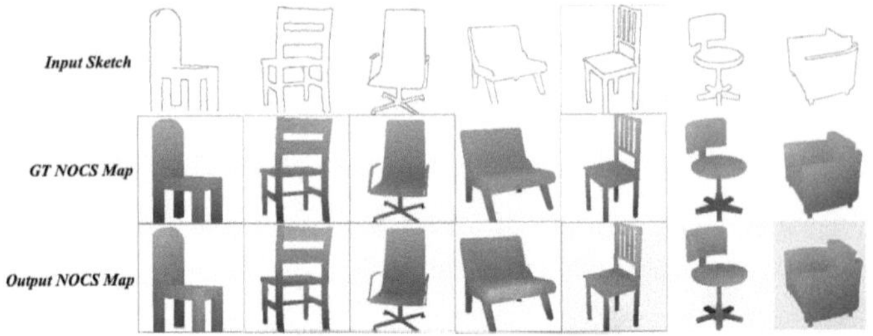

Fig. 5. Results of Sketch-to-NOCS map generation.

that correspond to sketches, as shown in Fig. 4. The resulting dataset, named *S2N-ShapeNet*, includes three object categories: chair, car, and airplane, commonly used in related works. Tens of thousands of 3D assets from ShapeNet-CoreV2 are utilized, with 20 views rendered for each object, five of which are randomly selected for training and testing. Text prompts are sourced from the Text2Shape [30], which provides detailed descriptions for chairs. For cars and airplanes, we use the category names as prompts.

Evaluation Metrics. We use two standard evaluation metrics to assess the quality of the reconstructed 3D point cloud: Chamfer Distance (CD) and Earth Mover's Distance (EMD) [31]. Additionally, to ensure the generated 3D model closely matches the input sketch, we project the generated shape into the ground truth view and compute the 2D IoU score between the projected silhouette and the ground truth silhouette.

Implementation Details. We train the sketch viewpoint perception network on two NVIDIA A100 40GB GPU cards with a batch size of 128, and the ControlNet-based DiffS-NOCS model with a batch size of 16, using Stable Diffusion 2.1 as the foundation model for multi-view diffusion model. In the training phase, the learning rate is set to 1×10^{-5}. And during inference, the DDIM steps for generating NOCS map images are set to 50.

Table 1. Comparison of single-view and multi-view sketch-point cloud reconstruction performance.

Method	Category								
	CD ↓			EMD ↓			2D IoU ↑		
	Chair	Car	Airplane	Chair	Car	Airplane	Chair	Car	Airplane
LAS-Diffusion [1]	3.265	3.505	2.577	11.13	11.64	10.81	0.664	0.638	0.493
Sketch2Mesh [25]	2.745	2.495	N/A	9.39	7.85	N/A	0.726	0.840	N/A
Sketch2Model [26]	2.894	2.579	1.949	10.30	10.22	9.07	0.637	0.741	0.645
3D-R2N2 [27] (1 view)	3.079	3.129	2.147	9.75	8.96	6.94	0.618	0.697	0.566
Ours (1 view)	**2.304**	**2.316**	**1.318**	**8.96**	**7.18**	**6.34**	**0.832**	**0.921**	**0.779**
3D-R2N2 (2 views)	2.963	2.923	1.798	9.52	7.83	6.90	0.723	0.814	0.613
3D-R2N2 (3 views)	2.649	2.871	1.460	9.27	7.52	6.92	0.745	0.839	0.642
3D-R2N2 (5 views)	2.508	2.450	1.239	9.19	7.31	6.52	0.764	0.887	0.674
Ours (2 views)	**1.915**	**1.958**	**1.080**	**8.82**	**7.07**	**6.28**	**0.836**	**0.938**	**0.791**
Ours (3 views)	**1.657**	**1.644**	**1.149**	**8.31**	**6.82**	**6.23**	**0.848**	**0.954**	**0.827**
Ours (5 views)	**1.324**	**1.732**	**0.674**	**8.05**	**6.59**	**6.15**	**0.875**	**0.972**	**0.854**

Table 2. Quantitative evaluations on the ProSketch dataset.

Method	CD ↓	EMD ↓	2D IoU ↑
LAS-Diffusion [1]	2.936	10.07	0.698
Sketch2Mesh [25]	6.749	12.37	0.604
Sketch2Model [26]	5.825	11.72	0.557
Ours	**2.853**	**9.95**	**0.728**

4.2 Evaluation Results

Quantitative Comparison. (1) **Single-View Reconstruction.** For mesh-represented methods, meshes are converted to point clouds, sampled to match our output size, and scaled to a unit diagonal bounding box. For 3D-R2N2, surface voxels are extracted, converted to points, and scaled accordingly. Table 1 shows that our method outperform all baselines in all categories on synthetic sketch dataset. We also test the generalization ability of our model on a hand-drawn sketch dataset ProSketch-3DChair [32] without fine-tuning. The statistics results in Table 2 demonstrate our method are much more faithful to the input sketch. (2) **Multi-View Reconstruction.** We compare our model with 3D-R2N2. Both methods are trained on random 5-view sketch-NOCS map pairs per batch and evaluated with up to 5 views at inference. Table 1 shows that our method outperforms 3D-R2N2 in all metrics, demonstrating better geometric consistency and shape matching.

Qualitative Comparison. Fig. 6 and Fig. 7 show the qualitative comparison on the chair category. Our method outperforms all baselines in shape recovery and

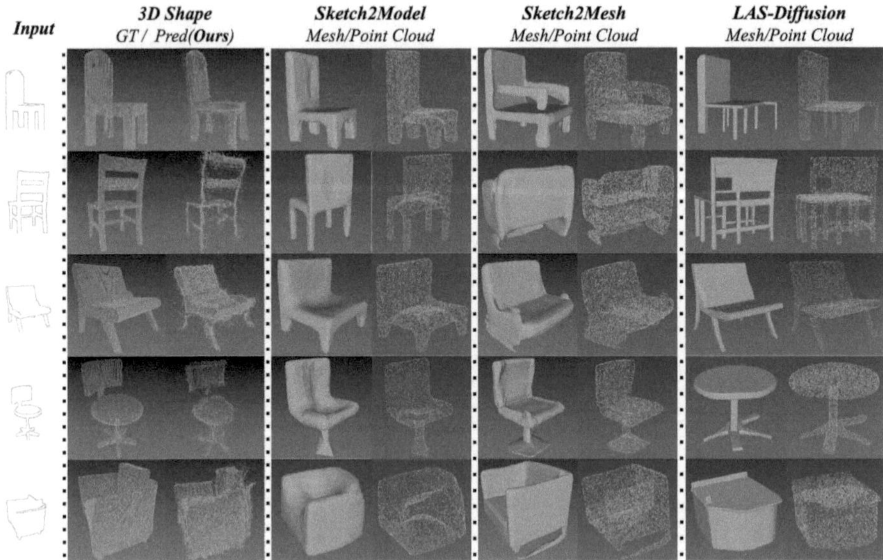

Fig. 6. Qualitative comparison of different models on synthetic chair sketches.

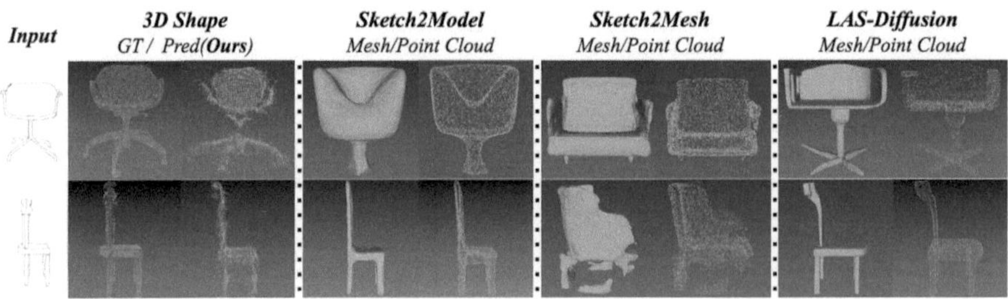

Fig. 7. Reconstruction results on hand-drawn chair sketches [32].

Table 3. Ablation study on chair category. The table illustrates the difference in model performance after removing sketch viewpoint encoder module. SVE denotes the Sketch Viewpoint Encoder.

Methods	CD ↓	EMD ↓	2D IoU ↑
w/o SVE	2.677	9.64	0.804
Ours	**2.304**	**8.96**	**0.832**

geometry preservation. Particularly for detailed sketches with complex shapes, DiffS-NOCS captures geometric features more accurately. This is because our model fully utilizes the spatial alignment of input sketch and output point cloud, via generated NOCS map. The NOCS maps generated from the sketches are shown in Fig. 5. And more qualitative comparisons of car and airplane categories are provided in Fig. 8.

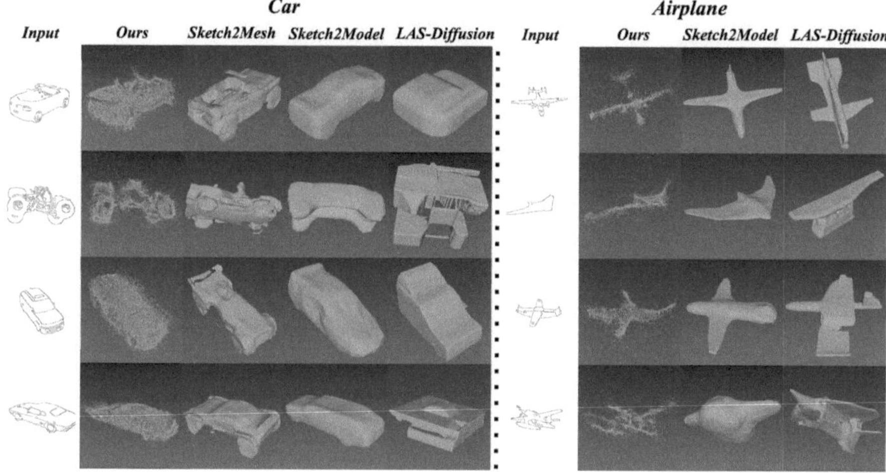

Fig. 8. More qualitative results of synthetic car and airplane sketches.

Table 4. Ablation study on multi-view decoder.

Category	Model	2 views	3 views	5 views
Chair	Single-View(D_{LDM})	2.127	1.972	1.924
	Multi-View(D_{MV})	**1.915**	**1.657**	**1.324**
Car	Single-View(D_{LDM})	2.009	1.782	**1.653**
	Multi-View(D_{MV})	**1.958**	**1.644**	1.732
Airplane	Single-View(D_{LDM})	1.157	**1.019**	0.981
	Multi-View(D_{MV})	**1.080**	1.149	**0.674**

4.3 Ablation Study and Analysis

Design of Sketch Viewpoint Encoder. Here we examine the effectiveness of the design of the sketch viewpoint encoder. The results are shown in Table 3. It can be seen that SVE module is beneficial.

Importance of Multi-view Decoder. As shown in Table 4, increasing the number of views significantly enhances reconstruction geometry. The multi-view decoder further improves the results by aggregating features with permutation equivariant layers, which effectively capture geometric relationships across different viewpoints. This highlights the critical role of multi-view decoder in achieving higher accuracy and robustness in the cross-modal 3D reconstruction task.

5 Conclusion

In this paper, we propose a diffusion-based method for sketch-to-point cloud reconstruction, converting sketches into NOCS maps with viewpoint awareness. Based on a ControlNet-inspired architecture, firstly, we train a viewpoint encoder to extract viewpoint features, which, combined with contour features from the Stable Diffusion Encoder, improve decoding performance. Then, a multi-view decoder facilitates cross-view information exchange, ensuring 3D consistency during generation. Our method excels in both single-view and multi-view reconstruction tasks, effectively handling hand-drawn sketches. Unlike 3D-based approaches, our method operates entirely in 2D using a controlled diffusion model, reducing both training and inference costs.

References

1. Zheng, X.-Y., Pan, H., Wang, P.-S., et al.: Locally attentional SDF diffusion for controllable 3D shape generation. ACM Trans. Graph. (ToG) **42**(4), 1–13 (2023)
2. Kong, D., Wang, Q., Qi, Y.-G.: A diffusion-refinement model for sketch-to-point modeling. In: Proceedings of the Asian Conference on Computer Vision, pp. 1522–1538 (2022)
3. Zhou, L., Du, Y., Wu, J.: 3D shape generation and completion through point-voxel diffusion. In: Proceedings of the IEEE/CVF International Conference on Computer Vision, pp. 5826–5835 (2021)
4. Choe, J., Im, S., Rameau, F., et al.: VolumeFusion: deep depth fusion for 3D scene reconstruction. In: Proceedings of the IEEE/CVF International Conference on Computer Vision, pp. 16086–16095 (2021)
5. Wu, J., Wang, Y., Xue, T., et al.: MarrNet: 3D shape reconstruction via 2.5D sketches. In: Advances in Neural Information Processing Systems, vol. 30 (2017)
6. Wang, H., Sridhar, S., Huang, J., et al.: Normalized object coordinate space for category-level 6D object pose and size estimation. In: Proceedings of the IEEE/CVF Conference on Computer Vision and Pattern Recognition, pp. 2642–2651 (2019)
7. Sridhar, S., Rempe, D., Valentin, J., et al.: Multiview aggregation for learning category-specific shape reconstruction. In: Advances in Neural Information Processing Systems, vol. 32 (2019)
8. Sohl-Dickstein, J., Weiss, E., Maheswaranathan, N., Ganguli, S.: Deep unsupervised learning using nonequilibrium thermodynamics. In: International Conference on Machine Learning, pp. 2256–2265 (2015)
9. Ho, J., Jain, A., Abbeel, P.: Denoising diffusion probabilistic models. Adv. Neural. Inf. Process. Syst. **33**, 6840–6851 (2020)
10. Song, Y., Sohl-Dickstein, J., Kingma, D.P., et al.: Score-based generative modeling through stochastic differential equations. *arXiv preprint*arXiv:2011.13456 (2020)
11. Goodfellow, I., Pouget-Abadie, J., Mirza, M., et al.: Generative adversarial networks. Commun. ACM **63**(11), 139–144 (2020)
12. Wang, S.-Y., Bau, D., Zhu, J.-Y.: Sketch your own GAN. In: Proceedings of the IEEE/CVF International Conference on Computer Vision, pp. 14050–14060 (2021)
13. Saharia, C., Chan, W., Saxena, S., et al.: Photorealistic text-to-image diffusion models with deep language understanding. Adv. Neural. Inf. Process. Syst. **35**, 36479–36494 (2022)
14. Rombach, R., Blattmann, A., Lorenz, D., et al.: High-resolution image synthesis with latent diffusion models. In: Proceedings of the IEEE/CVF Conference on Computer Vision and Pattern Recognition, pp. 10684–10695 (2022)

15. Zhang, L., Rao, A., Agrawala, M.: Adding conditional control to text-to-image diffusion models. In: Proceedings of the IEEE/CVF International Conference on Computer Vision, pp. 3836–3847 (2023)
16. Dhariwal, P., Nichol, A.: Diffusion models beat GANs on image synthesis. Adv. Neural. Inf. Process. Syst. **34**, 8780–8794 (2021)
17. Ho, J., Saharia, C., Chan, W., et al.: Cascaded diffusion models for high fidelity image generation. J. Mach. Learn. Res. **23**(47), 1–33 (2022)
18. Kong, D., Yang, H., Luo, Y., et al.: D-STAR: diffusion-based sparse tomographic angular recovery for isotropic-resolution photoacoustic imaging. IEEE Trans. Med. Imaging (2025)
19. Nichol, A., Dhariwal, P., Ramesh, A., et al.: GLIDE: towards photorealistic image generation and editing with text-guided diffusion models. arXiv preprint arXiv:2112.10741 (2021)
20. Gu, S., Chen, D., Bao, J., et al.: Vector quantized diffusion model for text-to-image synthesis. In: Proceedings of the IEEE/CVF Conference on Computer Vision and Pattern Recognition, pp. 10696–10706 (2022)
21. Wang, Y., Chen, X., Ma, X., et al.: LAVIE: high-quality video generation with cascaded latent diffusion models. Int. J. Comput. Vis. **133**(5), 3059–3078 (2025)
22. Gupta, A., Yu, L., Sohn, K., et al.: Photorealistic video generation with diffusion models. European Conference on Computer Vision, pp. 393–411 (2024)
23. Luo, S., Hu, W.: Diffusion probabilistic models for 3D point cloud generation. In: Proceedings of the IEEE/CVF Conference on Computer Vision and Pattern Recognition, pp. 2837–2845 (2021)
24. Kingma, D.P., Welling, M.: Auto-encoding variational Bayes. arXiv preprint arXiv:1312.6114 (2013)
25. Guillard, B., Remelli, E., Yvernay, P., Fua, P.: Sketch2Mesh: reconstructing and editing 3D shapes from sketches. In: ICCV, pp. 13003–13012 (2021)
26. Zhang, S.-H., Guo, Y.-C., Gu, Q.-W.: Sketch2model: view-aware 3D modeling from single free-hand sketches. In: Proceedings of the IEEE/CVF Conference on Computer Vision and Pattern Recognition, pp. 6012–6021 (2021)
27. Choy, C.B., Xu, D., Gwak, J.Y., Chen, K., Savarese, S.: 3D-R2N2: a unified approach for single and multi-view 3D object reconstruction. In: Leibe, B., Matas, J., Sebe, N., Welling, M. (eds.) ECCV 2016. LNCS, vol. 9912, pp. 628–644. Springer, Cham (2016). https://doi.org/10.1007/978-3-319-46484-8_38
28. He, K., Zhang, X., Ren, S., Sun, J.: Deep residual learning for image recognition. In: Proceedings of the IEEE/CVF Conference on Computer Vision and Pattern Recognition, pp. 770–778 (2016)
29. Chang, A.X., Funkhouser, T., Guibas, L., et al.: ShapeNet: an information-rich 3D model repository. arXiv preprint arXiv:1512.03012 (2015)
30. Chen, K., Choy, C.B., Savva, M., et al.: Text2shape: generating shapes from natural language by learning joint embeddings. In: Computer Vision–ACCV 2018: 14th Asian Conference on Computer Vision, pp. 100–116. Springer (2019)
31. Rubner, Y., Tomasi, C., Guibas, L.J.: The earth mover's distance as a metric for image retrieval. In: International Journal of Computer Vision, vol. 40, pp. 99–121 (2000)
32. Zhong, Y., Qi, Y., Gryaditskaya, Y., et al.: Towards practical sketch-based 3D shape generation: the role of professional sketches. IEEE Trans. Circuits Syst. Video Technol. **31**, 3518–3528 (2020)

ICPCC: Importance-Aware Crops Point Cloud Compression

Haonan Wang(✉), Haifeng Xia, and Siyu Xia

Advanced Ocean Institute, Southeast University, Nanjing 210096, China
{220234867,hfxia,xsy}@seu.edu.cn

Abstract. In the context of smart agriculture, effective monitoring of crop growth requires a 3D point cloud compression method that preserves detailed features of the primary plant structures while suppressing less relevant background information. However, achieving this balance is challenging due to the uniform treatment of spatial regions in conventional compression schemes. To address this need, we propose a resource-efficient importance-aware adaptive compression framework for point clouds. Specifically, after performing semantic segmentation on the raw point cloud, we quantify the semantic importance of each segmented region and map the importance scores to adaptive compression ratios. These ratios are then embedded into the latent representation during encoding and parsed during decoding to guide the reconstruction precision. This enables a more efficient allocation of bits to semantically critical regions. We validate the effectiveness of the proposed method on both our self-collected crop dataset and the publicly available Pheno4D dataset, demonstrating its feasibility and improved performance in balancing compression rate and reconstruction accuracy.

Keywords: Point cloud compression · Agricultural point cloud · Importance perception

1 Introduction

Point clouds have become one of the most widely adopted 3D representations in a variety of fields, including autonomous driving, embodied intelligence, and smart agriculture [2,3,31]. With the rapid advancement of sensing technologies, modern acquisition devices are now capable of capturing increasingly detailed and geometrically rich point clouds [11,35]. However, the resulting data is often highly complex and large in volume, which poses significant challenges for storage and real-time transmission. To address these issues, researchers have proposed a wide range of point cloud compression techniques [9,14]. Over time, the performance of such methods has matured, and current compression ratios are approaching their limits. As a result, pursuing marginal improvements in compression performance is becoming less meaningful, particularly in application-driven contexts.

In smart agriculture, for example, there is often a need for real-time monitoring of plant growth [24,25]. As is shown in Fig. 1, the objective is to preserve

C. Wallraven et al. (Eds.): ACPR 2025, LNCS 16174, pp. 308–323, 2026.
https://doi.org/10.1007/978-981-95-4395-3_22

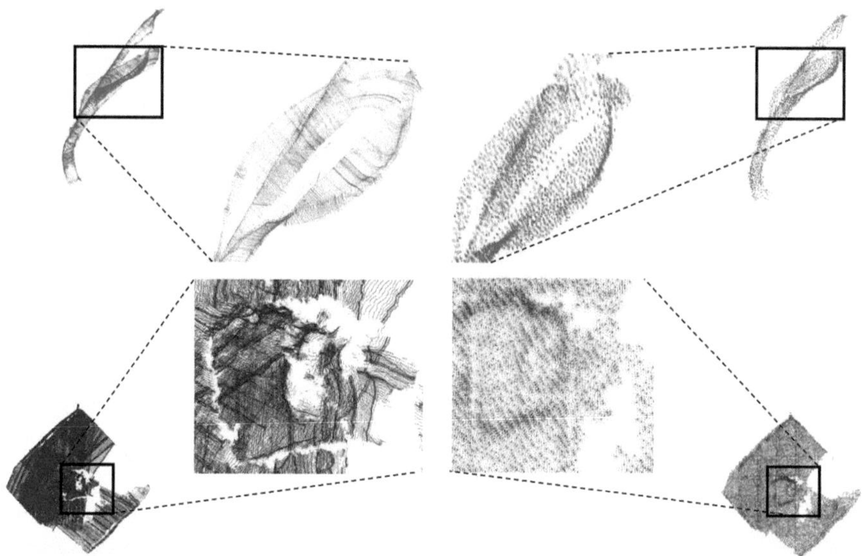

Fig. 1. In agricultural scenarios, there is a practical need to preserve fine details of plants or foliage. As illustrated, the left shows the original point cloud, while the right presents reconstructions under varying compression ratios. The method adopts an importance-aware adaptive compression strategy consistent with human visual perception, preserving fine details in semantically important regions such as crops, while retaining only coarse structures in less relevant areas such as soil.

crop regions with higher fidelity—preserving regions with higher fidelity through reduced compression—while aggressively compressing less critical areas such as soil, even at the cost of structural inconsistency relative to the original point cloud [21]. In these scenarios, it is more critical to retain the geometric and semantic details of crops, whereas background regions can tolerate higher loss. This motivates the development of compression methods that are not only efficient but also importance-aware [32].

In this work, we propose an importance-aware 3D point cloud compression framework. The key idea is to assess the relative importance of different regions within a point cloud through a multi-geometry-aware importance perception mechanism. The contributions of our paper are summarized as follows:

(1) Building upon an existing autoencoder architecture, we first segment the crop point cloud before encoding. We then quantitatively evaluate the importance of each segmented region based on multiple geometric features.

(2) These importance scores are mapped to a compression ratio matrix, which guides the downsampling rates during the encoding stage and is also incorporated into the entropy coding process to form the final bitstream. During decoding, this information is parsed and utilized to assist in the reconstruction of the point cloud.

(3) We perform comprehensive experiments and ablation studies on crop-related point cloud datasets to validate the effectiveness of our approach and the impact of each component.

2 Related Work

2.1 Point Cloud Analysis

Unlike 2D images, 3D point clouds are inherently unordered, sparse, irregular, and lack an explicit grid structure, making it difficult to apply traditional convolutional neural networks (CNNs) effectively. To address these issues, early methods often voxelized point clouds to enable 3D convolutions, but this leads to high memory usage and loss of detail.

Recent approaches process point clouds directly. PointNet [17] introduced a simple and effective framework using symmetric functions to handle unordered inputs. PointNet++ [18] extended this by capturing local structures through hierarchical grouping. DGCNN [30] improved on this by building dynamic graphs and learning edge features, which better represent local geometry. More recently, transformer-based methods such as Point Transformer [36] have been proposed to model long-range dependencies with attention mechanisms. Newer models like PointNeXt [19] and Point-BERT [34] further improve performance using residual learning and pretraining strategies, achieving state-of-the-art results on benchmarks like ModelNet40 and ScanNet.

2.2 Point Cloud Compression

Traditional point cloud compression algorithms [12,22] typically utilize spatial redundancy through structures like kd-trees and octrees to reduce storage and transmission costs. Although efficient, such hand-crafted methods often struggle to capture complex data-driven patterns.

Inspired by the success of deep learning in image and video compression [1,13], recent research has explored point cloud compression based on learning [20,28]. These methods, often based on autoencoder architectures, offer improved flexibility and better trade-offs between compression efficiency and reconstruction fidelity by learning compact latent representations. DPCC [4] preserves local point density to reduce structural distortion, emphasizing spatial structure. This complements our method, which adapts compression based on semantic importance.

Further advances introduce semantics-aware compression [5,33], which allocates bits according to the semantic importance of different regions, which is crucial for applications such as autonomous driving and digital twins.

Building on this idea, this paper focuses on an importance-aware compression framework that adjusts compression granularity based on semantic significance, achieving efficient representation without sacrificing reconstruction quality or compression ratio.

2.3 Point Cloud Importance Perception

Identifying perceptually or semantically important regions within point clouds is critical for tasks such as compression, rendering, and transmission [10]. Early methods typically rely on a single hand-crafted geometric feature to estimate local importance [15,16]. These approaches are computationally efficient but are often limited in capturing high-level contextual relevance.

More recently, learning-based approaches have been introduced to better model point-wise importance using data-driven strategies. PCGCv2 [27] integrates importance estimation within a compression network, while methods such as PointCloudSaliency [37] and DeepView [6] employ supervised or unsupervised learning to predict saliency maps based on task-driven objectives. However, compared to deep learning approaches, traditional geometry-based methods offer clearer interpretability by directly linking significance scores to measurable spatial properties.

In contrast to existing methods that rely on either a single geometric criterion or high-cost neural models, this paper focuses on multigeometry-aware importance estimation. By incorporating multiple geometric cues (e.g., curvature and density), our method captures a richer understanding of structural significance. Compared to single-feature baselines, it achieves more accurate importance predictions, and while it may not match the peak performance of deep models, it provides a resource-efficient alternative suitable for real-time or embedded applications.

3 Methodology

The proposed importance-aware point cloud compression framework shown in Fig. 2 builds upon a density-preserving deep compression model using an enhanced symmetric autoencoder. This model downscales the input point cloud while extracting local geometric features, applies entropy coding at the bottleneck, and reconstructs the cloud via feature-guided, stage-wise upsampling.

Prior to compression, the full point cloud P_0 is semantically segmented into parts $P_{s1}, P_{s2}, \ldots, P_{sn}$, ensuring intra-segment consistency and inter-segment distinction. Each segment's importance is quantified through multi-geometry feature analysis and then incorporated into the encoder, allowing adaptive compression—allocating more bits to critical regions while reducing redundancy elsewhere.

For each segment, an importance score imp_score_i is computed based on geometric features like density, roughness, curvature, and flatness. These scores are normalized using log-softmax to determine relative compression ratios, which control encoding downsampling and guide reconstruction during decoding.

3.1 Modified PointNet++ Segmentation Module

To ensure semantic consistency and structure-aware compression, the input point cloud $\mathbf{P}_0 = \{p_i \in \mathbb{R}^3\}_{i=1}^N$ (with optional color or intensity features) is first

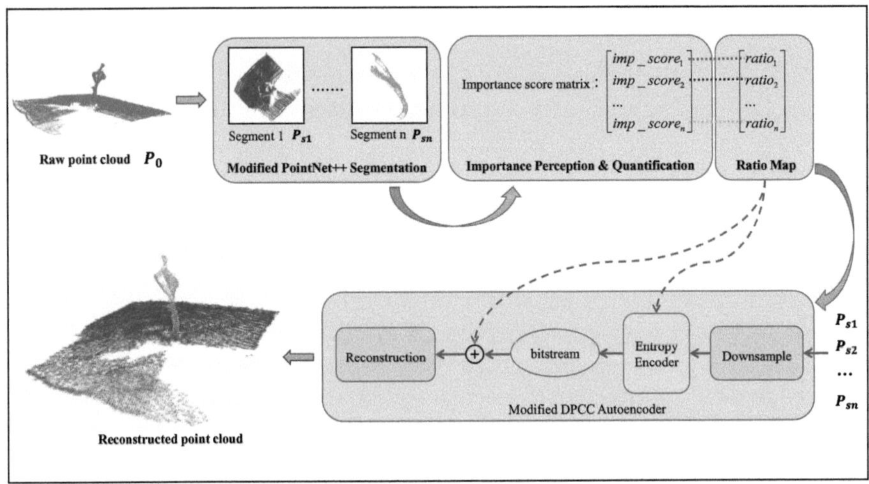

Fig. 2. Our pipeline first segments the input point cloud into multiple regions using a modified PointNet++ segmentation network. An importance-aware quantization module then computes an importance score matrix, which is subsequently mapped to a compression ratio matrix. This matrix guides the downsampling process in the autoencoder and is also embedded into the entropy encoder to form the bitstream. More details are shown in Fig. 3.

processed by a semantic segmentation module based on a PointNet++ backbone. The network hierarchically extracts features and segments the point cloud into semantically meaningful regions $(P_{s1}, P_{s2}, \ldots, P_{sn})$, each corresponding to a distinct class. To support supervised segmentation, we utilize the color or intensity information present in part of the dataset as proxy semantic labels. These enhanced features guide the network in learning class-discriminative representations. For unlabeled point clouds, we adopt a semi-supervised segmentation strategy to mitigate the lack of explicit annotations. Specifically, we employ consistency regularization [7,26], which enforces that the network produces similar predictions under different perturbations or augmentations of the same point cloud, such as random rotations, jittering, or dropout of points. This encourages the model to learn stable, semantically meaningful features even without labels. In addition, we incorporate spatial context modeling via neighborhood affinity graphs [8,29], where each point aggregates information from its local neighborhood weighted by feature similarity. This mechanism allows the network to capture local geometric and semantic relationships, helping infer plausible boundaries in regions with missing or noisy labels. Together, these strategies enable effective semi-supervised segmentation by leveraging both data-driven invariances and local structural priors. However, segmentation quality may degrade under severe occlusions or plant overlaps, which can propagate errors to the compression stage. Addressing this limitation requires integrating more robust segmentation models or uncertainty-aware compression mechanisms, allowing the network to generalize semantic boundaries even in the absence of explicit supervision.

3.2 Importance Perception and Quantification Module

Overview. After the point cloud has been segmented into individual segments by the segmentation module, it is essential to develop an effective method for accurately evaluating the semantic significance of each segment. This process should aim to quantify the importance of each segment while optimizing computational efficiency and minimizing processing time.

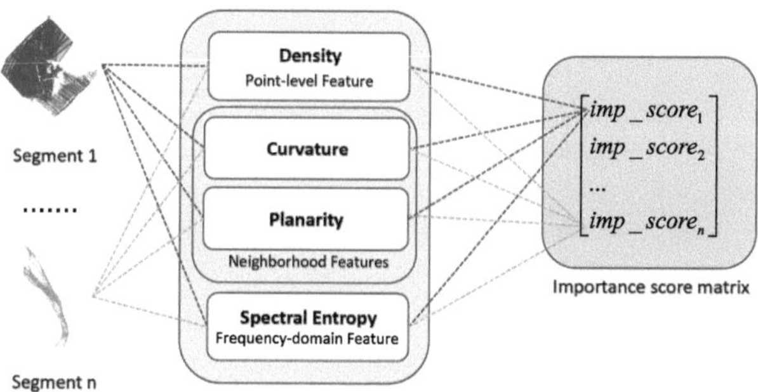

Fig. 3. For each segmented region, we compute four types of neighborhood, frequency-domain, and geometric feature parameters, which are then integrated to form the overall importance score matrix for the point cloud.

Quantification of Importance. As shown in Fig. 3, we quantify segment importance using four features: **Density**, **Curvature**, **Planarity**, and **Spectral Entropy**. Density measures local point concentration, Curvature and Planarity are derived from neighborhood covariance, and Spectral Entropy captures frequency-domain complexity. Segments with higher density, curvature, and entropy but lower planarity are considered more geometrically complex and thus more important, while the opposite indicates likely background regions like ground or walls.

Point-level Feature. For the segmented point cloud segments $(P_{s1}, P_{s2}, \ldots, P_{sn})$, the point density, as a point-level feature, provides an intuitive and interpretable measure to distinguish the relative importance among different segments. The point density of each segment can be quantitatively calculated using the following formula:

$$Den_i = \frac{n_i}{V_i}, \quad \text{where} \quad V_i = \prod_{d=1}^{3} \left(\max(p_j^d) - \min(p_j^d) + \varepsilon\right) \tag{1}$$

where Den_i represents the point density of the i-th segmented point cloud segment; n_i represents the total number of points contained in this segment; V_i is the volume of the axis-aligned bounding box enclosing the segment's points, computed as the product over each spatial dimension $d \in \{1, 2, 3\}$ of the range between the maximum $\max(p_j^d)$ and minimum $\min(p_j^d)$ coordinate values of points p_j within the segment; and ε is a small positive constant added to prevent division by zero.

Neighborhood Features. The neighborhood features of a point cloud are typically consistent with its geometric characteristics and can be more intuitively quantified using the covariance matrix of the local neighborhood and its corresponding eigenvalues. Given a point $p_i \in \mathbb{R}^3$, let its k-nearest neighborhood be represented as $\mathcal{N}(p_i)$. The centered coordinates of the neighborhood points are defined as:

$$\tilde{p}_j = p_j - \mu_i, \quad \text{where} \quad \mu_i = \frac{1}{k} \sum_{p_j \in \mathcal{N}(p_i)} p_j \tag{2}$$

The covariance matrix of the neighborhood is then computed as:

$$C_i = \frac{1}{k} \sum_{p_j \in \mathcal{N}(p_i)} \tilde{p}_j \tilde{p}_j^T \tag{3}$$

where let the eigenvalues of C_i be ordered as $\lambda_1 \leq \lambda_2 \leq \lambda_3$. Based on the three eigenvalues, the quantitative measures of **Curvature** and **Planarity** can be derived. The corresponding formulas are as follows:

$$Cur_i = \frac{\lambda_1}{\sum_{j=1}^{3} \lambda_j + \varepsilon} \tag{4}$$

$$Pla_i = \frac{\lambda_2 - \lambda_1}{\lambda_3 + \varepsilon} \tag{5}$$

where Cur_i represents the local surface variation, with higher values indicating sharper or more curved regions, while Pla_i measures the degree of planarity of the local neighborhood. The terms $\lambda_1, \lambda_2, \lambda_3$ are the ordered eigenvalues of the covariance matrix ($\lambda_1 \leq \lambda_2 \leq \lambda_3$), and ε is a small positive constant added for numerical stability.

Frequency-Domain Feature. For the frequency-domain features of point clouds, a local spectral representation can be constructed by computing the normalized graph Laplacian and its eigenvalues. Specifically, for the neighborhood of each point, a weighted graph $G_i = (V_i', E_i)$ is constructed, where V_i' represents the set of neighboring points and E_i represents the edges encoding their pairwise geometric relationships. The adjacency matrix W is generated using a Gaussian kernel function. The graph Laplacian matrix is then defined as:

$$L = I - D^{-1/2} W D^{-1/2} \tag{6}$$

where D is the degree matrix and L is the symmetric normalized Laplacian matrix. By solving for the eigenvalues of L, represented as $\gamma_1 \leq \gamma_2 \leq \cdots \leq \gamma_m$, the following spectral features can be extracted:

$$Spe_i = -\sum_{j=1}^{m} \tilde{\gamma}_j \log(\tilde{\gamma}_j), \quad \text{where} \quad \tilde{\gamma}_j = \frac{\gamma_j}{\sum_{j=1}^{m} \gamma_j} \tag{7}$$

where the spectral entropy Spe_i quantifies the distribution of spectral energy, with higher values indicating greater irregularity or structural complexity in the local frequency-domain. Note that the neighborhood used for constructing the graph G_i is identical to the k-nearest neighbors employed for the covariance matrix computation, ensuring geometric and spectral features share the same local context. The edge weights w_{jk} in W are computed via a Gaussian kernel $\exp(-\|p_j - p_k\|^2/\sigma^2)$, where σ is set as the mean distance to the nearest neighbor across the entire point cloud.

Feature Aggregation and Normalization. To obtain segment-level features from point-level computations, we aggregate curvature, planarity, and spectral entropy by averaging over all points within each segment P_{si}:

$$\overline{Cur}_i = \frac{1}{n_i} \sum_{p \in P_{si}} Cur_p, \quad \overline{Pla}_i = \frac{1}{n_i} \sum_{p \in P_{si}} Pla_p, \quad \overline{Spe}_i = \frac{1}{n_i} \sum_{p \in P_{si}} Spe_p \tag{8}$$

Density (Den_i) remains inherently at segment-level. All features are min-max normalized to $[0, 1]$ across the entire point cloud:

$$\hat{F}_i = \frac{F_i - F_{\text{min}}}{F_{\text{max}} - F_{\text{min}}} \tag{9}$$

where $F \in \{Den, \overline{Cur}, \overline{Pla}, \overline{Spe}\}$, and $F_{\text{min}}/F_{\text{max}}$ are the global extrema of feature F over all segments. This ensures equal weighting in the importance score.

Integrated Scoring Function. After segmentation, each region is analyzed using four normalized features: density, curvature, planarity, and spectral entropy. These are integrated into the following scoring function:

$$imp\_score_i = \frac{Den_i \cdot Cur_i \cdot Spe_i}{Pla_i + \epsilon} \tag{10}$$

where the parameter imp_score_i represents the quantitative importance score of the i-th point cloud cbuit. ϵ is a small constant to avoid division by zero. A higher score indicates greater structural or semantic importance of the segment. And the parameter will be transported to the next module to get importance-aware adaptive compression ratios.

The normalized features $\hat{Den}_i, \hat{Cur}_i, \hat{Spe}_i, \hat{Pla}_i \in [0, 1]$ imply $imp\_score_i \geq 0$ with no strict upper bound. However, $\hat{Pla}_i > 0$ (ensured by ϵ) and the product $\hat{Den}_i \cdot \hat{Cur}_i \cdot \hat{Spe}_i \leq 1$ typically constrain scores to $[0, 10^3]$ in practice. Extreme values beyond $[10^{-3}, 10^{3}]$ occur in $< 0.5\%$ of cases and do not affect compression ratio assignment, which relies on relative ordering.

This multiplicative-divisive design is heuristic but motivated by the complementary roles of each feature: density captures point concentration, curvature and entropy reflect local irregularity, while planarity penalizes over-simplified regions. The multiplicative combination highlights regions simultaneously complex across multiple dimensions. Nevertheless, we acknowledge its heuristic nature and propose incorporating data-driven learning or semantic priors in future work to capture richer contextual information (e.g., crop disease patterns) and improve robustness in noisy environments.

3.3 Compression Ratio Mapping Module

After getting the importance scores $imp\_score_1, imp\_score_2, \ldots, imp\_score_n$, we compute compression ratios using log-softmax normalization:

$$r_i = \frac{\exp(\log(ImpScore_i))}{\sum_{j=1}^{N} \exp(\log(ImpScore_j))} = \frac{ImpScore_i}{\sum_{j=1}^{N} ImpScore_j}$$

to ensure the most important segment receives a ratio of 1, we perform max normalization:

$$\tilde{r}_i = \frac{r_i}{\max\limits_j r_j}, \quad \tilde{r}_i \in (0, 1], \quad \max(\tilde{r}_i) = 1$$

which ensures an adaptive, interpretable, and differentiable allocation of compression ratios that reflect the semantic significance of each point cloud segment. The mapping strategy is suitable for integration into subsequent autoencoder architectures.

3.4 Autoencoder Compression Module

Our autoencoder backbone is adapted from DPCC, but instead of compressing the entire point cloud globally, we perform localized encoding and decoding on individual segments. This enables finer compression control and better preservation of key structures.

In the encoding stage, a downsampling process is applied to each point cloud segment. We define a base downsampling rate base_ds which corresponds to the downsampling rate when the importance-aware compression ratio $\tilde{r}_i = 1$. For other segments, the effective downsampling rate is modulated by scaling the base rate with $\tilde{r}_i$:

$$ds_i = base\_ds \times \tilde{r}_i, \quad \tilde{r}_i \in (0, 1] \tag{11}$$

where ds_i represents the downsampling rate for the i-th point cloud segment. This adaptive downsampling enables finer control over the spatial resolution of each segment according to its semantic importance.

Moreover, during the entropy coding stage, we introduce an adaptive compression control mechanism by concatenating the importance-aware compression ratio $\tilde{r}_i$—derived from Sect. 3.3—for each point cloud segment U_i into the corresponding compressed bitstream. Specifically, for each segment, the encoder outputs a latent representation $\mathcal{Z}_i$, which is quantized and entropy coded into a bitstream B_i. We then extend the bitstream by concatenating the importance ratio:

$$\hat{B}_i = \text{concat}(B_i, \tilde{r}_i) \tag{12}$$

where concat(·) represents bitwise concatenation. The appended ratio $\tilde{r}_i \in (0, 1]$ serves as a control token for regulating the *reconstruction fidelity* during decoding. At the decoder side, $\tilde{r}_i$ is first extracted from $\hat{B}_i$ and used to modulate the decoding process, such as adjusting the number of reconstructed points or the spatial resolution. The process can be formalized as:

$$\hat{U}_i = \text{Decoder}(\mathcal{Q}^{-1}(B_i), \tilde{r}_i) \tag{13}$$

where $\mathcal{Q}^{-1}(\cdot)$ represents inverse quantization, and Decoder(·) adapts its reconstruction behavior according to $\tilde{r}_i$. This mechanism ensures that more semantically important regions are reconstructed with higher precision, while less critical regions are compressed more aggressively, thus enabling efficient compression guided by semantic importance while maintaining high reconstruction fidelity for critical regions.

4 Experiment

In this section, we validate the effectiveness of our importance-aware 3D point cloud compression framework on crop datasets. Through comparative experiments, we demonstrate the superiority of our multi-geometry feature perception strategy. Furthermore, based on the implementation of importance-guided adaptive compression, our method achieves a notable improvement in both the compression ratio and the reconstruction accuracy of the point cloud

4.1 Setup

Dataset. Experiments are conducted on our self-collected crop dataset and the publicly available Pheno4D dataset [23]. Our dataset mainly contains 3D point clouds of soybean plants, covering stems, leaves, roots, and soil surfaces, with spatial coordinates for each point. Pheno4D [23] includes similar data for wheat and tomato plants, and some samples also provide light reflectance parameters, serving as color features. These attributes offer valuable cues for improving point cloud segmentation and interpretation.

Environment. Our experiments were conducted on an Ubuntu 18.04 system using Python 3.8 with the PyTorch framework. The training was accelerated with two NVIDIA RTX 3080 GPUs (totaling 20 GB of VRAM). We set the batch size to 1 and trained the model for 50 epochs.

Baseline. In the importance perception module, we compare our method with two representative baselines: a single geometric descriptor using PCA and a learning-based approach, PointNet++ Saliency [37]. In the final compression and reconstruction evaluation stage, we compare our method with DPCC [4].

Evaluation Metrics. We evaluate the performance of the importance-aware module in terms of accuracy, runtime, and GPU memory consumption. In addition, we assess the reconstruction quality using symmetric Chamfer Distance (CD) and point-to-plane PSNR, and evaluate compression efficiency through Bits per Point (Bpp).

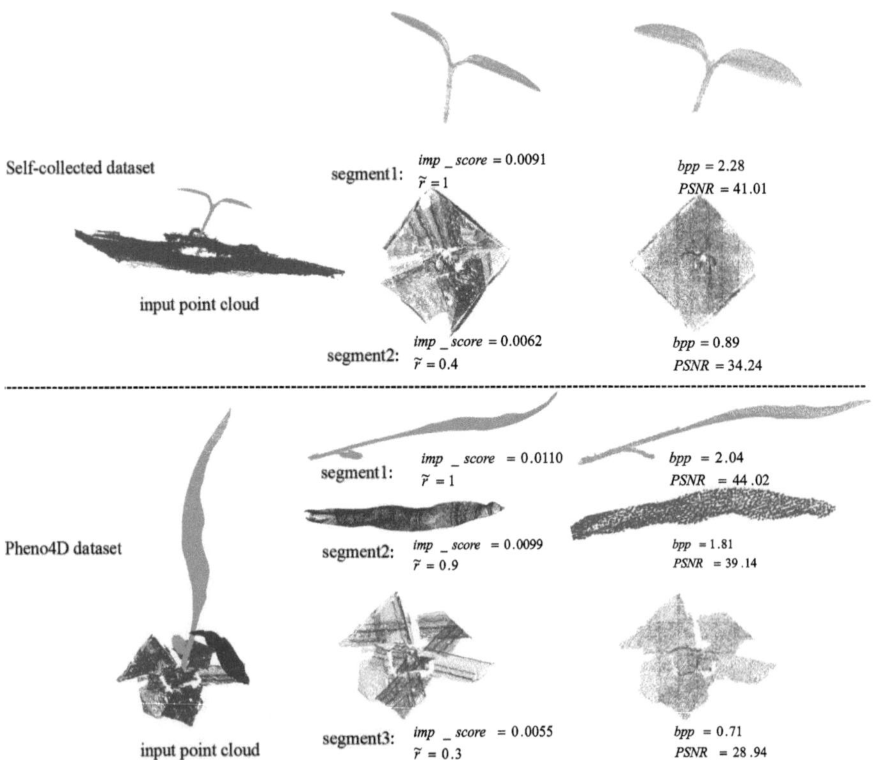

Fig. 4. Experimental results on crop point clouds. The results above are based on the self-collected crop dataset, while the results below are based on the Pheno4D dataset. Taking the latter as an example, the semantic importance ranks as: large leaves and stems > small leaves > ground. Accordingly, the bpp of the compressed point clouds follows the same order, while the PSNR is in reverse. Clearly, high-importance regions retain more details, whereas the ground only preserves coarse geometry, indicating the effectiveness of our method on agricultural datasets.

4.2 Results and Comparison

Importance Perception. Table 1 presents the experimental results related to point cloud importance perception. Compared to the conventional PCA-based method, our approach achieves significantly higher accuracy (+9.7% IoU) by leveraging both multi-geometry features and spectral entropy. While maintaining a much lower inference cost than deep learning-based PointNet++ saliency (less than half the runtime and memory), our method provides a competitive accuracy (82.1% vs. 84.7%), demonstrating its strong potential for real-time and resource-constrained point cloud compression scenarios. In summary, compared to single-geometry perception methods, our approach achieves a significant improvement in accuracy. In contrast to deep learning-based methods, our method maintains importance perception accuracy while substantially reducing computational time and resource consumption.

Compression and Reconstruction. Figure 4 provides an intuitive visualization of the network's compression performance on the agricultural dataset. Table 2 illustrates the performance comparison between the baseline DPCC model and our method, highlighting the results for different point cloud segments based on varying importance distributions. The above results demonstrate that our method achieves favorable compression performance for different segments of the point cloud with varying perceived importance. For regions with higher importance, although the Bpp increases slightly compared to the baseline, the reconstruction accuracy is significantly improved, indicating significantly improved preservation of critical structural details. Conversely, for regions with lower importance, the reconstruction accuracy decreases, but the Bpp reduces substantially, reflecting a notable saving in storage space. Moreover, when considering the point cloud as a whole, the strong internal consistency within each segment allows the combined bit rate to decrease while the overall reconstruction accuracy slightly improves. This confirms that our objective-to leverage importance awareness for compressing point clouds by preserving critical regions, reducing the footprint of less important parts, and enhancing overall performance-has been successfully achieved.

4.3 Ablation Study

For fair comparison, all ablation studies are conducted on Pheno4D with a fixed mean Bpp of 1.38. As shown in Table 3, a = min $ImpScore_i$, b = max $ImpScore_i$; CD[b, a] represents the range of Chamfer Distances. PSNR[a, b] and Bpp[a, b] are the same. Starting from a baseline using uniform segmentation, density-based importance, and linear compression mapping, we replace each component with our proposed PtSeg, IPQ, and CRM modules. Each module enhances importance-aware compression and improves overall performance.

Table 1. Comparison of Importance Perception Methods.

Methods	Accuracy	Runtime (ms)	Memory (MB)
PCA-based Geometric Metric	72.4% (IoU)	**8.3**	**180**
PointNet++ Saliency [37]	**84.7% (AUC)**	47.6	940
Ours (Multi-feature)	82.1% (IoU)	21.4	430

Table 2. Comparison of Compression Methods on Two Datasets.

Dataset	Methods	$\tilde{r}_i$	Chamfer Distance (10^{-2})	Bpp	PSNR
Self-collected	DPCC (baseline)		3.4	1.40	32.40
	Ours (max $ImpScore_i$)	1.0	**1.1**	2.11	**43.86**
	Ours (min $ImpScore_i$)	0.3	7.1	**0.65**	28.24
	Ours (mean $ImpScore_i$)	0.7	2.3	1.38	38.32
Pheno4D	DPCC (baseline)		2.5	2.20	38.54
	Ours (max $ImpScore_i$)	1.0	**0.7**	2.87	**47.66**
	Ours (min $ImpScore_i$)	0.2	5.3	**0.71**	25.12
	Ours (mean $ImpScore_i$)	0.6	2.1	2.01	40.89

4.4 Limitations and Potential Extensions

Although the proposed importance-aware point cloud compression framework achieves favorable results on agricultural datasets, several limitations should be acknowledged.

Limitations. The current method relies on handcrafted geometric and spectral features for importance estimation, which, while efficient and interpretable, may fail to capture complex semantic or contextual information in noisy or diverse environments. Moreover, the segmentation module assumes clear spatial separation between plant structures; in practice, overlaps and occlusions often degrade segmentation quality and affect compression accuracy. The current framework is restricted to static point clouds. Extending it to dynamic or time-varying crop growth data is an important future direction. One promising solution is to incorporate temporal consistency constraints into the importance scoring and compression ratio mapping, ensuring smooth fidelity allocation across consecutive frames. This extension would enable continuous agricultural monitoring and real-time growth analysis.

Potential Extensions. While we hypothesize applicability to domains such as digital heritage and industrial inspection, our current evaluation is limited to agricultural datasets. We plan to include cross-domain experiments in future work-for example, testing on cultural artifact scans or industrial defect datasets-to more rigorously validate the framework's generalizability. In digital heritage preservation, it can help retain fine details of cultural artifacts while compressing less relevant surroundings. Industrial inspection may also benefit by focusing on defect-prone areas with higher precision. Additionally, the framework's resource-efficient design makes it suitable for deployment on edge devices, enabling real-time processing in resource-constrained environments. Supporting temporal point clouds is another promising direction for applications involving dynamic scenes or continuous monitoring.

Table 3. The effectiveness of each component in our method.

Module	CD[b, a](10^{-2})	Mean CD(10^{-2})	PSNR[a, b]	Mean PSNR	Bpp[a, b]
Base	[2.3, 10.2]	2.61	[25.69, 35.21]	32.40	[0.53, 2.70]
+PtSeg	[1.8, 9.3]	2.02	[27.02, 38.59]	34.45	[0.58, 2.57]
+IPQ	[1.5, 8.0]	1.75	[28.11, 40.25]	37.01	[0.63, 2.32]
+CRM	[1.1, 7.1]	1.38	[29.24, 43.86]	38.32	[0.65, 2.11]

5 Conclusion

We introduced an importance-aware 3D point cloud compression framework that quantifies the importance of segments and applies adaptive compression ratios accordingly. The framework preserves crop structures while compressing background regions. Compared with prior works, it achieves a balance between accuracy and efficiency, suitable for smart agriculture. Future research will address current limitations by incorporating data-driven scoring, supporting dynamic point clouds, and validating cross-domain applicability.

Acknowledgements. This work was supported by National Natural Science Foundation of China (No. 62406068), the Natural Science Foundation of Jiangsu Province (No. BK20241299), Key Laboratory of Intelligent Processing Technology for Digital Music (Zhejiang Conservatory of Music), Ministry of Culture and Tourism under Grant 2023DMKLB003, the Big Data Computing Center of Southeast University, and Research Fund for Advanced Ocean Institute of Southeast University, Nantong (No. GP20010002).

References

1. Ballé, J., Laparra, V., Simoncelli, E.P.: End-to-end optimized image compression. arXiv preprint arXiv:1611.01704 (2016)
2. Cui, D., Liu, P., Liu, Y., Zhao, Z., Feng, J.: Automated phenotypic analysis of mature soybean using multi-view stereo 3d reconstruction and point cloud segmentation. Agriculture **15**(2), 175 (2025)

3. Guo, Z., Zhang, Y., Zhu, L., Wang, H., Jiang, G.: TSC-PCAC: voxel transformer and sparse convolution-based point cloud attribute compression for 3d broadcasting. IEEE Trans. Broadcast. (2024)
4. He, Y., Ren, X., Tang, D., et al.: Density-preserving deep point cloud compression. In: Proceedings of IEEE/CVF Conference on Computer Vision and Pattern Recognition (CVPR), pp. 2333–2342 (2022). https://doi.org/10.1109/CVPR52688.2022.00234
5. Huang, S.Y., Hsu, H.Y., Wang, F.: SPOVT: semantic-prototype variational transformer for dense point cloud semantic completion. In: Advances in Neural Information Processing Systems, vol. 35, pp. 33934–33946 (2022)
6. Irfan, M., et al.: Deepview: deep-learning-based users field of view selection in 360° videos for industrial environments. IEEE Internet Things J. **10**(4), 2903–2912 (2021)
7. Laine, S., Aila, T.: Temporal ensembling for semi-supervised learning. In: ICLR (2017)
8. Landrieu, L., Simonovsky, M.: Large-scale point cloud semantic segmentation with superpoint graphs. In: CVPR (2018)
9. Li, J., Wang, J., Chen, J., Xu, T.: Towards robust point cloud recognition with sample-adaptive auto-augmentation. IEEE Trans. Pattern Anal. Mach. Intell. (2025)
10. Li, Z., Wang, W., Wang, Z., Lei, N.: Point cloud compression via constrained optimal transport. In: 2024 IEEE International Conference on Multimedia and Expo (ICME), pp. 1–6. IEEE (2024)
11. Mari, D., Guarda, A.F., Rodrigues, N.M., Milani, S., Pereira, F.: Point cloud geometry scalable coding with a quality-conditioned latents probability estimator. In: 2024 IEEE International Conference on Image Processing (ICIP), pp. 3410–3416. IEEE (2024)
12. Mekuria, R., Blom, K., Cesar, P.: Design, implementation, and evaluation of a point cloud codec for tele-immersive video. IEEE Trans. Circuits Syst. Video Technol. **27**(4), 828–842 (2017)
13. Minnen, D., Ballé, J., Toderici, G.D.: Joint autoregressive and hierarchical priors for learned image compression. In: Advances in Neural Information Processing Systems, vol. 31 (2018)
14. Pang, J., Bui, K., Tian, D.: Pivot-net: heterogeneous point-voxel-tree-based framework for point cloud compression. In: 2024 International Conference on 3D Vision (3DV), pp. 1270–1279. IEEE (2024)
15. Park, Y.W., Klabjan, D.: Bayesian network learning via topological order. J. Mach. Learn. Res. **18**(99), 1–32 (2017)
16. Pauly, M., Gross, M., Kobbelt, L.P.: Efficient simplification of point-sampled surfaces. In: IEEE Visualization, 2002. VIS 2002, pp. 163–170. IEEE (2002)
17. Qi, C.R., Su, H., Mo, K., Guibas, L.J.: Pointnet: deep learning on point sets for 3d classification and segmentation. In: Proceedings of the IEEE Conference on Computer Vision and Pattern Recognition, pp. 652–660 (2017)
18. Qi, C.R., Yi, L., Su, H., Guibas, L.J.: Pointnet++: deep hierarchical feature learning on point sets in a metric space. In: Advances in Neural Information Processing Systems, vol. 30 (2017)
19. Qian, G., et al.: Pointnext: revisiting pointnet++ with improved training and scaling strategies. In: Advances in Neural Information Processing Systems, vol. 35, pp. 23192–23204 (2022)

20. Quach, M., Valenzise, G., Dufaux, F.: Learning convolutional transforms for lossy point cloud geometry compression. In: 2019 IEEE International Conference on Image Processing (ICIP), pp. 4320–4324. IEEE (2019)
21. Rui, Z., et al.: High-throughput proximal ground crop phenotyping systems - a comprehensive review. Comput. Electron. Agric. **224**, 109108 (2024)
22. Schnabel, R., Wahl, R., Klein, R.: Efficient ransac for point-cloud shape detection. In: Computer Graphics Forum, vol. 26, pp. 214–226. Wiley Online Library (2007)
23. Schunck, D., et al.: Pheno4d: a spatio-temporal dataset of maize and tomato plant point clouds for phenotyping and advanced plant analysis. PLoS ONE **16**(8), e0256340 (2021)
24. Song, J., Ma, B., Xu, Y., Yu, G., Xiong, Y.: Organ segmentation and phenotypic information extraction of cotton point clouds based on the cotsegnet network and machine learning. Comput. Electron. Agric. **236**, 110466 (2025)
25. Sun, X., et al.: Morphological estimation of primary branch length of individual apple trees during the deciduous period in modern orchard based on pointnet++. Comput. Electron. Agric. **220**, 108873 (2024)
26. Tarvainen, A., Valpola, H.: Mean teachers are better role models: weight-averaged consistency targets improve semi-supervised deep learning results. In: NeurIPS (2017)
27. Wang, J., Ding, D., Li, Z., Feng, X., Cao, C., Ma, Z.: Sparse tensor-based multiscale representation for point cloud geometry compression. IEEE Trans. Pattern Anal. Mach. Intell. **45**(7), 9055–9071 (2022)
28. Wang, J., Zhu, H., Liu, H., Ma, Z.: Lossy point cloud geometry compression via end-to-end learning. IEEE Trans. Circuits Syst. Video Technol. **31**(12), 4909–4923 (2021)
29. Wang, Y., Sun, Y., Liu, Z., Sarma, S.S., Bronstein, M.M., Solomon, J.M.: Dynamic graph CNN for learning on point clouds. In: ACM TOG (2019)
30. Wang, Y., Sun, Y., Liu, Z., Sarma, S.E., Bronstein, M.M., Solomon, J.M.: Dynamic graph CNN for learning on point clouds. ACM Trans. Graph. (tog) **38**(5), 1–12 (2019)
31. Xu, H., Zhang, X., Wu, X.: Fast point cloud geometry compression with context-based residual coding and INR-based refinement. In: Leonardis, A., Ricci, E., Roth, S., Russakovsky, O., Sattler, T., Varol, G. (eds.) ECCV 2024. LNCS, vol. 15126, pp. 270–288. Springer, Cham (2024). https://doi.org/10.1007/978-3-031-73113-6_16
32. Yang, B., Dong, Z., Liang, F., Mi, X.: Ubiquitous Point Cloud: Theory, Model, and Applications. CRC Press, Boca Raton (2024)
33. Young, S.I.: Radio: rate-distortion optimization for large language model compression. arXiv preprint arXiv:2505.03031 (2025)
34. Yu, X., Tang, L., Rao, Y., Huang, T., Zhou, J., Lu, J.: Point-BERT: pre-training 3d point cloud transformers with masked point modeling. In: Proceedings of the IEEE/CVF Conference on Computer Vision and Pattern Recognition, pp. 19313–19322 (2022)
35. Yuxiao, W., et al.: Pig back transformer: automatic 3d pig body measurement model. Smart Agric. **6**(4), 76 (2024)
36. Zhao, H., Jiang, L., Jia, J., Torr, P.H., Koltun, V.: Point transformer. In: Proceedings of the IEEE/CVF International Conference on Computer Vision, pp. 16259–16268 (2021)
37. Zheng, T., Chen, C., Yuan, J., Li, B., Ren, K.: Pointcloud saliency maps. In: Proceedings of the IEEE/CVF International Conference on Computer Vision, pp. 1598–1606 (2019)

FLUX-Font: Stylized Font Generation Based on Fine-Tuning Pre-trained Diffusion Transformer

Zheyu Li[1,2], Honglie Wang[1,2], Yan-Ming Zhang[1,2], and Cheng-Lin Liu[1,2](✉)

[1] State Key Laboratory of Multimodal Artificial Intelligence Systems, Institute of Automation of Chinese Academy of Sciences, Beijing, China
{lizheyu2025,wanghonglie2023}@ia.ac.cn, {ymzhang,liucl}@nlpr.ia.ac.cn
[2] School of Artificial Intelligence, University of Chinese Academy of Sciences, Beijing, China

Abstract. The generation of Chinese fonts presents both significant challenges and practical value. Despite numerous advances, how to generate high-quality font images with a few reference samples remains an open problem. Existing mainstream approaches typically rely on training small diffusion models from scratch, which is not only computationally intensive and time-consuming, but also prone to errors in glyph structure and inconsistencies in style when handling complex or rare character forms. To address these issues, this paper proposes FLUX-Font, a Chinese font generation method based on the pre-trained large diffusion model FLUX [1]. Particularly, FLUX-Font adopts LoRA-based fine-tuning as its core strategy and uses two separate LoRA modules to fine-tune the glyph and style networks, respectively. To further enhance the performance of the model and the quality of the generated outputs, we incorporate a character-aware loss function that leverages an OCR model to guide the optimization process, thus enhancing the structural stability of generated glyphs. Comprehensive experiments conducted on a benchmark font demonstrate that FLUX-Font consistently outperforms existing methods on various metrics while significantly reducing computational cost and training time. These findings suggest that FLUX-Font offers a promising and efficient approach for Chinese font generation under a few-shot setting.

Keywords: Font Generation · One-shot Image Generation · Flow Matching

1 Introduction

Text and images, as two distinct carriers and mediums of information exchange, play crucial roles in both everyday life and industrial production. The external visual form of text, its font, reflects individual writing habits and styles, which have important meaning in daily communication. Calligraphy, a high-threshold

C. Wallraven et al. (Eds.): ACPR 2025, LNCS 16174, pp. 324–338, 2026.
https://doi.org/10.1007/978-981-95-4395-3_23

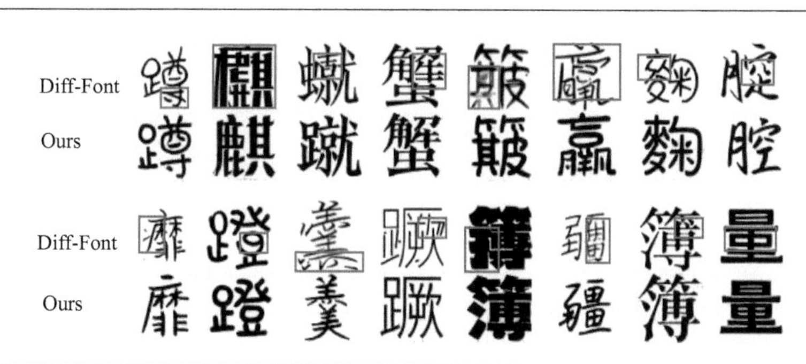

Fig. 1. Comparison results on complex characters show that Diff-Font suffers from stroke omissions/additions, local blur, and structural breakdown, whereas our model maintains structural integrity and visual clarity.

art form, also carries significant artistic value. Moreover, artistic fonts are widely used in commercial and industrial applications such as advertising design, font design, and book publishing due to their aesthetic appeal.

However, font design typically demands significant time and effort. As fonts reflect stylistic features, designing a complete font requires the creation of an entire font library. This is especially burdensome for languages like Chinese, which contains tens of thousands of basic characters. Even when only considering commonly used characters, there are still thousands-designing each one individually is extremely labor-intensive and time-consuming. Therefore, applying image generation techniques to font design has emerged as a promising direction-this task is known as font generation.

The offline font generation task aims to transform textual input into a specific visual form. Specifically, the objective is to use a model and a small number of style reference characters to generate other characters in the same style, thereby composing a complete font library. Taking Chinese as an example, the large number of characters and limited style reference samples make it crucial to maximize the model's ability to learn style from a few examples, framing the task as a few-shot learning problem. On the other hand, the high structural complexity of fonts means that even slight errors can significantly impact the semantic integrity of a character. Each Chinese character has a unique structure, which differentiates this task from other common generation tasks like face generation-although faces are diverse, they share a strong underlying structural consistency. For these reasons, offline stylized handwritten Chinese font generation is both highly meaningful and technically challenging.

In earlier studies, most font generation models were based on the GAN [5] framework, such as AGIS-Net [3], ZiGAN [26], DM-Font [2], and RD-GAN [10]. In recent years, diffusion-based models for font generation have emerged, demonstrating stronger generative capabilities and more precise style transfer, as seen in works like Diff-Font [6] and FontDiffuser [29]. However, the field of font generation still faces several key challenges: First, small models trained from scratch require extensive training time before acquiring even a basic understanding of glyph structure, which is inefficient for optimization and debugging. Second, when generating complex glyphs, issues such as missing or extraneous strokes can occur. Third, existing models often struggle with effective style transfer for fonts with large stylistic differences (as shown in Fig. 1).

To address these persistent challenges in font generation-such as limited style fidelity, poor structural accuracy, and high training costs-we propose FLUX-Font, a novel font generation framework that leverages the capabilities of diffusion models through fine-tuning. Specifically, FLUX-Font is built upon the pre-trained FLUX diffusion model [1], enabling it to inherit powerful generative priors learned from large-scale datasets.

Unlike conventional approaches that rely on training lightweight models from scratch, our method benefits from the robustness and expressiveness of the pre-trained diffusion backbone. This allows FLUX-Font to generate high-quality font images that are both structurally accurate and stylistically faithful, even with limited training data. Moreover, our model requires significantly less computational overhead compared to training a diffusion model from scratch, making it more practical and efficient for real-world applications.

In addition to fine-tuning, we introduce a character-aware loss function designed to explicitly preserve the detailed structure of glyphs during generation. This loss incorporates Optical Character Recognition (OCR) feedback to guide the model toward producing more stable and legible characters. By aligning the generated glyphs with their semantic content, the model learns to better capture the subtle nuances of different styles while maintaining consistent character identity.

In extensive experiments, FLUX-Font consistently outperforms existing small-scale font generation models across multiple metrics, demonstrating its superiority in both visual quality and structural consistency.

In summary, the main contributions of this work are as follows:

- We propose FLUX-Font, a Chinese font generation model based on fine-tuning the pretrained FLUX model. It achieves stable few-shot generation without the need for large-scale training. To the best of our knowledge, this is the first font generation model based on fine-tuning a pretrained model.
- Technically, we introduce two LoRA branches to the FLUX model to inject style and glyph conditions respectively, enabling fine-grained control over the generation process. By employing character recognition loss during training, the glyph correctness of text generation is further improved.
- Extensive experimental results show that FLUX-Font not only achieves superior generation quality compared to existing methods in font generation tasks, but also converges significantly faster during training due to its foundation on a pretrained model, greatly reducing the training time and computational cost.

2 Related Work

2.1 Chinese Font Generation

The font generation task, essentially a style transfer image generation task, has evolved in tandem with the development of generative model frameworks.

In the early stages, generative models mainly relied on deep neural networks to extract high-level features from images, with convolutional neural networks (CNNs) being representative. Gatys et al. [4] proposed an image style transfer model based on CNNs. However, due to the high structural detail requirements of Chinese characters, the model performed poorly in generating recognizable characters, with some being completely illegible.

As generative models advanced, frameworks such as Variational Auto-Encoders (VAE [11]), Generative Adversarial Networks (GAN [5]), and Diffusion Models (DM [8]) emerged, leading to iterative improvements in Chinese font generation frameworks.

Researchers proposed many specialized font generation models based on GANs. Tian et al. [21] introduced the zi2zi model, but it suffered from high training difficulty and could not meet the demands of few-shot scenarios. Yue Gao et al. [3] proposed AGIS-Net, which separates font features into glyph and style features to better handle complex character structures. Qi Wen et al. [26] introduced ZiGAN, adding a reverse mapping and consistency loss similar to CycleGAN [33] to the zi2zi model. These models handle a range of font styles but still struggle with complex Chinese characters.

Some models target local or component-level feature learning. J. Cha et al. [2] proposed DM-Font, introducing component reuse by encoding and storing features from different parts for reuse during character generation. Y. Huang et al. [10] proposed RD-GAN, with three modules dedicated to extracting radicals, rendering details, and constraining overall structure. Song Park et al. [15] introduced MX-Font, using multiple 'local experts' to encode local features and fuse them into style representations for image generation. Tang et al. [20] proposed FS-Font, selecting appropriate reference characters containing the required components based on the target glyph, extracting style features from multiple such references and combining them with content features encoded from the target character for final generation.

2.2 Diffusion Model

The Denoising Diffusion Probabilistic Model (DDPM [8]) generates images by a process of forward diffusion and reverse denoising. Song et al. [19] proposed DDIM, which extends DDPM to a non-Markovian setting, enabling predictions with larger time steps and reducing the number of sampling steps to dozens. Rombach et al. [18] introduced Stable Diffusion, moving the model from pixel space to latent feature space, removing high-frequency noise and detail to perform the diffusion process at the semantic level.

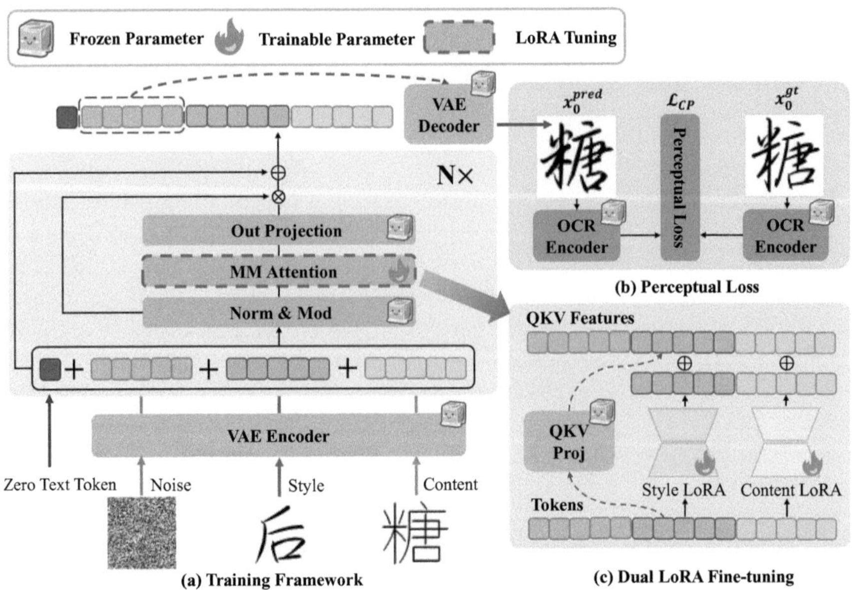

Fig. 2. Overview of the proposed method FLUX-Font. The figure illustrates the annotated framework, including the Dual LoRA [9] injection of style and content conditions, and the character-aware loss.

With the powerful generative capabilities of Diffusion Models, few-shot Chinese character generation has made new progress [17,24]. He et al. [6] proposed Diff-Font, introducing a character attribute encoder to encode properties such as content, style, strokes, and components into latent variables, which are then used as conditions in a diffusion model to generate characters from Gaussian noise. Yang et al. [29] introduced FontDiffuser, incorporating a multi-scale content aggregation (MCA) block and a style contrast refinement (SCR) module. Hua Li et al. [14] proposed HFH-Font, which supports one-step high-quality and high-resolution font image generation, facilitating subsequent vectorization into high-quality vector fonts.

Fine-tuning pretrained models has also gained prominence in scene text rendering, text editing, and other image generation tasks. Frameworks like GlyphControl [28] and AnyText [22], based on fine-tuning Stable Diffusion + ControlNet [30], have been proposed. Models such as EasyControl [32], FLUX-Text [12], and TextFLUX [27], based on the FLUX framework [16], demonstrate even more powerful generative capabilities.

3 Method

In this section, we introduce the technical details of our method. Based on the EasyControl model with several modifications, the model architecture is illustrated in Fig. 2. FLUX-Font is developed based on FLUX.1-dev, which is trained using Flow Matching. We fine-tune the original model with two LoRA modules, for injecting content and style information, respectively. In addition, we incorporate perceptual loss using the PP-OCRv3 [13] model. Since prompts are not required in this experiment, we use an all-zero vector as a substitute for the empty prompt.

3.1 Preliminary

The font generation task is defined as: given a content image $\mathbf{x}_c$ and a style reference image $\mathbf{x}_s$, the goal is to generate an image that preserves the content of $\mathbf{x}_c$ while matching the style of $\mathbf{x}_s$.

To achieve high-quality results, we use FLUX.1-dev as our base model, which is built on the Diffusion Transformer (DiT) architecture. Unlike traditional diffusion models that rely on U-Net, FLUX uses a pure Transformer backbone to better capture complex spatial and stylistic patterns.

At the input stage, the content and style images are concatenated along the spatial dimension to form a single input tensor that combines both structure and style. This tensor is then split into fixed-size patches (16×16), flattened, and projected into patch embeddings via a linear layer. Positional embeddings are added to retain spatial information.

A timestep embedding is also computed and passed through an MLP to match the embedding dimension. Instead of direct addition, it modulates the features in each Transformer block via scale-and-shift operations, conditioning the model on the denoising process.

Inside the Transformer, FLUX stacks multiple layers of multi-head self-attention, optional cross-attention, layer normalization, residual connections, and feed-forward networks. This design allows the model to effectively combine structural and stylistic cues and progressively generate high-quality font images during the diffusion process.

3.2 Flow Matching

Flow Matching is a generative modeling framework that learns a time-dependent velocity field to map one distribution to another using an ordinary differential equation (ODE). Unlike diffusion models that rely on multi-step denoising, Flow Matching directly models the continuous path between a known prior and the target distribution, improving efficiency and training stability.

During the denoising process, given a pair of random variables $\mathbf{x}_0 \sim p_{data}$ and $\mathbf{z}_1 \sim \mathcal{N}(0, I)$. Flow Matching defines an interpolated latent representation $\mathbf{x}_t \in [0, 1]$ as:

$$\mathbf{x}_t = (1 - \sigma_t)\mathbf{x}_0 + \sigma_t \mathbf{z}_1, \tag{1}$$

where σ_t is a monotonically increasing scalar function that controls the interpolation from $\mathbf{x}_0$ to $\mathbf{z}_1$.

The aim of Flow Matching is to train a neural network $\hat{\mathbf{v}}_\theta(\mathbf{x}_t, t, \mathbf{c})$ to predict the velocity vector that maps the intermediate sample $\mathbf{x}_t$ back to the trajectory defined by $(\mathbf{x}_0, \mathbf{z}_1)$. The training loss is defined as:

$$\mathcal{L}_{simple} = \mathbb{E}_{t,\mathbf{x}_0,\mathbf{z}_1}[\omega_t \cdot ||\hat{\mathbf{v}}_\theta(\mathbf{x}_t, t, \mathbf{c}) - (\mathbf{z}_1 - \mathbf{x}_0)||_2^2], \tag{2}$$

where $\hat{\mathbf{v}}_\theta(\mathbf{x}_t, t, \mathbf{c})$ is the predicted velocity field, ω_t is a time-dependent weighting function, $\mathbf{c}$ denotes optional conditional information, such as scene images, prompt embeddings, or attention masks.

During inference, a sample $\mathbf{z}_1 \sim \mathcal{N}(0, I)$ is drawn and evolved backward in time using the learned velocity field:

$$\frac{d\mathbf{x}_t}{dt} = \hat{\mathbf{v}}_\theta, \quad t \in [1, 0]. \tag{3}$$

This ODE is solved numerically to obtain $\mathbf{x}_t$, a sample from the target data distribution. Conditional inputs $\mathbf{c}$ can guide the generation process in conditional generation tasks.

3.3 LoRA Fine-Tuning

We fine-tuned the transformer network using two LoRA modules, which separately control the style and glyph conditions. We introduce conditional branches by concatenating tokens, including both content and style conditions. LoRA (Low-Rank Adaptation) is applied to fine-tune the pre-trained model. In the Diffusion Transformer framework, guided by the attention mechanism [23], the input consisting of noise $\mathbf{X}_n$, content condition $\mathbf{X}_c$, and style condition $\mathbf{X}_s$ is encoded as Query, Key, and Value vectors:

$$\mathbf{Q}^i = \mathbf{W}_\mathbf{Q}\mathbf{X}^i, \quad \mathbf{K}^i = \mathbf{W}_\mathbf{K}\mathbf{X}^i, \quad \mathbf{V}^i = \mathbf{W}_\mathbf{V}\mathbf{X}^i, \qquad i \in \{n, c, s\}. \tag{4}$$

However, since $\mathbf{W}_\mathbf{Q}, \mathbf{W}_\mathbf{K}, \mathbf{W}_\mathbf{V}$ are globally shared parameters, both content and style conditions would be processed identically, which is undesirable. To address this, we adopt a dual-LoRA fine-tuning strategy combined with masking to enable distinct encoding for content and style. Specifically, the LoRA mechanism for a Transformer linear projection is defined as:

$$\hat{\mathbf{W}}_\mathbf{m}^j = \mathbf{W}_\mathbf{m} + \Delta\mathbf{W}_\mathbf{m}^j, \qquad \mathbf{m} \in \{\mathbf{Q}, \mathbf{K}, \mathbf{V}\}, \quad j \in \{s, c\}. \tag{5}$$

$$\Delta\mathbf{W}^j = \mathbf{B}^j\mathbf{A}^j, \qquad j \in \{s, c\}. \tag{6}$$

where $\Delta\mathbf{W}$ represents the low-rank trainable adaptation, $\mathbf{A}_\mathbf{Q}, \mathbf{A}_\mathbf{K}, \mathbf{A}_\mathbf{V} \in \mathbb{R}^{r\times d}$ are LoRA down-projection weights, and $\mathbf{B}_\mathbf{Q}, \mathbf{B}_\mathbf{K}, \mathbf{B}_\mathbf{V} \in \mathbb{R}^{d\times r}$ are LoRA up-projection weights, r is the LoRA rank($r \ll d$).

To ensure separate encoding for content and style, we create two different LoRA branches and apply distinct masks to the input.

Given the inputs from the three branches $\mathbf{X}_n, \mathbf{X}_s, \mathbf{X}_c$ and their token lengths n_n, n_s, n_c, let the whole input to be:

$$\mathbf{X} = [\mathbf{X}_n; \mathbf{X}_s; \mathbf{X}_c]. \tag{7}$$

The content LoRA branch input $\mathbf{X}_{content\_only}$ and the style LoRA branch input $\mathbf{X}_{style\_only}$ are calculated respectively as:

$$\mathbf{X}_{content\_only} = \mathbf{X} \odot \mathbf{M}_{content}, \quad \mathbf{M}_{content} = [\mathbf{0}, \mathbf{0}, \mathbf{1}]. \tag{8}$$

$$\mathbf{X}_{style\_only} = \mathbf{X} \odot \mathbf{M}_{style}, \quad \mathbf{M}_{style} = [\mathbf{0}, \mathbf{1}, \mathbf{0}]. \tag{9}$$

Here, $\odot$ denotes element-wise multiplication, and the masks ensure that each LoRA branch only receives the relevant condition while zeroing out the others, effectively learning disentangled condition representations.

The **QKV** computation with the added mask is as follows:

$$\begin{aligned}
\mathbf{Q} &= \mathbf{W_Q X} + \Delta \mathbf{W}^s_\mathbf{Q} \mathbf{X}_{style_only} + \Delta \mathbf{W}^c_\mathbf{Q} \mathbf{X}_{content_only}. \\
\mathbf{K} &= \mathbf{W_K X} + \Delta \mathbf{W}^s_\mathbf{K} \mathbf{X}_{style_only} + \Delta \mathbf{W}^c_\mathbf{K} \mathbf{X}_{content_only}. \\
\mathbf{V} &= \mathbf{W_V X} + \Delta \mathbf{W}^s_\mathbf{V} \mathbf{X}_{style_only} + \Delta \mathbf{W}^c_\mathbf{V} \mathbf{X}_{content_only}.
\end{aligned} \tag{10}$$

Furthermore, although the concatenated token sequences in the attention layers already allow cross-attention between different branches (noise, style, and content), redundant computations-such as using style queries to attend to noise keys-may interfere with the training process. To achieve finer control over attention and enforce isolated self-attention and cross-attention among noise, style, and content tokens across different layers within the DiT framework, we introduce causal attention and a causal mask:

$$M(i,j) = \begin{cases} 0, & \text{if } i < n_n \text{ or } j < n_n (i \text{ or } j \text{ belong to noise branch}) \\ 0, & \text{if } i, j \text{ belong to the same branch (style or content)} \\ -\infty, & \text{otherwise} \end{cases} \tag{11}$$

The final attention computation is given by:

$$Attention(\mathbf{Q}, \mathbf{K}, \mathbf{V}) = Softmax(\frac{\mathbf{QK}^T}{\sqrt{d_k}} + M)\mathbf{V}. \tag{12}$$

3.4 Perceptual Loss

During inference, we observe that the model has achieved promising results in style extraction and fusion. However, it still struggles to preserve the structural integrity of glyphs. To improve the glyph quality of the generated images, we introduce a character-aware perceptual loss $\mathcal{L}_{CP}$ using the pre-trained PP-OCRv3 [13] model. The training objective is to ensure that the generated character images can still be correctly recognized by the OCR model as the original characters, preserving glyph shape and preventing stroke loss.

During the training phase, we first reconstruct $\mathbf{x}_0$ for each single-step noise prediction:

$$\hat{\mathbf{x}}_0 = \mathbf{x} - \sigma \cdot \hat{\epsilon}. \tag{13}$$

Then, $\hat{\mathbf{x}}_0$ is decoded through the VAE to obtain the predicted character image $\mathbf{x}_{pred}$. This image and the corresponding ground-truth character label $\mathbf{x}_{gt}$ are both fed into the pre-trained PP-OCRv3 model to extract feature maps $f_{pred}, f_{gt} \in \mathbb{R}^{h \times w \times c}$, and the perceptual loss is computed between them:

$$\mathcal{L}_{CP} = \frac{1}{hw}||f_{pred} - f_{gt}||_2^2. \tag{14}$$

After introducing the character-aware perceptual loss, the final training objective consists of two components: the diffusion reconstruction loss and the perceptual loss. Assuming a unified weighting, the final objective can be written as:

$$\mathcal{L}_{total} = \mathcal{L}_{simple} + \alpha \cdot \mathcal{L}_{CP}, \tag{15}$$

where α is a predefined hyperparameter.

4 Experiments

4.1 Dataset and Quantitative Metrics

Chinese Character Dataset. We constructed a database containing 450 Chinese fonts, with each font covering 6,625 unique Chinese characters. Among them, 400 fonts are used as the training set, and the remaining 50 fonts are used as the test set. For each font, we randomly partition the 6,625 characters into two subsets: 5,000 characters that are seen during training (Unseen Font Seen Character, UFSC), and 1,625 characters that are unseen during training (Unseen Font Unseen Character, UFUC).

Quantitative Evaluation Metrics. In our quantitative evaluation, we adopt SSIM [25], L1 distance, FID [7], and LPIPS [31] as the evaluation metrics to assess generation quality.

4.2 Implementation Details

We use FLUX.1-dev as the pre-trained model. During training, we use four A6000 GPUs (each with 48GB of memory). The image size is set to 64×64, the batch size is 16, and the learning rate is 1e−4. The first stage of training runs for 300,000 steps, and the second stage, which incorporates character-aware loss, runs for an additional 210,000 steps. During the inference stage, we set the number of inference steps to 25.

Table 1. Quantitative comparison of different models on UFSC, UFUC, and ALL character sets across Easy, Hard, and Average font categories. Bold numbers indicate the best performance.

Models		easy				hard				average			
		FID↓	L1↓	SSIM↑	LPIPS↓	FID↓	L1↓	SSIM↑	LPIPS↓	FID↓	L1↓	SSIM↑	LPIPS↓
UFSC	FontDiffuser	27.2157	**0.1511**	**0.5187**	**0.1046**	80.5340	**0.2028**	0.3481	**0.1840**	54.4190	**0.1775**	0.4317	**0.1452**
	Diff-Font	28.8294	0.2090	0.3563	0.1607	71.7494	0.2274	0.3071	0.2097	50.2894	0.2182	0.3317	0.1852
	SD+ControlNet	110.7103	0.2006	0.3647	0.1994	176.8065	0.2404	0.3273	0.2192	144.7599	0.2211	0.3454	0.2096
	FLUX-Font	**24.6825**	0.1680	0.5053	0.1374	**70.8442**	0.2317	**0.3778**	0.2437	**48.2344**	0.2005	**0.4417**	0.1916
UFUC	FontDiffuser	30.7328	**0.1548**	**0.5068**	**0.1060**	84.6479	**0.2042**	0.3446	**0.1845**	58.2405	**0.1800**	0.4240	**0.1460**
	Diff-Font	34.4056	0.2079	0.3595	0.1572	78.1819	0.2276	0.3076	0.2077	56.2938	0.2178	0.3358	0.1825
	SD+ControlNet	–	–	–	–	–	–	–	–	–	–	–	–
	FLUX-Font	**28.6399**	0.1734	0.4940	0.1418	**74.8498**	0.2337	**0.3742**	0.2456	**52.2163**	0.2042	**0.4329**	0.1947
ALL	FontDiffuser	26.7918	**0.1520**	**0.5158**	**0.1050**	79.9257	**0.2032**	0.3472	**0.1841**	53.9009	**0.1781**	0.4298	**0.1454**
	Diff-Font	27.8855	0.2087	0.3571	0.1599	70.7662	0.2275	0.3072	0.2092	49.3259	0.2181	0.3322	0.1845
	SD+ControlNet	110.7103	0.2006	0.3647	0.1994	176.8065	0.2404	0.3273	0.2192	144.7599	0.2211	0.3454	0.2096
	FLUX-Font	**24.1312**	0.1694	0.5048	0.1385	**70.1916**	0.2322	**0.3769**	0.2442	**47.6314**	0.2014	**0.4396**	0.1924

4.3 Comparison Methods

We compare our method with the two most effective models in the field: FontDiffuser [29] and Diff-Font [6], representing small models trained from scratch. Both models are trained on our constructed dataset for fair comparison. Additionally, we fine-tune the large pretrained model Stable Diffusion v1.5 (SD1.5) using ControlNet [30] on the same dataset to evaluate the impact of pretraining on generation performance. To ensure that the model fits well on the dataset, we train it from scratch on the constructed dataset.

To further compare the training efficiency between our method and scratch-trained small models, we evaluate model checkpoints of FontDiffuser, Diff-Font, and our method (FLUX-Font) under the same batch size and at equivalent training steps.

4.4 Quantitative Evaluation

Quantitative results are presented in Table 1. To facilitate further analysis, we divide all fonts evenly into two categories-Easy and Hard-based on their FID scores. Additionally, we classify characters into two groups: UFSC (unseen fonts with seen characters during training) and UFUC (unseen fonts with unseen characters). FLUX-Font outperforms Diff-Font across almost all metrics and consistently achieves lower FID scores than FontDiffuser. This advantage becomes more pronounced as the font style complexity increases, highlighting the superior generalization capability of large-scale models. Compared to the fine-tuning-based SD approach, FLUX-Font demonstrates significantly better performance on all metrics, indicating that the generative power of the base pretrained model plays a crucial role in determining the final model quality.

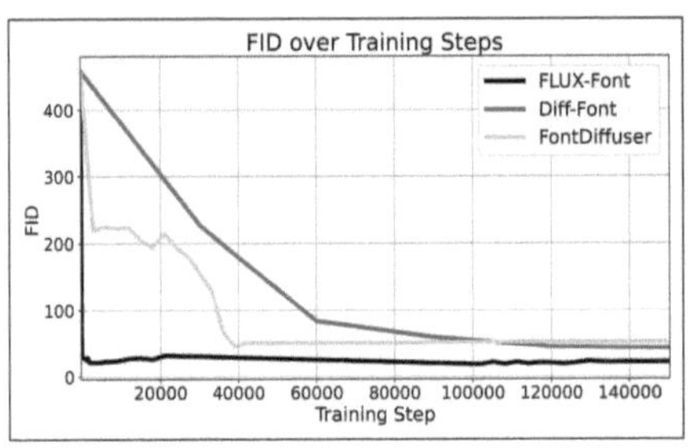

(a) FID curves with linear step axis.

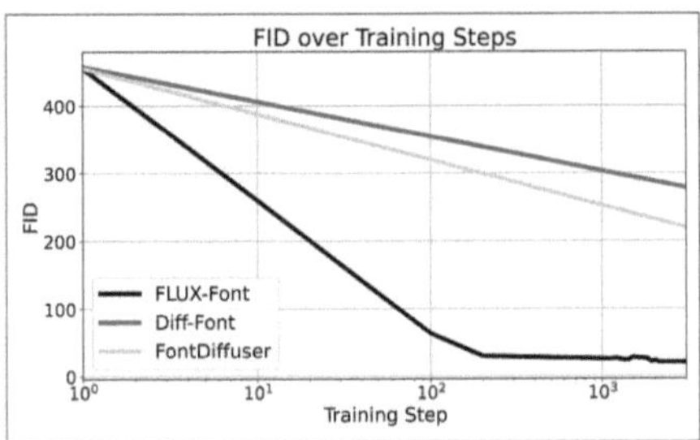

(b) FID curves with logarithmic step axis.

Fig. 3. FID reduction curves during training for three models on the same single-font generation task. The x-axis represents training steps in (a) linear and (b) logarithmic scale.

4.5 Training Speed Comparison

To compare the training speed of the three models, we recorded the training checkpoints every 30,000 steps. Additionally, within the first 030,000 steps, we recorded checkpoints every 3,000 steps. For FLUX-Font, due to its rapid performance improvement, we further recorded checkpoints every 100 steps within the first 3,000 steps. For each checkpoint, we generated a complete set of characters in the same font and calculated the corresponding FID scores.

As shown in Fig. 3, FLUX-Font achieves rapid convergence within the first 1,000 training steps, significantly faster than both FontDiffuser and Diff-Font.

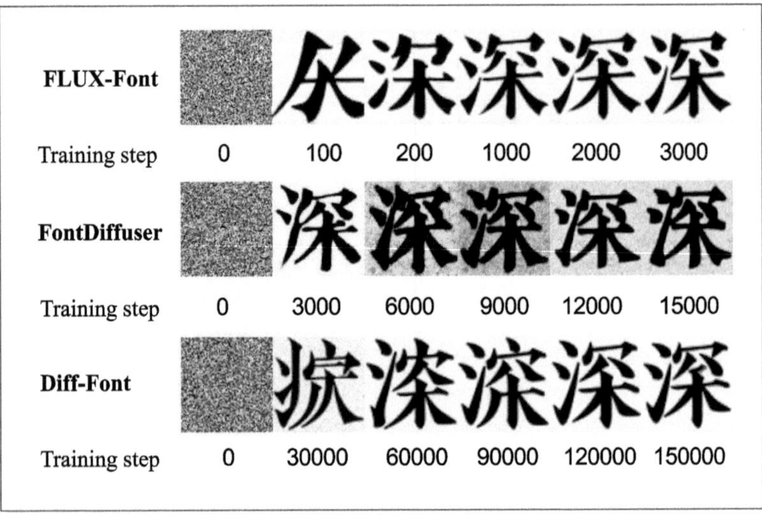

Fig. 4. Qualitative comparison of glyph generation quality at different training steps for FLUX-Font, FontDiffuser, and Diff-Font.

The visual comparison is shown in Fig. 4. It can be observed that FLUX-Font completes the glyph learning process within the first 1,000 training steps, and is already capable of generating reasonably high-quality Chinese characters. In contrast, FontDiffuser still exhibits minor stroke additions at 3,000 steps, and only gradually removes noise in the subsequent steps. Diff-Font, however, suffers from persistent structural issues throughout the recorded 100,000 steps, and even at 150,000 steps, unwanted stroke additions can still be seen.

This faster convergence not only demonstrates its superior learning efficiency but also leads to a substantial reduction in training resource consumption.

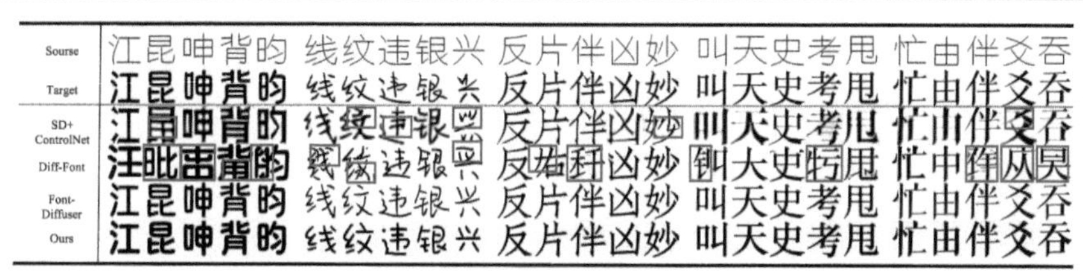

(a) Easy-style font with simple characters.

(b) Easy-style font with complex characters.

(c) Hard-style font with complex characters.

Fig. 5. Qualitative comparison under different style and glyph conditions. (a) Easy-style font with simple characters. (b) Easy-style font with complex characters. (c) Hard-style font with complex characters.

4.6 Qualitative Comparison

The qualitative comparison is shown in Fig. 5. In this comparison, we categorize the test cases into three groups based on font and character complexity: (1) easy-style fonts with simple characters Fig. 5a, (2) easy-style fonts with difficult characters Fig. 5b, and (3) hard-style fonts with difficult characters Fig. 5c. The classification of font style difficulty is consistent with the quantitative evaluation, while character difficulty is determined by stroke count-specifically, the top 1,000 characters with the most strokes (out of 6,625) are designated as difficult characters.

From the results, we observe that SD+ControlNet produces lower-quality generations overall. Diff-Font demonstrates strong style representation ability but tends to confuse structures when generating simple characters. FontDiffuser performs well in preserving glyph shapes but lags behind our method, FLUX-Font, in capturing fine stylistic details such as stroke texture. FLUX-Font achieves the best visual consistency with the reference styles.

5 Conclusion

In this paper, we propose FLUX-Font, a Chinese offline font generation method based on large pre-trained models. Built upon the pre-trained model FLUX, our approach employs the LoRA fine-tuning strategy with a dual LoRA mechanism to control both content and style, enabling more refined guidance during the font generation process. Compared to traditional models trained from scratch, FLUX-Font leverages the prior knowledge of large pre-trained models and applies lightweight fine-tuning through LoRA modules, significantly reducing training complexity and computational cost while maintaining high generation quality and effective style transfer. Furthermore, a character-aware loss is introduced to enhance glyph recognizability. Experimental results demonstrate that these strategies improve the generation performance, particularly in terms of style diversity, structural accuracy, and perceptual quality.

Acknowledgements. This work has been supported by the National Natural Science Foundation of China (NSFC) grant 62276258.

References

1. Black Forest Labs: FLUX (2024). https://github.com/black-forest-labs/flux. Accessed 21 June 2025
2. Cha, J., Chun, S., Lee, G., Lee, B., Kim, S., Lee, H.: Few-shot compositional font generation with dual memory. In: Vedaldi, A., Bischof, H., Brox, T., Frahm, J.-M. (eds.) ECCV 2020. LNCS, vol. 12364, pp. 735–751. Springer, Cham (2020). https://doi.org/10.1007/978-3-030-58529-7_43
3. Gao, Y., Guo, Y., Lian, Z., Tang, Y., Xiao, J.: Artistic glyph image synthesis via one-stage few-shot learning. ACM Trans. Graph. (ToG) **38**(6), 1–12 (2019)

4. Gatys, L.A., Ecker, A.S., Bethge, M.: Image style transfer using convolutional neural networks. In: Proceedings of the IEEE Conference on Computer Vision and Pattern Recognition, pp. 2414–2423 (2016)
5. Goodfellow, I., et al.: Generative adversarial networks. Commun. ACM **63**(11), 139–144 (2020)
6. He, H., et al.: Diff-font: diffusion model for robust one-shot font generation. Int. J. Comput. Vision **132**(11), 5372–5386 (2024)
7. Heusel, M., Ramsauer, H., Unterthiner, T., Nessler, B., Hochreiter, S.: GANs trained by a two time-scale update rule converge to a local nash equilibrium. In: Advances in Neural Information Processing Systems, vol. 30 (2017)
8. Ho, J., Jain, A., Abbeel, P.: Denoising diffusion probabilistic models. In: Advances in Neural Information Processing Systems, vol. 33, pp. 6840–6851 (2020)
9. Hu, E.J., et al.: LoRa: low-rank adaptation of large language models. In: International Conference on Learning Representations (ICLR). arXiv preprint arXiv:2106.09685 (2022)
10. Huang, Y., He, M., Jin, L., Wang, Y.: RD-GAN: few/zero-shot Chinese character style transfer via radical decomposition and rendering. In: Vedaldi, A., Bischof, H., Brox, T., Frahm, J.-M. (eds.) ECCV 2020. LNCS, vol. 12351, pp. 156–172. Springer, Cham (2020). https://doi.org/10.1007/978-3-030-58539-6_10
11. Kingma, D.P., Welling, M.: Auto-encoding variational bayes. arXiv preprint arXiv:1312.6114 (2013)
12. Lan, R., Bai, Y., Duan, X., Li, M., Sun, L., Chu, X.: Flux-text: a simple and advanced diffusion transformer baseline for scene text editing. arXiv preprint arXiv:2505.03329 (2025)
13. Li, C., et al.: Pp-ocrv3: more attempts for the improvement of ultra lightweight OCR system. arXiv preprint arXiv:2206.03001 (2022)
14. Li, H., Lian, Z.: HFH-font: few-shot Chinese font synthesis with higher quality, faster speed, and higher resolution. ACM Trans. Graph. (TOG) **43**(6), 1–16 (2024)
15. Park, S., Chun, S., Cha, J., Lee, B., Shim, H.: Multiple heads are better than one: few-shot font generation with multiple localized experts. In: Proceedings of the IEEE/CVF International Conference on Computer Vision, pp. 13900–13909 (2021)
16. Peebles, W., Xie, S.: Scalable diffusion models with transformers. In: Proceedings of the IEEE/CVF International Conference on Computer Vision, pp. 4195–4205 (2023)
17. Ren, M.S., Zhang, Y.M., Chen, Y.: Decoupling layout from glyph in online Chinese handwriting generation. In: International Conference on Learning Representations (ICLR) (2025)
18. Rombach, R., Blattmann, A., Lorenz, D., Esser, P., Ommer, B.: High-resolution image synthesis with latent diffusion models. In: Proceedings of the IEEE/CVF Conference on Computer Vision and Pattern Recognition, pp. 10684–10695 (2022)
19. Song, J., Meng, C., Ermon, S.: Denoising diffusion implicit models. arXiv preprint arXiv:2010.02502 (2020)
20. Tang, L., et al.: Few-shot font generation by learning fine-grained local styles. In: Proceedings of the IEEE/CVF Conference on Computer Vision and Pattern Recognition, pp. 7895–7904 (2022)
21. Tian, Y.: zi2zi: Master Chinese calligraphy with conditional adversarial networks, **3**(2) (2017). [Internet] https://github.com/kaonashi-tyc/zi2zi
22. Tuo, Y., Xiang, W., He, J.Y., Geng, Y., Xie, X.: Anytext: multilingual visual text generation and editing. arXiv preprint arXiv:2311.03054 (2023)

23. Vaswani, A., et al.: Attention is all you need. In: Advances in Neural Information Processing Systems, vol. 30 (2017)
24. Wang, H., Ren, M., Zhang, Y.M., Yin, F., Liu, C.L.: Template-guided cascaded diffusion for stylized handwritten Chinese text-line generation. In: International Conference on Document Analysis and Recognition (2025)
25. Wang, Z., Bovik, A.C., Sheikh, H.R., Simoncelli, E.P.: Image quality assessment: from error visibility to structural similarity. IEEE Trans. Image Process. **13**(4), 600–612 (2004)
26. Wen, Q., Li, S., Han, B., Yuan, Y.: ZiGAN: fine-grained Chinese calligraphy font generation via a few-shot style transfer approach. In: Proceedings of the 29th ACM International Conference on Multimedia, pp. 621–629 (2021)
27. Xie, Y., et al.: Textflux: an OCR-free DIT model for high-fidelity multilingual scene text synthesis. arXiv preprint arXiv:2505.17778 (2025)
28. Yang, Y., et al.: Glyphcontrol: glyph conditional control for visual text generation. In: Advances in Neural Information Processing Systems, vol. 36, pp. 44050–44066 (2023)
29. Yang, Z., Peng, D., Kong, Y., Zhang, Y., Yao, C., Jin, L.: Fontdiffuser: one-shot font generation via denoising diffusion with multi-scale content aggregation and style contrastive learning. In: Proceedings of the AAAI Conference on Artificial Intelligence, vol. 38, pp. 6603–6611 (2024)
30. Zhang, L., Rao, A., Agrawala, M.: Adding conditional control to text-to-image diffusion models. In: Proceedings of the IEEE/CVF International Conference on Computer Vision, pp. 3836–3847 (2023)
31. Zhang, R., Isola, P., Efros, A.A., Shechtman, E., Wang, O.: The unreasonable effectiveness of deep features as a perceptual metric. In: Proceedings of the IEEE Conference on Computer Vision and Pattern Recognition, pp. 586–595 (2018)
32. Zhang, Y., Yuan, Y., Song, Y., Wang, H., Liu, J.: Easycontrol: adding efficient and flexible control for diffusion transformer. arXiv preprint arXiv:2503.07027 (2025)
33. Zhu, J.Y., Park, T., Isola, P., Efros, A.A.: Unpaired image-to-image translation using cycle-consistent adversarial networks. In: Proceedings of the IEEE International Conference on Computer Vision, pp. 2223–2232 (2017)

MC2SC: Signal Transformation for Multi-channel Signal Processing

Sunil Kumar Kopparapu(✉)

TCS Research, Tata Consultancy Services Limited, Mumbai, India
sunilkumar.kopparapu@tcs.com
http://www.tcs.com

Abstract. In this paper, we propose a signal transformation, using basic signal processing, to combine the individual time synchronised channels of a low-bandwidth multi-channel signal, like the EEG into a single-channel high-bandwidth signal, like audio. Further the signal transformation is bi-directional, namely the multi-channel signal can be reconstructed back from the single-channel signal. As a motivation, such a transformation when applied to EEG signals (a) allows processing a multi-channel signal as a single-channel, and (b) allows the use of single-channel pre-trained models, for multi-channel signal processing and analysis. We demonstrate the usefulness of the proposed signal transformation on a publicly available EEG dataset.

1 Introduction

Electroencephalography (EEG) is a method to record the spatial electrical activity of the brain non-intrusively. Typically the instrument used to record EEG has several electrodes mounted on a cap which when placed on the head can sense the electrical activity of the brain at the location or in the spatial vicinity of the electrode. Each electrode captures the brain activity underneath the electrode at a low sampling rate, typically between 250 and 1000 Hz. As a consequence if one uses an EEG instrument with n electrodes, there are n-channels of signals that are simultaneously recorded from each of electrode and are time synchronized. So any analysis on the EEG signal implies processing all the n electrode output signals together to exploit the property that these signal are time synchronized. This, EEG signal, can be considered as an example of a multi-channel signal.

There are several disadvantages and challenges when processing multi-channel signals, like EEG. For example, to mention a few, (a) multi-channel data involves multiple signals recorded simultaneously, which makes it more difficult to identify relevant patterns and interpret results compared to single-channel signals, (b) processing and analyzing multi-channel data requires more computational resources and time longer processing times, (c) different channels may be correlated due to shared sources of brain activity or artifacts, throwing up challenges during analysis, use of techniques to disentangle the signals, (d)

C. Wallraven et al. (Eds.): ACPR 2025, LNCS 16174, pp. 339–354, 2026.
https://doi.org/10.1007/978-981-95-4395-3_24

interpretation of results from multi-channel EEG can be difficult, relating the observed activity in different channels to specific cognitive processes or brain regions, (e) lack of standardization in terms of the number of electrodes used to record EEG data or the sampling rate at which the signal is digitized leads to variability in results across studies; making it difficult to compare findings or even build pre-trained foundational models as is common in single-channel signals like audio and speech, (f) a risk of overfitting models to the data, especially if the number of data samples is not sufficiently large relative to the number of channels, leading to poor generalization while analyzing unseen data, and (g) visualizing multi-channel EEG data requires methods to represent both the spatial and temporal aspects in a way that is interpretable. In this paper, we propose a simple yet effective *signal transformation* that overcomes some of these disadvantages of processing and analyzing a multi-channel signal. The proposed transformation allows for representation of a multi-channel signal as a single-channel signal where the transformed signal retains the properties of the original multi-channel signal, making the transformation reversible. The single-channel signal not only allows for better visualization of the signal, but also allows for use of pre-trained foundational models that are available in plenty for single-channel signals, like speech and audio.

The multi-channel EEG signals are low-frequency (low-bandwidth), ranging from 0.1 Hz to about 100 Hz, signals. For the purposes of brain activity analysis, EEG signals are typically divided into different frequency bands, namely, δ, θ, α, σ, β, and γ. These frequency bands are essential in EEG signal processing to understand different brain states and activities. Analyzing and processing multi-channel EEG data often requires specialized knowledge and training in signal processing, and neuroscience.

It is well known, from basics of signal processing literature that signals need to be sampled at twice the maximum frequency present in the signal (also called the Nyquist rate [8]) to preserve the signal characteristics. Since the frequency bands of interest (0.1 to 100 Hz) are low, most EEG instruments sample the brain activities at rates, typically in the range of 250 to 1000 Hz. Observe, in contrast, music, speech and audio signals are sampled at 44.1 kHz for CD quality and typical sampling rates used in speech and audio signal processing is either 8 or 16 kHz. Formally, the Nyquist rate is a fundamental concept in signal processing, which refers to the minimum rate at which a signal must be sampled to accurately represent the signal without losing any information in terms of fidelity. Specifically, the Nyquist rate is twice the highest frequency (bandwidth) of the signal [8]. Our motivation to explore a method for transforming a multi-channel low-bandwidth signal into a single-channel high-bandwidth signal comes from two key observations:

1. Lack of Pre-trained Models for Low-bandwidth multi-channel EEG: There are currently no large pre-trained models specifically designed for low-bandwidth EEG signals. This is largely due to the lack of standardization in multi-channel EEG data, which varies both in terms of the number of electrodes used and the sampling rates.

2. Availability of Pre-trained Models for High-bandwidth single-channel Signal: In contrast, there are several well-established pre-trained foundational models, such as VGGish, that are available for high-bandwidth single-channel audio signals. These models can be leveraged for various applications, making them highly useful.

By developing a mechanism to transform a low-bandwidth multi-channel EEG signal into a single-channel high-bandwidth signal, we aim to bridge this gap and potentially enable the use of existing pre-trained models for EEG analysis. Focusing on the question, *"Can we use existing pre-trained single-channel (audio or speech) models to analyze or process multi-channel (EEG) signals?"*, in this paper, we propose a transformation, based on simple signal processing, that allows representing a multi-channel low-bandwidth EEG signal as a single-channel high-bandwidth signal. The proposed transformation is bi-directional (reversible) meaning that the single-channel high-bandwidth signal can be converted back into the original multi-channel low-bandwidth EEG signals without any loss of information. This is the main contribution of the paper. The rest of the paper is organized as follows. We describe the proposed transformation to convert a multi-channel low-bandwidth signal into a single-channel high-bandwidth signal in Sect. 2, we show in Sect. 3 the utility of such a transformation by conducting a set of experiments on a publicly available EEG dataset for odour and subject classification. We conclude in Sect. 4 and provide future directions.

2 Multi-channel to Single-Channel (MC2SC) Transform

Consider a p-channel EEG signal (multi-channel, p electrodes), of duration T (in seconds) sampled at a sampling frequency of f_s Hz. Let $\{e_i[n = 1, \cdots, N]\}_{i=1}^{p}$ denote the p-channel EEG signal where $e_i[n]$ denotes the nth sample in the ith channel and $N = T \times f_s$. The maximum frequency component in $e_i[n]$ is $(f_s/2)$ which is also the bandwidth occupied by each of the individual p-channel's. Note that the cumulative bandwidth of the p-channel EEG signal, if one were to stack the p-channel's one on top of other is $(p \times f_s/2)$, though each individual channel has a bandwidth of $(f_s/2)$. The essential idea of the proposed signal transformation is to *transform* the p-channel EEG signals into a single-channel signal while retaining the individual characteristics of all the p channels of the p-channel EEG signal.

Consider $s[n']$ to be the transformed signal, sampled at a sampling frequency of F_s, namely, the bandwidth of $s[n']$ is $(F_s/2)$. We now describe a process to transform $\{e_i[n : 1, \cdots, N]\}_{i=1}^{p}$, the p-channel EEG signal, each channel having a bandwidth of $(f_s/2)$ into a single-channel $s[n']$ having a bandwidth of $(F_s/2)$, namely,

$$\{e_i\}_{i=1}^{p} \Longleftrightarrow s. \tag{1}$$

Note that the transformation is bi-directional, namely, we are able to reconstruct $\{e_i\}_{i=1}^{p}$ from s when there is a priori knowledge of how s was obtained from $\{e_i\}_{i=1}^{p}$. The complete implementation of constructing s from $\{e_i\}_{i=1}^{p}$ is shown in Algorithm 1. We now describe, in detail, the transformation process based on simple signal processing. There are essentially four steps in the transformation process.

Step #1 For each of the p channels, we compute the well known Fast Fourier Transform (FFT) as shown in Line 9, Algorithm 1, namely,

$$e_i[n] \xrightarrow{FFT} E_i[k] \quad \text{where,} \quad E_i[k] = \sum_{n=0}^{N-1} e_i[n] \exp^{-j\frac{2\pi}{N}kn}, \tag{2}$$

for $k = 0, \cdots, (N-1)$ and has the same number of samples as e_i. Note that the maximum frequency component in E_i is $(f_s/2)$ and the kth sample, $E_i[k]$ corresponds to the amplitude of the frequency component $\left(k \times \left(\frac{f_s/2}{(N-1)}\right)\right)$ Hz in the signal e_i.

Step #2 Now we *stretch* E_i so that the stretched $E_i^{stretch}$ has a maximum frequency of $(F_s/2p)$. This is essentially an index stretching operation, where we take $E_i[k]$ where k runs from $1, \cdots, N$ and map those indices to a new set of indices, namely, k' which runs from $1, \cdots, \alpha N$, where $\alpha = (F_s/2p)$. As captured in Line 11, Algorithm 1, the frequency domain signal $E_i[k]$ is re-indexed to construct $E_i^{stretch}[k']$, namely,

$$E_i[k] \xrightarrow{k'=\alpha k} E_i^{stretch}[k'] \tag{3}$$

where $\alpha = (F_s/2p)$ and $k = 0, \cdots, (N-1)$. Note that the N samples in E_i would result in αN samples in $E_i^{stretch}$, namely, $k' = 0, \cdots, \alpha(N-1)$. Observe that the value of $E_i^{stretch}[k']$ is the same as the value of the kth sample, $E_i[k]$. However, $E_i^{stretch}[k']$ corresponds to the frequency component $\left(\alpha \times k \times \left(\frac{f_s/2}{(N-1)}\right)\right)$ Hz while $E_i[k]$ corresponds to the frequency component $\left(k \times \left(\frac{f_s/2}{(N-1)}\right)\right)$ Hz. While the maximum frequency component in $E_i[k]$ is $(f_s/2)$, the maximum frequency component in $E_i^{stretch}$ is $(F_s/2p)$ This makes sure that when all the p-channels are stacked together, the combined bandwidth of the p-channel's is $(F_s/2)$. The process of stretching or reindexing from the implementation perspective is best understood with the help of Algorithm 1.

Step #3 We now concatenate or stack the p-channels of $\{E_i^{stretch}[k']\}_{i=1}^p$ on top of one another as shown in Fig. 2 to form a single-channel signal of bandwidth $(F_s/2)$. Namely,

$$\{E_i^{stretch}[k']\}_{i=1}^p \xrightarrow{\text{stack}} S[k']. \tag{4}$$

Note that we could stack the p-channels in $p!$ different ways. However, in our implementation, without loss of generality, we choose to stack the p-channels such that the $(i+1)^{th}$ channel was stacked on top of the ith channel as shown in Fig. 2. Line 12 to 21 in Algorithm 1 captures the implementation of the stacking $\{E_i^{stretch}[k']\}_{i=1}^p$ to construct $S[k']$.

Step #4 As the last step in the signal transformation process we compute the inverse FFT (IFFT) of $S[k']$ to construct the time domain signal $s[n']$ (Line 23, Algorithm 1), namely,

$$S[k'] \stackrel{IFFT}{\longrightarrow} s[n'] \quad \text{where,} \quad s[n'] = \frac{1}{N}\sum_{k'=1}^{N} S[k'] \exp^{j\frac{2\pi}{N}k'n'}. \tag{5}$$

Note that the bandwidth of the time domain single-channel signal $s[n']$ is $(F_s/2)$.

Figure 1 shows the ith channel of the EEG signal $e_i[n]$ (top), and its spectral representation $E_i[k]$ (middle) and the stretched version of $E_i[k]$, namely, $E_i^{stretch}[k']$ (bottom). For visual clarity, we use spectrogram of the signals $e_i[n]$ instead of showing the frequency domain signal $E_i[k]$. Figure 2 shows the complete process of constructing a higher bandwidth single-channel signal from low bandwidth multi-channel signals, namely,

$$\overbrace{\{e_i[n]\}_{i=1}^{p} \stackrel{FFT}{\longrightarrow}}^{\text{Step\#1}} \underbrace{\{E_i[k]\}_{i=1}^{p} \stackrel{k'=\alpha k}{\longrightarrow}}_{\text{Step\#2}} \overbrace{\{E_i^{stretch}[k']\}_{i=1}^{p} \stackrel{\text{stack}}{\longrightarrow}}^{\text{Step\#3}} \underbrace{S[k'] \stackrel{IFFT}{\longrightarrow} s[n']}_{\text{Step\#4}}. \tag{6}$$

The implementation of the process of transforming a multi-channel signal into a single-channel signal (6) is captured in Algorithm 1. As mentioned earlier, the transformation process uses fairly well known signal processing techniques and is is self-explanatory. However, we would like to mention that $\texttt{linspace}(0, f_s, N')$ (Line 6) is a well known `NumPy` function that generates N' evenly spaced values between 0 and f_s. The whole process of stacking or reindexing (4) is implemented as shown from Line 12 to 21 which allows to transfer the amplitude associated with the stretched i^{th} (Line Line 11) channel frequency of the EEG signal to the *closest* frequency available in the desired signal, S obtained using (Line 6) described earlier.

It should be noted that by reversing the sequence of operations seen in (6), we can get back $\{e_i[n]\}_{i=1}^{p}$ from $s[n']$. Namely,

$$s[n'] \stackrel{FFT}{\longrightarrow} \underbrace{S[k']}_{(F_s/2)} \stackrel{\text{unstack}}{\longrightarrow} \{\underbrace{E_i[k']}_{(F_s/2p)}\}_{i=1}^{p} \stackrel{k=(1/\alpha)k'}{\longrightarrow} \{\underbrace{E_i[k]}_{(f_s/2)}\}_{i=1}^{p} \stackrel{IFFT}{\longrightarrow} \{e_i[n]\}_{i=1}^{p} \tag{7}$$

Typical values of f_s is around 250 Hz (EEG signal) while typical F_s is 8 or 16 kHz (audio). We hypothesize that $s[n']$ constructed as described in this section represents all the information in the p channel's, namely, $\{e_i[n]\}_{i=1}^{p}$ in a single-channel signal, namely, $s[n']$. The process of this multi-channel to single-channel transformation allows one to (a) process a single-channel signal $s[n']$ instead of processing all the p-channels $\{e_i[n]\}_{i=1}^{p}$, (b) make use of any of the known audio processing tools and algorithms, especially when F_s is chosen to be 8 or 16 kHz, and more importantly (c) allows the use of existing pre-trained models trained on single-channel signal.

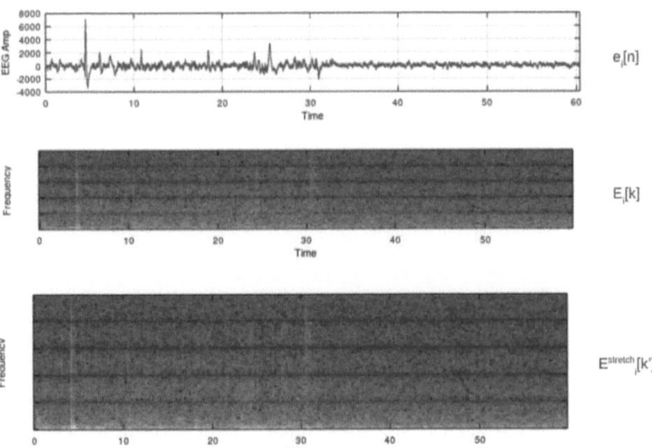

Fig. 1. Sample of a single-channel EEG signal of bandwidth $(f_s/2)$ (Top, e_i), spectral representation of e_i (Middle, E_i), and stretched spectral representation with bandwidth $(F_s/2p)$ (Bottom, $E_i^{stretch}$).

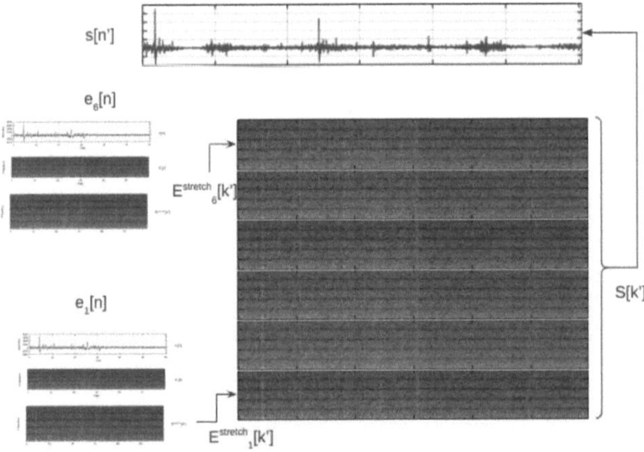

Fig. 2. $p = 6$ channel EEG with each channel having a bandwidth of $(f_s/2)$ is stretched to $E_i^{stretch}$ having a bandwidth $((f_s/2) * 6)$ and stacked into a single-channel signal (s) with bandwidth $(F_s/2)$. Implementation details in Algorithm 1.

Fortunately, unlike multi-channel signals, there are quite a few pre-trained models for single-channel signals. For example, VGGish [4] is a popular pre-trained model that has been used for audio classification tasks, YAMNet [11] is another pre-trained deep learning model for sound event detection, DeepSpeech [3] and Wav2Vec [12] are popular pre-trained models used for speech recognition tasks. While almost all of the pre-trained models have not been trained on EEG *like* data, we reckon that they can be used to extract embeddings or features from the transformed signal s which can be treated as features corresponding to all the p channels of EEG, namely, $\{e_i\}_{i=1}^p$.

Algorithm 1. Constructing $s[n']$ from $\{e_i[n]\}_{i=1}^{p}$

procedure MULTI2SINGLE($\{e_i[1:N]\}_{i=1}^{p}, f_s, F_s$)
$\quad\quad$ ▷ f_s : sampling rate of e_i, N : number of samples
$\quad\quad$ ▷ F_s : sampling rate of desired signal s
$\quad t_{sec} = N/f_s$ ▷ t_{sec} : duration of e_i in seconds
$\quad f_{band} = F_s/2p$; ▷ f_{band} : bandwidth stretched e_i
$\quad freq[1:N] = [0:N-1] \times \frac{f_s}{(N-1)}$
$\quad\quad$ ▷ freq corresponding to N sample
$\quad N' = t_{sec} * F_s$; ▷ Samples in the single-channel
$\quad F_{desired}[1:N'] = \texttt{linspace}(0, F_s, N')$;
$\quad S[1:N'] = 0$; $s[1:N'] = 0$ ▷ Initialize
$\quad$ **for** $i = 1:p$ **do**
$\quad\quad E_i[1:N] = \text{FFT}(e_i[1:N])$ ▷ Eq (2); Step #1
$\quad\quad l_f = (i-1) * f_{band}$;
$\quad\quad f_{stretch}[1:N] = l_f + \left(freq[1:N] \times \frac{f_{band}}{f_s}\right)$
$\quad\quad\quad$ ▷ Eq (3); Stretching.
$\quad\quad$ **for** $j = 1:N$ **do** ▷ Eq (4); Stacking
$\quad\quad\quad min_v = 10^{10}; min_1 = -1; min_2 = -1$
$\quad\quad\quad$ **for** $k = 1:N'$ **do**
$\quad\quad\quad\quad$ **if** $(|F_{desired}[k] - f_{stretch}[j]| \le min_v)$ **then**
$\quad\quad\quad\quad\quad min_v \leftarrow |F_{desired}[k] - f_{stretch}[j]|$
$\quad\quad\quad\quad\quad min_1 \leftarrow j; min_2 \leftarrow k$
$\quad\quad\quad\quad$ **end if**
$\quad\quad\quad$ **end for**
$\quad\quad\quad S[min_2] = E_i[min_1]$;
$\quad\quad$ **end for**
$\quad$ **end for**
$\quad s[1:N'] = \text{IFFT}(S[1:N'])$ ▷ Eq (5); Construct s from S
end procedure

3 Experimental Analysis

We use the widely used, publicly available odour-EEG dataset (EEGDOT) [7] for training (a) odour-classification [10] system and (b) subject identification [9] system. The EEGDOT dataset consists of a 32 channel EEG signal recorded using the Cerebus system from 11 healthy individuals (8 males and 3 females), right-handed, aged 24.9 ± 3.0 years in response to 13 odour stimuli (rose, caramel, rotten smell, canned peaches, excrement, mint, tea, coffee, rosemary, jasmine, lemon, vanilla, and lavender). Two of the 32 channels are reference channels, making it, $p = 30$ usable channels for analysis. The electrodes for collecting EEG are arranged according to the international 10-20 system, and sampled at $f_s = 1$ kHz. Each sample collected was for a duration of 10 seconds ($N = 10000$ samples), called a trial. In total, EEGDOT dataset has 11 (Subjects) $\times$ 13 (odours) $\times$ 35 (trials) resulting in a total of 5005 30-channel EEG samples. We partition the EEGDOT dataset into non-intersecting $80:20$ train and test sets. The training set consists of 4004 samples while the remaining 1001 samples were used for test. We retained the split in all our experiments for consistency in experiments.

We converted the 30-channel ($p = 30$) EEG signal into a single-channel high bandwidth audio signal of $F_s = 16$ kHz as described in the previous section following Steps #1, #2, #3, and #4 implemented as mentioned in Algorithm 1. In the first set of experiments, using the single-channel high bandwidth (16 kHz) transformed signal, we extracted the spectrogram (for example, Fig. 1 (middle) is the spectrogram of the e_i) using 64 ms (1024 samples) as the window and 48 ms (768 samples) as the overlap. The resulting size of the spectrogram was 513×621, which is a representation of all the 30 EEG channels *simultaneously*. So each EEG trial was represented by a spectrogram matrix of size 513×621. We used a Convolutional Neural Network (CNN) architecture [5] as shown in Table 1 for the purpose of odour (13 class, 157945997 trainable parameters) and subject (11 class, 157945739 trainable parameters) classification. The CNN was implemented in `keras` and no hyper parameter tuning was done. As is common, 20% of the train data was used for the purposes of validation. So we had 3203, 801, 1001 samples for training, validation and test respectively with no overlap.

Table 1. 2D-CNN architecture used for [Odour] and Subject Classification. Using spectrogram features extracted from the transformed single-channel signal s.

Layer (type)	Output Shape	Param #
spectrogram (Conv2D)	(None, 511, 619, 32)	320
max_pooling2d (MaxPooling2D)	(None, 255, 309, 32)	0
conv2d (Conv2D)	(None, 253, 307, 64)	18496
max_pooling2d (MaxPooling2D)	(None, 126, 153, 64)	0
flatten (Flatten)	(None, 1233792)	0
dense (Dense)	(None, 128)	157925504
[odour] subject (Dense)	(None, *[13]* 11)	*[1677]* 1419

The CNN architecture (Table 1) with a batch size of 32 was run for 150 epochs for odour classification. The training and validation losses (Fig. 3a) and accuracy is shown in Fig. 3b. The test accuracy for 13 class odour classification was 51.85%. The CNN architecture (Table 1) with a batch size of 32 was run for 25 epochs for subject (11 class) classification. The training and validation losses are shown in Fig. 3c while the accuracy is shown in Fig. 3d for subject classification. The test accuracy for 11 class subject classification was 99.70%. As seen in Table 2, we achieve the best performance for both odour and subject classification when a single-channel s is used instead of the multi-channel $\{e_i\}_{i=1}^{30}$. Also seen in Table 2 are the performance of SVM (27.63%) and RF (29.85%) classifiers on hand crafted features for odour classification as reported in [10] and subject classification [9]. The total number of features used were 720 which included energy, entropy, discrete wavelet transform for each of the bands.

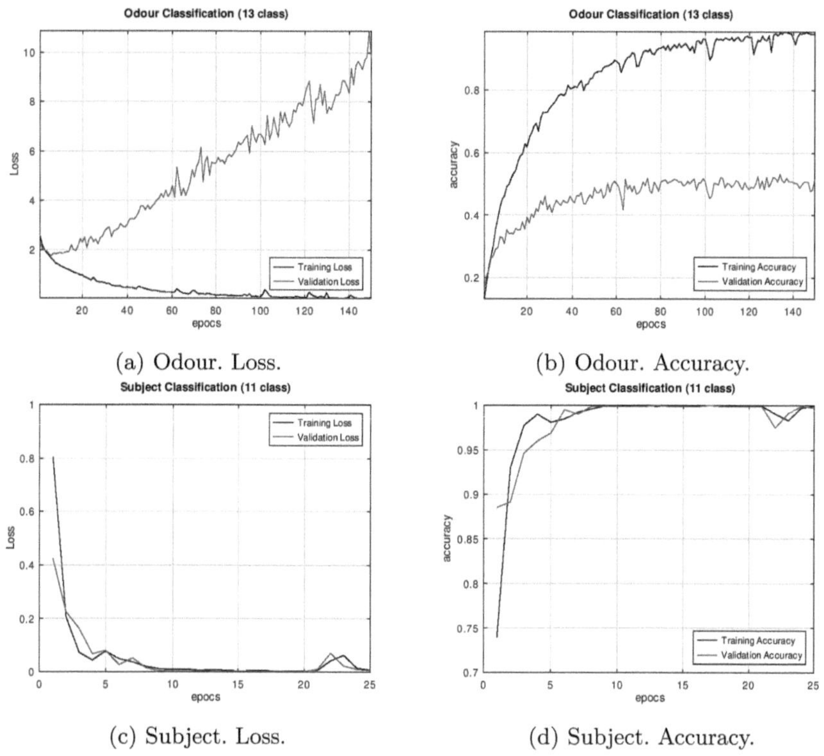

Fig. 3. Odour, Subject Classification. Train, Validation plots. For 2D-CNN architecture (Table 1) using spectrogram of the transformed signal as the input features.

Table 2. Odour and Subject Classification when the transformed single-channel (s) is used versus multi-channel signal ($\{e_i\}_{i=1}^{30}$) for different features and classifiers.

Signal	Features (size)	Classifier	Odour	Subject
s	Spectrogram (513×621)	2D-CNN	**51.85**	**99.70**
$\{e_i\}_{i=1}^{30}$	EEG features (720)	RF	29.85 [10]	97.94 [9]
$\{e_i\}_{i=1}^{30}$	EEG features (720)	SVM	27.63 [10]	93.55 [9]

As mentioned earlier, one of the benefits of transforming a multi-channel EEG signal into a single-channel high bandwidth signal is that it allows the use of existing pre-trained models trained on massive amounts of single-channel data. The use of pre-trained models allows to extract embeddings from these models which can be used as features rather than using handcrafted features for the downstream classification tasks. In the next set of experiments, we used `VGGish` [1] and `YAMNet` [2] pre-trained model to extract embeddings, because both of these models have been trained for acoustic or audio event detection. We discounted the use of other pre-trained models like `Wav2Vec` or `DeepSpeech` because they are specifically trained for human speech; we feel that the transformed EEG signal is closer to an acoustic event like signal compared to human speech.

The `VGGish` model gives an embedding of size 128 dimension at 1 Hz. As a consequence, the 10 second 30-channel EEG signal, transformed to a single-channel signal (s), had a representation in the form of a feature vector of size 10×128. We used a shallow 2D-CNN architecture as shown in Table 3(a). As seen in Table 4 the performance of the odour classification (2066571 trainable parameters) was 30.27% while the performance was 85.91% for subject classification (2066829 trainable parameters). In both the cases, we did not do any hyper-parameter turning and used a batch size of 32 and trained for 1000 epochs. The training and validation accuracy are shown in Fig. 4a and Fig. 4b for odour and subject classification respectively. Along similar lines, the `YAMNet` model resulted in an embedding of size 20×521, where 521 corresponds to the number of audio event classes that `YAMNet` was trained for. Using a shallow 2D-CNN as mentioned in Table 3(b) we trained for both odour (19097997 trainable parameters) and subject classification (19097739 trainable parameters). As seen in Table 4 the performance of a 2D-CNN architecture using `YAMNet` embeddings derived from the transformed signal (s) was 33.17% and 94.21% for odour and subject classification respectively. The performance for both odour and subject classification is better when `YAMNet` pre-trained model is used compared to when `VGGish` is used; the improvement when `YAMNet` pre-trained model is used shows a relative improvement of $\approx 9\%$ for both odour $\left(\left(\frac{33.17-30.37}{30.27}\right) \times 100\right)$ and subject $\left(\left(\frac{94.21-85.91}{85.91}\right) \times 100\right)$ classification. However, as seen in Table 4, while the performance, when a pre-trained model is used, is not as good as when the spectrogram features (513×621) of s is used, it nevertheless demonstrates the effective use of existing pre-trained audio models, even though they have not been explicitly trained to process and thereby extracting features low bandwidth multi-channel EEG signals. It should be noted that one of the challenges in processing EEG signals is not only the ability to select as appropriate channel or a set of channels (from the multi-channel signal data) but also the ability to determine the right set of hand-crafted features that best suit the task. Using pre-trained models on the transformed signal s eliminates this challenge. This experimental result demonstrates the effective use of pre-trained models to enable building shallow machine learning models (compare the architecture in Table 1 and Table 3) for odour and subject classification.

For the purpose of comparison, we use the original 30-channel EEG signal to extract spectrogram for each of the 30 EEG channels separately using `librosa`'s short term Fourier transform, to obtain 30 spectrograms of dimension 62 freqency bins $\times$ 141 time frames, in effect we had a $30 \times 62 \times 141$ tensor representing the EEG signal. We used a 3D-CNN (see Table 5) architecture consisting of 2, convolution followed by average pooling layers followed by Flatten, Dense, BatchNormaization, Dropout(0.5) and Dense layers to train a model for odour and subject classification. We used the default hyper-parameters with a batch size of 32 and 100 epochs. The performance for odour and subject classification was 26.17% and 96.1% respectively (see Table 6). Clearly, deriving spectrogram

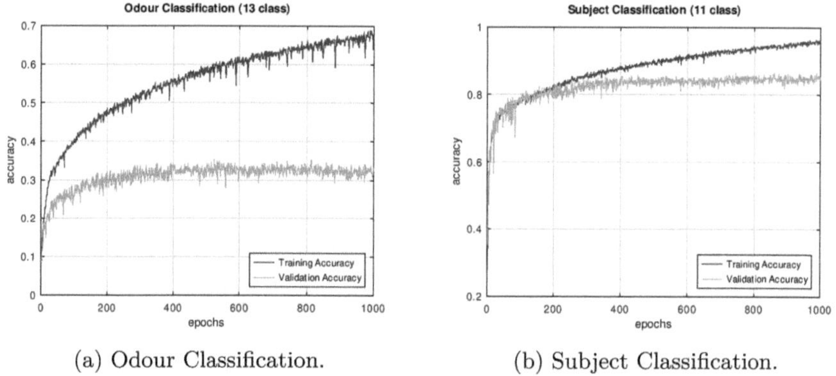

(a) Odour Classification. (b) Subject Classification.

Fig. 4. Odour and Subject classification train and validation accuracy plots for 2D-CNN architecture (Table 1(a)) using `VGGish` embeddings.

Table 3. Shallow 2D-CNN architecture using (a) `VGGish` embeddings and (b) `YAMNet` embeddings derived from the transformed single-channel signal s.

Layer (type)	Output Shape	Param #
vggish (Conv2D)	(None, 8, 126, 64)	640
max_pooling2d_2 (MaxPooling2D)	(None, 4, 63, 64)	0
flatten_1 (Flatten)	(None, 16128)	0
dense_1 (Dense)	(None, 128)	2064512
[odour] subject (Dense)	(None, [13] 11)	[1677] 1419

(a) 2D-CNN architecture with `VGGish` embeddings.

Layer (type)	Output Shape	Param #
yamnet (Conv2D)	(None, 18, 519, 64)	640
max_pooling2d_2 (MaxPooling2D)	(None, 9, 259, 64)	0
flatten_1 (Flatten)	(None, 149184)	0
dense_1 (Dense)	(None, 128)	19095680
[odour] subject (Dense)	(None, [13] 11)	[1677] 1419

(b) 2D-CNN architecture with `YAMNet` embeddings.

features from the transformed single-channel signal (s) performs better (99.70%) than the same spectrogram features derived from the original multi-channel $\{e_i\}_{i=1}^{30}$ signal (96.10%) for subject classification. Similar enhanced performance is observed for odour classification, compare 51.85% to 26.17% (Table 6). This enhanced performance can be attributed to the proposed signal transformation process that allows the deep learning architecture to *view all the* 30*-channels*

Table 4. Odour and Subject Classification using the transformed single-channel signal (s) to demonstrate the use of existing pre-trained single-channel models (`VGGish` and `YAMNet`.

Signal	Features (size)	Classifier	Odour	Subject
s	Spectrogram (513×621)	2D-CNN	**51.85**	**99.70**
s	`VGGish` (10×128)	2D-CNN	30.37	85.91
s	`YAMNet` (20×521)	2D-CNN	33.17	94.21
s	`VGGish` (1280)	RF	38.26	87.01
s	`VGGish` (1280)	SVM	16.98	68.53
s	`YAMNet` (10420)	RF	38.66	93.91
s	`YAMNet` (10420)	SVM	25.77	88.71

Table 5. 3D-CNN Architecture used with $\{e_i\}_{i=1}^{30}$. Total trainable parameters for odour and subject classification is 12083277 and 12082251 respectively.

Layer (type)	Output Shape	Param #
conv3d (Conv3D)	(None, 28, 60, 139, 32)	896
average_pooling3d (AveragePooling3D)	(None, 14, 30, 69, 32)	0
conv3d_1 (Conv3D)	(None, 12, 28, 67, 64)	55360
average_pooling3d_1 (AveragePooling3D)	(None, 6, 14, 33, 64)	0
conv3d_2 (Conv3D)	(None, 4, 12, 31, 128)	221312
max_pooling3d (MaxPooling3D)	(None, 2, 6, 15, 128)	0
flatten (Flatten)	(None, 23040)	0
dense (Dense)	(None, 512)	11796992
batch_normalization (BatchNormalization)	(None, 512)	2048
dropout (Dropout)	(None, 512)	0
[odour] subject (Dense)	(None, [13] 11)	[6669] 5643

Table 6. Odour and Subject Classification using spectrogram derived from the transformed signal s and the original multi-channel signal $\{e_i\}_{i=1}^{30}$.

Signal	Features (size)	Classifier	Odour	Subject
s	Spectrogram (513×621)	2D-CNN	**51.85**	**99.70**
$\{e_i\}_{i=1}^{30}$	Spectrogram ($30 \times 62 \times 141$)	3D-CNN	26.17	96.10

together as a single unit rather than have them viewed as a stack of 30 spectrograms.

To sum up the experimental observations as seen from Table 2, Table 4, and Table 6,

1. The best performance for odour (subject) classification is 51.85% (99.70%) is obtained using the spectrogram features extracted from the single-channel transformed signal (s) using a 2D-CNN architecture. The improved performance compared to any features (spectrogram or handcrafted) extracted from the 30 individual EEG channels (e_i) demonstrates the usefulness of transforming a multi-channel low-bandwidth signal into a single-channel signal.
2. While both `YAMNet` and `VGGish` are pre-trained models that are used for audio classification tasks, the use of `YAMNet` embeddings show better performance compared to use of `VGGish` embeddings across different classifiers for both odour and subject classification tasks (Table 4). While the relative improvement in performance is around 8–9% for 2D-CNN and RF classifiers it is much higher (34% for subject and 51% for odour classification) for SVM classifier.
3. The performance of both odour and subject classification task using embeddings derived from pre-trained models (`VGGish`, `YAMNet`) from the transformed signal (s) is lower compared to the using spectrogram as features extracted from either s or $\{e_i\}_{i=1}^{30}$. This is to be expected because the spectrograms are in some sense a better representation of the signal compared to the embeddings extracted from pre-trained models which have been trained on audio signals that are different from the EEG signals.
4. The best performance using pre-trained models is achieved using `YAMNet` embeddings + 2D-CNN for subject classification (94.21%) and `YAMNet` embeddings + RF for odour classification (38.66%) as seen in Table 4.
5. Use of `YAMNet` or `VGGish` features demonstrate superior performance (except SVM classifier) compared to extracting hand crafted features from all the 30 EEG channels (Tables 2 and 4). This demonstrates that the features extracted as embedding from the single-channel signal (s) using models not specifically trained for EEG signals perform better than even the hand-crafted signal derived from the multi-channel signal (e_i).
6. The difference in performance between odour (best 51.85%) and subject (best 99.70%) classification can be attributed to the EEGDOT data. Figure 5 shows the t-SNE plot [6] for the training data; better clustered for subject (Fig. 5b) than for odour (Fig. 5a) correlates with the poorer performance for odour classification.

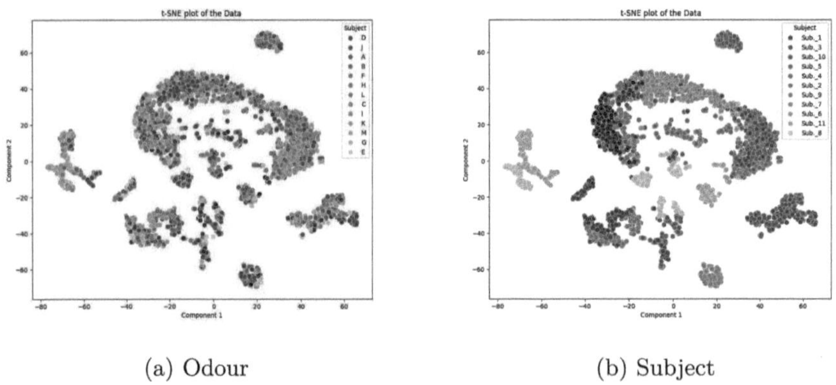

(a) Odour (b) Subject

Fig. 5. t-SNE plot of the Training data used for (a) odour classification, (b) for subject classification (better clustering).

4 Conclusions

In this paper, we proposed a simple yet effective signal processing method to transform a multi-channel low bandwidth EEG signal into a single-channel high bandwidth signal. The signal transformation is such that it retains all the properties of the original multi-channel signal in the single-channel signal; further the transformation is bi-directional, meaning it allows for reconstructing the multi-channel signal for the single-channel signal. This is the main contribution of this paper. We motivated the need for such a transformation, primarily because the signal transformation allows for a comprehensive, time synchronized view of the multi-channel signal in a single-channel waveform. This is useful, especially in an end-to-end deep learning setup, because there is no extra burden on the end-to-end deep learning setup to *learn the association between different channels* in the multi-channel signal. Single-channel representation derived from the multi-channel signal allows for all the channels to be simultaneously available for processing. Another motivation is that this transformation enables exploit the use of existing pre-trained single-channel acoustic models especially because of the absence of any such pre-trained models for multi-channel signals like EEG. Experimental results show that the single-channel high bandwidth signal is able to retain the properties of the EEG signal very effectively; indicated by the superior performance for both odour and subject classification compared to hand crafted features extracted from multi-channel EEG signal.

4.1 Discussion

While we have experimented with varying number of convolution layers, different convolution sizes, and varying number of nodes in the dense layers and presented the best performing architectures, we have not experimented with hype-parameter tuning. There is plenty of scope for further experimentation using different deep learning architectures and hype-parameter tuning. However, as emphasized earlier, the focus of this paper was on demonstrating that a simple signal processing transformation allowed for a better representation of a multi-channel signal.

The use of pre-trained models trained on acoustic data for acoustic event detection of classification task in the context of EEG data does throw up several questions including the relevance of these pre-trained models for EEG data processing. However, listening to the transformed signal (s) derived from (e_i) made us believe that the transformed signal might have some relevance to acoustic events. The experimental results seem to demonstrate that the pre-trained models are able to extract embeddings that seem to capture the odour and the subject characteristics in the transformed signal. As future work, the single-channel data is neither speech nor audio but converting EEG multi-channel data into a single-channel data, as mentioned in this paper, might allow building models which best work for EEG data.

While both the pre-trained models have been trained for downstream acoustic event detection or classification, it is not clear why one works better than the other. While the focus in this paper was to use the pre-trained models as a black box to extract embeddings or features and not to looking at the architecture or training of the pre-trained models, as future work, it might be a good idea to understand and correlate the performance of odour and subject classification to the architecture and training data associated with the pre-trained model.

References

1. Google: VGGish model checkpoint (2017). https://storage.googleapis.com/audioset/vggish_model.ckpt
2. Google: YAMNet model (2020). https://www.kaggle.com/models/google/yamnet/tensorFlow2/yamnet/1, https://tfhub.dev/google/yamnet/1
3. Hannun, A., et al.: Deep speech: scaling up end-to-end speech recognition. arXiv preprint arXiv:1412.5567 (2014)
4. Hershey, S., et al.: CNN architectures for large-scale audio classification. In: 2017 IEEE International Conference on Acoustics, Speech and Signal Processing (ICASSP), pp. 131–135. IEEE (2017)
5. LeCun, Y., Bottou, L., Bengio, Y., Haffner, P.: Gradient-based learning applied to document recognition. Proc. IEEE **86**(11), 2278–2324 (1998)
6. van der Maaten, L., Hinton, G.: Visualizing data using t-SNE. J. Mach. Learn. Res. **9**, 2579–2605 (2008)
7. Meng, Q.H., Hou, H.R.: Olfactory EEG datasets: EegDot and EegDoc (2022). https://doi.org/10.21227/59nx-6g46
8. Nyquist, H.: Certain topics in telegraph transmission theory. Trans. Am. Inst. Electr. Eng. **47**(2), 617–644 (1928)
9. Pandharipande, M., Chakraborty, R., Kopparapu, S.K.: Modeling of olfactory brainwaves for odour independent biometric identification. In: 2023 31st European Signal Processing Conference (EUSIPCO), pp. 1140–1144 (2023). https://doi.org/10.23919/EUSIPCO58844.2023.10290059

10. Pandharipande, M., Tiwari, U., Chakraborty, R., Kopparapu, S.K.: Tempo-spectral EEG biomarkers for odour identification. In: 45th Annual International Conference of the IEEE Engineering in Medicine and Biology Society, EMBC 2023, Sydney, Australia, 24–27 July 2023, pp. 1–4. IEEE (2023). https://doi.org/10.1109/EMBC40787.2023.10340395
11. Plakal, M., Ellis., D.: Yamnet: a pretrained deep net for classifying audio events (2019). https://github.com/tensorflow/models/tree/master/research/audioset/yamnet
12. Schneider, S., Baevski, A., Collobert, R., Auli, M.: wav2vec: Unsupervised pre-training for speech recognition. In: Proceedings of the 2019 Conference of the North American Chapter of the Association for Computational Linguistics (NAACL), pp. 7–12 (2019)

Efficient Isomorphic Mesh Generation from Point Clouds via Group-Wise Implicit Function Networks

Shoko Miyauchi[1(✉)], Hayata Emoto[2], and Ken'ichi Morooka[3]

[1] Kyushu University, Fukuoka 8190395, Japan
miyauchi@ait.kyushu-u.ac.jp
[2] Okayama University, Okayama 7008530, Japan
[3] Kumamoto University, Kumamoto 8608555, Japan

Abstract. Isomorphic meshes (IMs), which represent all 3D data using a common mesh structure, are one approach to representing 3D data suitable for statistical analysis and deep learning. Existing methods for generating IMs from point clouds include iMG, which suffers from a high computational cost, and DIT-based network, which has limited generalization capability to previously unseen object classes. In this study, we propose a novel method for IM generation that addresses these issues by combining the strengths of iMG and DIT-based network. Our method begins with a global deformation of a template mesh in a manner similar to iMG. Next, both the deformed template and the input point cloud are partitioned into multiple local regions and grouped based on shape similarity. An implicit function network is then applied to each group, using a model trained specifically for that group, following the strategy used in DIT-based network. Finally, all locally deformed regions are integrated to produce the final IM corresponding to the input point cloud. Experiments on 17 object classes demonstrate that the proposed method achieves faster mesh generation than iMG in 15 of them. Furthermore, in 6 classes, it outperforms iMG in both speed and accuracy. We also demonstrate that introducing parallel processing into our framework can further accelerate the mesh generation process.

Keywords: Isomorphic mesh · Point-to-mesh network · Implicit function network

1 Introduction

In computer vision, mesh models are an effective description method of 3D shapes compared with the direct use of the 3D point clouds. Therefore, various methods have been developed to generate surface meshes from point clouds [12,15,17,18]. Generally, the mesh models of objects obtained using the conventional methods have differing mesh structures even though the objects belong to the same class. As a result, we need additional processes to deal with mesh

C. Wallraven et al. (Eds.): ACPR 2025, LNCS 16174, pp. 355–369, 2026.
https://doi.org/10.1007/978-981-95-4395-3_25

models with different mesh structures, such as the determination of the correspondence between the models. One approach to this problem is the use of isomorphic meshes (IMs). IMs describe the surface meshes of all objects using a unified mesh structure, with the same number of vertices and identical edge connections, regardless of the object class. In comparison with the general mesh models, IMs allow for fast and reliable analyses that consider the commonality and variety of shapes among target objects. This capability is useful in applications such as real-time animations [1], deformation transfers [13], and the straightforward generation of statistical shape models [6]. Moreover, using IMs, all meshes can be represented as fixed-dimensional vectors. This unified representation enables modern deep neural networks (DNNs) of various architectures to process surface models efficiently and without additional pre-processing.

Various methods for generating IMs have been proposed [9,16]. The IM generator (iMG) [9] generates IMs for input point clouds by deforming a spherical reference mesh. To achieve the deformation, iMG trains many multilayer perceptrons (MLPs) for each input point cloud. Therefore, it requires a significant amount of computation time for the mesh generation. In addition, because MLPs are trained using only the input point cloud, the accuracy of shape restoration is significantly degraded when the input point cloud contains a lot of noise.

The DIT-based network [8] enables faster IM generation than iMG by extending the deep implicit template (DIT) framework [19], which represents 3D object shapes using implicit functions. DIT learns the average shape of objects in a class, known as the template shape, and enables point correspondences between input point clouds via their signed distance fields (SDFs). To generate IMs, the DIT-based network introduces two additional steps. First, it constructs a template mesh by applying iMG to the template shape of each class. Second, it generates an IM for a given input by deforming the template mesh using an inverse warping function. Unlike iMG, this method directly outputs an IM using a pre-trained network without additional training during inference, resulting in significantly faster generation of IMs. It also remains robust even when the input point cloud contains noise. However, the method assumes the class of the input is known, and its performance is not guaranteed for unseen classes.

In this study, we propose a novel method, efficient IM generator (EiMG), for IM generation that combines the strengths of iMG and the DIT-based network to address the limitations of existing approaches. Figure 1 shows an overview of the EiMG. The EiMG begins by globally deforming a template mesh in a manner similar to iMG. Then, both the deformed template and the input point cloud are divided into multiple local regions, which are grouped based on shape similarity. For each group, an implicit function network trained specifically for that group is applied, following the group-wise modeling strategy inspired by the DIT-based network. Finally, all locally reconstructed regions are integrated to produce the final IM corresponding to the input point cloud. Unlike the DIT-based network, which uses a single implicit function to represent the entire shape of an object, our approach learns group-wise implicit function networks for shape-similar local regions. This enables the model to generalize to objects of

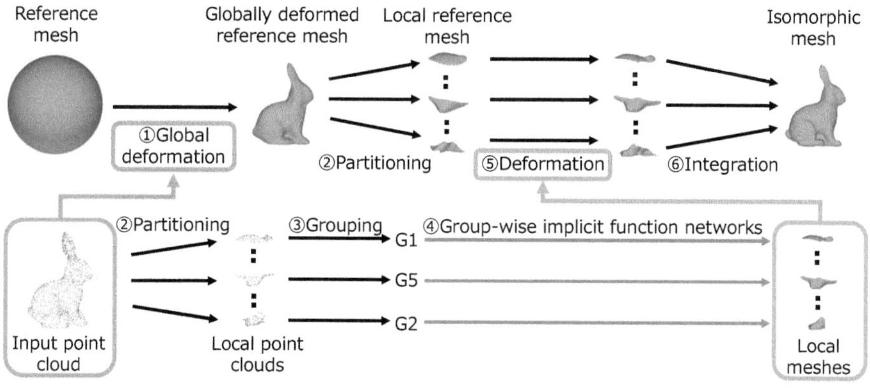

Fig. 1. An overview of the proposed method (EiMG)

unknown classes without relying on class labels. By replacing the region-specific MLPs used in iMG with these group-wise implicit function networks, the EiMG achieves efficient and accurate generation of IMs even for input point clouds from previously unseen classes.

The main contributions of this paper are as follows:

- We propose a novel method for IM generation that combines the global deformation strategy of iMG and the group-wise modeling approach inspired by the DIT-based network.
- Our method learns multiple implicit function networks, each specialized for a local region grouped by shape similarity, enabling robust and accurate reconstruction without requiring prior knowledge of object classes.
- By replacing the region-specific MLPs in iMG with group-wise implicit function networks, the proposed method significantly reduces computational cost while maintaining high reconstruction accuracy.
- Experimental results on 17 object classes show that our method achieves faster mesh generation than iMG in most classes and outperforms it in both speed and accuracy for several classes.

2 Related Works

In recent years, numerous neural network-based methods for generating meshes from point clouds have been proposed [7,10,12]. These methods differ in several aspects. Some require pre-training, while others do not. There are also approaches that utilize implicit function representations. However, most of these methods primarily focus on surface reconstruction and do not directly address the generation of IMs with unified mesh structures.

The Deep Implicit Template (DIT) method [19] achieves high-accuracy shape recovery by learning dense correspondences among 3D shapes in an unsupervised manner. Building on DIT, an NDF-based method [14] enables the generation of IMs within a single object class by introducing neural diffeomorphic flows. Nevertheless, both methods are limited to known object classes and do not generalize well across multiple classes. In contrast, the DIT-based network [8] enables the generation of IMs across object classes by integrating iMG and an inverse warping function into DIT. However, the DIT-based network assumes the class of the input is known, and its performance is not guaranteed for unseen classes.

Several approaches directly can generate IMs from point clouds while maintaining consistent mesh topologies across different objects. Among these, AtlasNet [4] and Voxel2Mesh [16] are based on pre-trained networks. AtlasNet reconstructs surfaces by dividing the input point cloud into local regions and mapping 2D planar points to 3D space using multilayer perceptrons (MLPs). It can also generate IMs without partitioning, though with reduced accuracy. Moreover, AtlasNet requires large-scale dataset pre-training and does not explicitly address noise or missing data.

Voxel2Mesh deforms a reference mesh by leveraging features extracted from voxel inputs and applies patch subdivision to improve reconstruction fidelity. However, this subdivision alters the mesh topology, preventing the generation of IMs. Although IMs can be generated without subdivision, the shape reconstruction accuracy tends to decrease significantly.

In contrast, Point2Mesh [5] and iMG [9] do not require pre-training and directly deform a reference mesh based on the input point cloud. Point2Mesh employs patch subdivision to enhance accuracy, but this results in variation in mesh structure depending on the input. Without subdivision, IMs can be generated, though with lower reconstruction accuracy. Similarly, iMG achieves high reconstruction accuracy by gradually deforming a spherical reference mesh through multiple MLPs trained for each input point cloud. While this approach avoids the need for dataset-level training, it incurs a high computational cost and is sensitive to input noise and missing data.

3 Efficient IM Generator (EiMG)

The EiMG consists of six steps, each corresponding to ① to ⑥ in Fig. 1:

- Step 1 A global deformation is applied to a template mesh using a technique similar to iMG.
- Step 2 Both the deformed template mesh and the input point cloud are partitioned to obtain local reference meshes and local point clouds.
- Step 3 The local point clouds are then grouped based on shape similarity.
- Step 4 For each group, a pre-trained implicit function network is used to reconstruct a local mesh from the corresponding local point cloud.
- Step 5 Each local template mesh is subsequently deformed to match the reconstructed local mesh while preserving the mesh structure.
- Step 6 The deformed local template meshes are integrated to produce the final IM.

The following sections describe the details of each step in the proposed method.

3.1 Global Reference Mesh Deformation [9]

The global deformation of the reference mesh is performed using the global mapping strategy from iMG. The reference mesh is initialized by subdividing a regular icosahedron with a circumscribed radius of 1 into a desired resolution. It is represented by a set of vertices and triangular patches, where each vertex is defined by its 3D coordinates, and each triangle is represented by the indices of its three constituent vertices.

The global mapping is achieved by training a multilayer perceptron (MLP) ϕ that maps points sampled from the reference mesh to the input point cloud $\boldsymbol{\Pi}$. Specifically, a set of sampled points $\boldsymbol{S}$, equal in size to $\boldsymbol{\Pi}$, is sampled from the surface of the reference mesh. Each sampled point $\boldsymbol{s} \in \boldsymbol{S}$ is fed into the MLP, which is trained so that its output $\phi(\boldsymbol{s})$ matches the corresponding target point $\boldsymbol{\pi} \in \boldsymbol{\Pi}$, assigned based on the minimum Sinkhorn-regularized distance [3]. The loss function is defined as the mean squared error (MSE) between $\boldsymbol{s}$ and its corresponding point $\boldsymbol{\pi}$:

$$L_{glo}(\boldsymbol{S}, |\boldsymbol{\Pi}) = \frac{1}{|\boldsymbol{\Pi}|} \sum_{\boldsymbol{s} \in \boldsymbol{S}, \boldsymbol{\pi} \in \boldsymbol{\Pi}} \|\phi(\beta_1 \boldsymbol{s}) - \boldsymbol{\pi}\|. \tag{1}$$

where β_1 is a scaling factor empirically determined for each object. The point correspondences are updated during training. After training, the vertices of the reference mesh are replaced with their mapped positions using ϕ, resulting in a globally deformed reference mesh.

3.2 Partitioning of Input Point Cloud and Globally Deformed Reference Mesh

The input point cloud $\boldsymbol{\Pi}$ is partitioned into N_L local point sets $\boldsymbol{X}_i$ using overlapping spherical regions. The globally deformed reference mesh is partitioned in the same manner to obtain N_L local reference meshes $\boldsymbol{L}_i^{(1)}$. This spherical partitioning ensures that all points originally assigned to each region remain within that region even after rotational alignment.

To partition the input point cloud, a bounding box that tightly encloses the entire point cloud is first computed. This bounding box is then uniformly divided into cubic cells of size $l \times 1 \times l$. The minimum length among the width, height, and depth of the bounding box is denoted as l_{min}. Next, the aspect ratios of the width, height, and depth are calculated, and the difference between their maximum and minimum values is determined. The cell size l is then set according to this difference: $l = \frac{l_{\text{min}}}{2}$ if the difference is 4 or greater, $l = \frac{l_{\text{min}}}{4}$ if it is between 2 and 4, and $l = \frac{l_{\text{min}}}{5}$ if it is less than 2. Finally, a spherical region of radius $\frac{\sqrt{3}}{2}l$ is placed at the center of each cube. Determining l based on the maximum aspect ratio difference prevents excessive subdivision for objects with large aspect ratio differences, such as thin structures.

For each spherical region, a 5th-order polynomial surface is fitted to the enclosed point cloud. If the fitting error exceeds a threshold τ_e, the corresponding cell is subdivided into n^3 sub-cubes, each enclosed by a new sphere. This process continues by incrementing n until all fitting errors fall below τ_e or the number of points within any sphere drops less than or equal to 10. The point sets enclosed in each final spherical region are defined as the local point clouds $\boldsymbol{X}_i$. Since adjacent spheres overlap, points near their boundaries belong to multiple local sets.

Next, the globally deformed reference mesh is partitioned into local reference meshes $\boldsymbol{L}_i^{(1)}$ using the same spherical regions. For each region, the subset of vertices $\boldsymbol{V}_i$ and their associated triangular patches $\boldsymbol{\mathcal{P}}_i$ enclosed within the i-th sphere are extracted. To avoid the inclusion of isolated vertices in $\boldsymbol{V}_i$, if a vertex is not part of any triangle in $\boldsymbol{\mathcal{P}}_i$, the surrounding triangles are examined. If a triangle includes only one vertex outside $\boldsymbol{V}_i$, that vertex and the triangle are added to $\boldsymbol{V}_i$ and $\boldsymbol{\mathcal{P}}_i$, respectively. If multiple such candidates exist, the one forming the most triangles with existing $\boldsymbol{V}_i$ vertices is selected. If no triangle satisfies this condition, the isolated vertex is removed from $\boldsymbol{V}_i$.

Furthermore, to ensure that all vertices of the globally deformed reference mesh are included in at least one local reference mesh, any unassigned vertex is handled separately. Each such vertex is added to the vertex set $\boldsymbol{V}_j$ of the local reference mesh $\boldsymbol{L}_j^{(1)}$, to which its nearest neighbor belongs. If any triangular patch from the original reference mesh can be formed using the added vertex and adjacent vertices in $\boldsymbol{V}_j$, it is added to $\boldsymbol{\mathcal{P}}_j$. If no such patch exists, the vertex is treated as an isolated point in $\boldsymbol{V}_j$ and processed using the same method described in the previous paragraph. Due to the overlapping partitioning, the local reference meshes $\boldsymbol{L}_i^{(1)}$ share common vertices and triangles at their boundaries, facilitating seamless integration in later steps.

3.3 Grouping of Local Point Clouds

For each local point set $\boldsymbol{X}_j$, a local coordinate transformation and alignment are first performed. Then, PointNet [11] is used to extract shape features, which are subsequently used for classification.

In the alignment process, $\boldsymbol{X}_j$ is first translated so that the center of the enclosing sphere becomes the origin of the local coordinate system. It is then uniformly scaled so that the radius of the enclosing sphere becomes 1. Afterward, the average normal vector of the points in $\boldsymbol{X}_j$ is computed and the point set is rotated so that this vector aligns with the z-axis of the local coordinate system.

The transformed local point set is input to PointNet [11] to extract a 1,024-dimensional shape feature vector. These features, computed from all local point sets in the training data, are clustered using the x-means algorithm, and the resulting clusters are used as local point set groups.

During inference, the shape feature of a given local point set is extracted in the same manner, and its distance to each cluster centroid is calculated. The local point set is then assigned to the group corresponding to the nearest centroid.

3.4 Local Mesh Generation Using Group-Wise Implicit Function Network

To generate each local mesh model $\boldsymbol{D}_i$, we employ a module of the DIT-based network [8] as an implicit function network, trained exclusively on the training data belonging to the same group as the target local point set. Specifically, the DIT component of the DIT-based network was used as the implicit function network. Given the signed distance field (SDF) of a local point set $\boldsymbol{X}_i$, a set of vertices sampled from the SDF is fed into the network, which then outputs a mesh model $\boldsymbol{D}_i$ that captures the geometry of $\boldsymbol{X}_i$. Adjusting the number of vertices sampled from the SDF allows for controlling the trade-off between the generation time and the reconstruction accuracy of the IMs.

The training procedure for each group-wise implicit function network is as follows. First, for each local point set in the training data, an SDF is constructed using normal vectors estimated from the point set. Then, the implicit function network corresponding to each group is trained using the SDFs of all training local point sets belonging to that group.

During inference, the group to which a given local point set belongs is determined using the procedure described in Sect. 3.3. The SDF is then computed from the input point set, and the group-specific implicit function network takes this SDF as input to produce a local mesh model $\boldsymbol{D}_i$.

3.5 Deformation of Local Reference Meshes

Each local mesh model $\boldsymbol{D}_i$ $(i = 1, \ldots, N_L)$ is first transformed from its local coordinate system to the world coordinate system. It is then refined by retaining only the triangular patches located within the spherical region used for partitioning in Sect. 3.2. This step removes extraneous mesh fragments generated in regions not covered by the original local point set.

The local mesh models are generated in different local coordinate systems due to the alignment process described in Sect. 3.3. To integrate these meshes into a single IM, the inverse of the alignment transformation is applied to each local mesh model, bringing all models into a consistent world coordinate system.

Since the local meshes in Sect. 3.4 are produced from signed distance fields (SDFs) defined within a cubic space, they may contain triangles in regions where no input points exist. To address this issue, the triangular patches located outside the corresponding spherical region are removed. This ensures that the spatial extent of each local mesh model matches its corresponding local point set.

After refinement, each local reference mesh is deformed to approximate the shape of its corresponding local mesh model while preserving the mesh topology. Specifically, twice as many surface points as the number of vertices in the local mesh are uniformly sampled. Then, each vertex of the local reference mesh is replaced with the position of its nearest sampled surface point. The deformed local reference mesh is denoted as $\boldsymbol{L}_i^{(2)}$.

3.6 Integration of Local Reference Meshes

The final IM is generated by integrating the deformed local reference meshes $\boldsymbol{L}_i^{(2)}$ obtained in Sect. 3.5. As described in Sect. 3.1, overlapping regions exist between adjacent local reference meshes. Consequently, a single vertex of the original reference mesh may correspond to multiple deformed positions, referred to as candidate positions, in these overlapping areas. To achieve smooth integration, a unified vertex position must be computed from these candidate positions. This is accomplished by assigning weights to each candidate position and computing a weighted average to determine the final vertex position in the overlapping regions.

Specifically, each deformed local reference mesh $\boldsymbol{L}_i^{(2)}$ is inverse-mapped onto its original spherical representation, yielding $\boldsymbol{L}_i^{(0)}$. For $\boldsymbol{L}_i^{(0)}$, the Euclidean distance g is then calculated as the distance from the centroid of $\boldsymbol{L}_i^{(0)}$ to its farthest vertex. For each vertex in $\boldsymbol{L}_i^{(0)}$, the geodesic distance to the centroid is computed, and the corresponding weight is defined as 1 minus the ratio of the geodesic distance to g.

In overlapping regions, the final vertex position is computed as the weighted average of all candidate positions. In non-overlapping regions, the vertex positions of the deformed local reference mesh are directly used as the final positions. Replacing all vertices of the globally deformed reference mesh with these final positions generates the final IM.

4 Experiment and Discussion

To validate the effectiveness of the proposed method, we conducted experiments to generate isomorphic meshes (IMs) from input point clouds. We compared our method against four existing methods: iMG [9], Point2Mesh [5], AtlasNet [4], and Voxel2Mesh [16]. For the iMG baseline, we evaluated the trade-off between reconstruction accuracy and computation time. To examine the impact of local region partitioning on reconstruction accuracy, we also compared the proposed method with the DIT-based network, which does not incorporate such partitioning, in terms of both reconstruction accuracy and computation time for the Sofa class. In these experiments, the number of sampled points from the SDF in Sect. 3.4 was fixed at 2000.

Additionally, we investigated how varying the number of sampled points from the SDF affects both the reconstruction accuracy and the computation time. We also evaluated the effect of introducing parallel processing into our method.

The reconstruction accuracy of the IMs is evaluated using the point-to-mesh (PM) distance [9], defined as the average of the distances from the generated mesh to the ground truth mesh $\boldsymbol{G}$ and vice versa. A lower PM distance indicates higher reconstruction accuracy. All experiments were conducted using a spherical reference mesh with 2,562 vertices on a desktop computer equipped with an AMD Ryzen 7 5800X 8-core CPU and an NVIDIA GeForce RTX 3060 Ti GPU. The datasets used are described below, followed by detailed results and analysis.

Table 1. Training dataset

Class	Airplane	Bench	Cabinet	Car	Cellphone	Chair	Firearm
No. of objects	3,236	1,452	1,257	5,996	841	5,421	1,897
Class	Lamp	Monitor	Sofa	Speaker	Table	Watercraft	
No. of objects	1,854	874	2,538	1,294	6,807	1,551	

4.1 Dataset

In this experiment, we used 35,018 objects from 13 classes in the ShapeNet dataset [2] (Airplane, Bench, Cabinet, Car, Cellphone, Chair, Firearm, Lamp, Monitor, Sofa, Speaker, Table, and Watercraft) as training data. Each object is represented by a point cloud consisting of 30,000 points, and the number of objects per class is summarized in Table 1. Using the proposed method, the 35,018 objects were divided into 7,555,003 local point sets, from which 75,550 were randomly selected for training.

To evaluate shape restoration accuracy for both seen and unseen classes, we used a total of 73 objects as test data. For the seen classes, five objects not used in training were selected from each of the 13 ShapeNet classes. For the unseen classes, we selected five objects from the Bottle class in ShapeNet and three CAD objects (Rabbit, Max Plank, and Box). The ShapeNet objects were scaled to fit within a unit sphere of diameter of diameter 1 [mm], while the CAD models were scaled to fit within a bounding box of 100 [mm] per side.

4.2 Comparison of Shape Restoration Accuracy with Existing Methods

Table 2 summarizes the average shape restoration accuracy for each method, including the averages for seen classes, the unseen ShapeNet class (bottle), and three unseen CAD objects. The accuracy values for Point2mesh, AtlasNet, and Voxel2mesh are taken from [9], where experiments were conducted on the same dataset used in this study. For detailed experimental settings, refer to [9]. Figure 2 shows examples of IMs generated by iMG and EiMG (the proposed method).

From Fig. 2, the proposed method generates IMs that capture fine geometric details of the input point clouds, similar to those generated by iMG. However, in some cases, such as the Monitor class (9th column), the proposed method introduces dents on flat surfaces. This issue arises when, during the partitioning of the input point cloud, point clouds forming two discontinuous surfaces are included within the same local region. In such cases, the implicit function network generates only one of the surfaces, causing dents as shown in Fig. 2. This issue may be resolved by adding a further partitioning process or by improving the accuracy of local mesh generation using the implicit function network.

Table 2 shows that the proposed method consistently achieved shape restoration accuracy that was either on par with or second only to iMG across all test

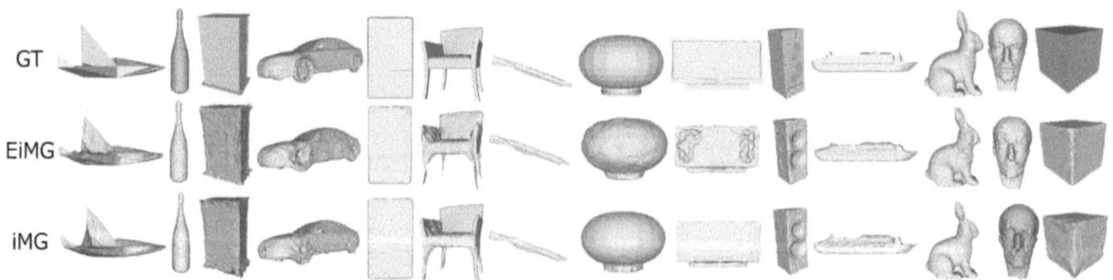

Fig. 2. Examples of ground-truth meshes and IMs generated by iMG and EiMG (the proposed method).

data. Among the 14 ShapeNet classes, the proposed method attained equal or the highest accuracy in 7 classes (Airplane, Bench, Bottle, Car, Firearm, Table, Watercraft). For classes where accuracy was lower than iMG, such as the edges of Cabinets and armrests of Chairs, the local mesh models showed reduced shape restoration accuracy due to their thin structures. Additionally, although local mesh models achieved high accuracy for features like the corners of Speaker and Box, the neck of Rabbit, and the nose of Max Plank, edge collapse in the local reference mesh models led to lower final accuracy. Future work will focus on improving the accuracy of local mesh generation and refining the deformation method of local reference meshes to better handle such challenging shapes.

4.3 Comparison of Inference Time

We compared the computation time required to generate IMs using the proposed method and iMG, the most accurate method for unseen classes and the basis of our approach. Table 2 shows the average of computational times for all testing data.

Like iMG, the proposed method partitions the reference mesh and input point cloud into local regions and performs region-wise deformation. However, because the deformation is executed using a pretrained network, the average computation time is reduced to 553.28 s, compared to 1216.95 s with iMG. In particular, for the Bench, Bottle, Car, Firearm, Table, and Watercraft classes, the proposed method generated IMs faster than iMG while maintaining comparable or superior accuracy.

For the Cellphone class, computation time increased to 964.87 s, which is the only case where it exceeds that of iMG (957.53 s). This is due to its thin geometry, which leads to more local regions during partitioning, as described in Sect. 3.2. Future work will consider more efficient partitioning methods that take into account the global shape of the input.

4.4 Evaluation of the Contribution of Local Partitioning

The proposed method generates IMs by partitioning the point cloud into multiple local regions and applying the implicit function network to each region.

Table 2. PM distances ([$\times 10^{-2}$ mm]) and computation times ([*sec*]) of IMs generated by the five methods. The best accuracy values are highlighted in bold, and the second-best values are indicated by underlining.

Method	Seen avg. (13 ShapeNet classes)	Unseen avg. (Bottle, ShapeNet)	Unseen avg. (3 CAD objects)	Computational time
EiMG (Proposed)	<u>0.23 ± 0.08</u>	$\mathbf{0.25 \pm 0.11}$	<u>32.67 ± 4.93</u>	$\mathbf{553.28 \pm 139.35}$
iMG	$\mathbf{0.20 \pm 0.09}$	<u>0.25 ± 0.15</u>	$\mathbf{15.71 \pm 2.36}$	<u>1216.95 ± 442.75</u>
Point2mesh	0.24 ± 0.08	0.32 ± 0.05	37.93 ± 10.43	-
AtlasNet	0.41 ± 0.13	0.67 ± 0.16	175.55 ± 10.86	-
Voxel2mesh	0.88 ± 0.26	0.45 ± 0.09	272.04 ± 49.58	-

To evaluate the effect of partitioning on shape restoration accuracy, we compared the reconstruction accuracy and computation time between the proposed method with partitioning and the DIT-based network without partitioning.

The DIT-based network requires training a network for each class. In this experiment, we selected the Sofa class from the dataset described in Sect. 4.1 and trained a DIT-based network using 1,631 Sofa training samples. For testing, five Sofa objects were used as described in Sect. 4.1.

The proposed method achieved a shape restoration accuracy of $(0.29 \pm 0.10) \times 10^{-2}$ [mm], whereas the DIT-based network yielded $(1.49 \pm 0.24) \times 10^{-2}$ [mm]. These results show that the proposed method provides higher shape restoration accuracy. From Fig. 3, the DIT-based network suffers from significant accuracy degradation when the target shape differs substantially from the template. In contrast, the proposed method successfully reconstructs complex areas, such as the space under the legs and the cushions, which are not captured by the DIT-based network. This indicates that our method can generate IMs that more effectively capture the detailed shape features of target objects.

In terms of computation time, the DIT-based network required 73.94 ± 0.36 s, while the proposed method took 507.19 ± 67.45 s, making the DIT-based method approximately 6.9 times faster. This difference arises because the DIT-based network optimizes a single latent variable for the entire input point cloud, whereas the proposed method must optimize a separate latent variable for each local point set obtained via partitioning. However, since local point sets are processed independently, parallelization can be applied to reduce total computation time, as discussed in Sect. 4.6.

4.5 Trade-Off Analysis Between Accuracy and Computation Time Across Sampling Numbers

To evaluate the effect of the SDF sampling number in Sect. 3.4, we analyzed how varying this number impacts the computation time and shape restoration accuracy of IM generation. Figure 4 shows the average accuracy and computation time for 70 test samples from 14 ShapeNet classes using sampling numbers of 500, 1000, 2000, and 8000. For reference, the average reconstruction accuracy

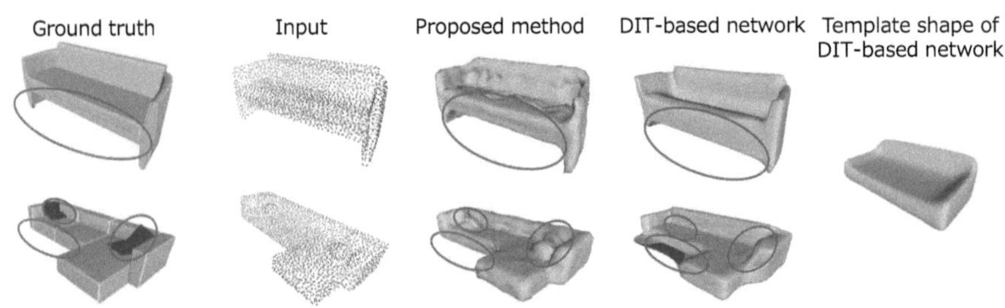

Fig. 3. Ground-truth meshes, input point clouds, and IMs generated by the proposed method and the DIT-based network for two Sofa objects, along with the single template shape used by the DIT-based network.

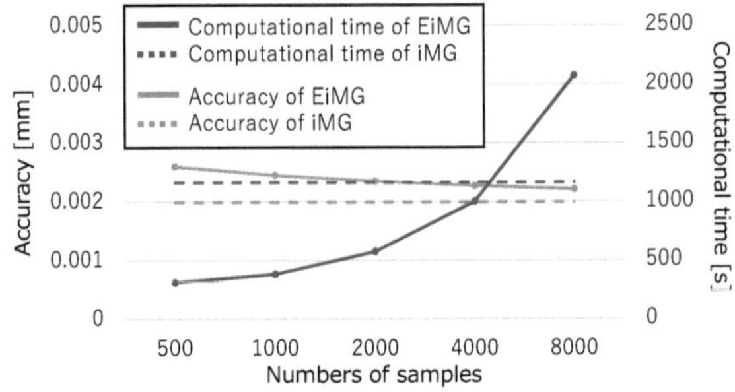

Fig. 4. Average shape restoration accuracy and computation time for ShapeNet's 14-class test data with varying numbers of samples. (Color figure online)

(orange dashed line) and computation time (blue dashed line) of iMG are also included.

The results indicate that increasing the sampling number improves accuracy gradually but significantly increases computation time. While the proposed method is slightly less accurate than iMG (by 0.022×10^{-2} [mm]), reducing the sampling number to 500 shortens computation time to 314.64 s.

Next, we highlight the results for four classes (Bench, Car, Table, and Watercraft), for which the proposed method achieved both higher accuracy and faster computation than iMG. The corresponding results are presented in Fig. 5 and 6. In particular, for Bench and Table, higher sampling numbers enhance the reconstruction of edge details, especially in regions highlighted by the red and blue circles in Fig. 6. In summary, increasing the number of samples from the SDF contributes to higher reconstruction accuracy, but introduces a trade-off with computation time.

4.6 Evaluation of Parallel Processing Effects

In the proposed method, Step 4, which generates local mesh models, is independently executed for each group, allowing for potential acceleration through

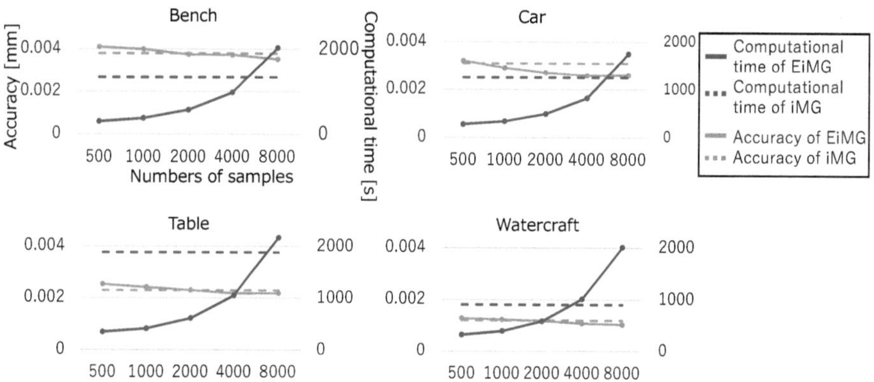

Fig. 5. Average shape restoration accuracy and computation time for the Bench, Car, Table, and Watercraft classes with varying numbers of samples.

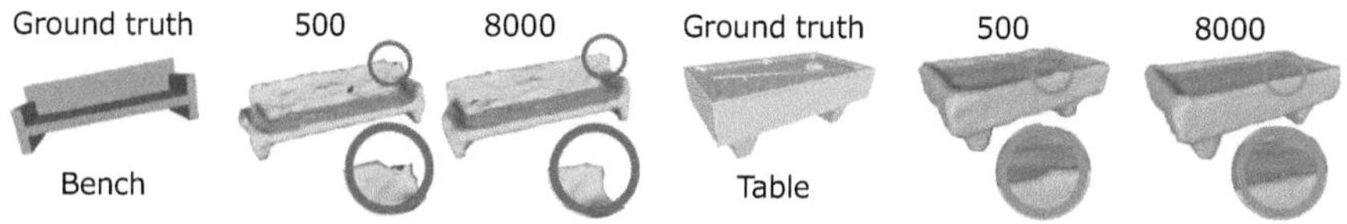

Fig. 6. Examples of IMs generated by the proposed method for the Bench and Table classes with sampling sizes of 500 and 8000.

parallel processing. This experiment compares computation times on a workstation equipped with four GPUs (CPU: AMD Ryzen Threadripper Pro 3975WX 32-core × 64; GPU: NVIDIA RTX A6000), running Step 4 sequentially on a single GPU versus in parallel across all four GPUs. The sampling number in Sect. 3.4 was set to 8000.

Table 3 shows the time for Step 4 alone (second row), the time for all other steps (third row), and the total computation time (fourth row). Note that processing time excluding Step 4 was measured on the system used in other experiments. All computational times represent averages over the test dataset.

Table 3 shows that parallelization speeds up Step 4 by 3.0 times and accelerates total processing time by 2.5 times. This demonstrates that parallel processing can significantly reduce computation time without compromising reconstruction accuracy.

Table 3. IM generation times with and without parallel processing (PP) [*sec*]

	Without PP (single GPU)	With PP (four GPUs)
Step 4	1176.75	389.92
Excluding Step 4	141.28	142.16
Total	1318.03	532.08

5 Limitation

While the proposed method demonstrates improved efficiency and accuracy, it still faces certain limitations. For some object shapes, increasing the number of partitions can significantly raise computational cost. Moreover, when disconnected surfaces are grouped into a single region during partitioning, we observed a decline in shape restoration accuracy. Furthermore, since evaluations so far have been limited to noise-free data, validation on more realistic datasets with noise and missing data remains necessary.

6 Conclusion

In this study, we proposed EiMG, a novel method for IM generation that combines the strengths of two existing approaches: iMG [9], which excels in accuracy but suffers from high computational cost, and DIT-based network [8], which is faster but less generalizable. The proposed method first globally deforms a template mesh, then partitions and groups both the deformed mesh and input point cloud based on shape similarity. Each group is refined using a specialized implicit function network, and the results are integrated into the final IM. Through experiments on 17 object classes, we demonstrated that EiMG generates IMs faster than iMG in 15 classes. Moreover, for 6 of those classes, it outperforms iMG in both speed and restoration accuracy. We also showed that incorporating parallel processing can further accelerate mesh generation.

To address the limitations mentioned in Sect. 5, future work will focus on improving the partitioning strategy and enhancing restoration accuracy in regions that include multiple or disconnected surfaces. Through these improvements, we aim to further increase both the restoration accuracy and efficiency of the proposed method. Furthermore, evaluating the accuracy of the proposed method on input point clouds containing noise and missing data remains a future task to assess its practical applicability.

Acknowledgements. This work was supported by JST ACT-X under Grant JPMJAX190T, JST AIP Acceleration Research JPMJCR23U4, and JSPS KAKENHI Grant Number JP25K21621, Japan.

References

1. Casas, D., Tejera, M., Guillemaut, J.-Y., Hilton, A.: Parametric control of captured mesh sequences for real-time animation. In: Allbeck, J.M., Faloutsos, P. (eds.) MIG 2011. LNCS, vol. 7060, pp. 242–253. Springer, Heidelberg (2011). https://doi.org/10.1007/978-3-642-25090-3_21
2. Chang, A.X., et al.: ShapeNet: an information-rich 3D model repository. arXiv preprint arXiv:1512.03012 (2015)
3. Cuturi, M.: Sinkhorn distances: lightspeed computation of optimal transport. In: Advances in Neural Information Processing Systems, vol. 26, pp. 2292–2300 (2013)

4. Groueix, T., Fisher, M., Kim, V.G., Russell, B.C., Aubry, M.: A papier-mâché approach to learning 3D surface generation. In: Proceedings of the IEEE Conference on Computer Vision and Pattern Recognition, pp. 216–224 (2018)
5. Hanocka, R., Metzer, G., Giryes, R., Cohen-Or, D.: Point2Mesh: a self-prior for deformable meshes. arXiv preprint arXiv:2005.11084 (2020)
6. Heimann, T., Meinzer, H.P.: Statistical shape models for 3D medical image segmentation: a review. Med. Image Anal. **13**(4), 543–563 (2009)
7. Lei, H., Leng, R., Zheng, L., Li, H.: CircNet: meshing 3D point clouds with circumcenter detection. arXiv preprint arXiv:2301.09253 (2023)
8. Miyauchi, S., Itaya, K., Morooka, K.: Generation of semantic isomorphic mesh using implicit function representation. Technical report, SSRN (2025). https://doi.org/10.2139/ssrn.5205387. https://ssrn.com/abstract=5205387
9. Miyauchi, S., Morooka, K., Kurazume, R.: Isomorphic mesh generation from point clouds with multilayer perceptrons. IEEE Trans. Vis. Comput. Graph. **31**(03), 1647–1663 (2025)
10. Potamias, R.A., Ploumpis, S., Zafeiriou, S.: Neural mesh simplification. In: Proceedings of the IEEE/CVF Conference on Computer Vision and Pattern Recognition, pp. 18583–18592 (2022)
11. Qi, C.R., Su, H., Mo, K., Guibas, L.J.: PointNet: deep learning on point sets for 3D classification and segmentation. In: Proceedings of the IEEE Conference on Computer Vision and Pattern Recognition, pp. 652–660 (2017)
12. Rakotosaona, M.J., Guerrero, P., Aigerman, N., Mitra, N.J., Ovsjanikov, M.: Learning Delaunay surface elements for mesh reconstruction. In: Proceedings of the IEEE/CVF Conference on Computer Vision and Pattern Recognition, pp. 22–31 (2021)
13. Sumner, R.W., Popović, J.: Deformation transfer for triangle meshes. ACM Trans. Graph. (TOG) **23**(3), 399–405 (2004)
14. Sun, S., Han, K., Kong, D., Tang, H., Yan, X., Xie, X.: Topology-preserving shape reconstruction and registration via neural diffeomorphic flow. In: Proceedings of the IEEE/CVF Conference on Computer Vision and Pattern Recognition, pp. 20845–20855 (2022)
15. Ummenhofer, B., Koltun, V.: Adaptive surface reconstruction with multiscale convolutional kernels. In: Proceedings of the IEEE/CVF International Conference on Computer Vision, pp. 5651–5660 (2021)
16. Wickramasinghe, U., Remelli, E., Knott, G., Fua, P.: Voxel2Mesh: 3D mesh model generation from volumetric data. In: Medical Image Computing and Computer Assisted Intervention-MICCAI 2020: 23rd International Conference, Lima, Peru, 4–8 October 2020, Proceedings, Part IV 23, pp. 299–308. Springer (2020)
17. Williams, F., Trager, M., Bruna, J., Zorin, D.: Neural splines: fitting 3D surfaces with infinitely-wide neural networks. In: Proceedings of the IEEE/CVF Conference on Computer Vision and Pattern Recognition, pp. 9949–9958 (2021)
18. Zhang, J., Yao, Y., Quan, L.: Learning signed distance field for multi-view surface reconstruction. In: Proceedings of the IEEE/CVF International Conference on Computer Vision, pp. 6525–6534 (2021)
19. Zheng, Z., Yu, T., Dai, Q., Liu, Y.: Deep implicit templates for 3D shape representation. In: Proceedings of the IEEE/CVF Conference on Computer Vision and Pattern Recognition, pp. 1429–1439 (2021)

Real-Time, Multi-center, Dual-Task-Based Cognitive Impairment Screening with Graph Convolutional Neural Networks

Ákos Godó[1(✉)], Shuqiong Wu[1], Manabu Ikeda[2], Shunsuke Sato[3], Yuto Satake[4], Maki Suzuki[5], Kazue Shigenobu[5,6], Daiki Taomoto[2], and Yasushi Yagi[1]

[1] The University of Osaka, 8-1 Mihogaoka, Ibaraki, Osaka 567-0047, Japan
{godo,wu,yagi}@yy.d3c.osaka-u.ac.jp

[2] Department of Psychiatry, Graduate School of Medicine, The University of Osaka, 2-2 Yamadaoka, Suita, Osaka 565-0871, Japan
{mikeda,taomotodaiki}@psy.med.osaka-u.ac.jp

[3] Health and Counseling Center, The University of Osaka, Osaka, Toyonaka, Japan

[4] Division of Psychiatry, University College London, Maple House, 149 Tottenham Ct Rd, London W1T 7NF, England

[5] Department of Behavioral Neurology and Neuropsychiatry, United Graduate School of Child Development, The University of Osaka, 2-2 Yamadaoka, Suita, Osaka 565-0871, Japan
{msuzuki,kamae}@psy.med.osaka-u.ac.jp

[6] Asakayama General Hospital, Sakai, 3-3-16 Imaikecho, Sakai, Osaka 590-0018, Japan

Abstract. Early detection of dementia, particularly during the preceding mild cognitive impairment (MCI) stage, remains a critical challenge due to its subtle behavioral symptoms. While recent advances have combined deep learning with simple behavioral assessments to promising results, most existing approaches lack full automation, real-time capability, and robustness across diverse environments. We introduce a real-time, fully automated, multi-center cognitive screening system based on the dual-task paradigm, powered by a gait-based graph convolutional neural network. Designed for online operation, our system performs continuous assessment during motor and cognitive tasks, while simultaneously collecting data for iterative offline refinement of the underlying classification model. To ensure real-world applicability, we gathered 660 samples from five locations, encompassing a range of subjects, physical environments and camera hardware. The resulting data heterogeneity is overcome through a robust selection of standardized modalities, applying augmentation techniques specific to the periodicity of gait, and employing transfer learning to adapt across devices. We achieved strong performance with a sensitivity of 0.9394 and specificity of 0.9065, demonstrating the system's robustness and accuracy in multi-center settings.

This work was supported in part by the Japan Agency for Medical Research and Development (AMED) under Grant JP25uk1024001.

C. Wallraven et al. (Eds.): ACPR 2025, LNCS 16174, pp. 370–386, 2026.
https://doi.org/10.1007/978-981-95-4395-3_26

Keywords: Real-time screening · Mild cognitive impairment (MCI) · Dementia · Dual-task · Graph convolutional neural networks

1 Introduction

Dementia is a progressive neurodegenerative condition characterized by cognitive decline that eventually impairs independent living. Although it is not a normal part of aging, dementia affects over 55 million people globally [9], predominantly among the aging population. Dementia is preceded by mild cognitive impairment (MCI), where cognitive and memory issues arise but independence is largely preserved [1], making early detecting challenging due to its subtle symptoms.

Timely intervention during the MCI stage can slow progression to dementia [20], whether through behavioral therapy [25] or pharmacological treatments, including recently approved drugs such as Lecanemab [8]. This underscores the urgent need for fast and efficient early detection methods.

Behavioral assessments, such as the dual-task paradigm, are a possible approach for early detection. During a dual-task assessment, participants perform a motor task and a cognitive task, first separately then simultaneously. Involving gait in the motor task is effective, as the degree of gait disruption during the dual-task phase has been shown to correlate strongly with cognitive impairment [2,18].

In this study, we present an automated, real-time cognitive impairment screening system based on the dual-task paradigm, relying on a gait-based graph convolutional neural network (GCNN) as the classifier. The system serves two purposes: (1) provide an immediate classification of cognitive state during an assessment session, and (2) continuously collect session data from multiple assessment sites to refine and improve the underlying classification model offline. Using the collected data, the system is iteratively updated with a more accurate and generalizable classifier (Fig. 1).

Our contributions can be summarized as follows:

1. We present a low-cost, automated, real-time cognitive impairment screening system based on the dual-task paradigm. We collect a multi-center dataset comprising 660 samples from five sites using two different camera types (Kinect V2 and generic USB cameras).
2. We address domain shift caused by multi-site and multi-device data collection through input standardization, modality selection, data augmentation, and transfer learning, enabling strong generalization across centers.
3. Our GCNN classifier achieves high diagnostic accuracy under a 5-fold cross-validation testing setup, with an average sensitivity of 0.9394 and specificity of 0.9065, demonstrating the system's potential for accurate, real-time cognitive screening at scale.

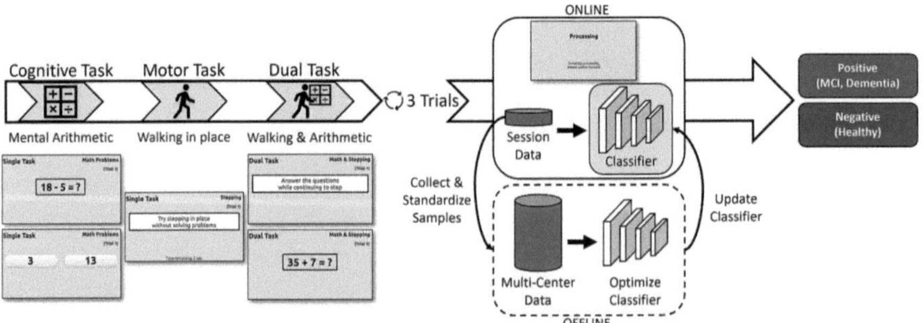

Fig. 1. Overview of the proposed real-time assessment system. Session data collected from 3 consecutive trials of cognitive, motor and dual-tasks is used for immediate assessment of MCI/dementia labels using a GCNN classifier. Session data from multiple centers and recording devices is collected for offline refinement of the classifier.

2 Related Work

2.1 Cognitive Assessment Technology

Paper-based test approaches are the go-to method for cognitive assessments in a clinical setting. The Mini Mental State Examination (MMSE) is a popular example [10]. It assigns a score between 0–30 based on answers to pre-determined questions. Scoring between 27 and 24 points suggests MCI, and scoring under 23 points suggests dementia. Such methods are cost effective, but the answers can be memorized [29], known as the practice effect (PE), which can influence results. Scores are also affected based on the evaluator, often leading to inconsistencies [29].

MMSE takes between 5 to 10 min to administer and has a sensitivity of 81% and specificity of 89% when detecting dementia, with a reduced sensitivity of 45% and specificity of 65% when detecting MCI [26]. MCI cases, particularly those in the early stages, are difficult to detect even for professional clinicians because the brain changes at this phase are often too subtle to be easily recognized resulting in an easily misclassifiable borderline class [4].

Recently, behavioral assessments, especially those involving gait have gained attention. Gait is strongly tied to cognition [18] and it has been shown that the slowing of gait precedes cognitive decline by several years [23]. One such behavioral assessment is the dual-task paradigm. Various dual-task based approaches exist in conjunction with a motor task involving gait [2,17].

Screening performance of dual-task-based assessments depends on the processing method. Extracting the pose sequence of motor tasks and leveraging the graph structure of the skeleton via a spatio-temporal graph convolutional network is a successful approach [15,30]. Our previous work [12] recognized the periodicity of gait, extracting motion periods and applying a custom GCNN architecture, the Phase-Aligned Periodic Graph Convolutional Network (PPGCN), to effectively handle the period-extracted gait modality. Compared with other dual-task-based work [15,30] PPGCN demonstrated the importance of gait periodicity for cognitive impairment detection.

General applicability of the above NN-based methods is hampered by dataset limitations (single recording device and/or environment; limited number of subjects) and performance requirements: NN-based methods target fast offline inference using high-performance GPU for which does not match real-time, screening conditions with affordable computers [12,15,21,30].

2.2 Multi-center Problem

To achieve unbiased high performance with adequate generalization capability, machine learning models are trained on large and diverse datasets. The required number and diversity of samples often far exceeds the number of subjects available at a single data collection location (center), especially for clinical data. This leads to the necessity of gathering data from multiple centers [13,14].

Difference in conditions, equipment and annotators across centers imposes a warehousing (especially regarding the protection of personal information) and standardization overhead [11,24]. The balance of sensitivity and specificity underlying the accuracy is important to guarantee a fair classifier. Even having standardized the data, the heterogeneity of data coupled with center-specific conditions may introduce noise or biases to the collected dataset degrading machine learning model performance [27]. MMSE performs significantly worse when multiple centers are involved with a reduced sensitivity of 54% and a specificity of 80% [5].

To overcome data heterogeneity, Chang et al. take a generative approach [7] by synthesizing samples for multiple centers which allows downstream machine learning models to observe samples as if they were generated in centers different from the one the sample was collected at. On the other hand, Seoni et al. argue that just by standardizing data via pre-processing and collecting data using multiple devices as well as from multiple centers, machine learning models can provide more robust insights [22]. They warn, however, that unless care is taken during data pre-processing and standardization, inconsistencies may hamper performance and introduce bias. Furthermore, Campello et al. claim [6] that collecting a multi-center and multi-device dataset significantly increases model generalizability for future, yet unseen devices.

3 Methods

3.1 Dual-Task-Based Assessment System

Following the work of Matsuura et al. [17] and improving on our previous method [12], we designed a dual-task-based cognitive impairment assessment system for real-time prediction of MCI/dementia. During a session, subjects are presented mental arithmetic problems as the cognitive task (Fig. 2a), and are instructed to walk in place for the motor task (Fig. 2b). Mental arithmetic problems consist of simple addition and subtraction questions of two positive operands in the

0–99 range, ensuring the result is positive when randomly generating the questions. The generated nature of questions solves the PE problem often present in cognitive modalities of assessments.

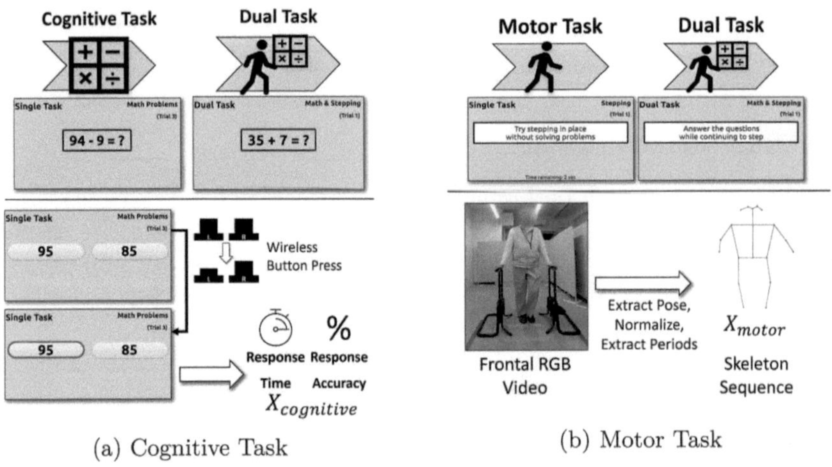

(a) Cognitive Task (b) Motor Task

Fig. 2. (a) During the cognitive and dual tasks subjects are instructed to solve mental arithmetic problems by selecting one of two possible answers. The average response time and accuracy during both tasks is stored as the cognitive modality $X_{cognitive}$. (b) During the motor and dual tasks subjects are instructed to walk in place. From the frontal RGB video recorded during the session, pose extraction, normalization and period extraction [16] is performed in real time to get the motor modality X_{motor}

In a significant advancement over our previous work [12] which was wholly offline and required a GPU for inference, our proposed new system handles online assessment without the need for expensive resources. It runs on a mid-range multi-core CPU, does not require a GPU, and uses less than 4 gigabytes of memory to perform real-time pose extraction as well as classification. It supports generic USB cameras as opposed to the prior version's strict Kinect V2 requirement and supports wireless push-button input through bluetooth human interface devices.

Data is recorded during three loops of the cognitive, motor and dual-tasks, as research from Wu et al. showed that data from multiple consecutive trials increase detection accuracy [28]. From the collected session data, a NN-based classification model provides a real-time prediction regarding the subject's cognitive impairment. Similarly to MMSE, a session takes approximately 8 min to administer. The recorded session data is collected from multiple centers to be used offline for further optimizing the performance of the underlying classification model (Fig. 1).

The data raw data collected during a session consists of frontal RGB video of the subject recorded during the entire session as well as the generated mental arithmetic questions, presented possible answers, the selected answers, and response times. Following the findings of Campello et al. [6], we collect data at multiple sites using different camera devices: Microsoft Kinect V2 and a generic USB camera.

3.2 Data Standardization

We aimed to overcome the data inhomogeneity stemming from multiple collection locations by standardizing the recorded data as well as by deriving modalities less affected by the variation in recording conditions from the raw data.

To reduce data heterogeneity introduced by using different cameras we utilize the skeleton sequences instead of the raw RGB video. First, the recorded RGB video was standardized to have 960×540 pixels resolution at 30 frames per second for all locations and cameras. Human pose is extracted using the RTMPose [19] pose-extraction pipeline from the RGB frames of the walking-in-place and dual-tasks (Fig. 2b).

We recognize that the placement of the camera and the subject's relative position to it introduce the following factors (Fig. 3) affecting the extracted skeleton sequence:

1. Translation: if the subject is not centered in the frame, it introduces an offset to the extracted joint co-ordinates.
2. Scale: subjects' distance from the camera results in a scale difference when projected onto the image plane.
3. Rotation: if the camera is not level, the extracted pose will be rotated as well.

If a center is biased towards a specific label, the translation, scale and rotation parameters of the recording may strongly correlate with the labels of the collected data, introducing a biased spurious correlation into the dataset, which negatively impacts the generalization capability of the classifier.

Following our prior work [12], we translate and rescale the skeleton sequences to move the hip to the origin and to make the spine unit length. The skeleton sequences are interpolated to 10 frames per second and the joint motion periods are extracted using SelfDTW [16]. These preprocessing steps introduce scale and translation invariance but do not yet solve the issue of rotation.

To solve the issue of rotation, we standardize the rotation of skeleton sequences by rotating the pose so the spine is parallel with the Y axis on a reference frame where the subject is static (the final frame of the mental arithmetic task). The calculated rotation is applied to the extracted skeleton sequence frame-by-frame, removing rotation caused by a non-level camera but retains the rotation introduced by the subject's motion during the motor and dual task (Fig. 3).

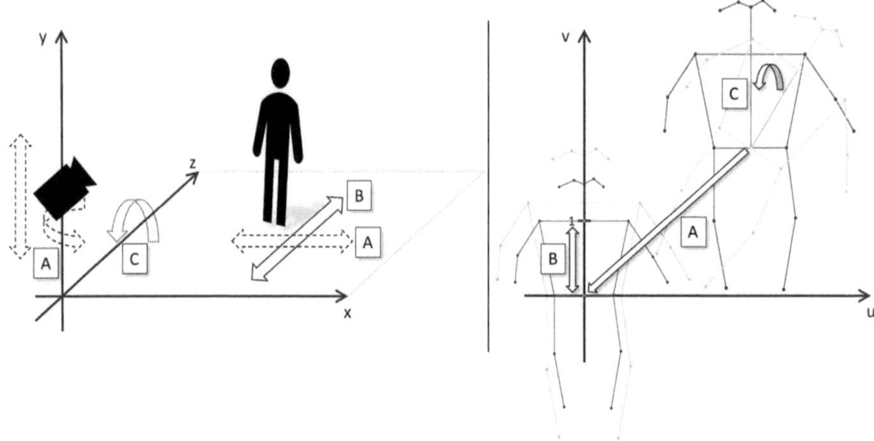

Fig. 3. The subject's distance (solid arrow), relative position (dashed arrows) in the frame and camera tilt (dotted arrow) varies across centers. These effects introduce translation (A), scale (B) and rotation (C) to the extracted skeleton sequences which increase data heterogeneity. To overcome this, in addition to the translation (A) and scaling (B) normalization steps detailed in [12], the extracted pose is rotated (C) so that the spine is parallel to the vertical axis.

The cognitive modality is not affected by the multi-center problem (Fig. 2a) because the mental arithmetic questions are generated using standardized parameters at every location.

3.3 Classification Problem Definition

The objective of the classifier is to predict whether a subject suffers from cognitive impairment based on the data recorded during a session with our dual-task-based assessment system. The measurements are conducted at multiple locations and using different camera devices which leads to increased data heterogeneity, making it more challenging to construct a single model capable of reliably predicting cognitive impairment.

We define the problem as a binary classification problem, where healthy subjects are to be classified as negative and subjects with cognitive impairment (MCI and dementia) are to be classified as positive. Given standardized motor X_{motor} and cognitive $X_{cognitive}$ input modalities derived from the data collected from multiple centers and recording devices, the task of the classifier is to predict the ground truth label $\hat{y} \in \{0, 1\}$. $\hat{y} = 0$ if the subject is healthy and $\hat{y} = 1$ if the subject suffers from MCI or dementia. The classifier outputs $y \in [0, 1]$, the probability of the subject suffering from cognitive impairment. If $y > 0.5$, a positive (suffers from MCI or dementia) prediction is assigned to the subject, otherwise if $y <= 0.5$ the prediction is negative (healthy). It is important to note that the magnitude of the predicted y value does not correspond to the severity of cognitive impairment.

3.4 Classification Model

For feature extraction and for the prediction of y from the inputs X_{motor} and $X_{cognitive}$, we rely on the PPGCN pipeline [12], a graph convolutional neural network exploiting the periodicity of gait.

$X_{motor} \in \Re^{(N_{trials} \times N_{dims}) \times N_{periods} \times N_{phase} \times N_{joints}}$ is the two-dimensional skeleton sequence extracted from the recorded RGB frames, where $N_{trials} = 3$ is the number of repeats of tasks during an experiment, $N_{dims} = 2$ is dimensionality of the pose sequence, $N_{periods} = 10$ is the number periods extracted, $N_{phase} = 50$ is the number of phase samples by SelfDTW [16], and $N_{joints} = 17$ is the number of joints in the skeleton sequence extracted by RTMPose [19].

The cognitive modality, $X_{cognitive}$ consists of the average response time and accuracy for the single mental arithmetic task and the dual task calculated from the collected answer data (Fig. 2a). $X_{cognitive} \in \Re^{+^{N_{trials} \times 4}}$ contains four features per trial: average response times and response accuracy for the mental arithmetic and dual tasks.

3.5 Categorical Feature Distance Loss

The binary pairwise feature distance loss of the PPGCN pipeline has been enhanced to be a categorical feature distance loss aware of the underlying healthy, MCI and dementia labels. The motor modality features F, extracted from X_{motor} are separated into sub-batches of $F^c, c \in C = \{\text{Healthy, MCI, Dementia}\}$, corresponding to features of each label. A sub-batch F^c is designated to be positive, F^{c+}, with the negative sub-batch $F^{c-} = F^{C'}$ being the remaining c' class features: $C' = \{c' | c' \in C, c' \neq c\}$. The sub-batches are used to maximize the pairwise cosine similarity L^c_{same} of both F^{c+} and F^{c-} individually as well as minimize it for the opposing labels of F^{c+} and F^{c-} simultaneously in L^c_{opp}, as defined in Eqs. 1, 2, 3, and 4.

$$L^c_{same} = \frac{L^{c+}_{same}}{\|F^{c+}\|(\|F^{c+}\| - 1)} + \frac{L^{-}_{same}}{\|F^{c-}\|(\|F^{c-}\| - 1)} \tag{1}$$

$$L^{c+}_{same} = \sum_i \sum_j 1 - \frac{\mathbf{F^{c+}_i} \mathbf{F^{c+}_j}}{\|\mathbf{F^{c+}_i}\| \|\mathbf{F^{c+}_j}\|} \quad \text{where } i, j \in [1, \|F^{c+}\|], i \neq j \tag{2}$$

$$L^{c-}_{same} = \sum_i \sum_j 1 - \frac{\mathbf{F^{c-}_i} \mathbf{F^{c-}_j}}{\|\mathbf{F^{c-}_i}\| \|\mathbf{F^{c-}_j}\|} \quad \text{where } i, j \in [1, \|F^{c-}\|], i \neq j \tag{3}$$

$$L^c_{opp} = \frac{1}{\|\mathbf{F^{c+}}\| \|\mathbf{F^{c-}}\|} \sum_i \sum_j \frac{\mathbf{F^{c+}_i} \mathbf{F^{c-}_j}}{\|\mathbf{F^{c+}_i}\| \|\mathbf{F^{c-}_j}\|} \tag{4}$$

$$\text{where } i \in [1, \|F^{c+}\|], j \in [1, \|F^{c-}\|]$$

The final feature loss is calculated as the average of each c label loss component: $L_{same} = \frac{1}{|C|}\sum_c L^c_{same}$ and $L_{opp} = \frac{1}{|C|}\sum_c L^c_{opp}$. This extension fits into the formulation of the final training loss L from [12], as defined in Eq. 5.

$$L = \frac{(\alpha+\beta)L_{BCE} + \alpha L_{same} + \beta L_{opp}}{2\alpha + 2\beta} \tag{5}$$

where L_{BCE} is the supervised Binary Cross-Entropy task loss and $\alpha = 9.0233$, $\beta = 8.7723$ (determined via the Optuna hyperparameter optimization framework [3]) are the coefficients of L_{same} and L_{opp}, respectively.

3.6 Data Augmentation

Due to the limited amount of samples collected as well as imbalance being present in dataset labels, in addition to increasing the number of samples available for training the classifier, our goal with data augmentation is to balance the number of positive and negative samples. Wishing to augment the dataset by a factor of K, we exploit the periodicity of X_{motor} and apply a shift K times across the period dimension.

Given a target augmentation factor $K \leq N_{period}$ (larger values would not produce new data), the magnitudes of the applied period shifts i can be expressed as $i \in \{ns|n \in \mathbb{N},\ \text{ns} < N_{period}\}$, where s is the stride of the shift magnitudes, defined as $s = \lceil \frac{N_{period}}{K} \rceil$. It can be seen that this approach maximizes the difference between the applied shift magnitudes for any desired $K > 1$ which in turn maximizes the difference between newly generated and original samples which benefits the data augmentation process.

X_{motor} is augmented into X'_{motor} by applying translation with modulo to its period dimension of $X_{motor_{period}} = \{p_1, p_2, ..., p_{N_{period}}\}$ as described in Eq. 6.

$$X'_{motor_{period}}(j) = X_{motor_{period}}(j - i)_{mod N_{period}} \tag{6}$$

where $X_{motor_{period}}(j) = p_j, j \in 1, ..., N_{period}, i \in \{ns|n \in \mathbb{N}, ns < N_{period}\}$

To illustrate, if $K = 2$, then $s = 5$ and the shift magnitudes will be $i \in \{0, 5\}$. One half of the augmented dataset will be the original data, another half will be shifted by 5 periods.

The data augmentation process also utilizes the underlying healthy, MCI and Dementia labels. Healthy samples are shifted $K_{Healthy}$, MCI samples K_{MCI}, and dementia samples $K_{Dementia}$ times.

4 Experiments

4.1 Dataset

We collected data from 660 subjects in five centers (Locations A, B, C, D, E), using two camera devices: Microsoft Kinect V2, and a generic USB camera. Each sample is the skeleton sequence and mental arithmetic scores of a subject recording during a session (three loops of the cognitive, motor and dual-tasks) recorded with our dual-task system.

Healthy subjects are labeled as negative, subjects with MCI or dementia (limited to Alzheimer's disease dementia and dementia with Lewy bodies), annotated by geriatric psychiatrists based on subjects' diagnoses. This study was approved by the Ethics Committees of Osaka University Hospital (Study Number 21236(T9)-10, Suita, Japan). Subjects deemed to be at health risk for participation were excluded in accordance with the study protocol. Patients are excluded if they have dementia due to medication or cerebrovascular disease, suffer from severe medical conditions, have co-occurring psychiatric disorders such as schizophrenia, mood disorders, or substance abuse, or if the attending physician considers them unsuitable for participation. Informed consent was obtained from all participants.

The majority of the data has been recorded using the proprietary Microsoft Kinect V2 camera, which has been phased out in favor of a generic USB camera version due its obsolescence. Each location has significant bias in both the recording device used and in class labels (Table 1).

Table 1. Sample counts per recording device and collection location

	Loc. A	Loc. B	Loc. C	Loc. D	Loc. E
Kinect V2	249	0	214	0	0
USB Camera	0	78	34	52	33

We observed degradation in online prediction accuracy between samples collected with different cameras. As such, our goal is to mitigate the detrimental effect of data heterogeneity due to using different camera devices. To achieve this, we split the dataset into subsets based on the recording device. The resulting Kinect V2 dataset contains 463 samples, 249 of which are negative and 214 positive collected from two centers (Table 2). This dataset is an extension of the dataset used in our previous work [12] containing 71 additional positively labeled (41 MCI, 30 dementia) subjects to improve dataset balance.

Table 2. Distribution of subject sex and label counts per location for Kinect V2 samples

	Healthy	MCI	Dementia	Male	Female	Total
Loc. A	249	0	0	107	142	249
Loc. C	0	98	116	79	135	214

The USB camera dataset collected with exclusively with our presented new system contains 197 samples, 78 of which are negative and 119 of which are positive, collected from four centers, with one in common with the Kinect V2 subset (Table 3). The distribution of sex and healthy/MCI/dementia labels for Kinect V2 and USB camera samples are listed in Table 4.

Table 3. Distribution of subject sex and label counts per location for USB camera samples

	Healthy	MCI	Dementia	Male	Female	Total
Loc. B	78	0	0	30	48	78
Loc. C	0	26	8	14	20	34
Loc. D	0	4	48	17	35	52
Loc. E	0	12	21	7	26	33

Table 4. Distribution of subject sex and label counts for Kinect V2 and USB camera samples

	Kinect V2		USB Camera	
	Female	Male	Female	Male
Healthy	142	107	48	30
MCI	62	36	26	14
Dementia	73	43	56	24

4.2 Experimental Settings

To train, validate and test the classifier model, we separate both the Kinect V2 and USB camera datasets (Table 5) into five folds, balanced according to multiple criteria, in order of priority: the cognitive impairment label (healthy, MCI or dementia), MMSE score, sex and age.

In this setup one fold is selected to be the test set, while three of the remaining four are used as training data and the remaining fold as the validation set. For each test set, four models are trained with a rotating validation set, each tested using the same test set. Then, the next fold is selected as the test set and the above steps are repeated until all folds have been used as the test set. This results in 20 classifiers, four (models I, II, III and IV) for each test set.

The augmentation factors K were chosen using grid search in the $[0, 5]$ range. For the Kinect V2 samples $K_{Healthy} = 2$, $K_{MCI} = 5$, $K_{Dementia} = 4$, for the USB camera data, $K_{Healthy} = 5$, $K_{MCI} = 5$, $K_{Dementia} = 1$ produced the best results. The pre- and post-augmentation sample counts are listed in Table 6. Additionally, batches are sampled evenly so that an equal amount of Healthy, MCI and dementia labeled samples are included, with minority labels randomly oversampled during an epoch to achieve this. Data augmentation is applied to the training set only, validation and test sets are not augmented.

Table 5. Distribution of label and sex per fold for Kinect V2 and USB camera samples

	Kinect V2					USB Camera				
	Fold 1	Fold 2	Fold 3	Fold 4	Fold 5	Fold 1	Fold 2	Fold 3	Fold 4	Fold 5
Healthy	50	50	50	50	49	16	16	16	15	15
MCI	20	20	19	19	20	8	8	8	9	8
Dementia	23	23	24	23	23	16	16	15	15	16
Male	56	55	55	55	56	26	26	26	25	26
Female	37	38	38	37	36	14	14	13	14	13

Table 6. Label counts pre- and post-augmentation

	Original			Augmented		
	Healthy	MCI	Dementia	Healthy	MCI	Dementia
Kinect V2	249	98	116	498	490	464
USB Camera	78	40	78	390	200	78

First, we show the performance of PPGCN [12] classifiers trained, validated and tested using only Kinect V2 data to serve as a baseline. To demonstrate the degraded performance on USB camera samples, and to confirm that it is due to data heterogeneity arising from the use of multiple camera devices, we measure USB camera sample performance using a classifier trained only on Kinect V2 data.

Then, we optimize the classifiers using USB camera samples. Due to significantly fewer USB camera samples being available than Kinect V2 samples, we take a transfer learning approach, allowing the classifier to adapt already learnt features from the Kinect V2 dataset to the USB camera data.

Classifier performance is evaluated by measuring the accuracy (Eq. 7). For deeper analysis, sensitivity or true positive rate (TPR, Eq. 8) and specificity or true negative rate (TNR, Eq. 9) are also calculated.

$$\text{Accuracy} = \frac{\text{TPR} + \text{TNR}}{2} \tag{7}$$

$$\text{Sensitivity} = \text{TPR} = \frac{\text{TP}}{\text{TP} + \text{FN}} \tag{8}$$

where TP: True Positives, FN: False Negatives.

$$\text{Specificity} = \text{TNR} = \frac{\text{TN}}{\text{TN} + \text{FP}} \tag{9}$$

where TN: True Negatives, FP: False Positives.

Since sensitivity is the key metric for performance as it corresponds to the classifer's performance for detecting MCI and dementia, model selection is performed based on the highest sensitivity with specificity as the tie-breaker.

4.3 Ablation Studies

To evaluate the impact of the proposed data standardization and augmentation procedures we conduct ablation studies by disabling both the spine rotation normalization and the period-shift data augmentation (setting to $K_{Healthy} = 1$, $K_{MCI} = 1$, $K_{Dementia} = 1$) both one-at-a-time and simultaneously.

5 Results and Discussion

Table 7. Overview of results, per dataset used for training and testing

Dataset		Performance		
Training	Testing	Sensitivity	Specificity	Accuracy
PPGCN [12] (Baseline)	USB Camera	0.4663 ± 0.0842	0.9840 ± 0.0080	0.7251 ± 0.0409
Kinect V2	Kinect V2	0.9493 ± 0.0408	0.6914 ± 0.0556	0.8203 ± 0.0432
Kinect V2	USB Camera	0.8930 ± 0.0924	0.5785 ± 0.1271	0.7358 ± 0.0544
USB Camera (Transfer Learning)	**USB Camera**	**0.9394 ± 0.0496**	**0.9065 ± 0.0576**	**0.9230 ± 0.0268**

Average 5-fold cross-validation accuracy of the baseline PPGCN model in a multi-center setting is 0.7251. After training on the extended Kinect V2 dataset, the classification model achieves an accuracy of 0.8203, with a sensitivity of 0.9493 and specificity of 0.6914. Testing this model directly on the USB data results in a degraded accuracy of 0.7358, as well as an increased bias towards a specificity of 0.8930 versus 0.5785 specificity.

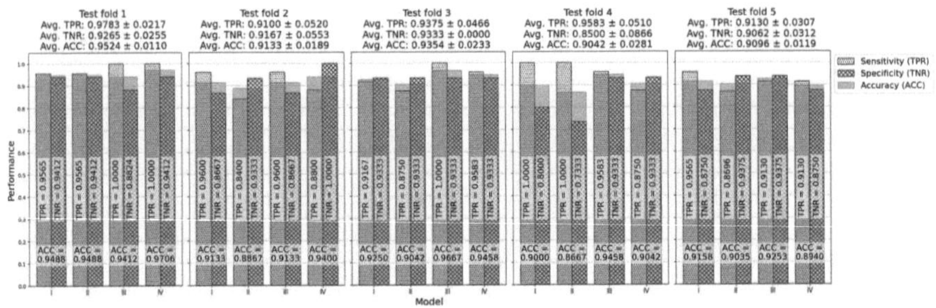

Fig. 4. Five-fold cross-validation results after transfer learning on the USB camera data set showing the measured sensitivity (TPR) and specificity (TNR) and accuracy (ACC) of models I, II, III, IV for each test fold.

Transfer learning with USB samples improves average classifier accuracy to 0.9230. Per-model breakdown of 5-fold cross-validation results for the USB camera data set are detailed in Fig. 4. The classifiers achieve a combined AUC of 0.9642 (Fig. 5).

Ablation experiment results (Table 8) show that the classifier performs best with both data augmentation and spine rotation normalization enabled.

Table 8. Effects of data augmentation and spine rotation normalization

Augmentation	Rotation	Sensitivity	Specificity	Accuracy
On	On	0.9394 ± 0.0496	0.9065 ± 0.0576	0.9230 ± 0.0268
On	Off	0.9370 ± 0.0473	0.8576 ± 0.0749	0.8973 ± 0.0361
Off	On	0.9496 ± 0.0407	0.8156 ± 0.1086	0.8826 ± 0.0512
Off	Off	0.9280 ± 0.0683	0.7694 ± 0.1267	0.8487 ± 0.0592

Per-location breakdown of results shows 0.9065 specificity for Location B and sensitivities are 0.9021, 0.9650, 0.9722 for Locations C, D, and E, respectively (Table 9). Average specificity for the healthy class is 0.9065, and average sensitivity for MCI and dementia labels is 0.9035 and 0.9597, respectively (Table 10).

Table 9. USB camera data sensitivity and specificity per location

	Sensitivity	Specificity
Loc. B	N/A	0.9065 ± 0.0576
Loc. C	0.9021 ± 0.0876	N/A
Loc. D	0.9650 ± 0.0499	N/A
Loc. E	0.9722 ± 0.0569	N/A

Our observations of reduced cognitive impairment detection performance on USB data during the system's online operation, are confirmed by the baseline PPGCN's as well as the Kinect V2-trained model's reduced accuracy when tested with the newly collected USB samples (Table 7). We successfully overcome this domain gap by applying transfer learning to the baseline model.

The proposed period-shift augmentation most significantly contributes to increased performance, further emphasizing the importance of the periodicity of gait for tasks involving it. Spine angle normalization also improves overall performance (Table 8) and reduces bias.

Compared to the average MMSE sensitivities of 81% for dementia and 45% for MCI [26], our assessment is more accurate while requiring the same time to administer. Furthermore, it is immune to PE and generalizes well across multiple centers. Further data collection will improve the fineness of the measured results and enable the training of even more robust classifiers for multi-center settings.

The selected model, model IV of test fold 1 (Fig. 4) achieves an accuracy of 0.9706 and an AUC of 0.9817. Updating our system with this classifier will further improve its real-time cognitive impairment detection capabilities.

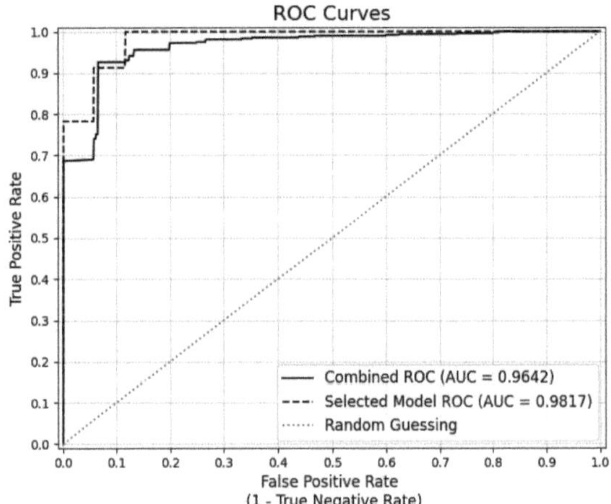

Fig. 5. ROC curve of all classifiers combined and of the selected model (test fold 1, model IV) after transfer learning on the USB camera data set.

Table 10. USB camera data sensitivity and specificity per label

	Sensitivity	Specificity
Healthy	N/A	0.9065 ± 0.0576
MCI	0.9035 ± 0.0930	N/A
Dementia	0.9597 ± 0.0532	N/A

6 Conclusion

In this work we presented a real-time dual-task-based cognitive impairment assessment system. Our system can perform assessment online using a gait-based GCNN architecture to predict the subject's cognitive state. The data collected from assessment sessions is regularly used to update the system offline with a better performing classifier.

We presented the performance improvements of the latest offline update. Performance significantly improved after addressing data heterogeneity due to multiple centers and different camera devices. The classifiers achieved an average sensitivity of 0.9394 and an average specificity of 0.9065 in a 5-fold cross-validation setup across multiple data collection centers.

Acknowledgement. We are grateful to all participants for their cooperation in the data collection process.

References

1. What Is Mild Cognitive Impairment? | Alzheimers.gov. https://www.alzheimers.gov/alzheimers-dementias/mild-cognitive-impairment. Accessed 12 May 2025
2. Åhman, H.B., Cedervall, Y., Kilander, L., et al.: Dual-task tests discriminate between dementia, mild cognitive impairment, subjective cognitive impairment, and healthy controls - a cross-sectional cohort study. BMC Geriatr. **20**(1), 258 (2020). https://doi.org/10.1186/s12877-020-01645-1
3. Akiba, T., Sano, S., Yanase, T., Ohta, T., Koyama, M.: Optuna: a next-generation hyperparameter optimization framework. In: KDD '19: Proceedings of the 25th ACM SIGKDD International Conference on Knowledge Discovery & Data Mining, pp. 2623–2631. Association for Computing Machinery, New York, NY, USA (2019https://doi.org/10.1145/3292500.3330701
4. Anderson, N.D.: State of the science on mild cognitive impairment (MCI). CNS Spectr. **24**(1), 78–87 (2019). https://doi.org/10.1017/S1092852918001347
5. Arevalo-Rodriguez, I., Smailagic, N., et al.: Mini-Mental State Examination (MMSE) for the early detection of dementia in people with mild cognitive impairment (MCI). Cochrane Database of Systematic Reviews (7) (2021). https://doi.org/10.1002/14651858.CD010783.pub3
6. Campello, V.M., Gkontra, P., Izquierdo, C., et al.: Multi-centre, multi-vendor and multi-disease cardiac segmentation: The M&Ms challenge. IEEE Trans. Med. Imaging **40**(12), 3543–3554 (2021). https://doi.org/10.1109/TMI.2021.3090082
7. Chang, Q., Yan, Z., Zhou, M., Qu, H., He, X., Zhang, H., et al.: Mining multi-center heterogeneous medical data with distributed synthetic learning. Nat. Commun. **14**(5510), 1–16 (2023). https://doi.org/10.1038/s41467-023-40687-y
8. van Dyck, C.H., Swanson, C.J., et al.: Lecanemab in Early Alzheimer's Disease. N. Engl. J. Med. (2023). https://doi.org/10.1056/NEJMoa2212948
9. Evans-Lacko, S., Aguzzoli, E., Read, S., Comas-Herrera, A., Farina, N.: World Alzheimer Report 2024: Global Changes in Attitudes to Dementia. Alzheimer's Disease International, London, United Kingdom (2024)
10. Folstein, M.F., Folstein, S.E., McHugh, P.R.: Mini-mental state: a practical method for grading the cognitive state of patients for the clinician. J. Psychiatr. Res. **12**(3), 189–198 (1975)
11. Fu, A., Shen, T., Roberts, S.B., et al.: Optimizing the efficiency and effectiveness of data quality assurance in a multicenter clinical dataset. J. Am. Med. Inform. Assoc. **32**(5), 835–844 (2025). https://doi.org/10.1093/jamia/ocaf042
12. GodÃ, Ã., Wu, S., Okura, F., et al.: Ppgcn: Phase-aligned periodic graph convolutional network for dual-task-based cognitive impairment detection. IEEE Access **12**, 37679–37691 (2024). https://doi.org/10.1109/ACCESS.2024.3371517
13. Gong, Z., Xu, T., Peng, N., Cheng, X., Niu, C., Wiestler, B., et al.: A multi-center, multi-parametric MRI dataset of primary and secondary brain tumors. Sci. Data **11**(789), 1–6 (2024). https://doi.org/10.1038/s41597-024-03634-0
14. Jha, D., Tomar, N.K., Sharma, V., et al.: Polypdb: A curated multi-center dataset for development of ai algorithms in colonoscopy. CoRR **abs/2409.00045** (2024). https://doi.org/10.48550/arXiv.2409.00045
15. Liu, J., Wu, S., Okura, F., et al.: Two-stream graph convolutional networks with task-specific loss for dual-task gait analysis. In: 2023 EMBC, pp. 1–4 (2023https://doi.org/10.1109/EMBC40787.2023.10339953
16. Makihara, Y., Aqmar, M., et al.: Phase estimation of a single quasi-periodic signal. Signal Processing, IEEE Transactions on **62**(8), 2066–2079 (2014). https://doi.org/10.1109/TSP.2014.2306174

17. Matsuura, T., Sakashita, K., Grushnikov, A., et al.: Statistical analysis of dual-task gait characteristics for cognitive score estimation. Sci. Rep. **9**(19927), 1–12 (2019). https://doi.org/10.1038/s41598-019-56485-w
18. Morris, R., Lord, S., Bunce, J., et al.: Gait and cognition: mapping the global and discrete relationships in ageing and neurodegenerative disease. Neurosci. Biobehav. Rev. **64:326-45.** (2016). https://doi.org/10.1016/j.neubiorev.2016.02.012
19. Open-MMLab: Rtmpose: Real-time multi-person pose estimation based on mmpose. https://github.com/open-mmlab/mmpose/. Accessed 12 May 2025
20. Santacruz, K.S., Swagerty, D.: Early Diagnosis of Dementia. Am. Fam. Physician **63**(4), 703–714 (2001). https://www.aafp.org/pubs/afp/issues/2001/0215/p703.html
21. Seifallahi, M., Galvin, J.E., Ghoraani, B.: Curve walking reveals more gait impairments in older adults with mild cognitive impairment than straight walking: a kinect camera-based study. J. Alzheimer's Disease Reports **8**(1), 423–435 (2024). https://doi.org/10.3233/ADR-230149
22. Seoni, S., Shahini, A., Meiburger, K.M., et al.: All you need is data preparation: a systematic review of image harmonization techniques in Multi-center/device studies for medical support systems. Comput. Methods Programs Biomed. **250**, 108200 (2024). https://doi.org/10.1016/j.cmpb.2024.108200
23. Skillbäck, T., Blennow, K., Zetterberg, H., Skoog, J., Rydén, L., Wetterberg, H., et al.: Slowing gait speed precedes cognitive decline by several years. Alzheimer's Dement. **18**(9), 1667–1676 (2022). https://doi.org/10.1002/alz.12537
24. van Soest, J.P.A., Dekker, A.L.A.J., Roelofs, E., Nalbantov, G.: Application of Machine Learning for Multicenter Learning, pp. 71–97. Springer International Publishing, Cham (2015). https://doi.org/10.1007/978-3-319-18305-3_6
25. Tisher, A., Salardini, A.: A comprehensive update on treatment of dementia. Semin. Neurol. **39**(02), 167–178 (2019). https://doi.org/10.1055/s-0039-1683408
26. Tombaugh, T.N., McIntyre, N.J.: The mini-mental state examination: a comprehensive review. J. Am. Geriatr. Soc. **40**(9), 922–935 (1992)
27. Vrudhula, A., Kwan, A.C., Ouyang, D., Cheng, S.: Machine learning and bias in medical imaging: opportunities and challenges. Circ.: Cardiovasc. Imaging (2024). https://www.ahajournals.org/doi/full/10.1161/CIRCIMAGING.123.015495#sec-2
28. Wu, S., Matsuura, T., Okura, F., et al.: Detecting lower MMSE scores in older adults using cross-trial features from a dual-task with gait and arithmetic. IEEE Access **9**, 150268–150282 (2021)
29. Ya-Chen, L., Shu-Chun, L., En-Chi, C.: Practice effect and test-retest reliability of the mini-mental state examination-2 in people with dementia. BMC Geriatr. **22**(67), 1–8 (2022)
30. Yan, S., Xiong, Y., Lin, D.: Spatial temporal graph convolutional networks for skeleton-based action recognition. In: AAAI, pp. 7444–7452 (2018)

Ensemble-Based Progressive YOLOv11 Framework for Quantitative Analysis of Riverine Environments

Saomyaraj Jha[1(✉)], Anubhav Jain[2], Vivek Kumar[3], Dhruv Singhal[4], Partha Pratim Roy[5], and Alireza Alaei[6]

[1] Pandit Deendayal Energy University, Gandhinagar, India
saomyaraj812@gmail.com
[2] College of Engineering Roorkee, Roorkee, India
[3] National Institute of Technology, Raipur, India
vkumar.btech2022.bme@nitrr.ac.in
[4] S.D. College of Engineering and Technology, Muzaffarnagar, India
[5] Indian Institute of Technology Roorkee, Roorkee, India
partha@cs.iitr.ac.in
[6] Southern Cross University, Gold Coast, Australia

Abstract. Million tonnes of plastic waste from rivers and coastal communities enter the seas and oceans every year. Therefore, monitoring and reducing riverine pollution is vital for environmental sustainability and public health. As manual surveys and monitoring strategies are costly and ineffective, automated computer vision solutions have emerged in recent years. However, detecting and counting floating litter in real time is challenging due to water surface reflections, occlusions, and lighting variations. This paper introduces a three-phase progressive training strategy using YOLOv11-based object detection algorithms. Phase 1 is Progressive Model Training, which trains YOLOv11 variants sequentially with increasing capacity as it allows for earlier convergence on architectures that are simpler before the models scale up. Phase 2 is the Ensembling that captures the features of multiple variants and combines them. Phase 3, Test-Time Augmentation, evaluates each model on four resolutions, maximizing inference accuracy by selecting the best scale for each image. StrongSORT, by its refined appearance embeddings and motion-consistency associations was integrated into our pipeline on top of YOLO's detection to enhance per-object tracking and counting in live video, maintaining consistent object IDs even under partial occlusion and rapid water flow. The experimental results on our manually collected and annotated dataset show that the best model selected from our ensemble achieves a mAP@0.5 of 0.939, outperforming individual baseline variants.

Keywords: River Litter Detection · YOLOv11 · Progressive Training · Ensemble Learning · Test-Time Augmentation · StrongSORT

C. Wallraven et al. (Eds.): ACPR 2025, LNCS 16174, pp. 387–401, 2026.
https://doi.org/10.1007/978-981-95-4395-3_27

1 Introduction

1.1 Motivation

Riverine pollution through litter and debris disposal has become one of the most important environmental challenges of our time. Annual plastic production rose from 1.5 Mt in 1950 to over 400 Mt by 2022, and the vast majority of marine litter ($\approx$ 85%) is plastic [16]. Lebreton *et al.* estimated that inland rivers contribute significantly to marine plastic pollution, with $\sim 1,000$ rivers responsible for around $\sim$ 80% of the 0.82.7 million tonnes of plastic entering the oceans annually [11]. Microplastic pollution also contaminates the food web: Portuguese river studies found heavy concentrations in sediments and benthic invertebrates, with small organisms showing signs of malnutrition and digestive harm [18]. These results underscore the importance of riverine litter monitoring in sustainability efforts as early detection and removal of floating waste can block debris before it reaches marine environments [14]. The complexity of monitoring such vast and dynamic systems presents significant challenges that traditional manual methods cannot sufficiently address.

Traditional monitoring approaches have relied primarily on manual surveys and visual counting methods, which were labor-intensive, time-consuming, and often impractical for real-time surveillance of large river systems [19]. Manual river patrol methods face difficulties in detecting and handling floating objects due to the vast spatial coverage required, temporal variability in debris transport, and safety concerns associated with water-based monitoring activities [21]. These conventional approaches are further complicated by the high spatial and temporal heterogeneity in plastic debris distribution, requiring large sample sizes for statistical power to detect meaningful changes in abundance [19]. Environmental factors such as surface reflections, changing light, and occlusions from vegetation or water features add extra hurdles for automated aquatic monitoring and detection, making reliable object recognition far more difficult [9,13]. The dynamic nature of flowing water introduces motion blur and rapid changes in object positioning, while the diversity of floating debris presents classification challenges due to varying shapes, sizes, and optical properties [26]. To address these challenges, automated computer vision solutions have emerged in recent years [1]. However, existing approaches remain imperfect, and there is a substantial demand for more accurate and generalized methods in this domain [20].

1.2 Related Works

Initial automated detection systems for floating debris used traditional image processing techniques, including background subtraction, frame differencing, and basic image segmentation methods [13]. These approaches struggled with the complexity of aquatic environments, particularly regarding sunlight reflection, water plant occlusion, and significant scale differences between near and distant targets [9]. Early detection systems also relied on spectral indices and bio-optical modeling approaches, but these methods required extensive calibration and demonstrated sensitivity to changes in water optical properties [12].

Then, deep learning techniques have transformed riverine litter detection capabilities, with CNNs demonstrating superior performance over traditional methods. Wolf et al. developed specialized CNN architectures, including Plastic Litter Detector (PLD)-CNN with 83% accuracy for image classification and Plastic Litter Quantifier (PLQ)-CNN with 71% accuracy for macro-plastic subcategorization [23]. The YOLO family of object detection algorithms has emerged as a dominant approach for floating debris detection due to their real-time processing capabilities and robust performance. For instance, Ramya R. et al. applied YOLOv7 on 2,640 river images and reported F1 (≈ 0.93) and mAP@0.5 (≈ 0.93) [17]. Lin et al. introduced FMA-YOLOv5s (Feature Map Attention YOLOv5s) with mosaic augmentation and expanded their training set from 1,920 to 4,800 samples by compositing labeled debris onto clean river backgrounds and achieved 79.4% mAP at 42 FPS [9]. Chen and Zhu's lightweight YOLOv5 on the "Orca" river-garbage dataset reached 84.9% mAP@0.5 and 88.7% precision [3], while Maharjan et al. showed YOLOv5s attained 81% mAP@0.5 on UAV images of Mekong tributaries (with transfer-learned YOLOv4 at 83%) [10]. Studies have evaluated multiple CNN architectures for floating object detection, including SSD, Faster-RCNN Faster-RCNN with VGG16, MobileNetV2, and ResNet50 backbones, and various YOLO versions, with YOLOv5 demonstrating superior balance between accuracy and computational efficiency [21,26]. These evaluations also confirm that YOLO variants often outperform its predecessors in speed and accuracy when tuned appropriately. Zailan et al. reported an "optimized" YOLOv4 hitting 89.0% mAP@0.5 [25]. Advanced YOLO variants (including YOLOv9) have been tested in ensemble systems, though high baseline detection accuracies remain challenging due to complex water-surface dynamics [5,13].

Ensemble approaches for object detection have also gained prominence through methods such as Weighted Boxes Fusion (WBF), which combines predictions from multiple models to improve overall detection accuracy [5]. Recent implementations have successfully integrated multiple state-of-the-art detectors, including YOLOv9-e, YOLOR-W6, InternImage, and CO-DETR using ensemble techniques [5]. In addition to ensembling, other methods have been explored to further enhance detection performance. One such technique Test-time augmentation (TTA) is an effective heuristic that applies geometric/scale transforms at inference and averages the outputs. Kimura et al. noted that TTA effectively ensembles over input combinations to improve model generalization [8]. Progressive training or curriculum schemes have been explored to speed convergence, although few published works applied this to litter detection explicitly [8].

Object tracking has become essential for continuous monitoring applications, with DeepSORT establishing early benchmarks for multi-object tracking in video sequences. DeepSORT (Wojke et al. 2017) is a classic real-time tracker: it extends the SORT algorithm [2] by adding a deep appearance embedding, which greatly reduces identity switches in occlusion [22]. More recent work (Du et al. 2023) introduces StrongSORT, which improves DeepSORT by enhancing the detector and feature embedder and by adding an appearance-free linking step to fuse short tracklets without matching embeddings [4]. The evolution to StrongSORT has provided enhanced tracking capabilities through improved feature extraction, motion information processing, cost matrix optimization, and advanced post-processing techniques, including AFLink and GSI interpolation, for improved accuracy [4].

Existing riverlitter detection systems often struggle due to real-world variations in lighting, reflections, and occlusions, limitations commonly observed in domain generalization research. These systems frequently miss small debris, such as microplastics and foam, because standard detection methods exhibit low recall on tiny objects [24]. Moreover, trackers based on simplistic motion or appearance models tend to fail under rapid water flow and partial submersion, challenges identified in broader domain adaptation studies [15]. Therefore, we propose an ensemble-based progressive framework built on YOLOv11 [7] for automated detection and counting of diverse riverine macroplastics.

1.3 Contribution and Organization of Paper

In this work, we present a comprehensive framework for realtime detection, tracking, and counting of floating riverine litters. Our key contributions are:

1) We propose a threestage model training pipeline that incrementally scales from YOLOv11nano to YOLOv11large, enabling faster convergence on simpler architectures and more robust feature learning in larger models.
2) By ensembling multiple YOLOv11 variants and applying multiscale testtime augmentation (608, 640, 672, 704)px, we capture complementary detections across models and resolutions, pushing mAP@0.5 to 0.939 on our custom dataset by boosting precision, recall and F1 score.
3) We also integrated StrongSORT's refined appearance embeddings and motionconsistency association to maintain stable object identities under watersurface reflections, occlusions, and rapid flow, enabling accurate per-object counting in live video streams.

The rest of the paper is organized as follows: Sect. 2 explains methodology of the proposed approach followed by Sect. 3, which presents the dataset, experimental setup, and results. Finally, Sect. 4 concludes our key findings and suggests directions for future research.

2 Methodology

As shown in Fig. 1, our proposed real-time litter detection and tracking framework is composed of five components: (1) Data Acquisition and Preprocessing, (2) YOLO Architecture and Loss Function, (3) Proposed Training Strategy, (4) Baseline Model Final Aggregation, and (5) Real-time Tracking and Counting. Our proposed training strategy comprises three stages: (1) Progressive Model Training, (2) Ensemble Model Training, and (3) Test-Time Augmentation for inference. This framework is designed to maximize detection accuracy and robustness against environmental challenges such as reflections, occlusions, and variable lighting.

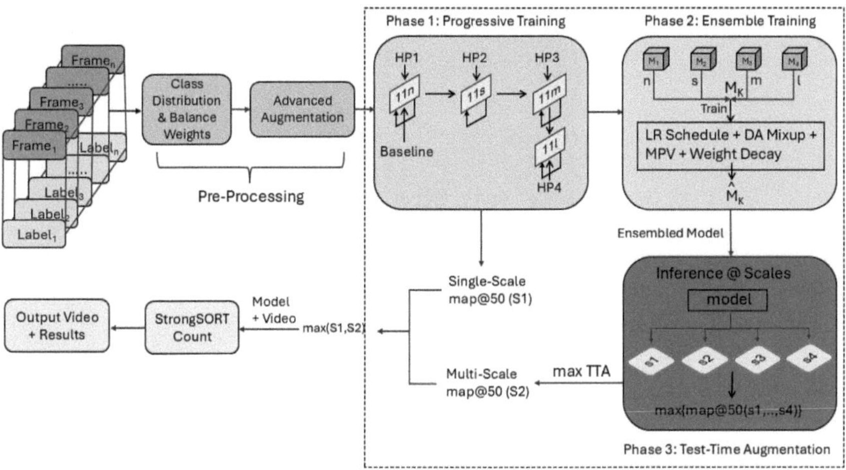

Fig. 1. Block diagram of our threestage training and inference pipeline, showing how images flow through (1) Progressive Model Training, (2) Ensemble with hyperparameter perturbations, and (3) TestTime Augmentation into final detections. In stage 1 we train four variants $v \in \{\mathrm{n, s, m, l}\}$ (nano, small, medium, large); in stage 3 we evaluate each model at four scales $s \in \{608, 640, 672, 704\}$px.

2.1 Data Acquisition and Preprocessing

The collected data is first manually annotated according to five predefined classes and then organized into frames with the corresponding labels. More details on this process can be found in Sect. 3.1.

Let $\mathcal{D} = \{(I_i, \{b_{ij}, c_{ij}\}_{j=1}^{n_i})\}_{i=1}^{N}$ denote the dataset of N images, where each image $I_i \in \mathbb{R}^{H_i \times W_i \times 3}$ has n_i annotated bounding boxes. Each box is represented by $b_{ij} = (x_{ij}, y_{ij}, w_{ij}, h_{ij})$ for $j = (1, \ldots, n_i)$, and $c_{ij} \in \{0, \ldots, C-1\}$ denotes the class index, where $C = 5$ is the total number of classes. We first resize all images to a canonical size $S \times S$ (640×640), producing $\tilde{I}_i = f_{\text{resize}}(I_i)$ where f_{resize} performs bilinear interpolation and then scale the boxes as follows:

$$\tilde{I}_i(u, v) = I_i\Big(\tfrac{u}{S}\, H_i,\ \tfrac{v}{S}\, W_i\Big), \quad u, v \in \{1, \ldots, S\}, \tag{1}$$

$$\tilde{b}_{ij} = \Big(\tfrac{x_{ij} W_i}{S},\ \tfrac{y_{ij} H_i}{S},\ \tfrac{w_{ij} W_i}{S},\ \tfrac{h_{ij} H_i}{S}\Big). \tag{2}$$

A normalization process is then applied by dividing all pixels by 255 ($\tilde{I}_i \leftarrow \frac{\tilde{I}_i}{255}$) to scale them to the $[0, 1]$ range, which enhances the learning capability of our proposed framework. To further improve generalization and help the network learn multi-scale features, we apply a modified *Mosaic* augmentation to increase the training dataset. Four images $\{\tilde{I}_{i_k}\}_{k=1}^{4}$ are randomly selected and combined into a single mosaic image $\hat{I}$ of size $2S \times 2S$:

$$\hat{I}(u,v) = \begin{cases} \tilde{I}_{i_1}(u,v), & 0 \le u < S,\ 0 \le v < S, \\ \tilde{I}_{i_2}(u,v-S), & 0 \le u < S,\ S \le v < 2S, \\ \tilde{I}_{i_3}(u-S,v), & S \le u < 2S,\ 0 \le v < S, \\ \tilde{I}_{i_4}(u-S,v-S), & S \le u < 2S,\ S \le v < 2S. \end{cases} \tag{3}$$

However, because our objects (river litter) can be small and spatially sparse, we restrict aggressive transformations that can excessively distort relative positions. To do so, we choose the mosaic center (x_c, y_c) to lie within the range $[\frac{S}{4}, \frac{3S}{4}] \times [\frac{S}{4}, \frac{3S}{4}]$, so that each image occupies roughly an equal quadrant. We also shift it by $(\Delta x_k, \Delta y_k)$, where $(\Delta x_1, \Delta y_1) = (0,0)$, $(\Delta x_2, \Delta y_2) = (0, -y_c)$, $(\Delta x_3, \Delta y_3) = (-x_c, 0)$, $(\Delta x_4, \Delta y_4) = (-x_c, -y_c)$ to preserve spatial consistency. The mosaic is then downsampled back to $S \times S$ via the following average pooling, so that $\bar{I} \in \mathbb{R}^{S \times S \times 3}$ becomes the final augmented image.

$$\bar{I} = \text{AvgPool}\big(\hat{I};\, \text{kernel} = (2,2),\, \text{stride} = (2,2)\big), \tag{4}$$

The corresponding boxes are also scaled by a factor of $\frac{1}{2}$ in both width and height when mapping from $\hat{I}$ to $\bar{I}$. This "conservative" mosaic ensures diverse scene composition while preserving object geometry for precise localization. Additionally, we apply the HSV color jitter to $\bar{I}$ by shifting the hue (H), scaling the saturation (S), and the value (V) by:

$$(H', S', V') = \big(H + \Delta_h,\ S\,\lambda_s,\ V\,\lambda_v\big), \tag{5}$$

where $\Delta_h \sim \mathcal{U}(-0.015, 0.015)$, $\lambda_s \sim \mathcal{U}(-0.7, 0.7)$, and $\lambda_v \sim \mathcal{U}(-0.4, 0.4)$. Finally, a horizontal flip is applied with probability $p_{\text{flip}} = 0.5$ by mapping $u \mapsto S-1-u$. The resulting images $\bar{I}$ and adjusted boxes are fed into the training dataset.

The class imbalance is also handled via inverse-frequency weights. Let n_i be the total number of examples in class i across the training set, and $N_{\text{total}} = \sum_{i=1}^{C} n_i$. We compute inverse-frequency weights using Eq. (6) so that $\sum_{i=1}^{C} \hat{w}_i = C$. During training, each positive example of class i is weighted by $\hat{w}_i$ in the classification loss. This avoids majority-class dominance and encourages the network to attend equally to rare classes (e.g., foam or polybags) that would otherwise be underrepresented.

$$w_i = \frac{N_{\text{total}}}{C\, n_i}, \quad \hat{w}_i = \frac{w_i}{\sum_{j=1}^{C} w_j} \times C, \tag{6}$$

2.2 YOLO Architecture and Loss Function

The core of our pipeline is the YOLOv11 object detector [7]. It divides the input image $\bar{I} \in \mathbb{R}^{S \times S \times 3}$ into an $S_{\text{grid}} \times S_{\text{grid}}$ grid. Each grid cell predicts B anchors, each contributing $(\hat{t}, \hat{x}, \hat{y}, \hat{w}, \hat{h}, \hat{\mathbf{p}})$, giving an output tensor of shape $\mathbb{R}^{S_{\text{grid}} \times S_{\text{grid}} \times \left(B(5+C)\right)}$.

We scale capacity across four variants: v11n (nano), v11s (small), v11m (medium), v11l (large). At each stage, we fine-tune pretrained weights using our training dataset and transfer learned weights from smaller to larger variants to accelerate convergence. YOLO's objective function consists of three terms, which are listed below.

(i) **Box regression loss** $\mathcal{L}_{\text{CIoU}}$: For the predicted box $\hat{b} = (\hat{x}, \hat{y}, \hat{w}, \hat{h})$ and groundtruth box $b = (x, y, w, h)$, the CIoU loss is computed by:

$$\mathcal{L}_{\text{CIoU}} = 1 - \text{IoU}(b, \hat{b}) + \frac{\rho^2(\mathbf{b}, \hat{\mathbf{b}})}{c^2} + \alpha\, v,$$

where $\rho(\cdot)$ is the Euclidean distance between box centers, c is the diagonal length of the smallest bounding box, v measures aspect-ratio consistency, and α balances these terms.

(ii) **Classification loss** $\mathcal{L}_{\text{cls}}$: a weighted binary crossentropy over each anchor's class predictions. For groundtruth onehot vector $\mathbf{y}$ and predicted logits $\hat{\mathbf{y}}$,

$$\mathcal{L}_{\text{cls}}(\mathbf{y}, \hat{\mathbf{y}}) = -\sum_{i=1}^{C} \hat{w}_i \Big[y_i \log\big(\sigma(\hat{y}_i)\big) + (1 - y_i) \log\big(1 - \sigma(\hat{y}_i)\big) \Big],$$

where $\sigma(\cdot)$ is the sigmoid activation function. Label smoothing can be applied by replacing $y_i \in \{0, 1\}$ with $\tilde{y}_i = y_i(1 - \epsilon) + 0.5\epsilon$ for $\epsilon > 0$.

(iii) **Objectness loss** $\mathcal{L}_{\text{obj}}$: enforces high objectness scores on positive anchors and low on negatives, formulated as binary crossentropy:

$$\mathcal{L}_{\text{obj}}(t, \hat{t}) = -\big[t \log\big(\sigma(\hat{t})\big) + (1 - t) \log\big(1 - \sigma(\hat{t})\big) \big],$$

where $t = 1$ denotes the presence of an object and $t = 0$ denotes the background.

The total loss for a single training batch is computed as follows:

$$\mathcal{L}_{\text{total}} = \lambda_{\text{box}} \sum_{\text{pos}} \mathcal{L}_{\text{CIoU}} + \lambda_{\text{cls}} \sum_{\text{pos}} \mathcal{L}_{\text{cls}} + \lambda_{\text{obj}} \sum_{\text{all}} \mathcal{L}_{\text{obj}}, \tag{7}$$

where λ_{box}, λ_{cls}, and λ_{obj} are loss weights. In our method, we set λ_{box} to a relatively high value (eight times the default) to highlight precise localization, whereas λ_{cls} remains unity, and λ_{obj} follows the default scaling.

2.3 Proposed Training Strategy

We propose a three-phase training strategy designed to systematically maximize object detection performance using YOLOv11 variants while maintaining training efficiency and generalization. Together, these stages optimize convergence efficiency, generalization, and accuracy: progressive scaling leverages depthadaptive feature learning, ensembling exploits stochastic diversity for stability and accuracy, and TTA ensures inference-time robustness. The details of each phase are discussed as follows:

Phase 1: Progressive Training. Instead of training each model variant in isolation, we adopt a progressive strategy.

Algorithm 1. Progressive Training of YOLOv11 Variants

Require: Variants $v \in \{\mathrm{n}, \mathrm{s}, \mathrm{m}, \mathrm{l}\}$
Ensure: Standard mAP $\mathrm{mAP}_v^{\mathrm{std}}$ for each v
for each variant v **do**
  Initialize YOLOv11v with pretrained weights
  Train using $\mathcal{L}_{\mathrm{total}}$ until convergence or early stopping
  Validate at scale S to get $\mathrm{mAP}_v^{\mathrm{std}}$
  if $v \neq \mathrm{x}$ **then** WHAT IS x as you said we have 4 YOLO models (n,s,m,l)
    Transfer weights from YOLOv11v to YOLOv11next(v) and fine-tune
  end if
end for

This sequential training acts as a form of curriculum learning, where models of increasing architectural complexity sequentially first learn general features on simpler architectures before refining them on more complex ones. Each stage uses the previous model's weights for warm-start initialization, allowing the larger models to converge faster with better generalization. This approach leads to a more stable training and accelerates convergence for larger and more powerful models.

Phase 2: Ensemble and Model Diversity. To further enhance performance and robustness, we create an ensemble of models.

Algorithm 2. Ensemble with Hyperparameter Perturbations

Require: Trained variants $\{\mathrm{n}, \mathrm{s}, \mathrm{m}\}$
Ensure: Ensemble metrics $\mathrm{mAP}^{\mathrm{ens}}_{\mathrm{max}}, \mathrm{mAP}^{\mathrm{ens}}_{.}, \sigma_{\mathrm{ens}}$
for $k = 1 \to 4$ **do**
  Apply perturbations to model M_k:
  Learning rate schedule: $\eta_k = \eta(1 + \Delta_k)$, Δ_k = small perturbation & η = base learning rate.
  Mosaic probability variation: Adjust the probability $p_{\mathrm{mosaic},k}$
  Mixup: $\bar{I}_{\mathrm{mix}} = \lambda \bar{I}_a + (1 - \lambda)\bar{I}_b$, $\lambda \sim \mathrm{Beta}(\alpha, \alpha)$, where α is small (e.g., 0.1).
  Weight decay: ω_k
  Train M_k independently
  Validate with TTA $\to \mathrm{mAP}_k^{\mathrm{TTA}}$
end for
Compute:

$$\mathrm{best\_emAP} = \max_{k \in \{1,2,3,4\}} \left(\mathrm{mAP}_k^{\mathrm{TTA}}\right),$$

$$\mathrm{mean\_emAP} = \frac{1}{4} \sum_{k=1}^{4} \mathrm{mAP}_k^{\mathrm{TTA}},$$

$$\mathrm{std\_emAP} = \sqrt{\frac{1}{4} \sum_{k=1}^{4} \left(\mathrm{mAP}_k^{\mathrm{TTA}} - \mathrm{mean\_emAP}\right)^2}.$$

This phase involves training the top-performing variants (n, s, m, l) with diversified hyperparameters and augmentations. This ensures that each model in the ensemble learns slightly different representations of the data. By training multiple models with varied configurations, we can more effectively explore the hyperparameter space. This process allows us to select a final model that is less susceptible to suboptimal local minima and demonstrates better generalization, which is especially useful for challenging datasets like river litter.

Phase 3: Test-Time Augmentation (TTA). To maximize inference accuracy, we apply Test-Time Augmentation. For a given trained model f_θ and a validation image I, we perform inference on multiple scaled versions of the image.

Algorithm 3. Test-Time Augmentation (TTA) for Inference

Require: Trained model f_θ, validation images $\{I\}$
Ensure: TTA-enhanced mAP@0.5 for each model
for each image I **do**
  Define scale set $\mathcal{S} = \{608, 640, 672, 704\}$
  for each scale $s \in \mathcal{S}$ **do**
    $m_s \leftarrow \text{mAP}_{0.5}(f_\theta, s) = \frac{1}{C}\sum_{i=1}^{C} \text{AP}_i(\hat{B}^{(s)}, B^{\text{gt}})$
  end for
  $\text{mAP}^{\text{TTA}}(f_\theta) \leftarrow \max_{s \in \mathcal{S}} m_s$
end for

AP_i is the average precision for class i comparing the set $\hat{B}^{(s)}$ of predicted boxes of class i against the ground-truth boxes B^{gt}. This procedure exploits scale invariance: some litter objects (e.g., small plastic fragments) may only be detectable at slightly higher resolutions, while others (e.g., large bottles) may be more clearly segmented at a lower scale. Taking the maximum mAP across scales ensures we capture each model's best possible performance under multi-scale inference.

2.4 Ensemble Inference Strategy

To address the challenge of finding the optimal model configuration, our ensemble approach focuses on training a diverse set of models, from which the best-performing one is selected for the final evaluation. In Phase 2, we train multiple YOLOv11 variants using different hyperparameters to ensure each model learns different feature representations.

However, during inference, we do not fuse the bounding box predictions from these models using techniques like Weighted Boxes Fusion (WBF) or Non-Maximum Suppression (NMS). Instead, our final reported metrics are the result of a best-model selection process. Each of the trained models in the ensemble is evaluated independently on the test dataset. The model that achieves the highest mean Average Precision (mAP@0.5) is designated as the final model. The performance metrics reported in Table 1 correspond to this single best model, which benefits from the comprehensive hyperparameter search inherent in our multi-model training pipeline. This strategy ensures we identify the most robust and accurate model from our diversified training phase.

2.5 Baseline Model and Final Aggregation

To quantify the gains of our approach, we train a baseline YOLOv11n using default augmentation (random horizontal flips only, no Mosaic) and default loss weights. Let θ_{base} denote these baseline weights. We evaluate $\text{mAP}_{0.5}^{\text{base}}$ on the test subset using single-scale inference (no TTA). This baseline mAP provides a reference point, illustrating how a minimal YOLO setup performs on the same data. Finally, we aggregate and define the overall best mAP using the following formulas:

$$\text{mAP}_{\text{max}}^{\text{prog}} = \max_{v}\Big\{\max\big(\text{mAP}_v^{\text{std}},\ \text{mAP}_v^{\text{TTA}}\big)\Big\}. \tag{8}$$

$$\text{mAP}_{\text{best}} = \max\{\text{mAP}_{\text{max}}^{\text{prog}},\ \text{mAP}_{0.5}^{\text{base}}\}. \tag{9}$$

All metrics, including per-variant losses, precision, recall, and mAP values, are recorded in a JSON report for reproducibility.

2.6 Real-Time Tracking and Counting

For the tracking and counting task, the optimized YOLOv11 detector is integrated with state-of-the-art tracking algorithms, specifically **StrongSORT** and **DeepSORT** [22]. The tracking-by-detection framework operates by first detecting all litter objects in a given video frame. For each detection, a state vector is generated:

$$x = [u, v, \gamma, h, u', v', \gamma', h'] \tag{10}$$

where u, v represent the object's position, γ, h represent its size or shape, and u', v', γ', h' denote the predicted changes in position and size based on motion. Next, a data association step links these new detections to existing object tracks. This association is driven by a combined metric that integrates motion, predicted by a Kalman filter [6], and appearance, using deep feature embeddings to re-identify objects even in the presence of temporary occlusions. Each successfully maintained trajectory is assigned a unique ID, and the total count of litters is derived from the number of unique IDs generated.

3 Experiment and Discussion

3.1 Dataset

A custom dataset comprising 1,200 images was constructed using video recordings captured with a *GoPro Hero 10* (23 MP) at 4K resolution and 24fps. Frames were extracted at 1fps and resized to 640×640 pixels prior to training. The dataset was collected from the Upper Ganga Canal, Roorkee, India. Each image was manually annotated for five litter categories: *Plastic*, *Polybag*, *Debris*, *Bottle*, and *Foam*. The dataset was divided into 80% for training and validation and 20% for testing.

3.2 Implementation Details

All models were trained for 200 epochs on a single NVIDIA A2000 GPU for 26 hrs using an automatic batch-size. Input images were resized to 640×640 and loaded with 8 workers. We used AdamW (initial learning rate 5×10^{-4}, weight decay 5×10^{-4}) with a cosine-style scheduler (lrf = 0.01) and a 3epoch warmup (momentum from 0.80 to 0.937, bias LR 0.1). Early stopping with patience 50 was applied based on validation mAP to maximize precision.

3.3 Quantitative Results

Table 1 summarizes detection performance across several existing methods and our proposed approach. We report the mAP at IoU 0.5 (mAP@0.5), precision, recall, and F1score. Legacy approaches, such as FMAYOLOv5s and PLDCNN, achieve mAPs between 0.80 and 0.90, but they often trade off recall or precision when detecting small debris. The baseline YOLOv11n improves overall balance (mAP@0.5 = 0.87, precision = 0.92, recall = 0.91, F1 = 0.82). Our progressive, ensemble, and TTA pipeline pushes mAP@0.5 up to 0.939 while maintaining high precision (0.94) and recall (0.96), giving an F1 = 0.89. This demonstrates the value of model diversity and multi-scale inference in challenging riverine environments.

Table 1. Performance comparison across different models

Model	mAP@0.5	Precision	Recall	F1
FMAYOLOv5s [9]	0.794	-	-	-
PLDCNN [23]	0.803	0.820	0.980	0.890
YOLOv4Transfer [10]	0.830	-	-	-
YOLOv5Orca [3]	0.849	0.887	0.787	-
YOLOv4Optimised [25]	0.890	-	0.86	0.80
YOLOv7 [17]	0.932	0.913	0.94	0.92
Baseline YOLOv11	0.861	0.928	0.910	0.820
Our Approach	**0.939**	**0.946**	**0.96**	**0.890**

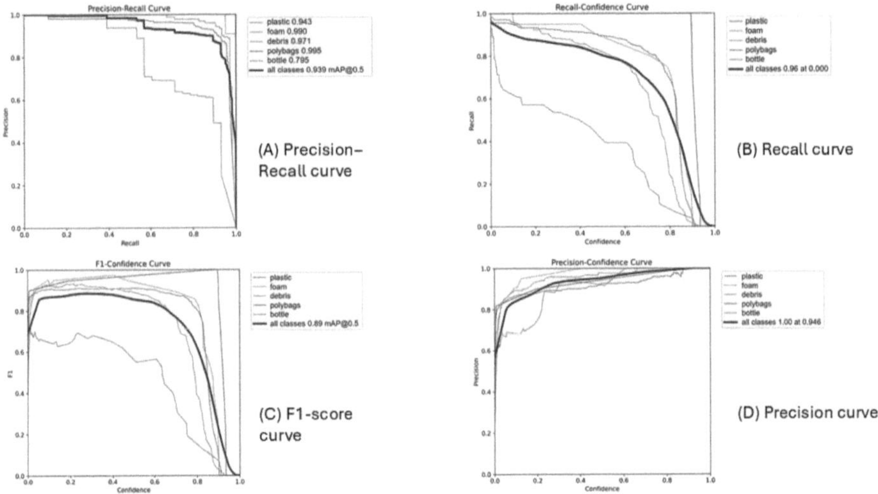

Fig. 2. Detection performance curves for our ensemble on the test set. (a) Precision-Recall curve, (b) Recall vs. confidence threshold, (c) F1-score vs. confidence threshold, and (d) Precision vs. confidence threshold; here mAP@0.5 refers to mean Average Precision at IoU 0.5.

Fig. 3. Live video tracking and counting of detected river litter using StrongSORT. Each colored box shows a unique object ID, and the upper-left inset reports cumulative counts $n_{\text{plastic}}, n_{\text{foam}}, \ldots, n_{\text{bottle}}$ over the frames. (Color figure online)

3.4 Qualitative Results

Figure 2 presents evaluation plots demonstrating the performance of the YOLOv12 model in detecting river litter across classes such as plastic, foam, debris, polybags, and bottles. The PrecisionRecall curve (A) shows high mAP@0.5 of 0.939, with strong results for polybags and debris. The Recall-

Confidence (B) and F1Confidence (C) curves indicate reliable detection across confidence thresholds, while the PrecisionConfidence curve (D) reflects high precision at increasing confidence levels, suggesting low false positives. These results validate the model's robustness and generalization across diverse waste types.

Figure 3 shows a qualitative output of the model on a live river video stream. The model tracks litter objects with consistent IDs and displays frame-wise statistics like object counts and active tracks in real time. This confirms the system's effectiveness for real-world deployment in river pollution monitoring.

4 Conclusion and Future Scope

We introduced a three-phase progressive training and ensemble pipeline for YOLOv11, achieving 0.9391 mAP@0.5 on five river-litter classes. By progressively training on YOLO models, we warm-start larger nets from simpler ones, which often leads to faster convergence and better initial weights. Ensembling multiple trained variants at test time allows the system to capture complementary detections (e.g., some models may better see small objects, others large ones) related to TTA but across model diversity. Finally, we apply TTA by scoring each image at multiple scales and keeping the best per-image detections. This explicitly boosts recall for objects that only appear clearly at certain resolutions. In tracking, using StrongSORT mitigates occlusions and smooths out spurious detections, giving stable counts.

As a result, our system substantially outperforms a single-model baseline. On our custom riverine dataset, the progressive ensemble achieved 93.91% mAP@0.5 vs 86.1% for the baseline YOLO11n. This accuracy is on par with prior reports (84.9% mAP for YOLOv5 on river garbage, or 79.4% for FMA-YOLOv5 on debris) while retaining real-time throughput. In short, by combining advances in model design, ensemble learning, multi-scale evaluation, and robust tracking, our method overcomes many limitations of past approaches. Future work includes full ensemble fusion at inference, domain adaptation to new waterways, adding extra large variant and new architecture from scratch.

Acknowledgment. This work was partially supported by the Southern Cross University Deputy Vice Chancellor (Research) Seed Grant, project number GLC: 31930. We gratefully thank Southern Cross University for their support.

References

1. Akkoyun, D.: Identification and detection of beach litter using computer vision techniques (2024)
2. Bewley, A., Ge, Z., Ott, L., Ramos, F., Upcroft, B.: Simple online and realtime tracking. In: 2016 IEEE International Conference on Image Processing (ICIP), pp. 3464–3468. IEEE (2016)
3. Chen, L., Zhu, J.: Water surface garbage detection based on lightweight yolov5. Sci. Rep. **14**(1), 6133 (2024)

4. Du, Y., et al.: Strongsort: make deepsort great again. IEEE Trans. Multimedia **25**, 8725–8737 (2023)
5. Duong, V.H., Nguyen, D.Q., Van Luong, T., Vu, H., Nguyen, T.C.: Robust data augmentation and ensemble method for object detection in fisheye camera images. In: Proceedings of the IEEE/CVF Conference on Computer Vision and Pattern Recognition, pp. 7017–7026 (2024)
6. Jain, K., Juthani, M., Jain, J., Nimkar, A.V.: Trashbusters: Deep learning approach for litter detection and tracking. arXiv preprint arXiv:2404.07467 (2024)
7. Khanam, R., Hussain, M.: Yolov11: An overview of the key architectural enhancements. arXiv preprint arXiv:2410.17725 (2024)
8. Kimura, M.: Understanding test-time augmentation. In: International Conference on Neural Information Processing, pp. 558–569. Springer (2021)
9. Lin, F., Hou, T., Jin, Q., You, A.: Improved yolo based detection algorithm for floating debris in waterway. Entropy **23**(9), 1111 (2021)
10. Maharjan, N., Miyazaki, H., Pati, B.M., Dailey, M.N., Shrestha, S., Nakamura, T.: Detection of river plastic using UAV sensor data and deep learning. Remote Sens. **14**(13), 3049 (2022)
11. Meijer, L.J., Van Emmerik, T., Van Der Ent, R., Schmidt, C., Lebreton, L.: More than 1000 rivers account for 80% of global riverine plastic emissions into the ocean. Sci. Adv. **7**(18), eaaz5803 (2021)
12. Mohsen, A., Kiss, T., Kovács, F.: Machine learning-based detection and mapping of riverine litter utilizing sentinel-2 imagery. Environ. Sci. Pollut. Res. **30**(25), 67742–67757 (2023)
13. Qiao, G., Yang, M., Wang, H.: A detection approach for floating debris using ground images based on deep learning. Remote Sens. **14**(17), 4161 (2022)
14. Qiao, G., Yang, M., Wang, H.: An annotated dataset and benchmark for detecting floating debris in inland waters. Sci. Data **12**(1), 385 (2025)
15. Rafi, T.H., Mahjabin, R., Ghosh, E., Ko, Y.W., Lee, J.G.: Domain generalization for semantic segmentation: a survey. Artif. Intell. Rev. **57**(9), 247 (2024)
16. Raju, M.P., et al.: A machine learning-based detection, classification, and quantification of marine litter along the central east coast of india. Front. Mar. Sci. **12**, 1604055 (2025)
17. Ramya, R., Jebathangam, J.: An effective object detection model to detect floating macroplastic debris on the waterways using yolo. In: 2025 International Conference on Inventive Computation Technologies (ICICT), pp. 524–529. IEEE (2025)
18. Rodrigues, C., A, R., N, S., Patricio Silva, A., Gravato, C., C.A., R.: Citizens' awareness and education for tackling microplastic contamination in freshwater ecosystems. In: Proceedings of the 17th International Conference on Environmental Science and Technology (CEST 2021), Athens, Greece. (09 2021)
19. Ryan, P.G., Moore, C.J., Van Franeker, J.A., Moloney, C.L.: Monitoring the abundance of plastic debris in the marine environment. Philos. Trans. Royal Society B: Biol. Sci. **364**(1526), 1999–2012 (2009)
20. Shen, C.: A transdisciplinary review of deep learning research and its relevance for water resources scientists. Water Resour. Res. **54**(11), 8558–8593 (2018)
21. Wei, P., et al.: Research on detection of floating objects on water surface based on faster-rCNN. In: 2024 IEEE 22nd International Conference on Industrial Informatics (INDIN), pp. 1–6. IEEE (2024)
22. Wojke, N., Bewley, A., Paulus, D.: Simple online and realtime tracking with a deep association metric. In: 2017 IEEE International Conference on Image Processing (ICIP), pp. 3645–3649. IEEE (2017)

23. Wolf, M., et al.: Machine learning for aquatic plastic litter detection, classification and quantification (aplastic-q). Environ. Res. Lett. **15**(11), 114042 (2020)
24. Xu, S., Zhang, M., Song, W., Mei, H., He, Q., Liotta, A.: A systematic review and analysis of deep learning-based underwater object detection. Neurocomputing **527**, 204–232 (2023)
25. Zailan, N.A., Azizan, M.M., Hasikin, K., Mohd Khairuddin, A.S., Khairuddin, U.: An automated solid waste detection using the optimized yolo model for riverine management. Front. Public Health **10**, 907280 (2022)
26. Zhang, J., Xiang, A., Cheng, Y., Yang, Q., Wang, L.: Research on detection of floating objects in river and lake based on AI intelligent image recognition. arXiv preprint arXiv:2404.06883 (2024)

Hierarchical Spatial Mamba Framework for Point Cloud Classification

Yajie Sun[1], Ali Zia[2], Zekun Long[1], Zhangchi Qiu[1], Wei Xiang[2], and Jun Zhou[1(✉)]

[1] School of Information and Communication Technology, Griffith University, Queensland, Australia
{yajie.sun,zekun.long,zhangchi.qiu}@griffithuni.edu.au, jun.zhou@griffith.edu.au

[2] School of Computing, Engineering and Mathematical Sciences, La Trobe University, Victoria, Australia
{a.zia,w.xiang}@latrobe.edu.au

Abstract. The unstructured, high-dimensional nature of point clouds poses challenges for effective feature extraction and classification. While transformer-based architectures excel at modelling complex spatial dependencies, they require substantial computational resources and large-scale pretraining. In contrast, the Mamba architecture, leveraging State Space Models (SSMs), offers greater computational efficiency and strong sequence modelling capabilities. However, its inherent linearity and temporal bias limit its ability to capture intricate spatial relationships essential for point cloud analysis. To address these limitations, we propose the Hierarchical Spatial Mamba Framework (HSMF), a novel architecture designed to enhance spatial feature learning for point cloud classification. HSMF integrates an Integrated Spatial Representation Module (ISRM) that systematically captures multi-scale geometric features at the surface, edge, and point levels, a Dynamic Scaling Learning Module (DSLM) that aggregates hierarchical spatial information through adaptive sampling, and a Mamba Backbone with Enhanced Spatial Locality that employs Morton curve-based reordering to preserve spatial coherence when mapping high-dimensional data into sequential formats compatible with SSMs. Experiments on ScanObjectNN and ModelNet40 demonstrate that HSMF achieves state-of-the-art performance, outperforming existing methods.

Keywords: Point cloud classification · hierarchical Mamba · spatial features · 3D computer vision

1 Introduction

Point cloud data is fundamental to high-resolution 3D spatial analysis and finds applications in autonomous driving [1–3], robotics [4–6], cultural heritage preservation [7–9], and geographic information systems [10,11]. However, its unstructured nature and high dimensionality pose significant challenges for tasks such as

C. Wallraven et al. (Eds.): ACPR 2025, LNCS 16174, pp. 402–417, 2026.
https://doi.org/10.1007/978-981-95-4395-3_28

classification, segmentation, and object recognition. Traditional methods often struggle to capture the complex spatial relationships inherent in point clouds, leading to inefficiencies in feature extraction and data interpretation [12].

Recent advancements have leveraged the capabilities of Vision Transformers (ViTs) to address these challenges. Models like Point-BERT utilize masked point modelling with auxiliary non-transformer components to enhance feature learning, while Point-MAE introduces masked autoencoders to improve self-supervised learning in point cloud tasks [13,14]. These transformer-based methods excel at capturing global dependencies but rely heavily on large-scale pretraining and demand significant computational resources, limiting their scalability in real-world applications.

To improve efficiency, the Mamba architecture has been proposed as an alternative, offering strong sequence modelling capabilities with reduced computational complexity. Mamba incorporates State Space Models (SSMs), which excel at modelling long-range dependencies and have shown promise in visual tasks like image processing, video analysis, and point cloud classification [15]. However, SSMs are inherently designed for temporal data and exhibit limitations when applied to spatial data due to their linear structure. This restricts their ability to capture complex local geometries and spatial relationships, which are critical for understanding point cloud semantics. Moreover, SSMs primarily focus on temporal state transitions rather than spatial dependencies, making them less effective for tasks that require detailed spatial reasoning.

To overcome the limitations of existing SSM-based methods in point cloud processing, we propose a novel architecture termed the **Hierarchical Spatial Mamba Framework** (**HSMF**), which augments spatial feature learning through structured geometric reasoning and efficient sequence modelling. Building upon the foundation laid by *PointMamba*, which introduced SSMs to unordered point cloud data, our framework advances the state of the art through three key innovations. First, we employ **Morton code-based spatial reordering**, a hierarchical space-filling transformation that better preserves local continuity and global coherence than the flat sorting strategies used previously, enabling more effective spatial reasoning within the Mamba backbone. Second, we develop an **Integrated Spatial Representation Module (ISRM)** that explicitly encodes geometric features across point-, edge-, and surface-level hierarchies–capturing multi-scale structural cues often overlooked by existing point-level embeddings. Third, we introduce a **Dynamic Scaling Learning Module (DSLM)** that adaptively samples and aggregates features at multiple spatial resolutions, thereby addressing spatial heterogeneity and varying point densities more robustly than conventional fixed-radius grouping. These components collectively form a principled framework for point cloud classification that effectively bridges the gap between sequence-based modelling and spatial learning.

The proposed HSMF comprises:

- **Integrated Spatial Representation Module (ISRM)**: Captures geometric features at surface, edge, and point levels to enrich local and contextual representations.
- **Dynamic Scaling Learning Module (DSLM)**: Aggregates multi-scale spatial features using adaptive sampling for improved robustness and generalisation.
- **Mamba Backbone with Enhanced Spatial Locality**: Leverages Morton curve-based reordering to preserve spatial structure when transforming point clouds into sequences compatible with SSMs.
- **Comprehensive empirical evaluation** on *ScanObjectNN* and *ModelNet40* demonstrates that HSMF achieves state-of-the-art performance, outperforming existing Transformer- and SSM-based baselines in classification accuracy.

The remainder of this paper is organised as follows. Section 2 reviews relevant literature on Transformer-based models, State Space Models, and spatial feature learning for point clouds. Section 3 presents the proposed HSMF architecture, detailing its three key components: the Integrated Spatial Representation Module, the Dynamic Scaling Learning Module, and the Mamba Backbone with Enhanced Spatial Locality. Section 4 reports experimental results on benchmark datasets, including ablation studies and comparative analysis. Finally, Sect. 5 concludes the paper and outlines potential directions for future work.

2 Related Works

Recent advances in 3D deep learning have introduced diverse architectural paradigms for point cloud classification. These approaches can be broadly grouped into three categories: Transformer-based models that emphasise global attention mechanisms, State Space Model (SSM)-based architectures that prioritise efficient long-range dependency modelling, and methods that focus on spatial feature extraction to capture fine-grained geometric structures. We briefly review each of these directions to highlight their strengths and limitations, and to motivate the design of our proposed HSMF framework.

2.1 Transformer-Based Point Cloud Learning

Transformer architectures have demonstrated strong capabilities in capturing long-range dependencies in visual and spatial data. In the context of point cloud classification, models such as Point Transformer [16] and PCT [17] leverage self-attention mechanisms to model both local and global relationships. However, their quadratic complexity with respect to the number of points significantly hampers scalability, especially when handling dense or large-scale point clouds.

To overcome these limitations, self-supervised Transformer models have been proposed. Point-BERT [13] introduces masked point modelling to pre-train point cloud representations, but relies on auxiliary networks like DGCNN for tokenization, increasing architectural complexity. PointMAE [14] reduces this dependence by adopting an end-to-end masked autoencoding approach, yet still inherits the inefficiencies of standard Transformers. More recently, PointGPT [18] proposes an autoregressive framework with a double masking strategy to improve sequential prediction. While it addresses issues of data disorder and sparsity, PointGPT suffers from slow inference and high sensitivity to masking configurations.

Overall, although Transformer-based methods offer powerful global modelling capabilities, they often neglect fine-grained local geometries and demand high computational resources and extensive pretraining.

2.2 State Space Models in Visual and 3D Learning

The Mamba architecture [19] introduces Selective State Space Models (SSMs) for efficient sequence modelling, enabling near-linear complexity in capturing long-range dependencies. Originally designed for temporal data, SSMs have shown promise in visual domains such as image and video analysis, where sequential structures can be imposed through scan-based ordering. Variants such as VMamba [20] and LocalMamba [21] extend this capability through local windowing and hierarchical scans, facilitating improved modelling of visual context in 2D tasks.

In the 3D domain, PointMamba [15] adapts Mamba to unordered point cloud data by imposing a sequential structure through a spatial reordering scheme. This enables compatibility with SSMs, but also introduces a modelling bias rooted in the temporal assumptions of traditional SSMs. Such biases can impair the representation of fine-grained spatial relationships, particularly in irregular or densely clustered point cloud regions. The imposed sequences often fail to preserve geometric locality, limiting the model's ability to reason effectively about spatial semantics.

To address these limitations, it is essential to reinterpret SSMs within a spatial context. We posit that spatial dependencies in point clouds can be reformulated as pseudo-sequential signals, provided that the reordering scheme preserves locality. Our framework adopts *Morton code*-based spatial indexing–a hierarchical, space-filling curve known for its ability to maintain proximity among neighbouring points in high-dimensional Euclidean space. This transformation allows us to exploit the computational advantages of Mamba while mitigating the spatial distortion introduced by naive linear ordering. When combined with structured spatial encoding modules, this approach enables SSMs to operate as effective spatial reasoning engines, rather than merely temporal predictors. Thus, our method establishes a principled adaptation of SSMs to spatial data, reconciling sequence modelling with the inherent structure of point clouds.

2.3 Spatial Feature Learning in Point Clouds

Spatial feature learning plays a crucial role in point cloud understanding. Traditional methods such as DGCNN [16] utilize edge convolutions to model local geometry by constructing dynamic graphs, while KPConv [26] applies deformable kernels to capture fine-grained geometric patterns. RS-CNN [27] further introduces relation-shape convolution to encode contextual geometric structures based on shape consistency. These methods focus on extracting features from point neighborhoods but often lack hierarchical feature abstraction across multiple geometric levels.

More recent works have explored hierarchical spatial encoding. For example, GBNet [30] employs geometric back-projection to integrate multi-view information for robust classification. However, many of these approaches either rely on fixed-scale groupings or lack explicit mechanisms to adapt to varying spatial densities.

To enhance spatial feature learning, our proposed HSMF integrates an Integrated Spatial Representation Module (ISRM) that captures surface-, edge-, and point-level features, enabling a richer encoding of local geometries. Moreover, the Dynamic Scaling Learning Module (DSLM) adaptively aggregates features at multiple spatial resolutions, addressing the shortcomings of fixed-radius sampling. These innovations allow HSMF to retain both geometric fidelity and global context while maintaining computational efficiency.

3 Hierarchical Spatial Mamba Framework

HSMF comprises three key components: an Integrated Spatial Representation Module (ISRM) for multi-scale feature extraction, a Dynamic Scaling Learning Module (DSLM) for hierarchical aggregation, and a Mamba Backbone with Enhanced Spatial Locality to improve spatial coherence during sequence modelling. This can be seen in Fig. 1

3.1 Integrated Spatial Representation Module

The ISRM systematically captures geometric features across three hierarchical levels: surface, edge, and point. Unlike traditional approaches that rely solely on Cartesian coordinates, this module enriches point features by embedding local geometric properties.

Surface-Level Features: Given a point cloud with m points, we define the set as $\mathbf{P} = \{\mathbf{p}_1, \cdots, \mathbf{p}_m\} \in \mathbb{R}^{m\times 3}$, where each point $\mathbf{p}_i = (x_i, y_i, z_i)$. For each point $\mathbf{p}_i$, q neighboring points $\mathbf{k}_j = (x_j, y_j, z_j)$ form a group $\mathbf{G}_i$. The surface-level feature captures the geometric displacement of neighbouring points relative to the central point, offering insight into local surface orientation. It is defined as:

$$f_i^{\text{surface}} = (x_i - x_j, y_i - y_j, z_i - z_j), \tag{1}$$

where each $(x_j, y_j, z_j) \in \mathbf{G_i}$ is a neighbour of point p_i.

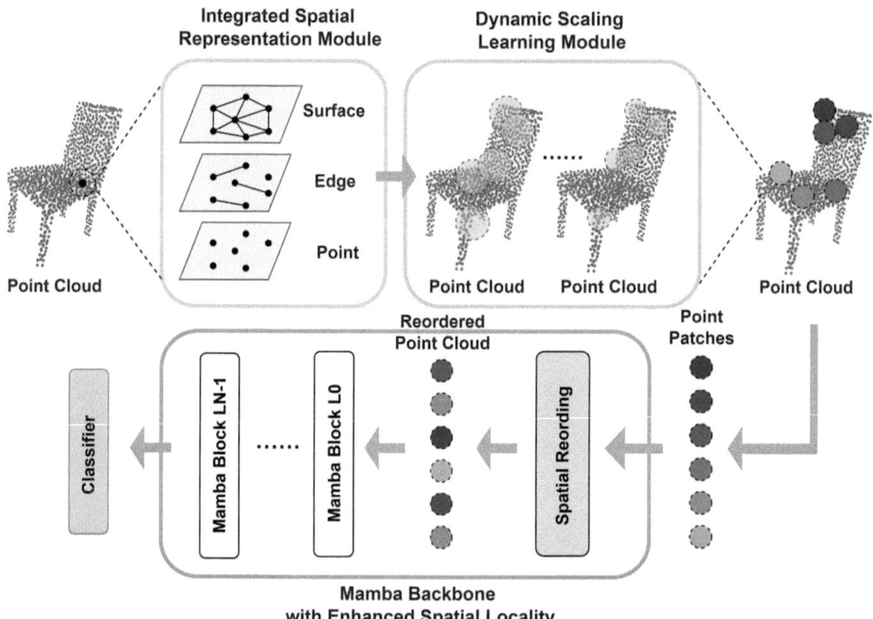

Fig. 1. Overall scheme of the hierarchical spatial Mamba framework. The model mainly consists of three parts: an integrated spatial representation module, a dynamic scaling learning module, and a Mamba backbone with enhanced spatial locality.

Edge-Level Features: Edge features capture local geometric variations by analyzing the consistency of normal vectors. For point $\mathbf{p}_i$, the normal vector is $\mathbf{f}_{p_i}$, and the normal vectors of its neighbors are $\mathbf{f}_{k_j}$. The angular difference from a neighboring point can be calculated. The mean $\bar{\theta}$ and variance σ^2 of these angular differences are used as edge features:

$$\mathbf{f}_{edge_i} = \begin{cases} \bar{\theta} = \frac{1}{q}\sum_{i=1}^{q} \cos^{-1}\left(\frac{\mathbf{f}_{p_i} \cdot \mathbf{f}_{k_j}}{\|\mathbf{f}_{p_i}\|\|\mathbf{f}_{k_j}\|}\right), \\ \sigma^{\mathbf{2}} = \frac{1}{q-1}\sum_{i=1}^{q}\left[\cos^{-1}\left(\frac{\mathbf{f}_{p_i} \cdot \mathbf{f}_{k_j}}{\|\mathbf{f}_{p_i}\|\|\mathbf{f}_{k_j}\|}\right) - \bar{\theta}\right]^2. \end{cases} \tag{2}$$

Point-Level Features: To encode relative spatial arrangements beyond Cartesian differences, we compute polar features that capture angular and radial distances between each point and its neighbours. In simple words, polar coordinates capture the relative spatial arrangement of points. For point $\mathbf{p}_i$ and its neighbor $\mathbf{k}_j$, the features are defined as:

$$\mathbf{f}_{point_i} = \begin{cases} \theta_{ij} = \tan^{-1}(\frac{|y_i - y_j|}{|x_i - x_j|}) \\ \rho_{ij} = \sqrt{(x_i - x_j)^2 + (y_i - y_j)^2 + (z_i - z_j)^2} \\ \varphi_{ij} = \cos^{-1}\left(\frac{|z_i - z_j|}{\rho_{ij}}\right). \end{cases} \tag{3}$$

Feature Aggregation: The extracted surface-, edge-, and point-level descriptors are integrated to form a unified spatial representation for each point. Specifically, a shared multi-layer perceptron, denoted as MLP($\cdot$), is applied independently to each feature type to enable non-linear transformation and feature projection. For a given point $\mathbf{p}_i$, the final enriched feature vector $\mathbf{F}_i$ is constructed by concatenating its original Cartesian coordinate features $\mathbf{f}_{c_i}$ with the aggregated hierarchical features, comprising surface-, edge-, and point-level descriptors, computed over its local neighbourhood:

$$\begin{aligned} \mathbf{F}_i = &\text{concat}\Bigg(\text{MLP}(\mathbf{f}_{c_i}), \sum_{j=1}^{q} \text{MLP}(\mathbf{f}_{surface_i}), \\ &\sum_{j=1}^{q} \text{MLP}(\mathbf{f}_{edge_i}), \sum_{j=1}^{q} \text{MLP}(\mathbf{f}_{point_i})\Bigg). \end{aligned} \tag{4}$$

After feature aggregation, we obtain an enriched point set $\mathbf{P}' \in \mathbb{R}^{m \times n}$, where $\mathbf{P}' = \{\mathbf{p}'_1, \cdots, \mathbf{p}'_m\}$ and each $\mathbf{p}'_i$ is a feature vector of dimension n.

3.2 Dynamic Scaling Learning Module

Following hierarchical feature enrichment, the processed point cloud data $\mathbf{P}'$ is passed to the Dynamic Scaling Learning Module (DSLM), designed to capture multi-scale geometric features through adaptive grouping and hierarchical aggregation. This module addresses the challenge of varying point densities and irregular spatial distributions in point clouds by dynamically adjusting the receptive fields.

To model local geometric structures at different scales, we define dynamic groups G_r^c, where each group consists of a central point c and its neighboring points within a radius r. To capture features across varying spatial resolutions, we form multi-scale groups $G_{r_1}^c, G_{r_2}^c, \dots, G_{r_\gamma}^c$ using a set of radii $\{r_1, r_2, \dots, r_\gamma\}$, where γ denotes the number of scales. This hierarchical grouping enables the model to capture both fine-grained local features and broader contextual information.

The central points $\{c_1, c_2, \dots, c_\beta\}$ are selected using the Farthest Point Sampling (FPS) algorithm to ensure uniform spatial coverage and maximize the diversity of sampled regions:

$$\mathbf{C} = \text{FPS}(\mathbf{P}'), \quad \mathbf{C} \in \mathbb{R}^{\beta \times n}, \tag{5}$$

where β is the number of sampled centers, and n is the feature dimension of each point. For each center c_i ($i = 1, \ldots, \beta$), the corresponding neighbors are identified within each radius r_k ($k = 1, \ldots, \gamma$) using the K-nearest neighbors (KNN) algorithm, ensuring robust local feature extraction regardless of point cloud sparsity.

This process results in $t = \beta \times \gamma$ dynamic groups, each representing a different spatial context. To embed these groups into a higher-dimensional feature space, we employ a Feedforward Neural Network (FFN) parameterized by α, which performs non-linear transformations to enhance feature discrimination:

$$\mathbf{S} = \mathrm{FFN}_{\alpha}(\mathbf{C}), \quad \mathbf{S} \in \mathbb{R}^{t \times d}, \tag{6}$$

where d denotes the embedding dimension, and α represents the learnable parameters of the FFN. This embedding captures hierarchical spatial dependencies, facilitating robust learning of both local and global geometric structures. The DSLM's dynamic scaling mechanism enables the framework to adaptively learn from diverse point cloud distributions, improving generalization across different datasets and tasks.

3.3 Mamba Backbone with Enhanced Spatial Locality

To preserve the spatial structure of point cloud data and mitigate the effects of point disorder, point patches are organized into coherent sequences based on their central points. This is achieved by encoding the coordinates of the central points into a one-dimensional space using the Morton Code [22], which effectively preserves spatial locality through a hierarchical space-filling curve. The encoded values are then sorted to determine the sequential order $\mathbf{O}$ of the central points, ensuring that spatial proximity is maintained in the sequence. The reordered central points $\mathbf{C}$ and their corresponding feature matrix $\mathbf{S}$ are defined as:

$$\begin{aligned} \mathbf{O} &= \mathrm{argmax}(\mathrm{MortonCode}(C)), \quad \mathbf{O} \in \mathbb{R}^{n \times 1}, \\ \mathbf{C}', \mathbf{S}' &= \mathbf{C}[\mathbf{O}], \mathbf{S}[\mathbf{O}], \quad \mathbf{C}' \in \mathbb{R}^{\beta \times n}, \quad \mathbf{S}' \in \mathbb{R}^{t \times dim}. \end{aligned} \tag{7}$$

Fed the $\mathbf{S}'$ as the input to the Mamba backbone with SSMs, a vector $\mathbf{V}$ can be obtained:

$$\mathbf{V} = \mathrm{Mamba}(\mathrm{SSM}(\mathbf{S}')), \quad \mathbf{V} \in \mathbb{R}^{t \times Dim}. \tag{8}$$

After Global Average Pooling (GAP), the representation of the final learned information can be defined as:

$$\mathbf{V}' = \mathrm{GAP}(\mathbf{V}), \quad \mathbf{V}' \in \mathbb{R}^{Dim}. \tag{9}$$

The number of classes contained in the dataset can be defined as cls, and w is a parameter that needs to be trained in the classifier, so the final classification result can be identified as:

$$\mathbf{Q} = \mathrm{Classifier}_{w}(\mathbf{V}'), \quad \mathbf{Q} \in \mathbb{R}^{cls}. \tag{10}$$

We applied Cross-Entropy as the loss function. The random gradient descent (SGD) algorithm is used to train all parameters.

4 Experiments

The proposed HSMF is evaluated on two benchmark datasets: ScanObjectNN [23] and ModelNet40 [24], focusing on point cloud classification tasks.

4.1 Implementation

Each point cloud sample is downsampled to 1,024 points for uniformity. In the spatial feature extraction phase, the number of nearest neighbors is set to $q = 8$ to capture rich local geometric structures. For the Dynamic Scaling Learning Module, the point cloud is partitioned into 512 point patches. We apply the K-nearest neighbors (KNN) algorithm with radii $r_1 = 0.2$ and $r_2 = 0.1$ to facilitate multi-scale feature aggregation. The extracted features are fused into 128 groups to align with the Mamba backbone's architecture. The Mamba model is configured with 12 layers, each comprising 384 hidden dimensions and 6 attention heads. Training is conducted using stochastic gradient descent with an initial learning rate of 0.0005 and a weight decay of 0.1. No external pretraining or data augmentation techniques are employed, underscoring the framework's robustness in learning from raw point clouds.

4.2 Performance on Benchmark Datasets

HSMF demonstrates a strong capability to learn geometric features in clean, controlled environments while exhibiting robust generalization to complex, real-world point cloud data. The following results provide empirical evidence of HSMF's effectiveness across diverse datasets, highlighting its adaptability and performance under varying conditions.

Classification on ModelNet40: Dataset consists of 12,311 clean 3D CAD models spanning 40 categories, widely used as a standard benchmark for point cloud classification. The dataset is characterized by noise-free, uniformly sampled objects, which allows models to focus on learning global geometric structures without interference from background clutter or occlusions. As shown in Table 1, HSMF achieves an accuracy of 93.8%, outperforming state-of-the-art methods such as PointMamba [15] and PointMAE [14].

While the performance improvements on ModelNet40 are relatively incremental compared to baseline models, they highlight HSMF's capacity for effective feature learning in clean, synthetic environments. Importantly, HSMF achieves these results without pretraining on large-scale datasets like ShapeNet, unlike many Transformer-based methods. This indicates that HSMF possesses strong inductive biases tailored for spatial data, enabling it to generalise effectively even with limited supervision. The framework's hierarchical feature representation contributes to learning both fine-grained local details and broader shape structures, which are crucial for high classification accuracy in synthetic datasets.

Table 1. Classification results on ModelNet40.

Method	Points	Acc. (%)
PointNet [12]	1k	89.2
PointNet++ [12]	1k	90.7
PointCNN [25]	1k	92.5
KPConv [26]	1k	92.9
DGCNN [16]	1k	92.9
RS-CNN [27]	1k	92.9
PCT [17]	1k	93.2
PVT [28]	1k	93.6
Transformer [13]	1k	91.4
Point-BERT [13]	1k	92.7
PointMAE [14]	1k	93.2
PointMamba [15]	1k	93.6
Ours	1k	**93.8**

Classification on ScanObjectNN: It is a challenging real-world dataset comprising approximately 15,000 objects across 15 categories, characterized by background clutter, occlusions, partial visibility, and noise, which significantly increase classification difficulty compared to ModelNet40. It includes three variants of increasing complexity: OBJ_ONLY (cleanly segmented objects), OBJ_BG (objects with background clutter), and PB_T50_RS (partial occlusions and noise). As shown in Table 2, HSMF achieves 91.24% accuracy on OBJ_BG and 85.56% on PB_T50_RS, outperforming state-of-the-art models such as PointMamba [15] and PointMAE [14]. HSMF achieves significant performance gains on ScanObjectNN variants, especially on the challenging PB_T50_RS variant demonstrate its strong generalization capabilities. Moreover, the relatively smaller performance drop between OBJ_ONLY and PB_T50_RS for HSMF compared to other models indicates superior resilience to noise and incomplete data. Unlike Transformer-based models that often rely heavily on pertaining or data augmentation, HSMF demonstrates strong inductive learning from scratch, making it a promising approach for real-world 3D vision applications.

4.3 Qualitative Comparison of Feature Attribution

To further illustrate the interpretability and effectiveness of our model, we conduct a qualitative comparison with PointMamba using Grad-CAM-based visualisation [32]. Figure 2 shows class activation maps on four representative object categories: chair, guitar, bed, and lamp. These maps highlight the spatial regions each model attends to during classification.

Table 2. Classification results on three variants of ScanObjectNN.

Methods	Points	OBJ_BG	OBJ_ONLY	PB_T50_RS
PointNet [12]	1k	73.3	79.2	68.0
SpiderCNN [29]	1k	77.1	79.5	73.7
PointNet++ [12]	1k	82.3	84.3	77.9
DGCNN [16]	1k	82.8	86.2	78.1
PointCNN [25]	1k	86.1	85.5	78.5
BGA-DGCNN [23]	1k	-	-	79.7
BGA-PN++ [23]	1k	-	-	80.2
GBNet [20]	1k	-	-	80.5
PRANet [31]	1k	-	-	81.0
Transformer [13]	1k	79.86	80.55	77.24
Transformer-OcCo [13]	1k	84.85	85.54	78.79
Point-BERT [13]	1k	87.43	85.54	83.07
Point-MAE [14]	1k	88.12	88.12	83.17
PointMamba [15]	1k	90.71	**88.47**	84.87
Ours	1k	**91.24**	88.43	**85.56**

For the chair, PointMamba primarily focuses on the seat and rear leg, overlooking important structural elements such as the backrest and front support. In contrast, our method captures a more holistic representation by assigning high importance to the backrest, seat, and all leg components, demonstrating a more comprehensive understanding of the object's geometry.

In the guitar example, while both methods highlight the central body as relevant, our model also emphasises the neck and headstock regions. These parts are essential for distinguishing guitars from objects with similar outlines, indicating better semantic awareness.

For the bed, PointMamba focuses mainly on the headboard, overlooking other crucial features. In comparison, our model highlights not only the headboard but also the bed frame and edges of the mattress. This broader attention allows for richer spatial context, which supports more accurate classification.

In the case of the lamp, PointMamba's attention is largely limited to the lampshade. Our model, however, activates across the full structure, including the base and support rod, thereby capturing the complete geometric composition of the object.

These comparisons demonstrate that our model consistently attends to spatially meaningful and diverse regions of each object, reflecting stronger spatial reasoning and more informative feature attribution.

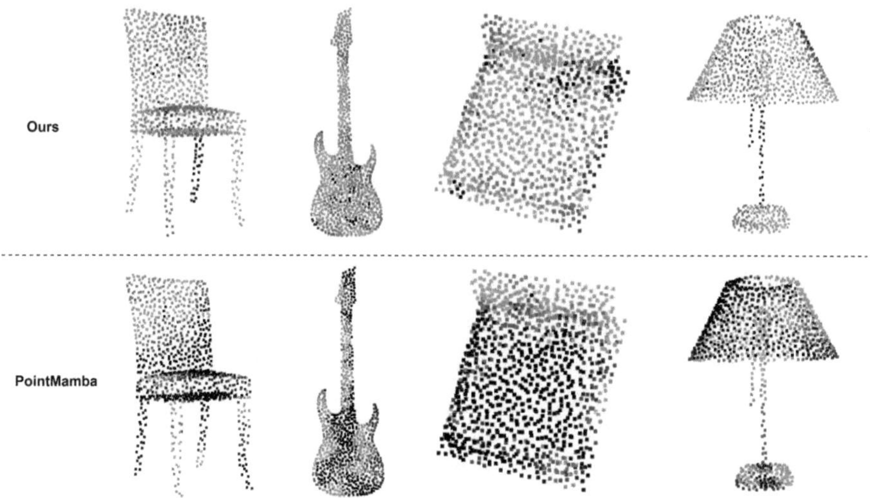

Fig. 2. Feature attribution comparison. Our method (top) identifies more diverse and structurally meaningful regions than PointMamba (bottom) across various object categories.

4.4 Ablation Studies

To evaluate the contributions of individual components in HSMF, we conduct ablation experiments on ScanObjectNN by systematically removing or modifying key modules and analyzing their impact on classification accuracy.

Effects of Spatial Features: Table 3 presents the impact of hierarchical spatial feature extraction in the Integrated Spatial Representation Module (ISRM). Using only point-level features (P) results in lower accuracy, while adding edge features (E) provides moderate improvement. The full model (P+E+S), which integrates surface features (S), achieves the highest accuracy across all dataset variants, demonstrating that hierarchical feature representation captures both fine-grained local and global geometric structures effectively. This confirms that each level contributes complementary information critical for robust object recognition.

Effect of Dynamic Scaling Learning: Table 4 evaluates the Dynamic Scaling Learning Module (DSLM) by testing different radius settings for feature aggregation. A single-scale approach (either 0.1 or 0.2) leads to suboptimal performance, as it limits the network's ability to capture geometric features across different spatial resolutions. Multi-scale configurations (0.2 + 0.1) achieve the best results, highlighting the importance of dynamically adjusting receptive fields to accommodate varying object structures and point densities. This confirms that adaptive multi-scale learning significantly improves classification performance, particularly in challenging real-world datasets.

Table 3. Integrated spatial representation module. "P", "E", and "S" represent the extraction of features from the point, edge, and surface levels, respectively.

Levels	OBJ_BG	OBJ_ONLY	PB_T50_RS
P	89.78	87.86	84.39
P+E	90.69	88.13	84.96
P+E+S	91.24	88.43	85.56

Table 4. Dynamic scaling learning module. 0.1 and 0.2 represent different radius sizes.

Scales	OBJ_BG	OBJ_ONLY	PB_T50_RS
0.1	90.12	87.02	84.32
0.2	90.04	87.13	84.44
0.2+0.2	90.68	87.89	85.01
0.2+0.1	91.24	88.43	85.56

Effect of Spatial Reordering with Morton Code: To enhance spatial locality in sequence modelling, we compared different point sorting methods within the Mamba Backbone. Traditional sorting techniques exhibited high sensitivity to point density and spatial distribution, leading to inconsistent performance across datasets. Implementing Morton Code Sorting, a hierarchical space-filling approach, improved classification accuracy by 2.6% by maintaining spatial coherence across point patches. This confirms that Morton Code Sorting effectively preserves geometric relationships, making it more adaptable to diverse 3D environments.

5 Conclusion

This paper presented the Hierarchical Spatial Mamba Framework (HSMF), a novel architecture that effectively bridges the efficiency of State Space Models (SSMs) with the spatial complexity of point cloud data. By integrating three key innovations, a Morton code-based spatial reordering scheme, a hierarchical Integrated Spatial Representation Module (ISRM), and an adaptive Dynamic Scaling Learning Module (DSLM), HSMF enables expressive and efficient feature learning across local and global spatial contexts. Experimental evaluations on ModelNet40 and ScanObjectNN demonstrate the strong generalisation capabilities of the proposed framework, outperforming several state-of-the-art baselines under both synthetic and real-world conditions. Notably, HSMF achieves these results without reliance on large-scale pretraining or complex data augmentation, highlighting its robustness and inductive efficiency. The ablation studies further confirm the contribution of each module, particularly the benefit of preserving spatial locality in SSM-compatible formats.

The broader applicability of HSMF extends to a variety of downstream 3D vision tasks, including segmentation, registration, and object detection in cluttered or resource-constrained environments. Nevertheless, several directions remain open. First, further exploration is needed to generalise the Morton reordering to anisotropic or highly non-uniform point clouds. Second, integrating HSMF into spatiotemporal pipelines (e.g., for action recognition or dynamic scene understanding) would test its scalability in more complex settings. Lastly, efficient deployment of HSMF on edge hardware through quantisation or pruning remains an important future goal for enabling real-time, low-power 3D processing.

Overall, this work contributes a principled, efficient, and generalisable architecture that expands the capabilities of SSMs for spatial reasoning in 3D vision, offering a promising step toward scalable and lightweight 3D understanding systems.

References

1. Kuang, H., Wang, B., An, J., Zhang, M., Zhang, Z.: Voxel-FPN: mlti-scale voxel feature aggregation for 3D object detection from LiDAR point clouds. Sensors **20**(3), 704 (2020)
2. Qian, R., Lai, X., Li, X.: 3D object detection for autonomous driving: a survey. Pattern Recogn. **130**, 108796 (2022)
3. Pravallika, A., Hashmi, M.F., Gupta, A.: Deep learning frontiers in 3D object detection: a comprehensive review for autonomous driving. IEEE Access (2024)
4. Song, C.H., Blukis, V., Tremblay, J., Tyree, S., Su, Y., Birchfield, S.: Robospatial: teaching spatial understanding to 2D and 3D vision-language models for robotics. In: Proceedings of the Computer Vision and Pattern Recognition Conference, pp. 15768–15780 (2025)
5. Aguiar, A.S., Dos Santos, F.N., Cunha, J.B., Sobreira, H., Sousa, A.J.: Localization and mapping for robots in agriculture and forestry: a survey. Robotics **9**(4), 97 (2020)
6. Checcucci, E., et al.: 3D imaging applications for robotic urologic surgery: an ESUT YAUWP review. World J. Urol. **38**, 869–881 (2020)
7. Yang, S., Xu, S., Huang, W.: 3D point cloud for cultural heritage: a scientometric survey. Remote Sensing **14**(21), 5542 (2022)
8. Cotella, V.A.: From 3D point clouds to HBIM: application of artificial intelligence in cultural heritage. Autom. Constr. **152**, 104936 (2023)
9. Crisan, A., Pepe, M., Costantino, D., Herban, S.: From 3D point cloud to an intelligent model set for cultural heritage conservation. Heritage **7**(3), 1419–1437 (2024)
10. Poux, F., Billen, R., Kasprzyk, J.-P., Lefebvre, P.-H., Hallot, P.: A built heritage information system based on point cloud data: HIS-PC. ISPRS Int. J. Geo Inf. **9**(10), 588 (2020)
11. Shan, P., Sun, W.: Research on 3D urban landscape design and evaluation based on geographic information system. Environ. Earth Sci. **80**(17), 1–15 (2021). https://doi.org/10.1007/s12665-021-09886-y
12. Qi, C.R., Yi, L., Su, H., Guibas, L.J.: PointNet++: deep hierarchical feature learning on point sets in a metric space. Adv. Neural. Inf. Process. Syst. **30**, 5099–5108 (2017)

13. Yu, X., Tang, L., Rao, Y., Huang, T., Zhou, J., Lu, J.: Point-BERT: pre-training 3D point cloud transformers with masked point modeling. In: Proceedings of the IEEE/CVF Conference on Computer Vision and Pattern Recognition (CVPR), pp. 19313–19322 (2022)
14. Wang, Y., Wang, W., Tay, F.E., Liu, W., Tian, Y., Yuan, L.: Masked autoencoders for point cloud self-supervised learning. In: European Conference on Computer Vision (ECCV), pp. 604–621. Springer, Cham (2022)
15. Liang, D., et al: PointMamba: a simple state space model for point cloud analysis. arXiv preprint arXiv:2402.10739 (2024)
16. Wang, Y., Sun, Y., Liu, Z., Sarma, S.E., Bronstein, M.M., Solomon, J.M.: Dynamic graph CNN for learning on point clouds. ACM Trans. Graph. (TOG) **38**(5), 1–12 (2019)
17. Guo, M.-H., Cai, J.-X., Liu, Z.-N., Mu, T.-J., Martin, R.R., Hu, S.-M.: PCT: point cloud transformer. Comput. Visual Media **7**(2), 187–199 (2021). https://doi.org/10.1007/s41095-021-0229-5
18. Chen, G., Wang, M., Yang, Y., Yu, K., Yuan, L., Yue, T.: PointGPT: auto-regressively generative pre-training from point clouds. Advances in Neural Information Processing Systems, vol. 36 (2024)
19. Gu, A., Dao, T.: Mamba: Linear-time sequence modeling with selective state spaces. arXiv preprint arXiv:2312.00752 (2023)
20. Liu, Y., et al.: VMamba: visual state space model. arXiv preprint arXiv:2401.10166 (2024)
21. Huang, T., Pei, X., Shao, Y., Wang, F., Qian, C., Xu, C.: LocalMamba: visual state space model with windowed selective scan. arXiv preprint arXiv:2403.09338 (2024)
22. Samet, H.: The quadtree and related hierarchical data structures. ACM Comput. Surv. (CSUR) **16**(2), 187–260 (1984)
23. Uy, M.A., Pham, Q.-H., Hua, B.-S., Nguyen, T., Yeung, S.-K.: Revisiting point cloud classification: A new benchmark dataset and classification model on real-world data. In: Proceedings of the IEEE/CVF International Conference on Computer Vision (ICCV), pp. 1588–1597 (2019)
24. Wu, Z., et al.: 3D ShapeNets: a deep representation for volumetric shapes. In: Proceedings of the IEEE Conference on Computer Vision and Pattern Recognition (CVPR), pp. 1912–1920 (2015)
25. Li, Y., Bu, R., Sun, M., Wu, W., Di, X., Chen, B.: PointCNN: convolution on X-transformed points. In: Advances in Neural Information Processing Systems, vol. 31 (2018)
26. Thomas, H., Qi, C.R., Deschaud, J.-E., Marcotegui, B., Goulette, F., Guibas, L.J.: KPConv: flexible and deformable convolution for point clouds. In: Proceedings of the IEEE/CVF International Conference on Computer Vision (ICCV), pp. 6411–6420 (2019)
27. Liu, Y., Fan, B., Xiang, S., Pan, C.: Relation-shape convolutional neural network for point cloud analysis. In: Proceedings of the IEEE/CVF Conference on Computer Vision and Pattern Recognition (CVPR), pp. 8895–8904 (2019)
28. Zhang, C., Wan, H., Shen, X., Wu, Z.: PVT: point-voxel transformer for point cloud learning. Int. J. Intell. Syst. **37**(12), 11985–12008 (2022)
29. Xu, Y., Fan, T., Xu, M., Zeng, L., Qiao, Y.: SpiderCNN: deep learning on point sets with parameterized convolutional filters. In: Proceedings of the European Conference on Computer Vision (ECCV), pp. 87–102 (2018)

30. Qiu, S., Anwar, S., Barnes, N.: Geometric back-projection network for point cloud classification. IEEE Trans. Multimed. **24**, 1943–1955 (2021)
31. Cheng, S., Chen, X., He, X., Liu, Z., Bai, X.: Pra-net: point relation-aware network for 3D point cloud analysis. IEEE Trans. Image Process. **30**, 4436–4448 (2021)
32. Selvaraju, R.R., Cogswell, M., Das, A., Vedantam, R., Parikh, D., Batra, D.: Grad-CAM: visual explanations from deep networks via gradient-based localization. Int. J. Comput. Vision **128**, 336–359 (2020)

Handwritten-Text-Image Editing with Diffusion Models and Attention-Based Matching

Yuteng Zhang and Koji Eguchi(✉)

Hiroshima University, Higashi-Hiroshima City, Hiroshima 739-8527, Japan
zytforb@outlook.com, eguchi@acm.org

Abstract. Advancements in diffusion models have significantly enhanced image-generation, with emerging applications extending into multimodal domains. However, persistent challenges in handwritten-text generation—particularly in maintaining typographic consistency and enabling precise modifications—remain unaddressed. This paper presents a novel diffusion model that leverages handwritten-glyph embeddings and attention-guided localization to achieve high-fidelity handwritten-text generation and editing. The proposed model consists of three key modules: (1) a handwritten-glyph-embedding module that incorporates style features and content features for text-control diffusion loss, (2) low-rank decomposition module that enables style-consistent modifications through optimized matrix injections, and (3) attention-guided localization module integrated with segmentation-based text-region detection for editable region detection. Experimental validation demonstrates substantial improvements over other existing methods: our attention-guided localization module achieved 20% higher mean reciprocal rank and 60% lower miss detection rate compared with conventional optical character recognition (OCR) models. In generation-quality assessment, the proposed model outperformed state-of-the-art baselines such as AnyText, showing improvement in learned perceptual image patch similarity and scale-invariant feature transform metrics. The proposed model enables interactive local editing while preserving non-target regions, establishing new benchmarks for style-consistent handwritten-text manipulation.

Keywords: Diffusion models · Handwritten-text Generation · Attention-guided Localization

1 Introduction

Diffusion models have achieved remarkable success in image synthesis. However, applying diffusion models to handwritten text remains challenging due to the discrete nature of text and the continuous nature of diffusion processes, often resulting in blurring, deformation, and reduced legibility.

Key challenges include the following.

C. Wallraven et al. (Eds.): ACPR 2025, LNCS 16174, pp. 418–432, 2026.
https://doi.org/10.1007/978-981-95-4395-3_29

1. **Discrete-continuous Gap:** Handwritten text exhibits discrete and intricate structures, whereas diffusion models operate in continuous latent spaces, making it difficult to accurately capture fine structural details.
2. **Limited Training Data:** Most diffusion models are trained on natural images and have limited exposure to the diverse styles and typographic nuances of handwritten text.
3. **Semantic and Visual Integration:** Generated text must be both legible and contextually coherent with its background—a challenge that traditional diffusion models often struggle to address.
4. **Inference Stability:** The iterative denoising process can undermine the structural integrity of handwritten characters.
5. **Inefficient Guidance:** Reliance on auxiliary cues (e.g., contrastive language-image pre-training (CLIP) or optical character recognition (OCR) corrections) increases complexity and may introduce inconsistencies.

To address these challenges, we propose a diffusion model for handwritten-text editing that incorporates three key modules:

1. A **handwritten-glyph embedding module** that integrates style and content features to enforce text-control diffusion loss, ensuring high-fidelity reproduction.
2. A **low-rank decomposition module** that facilitates style-consistent modifications through optimized matrix injections.
3. An **attention-guided localization module** that uses segmentation-based text-region detection for precise identification and targeted editing.

Our model, validated on the IAM [14] and CVL [10] datasets, achieved significant improvements, including a 20% increase in mean reciprocal rank (MRR) and 60% decrease in the miss detection rate (MDR) compared with traditional OCR-based models. Generation-quality evaluations demonstrated superior performance in both learned perceptual image patch similarity (LPIPS) and scale-invariant feature transform (SIFT) metrics.

The remainder of the paper is organized as follows. Section 2 reviews related work on diffusion-based generative models and text synthesis. Section 3 details our proposed diffusion model that includes the low-rank adaption (LoRA)-based fine-tuning strategy for handwritten-text editing. Section 4 presents our experimental evaluations on the effectiveness of the proposed model, and Sect. 5 concludes with potential future research directions.

2 Related Work

This section reviews advances in *text-image editing* and *text-image inpainting* along with several key techniques that serve as building blocks for our model. *Text-image inpainting* refers to the application of general inpainting methods—originally developed to restore or fill missing regions in images—to images that contain text [19]. In contrast, *text-image editing* aims to seamlessly replace or alter the text regions within an image while preserving the overall visual context.

We organize our related-work review as follows. We first highlight two representative text-editing models, **TextDiffuser** and **AnyText**, both of which leverage diffusion models to handle text in images. We next discuss an attention-based approach for text localization and explainability, which facilitates the detection of text regions through Transformer attention maps (ATTs). We then introduce one-shot diffusion mimicker (**One-DM**), a diffusion model specifically designed for one-shot handwritten-text generation, enabling style-specific text to be generated from minimal examples. Finally, we provide an overview of **LoRA**, a fine-tuning strategy that our proposed model uses to efficiently adapt large-scale diffusion models.

2.1 Text-Image-Editing Models

Studies have addressed the challenge of generating or editing text within images using diffusion models. Below, we discuss two state-of-the-art text-image-editing models in this area.

TextDiffuser TextDiffuser [4] was designed to generate clear and coherent text in images. While diffusion models excel at general image synthesis, they often face challenges in rendering text accurately. To address this issue, TextDiffuser uses a **two-stage generation process** that explicitly models text layout before synthesizing the final image as follows.

1. **Layout Generation Stage:** The goal with this stage is to determine the spatial layout of the text (e.g., bounding-box positions and sizes) on the basis of the input prompt. The process involves:
   (a) encoding the input text into an embedding using a CLIP text encoder [15],
   (b) predicting the bounding boxes of text regions autoregressively via a Transformer-based encoder-decoder, and
   (c) generating character-level segmentation masks to refine the layout details.
2. **Image Generation Stage:** Given the layout from the previous stage, the model generates an image that contains clear and legible text by
   (a) encoding the image into a four-dimensional latent space using a variational autoencoder [9],
   (b) using a U-Net-based diffusion model to iteratively denoise and reconstruct the image, and
   (c) optimizing the image quality through a combination of standard denoising loss and character-aware loss to ensure text legibility.

During inference, users can customize the generated text image by modifying the input prompt or adjusting layout parameters such as bounding-box positions and font sizes.

AnyText. AnyText [16] is a multilingual visual text generation and editing model based on diffusion models. While other diffusion models can generate high-quality images, the textual regions often exhibit blurring or distortion. To overcome this limitation, AnyText introduced a *text-control diffusion pipeline* comprising the following.

1. **Auxiliary Latent Module**: Generates text-specific latent features by integrating glyph information, positional cues, and masked image inputs.
2. **Text Embedding Module**: Leverages OCR models to encode stroke-level features and combines them with caption embeddings, ensuring that the generated text is seamlessly integrated with the image background.

AnyText incorporates two specialized losses, text-control diffusion loss and text perceptual loss, to improve the quality of text rendering across multiple languages.

2.2 One-Shot Diffusion Mimicker

Generating stylized text, such as handwriting, typically requires extensive training data or complex style-transfer methods. **One-DM** [5] addresses this challenge by enabling one-shot handwritten text generation, i.e., mimicking a specific style from a single reference image.

One-DM achieves this through the following techniques.

1. **High-frequency Style-feature Extraction**: Enhances style-specific details by extracting high-frequency components from the reference image using techniques such as Laplacian filtering.
2. **Style-enhancement Module**: Uses contrastive learning to robustly discriminate and refine style features, ensuring that subtle characteristics (e.g., slant, stroke width) are accurately captured.
3. **Gating Mechanism**: Suppresses background noise in the reference image, focusing the model on crucial style cues.
4. **Style-content Fusion via Self-attention**: Fuses the refined style features with content features using multi-head self-attention, ensuring that the generated text faithfully reflects the desired style.
5. **Conditional Diffusion Process**: Uses a diffusion model (e.g., denoising diffusion probabilistic model (DDPM) [6]) conditioned on both content and style features, using iterative denoising to produce high-quality handwritten-text images.

This one-shot capability significantly reduces the need for large datasets, enabling the generation of personalized handwritten-text images from minimal examples.

2.3 Attention Maps for Text Localization and Explainability

Transformer-based architectures have become central to multimodal tasks (e.g., visual question answering [1]) due to their strong contextual modeling capabilities. An inherent advantage of Transformers is that their attention weights can be used to understand which parts of the input the model focuses on. Chefer *et al.* [3] proposed a method for generating *attention heatmaps* (ATTs) by aggregating self-attention and cross-attention weights, thus enhancing the interpretability of vision-language models.

Fig. 1. Attention heatmap [3].

In practice, the ATT highlights the regions of an image that are most relevant to a given text query or prediction. By aggregating attention across multiple heads and layers, the resulting heatmap provides an intuitive visualization of the model's focus, which is particularly useful for localizing text within images. Figure 1 illustrates such an attention heatmap, where warmer colors indicate areas receiving higher attention.

2.4 LoRA for Efficient Fine-Tuning

Fine-tuning large pre-trained models is computationally expensive due to their extensive parameters. **LoRA** [7] offers a parameter-efficient alternative by freezing the pre-trained model weights and injecting trainable low-rank matrices into key layers. Mathematically, LoRA modifies a weight matrix $W_0 \in \mathbb{R}^{d \times k}$ as

$$W = W_0 + \Delta W, \quad \Delta W = AB,$$

where $A \in \mathbb{R}^{d \times r}$ and $B \in \mathbb{R}^{r \times k}$ with $r \ll \min(d, k)$.

By updating only the low-rank matrices, LoRA significantly reduces the number of trainable parameters, making fine-tuning more efficient without sacrificing performance. Our proposed model uses LoRA for it to adapt to the handwritten-text-image editing task, enabling rapid and resource-efficient specialization to the datasets for the target task while maintaining high fidelity in text rendering.

3 Proposed Model

In this section, we present our proposed diffusion model for handwritten-text-image editing, building on the analysis of related work and the contributions outlined in the introduction. The proposed model consists of three main modules:

1. **Text-localization Module:** This module automatically localizes text regions by leveraging the ATT method from Chefer *et al.* [3] together with a state-of-the-art handwritten OCR model [17].

2. **LoRA Fine-tuning:** Cropping and tagging are applied to handwritten-text datasets, followed by fine-tuning a LoRA-based model [7] to achieve high-fidelity generation of handwritten styles.
3. **Model Integration and Style Generation:** By integrating the handwritten-style-imitation model One-DM [5] with the image-editing model AnyText [16], we address the challenges of style inconsistency and lack of uniformity in handwritten-text editing that are commonly observed with current diffusion-based text-image-editing models.

The overall architecture of our proposed model is illustrated in Fig. 2. Initially, the original image and target word for modification are input into the text-localization module to obtain an appropriate mask. Next, the masked image, target word, LoRA weights, and a target text image generated by mimicking the original handwriting style are jointly fed into AnyText. Finally, an output image with consistent style and accurately modified text is generated.

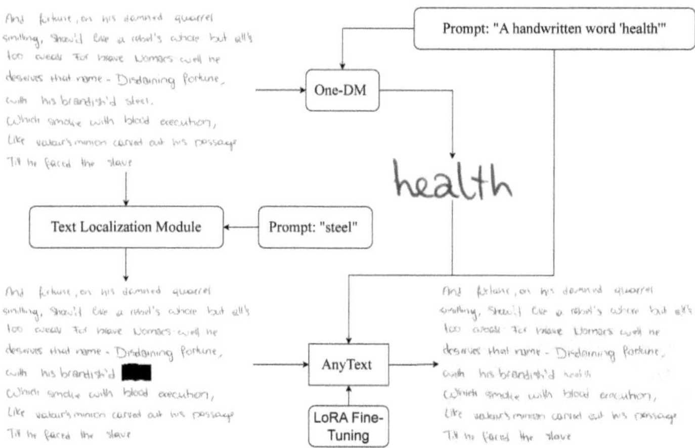

Fig. 2. Architecture of proposed model.

3.1 Text-Localization Module

This module consists of two parts. In the first part, an ATT is used to automatically obtain the approximate coordinates of the target word, as shown in Fig. 3. In the second part, an OCR model is used to extract the positions of all characters in the image (see Fig. 4).

Finally, by computing the intersection over union (IoU) between the coordinates from the ATT and those from the OCR model, the precise location of the target word is determined (see Fig. 5). While the ATT alone can identify the approximate area, it may not cover the complete target region. Conversely, the OCR model is capable of generating text boxes but may produce recognition errors (e.g., mistaking "steel" for "sfeel", as shown in Fig. 4). By leveraging both models concurrently, the overall localization accuracy significantly improves.

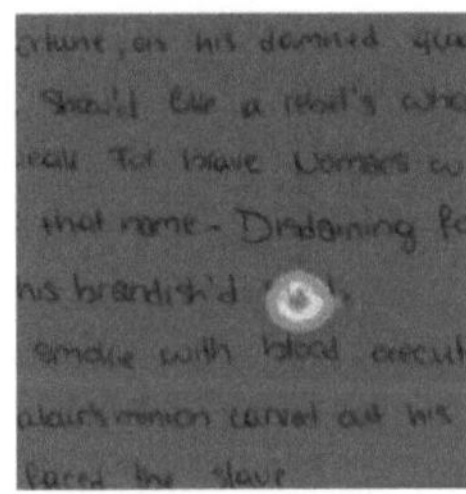

Fig. 3. ATT.

Fig. 4. Result of PGNet [17], a typical OCR model.

Fig. 5. Process of text-localization module.

3.2 LoRA Fine-Tuning

Cropping and Tagging. To recognize and modify handwritten words, we first conduct cropping and tagging on the handwritten-text-image datasets: IAM [14] and CVL [10].

Cropping and Tagging: To modify specific words in handwritten-text images, a high-quality word-level dataset is required. Accordingly, the following steps are applied:

1. **Word-Level Cropping:** Each image is segmented into word-level components on the basis of the available label information.
2. **Random Sampling:** 4% of the words are randomly selected from each image to reduce redundancy while maintaining diversity.
3. **Automatic Tagging:** WD14Tagger [2] is used to automatically assign tags to all images in the dataset.

Applying these procedures to the IAM [14] and CVL [10] datasets, as summarized below, results in high-quality datasets suitable for subsequent LoRA fine-tuning.

IAM Handwritten-Text-Image Dataset: The IAM dataset is widely used for handwritten text recognition (HTR) and handwriting analysis. It contains samples of handwritten English text collected between 1999 and 2002 and is commonly used for developing and evaluating offline HTR systems.

CVL Handwritten-text-image Dataset: The CVL dataset is extensively used in HTR, handwriting analysis, and writer identification. It comprises handwritten English and German text samples from various writers, playing a key role in tasks such as writer verification.

LoRA Fine-Tuning. We next describe the process of fine-tuning AnyText using LoRA (and outline the key techniques used during this process.

Aspect Ratio Bucketing (ARB): Although the input size of AnyText is fixed at 512×512, many word-level handwritten images are small and rectangular. To accommodate non-square aspect ratios, we introduce the ARB technique:

1. Compute the aspect ratio (width/height) for each image.
2. Classify images into predefined ARBs.
3. Assign each image to the closest matching bucket.

During fine-tuning, images within the same bucket are batched together to enhance computational efficiency. Dynamic padding is also applied to minimize redundant computation and optimize GPU utilization.

AdamW Optimizer: To optimize the fine-tuning process, we use AdamW (adaptive moment estimation with weight decay) [12], an enhanced version of Adam [8] that decouples weight decay from gradient computation. Since LoRA fine-tuning updates only the adapter layers, using a stable optimizer such as AdamW is crucial for effective learning.

Cosine Learning Rate Scheduler: The cosine learning rate scheduler gradually reduces the learning rate on the basis of a cosine function, resulting in smoother decay and improved convergence stability. The learning rate η_t at step t is given as

$$\eta_t = \eta_{\min} + \frac{1}{2}(\eta_{\max} - \eta_{\min})\left(1 + \cos\left(\frac{t}{T}\pi\right)\right),$$

where $\eta_{\max}$ is the initial learning rate, $\eta_{\min}$ is the final learning rate, and T is the total number of fine-tuning steps. This scheduler improves both generalization and stability during LoRA fine-tuning by ensuring a gradual reduction in the learning rate.

LoRA Parameters: AnyText accepts inputs of size 512×512, yet many word images exhibit non-square aspect ratios. To address this, ARB (bucket size of 64 units, minimum 64, maximum 512) is applied. We use AdamW with an initial learning rate of 2×10^{-4} and a cosine scheduler. On the basis of the setting of $r = 64$ in a previous study [7], we train the U-Net component of AnyText with a batch size of 6 over 10 epochs to obtain the LoRA weights, thus facilitating adaptation for handwritten-text generation.

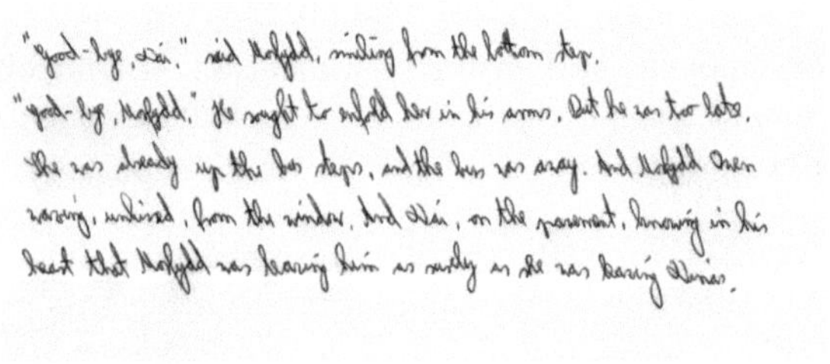

(a) Original handwritten example.

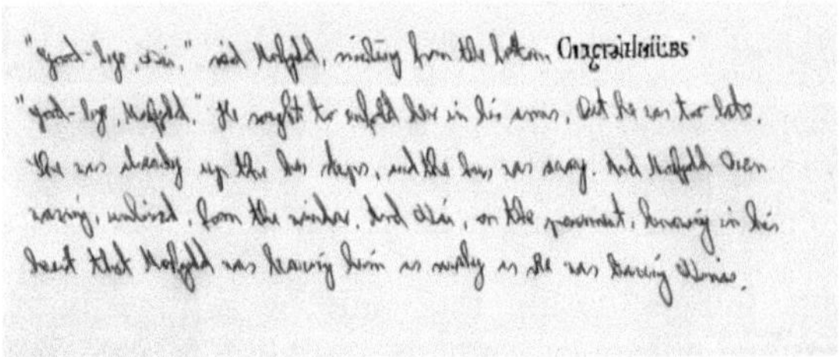

(b) Generated example using AnyText.

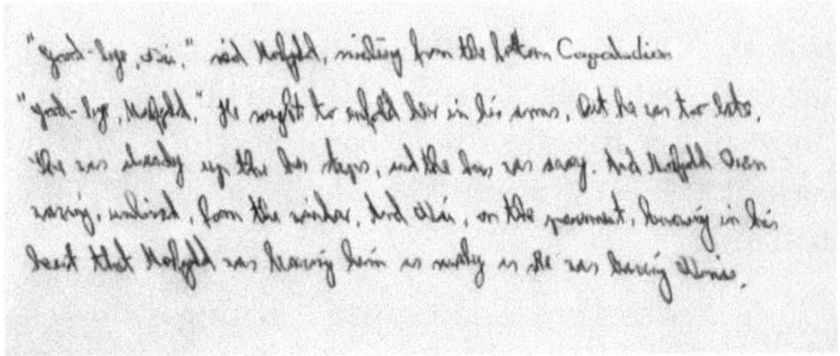

(c) Generated example using proposed model with LoRA fine-tuning.

Fig. 6. Original handwritten example and generated handwritten examples with modification of target word 'step'—located at end of first line from top—into 'congratulations' using AnyText and proposed model with LoRA fine-tuning.

3.3 Model Integration and Handwritten-Style Generation

Although AnyText can execute word-level modifications on handwritten images, its outputs sometimes exhibit inconsistencies in style. In certain cases, the modified region may show colors that do not match the original image or, more severely, the target text may be rendered in a printed font (see Fig. 6(b)). These issues undermine the consistency of the handwritten style, affecting the quality of the generated images.

We carefully observed that during target image generation, AnyText generates a stylistically target text image by using the glyph line, which is created by print font to guide the generation through the extraction of glyph features.

We hypothesize that this design is the primary reason for the printed output in handwritten text generation, as it prioritizes the structural consistency of printed text rather than the stylistic nuances of handwriting.

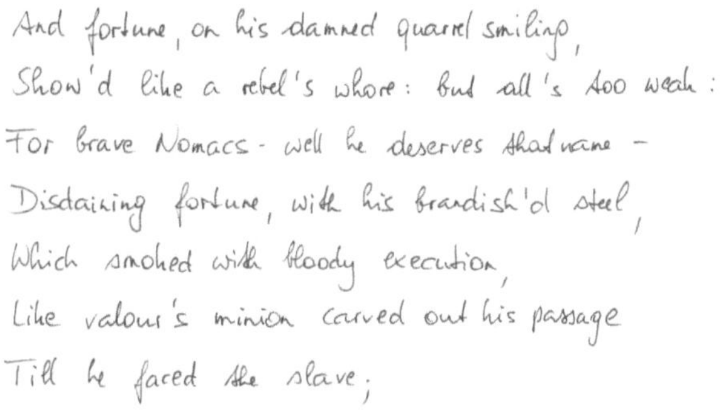

(a) Original handwritten example.

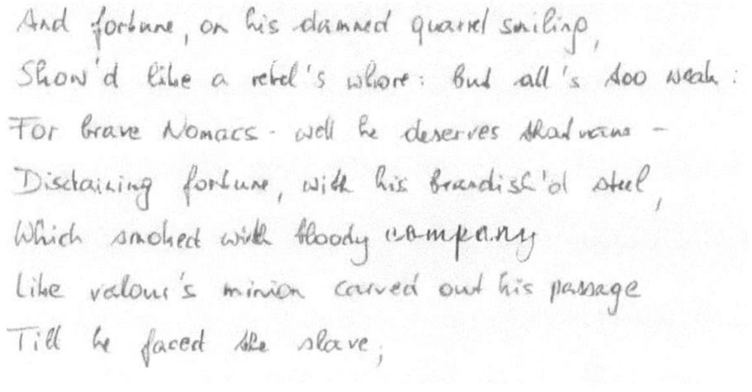

(b) Generated example using AnyText.

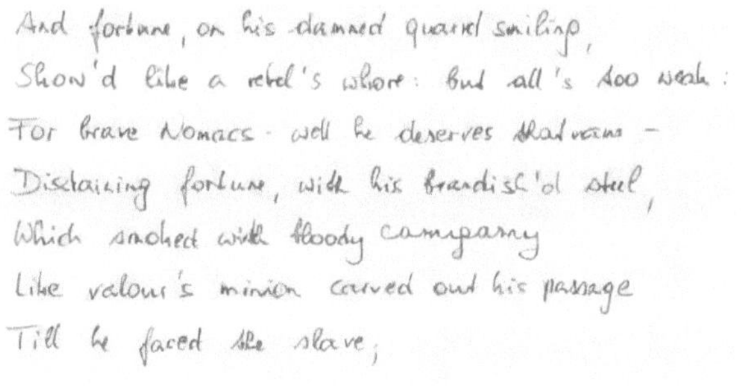

(c) Generated example using proposed model with LoRA fine-tuning.

Fig. 7. Original handwritten example and generated handwritten examples with modification of target word "execution"—located at end of third line from bottom—into "company" using AnyText and proposed model with LoRA fine-tuning.

To address this, we incorporate One-DM, which solely relies on the input handwritten-text image to mimic the handwriting style and generate the corresponding target text image. By replacing the printed target text with a target text image that faithfully imitates the original handwriting, we effectively resolve the style-inconsistency issue, as illustrated in Figs. 6 and 7.

4 Experiments and Results

To evaluate the effectiveness of the text-localization module of the proposed model, we selected 40 images each from the IAM [14] and CVL [10] datasets, resulting in a total of 80 images for quantitative evaluation. The OCR models involved in the quantitative evaluation were differentiable binarization (DB) [11] and point gathering network (PGNet) [17]. DB is an OCR model specialized in text detection, while PGNet is an end-to-end OCR model that integrates both text detection and recognition.

To evaluate the effectiveness of our proposed model as a whole, we conducted experiments on a subset of handwritten-text images from the IAM and CVL datasets. Specifically, we selected 50 images from each dataset, resulting in a total of 100 source images. For each source image, various modifications were carried out at different positions to generate approximately 50 output images per source. In total, 1940 images generated with the baseline AnyText [16] and 1940 images generated with our proposed model were collected for quantitative evaluation.

4.1 Evaluation Metrics

To assess the effectiveness of text localization and the quality of the text-image editing, we used the following evaluation metrics:

Metrics for Text Localization.

- **MRR:** MRR is a widely used metric in information retrieval, question answering, and recommendation systems to evaluate ranking effectiveness. In our study, we computed MRR on the basis of the IoU obtained from both the ATTs and OCR model, as well as the Jaccard distance from the OCR model. A higher MRR indicates that the correct target word is ranked higher in the result list, which reflects improved effectiveness in retrieving the desired text region.
- **MDR:** The MDR measures the proportion of target regions that the text localization method fails to detect. A lower MDR signifies stronger detection capabilities and enhanced overall performance. This metric is critical in scenarios where accurately identifying all occurrences of the target text is essential.

Metrics for Text-Image Editing

- **LPIPS** [18]**:** LPIPS is a metric that measures perceptual similarity by comparing deep features extracted from pre-trained networks, such as VGG or AlexNet. A lower LPIPS score indicates that the generated image is perceptually closer to the source image, meaning that the modifications are more seamlessly integrated, preserving the visual quality of the original image.

Table 1. Comparison of MRR and MDR for different methods. Boldface indicates optimal performance for each metric.

	MRR ⇑	MDR ⇓
ATT+PGNet	**0.9093**	0.2125
ATT+DB	0.8519	**0.0750**
PGNet	0.7017	0.1875

- **SIFT** [13]**:** SIFT is a feature detection and description algorithm that identifies and describes local keypoints in images, which are invariant to scale, rotation, and affine transformations. This metric compares these keypoints between the generated and source images to assess their similarity. Higher SIFT matching scores indicate better local consistency, meaning that the generated text or modifications maintain the handwriting style and visual structure in the specific regions where keypoints are detected.

4.2 Evaluation Results Based on MRR and MDR

The results in Table 1 indicate that incorporating ATTs improves MRR compared with using the OCR-based PGNet alone. Additionally, combining attention maps with DB enhances the MDR compared with the OCR-based PGNet. Thus, the combination of ATTs with DB strikes an optimal balance between MRR and the MDR.

4.3 Evaluation Results Based on LPIPS

We conducted the evaluation using LPIPS at both the overall image level and word level, as detailed below.

Overall LPIPS: Overall LPIPS is computed by treating the image as a whole. Each source image was compared with the set of images generated using both AnyText and our proposed model, and the average similarity was calculated over all comparisons. Table 2 lists the overall LPIPS scores for the CVL and IAM datasets, respectively. Our proposed model consistently achieved lower (better) LPIPS scores compared with AnyText across both datasets.

Table 2. Comparison of overall LPIPS scores. Boldface indicates optimal performance.

	CVL—Avg. ⇑	CVL—Std. Dev.	IAM—Avg. ⇑	IAM—Std. Dev.
Proposed	**0.02738**	0.005388	**0.01689**	0.004366
AnyText	0.02872	0.006568	0.01715	0.004126

Word-Level LPIPS: Since our task focuses on modifying only a small region of the image, the overall LPIPS score might be small, making it less indicative of local quality. To address this, we also computed a word-level LPIPS score. Specifically, source images were segmented into word regions on the basis of labels, and the LPIPS score was calculated between the corresponding regions in the generated images and source images. Table 3 presents the word-level LPIPS scores for the CVL and IAM datasets, confirming that our model consistently outperformed AnyText in perceptual similarity at the word level across both datasets.

Table 3. Comparison of word-level LPIPS scores. Boldface indicates optimal performance.

	CVL—Avg. ⇑	CVL—Std. Dev.	IAM—Avg. ⇑	IAM—Std. Dev.
Proposed	**0.4493**	0.04787	**0.4927**	0.05333
AnyText	0.4589	0.04435	0.4973	0.04893

4.4 Evaluation Results Based on SIFT

We also evaluated the local structural consistency using RGB-SIFT features combined with CLAHE (Contrast Limited Adaptive Histogram Equalization) [20]. CLAHE is used to enhance local contrast while preventing over-amplification of noise. RGB-SIFT is computed by extracting SIFT features from each of the R, G, and B channels separately and fusing them to produce a comprehensive descriptor that accounts for both local texture and color variations.

Table 4 reports the SIFT-matching scores for the CVL and IAM datasets, respectively. Higher SIFT scores indicate better local consistency between the generated and source images. Although our proposed model generally achieved higher SIFT scores compared with AnyText, a discrepancy was observed between the CVL and IAM datasets—likely due to the fact that the IAM dataset consists of grayscale images with less color information.

Table 4. Comparison of RGB-SIFT with CLAHE. Boldface indicates optimal performance in each experiment.

	CVL—Avg. ⇑	CVL—Std. Dev.	IAM—Avg. ⇑	IAM—Std. Dev.
Proposed	**56.18**	25.20	**43.54**	14.38
AnyText	54.93	23.471	43.53	13.98

The experimental results, summarized in Tables 2, 3, and 4, confirm that our model outperforms the baseline in both overall and word-level perceptual similarity, as well as in local feature matching. These results indicate the effectiveness of our model in enhancing the quality and consistency of handwritten-text-image editing.

5 Conclusions

We proposed a comprehensive model for editing handwritten-text images. Our model combines diffusion models with attention-based localization and LoRA fine-tuning to accurately identify and modify editable text regions. Experimental results indicate that our model improves text localization—achieving up to 20% higher MRR and 60% lower MDR compared with traditional OCR models—and enhances generation quality as measured using LPIPS and SIFT.

By combining ATTs with OCR, our model automatically detects target regions, while the fine-tuning on handwritten datasets via LoRA and the integration of the One-DM model with AnyText enable interactive, local editing that preserves non-target regions and maintains consistent handwritten style. With only the input image, target word, and desired output text, our model achieves high-fidelity handwritten-text manipulation, ensuring both accuracy in text localization and consistency in the overall handwriting style.

Despite these promising results, several limitations remain. The hybrid localization approach, while effective, still does not fully match the accuracy of manual annotations. In addition, the reliance on the baseline AnyText generation limits our model when AnyText fails to generate the correct target word.

Future work will focus on the following.

1. Enhancing the text-localization module through the development of more robust and adaptive techniques.
2. Constructing large-scale, diverse handwritten datasets to enable comprehensive training and improve model generalization.
3. Training an independent, large-scale model on the new dataset to reduce reliance on AnyText and further refine style consistency.

Overall, our proposed model establishes new benchmarks for style-consistent handwritten-text editing and opens up promising directions for future research in multimodal text generation.

Acknowledgements. This work was supported in part by the JSPS Grant-in-Aid for Scientific Research (Grant Number: 23K11231).

References

1. Agrawal, A., et al.: VQA: Visual question answering (2016). https://arxiv.org/abs/1505.00468
2. Anonymous: WD14 tagger (2023). https://github.com/toriato/stable-diffusion-webui-wd14-tagger
3. Chefer, H., Gur, S., Wolf, L.: Generic attention-model explainability for interpreting bi-modal and encoder-decoder transformers. In: Proceedings of the IEEE/CVF International Conference on Computer Vision (ICCV), pp. 397–406, October 2021
4. Chen, J., Huang, Y., Lv, T., Cui, L., Chen, Q., Wei, F.: TextDiffuser: diffusion models as text painters (2023). https://arxiv.org/abs/2305.10855

5. Dai, G., Zhang, Y., Ke, Q., Guo, Q., Huang, S.: One-shot diffusion mimicker for handwritten text generation (2024). https://arxiv.org/abs/2409.04004
6. Ho, J., Jain, A., Abbeel, P.: Denoising diffusion probabilistic models (2020). https://arxiv.org/abs/2006.11239
7. Hu, E.J., et al.: LoRA: low-rank adaptation of large language models (2021). https://arxiv.org/abs/2106.09685
8. Kingma, D.P., Ba, J.: Adam: a method for stochastic optimization (2017). https://arxiv.org/abs/1412.6980
9. Kingma, D.P., Welling, M.: Auto-encoding variational Bayes (2022). https://arxiv.org/abs/1312.6114
10. Kleber, F., Fiel, S., Diem, M., Sablatnig, R.: CVL database - an off-line database for writer retrieval, writer identification and word spotting, November 2018. https://doi.org/10.5281/zenodo.1492267
11. Liao, M., Wan, Z., Yao, C., Chen, K., Bai, X.: Real-time scene text detection with differentiable binarization (2019). https://arxiv.org/abs/1911.08947
12. Loshchilov, I., Hutter, F.: Decoupled weight decay regularization (2019). https://arxiv.org/abs/1711.05101
13. Lowe, D.G.: Distinctive image features from scale-invariant keypoints. Int. J. Comput. Vision **60**, 91–110 (2004)
14. Marti, U.V., Bunke, H.: The IAM-database: an English sentence database for offline handwriting recognition (2024). https://doi.org/10.57702/lyl7nrys
15. Radford, A., et al.: Learning transferable visual models from natural language supervision (2021). https://arxiv.org/abs/2103.00020
16. Tuo, Y., Xiang, W., He, J.Y., Geng, Y., Xie, X.: AnyText: Multilingual visual text generation and editing (2024). https://arxiv.org/abs/2311.03054
17. Wang, P., et al.: PGNet: real-time arbitrarily-shaped text spotting with point gathering network (2021), https://arxiv.org/abs/2104.05458
18. Zhang, R., Isola, P., Efros, A.A., Shechtman, E., Wang, O.: The unreasonable effectiveness of deep features as a perceptual metric (2018). https://arxiv.org/abs/1801.03924
19. Zhu, S., Fang, P., Zhu, C., Zhao, Z., Xu, Q., Xue, H.: Text image inpainting via global structure-guided diffusion models (2024). https://arxiv.org/abs/2401.14832
20. Zuiderveld, K.J., et al.: Contrast limited adaptive histogram equalization. Graphics Gems **4**(1), 474–485 (1994)

Heterogeneous Hierarchical Map Representation for Robotics Using Morse Smale Theory

Michael Law San[1,2(✉)], Romain Marie[1,2], and Ouiddad Labbani-Igbida[1]

[1] XLIM Research Institute, UMR CNRS 7252, University of Limoges, 123 Avenue Albert Thomas, 87000 Limoges, France
{michael.law_san,ouiddad.labbani-igbida}@unilim.fr

[2] 3iL Groupe, 43 rue de Sainte-Anne, 87015 Limoges, France
Marie@3il.fr

Abstract. This work presents a topological framework for scene representation and structural analysis based on Morse-Smale theory and persistent cohomology. By leveraging topological invariants, we construct a compact, hierarchical encoding of 3D environments from occupancy grid data. The method consists of computing a Morse-Smale complex on a distance-transformed occupancy grid to extract critical points and generate a topological skeleton of the scene. This representation is then hierarchically refined using merge trees, a topological structure that captures the connectivity and persistence of topological features of the explored environment across scales. The resulting representation is compact, sensor-agnostic, and well-suited for heterogeneous multi-robot systems. By capturing intrinsic spatial connectivity and hierarchical relationships, the framework defines a generic spatial grammar independent of predefined ontologies such as rooms or buildings. The framework also supports an adaptive stratification mechanism that reduces reliance on heuristics by using topological invariants to guide principled hierarchy construction. This enables robust, multiscale environmental understanding that adapts to structural complexity.

We validate our approach in simulated environments using Gazebo and ROS2, generating synthetic occupancy grids from diverse sensor modalities. Topological similarity, assessed via Wasserstein distance, has demonstrated the robustness of Morse-Smale merge trees under sensor variability, confirming their relevance for real-world multi-robot navigation and mapping applications.

Keywords: Topology representation · Multimodality · Robotics · Homology · Morse Smale Complex

1 Introduction

The increasing complexity of tasks assigned to robotic systems has led to the development of heterogeneous multi-robotic systems (HMRS), where multiple

C. Wallraven et al. (Eds.): ACPR 2025, LNCS 16174, pp. 433–445, 2026.
https://doi.org/10.1007/978-981-95-4395-3_30

robots with diverse sensing, dynamics, and cognitive capabilities collaborate to achieve common objectives. The multimodal nature of such systems enhances environmental understanding by leveraging complementary data from heterogeneous sensors and robots perspectives. However, this multimodality introduces significant challenges in data integration and representation. Consequently, one needs to overcome many challenges related to merging data of different forms, such as point clouds, pixel arrays, or time series, which also comes with inherent inconsistencies in scale, resolution, and noise characteristics. Furthermore, the observed environment often exhibits complex relationships, such as spatial adjacency, temporal correlations, or semantic hierarchies, which are typically captured partially and locally from various points of view.

To address these challenges, we propose the use of algebraic topology as a unifying formalism for modelling heterogeneous, multimodal data within HMRS. This enables us to build a representation that accommodates diversity in sensors and robot capabilities while preserving intrinsic spatial and structural relationships across multiple scales.

Related to this work is Benjamin Kuipers' seminal work [15] on the Spatial Semantic Hierarchy (SSH) that has been particularly influential in this domain and has been extended to Hybrid Spatial Semantic Hierarchy (HSSH) [4] by including relationship between large-scale and small-scale spatial representations. It offers a multi-layered framework that integrates qualitative and quantitative spatial knowledge, facilitating effective navigation and map-building in large-scale environments. More recently, authors [14] have argued that for higher level representation such as semantics and affordances, a hierarchical representation is almost required. Hierarchical representation offers a cognitive plausibility as it goes from general to more specific or vice versa, mirroring human cognition. The recent advances in spatial perception and multi-robot SLAM (Simultaneous Localisation and Mapping) demonstrate the increasing relevance of hierarchical and semantic representations in robotics. In [24], the authors introduce a 3D dynamic scene graph framework that integrates metric, topological, and semantic representations into a unified hierarchical structure. This approach enables robots to model their environments with a rich spatial understanding, capturing the relationships between objects, spaces, and dynamic elements. The approach was extended to distributed multi-robot systems for robust metric-semantic SLAM across multiple agents in [27]. The LayoutSLAM series [11,12] takes a complementary perspective by focusing on spatial regularities and object arrangements to improve map fidelity. They incorporate geometric features of object placement to jointly estimate layout and object maps in crowded environments.

The multiscale nature of spatial perception has also been approached by making use of the distance transform [19,22,23], which naturally encodes scale-space through level sets and operates across multiple scales of geometric significance. The medial axis [5], as the locus of local maxima in the distance field, offers a natural encoding of the distance transform. The computational aspects of the medial axis were studied by [10,17] for filtration and algorithmic simplification respectively. These insights find a topological counterpart in the Morse-Smale Complex (MSC) [7,20], which generalizes the distance transform using Morse theory on differentiable manifolds. The MSC captures the critical points and integral lines of scalar fields, yielding a topological skeleton that encodes structural features hierarchically. We refer the reader to [2,26] for further mathematical aspects of application of Morse theory on manifolds.

This work shares common ground with these works by aiming to unify multimodal spatial representations while addressing challenges related to heterogeneity in sensor data and robots. The main contribution is formulating Morse-Smale Merge Trees to model spatial relationships and capture hierarchical representations through deformation invariants. This yields a new robotics scene representation framework that is compact, sensor-agnostic, and scalable, unifying geometric and topological information.

2 Mathematical Prerequisites

The Morse-Smale complex provides a framework for analyzing the topology of Riemannian manifolds encoding geometric or physical properties. Given a differentiable manifold M and a Morse function $f : M \to \mathbb{R}$, the topological structure of M is characterized by the critical points of f and their connections, forming the Morse-Smale complex. This decomposition allows a multiscale representation of the manifold's topological features, such as connected components, cycles, and voids, formalized through k-homology groups $\mathcal{H}_k$. Below, will be a prerequisite for the definition and interpretation of methods used in Sect. 3.

Definition 1 (Simplicial Complex). *A simplicial complex K is a finite collection of simplices in $\mathbb{R}^N$ satisfying: (i) if $\sigma \in K$, then every face of σ is in K, and (ii) for any $\sigma, \tau \in K$, their intersection $\sigma \cap \tau$ is either empty or a common face of both.*

In this paper, we consider the geometrical realization of simplicial complexes as illustrated in Fig. 1. For a more abstract, purely combinatorial definition of simplicial complexes, where only the vertex connectivity is specified without reference to geometric embedding, we refer the reader to [13] for a comprehensive resource.

Fig. 1. Simplicial complexes generalize graphs to higher dimensions. Like graphs, they can be oriented to define directed structures and formalize algebraic operations such as boundary maps in homology theory.

In his seminal work [25], Stephen Smale studied gradient dynamical systems and laid the foundation for what is now known as Morse-Smale theory, though the term *Morse-Smale Complex* was not originally used. The notion of Morse-Smale complexes as explicit cell decompositions emerged more clearly in the computational topology literature, notably through the works of Forman [9] and Edelsbrunner et al. [7].

Definition 2 (Morse-Smale Complex). *Let $f : M \to \mathbb{R}$ be a Morse function on a smooth n-manifold M with Riemannian metric g. For each critical point $p \in Crit(f)$ of index k, define the stable and unstable manifolds:*

$$W^s(p) = \{x \in M \mid \lim_{t \to +\infty} \phi_t(x) = p\} \tag{1}$$

$$W^u(p) = \{x \in M \mid \lim_{t \to -\infty} \phi_t(x) = p\} \tag{2}$$

where ϕ_t is the flow of $-\nabla f$. The gradient $-\nabla f$ is ***Morse-Smale*** *if all stable and unstable manifolds intersect transversely. The* ***Morse-Smale complex*** *C is the CW-complex with k-cells given by the unstable manifolds $W^u(p)$ of index-k critical points, yielding the cellular decomposition $M = \bigsqcup_{p \in Crit(f)} W^u(p)$.*

The Morse-Smale complex provides both a topological decomposition of the manifold and a geometric realization of the gradient flow dynamics, which partitions the manifold into regions of uniform gradient flow.

In computational approaches, the smooth manifold M is approximated by a simplicial complex K through triangulation, and the smooth Morse function $f : M \to \mathbb{R}$ is discretized as a piecewise linear function $f_K : |K| \to \mathbb{R}$ defined on the vertices of K. Using discrete Morse theory [9], a combinatorial gradient field V is constructed on K to approximate the continuous gradient flow $-\nabla f$. The resulting Morse-Smale complex, which is a CW-complex, is then extracted from this discrete gradient field through flow computation algorithms. Thus, while the simplicial complex K serves as the computational substrate for discretising the problem, the output Morse-Smale complex retains its structure as a CW-complex which cells correspond to the discrete unstable manifolds $\{W_K^u(p) \mid p \in \text{Crit}(f_K)\}$. Edelsbrunner et al. [7] extended Morse-Smale theory to the discrete setting through a computational geometry approach by developing it for piecewise-linear 2-manifolds, later generalized to 3-manifolds in [8], building upon the foundational discrete curvature framework introduced by Banchoff [3]. While Banchoff's work established the geometric foundations by connecting discrete curvature measures to critical point theory on polyhedral surfaces, Edelsbrunner's contribution provides the algorithmic tools for constructing hierarchical Morse-Smale complexes and analyzing their topological structure in the discrete domains.

Definition 3 (Piecewise-Linear Manifold). *Morse theory is extended to piecewise linear Manifolds $(|K|, f)$, where $|K|$ is the geometrical realization of simplicial complexes as shown in Fig. 1, and f is a scalar function mapping simplices to $\mathbb{R}^n$.*

Then, the realization of a Morse Smale Complex C can be described on $(|K|, f)$, an illustration of this construction is provided in Fig. 2.

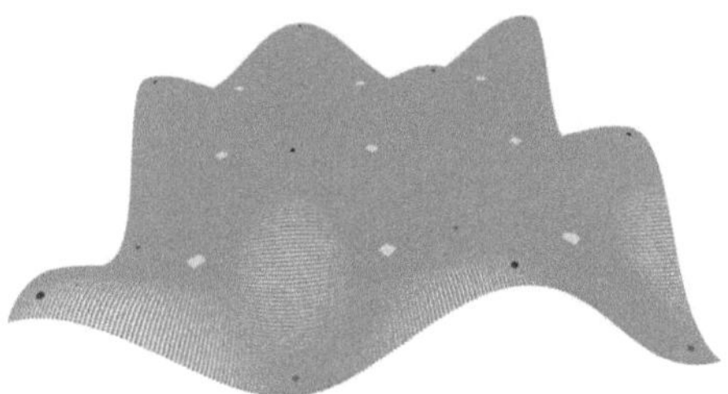

Fig. 2. Example of a discrete Morse-Smale Complex on a piecewise-linear manifold $(|K|, f)$ with $f : \mathbb{Z}^2 \to \mathbb{Z}$ defining a double sine wave surface. Red, yellow, and blue spheres represent minima, saddle points, and maxima respectively. Golden lines show geodesic integral lines connecting critical points, forming the Morse-Smale complex structure. (Color figure online)

3 Methodology

This section presents our approach for constructing sensor-agnostic topological representations of multi-modal data. The core contribution is the adaptation of merge trees to operate on Morse-Smale Complexes rather than scalar fields, enabling effective topogeometric encoding. Our methodology addresses three key challenges; (1) designing a unified representation that remains consistent across heterogeneous sensor modalities, (2) preserving salient topological features while achieving computational efficiency, and (3) encoding geometric information alongside topological structure. The following subsections detail our algorithmic framework, beginning with the theoretical foundations of the modified merge tree construction, followed by the stratification process. Figure 3 presents an overview of the proposed pipeline. Given a sensor observation $G_\tau \in \mathbb{R}^3$ at time τ, we consider G_τ as a discrete sampling of a manifold surface embedded in $\mathbb{R}^3$. This 3D representation may originate from various sensor modalities, such as data acquired from a 3D LiDAR, an RGB-D camera, or reconstructed using depth learning methods. We define the evolution of G_τ with respect to the parameter z, which, in this context, aligns with the direction of gravitational acceleration and represents altitude.

$$G[z] = \{e \in G_{a_i} | z \in Z\} \tag{3}$$

$$Z = \{z | E \in G_\tau\} \tag{4}$$

To mitigate sensor noise, we project $G[z]$ onto an occupancy grid that encodes free space. A second Morse function is then defined via a distance transform applied to this grid. Since the distance transform yields a discrete grid, it is represented as a piecewise linear (PL) manifold $(\mathcal{K}, f)$, where the vertices of $\mathcal{K}$ correspond to free cells, and the scalar function f assigns to each simplex the minimal Euclidean distance to the nearest occupied cell.

$$DT : G[z] \to PL[z] \tag{5}$$

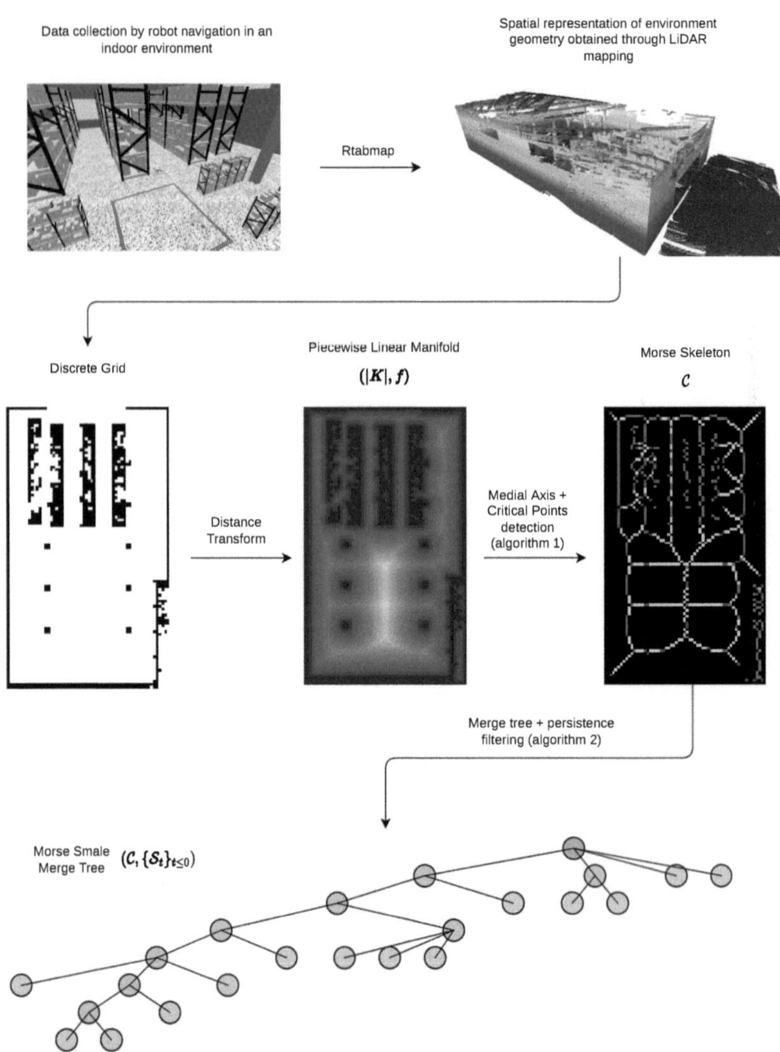

Fig. 3. Data flow through the computational pipeline for Morse-Smale merge tree construction on a single z-layer. From left to right: point cloud data from RTABMap is segmented by z-layer and processed via distance transform to assign scalar values to unoccupied voxels. The medial axis is computed and critical points are identified (red maxima and blue saddles similar to that in Fig. 2), followed by stratification to generate the corresponding merge tree. In the resulting merge tree, blue nodes represent internal nodes, green nodes denote leaves, and the red node indicates the root (Color figure online)

3.1 Morse-Smale Complex Representation

Following [7], critical points $\mathcal{H}_0$ are identified by analyzing the local neighborhood $St(u)$ of each vertex u in $\mathcal{K}$. As previously noted, $\mathcal{M}$ is heuristically equivalent to a corresponding Morse-Smale Complex, which allows for significant computational reduction by avoiding full recomputation and focusing on structurally relevant regions. The classification of critical points simplifies to:

$$c_0 \text{ if } DT(c) \leq h(p)|p \in St(c) \tag{6}$$

$$c_1 \text{ if } DT(c) \geq h(p)|p \in St(c) \tag{7}$$

$$c \in \mathcal{M} \tag{8}$$

Here, c_0 corresponds to a local maximum in the distance transform but a minimum in the Morse-Smale complex $\mathcal{M}$, acting as a saddle point on the underlying piecewise linear manifold $PL[z]$. In contrast, c_1 represents a maximum in both $\mathcal{M}$ and $PL[z]$.

The parameter ϵ serves as a hyperparameter that defines a contraction condition in Eq. 9, introduced to mitigate numerical artifacts in the computation.

$$c = p \text{ s.t. } p \in St(c), \text{ if } |h(c) - h(p)| \leq \epsilon \tag{9}$$

The matrix $MSC[z]$ obtained from Algorithm 1 is the combinatorial expression of the underlying vector field, following the same processing pipeline illustrated in Fig. 3.

3.2 Hierarchy Through Morse-Smale Merge Trees

Persistence diagrams provide the standard cohomological representation of topological features but fail to capture certain structural aspects that are preserved by merge trees [18]. Furthermore, we argue that merge trees are particularly well-suited for organizing multiscale information into an adaptive hierarchical structure. However, merge trees lack the n-dimensional cellular decomposition of Morse-Smale complexes, which is crucial for capturing the full geometric and topological structure. Hence, instead of performing subset level filtration on the scalar field where connectivity will be lost, we perform filtration on the Morse-Smale complex, preserving structural coherence throughout the hierarchy.

$$C_t = \{c \in C : f(c) \leq t\} \tag{10}$$

The adjacency structure of $\mathcal{C}_t$ is inherited from the original Morse-Smale complex $\mathcal{C}$: Two cells $c_i, c_j \in \mathcal{C}_t$ are adjacent if they share a boundary in the original complex. Let $\pi_0(\mathcal{C}_t)$ denote the set of connected components of the sublevel cell complex $\mathcal{C}_t$ defined with respect to this inherited adjacency relation. As the threshold parameter t increases, this yields a filtration:

$$C_{t_1} \subseteq C_{t_2} \subseteq \cdots \subseteq C \quad \text{for } t_1 < t_2 < \cdots \tag{11}$$

Algorithm 1. Morse-Smale Complex from Piecewise-Linear Manifolds

```
Require: Piecewise-linear manifold PL[z], hyperparameter ε ≥ 0
Ensure: Output matrix M representing a Morse-Smale Complex 𝒞
  ℳ ← ComputeMedialAxis(PL[z])                          ▷ Compute medial axis
  C ← ∅                                                  ▷ Initialize critical points set
  for c ∈ ℳ do                                           ▷ Only consider points on medial axis
      validPoint ← false
      for each p ∈ St(c) do                              ▷ Star of point c
          if |h(c) − h(p)| ≤ ε then                      ▷ Check numerical tolerance
              validPoint ← true
              C ← C ∪ {c}                                ▷ Add to critical points (c0 flows to c1)
              break                                      ▷ Exit inner loop once valid point found
          end if
      end for
  end for
  G_ℳ ← GetMedialAxisGraph(ℳ)                            ▷ Extract medial axis connectivity
  G ← (C, E) where E ← ∅                                 ▷ Initialize critical point graph
                    ▷ Use medial axis connectivity to reduce geodesic computations
  for each critical point c_i ∈ C do
      visited ← {c_i}                                    ▷ Track visited nodes
      queue ← GetNeighbors(c_i, G_ℳ)                     ▷ BFS from c_i
      while queue ≠ ∅ do
          c_j ← queue.pop()
          if c_j ∈ C and c_j ∉ visited then              ▷ Found another critical point
              γ_ij ← ComputeGeodesicOnMedialAxis(c_i, c_j, G_ℳ)
              geodesicLength ← length(γ_ij)              ▷ Length of geodesic between critical
  points
              E ← E ∪ {(c_i, c_j, geodesicLength)}       ▷ Add weighted edge
          end if
          visited ← visited ∪ {c_j}
          Add unvisited neighbors of c_j to queue
      end while
  end for
  n ← |C|                                                ▷ Number of critical points
  Initialize matrix M ∈ ℝ^{n×n} with zeros
  for each edge (c_i, c_j, w) ∈ E do
      M[i, j] ← w                                        ▷ Set matrix entry to signed flow connectivity
      M[j, i] ← −w                                       ▷ Anti-symmetric matrix for directed flow
  end for
  return MSC                                             ▷ Return signed flow connectivity matrix
```

This process induces a natural stratification of the clusters;

$$\mathcal{S}_t = \{S_1^{(t)}, S_2^{(t)}, \ldots, S_{k_f}^{(t)}\} \tag{12}$$

where each $S_i^t \subseteq \mathcal{C}$ represents a cluster of cells that merge at or before level t.

$$\mathcal{S}_{t_1} \succeq \mathcal{S}_{t_2} | t_1 < t_2 \tag{13}$$

That is, each cluster in $\mathcal{S}_{t_2}$ is a union of clusters from $\mathcal{S}_{t_1}$, for $t_1 < t_2$. The Morse-Smale Merge Tree denoted by $(\mathcal{C}, \{\mathcal{S}_t\}_{t\geq 0})$ defines a stratified space, where:

- Each stratum $\mathcal{S}_t$ is a partition of $\mathcal{C}$,
- The stratification respects the topological structure of the Morse-Smale complex,
- The hierarchy is consistent with the sublevel set filtration.

The construction of $(\mathcal{C}, \{\mathcal{S}_t\}_{t\leq 0})$ extends the Merge Tree algorithm introduced in [6], replacing the scalar field with the function $f(c)|c \in \mathcal{C}$.

1. **Initialize data structures:** Set up a Union-Find structure to track connected components and sort all cells in ascending order according to their function values.
2. **Process cells sequentially:** For each cell in sorted order, identify which previously processed adjacent cells it connects to by finding their component representatives.
3. **Handle merging cases:**
   (a) If the cell has no processed neighbours, initiate a new component
   (b) If the cell connects to a single component, create a merge node linking the new cell to that component
   (c) If the cell connects to multiple components, create a merge node that unifies all connected components along with the new cell.
4. **Update the tree structure:** For each merge event, create an internal node in the merge tree representing the merge operation and update pointers from active components to their associated tree nodes.
5. **Maintain connectivity:** Use Union-Find operations to merge identifiers and efficiently maintain a mapping from each active component to its corresponding node in the tree throughout the process.

3.3 Noise Removal

Due to sensor noise and numerical artifacts, spurious components are inevitably introduced into the merge tree. To mitigate this, we perform adaptive noise removal by analyzing the persistence gaps between merge events of clusters from Eq. 13. A gap factor γ regulates the sensitivity of the filtering process, i.e., smaller values of γ lead to more components being classified as noise, resulting in a simplified tree structure, while larger values preserve more low-persistence features. The full persistence-based filtering procedure is presented in Algorithm 2.

Algorithm 2. Persistence-based Noise Filtering

```
Require: Merge tree T, gap factor γ ∈ [0, 1]
Ensure: Filtered tree T′ with noise removed
  Compute persistence values: pers(c) = d_c − b_c for all components c
  Sort finite persistence values: p_1 ≤ p_2 ≤ ··· ≤ p_n
  Compute gaps: g_i = p_{i+1} − p_i for i = 1, ..., n − 1
  Find maximum gap: i* = arg max_i g_i
  Set threshold: τ = p_{i*} + γ · g_{i*}
  Initialize noise set: N = {c : pers(c) < τ and pers(c) ≠ ∞}
  for each node v in T (post-order) do
     if v ∈ N and v is leaf then
        Remove v from tree
     else if v ∈ N and |children(v)| = 1 then
        Promote child to replace v
     else if v ∈ N and |children(v)| > 1 then
        Create new merge node with filtered children
     else
        Keep v and filter its children recursively
     end if
  end for
  return T′
```

4 Results

In this section, We evaluate our approach on two synthetic environments obtained from the Gazebo Fuel repository [21]: a cluttered warehouse environment and an open-space environment with minimal obstacles. These scenarios are designed to showcase the method's applicability to both multiscale structure detection and multimodal data representation. For the input layer, we used RTABMap [16], which supports multiple sensor modalities including LiDAR, RGB-D cameras, and monocular/stereo visual sensors and incorporates corrections using an inertial measurement unit (IMU). We analyzed how varying the persistence gap parameter γ of the merge tree, influences the evolution of Wassertein distances across different altitude layers z for each sensor modality. In both environments. The occupancy grid was discretized into voxels of 0.5 m using the simulation framework provided by Gazebo.

5 Discussion

Figure 4 shows topological stability effectively discriminates between environmental types. Construction sites exhibit low Wasserstein distances near zero, reflecting large, coherent free spaces with stable topology. Warehouses show frequent high peaks, indicating fragmented structure where small filtering parameter changes cause significant topological reorganization. Increasing gap parameter γ from 0.1 to 0.9 does not monotonically decrease topological instability,

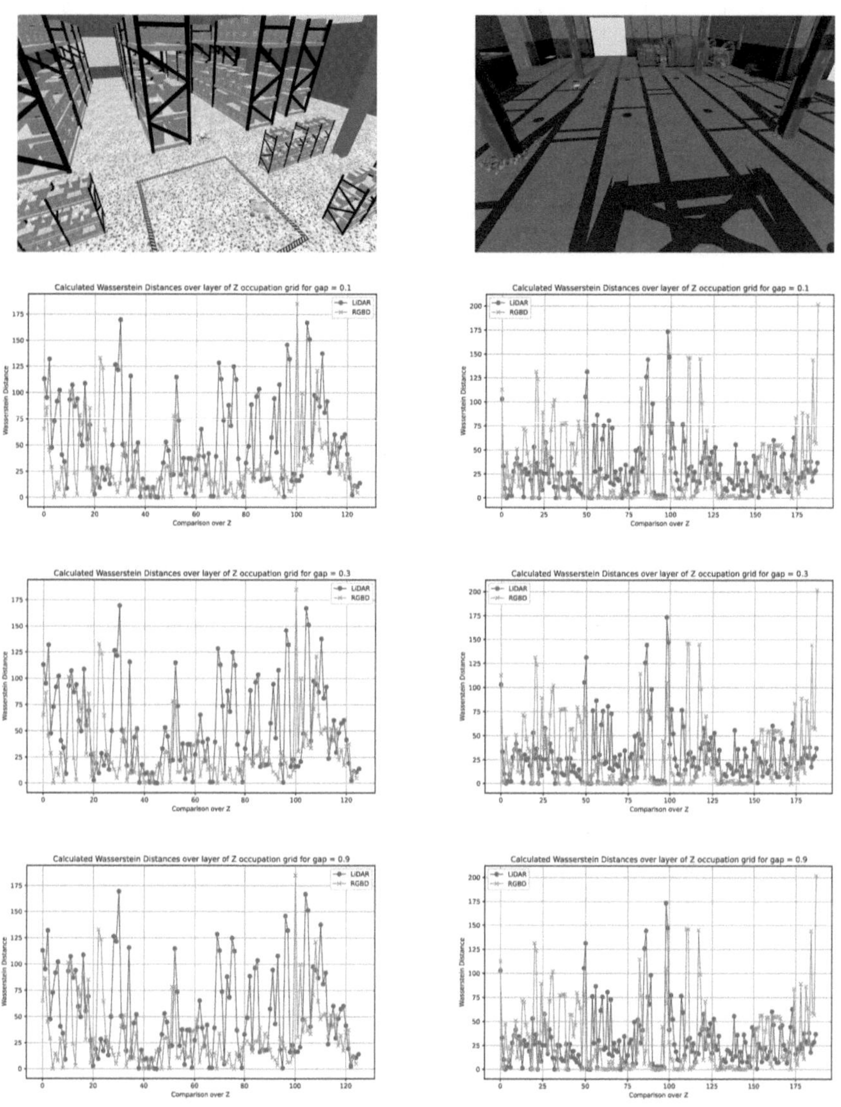

Fig. 4. The first column shows a cluttered environment in a warehouse, while the second column depicts a construction site with large open spaces. The persistence gap factor γ is set to 0.1, 0.3, and 0.9 for the first, second, and third rows, respectively.

suggesting clutter removal involves complex, scale-dependent mechanisms rather than simple noise reduction. Persistent topological peaks at higher γ values indicate that fine-scale *clutter* may represent structurally significant elements at coarser resolutions. Topological stability analysis captures intrinsic environmental properties beyond geometric complexity. Feature persistence under aggressive clutter removal reveals fundamental organizational principles within each environment. This suggests topological invariants provide robust environmental signatures for robotic mapping and planning that remain stable across different sensing conditions. A key insight is that the persistence filtering strategy $\tau = p_i + \gamma \cdot g_{i^*}$, where g_{i^*} is the largest merge tree gap, may compromise multiscale analysis by introducing scale bias. Features are evaluated relative to the dominant scale rather than local topological context, potentially suppressing meaningful structures at smaller or intermediate scales.

6 Conclusion

In this work, we proposed a topology-driven framework for scene representation based on Morse-Smale theory and persistence homology. By applying these techniques to occupancy grid data, we demonstrated efficient extraction, encoding, and comparison of topological features, providing an adaptive hierarchical representation supporting both multimodal integration and multiscale analysis. Future work should explore alternative persistence dimensions: (1) local gap distributions instead of global maximum gaps to better capture heterogeneous topological structures across environmental regions, and (2) fractal dimension-aware filtering that preserves self-similar patterns through scale-invariant persistence measures. Going further, one of the main challenges in robotics is enabling meaningful interaction with humans, where objects and relations between objects carry semantic significance. The 3d-scene graph framework [1] and its derived applications, offers a practical solution to this. Therefore, a promising direction involves considering a hybrid approach that involves the integration of Morse-Smale trees with 3D scene graphs as a structural scaffold, merging topological abstraction with semantic hierarchy.

References

1. Armeni, I., et al.: 3D scene graph: a structure for unified semantics, 3D space, and camera. In: Proceedings of the IEEE/CVF International Conference on Computer Vision, pp. 5664–5673 (2019)
2. Arnal, C., Cohen-Steiner, D., Divol, V.: Critical points of the distance function to a generic submanifold. arXiv preprint arXiv:2312.13147 (2023)
3. Banchoff, T.: Critical points and curvature for embedded polyhedra. J. Differ. Geom. **1**(3–4), 245–256 (1967)
4. Beeson, P., Modayil, J., Kuipers, B.: Factoring the mapping problem: mobile robot map-building in the hybrid spatial semantic hierarchy. Int. J. Robot. Res. **29**(4), 428–459 (2010)
5. Blum, H.: A transformation for extracting new descriptions of shape. Models for the perception of speech and visual form, pp. 362–380 (1967)
6. Carr, H., Snoeyink, J., Axen, U.: Computing contour trees in all dimensions. Comput. Geom. **24**(2), 75–94 (2003)
7. Edelsbrunner, H.: Zomorodian: hierarchical Morse-Smale complexes for piecewise linear 2-manifolds. Discrete Comput. Geom. **30**, 87–107 (2003)

8. Edelsbrunner, H., Harer, J., Natarajan, V., Pascucci, V.: Morse-Smale complexes for piecewise linear 3-manifolds. In: Proceedings of the Nineteenth Annual Symposium on Computational Geometry, pp. 361–370 (2003)
9. Forman, R.: Morse theory for cell complexes. Adv. Math. **134**(1), 90–145 (1998)
10. Fuseiller, G., Marie, R., Mourioux, G., Duno, E., Labbani-Igbida, O.: Enhancing distance transform computation by leveraging the discrete nature of images. J. Real-Time Image Proc. **19**(4), 763–773 (2022)
11. Gunji, K., et al.: Layoutslam++: simultaneous estimation of layout and object map based on geometric features of object placement. In: 2023 IEEE 19th International Conference on Automation Science and Engineering (CASE), pp. 1–8 (2023). https://doi.org/10.1109/CASE56687.2023.10260535
12. Gunji, K., et al.: Layoutslam: object layout based simultaneous localization and mapping for reducing object map distortion. In: 2022 IEEE/RSJ International Conference on Intelligent Robots and Systems (IROS), pp. 2825–2832 (2022). https://api.semanticscholar.org/CorpusID:255176781
13. Hatcher, A.: Algebraic topology. https://pi.math.cornell.edu/~hatcher/AT/AT+.pdf
14. Hughes, N., et al.: Foundations of spatial perception for robotics: hierarchical representations and real-time systems. Int. J. Robot. Res. 02783649241229725 (2024)
15. Kuipers, B.: The spatial semantic hierarchy. Artif. Intell. **119**(1–2), 191–233 (2000)
16. Labbé, M., Michaud, F.: RTAB-map as an open-source lidar and visual simultaneous localization and mapping library for large-scale and long-term online operation. J. Field Robot. **36**(2), 416–446 (2019)
17. Marie, R., Labbani-Igbida, O., Mouaddib, E.M.: The delta medial axis: a fast and robust algorithm for filtered skeleton extraction. Pattern Recogn. **56**, 26–39 (2016)
18. Morozov, D., Beketayev, K., Weber, G.: Interleaving distance between merge trees. Discret. Comput. Geom. **49**(22–45), 52 (2013)
19. Morse, B.S., Pizer, S.M., Liu, A.: Muitiscale medial analysis of medical images. Image Vis. Comput. **12**(6), 327–338 (1994)
20. Natarajan, V., Pascucci, V.: Volumetric data analysis using Morse-Smale complexes. In: International Conference on Shape Modeling and Applications 2005 (SMI 2005), pp. 320–325. IEEE (2005)
21. OpenRobotics: Gazebo fuel models (July). https://app.gazebosim.org/fuel/models
22. Pizer, S.M., Burbeck, C.A., Coggins, J.M., Fritsch, D.S., Morse, B.S.: Object shape before boundary shape: scale-space medial axes. J. Math. Imaging Vision **4**(3), 303–313 (1994)
23. Pizer, S.M., Siddiqi, K., Székely, G., Damon, J.N., Zucker, S.W.: Multiscale medial loci and their properties. Int. J. Comput. Vision **55**, 155–179 (2003)
24. Rosinol, A., et al.: Kimera: from slam to spatial perception with 3D dynamic scene graphs. Int. J. Robot. Res. **40**(12–14), 1510–1546 (2021)
25. Smale, S.: On gradient dynamical systems. Ann. Math. **74**(1), 199–206 (1961)
26. Song, A., Yim, K.M., Monod, A.: Generalized morse theory of distance functions to surfaces for persistent homology. Adv. Appl. Math. **166**, 102857 (2025)
27. Tian, Y., Chang, Y., Arias, F.H., Nieto-Granda, C., How, J.P., Carlone, L.: Kimera-multi: robust, distributed, dense metric-semantic slam for multi-robot systems. IEEE Trans. Robot. **38**(4) (2022)

Author Index

C. Wallraven et al. (Eds.): ACPR 2025, LNCS 16174, pp. 447–449, 2026.
https://doi.org/10.1007/978-981-95-4395-3

MIX
Papier aus verantwortungsvollen Quellen
Paper from responsible sources
FSC® C105338

If you have any concerns about our products,
you can contact us on
ProductSafety@springernature.com

In case Publisher is established outside the EU,
the EU authorized representative is:
Springer Nature Customer Service Center GmbH
Europaplatz 3, 69115 Heidelberg, Germany

Printed by Libri Plureos GmbH
in Hamburg, Germany